WESTERN CIVILIZATION VOLUME I

Eighth Edition

The Earliest Civilizations through the Reformation

Editor

William Hughes
Essex Community College

William Hughes is a professor of history at Essex Community College in Baltimore County, Maryland. He received his A.B. from Franklin and Marshall College and his M.A. from the Pennsylvania State University. He continued graduate studies at the American University and the Pennsylvania State University. Professor Hughes is interested in cultural history, particularly the role of film and television in shaping and recording history. He researched this subject as a Younger Humanist Fellow of the National Endowment for the Humanities, and he was a participant in the Image as Artifact project of the American Historical Association. He is author of the chapter on film as evidence in *The Historian and Film* (Cambridge University Press) and has written articles, essays, and reviews for *The Journal of American History, The New Republic, The Nation, Film and History, American Film,* and *The Dictionary of American Biography*. Professor Hughes also serves as an associate editor for *American National Biography,* a twenty-volume reference work to be issued by Oxford University Press.

Cover illustration by Mike Eagle

The Dushkin Publishing Group, Inc.
Sluice Dock, Guilford, Connecticut 06437

The Annual Editions Series

Annual Editions is a series of over 65 volumes designed to provide the reader with convenient, low-cost access to a wide range of current, carefully selected articles from some of the most important magazines, newspapers, and journals published today. Annual Editions are updated on an annual basis through a continuous monitoring of over 300 periodical sources. All Annual Editions have a number of features designed to make them particularly useful, including topic guides, annotated tables of contents, unit overviews, and indexes. For the teacher using Annual Editions in the classroom, an Instructor's Resource Guide with test questions is available for each volume.

VOLUMES AVAILABLE

Africa
Aging
American Foreign Policy
American Government
American History, Pre-Civil War
American History, Post-Civil War
Anthropology
Archaeology
Biology
Biopsychology
Business Ethics
Canadian Politics
Child Growth and Development
China
Comparative Politics
Computers in Education
Computers in Business
Computers in Society
Criminal Justice
Developing World
Drugs, Society, and Behavior
Dying, Death, and Bereavement
Early Childhood Education
Economics
Educating Exceptional Children
Education
Educational Psychology
Environment
Geography
Global Issues
Health
Human Development
Human Resources
Human Sexuality
India and South Asia

International Business
Japan and the Pacific Rim
Latin America
Life Management
Macroeconomics
Management
Marketing
Marriage and Family
Mass Media
Microeconomics
Middle East and the Islamic World
Money and Banking
Multicultural Education
Nutrition
Personal Growth and Behavior
Physical Anthropology
Psychology
Public Administration
Race and Ethnic Relations
Russia, the Eurasian Republics, and Central/Eastern Europe
Social Problems
Sociology
State and Local Government
Urban Society
Violence and Terrorism
Western Civilization, Pre-Reformation
Western Civilization, Post-Reformation
Western Europe
World History, Pre-Modern
World History, Modern
World Politics

Cataloging in Publication Data
Main entry under title: Annual editions: Western civilization, vol. I: The Earliest Civilizations through the Reformation.
    1. Civilization—Periodicals. 2. World history—Periodicals. I. Hughes, William, *comp.* II. Title: Western civilization, vol. I: The Earliest Civilizations through the Reformation.
901.9′05   82–645823   ISBN 1–56134–374–9

Eighth Edition

Printed in the United States of America

Printed on Recycled Paper

Editors/ Advisory Board

EDITOR

William Hughes
Essex Community College

ADVISORY BOARD

Robert Lembright
James Madison University

Charles R. Lilley
Northern Virginia Community
College

John Maxwell
West Virginia University

George Munro
Virginia Commonwealth University

Ronald Rader
The University of Georgia

Max Schoenfeld
University of Wisconsin
Eau Claire

Irvin D. Solomon
University of South Florida

Michael A. White
McLennan Community College

Arthur H. Auten
University of Hartford

Achilles Avraamides
Iowa State University

Beverly Blois, Jr.
Northern Virginia Community
College

Wendel Griffith
Okaloosa Walton Community
College

William R. Hanna
Humber College of Applied Arts
& Technology

Wallace Hutcheon
Northern Virginia Community
College

David Ibsen
Fullerton College

Bernard Klass
Los Angeles Pierce College

Members of the Advisory Board
are instrumental in the final
selection of articles for each
edition of Annual Editions. Their
review of articles for content,
level, currentness, and
appropriateness provides critical
direction to the editor and staff.
We think you'll find their careful
consideration well reflected in
this volume.

STAFF

Ian A. Nielsen, Publisher
Brenda S. Filley, Production Manager
Roberta Monaco, Editor
Addie Raucci, Administrative Editor
Cheryl Greenleaf, Permissions Editor
Deanna Herrschaft, Permissions Assistant
Diane Barker, Proofreader
Lisa Holmes-Doebrick, Administrative Coordinator
Charles Vitelli, Designer
Shawn Callahan, Graphics
Steve Shumaker, Graphics
Lara M. Johnson, Graphics
Laura Levine, Graphics
Libra A. Cusack, Typesetting Supervisor
Juliana Arbo, Typesetter

To the Reader

In publishing ANNUAL EDITIONS we recognize the enormous role played by the magazines, newspapers, and journals of the *public press* in providing current, first-rate educational information in a broad spectrum of interest areas. Within the articles, the best scientists, practitioners, researchers, and commentators draw issues into new perspective as accepted theories and viewpoints are called into account by new events, recent discoveries change old facts, and fresh debate breaks out over important controversies.

Many of the articles resulting from this enormous editorial effort are appropriate for students, researchers, and professionals seeking accurate, current material to help bridge the gap between principles and theories and the real world. These articles, however, become more useful for study when those of lasting value are carefully *collected, organized, indexed,* and *reproduced* in a *low-cost format*, which provides easy and permanent access when the material is needed. That is the role played by *Annual Editions*. Under the direction of each volume's *Editor*, who is an expert in the subject area, and with the guidance of an *Advisory Board*, we seek each year to provide in each ANNUAL EDITION a current, well-balanced, carefully selected collection of the best of the public press for your study and enjoyment. We think you'll find this volume useful, and we hope you'll take a moment to let us know what you think.

What exactly are we attempting to do when we set out to study the history of Western civilization?

The traditional course in Western civilization was often a chronological survey of sequential stages in the development of European institutions and ideas, with a cursory look at Near Eastern antecedents and a side glance at the Americas and other places where Westernization has occurred. Typically it moved from the Greeks to the Romans to the medieval period and on to the modern era, itemizing the distinctive characteristics of each stage, as well as each period's relation to preceding and succeeding developments. Of course, in a survey so broad (usually advancing from Adam to the atom in two brief semesters) a certain superficiality was inevitable. Key events whizzed by as if viewed in a cyclorama; often there was little opportunity to absorb and digest the complex ideas that have shaped our culture.

It is tempting to excuse these shortcomings as unavoidable. But to present a course on Western civilization that leaves students with only a jumble of events, names, dates, and places is to miss a marvelous opportunity. For the great promise of such a broad course of study is that it enables students to explore great turning points or shifts in the development of Western culture. Close analysis of these moments enables students to understand the dynamics of continuity and change over time. At best, the course can provide a coherent view of the Western tradition and even its interactions with non-Western cultures. It also offers opportunities for students to compare varied historical forms of authority, religion, and economic organization, to assess the great contests over the meaning of truth and reality that have sometimes divided Western culture, and even to reflect on the price of progress.

Of course, to focus exclusively on Western civilization can lead us to ignore non-Western peoples and cultures or else to perceive them in ways that some have labeled "Eurocentric." But contemporary courses in the history of Western civilization are rarely, if ever, mere exercises in European triumphalism. Indeed, they offer an opportunity to subject the Western tradition to critical scrutiny, to assess its accomplishments *and* its shortcomings. Few of us who teach the course would argue that Western history is the only history that contemporary students should know. Yet it should be an essential part of what they learn, for it is impossible to understand the modern world without some grounding in the basic patterns of the Western tradition.

As students become attuned to the distinctive traits of the West, they can develop a sense of the dynamism of history. They can begin to understand how ideas relate to social structures and social forces. They may come to appreciate the nature and significance of conceptual innovation and recognize how values often inspire inquiry. More specifically, they can trace the evolution of Western ideas about such essential matters as nature, humankind, authority, the gods, even history itself; that is, they learn *how* the West developed its distinctive character. And, as historian Reed Dasenbrock has observed, in an age that seeks greater multicultural understanding there is much to be learned from "the fundamental multiculturalism of Western culture, the fact that it has been constructed out of a fusion of disparate and often conflicting cultural traditions." Of course, the articles collected in this volume cannot deal with all these matters, but by providing an alternative to the synthetic summaries of most textbooks, they can help students better understand the diverse traditions and processes that we label Western civilization.

This book is like our history—unfinished, always in process. It will be revised biennially. Comments and criticism are welcome from all who use this book. To that end a postpaid article rating form is included at the back of the book. Please feel free to recommend articles that might improve the next edition. With your assistance, this anthology will continue to improve.

William Hughes
Editor

Contents

Unit 1

The Earliest Civilizations

Six articles discuss some of the dynamics of early civilizations. The topics include the development of social organization, the early Mediterranean world, and early civilization's relationship with the environment.

The concepts in bold italics are developed in the article. For further expansion please refer to the Topic Guide and the Index.

Unit 2

Greece and Rome: The Classical Tradition

Eleven articles focus on Greek and Roman societies. Religion, sports, education, and the impact of philosophy and exploration on the development of Hellenic society are discussed.

The concepts in bold italics are developed in the article. For further expansion please refer to the Topic Guide and the Index.

Unit 3

The Judeo-Christian Heritage

Six articles examine the impact that Jesus, Paul, politics, and clashing cultures had on the Judeo-Christian heritage.

The concepts in bold italics are developed in the article. For further expansion please refer to the Topic Guide and the Index.

Unit 4

Muslims and Byzantines

Four selections discuss the effects of Greek Hellenic
and Christian cultures on the development of the
Muslim and Byzantine worlds.

Unit 5

The Medieval Period

Eleven selections examine the medieval world. The topics include knighthood, trade exploration, education, and culture.

The concepts in bold italics are developed in the article. For further expansion please refer to the Topic Guide and the Index.

Unit 6

Renaissance and Reformation

Ten articles discuss the importance of trade and commerce on the development of the modern state, the role of art in Renaissance culture, and the emergence of religion.

The concepts in bold italics are developed in the article. For further expansion please refer to the Topic Guide and the Index.

The concepts in bold italics are developed in the article. For further expansion please refer to the Topic Guide and the Index.

Topic Guide

This topic guide suggests how the selections in this book relate to topics of traditional concern to students and professionals involved with the study of Western civilization. It is useful for locating articles that relate to each other for reading and research. The guide is arranged alphabetically according to topic. Articles may, of course, treat topics that do not appear in the topic guide. In turn, entries in the topic guide do not necessarily constitute a comprehensive listing of all the contents of each selection.

TOPIC AREA	TREATED IN:	TOPIC AREA	TREATED IN:
Afrocentrism	7. Out of Egypt, Greece	Historiography	7. Out of Egypt, Greece 10. Herodotus—Roving Reporter 14. Why Brutus Stabbed Caesar
Christianity	18. Jews and Christians in a Roman World 19. Who Wrote the Dead Sea Scrolls? 20. Who Was Jesus? 31. Ordeal by Fire 38. Jan Hus—Heretic or Patriot? 45. Luther: Giant of His Time 47. Explaining John Calvin	Islam	26. World of Islam 27. Rise of the Umayyad Dynasty 29. Golden Age of Andalusia
		Jews/Judaism	18. Jews and Christians in a Roman World 19. Who Wrote the Dead Sea Scrolls? 20. Who Was Jesus? 21. Jesus and the Teacher of Righteousness 29. Golden Age of Andalusia
Cities	1. Civilization and Its Discontents		
Commerce	28. Viking Saga 39. Jacques Coeur		
Crime	11. Love and Death in Ancient Greece	Justice	11. Love and Death in Ancient Greece
Culture	7. Out of Egypt, Greece 10. Herodotus—Roving Reporter 12. The Oldest Dead White European Males 18. Jews and Christians in a Roman World 24. Byzantium: The Emperor's New Clothes? 43. Hungary's Philosopher King: Matthias Corvinus 46. Forming of German Identity 48. That Others Might Read	Medieval Society	31. Ordeal by Fire 32. Lives of Medieval Women 33. Margery Kempe and the Meaning of Madness 37. How a Mysterious Disease Laid Low Europe's Masses
		Modern Society	39. Jacques Coeur
		Muslims	26. World of Islam 27. Rise of the Umayyad Dynasty 29. Golden Age of Andalusia
Ecology	6. Early Civilizations and Natural Environment	Nation-States	1. Civilization and Its Discontents
Economics	28. Viking Saga 39. Jacques Coeur	Philosophy	40. Machiavelli 43. Hungary's Philosopher King: Matthias Corvinus
Empires	5. Grisly Assyrian Record 13. Greek Gifts? 25. War by Other Means	Politics	1. Civilization and Its Discontents 4. Hatshepsut, Female Pharaoh 8. American Democracy through Ancient Greek Eyes 15. Nero, Unmaligned 40. Machiavelli
Exploration	28. Viking Saga 44. Columbus—Hero or Villain?		
Greek Society	11. Love and Death in Ancient Greece		

The Earliest Civilizations

Civilization is a relatively recent phenomenon in the human experience. But what exactly is civilization? How did it begin? How do civilized people differ from those who are not civilized? How is civilization transmitted?

Civilization, in its contemporary meaning, denotes a condition of human society marked by an advanced stage of artistic and technological development and by corresponding social and political complexity. Thus, civilized societies have developed formal institutions for commerce, government, education, and religion—activities that are carried out informally by precivilized societies. In addition, civilized people make much more extensive use of symbols. The greater complexity of civilized life requires a much wider range of specialized activities.

Symbolization, specialization, and organization enable civilized societies to extend greater control over their environments. Because they are less dependent than precivilized societies upon a simple adaptation to a particular habitat, civilized societies are more dynamic. Indeed, civilization institutionalizes change. In sum, civilization provides us with a wider range of concepts, techniques, and options to shape (for good or evil) our collective destinies.

In the West, the necessary preconditions for civilization first emerged in the great river valleys of Mesopotamia and Egypt. There we find the development of irrigation techniques, new staple crops, the introduction of the plow, the invention of the wheel, more widespread use of beasts of burden, improved sailing vessels, and copper metallurgy. These developments revolutionized society. Population increased and became more concentrated and more complex. The emergence of cities ("the urban revolution") marked the beginning of civilization.

Civilization combines complex, social, economic, and political structures with a corresponding network of ideas and values. The Sumerians organized themselves in city-states headed by kings who acted in the name of the local patron deity. The Egyptians developed a more centralized and authoritarian system based on loyalty to national god-kings. The Assyrians used force and intimidation to shape an international empire. Aspects of the earliest state structures are explored in "Civilization and Its Discontents" and "Grisly Assyrian Record of Torture and Death."

These early civilizations allowed for little individualism or freedom of expression. As historian Nels M. Bailkey notes in *Readings in Ancient History: Thought and Experience from Gilgamesh to St. Augustine* (1987), "Their thought remained closely tied to religion and found expression predominantly in religious forms." Elaborate myths recounted the deeds of heroes, defined relations between mankind and the gods, and generally justified the prevailing order of things. Thus, myths reveal something of the relationship between values and the social order in ancient civilizations. The link between beliefs and authority, particularly in Egypt, is treated in "Hatshepsut: The Female Pharaoh" and "Precincts of Eternity."

We are inclined nowadays to make much of the limitations of ancient systems of thought and authority. Yet the record of the Mesopotamians and Egyptians demonstrates, from the very beginning, civilization's potential for innovation and collective accomplishment. They developed writing and mathematics, monumental architecture, law, astronomy, art, and literatures rich with diversity and imagination. The record of ancient civilizations is full of cruelty and destruction, but it also includes an awakening concern for justice and righteousness. These early civilizations are notable, too, for their heroic efforts to bring nature under human control, an enterprise described in "Early Civilizations and the Natural Environment."

For a time the great river valleys remained islands of civilization in a sea of barbarism. The spread of civilization to rain-watered lands required that outlying areas find the means to produce a food surplus and develop the social mechanisms for transferring the surplus from farmers to specialists. The first condition was met by the diffusion of plow agriculture, the second by culture contacts that came about through conquest, trade, and migration. Along these lines, "Egypt and the Mediterranean World" explores contacts between Egypt and the Aegean civilizations.

Several satellite civilizations evolved into great empires; these further enhanced cultural exchange between diverse and dispersed societies. The problem of governing scattered and often hostile subjects required that conquerors create new patterns of authority. The establishment of empires like those of the Assyrians and Persians were not mere acts of conquest; they were innovations in government and administration.

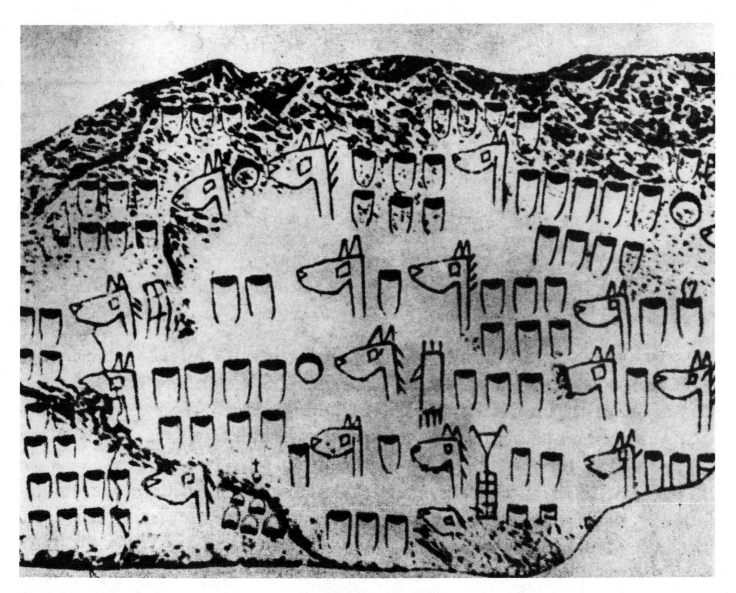

Looking Ahead: Challenge Questions

What accounts for the expansion of Mediterranean civilization during the Uruk period?

How did Egypt influence other Mediterranean cultures?

How did it come about that Egypt was ruled by a female pharaoh? How did her subjects react to this unusual situation?

What was the purpose of the temple at Karnak?

Describe the ecological impact of the earliest civilizations.

Civilization and Its Discontents

Why did the world's first civilization cut a swath across the Near East?

Bruce Bower

Investigators from the German Archaeological Institute in Cairo, Egypt, make an annual slog through the Nile Delta to the waterlogged site of Buto, the legendary ancient capital of Lower Egypt. Strategically located near the Mediterranean Sea, Buto was a major port during the 4th millennium B.C.—a poorly understood period of Egyptian history preceding the emergence of the pharaohs around 3100 B.C.

During four field seasons that began in 1983, the German researchers repeatedly drilled through the mud, sand and water-saturated soil covering Buto until they reached pottery fragments and other ancient debris. Since 1987, the investigators have siphoned off groundwater at the spot with diesel-driven pumps and then carefully dug into Buto's muddy

Courtesy, Metropolitan Museum of Art, Gift of Martin & Sarah Cherkasky, 1983

remains. Their dirty work is yielding important evidence not only about Lower Egypt's early days but also about the world's first civilization, which began developing in Mesopotamia around 5,400 years ago.

"We've found the first archaeological evidence of cultural unification in Egypt at the end of the 4th millennium B.C., before the first dynasty of pharaohs appeared," says project director Thomas von der Way. Excavations show that during the final stages of the predynastic era at Buto, local methods of pottery and stone-blade production were replaced by more advanced techniques that originated in Upper Egypt, which lay farther to the south. Apparently, Upper Egyptian invaders had conquered this prominent city and port, von der Way says.

Some of the Upper-Egyptian-style pottery is poorly made and probably represents the handiwork of Buto residents who were allowed to stay on and adapt to the new regime, he maintains. Those individuals were most likely commoners, von der Way says, adding, "Buto's ruling class and its followers might in fact have been wiped out."

Even more intriguing is evidence of close contact between Buto's Egyptian residents and the Sumerians of southern Mesopotamia (now southern Iraq), who fashioned the world's first full-fledged

civilization and state institutions during the last half of the 4th millennium B.C. Not only does pottery at Buto display Mesopotamian features, but clay nails uncovered at the delta site are nearly identical to those used to decorate temples at sites such as Uruk—the largest Sumerian settlement and the world's first city. In Mesopotamia, workers inserted the nails into temple walls and painted their heads to form mosaics. The researchers also found a clay cone at Buto that closely resembles clay decorations placed in wall niches inside Mesopotamian temples.

Scientists have long argued over ancient Egypt's relationship to early Mesopotamia. Much of the debate centers on Mesopotamian-style artifacts, such as cylinder seals and flint knife handles, found in 4th-millennium-B.C. graves situated on slopes above the Nile Valley near Buto. Traders who regularly traveled through Mesopotamia and Syria may have brought those artifacts to Egypt, says David O'Connor of the University of Pennsylvania in Philadelphia.

At Buto, however, Egyptians may have copied temple decorations shown to them by Sumerians more than 5,000 years ago, suggesting "direct and complex influences at work" between the two societies, O'Connor observes.

"It's not possible to trade architecture," von der Way asserts. "Direct personal contact between people from Lower Egypt and Mesopotamia led to the adoption of foreign architecture at Buto."

Buto fuels the growing recognition among archaeologists that early Mesopotamian civilization experienced an unprecedented expansion between 3400 and 3100 B.C. The expansion occurred during the latter part of a phase called the Uruk period (named after the major city of the time), which began around 3600

B.C. Excavations conducted over the past 15 years indicate that southern Mesopotamian city-states, each consisting of one or two cities serving as political hubs and providing goods and services to thousands of people living in nearby farming villages, established outposts in neighboring territories lying within modern-day Iraq, Iran, Syria and Turkey. Even artifacts recovered at sites in the Transcaucasus of the Soviet Union show signs of Sumerian influence.

Such discoveries leave investigators pondering what made the Sumerians such hard-chargers in a world largely made up of subsistence farmers.

Many subscribe to the view of Robert McCormick Adams of the Smithsonian Institution in Washington, D.C., who calls the Uruk expansion "the first urban revolution." Adams says the economic demands of burgeoning Mesopotamian cities led to a great transregional civilization in the Near East.

Others, such as Henry T. Wright of the University of Michigan in Ann Arbor, contend the term "urban revolution" masks the fundamental significance of the Uruk expansion—the introduction, for the first time anywhere, of political states with a hierarchy of social classes and bureaucratic institutions that served powerful kings.

"Whatever the case, it was a revolutionary time, a moment of extraordinary innovations in art, technology and social systems," Adams says. For instance, in the late 4th millennium B.C., Mesopotamia witnessed the emergence of mass-produced pottery, sculpture as an art form and the harnessing of skilled craftsmen and pools of laborers by an administrative class to produce monumental buildings. The world's earliest clay tablets, portraying simple labels and lists of goods with pictographic symbols, also appeared, foreshadowing the birth of fully expressive writing around 3000 B.C.

The Mesopotamian revolution paved the way for modern societies and political states, Wright observes. "A number of competing formulations of what was driving the Uruk expansion have been proposed and must be tested with new archaeological studies," he says.

Perhaps the most controversial of these theories, proposed by Guillermo Algaze of the University of Chicago's Oriental Institute, holds that

Map shows modern-day Baghdad and several 4th-millennium B.C. Uruk sites in Mesopotamia and nearby regions.

advanced societies in southern Mesopotamia were forced to expand northward, beginning around 5,400 years ago, to obtain scarce resources desired by powerful administrators and social elites.

These northern regions held items crucial to the growth of the incipient civilization, including slaves, timber, silver, gold, copper, limestone, lead and bitumen (an asphalt used as a cement and mortar), Algaze argues in the December 1989 CURRENT ANTHROPOLOGY. To guarantee a reliable flow of imports, Sumerian settlers colonized the plains of southwestern Iran and established outposts at key points along trade routes traversing northern Mesopotamia, he suggests.

Excavations at a number of ancient villages in southwestern Iran indicate the area was "part and parcel of the Mesopotamian world" by the end of the Uruk period, Algaze notes. Cultural remains, such as ceramic pottery, record-keeping tablets, engraved depictions of religious offerings and architectural styles, are strikingly similar at sites in the Iranian plains and southern Mesopotamia, he says. Apparently, Sumerians colonized "a fertile and productive area that was only lightly settled and could surely mount only minimal resistance."

Uruk-period cities and smaller settlements also popped up farther to the north, especially where east-west trade routes intersected with the Tigris and Euphrates rivers, Algaze argues. A good example is the Uruk city of Habuba Kabira, which lies along the upper Euphrates in what is now Syria. Habuba Kabira once encompassed at least 450 acres, according to estimates based on Algaze's assessment of the site. Cultural remains in its metropolitan core and in clusters of sites outside its huge defensive wall are identical to those found in southern Mesopotamia. With its neatly planned residential, industrial and administrative quarters, Habuba Kabira was well situated to control the flow of trade goods through the region, Algaze says.

Although Sumerians produced surplus grain, leather products, dried fish, dates and textiles for export, they most likely took more from colonized areas and northern traders than they gave in re-

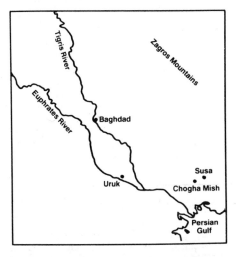

turn, Algaze maintains. The influx of imports, he says, added new layers of complexity to Mesopotamia's urban centers as fresh legions of administrators scurried to coordinate distribution of the bounty.

Sumerian city-states, of which there were at least five, almost certainly engaged in fierce competition and warfare for imported goods, Algaze says. Cylinder seals from various southern Mesopotamian sites, depicting military scenes and the taking of prisoners, reflect these rivalries.

Cylinder seals are engraved stone cylinders that were used to roll an impression onto clay seals for documents and bales of commodities. A variety of scenes, often including domestic animals, grain, deities and temples, are found on the seals.

Algaze's assertion that the Uruk expansion was primarily fueled by an urgent need for resources available only in foreign lands is receiving much attention, and a good deal of criticism, in the archaeological community.

Piotr Steinkeller of Harvard University contends that, contrary to Algaze's argument, southern Mesopotamians did not need to establish such a far-flung network of settlements to obtain such resources, which were available in the foothills of the nearby Zagros mountains. The Uruk expansion was purely a commercial venture aimed at making a profit, Steinkeller asserted at December's annual meeting of the American Institute of Archaeology in Boston.

"The Sumerians wanted to become middlemen in international trade networks and reap big profits," he says. "They weren't forced to expand because of internal growth."

1. THE EARLIEST CIVILIZATIONS

In Steinkeller's scenario, Uruk migrants did not colonize new territories. Instead, they forged intricate trade agreements with foreign communities to divvy up local and imported goods.

Both colonization and commerce are difficult to pin down through archaeological research, observes Adams of the Smithsonian Institution. "There's no evidence for goods moving in a private-enterprise sense during the Late Uruk period," Adams asserts. At most, he says, valuable items may have been exchanged between distant royal palaces or religious temples.

"Today we tend to treat economics as a separate domain," he says. "But in Uruk times, the economy probably wasn't separated from politics and religion."

Indeed, says Carl C. Lamberg-Karlovsky of Harvard University, religious beliefs may have exerted an important influence on the Uruk expansion. Southern Mesopotamians believed their temple gods owned the land and humans were its stewards. Thus, Uruk city-states may have pursued a type of "manifest destiny" he suggests, claiming nearby lands in the name of their deities.

Harvey Weiss of Yale University downplays religious factors. He contends that the emergence of social classes—particularly elite groups seeking exotic items to signify their elevated status—may lie at the heart of the Uruk expansion.

Weiss says archaeologists lack substantial evidence for extensive imports during the Uruk period, with the exception of copper and the semiprecious stone lapis lazuli.

"It's a good bet the Sumerians were acquiring foreign materials that weren't necessary for their survival," he says. "Newly emerging social elites defined what types of exotica were imported."

However, he adds, it is far from clear what types of social classes characterized Sumerian civilization and why they emerged at that time.

Knowledge about Sumerian settlements built before 3400 B.C. is similarly scant, observes Wright of the University of Michigan. "The Uruk expansion must have started earlier and been more complex than Algaze assumes," he argues.

While Algaze proposes that long-distance trade resulted in the explosive growth of Sumerian city-states, Wright argues just the opposite. As he sees it, competitive city-states attempted to control ever-larger territories, and trade was an outgrowth of their political jousting.

In a fundamental challenge to this already-diverse collection of views, Gregory A. Johnson of the City University of New York, Hunter College, questions the whole notion of a strong, expanding Sumerian civilization in Uruk times. Instead, he contends, the period was one of political collapse and fragmentation.

Johnson says the Sumerian colonists described by Algaze were most likely a group of refugees, initially consisting of administrative elites who had been defeated in the political power struggles that flared up in budding city-states.

"Why were Uruk outposts established in distant areas fully equipped with household utensils, administrative paraphernalia, husbands, wives, children, sundry relatives, animals, architects, artisans—all the comforts of home? Perhaps things at home were not that comfortable," he suggests.

If, as Algaze argues, traders founded communities such as Habuba Kabira, they could easily have adapted to local ways of life without taking with them everything but the kitchen hearth, Johnson points out. Refugees, however, are more likely to recreate the lives they were forced to leave behind.

And masses of Mesopotamians indeed left their lives behind. Populations declined sharply in many southern Mesopotamian cities and their surrounding villages at the end of the 4th millennium B.C. Surveys conducted by Johnson and others indicate the abandonment of nearly 450 acres of occupied areas representing as many as 60,000 people.

The populations of inhabited areas of seven major Sumerian cities dropped by an average of 51 percent in the last few centuries of the Uruk period, Johnson notes. Only at the city of Uruk have archaeologists documented significant expansion during that time.

Moreover, widespread abandonment of settlements on Iran's Susiana plain created an uninhabited, 9-mile-wide "buffer zone" between two large Late Uruk communities known as Susa and Chogha Mish. What once had been a single state in its formative stages was thus sliced in half, Johnson says. The buffer zone probably became the site of intense warfare between administrative elites from the two sides, who wrestled for control of rural labor and agriculture on the plain. Some Sumerian cylinder seals portray political conflicts of this type rather than economic rivalries, he asserts. Susa gained the upper hand and remained an urban center into the 3rd millennium B.C., while Chogha Mish became a ghost town.

Johnson says competing political factions undoubtedly plagued other nascent states, creating a reservoir of disgruntled Sumerians with plenty of incentive to haul their belongings to distant greener pastures.

Further archaeological work, particularly in areas remote from the intensively surveyed river sites, may clarify some of the controversy surrounding the rise and rapid fall of the world's first civilization. But a consensus will be difficult to dig out of the ground.

"Quite frankly, no one has come up with a good explanation for the Uruk expansion," concedes Weiss. "It remains a great mystery."

Egypt and the Mediterranean World

Gaballa Aly Gaballa

Gaballa Aly Gaballa, of Egypt, is Professor of Egyptology at Cairo University. He was formerly visiting Professor at the Mohamed V University (Morocco), at the University of Central Florida (USA), and at the University of Kuwait. He is the author of two books published in English, Narrative in Egyptian Art, *(1976) and* The Memphite Tomb—Chapel of Mose *(1977), and of many articles.*

Historic Egypt emerged as a unified country, with its own system of writing, towards the end of the fourth millennium B.C. It rapidly became the seat of a brilliant civilization in which flourished philosophy and literature, architecture and art, science and medicine, administration and social organization. From ancient times, thanks to the country's situation on the Mediterranean coast, the Egyptians made increasingly numerous contacts with Europe. The contribution made by Egypt to Western culture enriched civilization as a whole.

Around the same time, the Minoan civilization (named after Minos, the legendary king), came into being on the shores of the Aegean, centred on the island of Crete.

Although the Mediterranean was no obstacle between Egypt and the Aegean, contacts between Egyptian and Aegean traders and emissaries were made first of all in the Phoenician coastal ports, Byblos in particular. Egyptian trading vessels no doubt set sail from these ports to Crete, and called at Cyprus, Rhodes, Karpathos and Kasos before returning directly to Egypt (some 270 nautical miles from Crete), carried along by the north winds that blow in summer. The voyage then took three days and two nights.

There is no lack of archaeological evidence for relations between the two peoples. Many Egyptian cylindrical stone jars have been found in Crete and eventually the Cretans adopted the Egyptian technique of manufacturing these jars. On the island of Kithira, an alabaster vase has been found bearing the name of an Egyptian king of the Fifth Dynasty (c. 2465–2323 B.C.). From the twenty-second century B.C., Egyptian writings began to mention Kaftiou, an Egyptian adaptation of the Semitic name for Crete, Caphtor, which also appears in the Bible.

At the beginning of the second millennium B.C., there was a thriving trade between Middle Kingdom Egyptians and Cretans of the period known as Middle Minoan. Many Egyptian objects from that era, including everyday utensils, scarabs used as seals and a diorite statuette, have been found in Crete, while Minoan pottery in the Kamares style, and silver vases showing an Aegean influence, have been discovered in a temple near Luxor.

Around 1500 B.C., Egypt cast off the yoke of the Hyksos[1] and emerged from its traditional isolationism to become an international power, strengthened by a series of military victories. Phoenicia and Syria fell under its sway, and the Egyptian fleet controlled the Phoenician ports, probably extending its influence as far as Cyprus. This Egyptian presence created a new situation in the eastern Mediterranean basin. The Aegeans of the Late Minoan period and the Mycenaeans of Hellas[2] had thereafter to deal directly with the Egyptians if their merchant ships were to have access to the traditional markets of Palestine and Syria. In all probability, the Cretans and the Mycenaeans came to an agreement with the powerful Pharaoh Tuthmosis III (c. 1479–1425 B.C.) The tomb of his vizier Rekhmire, at the necropolis of Thebes, depicts Cretan emissaries bearing tribute from their island. The Egyptian inscription describes the scene:

"The arrival of the princes from Kaftiou and the islands in the midst of the sea, submissive and with bowed heads before the might of His Majesty Tuthmosis III". There is every reason to believe that these "islands in the midst of the sea" were those of the eastern Mediterranean and the city of Mycenae in the Peloponnese.

Brown-skinned Aegeans, wearing brightly coloured loincloths and with thick manes of hair hanging to their shoulders or worn in one or more plaits bound around their foreheads, became a familiar sight to the Egyptians as they threaded through the streets of Thebes to bear their gifts, called "tribute" by the Egyptians, to Pharoah: large, ornate goblets with handles shaped like animals, or elongated vases with small handles, decorated with floral motifs or horizontal polychrome lines.

Towards the middle of the fifteenth century B.C., the Cretan civilization foundered, probably as a result of internal power struggles. Small wonder, then, that the name of Kaftiou should have disappeared from Egyptian sources after the end of that century. However the expression "islands in the midst of the sea" continues to occur frequently in these writings, before disappearing, in its turn, in the twelfth century B.C., when successive waves of the barbarians known to the Egyptians as the "sea peoples" were surging into the Peloponnese peninsula and wreaking havoc. These hordes crossed Anatolia (where they annihilated the Hittites) and Greece, and advanced on Egypt overland across Syria and by sea via the Mediterranean islands. But they were repelled by such powerful Pharaohs as Ramesses II, Merneptah and Ramesses III, who saved Egypt from destruction on a massive scale.

The Greek presence in Egypt made itself felt in the early seventh century

Reprinted with permission from *The Unesco Courier,* September 1988, pp. 30-32.

B.C. through mercenaries serving in the Egyptian armies and merchants who set up trading posts in various towns of the Delta. Greek philosophers, historians and geographers followed them, dazzled by Egyptian civilization with its gigantic monuments, its beliefs and its wealth of knowledge.

The Greek astronomer, philosopher and mathematician, Thales of Miletus, is said to have brought back the 365-day solar calendar from Egypt at the end of the seventh century B.C. The Athenian statesman Solon (c. 640–560 B.C.) visited Egypt at the time when, according to Herodotus, the Sixteenth-Dynasty king Amasis II promulgated a law under which each Egyptian was obliged to make an annual declaration of income and return it to the governor of the province. Any person guilty of illicit gains was condemned to death. Solon had an identical law adopted in Athens. Another Greek historian, Diodorus of Sicily, recounts that Lycurgus (legendary king of Sparta) drew inspiration from Egyptian legislation, as did Plato.

Egypt's influence on early Greek art is evident, too. The *kouros* figure of a young man, characteristic of archaic statuary, has an Egyptian air about it. The tall, slim youth stands with his left leg forward, his arms held straight by his sides and his hands clenched. This type of statue not only imitates the attitudes of Egyptian figures, but also abides by the traditional rules governing Egyptian art, in particular the "rule of proportion" that its creators had been applying for over 2,000 years. The human body was originally divided into 18 equal squares, and into 21 from the Saite[3] period (seventh century B.C.), when the unit of measurement of length, the cubit, was modified. Diodorus of Sicily relates that in the sixth century B.C. Telekles and Theodorus, two famous Greek sculptors, drew on that tradition for a statue of Apollo by dividing the body into $21^{1}/_{4}$ squares.

Over the centuries, the Greeks became increasingly involved in the history of Egypt. In 332 B.C., the country was conquered by Alexander the Great, and a Macedonian Dynasty was founded which governed the country for some three centuries. Egypt became part of the Hellenistic world encompassing the eastern basin of the Mediterranean. Alexandria, the new Egyptian capital founded by the Greeks, brought fresh prestige to Hellenism through its writers, geographers, historians, architects and astronomers.

When the Roman general Marcus Antonius, ally of Cleopatra VII, lost the battle of Actium in 31 B.C., Egypt became a Roman province. As the granary of Rome it helped to supply the Roman army during its major conquests.

As regards religion, the cult of Isis and Osiris (Serapis, in its Ptolemaic form), and of their son Horus-Harpocrates, was widely adopted in the Graeco-Roman world. The legend of Osiris, based on belief in the afterlife of the soul in a better world, has strong popular appeal, since it promises salvation to all, a concept lacking in the official worship of the Greek and Roman divinities. To the Greeks, Isis was the incarnation of destiny, since she succeeded in freeing herself from the control of the gods and thereby acquired absolute power. The Isis cult in Rome competed with the Roman religion and emperor-worship. Moreover, the Osirian triad foreshadowed the Christian trinity. Before the advent of Christianity, Isis-worship in Europe became as prevalent as the later cult of the Virgin Mary.

The world also owes the invention of the calendar and the alphabet to the ancient Egyptians.

Like other peoples, the Egyptians first devised a dating system which divided time into lunar years of 354 days. But before long they realized that it was not sufficiently accurate and was unsuited to the organization of their complex bureaucratic system, so it fell into disuse except for the celebration of certain religious events. Around 3000 B.C. they invented a solar calendar of 365 days divided into twelve months of thirty days each, to which at the end of the year were added five extra, or "epagomenal", days. The Egyptians knew that their year was six hours shorter than the solar year ($365^{1}/_{4}$ days), but for a long time they did nothing to remedy this discrepancy. Only under Greek rule did they begin to add one day to the official year every four years, to bring it into alignment with the solar year. That calendar was adopted by Julius Caesar and imposed in Rome from 45 B.C. The Julian calendar was used in Europe and the West until, at the end of the sixteenth century, it was refined by Pope Gregory XIII and, as the Gregorian calendar, became known throughout the world.

Towards the end of the fourth millennium B.C., the Egyptians invented a system of writing which used hieroglyphic signs, i.e. pictures, rather than letters. These pictures were chosen, not for their meaning, but for the sounds that they represented.

It is true that the modern European alphabet is derived from the Graeco-Roman alphabet, which is directly based on the Phoenician alphabet. But what system of writing influenced the Phoenicians? The oldest Semitic texts known to us date back to the fifteenth century B.C. They were discovered in the Sinai desert, and contain Semitic terms transcribed with signs that resemble hieroglyphs. It is very likely that this Semitic writing was based on hieroglyphs, using a system of pictured sounds, and that it developed over several centuries into the Phoenician alphabet, in which each sound is represented by a single letter. It seems probable, therefore, that the alphabet, one of the greatest achievements of the human mind, is of Egyptian origin.

NOTES

1. Asiatic invaders of northern Egypt who ruled as the Fifteenth Dynasty (c. 1640–1532 B.C.).
2. Greeks of the classical period called their country Hellas and themselves Hellenes.
3. Named after the Twenty-Sixth Dynasty (644–525 B.C.) capital city, Saïs, in the Nile Delta. *Editor.*

Precincts of Eternity

Jean-Claude Golvin

Jean-Claude Golvin, of France, is a research director at the French National Centre for Scientific Research (CNRS). He is currently director of the Franco-Egyptian Centre at Karnak and of the CNRS permanent mission in Egypt. His publications include Les bâtisseurs de Karnak *(with Jean-Claude Goyon, 1987) and* Amphithéâtres et bladiateurs *(with Christian Landes, 1990).*

The sites of Pharaonic temples were chosen in accordance with a tradition whose origins are sometimes lost in the mists of time. The great temple of Amon-Re at Karnak, for instance, marked the spot where the first mound emerged from the waters of *noun* (the primordial ocean), a pointed knoll which the god Amon caused to rise at the beginning of the world and around which he continued to shape his creation. The very name of the god (*Imm*, Amon) means "the hidden one", in other words, he who might assume any shape or size and who was present in the inmost depths of all creatures and all the material world.

The Egyptians thought, however, that the forces of evil, over which the god alone could triumph, could not be defeated once and for all. It was therefore vital to encourage Amon to fight them constantly and regularly to perform anew his act of creation. Such was the underlying significance of the devotions offered to him in all the temples. Through suitable offerings, made at the proper times and under ritual conditions laid down in detail, an attempt was made to keep the god in the frame of mind needed to ensure that the universe remained in a state of balance.

A tiny part of the divine substance was concentrated in a small gold statuette barely more than a cubit high (52 cm), placed in a kind of monolithic granite shrine (the *naos*) capped by a pyramidal form and provided with wooden shutters which could be opened. The Egyptian temple was not a place of worship where large numbers of the faithful could gather, but god's home on Earth, a dark and mysterious dwelling accessible only to officiating priests and to the first among them, the Pharaoh, who enjoyed the rare privilege of being able to gaze upon the god's face.

The most important part of the temple, where the tremendous energy needed to uphold creation (the divine statuette) was stored, was also, paradoxically, the smallest part. The successive monumental encasements in which it was set were intended to protect it from any aggression or harmful influence. The statuette and the *naos,* which served as the first encasement, were located in a small dark chamber, the sanctuary. They were flanked by the private apartments of the god which possessed all the attributes of a sumptuous palace and where he lived and reigned like an earthly king. The only function of the priests was to be his faithful servants.

The god was worshipped daily just as though he were a person of flesh and blood. Ritual acts, chants and prayers accompanied the various parts of this recurring ceremonial. In the morning the officiating priest broke the clay seal affixed at the end of the previous day. He thus released the cord that held the wooden shutters closed, affording access to the divine statue. He then proceeded to wash and dress the god and to ensure throughout the day that the necessary offerings of food were made to him. The god was believed to feast on the essence of these provisions which were subsequently sent to the royal altars and then to the priests, for whom more material forms of satisfaction were appropriate.

Many other temples in Egypt, including the famous temple at Luxor, were dedicated to Amon. How could the same god, who was proclaimed to be unique in hymns and prayers, be in several different places at the same instant? To the Egyptians there was no contradiction here. In reality, the statues of Amon placed in the heart of the sanctuaries served simply as points of "concentration" and "emergence" for this omnipresent god.

Some cities also honoured other gods, but their temples have not been so well preserved. The great sanctuary of Heliopolis, dedicated to Re, has been almost entirely destroyed, while those of Ptah at Memphis or Thoth at Hermopolis, which have greatly suffered from erosion, cannot compete with the impressive ruins at Karnak.

KARNAK, A DYNASTIC TEMPLE

The temple of Amon-Re at Karnak was probably founded in the twentieth century BC, during the reign of Sesostris I (1971–1929 BC). It steadily grew in size, ending up as a colossal complex of buildings forming a four-sided figure measuring 600 metres from corner to corner. It assumed such proportions and underwent so many metamorphoses because it became the great dynastic temple of Egypt to which each Pharaoh came to find the source of his legitimacy. Hardly had he assumed office than the new sovereign had a building put up for his divine father, Amon, in order to secure further benefits from him. A system of give-and-take was thus established between the god and the king, which underpinned the country's stability. Each monument, which was first and foremost an offering, might very well be destroyed in the next reign by a king who wished in his turn to perform a notable act. The dismantled stones were used again in new monuments.

Karnak is thus the product of a long history of destructions, additions and al-

Reprinted with permission from *The Unesco Courier,* November 1990, pp. 15-17.

11

terations, and its foundations and thick walls are consequently made up of thousands of stone blocks, scattered around and jumbled together. These are patiently being restored to their former positions and studied by archaeologists seeking to reconstitute the original form of the vanished monuments.

A form which, in itself, has nothing special about it: all the temples of ancient Egypt resembled one another. In front of the sanctuary were rooms paved with huge flagstones. At the entrance to the hypostyle (pillared) halls set along the main axis of the temple there were great stone doors framed by two massive towers symbolizing the two mountains at the confines of the land of Egypt: the Arabian chain in the east and the Libyan chain in the west. The doors and towers together formed a structure known as a pylon which marked the boundaries of a sacred place. Before the doorways huge wooden poles were adorned with banners that waved in the wind, revealing the movements of the "divine breath" through the world.

The general orientation of the temples was also a matter of deliberate choice. The main axis of the temple of Amon-Re followed the east-west course of the sun. It was intersected by a second perpendicular axis, running from south to north like the Nile. This royal axis, followed only by solemn processions, consisted of a series of courtyards and pylons preceded by colossal statues of the royal dynasty, which expressed in material form the eternal presence of the sovereign in the temple.

The way in which scenes were set out on the walls was patterned on the world in which the Egyptians lived. The bottom was bordered by geographical sequences in which the Nile gods alternated with the goddesses of the countryside and figures symbolizing the different administrative districts of the country, known as nomes. The ceiling was decorated with motifs inspired by astral themes: stars, constellations, zodiacs or representations of the sun's celestial course within the body of the goddess of the sky, Nut.

A PRECISE SYSTEM OF SYMBOLS

The bas-reliefs on the walls indicated the function of each room. Divinities and plants that were emblematic of the north (the Nile delta, Lower Egypt) were placed on the northern side and those relating to the south (the Nile valley or Upper Egypt) on the southern side. Along the axis of the high cornices projecting out from over the doors the disk of the sun could be seen, protected by two upright cobras facing in opposite directions. The sun's celestial course was portrayed by the unfolding of two large wings. Inside the rooms were religious scenes depicting the essential ritual acts that were accomplished with the participation of divinities, the king and priests—offerings, processions, acts of consecration, acts performed on the occasion of coronations or jubilees. On the outside, scenes were portrayed that showed the exploits achieved during the reign: the slaughtering of enemies, conquests and battles.

The founding of a temple was marked by ceremonies in which the succession of building operations was accompanied by symbolic acts. Many scenes depict the king marking out the layout of the temple with string, scooping out the first furrow with a hoe, purifying the foundations with natron, laying the cornerstones with the help of a lever and finally presenting the dwelling to his master, Amon-Re.

The temple was thus ushered into existence like a living being. In one corner of the temple a "foundation deposit" was buried. This was a collection of objects comprising scale models of tools, representations of offerings (glazed earthenware lettuces, ox legs and heads and sacrificed geese) and briquettes marked with the name of the king who had founded the temple. These deposits are a boon to archaeologists as they serve as the equivalent of birth certificates, enabling them to assign a date to the building of a temple.

Other temples formed part of a complex designed to ensure the dead Pharaoh's survival in the hereafter. Human beings were considered by the ancient Egyptians to have several components: the body, which was the material covering of the human spirit (which was mummified in an attempt to preserve it), but also the Ba (the soul), the Akh (the immortal principle), the shadow and the Ka (the life-force). The Ka of the king was the very embodiment of his royal rank, of the indestructible, cosmic part of his being, and after his death joined up with that of his divine ancestors.

The pyramid was associated with the royal tomb, both in its form, which was a symbolic reminder of the original mound and hence of the birth of the world, and through its alignment with the four cardinal points with, inside or outside as the case may be, its flights of steps. It thereby enabled the king to ascend to heaven, or in other words to eternity. Continually reborn like the morning star which rises every day in the east, he was then assured of living for "millions of years".

Hatshepsut

The Female Pharaoh

Continuing our look at women in ancient Egypt, **John Ray** *considers the triumphs and monuments of Queen Hatshepsut, the only female Pharaoh.*

John Ray

John Ray is Herbert Thompson Reader in Egyptology at Cambridge University.

The Pharaoh of ancient Egypt is normally described as the typical example of a divine ruler. The reality was more complex than this, since the Pharaoh seems to have been a combination of a human element and a divine counterpart. This duality is expressed not only in the ruler's titles, which often have a double aspect to them, but also in the king's names. Every Pharaoh had a human name, given to him at birth and used in intimate contexts throughout his life. These names are the ones by which we know them. Since such names tended to repeat themselves in families, we now need to distinguish kings with the same name by numbers. In addition, there was a throne-name, conferred at the accession and containing the immortal form of the ruler's divinity. The king was an embodiment of the sungod, an eternal prototype, and the human frailties of the individual ruler did not affect this embodiment: a convenient system, surely, for having the best of both worlds when it comes to government. The Pharaoh was essentially an icon, much as the imperial Tsar was an icon, and even the president of the United States sometimes appears to be.

How far can icons be stretched? Pharaoh was the manifestation of the sun in time and place: he could be old, young, athletic, gay, incompetent, boring, alcoholic or insane, but he would still be Pharaoh. Examples of all these types are known, or hinted at in the sources. But could he be female? The theoretical answer to this question may have been 'yes', since there are several ancient Egyptian texts describing creator-gods with both male and female attributes, but it was one thing to concede an abstract possibility and another to welcome its embodiment. Female rulers are attested in the long history of dynastic Egypt, and later tradition puts the names of queens at or near the end of both the Old Kingdom (*c.* 2200 BC) and the Middle Kingdom, some five centuries later. (The Old Kingdom one, Nitocris, later attracted considerable legends, and appears prominently in Herodotos). However, the important point was that tradition placed these queens at the end of their particular dynasties: female Pharaohs were unnatural, and meant decline and retribution. Egyptian society gave remarkable freedoms and legal rights to women—far more than in the rest of the Near East or in the classical world—but limits were limits, even by the Nile.

Egypt was, and is, a Mediterranean country, where the most powerful man can frequently be reduced to confusion and paralysis by a remark from his mother, but women were limited to their sphere: if they had no other title, they could always be honoured as 'lady of the house'. If they stayed within this domain, they could expect to retain status and protection. Agriculture beside the Nile was intensive, and this meant that women's contributions were essential, as opposed to the more nomadic societies of the Near East, where females were often seen as an encumbrance. Many Egyptian women may not have thought their position a bad bargain; pregnancy and childbirth were expected but dangerous, and support outside the family was unknown

A granite head of Tuthmosis III, the sidelined young Pharaoh who took revenge on his over-assertive aunt by erasing her inscriptions after her death.

Hatshepsut's standard bearer is followed by men carrying herbs and spices from the Punt expedition, underlining the possibility that its motive was economic.

(Below) Loading up the Egyptian ships at Punt (from Howard Carter's drawings at the turn-of-the-century of the Deir el-Bahri reliefs): among the 'booty' were the frankincense trees that stood in front of Hatshepsut's temple.

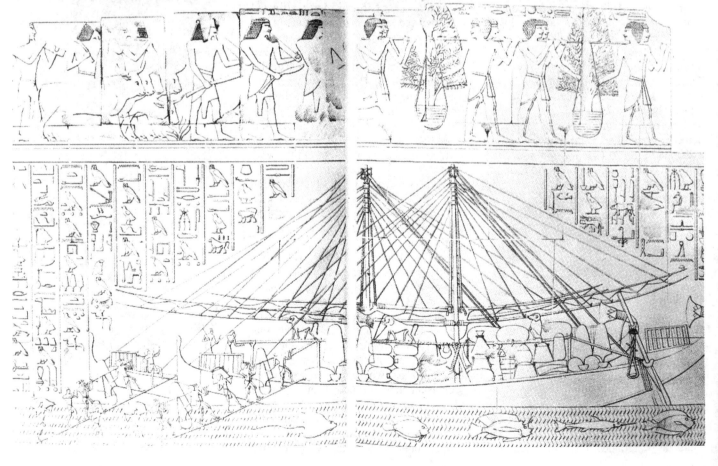

and perhaps impossible. Security, and the real possibility of influence over the holders of power, may not have seemed so poor a prospect, especially if a woman produced a son or two, while divorce and inheritance rules for females were relatively favourable. Why break the mould?

The early part of the Eighteenth Dynasty is often known as the Tuthmosid period, after the name of its principal rulers. Tuthmosis I (c. 1525–512 BC, although another reckoning would lower these dates by twenty-five years) was a warrior ruler, who took on the scattered principalities of Lebanon and Syria and carried his arms far beyond the Euphrates, setting up a victory stela on the banks of what the Egyptians described as the 'topsy-turvy' river, since it flowed the opposite way to the Nile. In retrospect, this is the beginning of something resembling an Egyptian empire in Asia, a subject which was to preoccupy foreign policy throughout the next two dynasties. However, retrospect is a one-way street, and contemporaries may have thought that one show of force was enough. It may equally be that the modern concept of empire is an anachronism

for the period; 'sphere of influence' might be a closer guide to Egyptian thinking. Tuthmosis I was followed by another Tuthmosis, a Pharaoh of whom little is known and arguably little worth knowing. However, he was married to Hatshepsut.

Hatshepsut was Tuthmosis II's half-sister (marriage to close relatives was not a problem in the Tuthmosid royal family, and this may explain the prominence given to queens in the early years of the dynasty; all were equally descended from the dynasty's heroic founder). However, it is likely that the king was worried about his wife's ambitions; her name, after all, meant 'Foremost of the noble ladies'. On his premature death (c. 1504 BC) he and Hatshepsut had produced only a daughter, Nefrure, and the official successor was Tuthmosis III, a young son by one of the king's minor wives. Clearly the boy was in need of a regent. His aunt thought herself qualified for the job; more importantly, she had convinced enough others of the same truth that she was able to stage a coup. She and Tuthmosis III were declared joint Pharaohs. There were precedents for this in earlier dynasties, and this may

have gone some way towards blurring the innovatory fact that one of the co-regents was not male. In a few early scenes she is shown dutifully following her partner, but this soon changes. This was to be a co-regency that was far from equal. For the next twenty-two years it would be 'goodnight from her, and goodnight from her'. The reign of Hatshepsut had begun, and her throne-name was Maatkare, 'Truth (a female principle which also embodies the ideas of justice and harmony) is the genius of the sun-god'.

There is a sense in which all history is about the meanings of words, and it is certainly true that to change history involves colliding with the language in which it is expressed. Hatshepsut does this. Traditional Pharaohs were the embodiment of the god Horus; Hatshepsut is also Horus, but the epithets she adds in hieroglyphs are grammatically in the feminine forms. Furthermore, she describes herself as 'The she-Horus of fine gold', fine gold (electrum) being an amalgam of this metal with the rarer and more valuable silver. It is as if she were to style herself the platinum goddess. Like other Pharaohs, she regularly refers to herself as 'His Majesty' (a closer rendering might be 'His Person'). However, the word for majesty is turned into a new feminine equivalent. One is reminded of Elizabeth I of England, with her doctrine of the dual body of the monarch, one of which happens to be female. Rewriting language in the light of gender is not a twentieth-century discovery. It did not work in ancient Egypt (and it might not work now), but the attempt was none the less made. The changes either originated with the queen, or were approved by her, and they must correspond with her thinking. In conven-

A touch of the exotic—the 'fat lady' of Punt and her husband—one of the observations of Hatshepsut's artists from the walls of her temple on the expedition sponsored by the queen in years 8-9 of her reign.

1. THE EARLIEST CIVILIZATIONS

tional temple scenes, where the icon of a traditional Pharaoh is necessary, she appears as a male ruler. In sculpture, on the other hand, she is shown as female but imperial, with the typical Tuthmosid face and arched profile. Her portraits are unmistakable.

A characteristic of Hatshepsut is her preoccupation with historical context. It is as if she is trying to define her own role in events, to justify her intervention on to the stage and to issue a challenge at the same time. In a deserted valley in Middle Egypt, in the eastern cliffs about 175 miles south of modern Cairo, is an unusual rock-cut temple known by its classical name of Speos Artemidos, the grotto of Artemis. The goddess in question was known to the Egyptians as Pakhet, an obscure deity with the attributes of a lioness. On the facade of this temple is a long dedication, put there by Hatshepsut and her artists, designed, as she tells us, to 'record the annals of her supremacy for ever'. In this text she announced the theme of her reign, which is no less than a complete rebuilding of the land of Egypt. Solar imagery abounds in the text, and Hatshepsut is described without any attempt at modesty as the one predestined since the moment of creation to restore the ritual purity of the temples, to recapture the perfection of the world's origins:

I raised up what was dismembered, even from the time when the Asiatics were in the midst of (the Delta), overthrowing what had been created. They ruled in ignorance of Re (the sun-god), and acted not by divine command, until my august person.

This is a reference both to the resurrection of the god Osiris and to the occupation of Egypt by the alien Hyksos, which had preceded the Eighteenth Dynasty: an episode which was shameful, but by no means as barbaric as Hatshepsut makes out. Nor did it last as long as she pretended. This combination of historical perspective and return to religious purity is characteristic of Hatshepsut. Since her position as Pharaoh was unorthodox, an appeal to fundamentalism was necessary to correct the balance. This may well have corresponded to her own thinking, and need not be merely cynical.

Determination to rewrite history is also seen in the official version of the queens proclamation and accession, where the choice of her as ruler is made, not by inheritance or acclamation, but by the oracle of the god Amun, leader of the

Egyptian pantheon and ruler of the royal city of Thebes. An oracle of this sort probably happened, since it is suspiciously convenient and could easily have been arranged by the queen's followers after her seizure of power. What

is more important is that the queen is cutting out any human medium, and going straight for an identification with the divine. As Pharaoh, she had this identification automatically, and there would normally be no need to labour the

Careful courtier: Senenmut, Hatshepsut's steward and one of the queen's closest advisers, shown here as a tutor cradling her daughter, the princess Nefrure.

point. Hatshepsut is not normal, and she labours the point for all it contains, here and in her other inscriptions. The platinum goddess can be seen as the Egyptian equivalent of Gloriana, the mythical transformation of Elizabeth I. This is a comparison to which we will return.

One feature of Hatshepsut's reign is often noted: the apparent lack of military activity. There is evidence for minor campaigns in Nubia, and the period is not a complete blank, but the frantic action of the previous reign is lacking. This is sometimes explained as a deliberate attempt by Hatshepsut to adopt a pacifist and feminine approach to politics. This is so completely out of line with what can be deduced about her character that it cannot convince. Female rulers can be as warlike as any man, especially if they feel that they have something to prove. A more likely reason is that Hatshepsut could not trust the army. If she led a campaign herself, even if this were politically acceptable, what would happen if she lost? A female commander would be the natural thing to blame for defeat. If the army won, it might start agitating for more victories, and for a greater role for the queen's nephew, who would gain status as he grew in years. The whole subject was best avoided, especially if Tuthmosis I had already made the point that Egypt was the leading power in Asia. Some things could be left as they were.

If the army could not be used on a large scale, an outlet must be found elsewhere. This is one of the purposes behind the famous expedition to the land of Punt, which occupied the eighth and ninth years of her reign. The location of Punt is unknown, though it may have been Eritrea or part of Somalia, or somewhere further south, but it was the home of the frankincense-tree. The adventure is recorded on the walls of the queen's masterpiece, the great temple in the cliffs of Deir el-Bahri in western Thebes, the modern Luxor. Exquisite reliefs show the departure of the expedition, the arrival at the exotic land beyond the sea, the lading of Hatshepsut's ships with the produce of Punt, and the preparations for the voyage home.

The event was not simply a foraging mission, since it was accompanied by artists to record the flora and fauna of the Red Sea and of the African coast. It can almost be described as the beginning of comparative anthropology, even if the climax—the appearance of the grossly overweight queen of Punt accompanied by a donkey—has an element of the ridiculous about it. Part of the expedition found its way back to Egypt by way of the upper Nile, while five shiploads, including incense-trees, returned by sea. Walter Raleigh would probably have enjoyed Punt, although the reasons for the voyage are not entirely clear. It may have been imperial prospecting, although this is unlikely at this early stage in the dynasty. Perhaps it was economic, an attempt to corner part of the lucrative incense-trade for Egypt. It was certainly an exercise for an underemployed army, and it was propaganda for the queen as provider of the exotic. Perhaps it was also fun.

The roots of the incense-trees can still be seen before the Deir el-Bahri temple, where they were planted and where they perfumed the night air. The temple has been excavated slowly over the past century (its scenes were first copied by a young draughtsman named Howard Carter), and its plan is now clear. No one who walks the path over the mountain from the Valley of the Kings and looks down at the other side can ignore the series of terraces below, built into the western cliffs. It is one of the most dramatic sights in Egypt. The variety of its scenes, all showing the slightly austere elegance that is common to Tuthmosid art, the balance between light and shade which is necessary in such an exposed site, and the originality of its design make the building unique. Perhaps to contemporaries it was too unique; certainly the concept was never recreated. Manuals of classical architecture tell us that the Doric column was developed in Greece around the seventh century BC. The north colonnade of Deir el-Bahri was composed of them, eight centuries earlier.

Part of the temple was devoted to the divine birth of Hatshepsut, another piece of mythology which normal Pharaohs did not need to use. The god Amun himself desired to create his living image on earth, to reveal his greatness and to carry out his plans. He disguised himself as Tuthmosis I, went one day to see the queen, and the result, in due course, was Hatshepsut. Amun did not mind that his image was female, so why should anyone else?

Similar themes are explored in a rather strange medium, an inscribed pair of granite obelisks which the queen set up in her sixteenth year before the temple of Amun at Karnak opposite Deir el-Bahri. The entire work, she tells us, took seven months. Obelisks in Egyptian thinking were a representation of the first ray of light which inaugurated the creation, or what we would now call the Big Bang. In the text Hatshepsut knows the mind of God: she was present with the creator at the beginning, she is the luminous seed of the almighty one, and she is 'the fine gold of kings'—another reference to electrum. This metal was even used to coat the obelisks, to make her splendour visible. Her sense of posterity, and the force of her personality, are clear from the words she uses:

> Those who shall see my monument in future years, and shall speak of what I have done, beware of saying, 'I know not, I know not how this has been done, fashioning a mountain of gold throughout, like something of nature' . . . Nor shall he who hears this say it was a boast, but rather, 'How like her this is, how worthy of her father'.

She also tells us that her obelisks were situated by the gateway of Tuthmosis I, since it was he who began the obelisk habit. This preoccupation with the father is not accidental. Pharaoh was Pharaoh because his father had been Pharaoh; in Egyptian mythology, he was Horus to his predecessor's Osiris, one god ruling on earth while the other reigned over the netherworld. However, this was conventional, and orthodox Pharaohs did not need to make it explicit. Hatshepsut, the female Horus, was not orthodox. Her kingship depended on mythological props, and also on political ones; in fact, she would not have made a distinction between the two. But there may well be a third element at work, a personal one.

Tuthmosis I is prominent in many of her inscriptions, far more than is necessary. His sarcophagus was even discovered in his daughter's tomb, where it had been transferred from his own. Clearly she intended to spend eternity with the man who had been her father on earth. She left her husband, Tuthmosis II, where he was lying in the Valley of the Kings, and her inscriptions never mention him, even though he was presumably the parent of her child. This is a trait which prominent females sometimes show. Anna Freud turned herself into Sigmund's intellectual heir, Benazir Bhutto makes a political platform out of her father's memory, and one is reminded of a recent British prime minister whose entry in *Who's Who* included a father but no mother. Did Tuthmosis I ever call his daughter 'the best man in the dynasty', and is this why Hatshepsut shows no identification with other women? This is not entirely hypothetical: among Hatshepsut's inscriptions is an imaginative reworking of an episode when she was young, in which her father proclaims her his heir before the entire palace. Such a text could have been based on a coming-of-age ceremony, or even a chance remark to an impressionable child.

Hatshepsut was determined to hold on to power, and the way she achieved this is clear. After the gradual disappearance of her father's advisers, almost all her supporters are new men (women she could not have appointed, even if she had had a mind to). They owed nothing to the traditional aristocracy, little to conventional patronage: they were 'one of us'. They were hers, and if she fell, they would fall also. Their tombs are still visible in the cliffs above Deir el-Bahri. They are easily distinguished by the terraced effect of their facades, which resemble the royal temple; even in their architecture they showed whose men they were. This must have been a court where many lesser lights danced attendance on the sun-queen.

The most prominent courtier of Hatshepsut's reign is Senenmut. He dominates the temple of Deir el-Bahri, where he seems to be an overall but ill-defined master of works. His figure even appears in small niches in some of its chapels, worshipping the god Amun and his royal mistress. These niches are hidden behind the doors, but the gods would have known what was in them, and so probably did Hatshepsut. This must have been done with her approval. Senenmut's place in the royal household is confirmed by his position as tutor to the queen's daughter Nefrure, and statues survive showing Senenmut crouching in the

guise of a patient client, while the head of the royal infant peeps out from between his knees. Senenmut was given permission to be buried within the precincts of the great temple, an unprecedented honour.

Around the seventh year of the reign Senenmut's mother died, and she too was interred in the temple. Senenmut exhumed the body of his father at the same time, and reburied him in splendour alongside her and other members of his family. The father had no title (otherwise the Egyptians, who were obsessed with titles, would not have failed to mention it), and his original burial was tantamount to a pauper's. Senenmut must have come from a small town along the Nile, and rose to prominence entirely through merit and the queen's patronage. This sheds unexpected light on what could happen in ancient Egypt. Senenmut seems never to have married. Perhaps he did not dare to; did not Walter Raleigh fall from grace as soon as he married one of Gloriana's maids?

Recently evidence has emerged that the reign of Hatshepsut could inspire distinctly tabloid reactions. Some years ago, in an unfinished tomb above the Deir el-Bahri temple, a series of graffiti were found. One of these is a feeble drawing of Senenmut, but on another wall there is a sketch showing a female Pharaoh undergoing the attentions of a male figure, in a way that implies her passive submission. This may be a contemporary comment on the relationship between Senenmut and the queen, or it may be a later satire on the notion of an impotent female Pharaoh, or it may simply be the fantasy of a little man for something he could never attain, rather on the lines of the stories which later circulated about Cleopatra or Catherine the Great. If the scene is genuine, it is extremely interesting, even if its meaning is less explicit than its drawing.

The queen died on the tenth day of the sixth month of the twenty-second year of her reign (early February 1482 BC). She was perhaps fifty. Tuthmosis III, so long cooped up, became sole Pharaoh and immediately led his army into Syria, where in seventeen campaigns he restored Egyptian overlordship of the Near East. At some point, though not for some years, he began a proscription of his aunt's memory. Probably he chose to wait until Senenmut and her other supporters had passed away. Perhaps he remained in awe of her. Her inscriptions were erased, her obelisks surrounded by a wall, and her monuments forgotten. Her name does not appear in later annals, which is why we refer to Tuthmosis by a Greek transcription, while hers is missing. The bodies of many of the New Kingdom Pharaohs survive, and are now in the Cairo Museum. As far as we know, hers is not among them. What we do know about her has been gained by excavation and careful epigraphy over the past hundred years. Perhaps this is as it should be, since the late twentieth century is a better time than most to think about the meaning of her reign. Will the feminist movement rediscover her, or will she be uncomfortable for us, as she was for some of her contemporaries?

FOR FURTHER READING:

Cambridge Ancient History (3 edn., vol. II, 1973, ch.9); Peter F. Dorman, *The Monuments of Senenmut* (Kegan Paul International, 1988); Miriam Lichtheim, *Ancient Egyptian Literature II* (California, 1976); Donald B. Redford, *History and Chronology of the Eighteenth Dynasty of Egypt* (Toronto, 1967) and the same author's *Egypt, Canaan, and Israel in Ancient Times* (Princeton, 1992); John Romer, *Romer's Egypt* (Rainbird, 1982); Edward F. Wente, 'Some Graffiti from the Reign of Hatshepsut', *Journal of Near Eastern Studies 43* (1984).

Grisly Assyrian Record of Torture and Death

Erika Bleibtreu

Assyrian national history, as it has been preserved for us in inscriptions and pictures, consists almost solely of military campaigns and battles. It is as gory and bloodcurdling a history as we know.

Assyria emerged as a territorial state in the 14th century B.C. Its territory covered approximately the northern part of modern Iraq. The first capital of Assyria was Assur, located about 150 miles north of modern Baghdad on the west bank of the Tigris River. The city was named for its national god, Assur, from which the name Assyria is also derived.

From the outset, Assyria projected itself as a strong military power bent on conquest. Countries and peoples that opposed Assyrian rule were punished by the destruction of their cites and the devastation of their fields and orchards.

By the ninth century B.C., Assyria had consolidated its hegemony over northern Mesopotamia. It was then that Assyrian armies marched beyond their own borders to expand their empire, seeking booty to finance their plans for still more conquest and power. By the mid-ninth century B.C., the Assyrian menace posed a direct threat to the small Syro-Palestine states to the west, including Israel and Judah.

The period from the ninth century to the end of the seventh century B.C. is known as the Neo-Assyrian period, during which the empire reached its zenith. The Babylonian destruction of their capital city Nineveh in 612 B.C. marks the end of the Neo-Assyrian empire, although a last Assyrian king, Ashur-uballit II, attempted to rescue the rest of the Assyrian state, by then only a small territory around Harran. However, the Babylonian king Nabopolassar (625–605 B.C.) invaded Harran in 610 B.C. and conquered it. In the following year, a

final attempt was made by Ashur-uballit II to regain Harran with the help of troops from Egypt, but he did not succeed. Thereafter, Assyria disappears from history.

We will focus here principally on the records of seven Neo-Assyrian kings, most of whom ruled successively. Because the kings left behind pictorial, as well as written, records, our knowledge of their military activities is unusually well documented:

1. Ashurnasirpal II—883–859 B.C.
2. Shalmaneser III—858–824 B.C.
3. Tiglath-pileser III—744–727 B.C.
4. Sargon II—721–705 B.C.
5. Sennacherib—704–681 B.C.
6. Esarhaddon—680–669 B.C.
7. Ashurbanipal—668–627 B.C.

Incidentally, Assyrian records, as well as the Bible, mention the military contracts between the Neo-Assyrian empire and the small states of Israel and Judah.

An inscription of Shalmaneser III records a clash between his army and a coalition of enemies that included Ahab, king of Israel (c. 859–853 B.C.). Indeed, Ahab, according to Shalmaneser, mustered more chariots (2,000) than any of the other allies arrayed against the Assyrian ruler at the battle of Qarqar on the Orontes (853 B.C.). For a time, at least, the Assyrian advance was checked.

An inscription on a stela from Tell al Rimah in northern Iraq, erected in 806 B.C. by Assyrian king Adad-nirari III, informs us that Jehoahaz, king of Israel (814–793 B.C.), paid tribute to the Assyrian king: "He [Adad-nirari III of Assyria] received the tribute of Ia'asu the Samarian [Jehcahaz, king of Israel], of the Tyrian (ruler) and the Sidonian (ruler)."[1]

From the inscriptions of Tiglath-pileser III and from some representations on the reliefs that decorated the walls of his palace at Nimrud, we learn that he too conducted a military campaign to the

west and invaded Israel. Tiglath-pileser III received tribute from Menahem of Samaria (744–738 B.C.), as the Bible tells us; the Assyrian king is there called Pulu (2 Kings 15:19–20).

In another episode recorded in the Bible, Pekah, king of Israel (737–732 B.C.), joined forces with Rezin of Damascus against King Ahaz of Judah (2 Kings 16:5–10). The Assyrian king Tiglath-pileser III successfully intervened against Pekah, who was then deposed. The Assyrian king then placed Hoshea on the Israelite throne. By then Israel's northern provinces were devastated and part of her population was deported to Assyria (2 Kings 15:29).

At one point, Israel, already but a shadow of its former self and crushed by the burden of the annual tribute to Assyria, decided to revolt. Shalmaneser V (726–722 B.C.), who reigned after Tiglath-pileser III, marched into Israel, besieged its capital at Samaria and, after three years of fighting, destroyed it (2 Kings 18:10). This probably occurred in the last year of Shalmaneser V's reign (722 B.C.). However, his successor, Sargon II, later claimed credit for the victory. In any event, this defeat ended the national identity of the northern kingdom of Israel. Sargon II deported, according to his own records, 27,290 Israelites, settling them, according to the Bible, near Harran on the Habur River and in the mountains of eastern Assyria (2 Kings 17:6, 18:11).

Later, in 701 B.C., when King Hezekiah of Judah withheld Assyrian tribute, Sargon II's successor, Sennacherib, marched into Judah, destroying, according to his claim, 46 cities and besieging Jerusalem. Although Sennacherib failed to capture Jerusalem (2 Kings 19:32–36), Hezekiah no doubt continued to pay tribute to Assyria.

The two principal tasks of an Assyrian king were to engage in military exploits and to erect public buildings. Both of these tasks were regarded as religious duties. They were, in effect, acts of obedience toward the principal gods of Assyria.

The historical records of ancient Assyria consist of tablets, prisms and cylinders of clay and alabaster. They bear inscriptions in cuneiform—wedge-shaped impressions representing, for the most part, syllables. In addition, we have inscribed obelisks and stelae as well as inscriptions on stone slabs that lined the walls and covered the floors of Assyrian palaces and temples.

In all of these inscriptions, the king stands at the top of the hierarchy—the most powerful person; he himself represents the state. All public acts are recorded as his achievements. All acts worthy of being recorded are attributed only to the Assyrian king, the focus of the ancient world.

The annals of the kings describe not only their military exploits, but also their building activities. This suggests that the spoil and booty taken during the military campaigns formed the financial foundation for the building activities of palaces, temples, canals and other public structures. The booty—property and people—probably provided not only precious building materials, but also artists and workmen deported from conquered territories.

The inscriptional records are vividly supplemented by pictorial representations. These include reliefs on bronze bands that decorated important gates, reliefs carved on obelisks and some engravings on cylinder seals. But the largest and most informative group of monuments are the reliefs sculpted into the stone slabs that lined the palaces' walls in the empire's capital cities—Nimrud (ancient Kalah), Khorsabad (ancient Dur Sharrukin) and Kuyunjik (ancient Nineveh).

According to the narrative representations on these reliefs, the Assyrians never lost a battle. Indeed, no Assyrian soldier is ever shown wounded or killed. The benevolence of the gods is always bestowed on the Assyrian king and his troops.

Like the official written records, the scenes and figures are selected and arranged to record the kings' heroic deeds and to describe him as "beloved of the gods":

"The king, who acts with the support of the great gods his lords and has conquered all lands, gained dominion over all highlands and received their tribute, captures of hostages, he who is victorious over all countries."[2]

The inscriptions and the pictorial evidence both provide detailed information regarding the Assyrian treatment of conquered peoples, their armies and their rulers. In his official royal inscriptions, Ashurnasirpal II calls himself the "trampler of all enemies . . . who defeated all his enemies [and] hung the corpses of his enemies on posts."[3] The treatment of captured enemies often depended on their readiness to submit themselves to the will of the Assyrian king:

"The nobles [and] elders of the city came out to me to save their lives. They seized my feet and said: 'If it pleases you, kill! If it pleases you, spare! If it pleases you, do what you will!' "[4]

In one case when a city resisted as long as possible instead of immediately submitting, Ashurnasirpal proudly records his punishment:

"I flayed as many nobles as had rebelled against me [and] draped their skins over the pile [of corpses]; some I spread out within the pile, some I erected on stakes upon the pile . . . I flayed many right through my land [and] draped their skins over the walls."[5]

The account was probably intended not only to describe what had happened, but also to frighten anyone who might dare to resist. To suppress his enemies was the king's divine task. Supported by the gods, he always had to be victorious in battle and to punish disobedient people:

"I felled 50 of their fighting men with the sword, burnt 200 captives from them, [and] defeated in a battle on the plain 332 troops. . . . With their blood I dyed the mountain red like red wool, [and] the rest of them the ravines [and] torrents of the mountain swallowed. I carried off captives [and] possessions from them. I cut off the heads of their fighters [and] built [therewith] a tower before their city. I burnt their adolescent boys [and] girls."[6]

A description of another conquest is even worse:

"In strife and conflict I besieged [and] conquered the city. I felled 3,000 of their fighting men with the sword . . . I captured many troops alive: I cut off

of some their arms [and] hands; I cut off of others their noses, ears, [and] extremities. I gouged out the eyes of many troops. I made one pile of the living [and] one of heads. I hung their heads on trees around the city."[7]

The palace of Ashurnasirpal II at Nimrud is the first, so far as we know, in which carved stone slabs were used in addition to the usual wall paintings. These carvings portray many of the scenes described in words in the annals.

From the reign of Shalmaneser III, Ashurnasirpal II's son, we also have some bronze bands that decorated a massive pair of wooden gates of a temple (and possibly a palace) at Balawat, near modern Mosul. These bronze bands display unusually fine examples of bronze repoussé (a relief created by hammering on the opposite side). In a detail, we see an Assyrian soldier grasping the hand and arm of a captured enemy whose other hand and both feet have already been cut off. Dismembered hands and feet fly through the scene. Severed enemy heads hang from the conquered city's walls. Another captive is impaled on a stake, his hands and feet already having been cut off. In another detail, we see three stakes, each driven through eight severed heads, set up outside the conquered city. A third detail shows a row of impaled captives lined up on stakes set up on a hill outside the captured city. In an inscription from Shalmaneser III's father, Ashurnasirpal II, the latter tells us, "I captured soldiers alive [and] erected [them] on stakes before their cities."[8]

Shalmaneser III's written records supplement his pictorial archive: "I filled the wide plain with the corpses of his warriors. . . . These [rebels] I impaled on stakes.[9] . . . A pyramid (pillar) of heads I erected in front of the city."[10]

In the eighth century B.C., Tiglath-pileser III held center stage. Of one city he conquered, he says:

"Nabû-ushabshi, their king, I hung up in front of the gate of his city on a stake. His land, his wife, his sons, his daughters, his property, the treasure of his palace, I carried off. Bit-Amukâni, I trampled down like a threshing (sledge). All of its people, (and) its goods, I took to Assyria."[11]

Such actions are illustrated several times in the reliefs at Tiglath-pileser's palace at Nimrud. These reliefs display an individual style in the execution of details that is of special importance in tracing the development of military techniques.

Perhaps realizing what defeat meant, a king of Urartu, threatened by Sargon II, committed suicide: "The splendor of Assur, my lord, overwhelmed him [the king of Urartu] and with his own iron dagger he stabbed himself through the heart, like a pig, and ended his life."[12]

Sargon II started a new Assyrian dynasty that lasted to the end of the empire. Sargon built a new capital named after himself—Dur Sharrukin, meaning "Stronghold of the righteous king." His palace walls were decorated with especially large stone slabs, carved with extraordinarily large figures.

Sargon's son and successor, Sennacherib, again moved the Assyrian capital, this time to Nineveh, where he built his own palace. According to the excavator of Ninneveh, Austen Henry Layard, the reliefs in Sennacherib's palace, if lined up in a row, would stretch almost two miles. If anything, Sennacherib surpassed his predecessors in the grisly detail of his descriptions:

"I cut their throats like lambs. I cut off their precious lives (as one cuts) a string. Like the many waters of a storm, I made (the contents of) their gullets and entrails run down upon the wide earth. My prancing steeds harnessed for my riding, plunged into the streams of their blood as (into) a river. The wheels of my war chariot, which brings low the wicked and the evil, were bespattered with blood and filth. With the bodies of their warriors I filled the plain, like grass. (Their) testicles I cut off, and tore out their privates like the seeds of cucumbers."[13]

In several rooms of Sennacherib's Southwest Palace at Nineveh, severed heads are represented; deportation scenes are frequently depicted. Among the deportees depicted, there are long lines of prisoners from the Judahite city of Lac-hish; they are shown pulling a rope fastened to a colossal entrance figure for Sennacherib's palace at Nineveh; above this line of deportees is an overseer whose hand holds a truncheon.

Sennacherib was murdered by his own sons. Another son, Esarhaddon, became his successor. As the following examples show, Esarhaddon treated his enemies just as his father and grandfather had treated theirs: "Like a fish I caught him up out of the sea and cut off his head,"[14] he said of the king of Sidon; "Their blood, like a broken dam, I caused to flow down the mountain gullies";[15] and "I hung the heads of Sanduarri [king of the cities of Kundi and Sizu] and Abdimilkutti [king of Sidon] on the shoulders of their nobles and with singing and music I paraded through the public square of Nineveh."[16]

Ashurbanipal, Esarhaddon's son, boasted:

"Their dismembered bodies I fed to the dogs, swine, wolves, and eagles, to the birds of heaven and the fish in the deep. . . . What was left of the feast of the dogs and swine, of their members which blocked the streets and filled the squares, I ordered them to remove from Babylon, Kutha and Sippar, and to cast them upon heaps."[17]

When Ashurbanipal didn't kill his captives he "pierced the lips (and) took them to Assyria as a spectacle for the people of my land."[18]

The enemy to the southeast of Assyria, the people of Elam, underwent a special punishment that did not spare even their dead:

"The sepulchers of their earlier and later kings, who did not fear Assur and Ishtar, my lords, (and who) had plagued the kings, my fathers, I destroyed, I devastated, I exposed to the sun. Their bones (members) I carried off to Assyria. I laid restlessness upon their shades. I deprived them of food-offerings and libations of water."[19]

Among the reliefs carved by Ashsurbanipal were pictures of the mass deportation of the Elamites, together with severed heads assembled in heaps. Two Elamites are seen fastened to the ground while their skin is flayed, while others are having their tongues pulled out.

There is no reason to doubt the historical accuracy of these portrayals and descriptions. Such punishments no doubt helped to secure the payment of tribute—silver, gold, tin, copper, bronze, and iron, as well as building materials including wood, all of which was necessary for the economic survival of the Assyrian empire.

In our day, these depictions, verbal and visual, give a new reality to the Assyrian conquest of the northern kingdom of Israel in 721 B.C. and to Sennacherib's subsequent campaign into Judah in 701 B.C.

NOTES

1. Stephanie Page, "A Stela of Adad-nirari III and Nergal-eres from Tell al Rimah," *Iraq* 30 (1968), p. 143.

2. Albert Kirk Grayson, *Assyrian Royal Inscriptions,* Part 2: *From Tiglath-pileser I to Ashur-nasir-apli II* (Wiesbaden, Germ.: Otto Harrassowitz, 1976), p. 165.

3. Ibid., p. 120.

4. Ibid., p. 124.

5. Ibid.

6. Ibid., pp. 126–127.

7. Ibid., p. 126.

8. Ibid., p. 143.

9. Daniel David Luckenbill, *Ancient Records of Assyria and Babylonia,* 2 vols. (Chicago: Univ. of Chicago Press, 1926–1927), vol. 1, secs. 584–585.

10. Ibid., vol. 1, sec. 599.

11. Ibid., vol. 1, sec. 783.

12. Ibid., vol. 2, sec. 22.

13. Ibid., vol. 2, sec. 254.

14. Ibid., vol. 2, sec. 511.

15. Ibid., vol. 2, sec. 521.

16. Ibid., vol. 2, sec. 528.

17. Ibid., vol. 2, secs. 795–796.

18. Ibid., vol. 2, sec. 800.

19. Ibid., vol. 2, sec. 810.

Early Civilizations and the Natural Environment

J. Donald Hughes

J. Donald Hughes holds a Ph.D. in history from Boston University and has taught ancient history at the University of Denver since 1967.

Cities, temples, palaces, and tombs of once-flourishing societies now lie in ruins throughout the Middle East. Here people first developed high civilizations, and here, in a particularly telling way, the surviving evidence shows that the course of history is not always that of upward human progress. The rise of civilizations depended upon the increasing ability of people to use and control their natural environment, and the downfall of these same civilizations was due to their failure to maintain a harmonious balance with nature. They suffered a true ecological disaster: not simply a change in climate—for people have weathered climatic changes before and prospered—but a disaster of their own making. This chapter will examine the successes and failures of the Mesopotamians and Egyptians in their relationships to the ecosystems in which they lived.

Mesopotamia, the broad plain of the Euphrates and Tigris rivers, borders the Mediterranean Basin on the east, and at one point north of Antioch in modern Turkey, the Euphrates comes within 90 miles of the Mediterranean coast. But the climate of Mesopotamia is very dry, with an annual rainfall of only six to eight inches. Summer temperatures of 120 degrees in the shade are not uncommon, and 137 degrees has been recorded. Most life in Mesopotamia is dependent on the water brought down from the mountains by the two rivers. The twin rivers begin in the snows of the Armenian mountains, which reach an elevation of almost seventeen thousand feet at Mount Ararat, and flow down into the head of the

Persian Gulf, a distance of 1150 miles for the Tigris and 1780 miles for the more circuitous Euphrates. A major tributary stream, the Karun, flows down from the Persian mountains. The plain is an alluvial deposit of sand and silt brought down by the rivers in past geological times, and the process is still going on. This undoubted fact once caused historians to believe that at the time of the earliest civilizations in Mesopotamia, the Persian Gulf extended much further northwest, providing Sumerian cities with a seacoast, and many maps in ancient history textbooks show it that way. But careful studies by geologists in the area have shown that in spite of the sediment still being brought down by the rivers, the land area in the delta region has not increased, because lower Mesopotamia has been undergoing periods of geological subsidence.[1] The coastline today, with minor variations, is in about the same position as it was 5,000 years ago.

The world's first cities, which arose in Mesopotamia and nearby, were made possible by a changed relationship between human beings and the environment, based on a new agriculture using two important inventions: systematic irrigation and the plow. The fertile, sandy, easily turned Mesopotamian soil made the plow useful. The rivers provided the essential water, but with a flow so undependable that control by major irrigation works was demanded. The new agriculture enabled a much larger human population to live in a given area, and an increasing portion of the population, freed from the need to work the soil, could take up specialized occupations.

The earliest cities seem to have shared some of the problems which have become so annoying in their modern counterparts. Babylon, in its day the largest city of the area, had a city wall ten miles long, and even including its suburbs was consequently only of moderate size by

modern standards. The evidence of narrow streets and small rooms in houses huddled within the compass of defensible walls tells us that crowding in ancient cities was extreme. Garbage accumulated in the houses, where the dirt floors were continually being raised by the debris, and human wastes were rarely carried further than the nearest street. The water supply, from wells, rivers, and canals, was likely to be polluted. Life expectancy was short, due in part to the high infant mortality. Flies, rodents, and cockroaches were constant pests. Even air pollution was not absent. In addition to dust and offensive odors, the atmosphere filled with smoke on calm days. Even today, in large preindustrial cities such as Calcutta the smoke of thousands of individual cooking fires, in addition to other human activities, produces a definite pall of smoke and dust which seldom dissipates for long. Under these unhealthy conditions, the death rate must have been high in Mesopotamian cities.

As an alluvial land, the Mesopotamian plain had no stone or deposits of metallic ore, and these had to be brought in from the mountains or imported from other countries. While this encouraged the early development of trade, it also meant that the inhabitants had to use the native materials, swamp reeds and clay, for ordinary construction. They built mighty works of baked and unbaked clay bricks—temples, shrines raised on lofty ziggurats, palaces, and walled cities—but the system of canals and other irrigation works is their most remarkable achievement. Incidentally, it is interesting to note that petroleum, the most important natural resource of modern Iraq, did not escape their notice. They used the oil which oozed forth in some places as fuel for their lamps and bitumen for waterproofing their boats.

The attitude of the peoples of Mesopotamia toward nature, from early Sum-

From *Ecology in Ancient Civilizations* by J. Donald Hughes, Chapter 4, pp. 29-42. Published by the University of New Mexico Press, 1975. © 1975 by J. Donald Hughes. Reprinted by permission of the author.

erian writings down through the Akkadian and Assyrian literatures, is marked by a strong feeling of battle. Nature herself was represented in Mesopotamian mythology as monstrous chaos, and it was only by the constant labors of people and their patron gods that chaos could be overcome and order established. Mesopotamian gods, though they retained their earlier character as nature deities to some extent, were primarily figures which sanctioned order, guarded the cities, upheld government and society, and encouraged the construction of works which would reproduce on earth the regularity of heaven. The order of heaven was quite apparent to the Mesopotamians, who developed both astrology and astronomy to a high degree and noticed that the motions of the moon and sun, stars and planets are constant and predictable. The labors of the Mesopotamian hero-god Enlil, or Marduk, in slaying the primeval monster of chaos, Tiamat, and creating the world out of her sundered body, reflected the labors of the Mesopotamians themselves, who built islands in the swamps, raised their cities above the flood plains, and irrigated desert stretches with an orderly series of well-maintained canals. They planned their cities so that the major streets of Babylon, for example, crossed each other at right angles in a regular grid pattern, and they laid out their canals in the same way wherever possible. Left to itself, Mesopotamia would have remained a land at the mercy of the capricious river and the merciless sun, in a precarious, shifting balance between tangled marsh and parched desert. But careful works of irrigation conquered sections of that land and won rich sustenance from its basic fertility. Thus a Mesopotamian king could list the construction of a new canal, along with the defeat of his enemies in battle, as the major events of a year of his reign.

Mesopotamians had a well-developed sense of the distinction between the tame and the wild, between civilization and wilderness. The proper effort of mankind toward wild things, they believed, is to domesticate them. They did this with such native animals as the donkey and the water buffalo, in addition to keeping the cows, pigs, sheep, and goats already known to their ancestors. They learned the uses of the palm tree and planted it widely. Animals which could not be truly domesticated were hunted—some, like the lion, to extinction. In the Epic of

Gilgamesh, Enkidu was presented as a man of the wild, a friend and protector of beasts. But when he had been tamed by womanly wiles, his former animal friends feared and fled from him. One of the great feats of Gilgamesh and his now-tamed companion was the slaying of Humbaba, the wild protector of the cedar forests in the west, and the seal set upon the defeat of Humbaba was the subjugation of the wilderness; the trees were felled for human use. This ancient legend described an actual ecological event; the cedars of Lebanon, after centuries of exploitation and export to all the surrounding lands, were completely destroyed except for a few small groves, leaving their mountain slopes open to severe erosion.

The Mesopotamians also displayed curiosity toward and interest in the natural environment. They compiled many lists, which survive on clay tablets, of animals, plants, and minerals. These might be regarded as a step toward genuine scientific classification. However, the lists always classify natural things on the basis of the uses to which they were put by man. Mesopotamian thought was intensely practical and anthropocentric. This principle was illustrated in a Sumerian legend which told how the god Ninurta fought a war in which some stones helped him and others opposed him. Ninurta rewarded the former by making them jewels and semiprecious stones, while the latter he punished by making them into paving stones and thresholds, trodden under foot by people.

The Mesopotamian fondness for building high ziggurats and towers has been seen as a compensation for the flatness of the land by people who had moved in from hilly regions and longed for the forests and mountains of their former homes. This motive might have been felt by the first generation or two of invaders in the country, who came from the mountains, and the persistence of the same forms among their descendants could be explained by the almost universal conservatism of religious architecture. The mountainlike appearance of ziggurats and palaces in Mesopotamia was undoubtedly emphasized by the trees, shrubs, and vines which were planted on them. Archaeologists have noticed that ziggurats were provided with interior channels to drain the water which seeped down from the carefully watered plants on top. So striking were they in appearance that they were among the wonders

of the ancient world, the Hanging Gardens of Babylon. Kings enjoyed collecting plants and animals from distant parts of the world to add interest to their gardens, which became botanical and zoological parks as a result. Some things discovered in this way may well have been adapted to agriculture; perhaps the grapevine and olive tree first came to Mesopotamia as gifts of specimens to a royal garden. Domestication seems to have been a key idea in royal collecting. One king had a pet lion who was supposed to have fought beside him in battle against his enemies.

The cities of Mesopotamia have been desolate mounds for a score of centuries, and only a poor remnant of the "Fertile Crescent," that green, cultivated area which once arched across the Middle East from Sumeria to Palestine, is visible in photographs taken from space today. This disaster is due not simply to changing climate or the devastating influences of war, though both of these have had important effects. It is a true ecological disaster, due partly to the difficulty of maintaining the canals and keeping them free of silt, but more importantly to the accumulation of salt in the soil. Irrigation water, carried over large areas, was allowed to evaporate with insufficient drainage, and over the centuries in this land of low humidity and scanty rain, the salts carried in by the water concentrated. Such areas had to be abandoned, while new sections were brought under irrigation and cultivation until they in turn suffered the same salinization. A similar process occurs in many places where deserts have been irrigated, as in the Imperial Valley of California today, where the best efforts of modern technology have barely been able to combat it. Salt would not have accumulated in well-drained soil, but in Mesopotamia the problem of drainage was especially difficult. Silt and mud carried by the rivers and canals settled out rapidly, so that constant dredging was necessary to keep the canals flowing. Excavated mud piled up along the sides of the canals to a height of thirty feet or more, serving as a barrier to drainage. Eventually the river level was raised well above the surrounding country. The natural remedy to this, flooding and a major shift in the course of the rivers, was catastrophic whenever it happened.

It is significant that the first urban societies were also the first societies to abandon a religious attitude of oneness with nature and to adopt one of separation. The dominant myth and reality in Mesopotamia was the conquest of chaotic nature by divine-human order. Such societies, it must be noted, were ultimately unsuccessful in maintaining a balance with their natural environment.

Far to the east of Mesopotamia, but in contact with it, another civilization flourished in the Indus River Valley. It is mentioned here because many scholars say that it fell because of mistreatment of its fragile semidesert environment. While Mesopotamian cities were built largely of sun-dried clay bricks, the Indus Valley cities used baked bricks almost exclusively, and great quantities of wood were required to fire them. This, combined with other uses of wood, produced widespread deforestation, while grazing of cattle, goats, and sheep further reduced the vegetative cover. The results included desiccation, flooding, and erosion. Some authors also theorize that the dust blown from the dried, denuded land produced a permanent layer of dusty haze in the atmosphere over the Indus Valley, which actually altered the climate by causing a temperature gradient that shifted the monsoon rains to the east, out of the area, and also caused premature seeding of the clouds which did develop in the area, further reducing the rainfall. Other scholars postulate a series of disastrous floods, which could also have been caused by deforestation.

The attitude of the Indus Valley people toward nature is virtually unknown. They did represent animals on their stamp seals, but their language has not yet been deciphered. Whatever their attitude, their practices may have made them a prime early example of the principle that human societies which fail to live in harmony with the natural environment eventually disappear or change beyond recognition.

Without the Nile River, Egypt would be part of the Sahara Desert. The facts of Egypt's climate speak for themselves. The average annual rainfall at Cairo is one inch, and southward in Upper Egypt there may be one shower every two or three years. The average temperatures are typical of the desert belt; in the valley they vary from about 50 degrees to 110 degrees on the average, while on the adjoining desert the range is even more extreme, varying from below freezing to above 120 degrees.

The Nile is the world's longest river. Rising in the mountains of Ethiopia and the lakes of East Africa, it flows northward through the swamps of the southern Sudan and then begins its course as an exotic river in the desert. Its total length is thirty-five hundred miles. Spring and summer rains on the headwaters of the Blue Nile and its tributaries, which always occurred at the same time of the year, reaching their height in September, fed the annual floods of the Nile, which brought both moisture and new alluvial soil to the fields of Egypt and were one of the major environmental influences in that country. During flood stage, the Nile usually carried fifty times as much water as at its lowest stage.

The contrast between the land watered by the Nile and the desert which borders it is abrupt and extreme. The ancient Egyptians recognized this, dividing the earth into two parts, the fertile black land of Egypt and the dry red land of the hostile desert. The black land, in turn, had two major divisions, the long, narrow strip of Upper Egypt, from one to thirteen miles wide, often guarded by high cliffs, and the broad delta of Lower Egypt, containing two-thirds of the arable land of the country.

In very ancient times, much of the black land was covered by marshes which supported an amazing variety of plant and animal life, including millions of water birds in the Biblical "land of whirring wings."[2] The Egyptian crocodile and hippopotamus are only the best known of the vast assemblage of wild animals. The marshes also provided the papyrus reed, subject to many uses, including the manufacture of paper.

The agricultural civilization of Egypt depended on harnessing the Nile's annual flood and distributing its waters and its fertile load of silt through the fields by a series of canals and basins with the use of the shadoof, a simple water-lifting machine consisting of a bucket with an arm and counterweight attached. The Nile's flood was regular and predictable, although its height varied from year to year, a very low Nile producing drought and famine and a very high Nile devastating the works of man and even eroding the soil. Still, most years brought a moderate, useful flood.

Egyptian attitudes toward nature reflect the dependable periodicity of their natural environment. Their gods were deities of nature, intimately sharing the characteristics of the animals and plants which were their attributes. Ra, the sun god, was worshiped beyond the others. His movements were regular, and all nature responded to them. When he rose, day came and life flourished, and when he set, the Egyptians associated the failing light with death, but a new dawn inevitably followed. The Egyptians calculated the solar year of 365 days, and noticed that the Nile's flood depended on the sun's cycle. Another major god, Osiris, represented the dying and rising vegetation, intimately associated with the Nile and the sun. All Egyptian gods represented aspects of the natural world, and most of them were conceived as friendly to mankind.

In the temples and sacred precincts, the Egyptians protected animals and plants which embodied the presence of gods, and often gave them divine honors. For example, crocodiles sacred to the god Sebak were kept in the lake at Shedet, fed with offerings, and even decorated with jewelry. Other animals were generally venerated throughout Egypt, such as the cat of Bubastis and the ibis of Thoth. To the Egyptians, all nature was animate and filled with gods. In the paintings, sculpture, and objects of daily life made by them, an artistic joy in nature can be sensed. Their hieroglyphics include many animals, birds, and plants, often represented with great attention to natural detail. Columns bore capitals representing the lotus and papyrus plants. Egyptian poems enumerate and glorify the appearance and workings of the natural world.

All beasts are content with their
  pasturage;
Trees and plants are flourishing.
The birds which fly from their nests,
Their wings are stretched out in praise
  to thy spirit.[3]

This poem comes from the time of Ikhnaton the montheist, when art and literature emphasized the natural, but the Amarna period (named after Ikhnaton's residence city) in this respect simply reasserted a tendency which was present in Egypt from the earliest surviving evidence.

Thus it is not surprising to discover that well-to-do Egyptians loved gardens, that they planned them carefully with symmetrical beds of flowers and shallow pools of water, and that they collected vegetables, herbs, vines, and fruit and shade trees to plant in them.

Practical knowledge of the workings of those parts of the environment directly useful to them the Egyptians had in abundance, and with it they maintained a flourishing agriculture throughout their history, except for the worst periods of invasion and internal unrest. Then the canals might go unrepaired and the desert and swamp readvance at the expense of the cultivated fields.

Egyptian science is known from treatises on mathematics, astronomy, and medicine. The medical writings include some directions regarding the use of plants and drugs in treating ailments.

The history of the Egyptian environment in antiquity is marked by a great reduction in the numbers and abundance of wildlife. This was primarily due to the conversion of marshes into fields, but partially also due to hunting. Egyptians from the pharaoh on down hunted water birds and animals in the remaining wetlands, and pursued lions, wild cattle, deer, and antelope in the nearby desert. Today even once-abundant species are seldom seen.

As Egypt was never forested, most wood had to be imported from Lebanon or the Upper Nile. The chief material for major construction, stone, was abundant in Egypt and widely quarried. Copper and tin were mined in Sinai and other desert margins or imported from abroad.

The regularity of the Nile saved Egypt from some of the problems of Mesopotamia. The floods provided annual drainage, and salinization was not widespread in Egypt. In fact, Egypt continued to produce food surpluses throughout the ancient period and was a major exporter of grain to Greece and Rome.

All told, the unique environment of Egypt tended to shelter it from some of the bad effects of ecological change felt elsewhere in the ancient world, and helped to ensure its long continuity as a relatively conservative civilization.

The Persians had a unique view of the natural world which gives them an important place in any consideration of ecology in ancient times. Their empire eventually stretched from India to Egypt and Greece, altering and influencing much of the Mediterranean Basin. The eastern neighbors of Mesopotamia, the Persians inhabited an arid, mountainous region where agriculture required extensive irrigation. For this purpose, the Persians developed underground channels, called *qanats,* through which water could flow from the aquifers without too much loss by evaporation. Cities had developed in this area before the arrival of the Persians themselves, and besides settled irrigation agriculture, many of the inhabitants practiced seminomadic herding of cattle.

The Persian religion, based upon an Indo-European pantheon of nature deities, developed a strong sense of reverence for the elements of the natural world. Earth, water, and especially fire were regarded as sacred in themselves, and much of Persian religion was concerned with the need to keep them free from ritual pollution. The Persians had many rules concerning cleanliness, and those who broke them could be severely punished. Water was to be kept in a state of pristine purity, whether it was flowing or standing in a lake or well. Sewage of any sort, whether urine or excrement, or even hair or fingernail parings, was not permitted to enter water, although water might itself be used as an agent of purification. The worst sort of pollution in Persian eyes resulted from contact with dead bodies of human beings or animals, and anyone seeing one of these in the water was duty bound to remove it and perform the necessary purifications. The earth was also sacred, and burial of dead bodies was considered the worst possible violation of the will of the gods. Since fire, an object of great veneration, could not be polluted either, bodies were simply exposed in rocky places or in special towers to be eaten by "unclean" animals such as wolves and vultures.

Along with the elements, the Persians worshiped sacred plants, animals, and stars. Certain human activities, such as agriculture, were regarded as acts of reverence to the earth which made the earth happy and fruitful. Domestic animals were given reverent care.

When the prophet Zoroaster reformed the Persian religion, he left intact the basic reverence for nature and the ritual maintenance of purity associated with it. He emphasized the dualism of Persian thought, however, including a certain ambivalence toward nature. While the elements are pure and must remain uncorrupted, the creatures of the earth are divided into two classes, good and evil. Ranged on the side of Ahura Mazda, the god of light and goodness, according to Zoroastrian thought, were all the good creatures, such as dogs, cattle, trees, and the sun itself, whose very rays helped to purify. On the other side, with Ahriman, the evil prince of darkness, were noxious creatures like wolves, snakes, demons of disease, and flies. Killing such creatures was regarded as an act of merit, so that condemned criminals were sometimes given the task of killing a certain number of them as a means of expiating their guilt.

In the Persian view, then, people were regarded as responsible for their actions in regard to the natural environment. They were seen as coworkers of the good Creator, charged with maintaining the purity and fruitfulness of the earth in defiance of the attempts of the forces of evil to pollute and destroy the earth and its good creatures.

It could be expected that people who observed the Persian religious rules would be healthier and cleaner than their neighbors in the ancient world, and this may have been the case. It would be nice to add that the Persian attitude of human responsibility toward the natural environment retarded the deterioration of the Persian landscape, but this does not seem to be true. The hillsides of Persia, like those of Lebanon, were deforested and subjected to erosion. Persian fields, like those of Mesopotamia, suffered salinization. Wildlife was gradually eradicated. Some of these results may be put down to the attitude of warfare toward the "evil" part of nature, and the belief that agriculture is invariably good. But more than this, the Persians illustrate a general principle of human ecology, that is, that a good attitude toward nature is not enough. Combined with a good attitude must be accurate knowledge of the workings of nature and the ability to control and direct human impact upon nature in channels which will help, rather than hinder, the balance of nature. The Persians' considerable experience with the natural environment is reflected in many of their wise rules. But they had no science worthy of the name, and their level of technology and social control, while high enough to be one of the wonders of the ancient world, was insufficient to put into effect the limited ecological insights which were contained in their religion.

Greece and Rome: The Classical Tradition

It has been conventional to say that, for the West, civilization began in Mesopotamia and Egypt, but that civilization became distinctly Western in Greece. These matters no longer go undisputed. "Out of Egypt, Greece" briefly summarizes conflicting viewpoints on whether Greek civilization derived from the older cultures of Egypt and the eastern Mediterranean.

The Greek ideals of order, proportion, harmony, balance, and structure—so pervasive in classical thought and art—inspired Western culture for centuries, even into the modern era. Their humanism, which made humans "the measure of all things," not only liberated Greek citizens from the despotic collectivism of the Near East, but also encouraged them, and us, to attain higher levels of creativity and excellence.

Though the Greeks did not entirely escape from the ancient traditions of miracle, mystery, and authority, they nevertheless elevated reason and science to new levels of importance in human affairs, and they invented history as we know it (see Carmine Ampolo's article on Herodotus). It was their unique sociopolitical system, the polis, that provided scope and incentives for Greek culture. Each polis was an experiment in local self-government. But to many, the Greek order was tainted because it rested on slavery and excluded women from the political process. Two selections, "American Democracy through Ancient Greek Eyes" and "The Martial Republics of Classical Greece," offer perspectives on the Greek political order. Kenneth Cavander discusses the place of Greek women in "Love and Death in Ancient Greece." Bernard Knox defends the ancient Greeks from their modern critics in "The Oldest Dead White European Males."

Yet for all its greatness and originality, classical Greek civilization flowered only briefly. The weaknesses of the polis system surfaced in the Peloponnesian War. During and after this long conflict between Athens and Sparta, the polis ceased to fulfill the lives of its citizens as it had in the past. The Greeks' confidence was shaken by events.

But it was not the war alone that undermined the civic order. The Greek way of life depended upon unique and transitory circumstances—trust, smallness, simplicity, and a willingness to subordinate private interests to public concerns. The postwar period saw the spread of disruptive forms of individualism and the privatization of life.

Above all, as H. D. F. Kitto has forcefully argued, the polis ideal, with its emphasis on public participation and the wholeness of life, eschewed specialization. "If one man in his time is to play all the parts," Kitto writes in *The Greeks* (Pelican, 1958), "these parts must not be too difficult for the ordinary man to learn. And this is where the polis broke down. Occidental man, beginning with the Greeks, has never been able to leave things alone. He must inquire, improve, progress; and Progress broke the polis."

Eventually, Alexander's conquests and the geographical unity of the Mediterranean enabled the non-Greek world to share Greek civilization. Indeed, a distinctive stage of Western civilization, the Hellenistic age, emerged from the fusion of Greek and Oriental elements. But, as Peter Green's "Greek Gifts?" indicates, some scholars question whether most Greeks respected or understood subject peoples and their cultures. At best the Hellenistic period was a time when new cities were built on the Greek model, a time of intellectual ferment and cultural exchange, travel and exploration, scholarship and research. At worst it was an era of amoral opportunism in politics and derivative styles in the arts.

Later, the Greek ideal survived Rome's domination of the Mediterranean. The Romans themselves acknowledged their debt to "conquered Greece." Modern scholars continue that theme, often depicting Roman culture as nothing more than the practical application of Greek ideals to Roman life. Yet the Romans were not merely soulless imitators of the Greeks. They were creative borrowers (from the Etruscans, as well as from the Greeks). Furthermore, they invented an effective system of imperial government and a unique conception of law. Their social order is described by Keith Hopkins in "Everyday Life for the Roman Schoolboy"; their political order (and our conceptualization of order in history) is illumined by Elie Kedourie's article on the murder of Caesar and Lionel Casson's piece on Nero. The decline of the Roman Empire is addressed in "Friends, Romans or Countrymen? Barbarians in the Empire."

The Romans bequeathed their language and law to Europe and preserved and disseminated Greek thought and values. The Greeks had provided the basis for the cultural unity of the Mediterranean; the Romans provided the political unity. Between them they forged and pre-

served many of the standards and assumptions upon which our tradition of civilization is built—the classical ideal.

Looking Ahead: Challenge Questions

What are the arguments for and against the assertion that Western civilization originated in Africa?

What was life like for Athenian wives?

What were the strengths and weaknesses of the histories by Herodotus?

What does Roman schooling reveal about broader aspects of social life in ancient Rome?

Were the barbarians, on balance, good or bad for the Roman Empire?

How has Nero been misjudged by history?

Out of Egypt, Greece

Seeking the roots of Western civilization on the banks of the Nile

Was Cleopatra black? Was Socrates? Did Nile legionnaires conquer the Aegean, setting the cradle of Western civilization in motion? For more than a generation African and African-American scholars have offered evidence that civilization was born on what Europeans called the Dark Continent. Led by the late Senegalese historian Cheikh Anta Diop, they have argued that Pythagorean theory, the concept of pi, geometric formulas and the screw and lever are only some of the patrimonies of Egypt, and not Greece as conventional wisdom holds. Western scholars gave these ideas about as much credence as they did spurious Soviet claims to have invented the telephone.

They didn't dispute the achievements of the great black kingdoms of west Africa in governance, social organization and economic sophistication. But they dismissed them as a sideshow in human civilization. And even if Egypt was pretty great . . . well, Egypt was not really Africa, cartographers notwithstanding. "Just as Africans were taken out of Africa, so Egypt has been taken out of Africa," says Barbara Wheeler, director of Africana Studies at Kean College in Union, N.J. But now the claims for Egypt, and Africa, have arrived front and center on the academic stage. Classics departments from Oxford to Harvard are embroiled in a red-hot debate over what role Egypt played in shaping the glory that was Greece. And that leads to an incendiary question: was Egypt "black"?

Perhaps it is mere coincidence that the scholar who has forced these questions onto the agenda has lighter skin and straighter hair than the west Africans who tried in vain to get the academy's attention. Martin Bernal is a professor of government at Cornell University, a scholar of modern China, Vietnam and Japan, a Briton whose father was the wartime adviser to Lord Mountbatten. In the 1970s a mid-life crisis sent him in search of his distant Jewish roots. His study of Hebrew and antiquity led him to Greece, and thence to Egypt. The result was the first of a projected four-volume series titled "Black Athena."

Published in 1987 and winner of the 1990 American Book Award, the 575-page work explores why European scholars beginning in the 18th century excised Egypt and Canaan from the family tree of Western civilization. Bernal's answer: the classicists were racists and anti-Semites. They could not stand the idea that their beloved Greece had been made "impure" by African and Semitic influence and so dismissed as mere myth the Greeks' own accounts of how Egyptian and Canaanite technology, philosophy and political theory shaped Aegean civilization.

Q. Did Nubians from east Africa sail on Phoenician fleets to the Western Hemisphere before 1492?

A. Sculpture dated 800 B.C., found in Mexico, has African features. It's good but not conclusive evidence.

In place of this ancient model, which had stood for 3,000 years, the classicists offered what Bernal terms the "Aryan model." This theory holds that Greek civilization began when (white) Indo-European speakers from the north swept down on the native (white) "pre-Hellenes" between the fourth and third millennium B.C. Most modern researchers say "there's no real question" that 19th-century academics were racist and anti-Semitic, as classicist Gregory Crane of Harvard University puts it. But not all agree that such personal beliefs tainted their scholarship.

The just published Volume II of "Black Athena" moves beyond its predecessor's ad hominem attacks to offer a bold alternative to the Aryan model. Marshaling mountains of evidence from linguistics, archeology and ancient documents, Bernal argues that between 2100 and 1100 B.C., when Greek culture was born, the people of the Aegean borrowed, adapted or had thrust upon them deities and language, technologies and architectures, notions of justice and polis. From where did they come? Egypt and the Phoenicians of Canaan, says Bernal. A sampling from his numbing barrage of evidence:

- **Ancient documents.** The Greeks wrote that their culture emerged (around 1500 B.C.) when Egyptians and Phoenicians civilized the Aegean natives. Herodotus wrote that "the names of nearly all the gods came to Greece from Egypt." Greek legends relate that Egyptian and Phoenician conquerors ruled all or parts of Greece until the 14th or 15th century B.C.; historians wrote that such great lawgivers as Lykourgos studied in Egypt and brought back the legal and political basis for the West's polities.

Bernal's critics treat the ancient texts more suspiciously. Greeks may well have traced their civilization to Egypt (Sparta used Egyptian pyramids as one of its symbols), they say, but only to claim legitimacy through an older civilization, and not because it reflected historical truth.

- **Archeology.** Scores of Egyptian objects, from coins and jewels to sculpture and earthenware, litter the Aegean from Crete to the Greek mainland. Palaces suddenly appeared on Crete in around 2000 B.C.—the first time this architectural style graced any land other than Egypt—at exactly the time when Crete abruptly switched from being a rural, farming state to an urban one like Egypt. Bernal says this sudden change could have occurred only through Egyptian colonization. Around 2750 B.C., the Greek city of Thebes built a pyramidlike structure resembling those on the Nile. Murals from buildings on Thera preserved in volcanic ash in 1628 B.C., show Egyptian influence. They depict a stratified society, scenes of the Nile River and African plants drawn according to Egyptian artistic convention.

Q. How advanced were west African empires?

A. They had cities, compasses and navigation charts, founded a university in Timbuktu, traded gold and slaves with north Africans and built great palaces.

The critics respond that such influences more likely reflect trade and cultural ties, not Egyptian conquest. No ancient generals left behind papyrus with their battle plans.

• **Linguistics.** Bernal is fluent in Greek, Hebrew, Coptic, Chinese, French, German, Japanese and Vietnamese; his grandfather wrote the definitive Egyptian grammar. He combines his own etymological analysis with secondary sources to argue that half of all Greek words are derived from Egyptian or Semitic. He traces scores of words to the Egyptian, including sword, wisdom, honor and king; the large number of Egyptian-derived words, says Bernal, argues for "massive and sustained Egyptian cultural influence" over a less developed population.

Because hardly any scholars share Bernal's virtuosity of language, very few can judge his thesis, which turns on such arcana as whether the Greek "Athena" is truly derived from the Egyptian "Nt." Those who can judge parts of it generally agree that Bernal's etymologies are plausible but insist that this could be the result of trade and cultural contact. "Most scholars say there is no real evidence of conquest or colonization," says historian James Mulhy of the University of Pennsylvania.

Who were these people, then, who left their mark on the childhood of Western civilization? For years many African scholars have argued that the answer is as plain as the Sphinx's face: Egypt was a black civilization. By inference, say some Afrocentrists, Euclid, Homer, Socrates and Egyptian royals from Tut to Cleopatra were African blacks.

Egypt almost certainly originated in the black African societies of the upper Nile, in what is now Ethiopia. Fossil skulls from the start of Egypt's Dynastic period (30th century B.C.) resemble people in northern Ethiopia today. Bernal is convinced that many pharaohs looked black. Among them: Menthotpe, who around 2100 B.C. reunited Egypt after 300 years of chaos, and Sesostris who 100 years later sent African regiments into the Levant, Turkey and perhaps southern Russia. There, Herodotus wrote, they settled on the eastern shore of the Black Sea.

But that does not mean that Egyptian civilization as a whole was black, as the term is understood today. Bernal says, and almost all scholars agree, that for 7,000 years Egypt has been populated by African, Asian and Mediterranean peoples. He notes that ancient carvings usually show Nefertiti with Caucasian features, and believes Cleopatra was Greek (her family traced its ancestry to Alexander's invading generals). Says Bernal, "It was a thoroughly mixed population that got darker and more Negroid the further up the Nile you went . . . though few Egyptians could have bought a cup of coffee in America's Deep South in 1954." He allows that a more accurate title of his work would have been "*African* Athena."

Other scholars attack the notion that Egypt was black. Classicist Frank Snowden, now at Georgetown University, spent his career (he is 80) researching ancient notions of race. Arguably America's greatest black classicist, he believes that when Herodotus, Aeschylus and Aristotle wrote of "black" Egyptians, they were referring only to their swarthier complexion. "Race as an intellectual construct didn't exist" for the ancients, agrees historian Gary Reger of Trinity College in Hartford, Conn. (In this they were smarter scientists than most people today: the concept of race has no biological validity, and genetic analysis shows that some "blacks" share more of their genes with "whites" than either do with members of their own "race.")

It was not too many years ago that anthropologists desperately sought to trace humankind's origins to anyplace but Africa. That debate has been settled in favor of an east African genesis, a resolution that struck at the heart of European biological arrogance. Bernal readily acknowledges that "the political purpose of 'Black Athena' is, of course, to lessen European cultural arrogance." He may not have done that yet, but he has clearly forced scholars to reexamine the roots of Western civilization.

Sharon Begley *with* Farai Chideya *and* Larry Wilson *in New York and bureau reports*

American Democracy Through Ancient Greek Eyes

Its capital city and seat of government is dominated by classical style and pose, but would 'the land of the free' be congenial territory to democracy's ancient progenitors today? Barry Strauss ponders the contrasts and the surprising similarities.

Barry Strauss

Barry Strauss is Associate Professor of History at Cornell University and author of Fathers and Sons in Athens *(Princeton and Routledge, 1993).*

Two thousand five hundred years after the founding of democracy in Athens, the United States of America is a larger, wealthier, and more powerful democracy than any Athenian could have imagined. But would an Athenian indeed consider America to be a democracy? If he could be restored to life and brought to Washington DC, would an Athenian visitor feel at home, even among the marble columns and the neo-classical façades? Would he judge the American government to embody 'the power of the 'people', as did Athens' *demokratia* (a compound of *demos,* 'people', and *kratos,* 'power')?

America a democracy? It is not merely the vast difference in size of territory and population between Athens and America that might make an ancient democrat reject the idea. At a size of about 1000 square miles, the American state of Rhode Island is no larger than Attica (as the territory of ancient Athens was called), but no Athenian would be any more the willing to consider Rhode Island a democracy. Nor would either the equality of women or the abolition of slavery or the ethnic and racial diversity of America be the crux of the problem for an Athenian. In early nineteenth-century America women could neither vote nor hold office, African slavery was widespread, and most free citizens

traced their ancestry from within the British Isles. Americans nonetheless considered their country a democracy, as did such European observers as Alexis de Tocqueville, whose visit to the States in 1831–32 furnished the material for his classic analysis, *De la démocratie en Amérique* (*Democracy in America*). An Athenian, however, might well have been unconvinced.

For him, the chief stumbling block would have been the American notion of representative democracy, which he would have considered an oxymoron, if not an impossibility. In Athens the people ruled not through representatives but directly. Their power was embodied in a popular assembly, a legislative and deliberative body open to all adult male citizens, as well as in jury courts, magistracies, and a Council that served as a sort of executive committee. Each of these institutions was large, thereby offering every one of Athens' adult male citizens (a number that fluctuated between c.25,000 and 50,000 in the two centuries of Athens' democratic regime) a chance to play at least a small part in self-government. Athenian ideology, moreover, emphasised participation and alternation in office. Take Athenian juries. Never composed of fewer than 201 men, they offered plenty of opportunity for participation to the pool of 6,000 jurors chosen at random each year. Seven hundred magistrates served annual terms in Attica (an additional number, varying in different eras, served abroad); most were chosen by lottery, thereby equalising opportunity between rich and poor. The

500 members of the Council, who also served annual terms, were selected by a combination of election and lottery.

Athenian insistence on direct democracy was not merely a constitutional detail. Direct popular participation in the government, rather, *was* democracy. The alternative, government by an elite, was considered to be not democracy but oligarchy, literally, 'rule by the few'. No matter how free the people were otherwise, Athenians did not consider them to be fully free unless they could govern themselves. Nor were the people deemed to enjoy full equality unless all adult male citizens had an equal opportunity to govern. Without such an opportunity, the Athenians believed, the government would be run not only by an élite but in the interests of an élite. Since the élite would generally be wealthier than ordinary people, the economic dimension was a key constituent of democracy.

Aristotle understood this well. As he put it, democracy is not only majority rule, but a regime run by poor and ordinary people in their own interests. Oligarchy is a regime run by an élite of wealthy people in their own interests.

The workings of American democracy have little in common with Athenian direct democracy. Legislation is carried out by the representatives of the people rather than by the people themselves. Magistrates are chosen by election or appointment, not lottery. Ordinary citizens may consider it their duty to be informed about public affairs and to vote, although a very large number of adult Americans rarely, if ever, vote.

Even those who do vote feel no responsibility to hold public office, as Athenians did: in America politics is a profession, the province of a few, just like law, engineering, or acting. Indeed, the American press usually judges whether a foreign government is truly a democracy by the presence or absence of free elections. Only the American jury system emphasises the direct empowerment of poor and ordinary people, who, as in Athens, sit in judgement on the élite. Only a small percentage of Americans actually do jury duty, however. Unlike Athenian courts, moreover, American courts are supervised by professionals, judges and lawyers, who are usually members of the élite; in Athenian courts, amateurs dominated the proceedings.

In constitutional terms, then, American government places power in the hands of far fewer people than Athenian government. Hence an Athenian might be less likely to judge America a democracy than an oligarchy.

The American Founding Fathers, moreover, would be neither surprised nor disturbed by that conclusion. The Founders tended, of course, to be admirers of Greek and Roman antiquity, but they were selective in their admiration. Having rebelled against the British crown, the revolutionary leaders of the thirteen British colonies of North America looked outside English history for models of behaviour. Ancient history, which loomed large in eighteenth-century American education, proved a rich source. The Founders looked to the republics of antiquity for models of martial ardour, public virtue, self-sacrifice, political pluralism, balanced and stable confederations, agrarian hardiness, and above all, love of liberty. They found Sparta a more appealing paragon than Athens, however, and the Roman Republic preferable to either. In fact, they evinced little love for Athenian democracy, which they considered to be unstable, prone to faction, and prey to demagogues. John Adams, for instance, thought its history of factional strife rendered Athenian democracy a system of government contrary to 'all human and divine benevolence'. Alexander Hamilton confessed to 'feeling sensations of horror and disgust' at the continual agitation and revolutions of 'the petty republics of Greece and Italy'. Thomas Jefferson praised America's 'introduction of this new principle of representative democracy', arguing that it 'renders useless'

almost all earlier political writings, including perhaps even Aristotle.

Pride in America's novelty and purity balanced the Founders' love of antiquity. The attitude resulted in part from the colonies' Puritan heritage of belief in special election as a chosen people doing the Lord's work, and in part from the sense of novelty and freshness of a frontier society. Hence, Samuel Adams of Massachusetts said that while America should be like Sparta, it should be a Christian Sparta. John Taylor of Virginia went a step further, emphasising the radical difference between the new American republic and its Greco-Roman antecedents; in America, he wrote, 'human character has undergone a moral change'.

It was not difficult, therefore, for the American Founders to reject Athens. They considered direct democracy as repugnant as the Athenians considered it essential, and for several reasons. First, having experienced what they considered to be tyranny under British colonial rule, the Founders had a considerable scepticism of direct governance of any kind. Hence their insistence on creating a federal government of checks and balances, where competition would limit the power of any one person or institution. The two chambers of the federal legislature, for example, the Senate and the House of Representatives would each balance the other, while the legislative branch as a whole would act as a counterweight to the executive branch, led by the president. Judicial review, provided by the courts, would enforce the constitution against encroachments by the legislative or the executive. The power of the individual states, moreover, would balance the power of the federal government.

Second, having effected a revolution against an ancient institution, the British crown, the Founders had a strong sense of the fragility of regimes. They worried intensely about the corrosive effect of factionalism. The corrective, they felt, would be a written constitution, difficult to amend, hence a factor for stability. Then too, they believed that a system of checks and balances would, in addition to other virtues, prevent faction—although America's subsequent history of vigorous party politics belies their hope.

Third, while some were considerably more egalitarian than others, none of the Founders was willing to entrust governmental power to poor people. Some looked to government by the rich, others

idealised the virtues of yeoman farmers, but none believed that political excellence was obtainable without a minimum of wealth and education. None was willing to allow the landless, the destitute, or the urban poor to vote, let alone to hold public office. Left to their own devices, ordinary people were too ignorant and excitable to offer good government: so the Founders believed. Prey to clever and unscrupulous demagogues, ordinary people needed the guidance and protection of 'some temperate and respectable body of citizens', as James Madison, at the time of the debate over the United States Constitution, described his proposed Senate. Until a constitutional amendment of the twentieth century, American Senators were chosen by state legislatures, not by popular election, rendering the Senate highly elitist—precisely a virtue that would greatly have aided democratic Athens, Madison thought. 'What bitter anguish would not the people of Athens have often escaped', he writes:

> if their government had contained so provident a safeguard [i.e., a Senate] against the tyranny of their own passions? Popular liberty might then have escaped the indelible reproach of decreeing to the same citizens the hemlock on one day and statues on the next.

No ancient Greek oligarch could have decried better the alleged flaws of democracy.

The ink had hardly dried on the Constitution, however, when 'popular liberty' began to break the bonds that Madison had tried to impose upon it. Over the past two centuries, America has grown far more democratic than the Framers would ever have wanted. As it currently exists, democracy in America lacks many of its original Madisonian checks on popular passions. The citizen body has expanded to include people whom the Framers might have considered dubious material for the fashioning of republican virtue: women, freed slaves and their descendants, immigrants from the four corners of the earth. Living in a largely rural country, Jefferson and many of his contemporaries praised agrarian virtues. What would they make of today's American electorate, which is overwhelmingly urban or suburban? Nor are there any property requirements for voting: standard in Madison's America, they were overthrown early in the nineteenth century. Suffrage is universal, office-holders are heterogeneous. Both women and the descendants of slaves serve as mayors of big cities, as state governors, US senators, and as justices of the US Supreme Court; only the presidency continues to elude them.

The barriers to the direct expression of American popular will have fallen considerably since the 1790s. Although the American president is chosen by a slate of electors from each state, the so-called electoral college has become a mere technicality as each state's electors are bound to support the candidate who wins a plurality of the popular vote in that state. On the state and local level, many judges are chosen by election rather than appointment. Sophisticated polling of public opinion makes it difficult for an elected official to ignore the voice of the people, not if he or she wants to be re-elected.

Not that checks and balances have been entirely removed from the American federal political system: indeed, compared to a parliamentary democracy, their continued importance is striking. Unlike a prime minister, the American president does not necessarily command a working majority in the legislature, as the results of congressional elections are independent of those of the presidential election. It is not unusual for one party to control the presidency and another to control the Congress. Each chamber of the legislature, moreover, is quite independent, meaning that a president has to find support in both the House of Representatives and the Senate in order to have a bill become law. Recent years, moreover, have seen a weakening of the ties of party loyalty. The end of the Cold War and its sense of emergency have brought a certain diminution in the prestige of the presidency. Hence, although Bill Clinton's Democratic party has majorities in both House and Senate,* it is no easy matter for him to have a legislative programme enacted. Nor can legislators in one chamber of Congress easily enact their programme without obtaining the support of the president; and without the support of the other chamber of Congress, they can enact nothing at all. Popular liberty, therefore, is indeed held in check, just as Madison would have wished.

Yet having written off America as an oligarchy, an Athenian might well have second thoughts. The closer he looked at America, particularly if he left the confines of Washington, the more similarities he might have detected between

ancient *demokratia* and modern democracy. Like Athens, the United States prides itself on freedom. Each society's ideologists grounded that freedom in an act of armed rebellion against foreign (or at least what was perceived as foreign) domination. America's national holiday is July 4th, celebrating the official declaration of the War of Independence against Britain (a nation now, ironically, both revered as the fountainhead of American culture and respected as America's closest ally). Athenian tradition celebrated both the failed aristocratic revolt of c. 515 BC against the tyranny that ruled Athens and the successful popular revolt against Sparta in 508/7 BC. The celebration of martial virtue as the guardian of freedom is to be found in both Athens and America. In Athens, military service was all-but universal, while America guarantees every citizen the right to bear arms—even, in recent years, in the face of unprecedented and at times anarchic violence. The notion of the independent American, armed against the threat of tyranny, runs deep in the national consciousness.

In large part because of its frontier legacy, America is a more violent society than was Athens. Yet Athens, no less than America, promoted an ideology according to which the ideal citizen would be active, not passive: enterprising, patriotic, vigorous, even, when need be, a busybody. Both Athenians and Americans have acquired a reputation for litigiousness. Neither society has shown much patience for strict libel laws or the protection of a politician's privacy.

Both Athens and America imagined themselves as open societies, offering asylum for refugees and economic opportunity for enterprising immigrants. Athenian immigrants, it is true, had virtually no chance of ever becoming citizens—a striking contrast to the universal citizenship of modern America. By the mid fifth-century BC, the Athenian democratic citizen body was largely a closed group. Athenian resident aliens or metics, as they were known, nonetheless attained great prosperity and a substantial amount of both individual and political freedom. Metics wrote speeches delivered by citizens in court and in the assembly. During the civil war of 404–403 BC metics fought and died for the democrats.

Like America, Athens was considered to be a highly cosmopolitan society, a babel of foreign voices, to the delight of

democrats and disgust of conservatives. The philosopher, Plato, no admirer of democracy, satirised Athens as resembling a multi-coloured coat, because of its diversity. Even worse, for him and like-minded thinkers, Athens was a society that prized equality.

Oligarchic Greeks looked down on Athenians for their easy-going and egalitarian manners. The benches of the Athenian assembly, critical sources state, were filled with boorish farmers and uneducated artisans and tradesmen. Athenians, one source reports, had the bad taste to let slaves walk the streets dressed like masters! America too has a strong egalitarian strain. Of many indices, consider only the scandal to refined opinion when, on the occasion of his inauguration as US president in 1829, Andrew Jackson opened the White House to ordinary citizens, never before admitted to such a celebration. 'Country men, farmers, gentlemen, mounted and dismounted, boys, women and children, black and white', entered the White House, as a contemporary reports, leaving china, crystal, and silk upholstery ruined in their wake.

Both societies particularly prize freedom of speech. Athenians focused on the right of every citizen to address the assembly. They recognised a more general freedom of speech, but they had nothing like the protection of the American Bill of Rights of 1791 (comprising the first ten amendments to the Constitution), which prohibits any federal legislation restricting the people's freedom of speech. The Bill of Rights goes further, moreover, by also guaranteeing the people's right to assemble peaceably and to petition and lobby their representatives in Congress. It prohibits the creation of an established religion, while protecting the people's freedom of religion more generally. Hence, freedom of speech is established more firmly and interpreted more broadly in the United States than in Athens.

None of this is to deny the enormous differences between Athenian and American democracy; indeed, the American freedom of religion merely highlights those differences. Modern Western liberalism emerged from the terrible wars of religion of the sixteenth and seventeenth centuries. Hence it places great emphasis on individual religious freedom, and on the separation of public and private more generally. An Athenian, by contrast, tended to turn to the polis, not the individual conscience, for ideological guidance.

Athenian religion, with its gods and festivals, was civic religion. There was no separation of church and state. Public and private were considered to be distinct, but the distinction was weaker than in modern democracy. Athenians were far more willing to intervene in private affairs than are contemporary democrats. Consider an extreme but revealing case, the trial of Socrates, who was executed in 399 BC for the crimes of not recognising the gods the city recognised, of having invented new gods and of having corrupted the youth. An American court would throw such charges out.

On the other hand, an Athenian court would dismiss the host of suits heard in American courts over the last generation, suits based on a seemingly open-ended notion of rights. The Athenian notion of 'rights' was attenuated in the first place, 'privilege' and 'duty' being far more important concepts in its political lexicon. In the second place, Athens had little room for the rectification of alleged discrimination against ethnic and racial minority groups, women, the handicapped, religious sects, the allergic, and now, even animals—whose demands for justice loom increasingly large in American justice and politics.

Perhaps the most striking difference between ancient and modern is capitalism. To be sure, certain similarities do exist between the ancient and modern economies. Athens, no more than America, practiced communism. Athenians evinced great respect for private property. Like Americans, they expected their government to provide a minimum of prosperity, especially for the poor. The poor looked to the Athenian state for employment in the navy and in such public works as building projects and the dockyards, as well as for reimbursement for jury duty, service in public office, and even for attending the theatre (in what was a kind of primitive welfare system). Yet Athens lacked the ideology as well as the technology for promoting modern economic growth. Athenians were relatively unacquisitive, and owned relatively few possessions. Unlike Americans, Athenians did not consider it the purpose of the polis to promote an ever-improving standard of living for its citizens. They might have been surprised to learn that 'the state of the economy' is generally considered the single most important issue in any American election.

The differences are indeed enormous. Yet one must not forget the thread of similarity that runs from ancient to modern democracy. Both Athens and America are societies that emphasise an ideology of equality and freedom, and the right of every citizen to have a say in the running of the country. An Athenian might dismiss America as an oligarchy. He would be astounded by the size and wealth of the United States and by the abolition of slavery. He would be distrustful of the freedom accorded women, and dismissive of the ever-greater number of 'rights' claimed by an ever larger number of people. And yet, when he encountered a group of American citizens openly criticising the government and organising a lobbying campaign to do something about it by fighting for their rights, the Athenian would probably nod in recognition and join right in.

---

*[Editor's note: In the 1994 congressional elections, the Republicans won control of both houses of Congress for the first time since 1954.]

FOR FURTHER READING:

Meyer Reinhold, *Classical Americana. The Greek and Roman Heritage In the United States* (Wayne State, 1984); Gordon S. Wood, *The Creation of the American Republic, 1776–1787* (W. W. Norton, 1972). The authors of the *Federalist Papers* (originally published 1788) especially James Madison (later sixth president of the United States) have much to say about the difference between the American constitution and ancient republics. Harry L. Watson, *Liberty and Power. The Politics of Jacksonian America* (Hill and Wang, 1990); Jonathan Rauch, *Kindly Inquisitors. The New Attacks on Free Thought* (Chicago, 1993); Ronald Takaki, *A Different Mirror: A History of Multicultural America* (Little, Brown, 1993).

The Martial Republics of Classical Greece

Paul A. Rahe

Paul Rahe is associate professor of history at the University of Tulsa. He has written extensively on classical antiquity, early modern political theory, and the American founding. He is the author of Republics Ancient and Modern: Classical Republicanism and the American Revolution *(1992).*

At the turn of this century, the Irish-American journalist Finley Peter Dunne wrote a column of political and social satire for a Chicago newspaper. On one occasion, he touched on the ancient world, attributing the following observation to his character, the sage of Halsted Street, Mr. Dooley:

I know histhry isn't thrue, Hinnissy, because it ain't like what I see ivry day in Halsted Sthreet. If any wan comes along with a histhry iv Greece or Rome that'll show me th' people fightin', gettin' dhrunk, makin' love, ge,ttin' marrid, owin' th' grocery man an bein' without hard-coal, I'll believe they was a Greece or Rome, but not befure. Historyans is like doctors. They are always lookin' f'r symptoms. Thos iv them that writes about their own times examines th' tongue an' feels th' pulse 'an makes a wrong dygnosis. Th' other kind iv histhry is a postmortem examination. It tells ye what a counthry died iv. But I'd like to know what it lived iv.

Mr. Dooley's complaint deserves mention because it reflects with great precision the difficulty faced by modern historians of antiquity and by their readers as well. Like Mr. Dooley, we are eager to know more about ancient domestic life—and not only about family quarrels, drinking bouts, love, marriage, and the never-ending struggle to make ends meet. But on these and related matters, we have very little reliable information. Indeed, what Mr. Dooley could see every day on Halsted Street in Chicago are the very things the ancients took great care to hide from one another—and ultimately from us.

The dearth of evidence regarding the private sphere does nothing to assuage our curiosity, but it may in itself be revealing. We may not be able to say what the Greek cities that flourished in the epoch stretching roughly from the eighth to the fourth centuries B.C. died of, but the relative silence of our informants regarding domestic affairs suggests that the citizens of the fully autonomous *polis* lived for something outside civilian life, a condition that Mr. Dooley and the residents of Halsted Street would have had trouble comprehending.

In their fundamental principles, modern liberal democracy and the ancient Greek *polis* stand radically opposed. The ancient city gave primacy not to the household and its attendant economic concerns but to politics and war: It was a republic oriented less toward the protection of rights than toward the promotion of virtue—first, by its very nature and, second, by its need to survive. Its cohesion was not and could not be a mere function of incessant negotiation and calculated compromise; it was and had to be bound together by a profound sense of moral purpose and common struggle.

One of America's Founding Fathers, Alexander Hamilton, captured the difference between the two regimes succinctly when he wrote in *The Federalist*, "The industrious habits of the people of the present day, absorbed in the pursuits of gain, and devoted to the improvements of agriculture and commerce are incompatible with the condition of a nation of soldiers, which was the true condition of the people of those [ancient Greek] republics." Hamilton's point is a simple one: The modern citizen is a civilian—a bourgeois family man or woman whose ancient counterpart was a warrior. Commerce defines the terms on which life is lived in modern, liberal polities. The ordinary citizen may not be a merchant himself, but the concerns of trade and industry regulate his labor with respect to time and govern the relations that unite him with his compatriots. By contrast, commerce was peripheral to the ancient economy. The ordinary Greek was a more or less self-sufficient peasant proprietor and he needed his fellow citizens as unpaid bodyguards against the city's slaves and for the defense of his family and land against foreigners far more than he needed them for any exchange of services and goods.

In antiquity, the model for political relations was not the contract but kinship. The ancient city was, like the household, a ritual community of human beings sharing in the flesh of animals sacrificed, then cooked at a common hearth. The citizens were bound together by the myth of common ancestry and linked by a veneration of the gods and the heroes of the land. The *polis* was not and could not be the household writ large, but as Plato makes clear in *The Republic,* this is what it tried to be. The city was not a circle of friends, but as both Plato and Aristotle imply, this is what it strove to become. The citizens were not tied to one another by a web of compromise. They were, as Augustine puts it, "united by concord regarding loved things held in common."

This fundamental like-mindedness was itself sustained by that steadfast adherence to tradition (*mos maiorum*) and that pious veneration of the ancestral (*ta*

From *The Wilson Quarterly*, Winter 1993, pp. 58-70. Adapted from *Republics Ancient and Modern: Classical Republicanism and the American Revolution* by Paul A. Rahe. © 1993 by the University of North Carolina Press. Reprinted by permission of the publisher.

patria) which the common civic rituals and legends were intended to foster. "The *polis* teaches the man." So wrote Simonides, the well-traveled poet from Iulis on Ceos. And when the Cyclops of Euripides' satyr play wants to know the identity of Odysseus and his companions, he asks whence they have sailed, where they were born, and what *polis* was responsible for their education (*paideia*). As long as the citizens were relatively isolated from outside influence, it mattered little, if at all, that the religious beliefs and rites of a particular city were irrational and incoherent. What mattered most was that the beliefs and rites peculiar to that city inspired in the citizens the unshakable conviction that they belonged to one another. And where it was difficult if not impossible to engender so profound a sense of fellow-feeling, as in colonies that drew their citizens from more than one metropolis, civil strife (*stasis*) was all too often the consequence. Put simply, the political community in antiquity was animated by a passion for the particular. The patriotism that gave it life was not a patriotism of universal principles, such as those enshrined in the Declaration of Independence, but a religion of blood and of soil.

Of course, the *polis* came into being in the first place because of the need for common defense. The word itself appears to be derived from an Indo-European term employed to designate the high place or citadel to which the residents of a district ordinarily retreated when subject to attack. But that high place was more than just a refuge. Even in the narrow, pristine sense of the word, the *polis* was also an enclosure sacred to the gods who lived within the city's walls. Thus, when a city pondered the establishment of a colony, it was customary for the founder (*oikistes*) to consult the oracle of Apollo at Delphi regarding the site. The failure to seek or a decision to ignore the advice of the god was thought likely to be fatal to the entire enterprise. In fact, the act of establishing a new community was itself an elaborate religious rite specified in detail by the laws. And in keeping with the divine origin and character of the new *polis,* the citizen designated as *oikistes* could expect to be buried with all solemnity in the central marketplace (*agora*), to be worshipped as a demigod and divine protector of the *polis* from the moment of his decease, and to be honored thereafter in

an annual festival complete with public sacrifices and athletic games.

The political community's sense of common endeavor was grounded in its particular *patrioi nomoi*—its ancestral customs, rites, and laws. These practices and institutions distinguished a city from similar communities and defined it even more effectively than the boundaries of the civic territory (*chora*) itself. If forced to abandon its *chora*, a *polis* could nonetheless retain its identity. The sage Heraclitus took this for granted when he wrote that "the people must fight for the *nomos* as if for the walls of the *polis.*" When a Greek city went to war the citizens battled not just to expand their dominion and to protect their wives, children, and land; they fought also to defend their *patrioi nomoi* and the entire way of life which these embodied.

This spirit carried over into the conduct of foreign affairs. Even where military cooperation was the only end sought, the Greeks tended to invest any confederacy they joined with moral and even religious foundations. This is why cities that formed such a connection often adopted each other's gods, founded a common festival, or sent delegations to share in each other's principal rites. In 428 B.C., when the Mytilenians were intent on securing aid from Sparta and its allies, they couched their request in terms that would find favor. "We recognize," they remarked, "that no friendship between private individuals will ever be firm and no community among cities will ever come to anything unless the parties involved are persuaded of each other's virtue and are otherwise similar in their ways: For disparate deeds arise from discrepancies in judgment."

Fifty-one years before, in a time of like trouble, the Spartans' Athenian rivals resorted to similar rhetoric. On the eve of the Battle of Plataea, the Spartans expressed fear that the citizens of Athens, their allies of the moment, would come to terms with the Persians. In response, the Athenians mentioned two reasons why they could not conceive of abandoning the struggle against the Mede. First, they explained, it was their duty to avenge the burning of their temples and the destruction of the images of their gods. "Then," they added, "there is that which makes us Hellenes—the blood and the tongue that we share, the shrines of the gods and the

sacrifices we hold in common, and the likeness in manners and in ways. It would not be proper for the Athenians to be traitors to these." In neither case was the presence of a shared enemy deemed adequate. Though separated by half a century, the two speeches were in accord: The only secure foundation for alliance was a common way of life.

The conviction so firmly stated by the Mytilenians and the Athenians contributed in a variety of ways to the actual making of policy. Cities with a common origin and extremely similar *nomoi* rarely went to war. The ordinary Greek colony, for example, generally had customs, rites, and laws closely akin to those of the mother city. Even when the two were fully autonomous, they usually maintained close ties, and the colony was expected to defer in most matters to the metropolis and to send a delegation with gifts of symbolic import to join in celebrating the principal festival of that community. The failure of a colony to perform what were seen as its moral obligations was deemed shocking in the extreme, and it could give rise to a bitterness that might easily overshadow the cold calculation of interests. As the historian Thucydides makes abundantly clear one cannot make sense of the origins of the Peloponnesian War (431–404 B.C.) without paying close attention to the deep-seated anger that shaped the Corinthians' policy towards their renegade colonists the Corcyraeans.

The forceful response that the Spartan expression of distrust elicited from the Athenians in 479 B.C. deserves a second glance. The great struggle against Persia did in fact bring home to the Hellenes all that they held in common—the blood and the tongue that they shared, the shrines of the gods and the public sacrifices, and their similarity in manners and ways. It was natural in the aftermath of that war particularly when the Great King of Persia started once again to meddle in Hellenic affairs, for some Greeks to begin to argue that wars within Hellas were not properly wars at all but examples of civil strife and, as such, reprehensible. But though such arguments were made, they had very little effect.

If the Greeks were nonetheless inclined to make war on each other it was at least in part because the disparate communities were never sufficiently similar in manners and in morals. What brought the citizens of a particular *polis* together set them apart from others; what united them as a people set them in opposition to outsiders. They held their land at the expense of slaves and foreigners, and they pursued the way of life peculiar to them in defiance of notions elsewhere accepted. When in Plato's *Republic* Polemarchus ("war-leader") defines justice as "doing good to friends and harm to enemies," he is merely reasserting on the personal level the grim civic ethic suggested by his name. In ancient Greece, patriotism went hand in hand with xenophobia. If "civil strife is not to thunder in the city," Aeschylus's divine chorus warns the Athenians, the citizens "must return joy for joy in a spirit of common love—and they must hate with a single heart."

The implications of all of this were not lost on the American Founding Fathers. Perhaps because of his own experience as a soldier Alexander Hamilton recognized the warlike demeanor of the ancient agricultural republics more clearly than many who have come after and this recognition played no small role in determining his adherence to James Madison's bold project of refashioning the disparate American states into an extended commercial republic. When confronted by the arguments of those who believed that no viable republic could be constructed on so vast a territory, Hamilton retorted that the American states were themselves already too large. Those who took such arguments seriously would have to choose between embracing monarchy and dividing the states "into an infinity of little, jealous, clashing, tumultuous commonwealths, the wretched nurseries of unceasing discord, and the miserable objects of universal pity or contempt."

On more than one occasion, the Greeks were forced to choose between the alternatives posed by Hamilton, and in all but the most difficult of circumstances most, if not all, preferred the jealousy, the tumult, the unceasing discord, and the excitement of life in the fully autonomous *polis* to the relative tranquillity promised in exchange for their absorption into a great empire. In considering the character of the *polis,* we must never lose sight of the permanence of conflict that afflicted Greek life. The ordinary Hellene would have nodded his approval of the opinion attributed by Plato to the lawgiver of Crete: "What most men call peace, he held to be only a name; in truth, for everyone, there exists by nature at all times an undeclared war among all the cities." Such was the human condition in Greece, where political freedom took precedence over commodious living.

Because the ancient city was a brotherhood of warriors and not an association of merchants, the principal task of legislation was the promotion of public-spiritedness and not the regulation of competing economic interests. It is revealing that, in Plato's *Republic,* a discussion of the best regime rapidly turns into a dialogue on character formation. Unfortunately, even under the best of circumstances, the nurturing of civic virtue was a difficult undertaking—one that called for the deliberate shaping of the citizens' passions and opinions. Even when everything has been done to ensure that the citizens have the same interests, there remains a tension between private inclination and public duty, between individual self-interest and the common good that is impossible fully to resolve. Death and pain are the greatest obstacles: They bring a man back upon himself, reminding him that when he suffers, he suffers alone. As a consequence, the quality which Plato and Aristotle called civic or political courage is rare: It is not by instinct that a man is willing to lay down his life for his fellow citizens. He must be made to forget the ineradicable loneliness of death. The fostering of courage, self-sacrifice, and devotion to the common good requires artifice, and this is why Plato's discussion of character formation rapidly turns into a dialogue on poetry and its chief subject: man's relations with the gods.

Even the most skeptical of the Greeks acknowledged the religious roots of that "reverence and justice" that served as the "regulators of cities" and the "bonds uniting" the citizens "in friendship." In Critias's satyr play *The Sisyphus,* the protagonist has occasion to discuss the origins of that cooperative capacity that makes political life possible. "There was a time," he notes, "when the life of human beings was without order and like that of a hunted animal: the servant of force. At that time, there was neither prize for the noble nor punishment for the wicked. And then human beings, so it seems to me, established laws in order that justice might be a tyrant and hold arrogance as a slave, exacting punishment if anyone stepped out of line." This stratagem worked well in most regards, but it was of limited effectiveness in one decisive respect—for "though the laws prevented human beings from committing acts of violence in the full light of day, men did so in secret." It required "a real man, sharp and clever in judgment," to find a remedy for this deficiency; when he finally appeared, he "invented for mortals dread of the gods, so that there would be something to terrify the wicked even when they acted, spoke, or thought entirely in secret." Critias's Sisyphus was by no means alone in making this assertion. In one fashion or another Aristotle, Isocrates, Polybius, Diodorus, Strabo, Quintus Mucius Scaevola, Marcus Terentius Varro, and Marcus Tullius Cicero all echo his claim.

The skepticism voiced by these luminaries was foreign to the ordinary Greek, but the political importance that these men ascribed to religion was not. The *polis* had a civic religion, and that religion was one of the chief sources of its unity and morale. For the Greeks, the gods were a constant presence. The Olympians might be thought to stand above the fray, but the gods and heroes of the land were taken to be the city's protectors, sharing in its glory and suffering its reverses. In Greece as well as in Rome, it was commonly believed that no town could be captured prior to the departure of its patron deities. For this reason, some cities chained their gods down, and it was an event of profound political importance when a citizen managed to discover abroad and remove to a final resting place within the territory of his own *polis* the bones of a hero. Securing and maintaining divine favor was vital. As a consequence, propitiation of the gods could never be simply a private matter; piety was a public duty.

Just as the piety of the citizens was thought to protect the city, so also their misdeeds could threaten its survival. Indeed, the whole community might be made to suffer for the sins of a single man. Pindar compares divine vengeance to "a fire on a mountainside: though begotten of a single seed, it removes a great forest entirely from sight." As a consequence, men were unwilling to take ship with an individual deemed guilty of offending the gods, and cities found it necessary to expel or even execute the impious and those who had polluted the community by murder, manslaughter, or some other infraction.

Just as patriotism required piety, so piety demanded patriotism. Treason was more than a political act, at least as politics is narrowly defined in modern times. The man who turned coat or simply abandoned his city in time of crisis betrayed not just his fellow citizens; he betrayed the gods as well. This explains why one peripatetic writer chose to list "offenses against the fatherland" under the category of "impiety." It also explains why the law of Athens equated treason with the robbing of temples. The Athenians dealt with the two crimes in a single statute that called not just for the guilty party's execution but also for the confiscation of his property and a denial to him of burial in his native soil.

To reinforce the conviction that the gods required of citizens a total devotion to the common good, the ancient cities resorted to the administering of oaths. Fortunately for us, an Athenian orator took the trouble to explain in detail the logic of this practice to the members of a jury. "The oath is the force holding the democracy together," he observed. "Our regime is composed of three elements: the magistrate, the juryman, and the private individual. Each of these is required to give his pledge, and quite rightly so. For many have deceived human beings and escaped notice, not only by eluding immediate dangers but also by remaining unpunished for their crimes through the rest of the time allotted to them. But no oath-breaker escapes divine notice; no man of this sort can avoid the vengeance that the gods exact. Even if a perjurer manages to escape retribution himself, his children and his entire family will fall upon great misfortunes." This religious understanding guided civic policy throughout all of Hellas.

Except during an emergency, it was probably not the norm for a community to exact from all of its citizens at once a pledge of their loyalty. It was common within the Greek cities to make provision for the military training of the young. Ordinarily, it seems to have been deemed sufficient that these youths be called upon to swear once and for all at the time of their initiation into manhood that they would stake their lives to protect the community, their fellow citizens, and the institutions they held in common.

The demands placed on the ordinary Greek soldier, or hoplite, and the moral support afforded him in his moment of trial went far beyond anything imagined by the average soldier today. As Aristotle emphasizes, mutual acquaintanceship was one of the features that distinguished the Greek *polis* from a nation. If the *polis* was to function properly, he suggests, it had to be "easily surveyed" so that the citizens might know each other's characters. Most of the cities were small towns, and in only a few did the citizen body exceed a few thousand. There was little, if any, privacy, and the citizen's entire existence was bound up with his participation in the religious and political affairs of the community. The Greek soldier was well-known to the men around him. He had spent the better part of his leisure time in their company: When not in the fields, he would leave the household to his wife and loiter about the blacksmith's shop, the palaestra, the gymnasium, or the marketplace, discussing politics and personalities, testing his strength and his wit against the qualities of his contemporaries, and watching the boys as they grew up. He lived for those hours when, freed from the necessity of labor, he could exercise the faculties—both moral and intellectual—that distinguished him from a beast of burden and defined him as a man. When deprived of reputation, he was deprived of nearly everything that really mattered. In classical Greece, the absence of a distinction between state and society was as much a practical as a theoretical matter: It meant that the citizen lived most of his life in the public eye, subject to the scrutiny of his compatriots and dependent on their regard. To be identified as a draft evader, accused of breaking ranks, or branded a coward and, in consequence, to be shunned or deprived of one's political rights could easily be a fate worse than death.

In time of war, the Greek citizen could not escape combat. No allowance was made for conscientious objection, there were no desk jobs, and slaves and metics performed whatever support functions the hoplite could not perform for himself. More often than not, he was fighting near his home in defense of his children and his land. And even when he was posted abroad, he was acutely aware that the city's safety and his family's welfare depended on the outcome of the struggle.

On the field of battle, this foot soldier would be posted alongside his fellow citizens as they advanced, shoulder to shoulder, marching in step—in some communities, to the tune of a flute. The phalanx was generally eight men deep, and it extended as far as the numbers and the terrain permitted. There was no place to hide. Ancient battles took place on open terrain, and this infantryman's behavior under stress would be visible to many, if not to all. For success, the modern army depends on the courage of the minority of men who actually fire their guns. The Greek phalanx depended on the effort of every man. The strength of this chain of men was no greater than that of its weakest link, for it took a breach at only one point for the formation to collapse. As a result, the behavior of a single hoplite could sometimes spell the difference between victory and rout. The man who betrayed his fellows, leaving them to die by breaking ranks, would not soon be forgiven and could never be forgotten. In a sense, he had spent his entire life preparing for this one moment of truth.

The process of preparation for that moment of truth required a great deal of time and effort. Toil undertaken for the sake of profit might be regarded as shameful, but toil undertaken for the sake of good order and victory in battle was honorable, and its avoidance was a source of unending shame. This fact explains the centrality of athletics in ancient Greek life. If the wealthy young men of the town spent their idle hours at the palaestra and the gymnasium, it was not simply or even chiefly because they were driven by narcissism. Indeed, their primary concerns were public, not private. In a tyranny such as the one established by Aristodemus at Cumae on the northern marches of Italy's Magna Graecia, there was to be no public sphere, and it might therefore seem prudent and even appropriate for the despot to do what he could to suppress the noble and manly disposition of the young by closing the gymnasiums and banning the practice of arms, by draping the young boys of the town in finery and keeping them out of the hot sun, and finally by sending them off, their long hair curled, adorned with flowers, and doused with perfume, to study with the dance masters and the players of flutes. But where the public sphere survived, this would never do. Republics needed real men, and citizens with the leisure in which to ready themselves for the ordeal of battle were expected to do so. "It is necessary, as Montesquieu observes, "to look on the Greeks as a society of athletes and warriors."

The historian Herodotus hammers away at the need for toil with particular vehemence. The manner in which he turns his description of the Battle of Lade into a parable is a case in point. In 499 B.C., the Greeks who inhabited the coastal communities of Asia Minor and the islands of the eastern Aegean had joined together in rebellion against their royal master, the Great King of Persia. A few years later, they sent naval contingents to the island of Lade, which lay off Miletus, the largest and most prosperous of the coastal towns. There, the rebels intended to make a concerted effort to prevent the Phoenician fleet of the Mede from regaining control of the sea and putting an end to their revolt. Upon the arrival of the various contingents, Dionysius of Phocaea reportedly addressed them in the following fashion: "Men of Ionia, our affairs—whether we are to be free men or slaves (and fugitive slaves at that)—stand balanced on a razor's edge. If, for the time being, you are willing to subject yourselves to hard work, you will have to submit to toil on the spot, but you shall be able to overcome those opposed to you and so go free. If, however, you prefer softness and disorder, I have no hope that you can avoid paying to the king the penalty for your revolt."

The Ionians initially took Dionysius's advice. According to Herodotus, they toiled for seven days from dawn to dusk, rowing their ships and practicing maneuvers under the Phocaean's direction. But because the men of the islands and coast were soft and unaccustomed to toil, many among them soon became ill, and in due course the rowers wearied of hardship and rebelled. Then they labored no more but instead erected tents on the island and took shelter there from the harsh rays of the sun. The Ionians paid dearly for their weakness. The Persian generals had promised to pardon any among the rebels who turned coat, and as a consequence of the rowers indolence and insubordination the Samian generals became persuaded that the cause was hopeless and elected to accept the king's offer. Thus, just as the battle began, the contingent from Samos—followed quickly by the triremes from Lesbos—sailed off, leaving the remaining Ionians to certain

defeat. Herodotus might have added that these men got precisely what they deserved, but he had no need to spell out his point.

Needless to say, toil, endurance, and good order were no less necessary for those destined to engage in combat on land. When Xenophon singles out farming as a profession likely to prepare men for war, he has more in mind than the fact that those who cultivate the soil have an interest in its defense. "The earth," his Socrates remarks, "supplies good things in abundance, but she does not allow them to be taken by the soft but accustoms men to endure the wintry cold and summer's heat. In exercising those who work with their own hands, she adds to their strength, and she makes men of those who, in farming, take pains, getting them up early and forcing them to march about with great vigor. For in the country as in the town, the tasks most fitting to the time must be done in season." Xenophon's Ischomachus even asserts that agriculture teaches generalship, noting that victory generally depends less on cleverness than on the thoroughness, diligence, and care exhibited by the sort of men who have learned from long experience the necessity of taking precautions.

Courage, strength, endurance, and diligence were vital, but they were not the only virtues demanded of the citizen-warrior in classical times. In certain crucial respects, the hoplite was quite unlike the heroes of *The Iliad*. He and his opponents fought not on their own but in formation. Therefore, he could not afford to be a berserker, driven by rage to run amok among the enemy host, for he could not break ranks to charge the enemy line without doing himself and his own side great harm. To achieve victory, the hoplite and his comrades had to display what the Greeks called *sophrosune*—the moderation and self-restraint expected of a man required to cooperate with others in both peace and war. Consequently, in considering the education to which young Greeks were customarily subjected, one would err in dwelling on athletic contests and military maneuvers to the exclusion of all else, for Greek boys were expected to toil at music as well. In fact, to judge by the remarks made by the greatest of the ancient philosophers, the study of music played a vital role in giving a young man the psychological preparation he needed for

the assumption of his duties as a citizen and soldier. In Plato's *Republic,* the interlocutors of Socrates take it for granted that education consists of gymnastic exercise and musical training. Initially, Socrates treats exercise at the gymnasium as a hardening of the body. But as the argument unfolds, he introduces another, more important consideration—the effect of that hardening on the soul, and the danger that guardians subjected to gymnastic training alone will be savage toward one another and toward their fellow citizens as well. Poetry set to music he presents as an instrument capable of moderating and harmonizing—in short, of civilizing—the all-important quality of spiritedness.

In *The Laws,* Plato's Athenian Stranger takes a similar tack, arguing at length—and with considerable psychological insight that participation in choral singing and dancing can habituate the young and the not so young to take pleasure in that which is good and to feel loathing and disgust when presented with that which is not. Even Aristotle thought such pursuits an antidote to the savagery bred of the ancient city's obsessive preoccupation with war. In fact, like his mentor, he was persuaded that a *polis* devoted to music and the arts would be a far healthier and saner polity than a community dedicated to conquest and imperial rule and consequently riven by political ambition and strife.

One of the more telling indications of the degree to which the warrior ethos permeated every aspect of Greek life is the prevalence of pederasty throughout Hellas. No ancient author gives us a full and detailed report of the conventions that guided Greek behavior in the various cities, and the surviving plays, courtroom harangues, philosophical dialogues, and vase representations that throw light on the elaborate code of homosexual courtship pertain chiefly to Athens. But though the evidence is fragmentary, the general pattern is clear: The Greeks seem to have practiced pederasty as a rite of passage marking a boy's transition to manhood and his initiation into the band of citizen-soldiers. And even where wooing adolescent boys was the fashion only among men of leisure, pederasty was conceived of by its many proponents as a reinforcement of those ties of mutual acquaintanceship that were universally recognized as the foundation of civil courage.

The pattern is evident in Ephorus's description of prevailing practice in the region of Greece where the *polis* as a religious and military community governed by constitutional forms seems first to have emerged. In Crete, the younger boys attended the men's mess with their fathers. Under the direction of the warden associated with that mess, those slightly older learned their letters, memorized the songs prescribed by the laws, and tested their strength against one another and against those associated with other messes. When the boys turned 17, the most distinguished among them gathered their less well-born contemporaries into herds, each collecting as large a personal following as possible. Fed at public expense and subject to their recruiter's father, they practiced hunting, participated in footraces, and—at appointed times—joined in battle against rival herds, marching in formation to the cadence of the flute and the lyre. This period of apprenticeship reached completion when a man of distinguished family took as his beloved the boy who had gathered the herd in the first place.

This ritual abduction marked the first stage in the process by which an aristocratic boy and his followers were prepared for initiation into manhood. Together, they were forcibly withdrawn from the community of ephebes, and for a transitional period they slipped off to the wilds. When they came back, they immediately took wives and joined the community of men.

Pederasty was evidently one of the central institutions of the martial communities of Crete, and it was probably from this island that the custom spread to the remainder of Greece. Concerning the other Hellenic cities we are less well informed, but all that we do know suggests that pederasty elsewhere served precisely the same function. Hunting, which was everywhere considered a form of training for war, and homosexual courtship appear to have been as closely connected in Athens as they were on Crete. On Thera, sodomy seems to have been linked with rituals honoring Apollo Delphinios and marking the boy's transition to manhood. At Thebes, when the beloved one was enrolled as a man, his lover conferred on him the hoplite panoply; in fourth-century Elis, as well as in Thebes, the couple would fight as a pair in the ranks. "It is the part of a prudent general," Onasander would later remark, to encourage his heavy infantrymen to take risks on behalf of those alongside them in the battle line by stationing "brothers next to brothers, friends next to friends, and lovers next to the boys they love."

Classical Hellas encompassed an array of independent communities stretching from the east coast of the Black Sea to the far reaches of the western Mediterranean. Language, literature, religion, culture, republican institutions, proximity to the sea, and diminutive size—these common characteristics made the ancient *poleis* much alike and very different at the same time. The last on this list of characteristics may well be the most important. Smallness in size gives rise to familiarity, and familiarity breeds contempt in more than one way. The defense of familiarity requires xenophobia, since all outside contact is a threat to the integrity of the community. The *polis* was akin to a party of zealots, and Alexander Hamilton was right when, in *The Federalist,* he described Hellas as "an infinity of little, jealous, clashing, tumultuous commonwealths." There was variety enough in the local circumstances and traditions of these apparently similar communities to set them incessantly at odds. And, strange to tell, the unity of the Greek world owed much to this very variety and to the conflicts it engendered. Radical particularity makes for a certain uniformity. Athenaeus, a Greek who wrote in the third century A.D., rightly made no distinction among *poleis* when he wrote that "the men of olden times thought courage the greatest of the political virtues," and what he had to say was as true for Rome as it was for the republics of Greece. Even where the institutions of the various cities were structurally different, the constant threat of war made them functionally similar.

As a type of community, the *polis* rested on its citizen militia and fell only when that militia was overwhelmed. The modern distinction between soldier and civilian did not pertain in the classical republics, and when that distinction emerged and the professional soldier became a figure of genuine importance—initially in Greece in the age of Philip of Macedon (359–36 B.C.) and Alexander the Great (336–23 B.C.), and again later at Rome in the time of Marius, Sulla, Pompey, and Caesar—freedom's existence became quite tenuous. Even where the city survived and retained a modicum of local autonomy, it did so on the sufferance of monarchs.

Something of the sort also could be said regarding the quasi-autonomous urban republics of the Middle Ages and the Renaissance. As Machiavelli makes clear in his *Art of War,* their failure to establish a militia capable of securing their defense rendered their retention of liberty largely a matter of chance. Indeed, it was only with the rise of popular armies at the time of the French Revolution that modern republicanism gained more than a foothold on the European continent. The degree to which the modern, democratic nation-state owes its solidarity, its sense of identity, and even its existence to the threat and experience of war cannot be overestimated. To date, at least, no lawgiver or state-builder has discovered what William James once termed a "moral equivalent of war."

Modern republicanism may be at odds with its ancient prototype in many particulars. But until such a moral equivalent has been discovered and deployed in practical, political form, Mr. Dooley's preoccupation with what could be seen every day on Halsted Street will render him and those similarly focused on domestic affairs as incapable of making a correct diagnosis of the modern condition as they are of understanding the history of ancient Greece and Rome. In the absence of a pacific equivalent of war, the breach between modernity and antiquity will remain incomplete and the martial republicanism of the classical Greeks will still be with us in one, crucial regard.

Herodotus

Roving reporter of the Ancient World

Carmine Ampolo

Carmine Ampolo, of Italy, teaches Greek history at the University of Pisa. He has carried out research on the origins of ancient Rome, on Greek politics and society, and on the relationship between myth and history. Among his published works are La citta antica *(1980; "The Ancient City") and, with M. Manfredini,* Le vite di Teseo et di Romolo *(1988; "The Lives of Theseus and Romulus").*

Herodotus of Halicarnassus, his *Researches* are here set down to preserve the memory of the past by putting on record the astonishing achievements both of our own and of other peoples . . . that the great deeds of men may not be forgotten . . . whether Greeks or foreigners: and especially, the causes of the war between them."*

In this introduction to his *Histories,* Herodotus (c. 490–425 BC) provides us with perhaps the earliest definition of the historian's aims and concerns. Some sixty years earlier, his precursor Hecataeus of Miletus, who had sought to inquire rationally into the mythical legends of the Greeks, explained his intentions in the following terms: "Thus speaks Hecataeus of Miletus: I write these things inasmuch as I consider them to be truthful; in fact, the legends of the Greeks are numerous and, to my mind, ridiculous." In this tetchy assertion of the author's role we can already see the two requirements of historiography in the Hellenic world: it must be written and it must be truthful.

With Herodotus the tone changes. He does not seek to give his own personal interpretation of what he relates, and

---

*Quotations from *Herodotus: The Histories,* translated by Aubrey de Sélincourt, Penguin Classics, 1954.

usually he compares the different versions of stories he has collected. He wants to talk about his researches, tell of his inquiries. History as he understands it is at once the gathering of information and the recounting of a story. He thus inaugurated the two main trends in Greek historiography for centuries to come. Sometimes one would be given prominence, sometimes the other, but the prime imperative was always truthfulness, even in the case of historians who attached very great importance to narrative.

THE ART OF STORYTELLING

When Herodotus describes his work as an "exposition of his researches, the narration of an inquiry", these ambivalent terms must be taken to mean both the oral transmission of a story and its written formulation. The blending of oral and written styles in the *Histories* can be explained by the fact that Herodotus would give public readings of the various stories *(logoi)* making up his work. This is confirmed by the allusions in the text to audience reaction, and by the circular structure of the writing.

This practice had a marked effect on the composition of the work, which may seem to be something of a patchwork, with its countless digressions that sometimes fit into one another like Chinese boxes or Russian dolls. More a painter than a sculptor, Herodotus excels in the art of storytelling and possesses the gift of enthralling his audience, whether listener or reader, by his descriptions of a detail, an episode or an individual.

He often tells a story which he has heard at second or third hand. For example, after describing the victory of the Athenians over the Persians at Marathon, he tells what happened to the Athenian soldier Epizelos, who lost his sight

while fighting in the battle, though nothing had hit him: "I am told that in speaking about what happened to him he used to say that he fancied he was opposed by a man of great stature in heavy armour, whose beard overshadowed his shield; but the phantom passed him by, and killed the man at his side." It would be a mistake to see this as Herodotus directly reporting what he has heard, but rather as an example of the mirror play that is a common feature of the *Histories:* Epizelos tells his story, others repeat it, Herodotus hears it and tells it in his turn.

This is not simply a taste for the fantastic or the marvellous, for which Herodotus is so often criticized, but a delight in intriguing and surprising his audience. He is able to arouse people's curiosity because his own is so great. He is interested in all kinds of out-of-the-way details, the customs of each people and all the wonders of the world, whether events, inventions or monuments like the pyramids of Egypt, the labyrinth above Lake Moeris and the walls of Babylon. In his quest for knowledge, Herodotus would travel and make inquiries of those who might have information about the countries visited—scholars, priests or people whose names are not recorded: "I learn by inquiry."

The reason for this passion for research emerges clearly in the introduction to the *Histories:* it is the historian's task to combat time, to preserve what he considers to be memorable. In the Greek cities and sanctuaries there were already "memorizers" *(mnemones)* responsible for recollecting and recording divine and human occurrences. But the historian's concerns are much loftier than the purely administrative, legal and religious functions of the *mnemones.* All the illustrious deeds and labours *(erga)* that he relates must retain their *kleos,* their aura of glory, their renown. In some ways Herodotus seems to carry on where the epic

Reprinted with permission from *The Unesco Courier,* March 1990, pp. 16-19.

poets left off. They recounted the deeds of heroes, the historian recounts the deeds of men.

The insatiable curiosity shown by Herodotus in his investigations and travels considerably broadened the scope of written history, which ceased to consist solely of myths, genealogical lists and ethno-historical material relating to particular peoples or communities. Although he wanted to preserve as much as possible, he had to select which of the facts to save. For the historian who takes as his subject "great and marvellous actions", not everything is memorable.

Herodotus was aware of the amount of space given in his *Histories* to the long parentheses of the storyteller. On one occasion he even confesses: "I need not apologize for the digression—it has been my plan throughout this work." To understand this attitude, we should not use modern criteria nor even refer to later Greek authors whose works, which were designed exclusively to be read, seem to be better constructed. In a work addressed primarily to listeners and only subsequently to readers, not only the form but the choice of material were determined by the exigencies of spoken communication. It is not enough for details to be historically revealing or admirable; they must also be entertaining and, whether glorious or despicable, arouse the curiosity of the narrator and strike a chord in the minds of his audience.

AN INVESTIGATOR AT WORK

What was Herodotus' raw material? Much of the *Histories* records the history and customs of peoples incorporated in the Persian empire (or those of peoples like the Scythians which were unsuccessfully fought by the empire) as well as facts about the Greek cities in the sixth and fifth centuries BC. The culmination is confrontation between the Greeks and the Persians, which accounts for less than half the work.

Herodotus does not speak of a single people, nor even of a single Greek city, nor of Greece in its entirety. He erects no barriers, shows no scorn. He does not really differentiate between the Greeks and other peoples, the "Barbarians". Born at a time which, under the influence of the Sophists, saw the development of cultural relativism, and originating from a region at the meeting-point of East and West, he showed curiosity, consideration and even respect for other cultures.

He nevertheless viewed them through Greek eyes. In keeping with a typically Hellenic way of seeing the foreigner as a reversed image of oneself, he depicted the behaviour of other peoples as the antithesis of that of the Greeks. Among the "strange practices" of the Egyptians, for example, he mentions that "women attend market and are employed in trade, while men stay at home and do the weaving. . . . Men in Egypt carry loads on their heads, women on their shoulders. . . ." His enumeration of their differences ends as follows: "In writing or calculating, instead of going, like the Greeks, from left to right, the Egyptians go from right to left—and obstinately maintain that theirs is the dexterous method, ours being left-handed and awkward."

This comparative method can be seen as a way of classifying and hence of understanding. But Herodotus also observes similarities, which he scrupulously notes, as in the case of the Spartans. Customs on the death of a king, he reports, "are the same in Sparta as in Asia", and "the Spartans resemble the Egyptians in that they make certain callings hereditary: town-criers (heralds), flute-players and cooks are all, respectively, sons of fathers who followed the same profession."

Although he does not go as far as Thucydides in saying that the Greeks lived formerly in the same way as the Barbarians today, and although he maintains a distance between the two worlds, he does not regard them as two monolithic blocks, one of which is in certain respects inferior to the other or culturally backward. Different though they may be, he acknowledges the many qualities of the Barbarians, considering, for example, that the Greek gods have Egyptian origins, that Egyptian civilization is older than that of the Greeks, and that the Persians have numerous virtues.

The *Histories* end with a revealing anecdote. To convince his people not to attempt to settle in more fertile lands, the Persian King Cyrus the Great declares to his troops that "soft countries breed soft men", pointing out that the Greeks have preferred to keep their freedom on a harsh land rather than to be slaves cultivating fertile plains for others. It is thus a Persian sovereign who enunciates a truth applying chiefly to the Greeks. Herodotus also sets among the Persians a discussion on the best form of government—democracy, oligarchy or monarchy. They are foreigners, enemies, but not completely different. They could even, in theory at least, be like the Greeks, in the same way that the Greeks in some respects resemble them.

Herodotus does not try to describe a series of mythical or historical events since their origins or even from one of the traditional milestones in Greek history, as other historians were to do after him. His field of study—the Median wars and the events that led up to them—covers a fairly recent period. That which is remote in time is left to poets and genealogists. He displays the same attitude towards Egypt, distinguishing what he has witnessed personally from the information he has collected from the Egyptians. If he consults Persian, Phoenician or Egyptian scholars about mythical episodes, such as the abduction of Helen and the Trojan War, it is mainly in order to retrace and understand the causes of the Median wars.

In choosing as his area of investigation recent history of which he could have direct knowledge, Herodotus had a decisive influence on the development of historiography. Thucydides, half a generation younger, would go even further than his great predecessor, directing his gaze to current events.

Love and Death in Ancient Greece

Catching him in the act, an obscure citizen of Athens slew his wife's lover. But was it a crime of passion—or premeditated murder?

Kenneth Cavander

Euphiletos was tired. He had been out in the country all day attending to business, and now he was home trying to get some sleep, and the baby was crying. His house was on two floors; the baby slept with a maid on the first floor; above, there was a combined living–dining– sleeping area for him and his wife. Euphiletos told his wife to go downstairs and nurse the baby. She protested that she wanted to be with him; she'd missed him while he was in the country—or did he just want to get rid of her so that he could make a pass at the maid, as he had the time he got drunk? Euphiletos laughed at that and at last his wife agreed to go downstairs and hush the child, but she insisted on locking the door to their room. Euphiletos turned over and went back to sleep. It never occurred to him to ask why his wife had gone through the charade of keeping him away from the maid, or why she had spent the rest of the night downstairs. But a few days later something happened that made him ask these questions, and by the end of the month a man was dead, killed in full view of a crowd of neighbors and friends.

This drama took place nearly two thousand five hundred years ago in ancient Athens. The characters were none of the brilliant and celebrated figures of the times—Socrates, Plato, Euripides, Aristophanes, Alcibiades—but members of the Athenian lower-middle class, obscure people who receded into the shadows of history. Their story is a soap opera compared to the grander tragedies being played out at the festivals of Di-

onysos in the theatre cut into the slopes of the Acropolis.

By a quirk of fate and an accident of politics the speech written for the murder trial that climaxes this story was the work of a man named Lysias. As a boy, Lysias sat in the company of Plato and Socrates, who often visited his father's house. As an adult, he was active in politics, and when a coup by the opposition party sent his family into exile, his property was confiscated and he narrowly escaped with his life. But a countercoup soon allowed him to return to Athens, and Lysias, now without a livelihood, had to find a profession.

He found one in the Athenian legal system. Athenian law was complex and attorneys were unknown; every citizen had to prosecute or defend himself in person. As a result, a class of professional legal advisers emerged that made a living supplying litigants with cogent, legally sound briefs. In time, Lysias became one of the most sought-after of these speech writers and several examples of his elegant and literate Greek style have been preserved, including the speech written for the defendant in this case.

Euphiletos, like many Athenians of modest means, lived in a small house in the city and commuted to the country to attend to his farm or market garden. He cannot have been well-off, for his house had the minimum number of slaves— one. Even a sausage seller or baker had at least one slave. Euphiletos had recently married and he was a trusting husband, so he said, giving his wife anything she asked for, never questioning her movements, trying to please her in

every possible way. The most exciting event in the marriage was the birth of their child, whom his wife nursed herself. But the most significant event was the death of his mother: the whole family attended the funeral and, although Euphiletos did not know it at the time, his marriage was laid to rest that day along with his mother.

After the birth of their child Euphiletos and his wife had rearranged their living quarters. It was too dangerous to carry the baby up and down the steep ladder to the upper floor every time the child needed to be washed or changed, so the family was split up. Euphiletos and his wife moved into the upper part of the house, while the baby, with the slave girl to look after it, stayed downstairs.

The arrangement worked well, and Euphiletos's wife often went down in the middle of the night to be with the baby when it was cranky. But on the evening of the day Euphiletos came back tired from the country, two things in addition to the little drama of the locked door struck him as unusual. One was his wife's makeup: it was only a month since her brother had died—yet he noticed that she had put powder on her face. And there were noises in the night that sounded like a hinge creaking. When his wife awakened him by unlocking the bedroom door the next morning, Euphiletos asked her about these sounds. She said she had gone next door to a neighbor's house to borrow some oil for the baby's night light, which had gone out. As for the makeup, when Euphiletos thought about it he remembered his wife saying how much she had missed him and how reluctantly she had left him to go down and take care of the baby. Reassured, he dismissed the whole episode from his mind and thought no more about it—until something happened to shatter this comforting domestic picture and rearrange all the pieces of the puzzle in quite a different way.

One morning, a few days later, Euphiletos was leaving his house when he was stopped in the street by an old woman. She apologized for taking his time. "I'm not trying to make trouble," she said, "but we have an enemy in common." The old woman was a slave. Her mistress, she said, had been having an affair, but her lover had grown tired of her and left her for another woman. The other woman was Euphiletos's wife.

"The man is called Eratosthenes," said the old slave. "Ask your maid about him. He's seduced several women. He's got it down to a fine art."

In the midst of his shock and anger Euphiletos revealed a streak of something methodical, almost detached, in his character. Instead of going straight to his wife or her lover, he proceeded like an accountant investigating an error in the books.

He retraced his steps to his house and ordered the maidservant to come with him to the market. His wife would see nothing unusual in this, for respectable married women did not go out shopping in fifth-century Athens. That was left to the men and the slaves. Halfway to the market Euphiletos turned aside and marched the girl to the house of a friend, where he confronted her with the old woman's story. The girl denied it. Euphiletos threatened to beat her. She told him to go ahead and do what he liked. He talked of prison. She still denied it. Then Euphiletos mentioned Eratosthenes' name, and she broke down. In return for a promise that she would not be harmed, she told Euphiletos everything.

Her story was bizarre as well as comic and macabre. It began at the funeral of Euphiletos's mother. Eratosthenes had seen Euphiletos's wife among the mourners and had taken a fancy to her. He got in touch with the maid and persuaded her to act as go-between. Whether it was a difficult or an easy seduction we don't know; but, as the old woman had said, Eratosthenes was a practiced hand.

This love affair, first planned at a funeral and then set in motion by proxy, was carried on mostly at Euphiletos's house when he was away in the country. On one occasion his wife may have contrived to meet her lover away from the house, for she had gone with Eratosthenes' mother to the festival of the Thesmophoria, one of several festivals celebrated in honor of feminine deities. During these festivals a woman could leave the seclusion of her own house without arousing suspicious comment.

The slave girl also told Euphiletos that on the night he came back tired from the country, her mistress had told her to pinch the baby to make it cry, which gave her an excuse to go downstairs. His wife's parade of jealousy, Euphiletos now realized, was an act, designed to provide her with a reason to lock the door on him. So while he was a temporary prisoner in his own bedroom, his wife was downstairs in the nursery with her lover, and the maid was keeping the baby quiet somewhere else.

In a crisis, a person will often revert to archetypal behavior. For the Greeks of the fifth century B.C. the Homeric poems provided a mythological blueprint for almost any life situation, and it is interesting to see how Euphiletos's next move re-created a scene out of the legends. In *The Odyssey* Homer tells the story of what happened when Hephaistos, the god of fire, found out that his wife, Aphrodite, had been sleeping with the war god, Ares. Hephaistos decided not to face Aphrodite with her infidelity; instead, he wove a magical net that was sprung by the two lovers when they climbed into bed together. Then, as they lay there trapped, Hephaistos invited the other Olympians to come and view the guilty pair, "and the unquenchable laughter of the gods rose into the sky." In his own mundane way, but without the magic net, Euphiletos would follow the example of Hephaistos. He made his slave promise to keep everything she had told him a secret; then, pretending to his wife that he suspected nothing, he went about his business as usual and waited for a chance to spring his trap.

The part of cuckold is a mortifying one to play, and it was particularly so in ancient Athens where the relative status of men and women was so unequal. A freeborn Athenian woman was free in little more than name. She could not vote, make contracts, or conduct any business involving more than a certain sum of money; legally she was little more than a medium for the transmission of property from grandfather to grand-children through the dowry she brought with her to her husband. Her husband, of course, was invariably chosen for her by her father or by the nearest male relative if her father was dead. Almost the only thing she could call her own was her reputation, which depended on good behavior, an unassertive demeanor, a life spent dutifully spinning, weaving, dyeing clothes, cooking, bearing and raising children, and, above all, on not interfering in the serious business of life as conducted by the men. In a famous speech in praise of the Athenian men who died during the Peloponnesian War, Pericles makes only one reference to women: according to Thucydides, who reports the speech in his history of the war, Pericles said that women should never give rise to any comment by a man, favorable or unfavorable. In the tragic dramas, moreover, women who offer their opinions unasked or who go about alone in public usually feel they have to apologize for behaving in such a brazen and immodest way.

Such was the official status of women. Unofficially, the women of ancient Athens found ways, as their sisters have done in every age and culture, to undermine the barriers of male prejudice. In Euripides' play *Iphigeneia at Aulis* (written within a year or two of Euphiletos's marriage), Agamemnon tries to assert his authority over his wife, Clytemnestra, in order to get her out of the way while he sacrifices his own daughter, Iphigeneia, to Artemis. Clytemnestra, with a show of wifely stubbornness that surely came out of the playwright's contemporary observation, refuses to be dismissed and finally cuts the conversation short by sending her husband about his business. In another play by Euripides, *Hippolytos,* there are some lines that might have been written specifically for Euphiletos himself to speak. Hippolytos, told that his stepmother, Phaidra, is in love with him, remarks scathingly: "I would have no servants near a woman, just beasts with teeth and no voice, [for] servants are the agents in the world outside for the wickedness women do."

Drink and sex are the traditional outlets for the oppressed. The comedies of Aristophanes are studded with snide references to the excessive drinking habits of women. According to Aristophanes, festivals such as the Thesmophoria were excuses for massive alcoholic sprees. More likely, these mystery cults were the safety valve for pent-up emotions, a chance to transcend the cruelly narrow boundaries imposed on women by their roles in a rigidly male society.

As for sex, women were the weaker vessel when it came to this human urge. In *Lysistrata* Aristophanes has the women wondering whether they can hold out long enough to bring the men to their knees. And in the legends that canonized popular wisdom on the subject there is a story about Zeus and Hera squabbling over who gets the greater pleasure out of sex—the man or the woman. When they finally appeal to Teiresias, the blind seer and prophet, who, as part man and part woman, ought to be able to settle the question for them, he duly reports that in the sexual act the woman, in fact, gets nine-tenths of the pleasure, and the man only one-tenth.

These scraps of myth and folklore, however, filtered through male fantasy as they are, reveal a sense of unease about women. In the Orestes myth, for instance, it is Clytemnestra who takes over the reins of government in the absence of Agamemnon, then murders him when he returns; and it is her daughter Electra who pushes a faltering Orestes into taking revenge for the slain king. A whole army of formidable heroines—Electra, Clytemnestra, Antigone, Hecuba, Andromache, Medea—marches through the pages of Greek drama. The Fates, the Muses, and the Furies are all women. None of these female figures is anything like the meek and passive drudge that the Greek woman of the fifth century was expected to be.

But were they real types, these mythological heroines, or were they phantom projections of male fears and desires, mother imagoes, castration anxieties dressed up as gods, embodiments of the part of a man he most wants to repress—his own irrational and emotional side, his moon-bound, lunatic aspects—thrust onto women because he dare not admit them in himself?

It is possible. Every mythologized figure embodies inner and outer worlds. We see what we wish to see, and the picture we perceive turns into a mirror. Were there actual women in Athens capable of organizing a fully functioning communistic state and pushing it through the assembly, like the Praxagora of Aristophanes' play *Ekklesiazousai?* Were there Electras and Clytemnestras and Medeas? If there were, they never reached the pages of the history books. We hear of Aspasia, Pericles' "companion" (the Greek word is *hetaira,* meaning "woman friend"), for whom he divorced his legal wife. But Aspasia was a member of the demimonde of "liberated" women who lived outside the social order, not necessarily slaves, but not full citizens either. They were often prostitutes, but some of them were cultured and educated, better traveled and more interesting to Athenian men than their own wives. Custom permitted one or more relationships with *hetairai* outside the marriage, but a *hetaira* had no legal claim on a man, and he could sell her or dispose of her any time he liked. Meanwhile, for the trueborn Athenian woman who wanted a more varied life than the one prescribed by convention, what was there? Gossip with the neighbors. The bottle. A festival now and then. A clandestine love affair.

Four or five days passed while Euphiletos brooded over the wrong done to him. Suppose a child was born from this liaison: who could tell whether it was his or Eratosthenes'? All kinds of complications might follow. But whatever he was feeling, Euphiletos managed to hide it from his wife. She never suspected that he knew anything at all.

Euphiletos had a good friend named Sostratos. Less than a week after his interview with the maid Euphiletos met Sostratos coming home from the country, and since it was late Euphiletos invited his friend to his house for supper. This casual meeting was to become important later at the trial. The two men went upstairs, ate and drank well, and had a pleasant evening together. By custom Euphiletos's wife was not present. After Sostratos had gone home Euphiletos went to sleep.

Some time in the middle of the night there was a knock on his door. It was the maid. Eratosthenes had arrived.

Leaving the maid to keep watch, Euphiletos slipped out a back way and went around the neighborhood waking up his friends. Some of them were out of town, but he managed to collect a small group who went to a nearby store and bought torches. Then they all trooped off to Euphiletos's house where they stood outside in the street holding the lighted torches while Euphiletos tapped on the door. Quietly the maid let him into the courtyard. He pushed past her into the room where his wife was supposed to be asleep with the baby. A few of Euphiletos's friends managed to crowd in behind him.

For a split second the scene must have been like a tableau out of Homer: Eratosthenes naked in bed, Euphiletos's wife in his arms, the two lovers trapped in the light of torches held by the neighbors.

Then Eratosthenes, still naked, sprang up. Euphiletos shouted at him, "What are you doing in my house?" and knocked him off the bed, pulled his wrists behind his back, and tied them.

Eratosthenes offered to pay Euphiletos any sum he named. Euphiletos had a choice: he could accept the bribe, or he could take a form of revenge allowed by law—brutalizing and humiliating Eratosthenes by such methods as the insertion of tough thistles up his rectum. There was also a third option open to him under the circumstances: since he had caught Eratosthenes in the act, and there were witnesses present, Euphiletos could kill him.

Euphiletos interrupted the other man's pleas. "I won't kill you," he said, and then, in the kind of logical twist the Greeks loved, he added, "but the law will."

And in the name of the law he killed Eratosthenes.

Athenian homicide law required the dead man's family, not the state, to bring charges of murder. Eratosthenes' family undertook the task, and approximately three months later Euphiletos found himself facing a jury of fifty-one Athenians in the court known as the Delphinion, located in the southeast corner of Athens, where cases of justifiable homicide were tried. Eratosthenes' family charged Euphiletos with premeditated murder on the grounds that he had sent his maid to lure Eratosthenes to the house; they may also have tried to prove that Eratosthenes was dragged into the building by force, or took refuge at the hearth before he was killed. In the speech he writes for Euphiletos, Lysias sets out to rebut all these charges.

Lysias puts into Euphiletos's mouth some ingenious legal arguments. The law (of which a copy is read to the court) says that a seducer caught in the act may be killed. "If you make it a crime to kill a seducer in this way," he argues, "you will have a situation in which a thief, caught burglarizing your house, will pretend that he is an adulterer in order to get away with a lesser crime." Lysias also refers the jury to the law on rape. Rape carries a lower penalty than seduction. Why? Because, theorizes Lysias, the rapist simply takes the woman's body, while the seducer steals her soul.

Nevertheless, in spite of Lysias's able and sophisticated defense, there is a flaw in Euphiletos's argument. His defense rests on the assumption that his action was unpremeditated, committed in the heat of the moment, under the shock and stress of finding his wife in bed with another man. That is surely the intent of the law, and Euphiletos goes to great lengths to prove he had not planned the encounter. He cites the dinner invitation to Sostratos, which, he says, is not the behavior of a man planning murder. But the rest of his story contradicts this. The signals by which the maid warned him that Eratosthenes had arrived and by which he let her know that he was waiting at the front door; the rounding up of friends to act as witnesses; the presence of the murder weapon on his person—all point to prior preparation. Euphiletos may prove to the jury's satisfaction that he did not lure Eratosthenes deliberately to his house that night, but he fails to prove that he was taken totally by surprise or that he tried to do anything to stop the affair before it reached that point. His action looks suspiciously like cold-blooded revenge executed under color of a law that forgives even violent crimes if they are committed in the heat of passion.

Neither the speech for the prosecution nor the testimony of witnesses has survived, so we do not know if the wife or the maid gave evidence. Though women were not allowed to appear as witnesses in court cases, the rules for murder trials may have been different. A slave could not testify at all, but a deposition could have been taken from her under torture and read to the court. On the other hand, Euphiletos may have wanted to avoid bringing the women into it: after all, they had been in league against him throughout the whole unhappy affair.

There is something touching in the alliance between the slave, an object without rights or status, and the wife, legally a free citizen but in reality a kind of slave too. The maidservant probably accepted a bribe from Eratosthenes, but all the same she had a moment of heroism when, threatened with a beating and prison, she refused to incriminate her mistress. Afterward, when she became Euphiletos's accomplice, there is an eerie reversal of the situation: the slave admits her master to the house in the same stealthy way that she had opened the door for her mistress's lover a few minutes earlier. But still, there was a moment when Euphiletos was the outsider, barred from his own house and his wife's arms, with only his rage and his group of male friends for company.

Finally there is the wife herself, the center of the drama and its most shadowy character. Apart from his grudging admission that she was thrifty and capable and a good housekeeper, Euphiletos tells us little about her. From what we know of Athenian marriage customs, we can guess that she was probably married at fourteen or fifteen to a virtual stranger and expected to keep house for this man who spent much of his time away from home on business. Was she satisfied with the trinkets that Euphiletos says he let her buy, and with all of the household duties and her young baby?

A small fragment survives from a lost play by Aristophanes in which a character says, "A woman needs a lover the way a dinner needs dessert." Euphiletos's wife was no Lysistrata, able to express her frustration and rebellion in some dramatic act of revolutionary will, but she did find a way to rebel all the same. It cost her dear. By Athenian law, if a man discovered that his wife had been raped or seduced, he was expected to divorce her. And from what we know of Euphiletos's character, we can be sure that he obeyed the law.

The Oldest Dead White European Males

A defense of ancient (and tarnished) Greece.

Bernard Knox

Bernard Knox is director emeritus of the Center for Hellenic Studies. A slightly different version of this essay was delivered at the National Endowment for the Humanities' Twenty-first Annual Jefferson Lecture in the Humanities in Washington, D.C.

I.

The species known as DWEM, which has only recently been isolated and identified, is already the focus of intense controversy. As usually happens to newly discovered species, it is even being broken down into subspecies; I am informed that a professor at a local university has recently offered a course in DWAM, that is, in Dead White American Males, with readings presumably in such writers as Thoreau, Emerson, and Mark Twain. I propose to discuss only the European type, and, in particular, its first appearance on the face of the planet.

My specimens are certainly dead. In fact, they have been in that condition longer than any other members of the species—for more than 2,500 years. Despite recent suggestions that they came originally from Ethiopia, they were undoubtedly white, or more exactly, a sort of Mediterranean olive. They invented the idea and gave us the name of Europe, fixing its imagined frontier at the long sea passage between the Black Sea and the Mediterranean, waters that Xerxes, the Great King of the Persians, crossed, Herodotus tells us, on his way from Asia to Europe. And they created a form of society in which, for all practical pur-

poses (which were, for them, war, politics, competitive athletics, and litigation), women played no part whatsoever.

I refer, of course, to the ancient Greeks, particularly to those of the eighth to the fourth centuries before the birth of Christ. Their assignment to the DWEM category is one of the accomplishments of modern multicultural and feminist criticism; and it is a declaration of their irrelevance. But previous ages spoke of them in very different terms. "We are all Greeks," wrote Shelley in 1822, "our laws, our literature, our religion, our arts, have their roots in Greece." There is some exaggeration here, especially in the matter of the Christian religion, which has deeper and wider roots in Hebrew Palestine than it does in Neoplatonic philosophy; Shelley, who had been expelled from Oxford for writing and circulating a pamphlet titled "The Necessity of Atheism," was not exactly an expert in this field. Still, by 1865 this identification with the ancient Greeks had advanced so far that, as Frank Turner put it in his fascinating book *The Greek Heritage in Victorian Britain:*

> The major commentator on Homer as well as a major translator of the poet, the chief critic and historian of Greek literature, the most significant political historians of Greece and the authors of the then most extensive commentaries on Greek philosophy either were or had recently been members of the House of Commons or the House of Lords.

The ancient Greeks were not seen just as roots, but as fully formed models of Victorian moral and intellectual culture. George Grote, the "intellectual and tactical leader of the philosophic radicals in the House of Commons," was the author of an influential *History of Greece,* in

which the Athenian assembly bears a startling resemblance to the House of Commons, with Pericles as prime minister and his opponent Thucydides the son of Melesias as leader of her majesty's loyal opposition. And William Ewart Gladstone, in the intervals of serving as president of the Board of Trade, colonial secretary, chancellor of the Exchequer, and four terms as prime minister, found time to write a series of books, one of them in three volumes, on Homer, in which he tried to prove that the Greeks, like the Jews, were a chosen people, entrusted by God with "no small share of those treasures of which the Semitic family of Abraham were to be the appointed guardians, on behalf of mankind, until the fullness of time should come." The Victorians appropriated the ancient Greeks, imagined them as contemporaries, and used their writings as weapons in their own ideological wars. If they had been attuned to modern advertising techniques, they might have reversed Shelley's claim and launched the slogan GREEKS 'R' US.

There was a reaction, of course. Scholars such as Jane Harrison, James Frazer, and Andrew Lang, drawing on the rather unreliable anthropological material available to them at the time (unreliable because most of it had been compiled by Christian missionaries who, like Gladstone, tried to detect premonitions of Christianity in what they regarded as the aberrations of the primitive mind), painted a very different picture of the religious ideas and practices of the Greeks. And historians developed a more acerbic view of the realities of Athenian democratic in-fighting: the ten-year sentence of exile imposed on Aristides the Just, the suicide in exile of Themistocles, who had saved Athens in the Persian War, the assassination of Ephialtes, the reformist colleague of Pericles, the temporary overthrow of the democracy by an oligarchic coup d'état in 411 B.C., and the reign of terror of the Thirty Tyrants, backed by victorious Spartan troops, in 404.

In 1938 Louis MacNeice, who was a professor of Greek at the University of London as well as, next to Auden, the finest poet of his generation, bade a melancholy farewell to "the glory that was Greece" in his poem "Autumn Journal." Contemplating the prospect of once more acting, to use his own phrase, as "impresario of the ancient Greeks," he sketched an ironic picture of the professor preparing his lectures on Greek civilization:

> The Glory that was Greece: put it in a
>   syllabus, grade it
> Page by page
> To train the mind or even to point a
>   moral
> For the present age:
> Models of logic and lucidity, dignity,
>   sanity,
> The golden mean between opposing
>   ills . . .

But then he suddenly turns his back on this familiar and comfortable prospect:

> But I can do nothing so useful or so
>   simple;
> These dead are dead
> And when I should remember the para-
>   gons of Hellas
> I think instead
> Of the crooks, the adventurers, the
>   opportunists
> The careless athletes and the fancy
>   boys,
> The hair-splitters, the pedants, the
>   hard-boiled sceptics
> And the Agora and the noise
> Of the demagogues and the quacks;
>   and the women pouring
> Libations over graves
> And the trimmers at Delphi and the
>   dummies at Sparta and lastly
> I think of the slaves.
> And how one can imagine oneself
>   among them
> I do not know;
> It was all so unimaginably different
> And all so long ago.

The Roman word for "poet," *vates,* also meant "inspired prophet," and in these lines MacNeice unconsciously anticipated, as poets often do, future developments. For in the fifty or so years since he wrote them, classical scholars have concentrated their attention on the dark underside of what the Victorians hailed as the Greek Miracle. There is

hardly an aspect of ancient Greek civilization that has not been relentlessly explored, analyzed, and exposed in its strangeness, it "otherness," to use a once fashionable term borrowed from the French existentialists, by scholars armed with the insights and methods of anthropology, sociology, psychology, psychoanalysis, structuralism, deconstruction, narratology, semiotics, and all the other proliferating weapons of the modern intellectual armory. If the Victorian vision of Greece could be summed up in the slogan GREEKS 'R' US, the modern critics could retort that GREEKS 'R' THEM, or more pointedly, GREEKS 'R' DWEM.

II.

The results, of course, have been mixed. It might be said of the new approaches to Greek culture and literature what Sophocles in a famous choral ode of the *Antigone* said of mankind in general: "Equipped with the ingenuity of its techniques, a thing subtle beyond expectation, it makes its way sometimes to bad, sometimes to good." In this re-evaluation of the Greek heritage, four areas are of special interest: anthropology, psychology, slavery, and the position of women.

One thing is certain: the strangeness, the "otherness," certainly exists. Many of the normal, routine practices of the ancient Greeks seem to us not just strange, but positively bizarre. One of the most common occurrences in any Greek epic text, for example, is a sacrifice. Sacrifice, for us, is a blandly metaphorical word: we talk of a "sacrifice play" in team sports, or more seriously, in the old formulas of the Christian communion service, "We offer and present unto thee O Lord ourselves, our souls and bodies, to be a reasonable, holy, and living sacrifice unto thee." And if we do think of sacrifice as a real ceremony, we are apt to see it in the romantic aura of Keats's "Ode on a Grecian Urn":

> Who are these coming to the sacrifice?
> To what green altar, O mysterious
>   priest,
> Lead'st thou that heifer lowing at the
>   skies,
> And all her silken flanks with garlands
>   dressed?

Keats stopped there; his urn didn't show what happened next. But Homer, more than once, gave the

full scenario. A domestic animal, the victim, makes its way toward the rough stone altar (it must not be coerced). The presiding sacrificer cuts a tuft of hair from its head and throws it onto the fire that has been lit well in advance; he then scatters barley meal over the animal. Another ministrant swiftly brings an ax down on the animal's neck, cutting the tendons, and the women who are present raise their ritual shriek (*ololuge* is the Greek onomatopoeic word for it). Another celebrant pulls back the animal's head and cuts its throat; the blood is caught in a bowl and splashed onto the altar.

The carcass is now hacked apart. The tough (and valuable) hide is ripped off and set aside. The thigh bones are stripped of flesh, wrapped in layers of fat, and decorated with small pieces of meat from the edible parts of the victim: this is the portion of the gods, and as it is thrown on the fire the thick bluish smoke goes up toward their dwelling place in the clouds. Meanwhile wine for the gods is poured out on the ground. The liver and the heart of the animal are toasted on the fire and eaten, as the serious business of roasting the flesh proper begins.

And all this hard and bloody work takes place in the glaring Aegean sun. The air is heavy with the odors of sweat, blood, burning fat, and the inedible offal of the animal that has been thrown away. And the flies—Homer speaks of them elsewhere as swarming round the milk pails in peace time, and in a more sinister context as feeding on the wounds of a dead warrior—the flies must have been there in swarms, covering the raw meat, stinging the butchers at their work.

It is not like anything we know, but for Homer's audience it was routine, normal, on a par with the launching of a boat, or the arming—or the death—of a warrior; and it was always described in the same formulaic language. All this ritual bloodletting and butchery, moreover, is not only the preliminary to a feast, it is also an act of worship of the Olympian gods.

For us, however, it is a puzzle: an elaborate pattern of behavior that seems at once naive—in its offering to the gods of the bones and fat decorated with some token tidbits of the edible meat—and sophisticated—in the careful ritualization that blunts the shock of the animal's violent death and tries to absolve the celebrants (through its pretense that the victim is willing) of any feeling of guilt.

It is the kind of puzzle that often faces anthropologists studying tribal customs in undeveloped countries. Indeed, much of the best modern work on Greek culture has in fact been based on an anthropological approach to the problems it presents.

As early as 1724, a French Jesuit called Joseph Lafitau, who had lived in Canada among the Indians, published a book in which he made the remarkable claim that though he had learned from classical authors many things that helped him understand the people he refers to as "savages," the reverse was also true: "The customs of the Savages afforded me illumination the more easily to understand and explain several matters to be found in ancient authors." This passage is cited by Pierre Vidal-Naquet, one of a brilliant group of French cultural historians who, in recent years, have used the insights and the techniques of modern anthropology to investigate the religious, moral, and political mentality of the ancient Greeks. Louis Gernet (1882–1962), little known in his lifetime, became famous after his student Jean-Pierre Vernant published a collection of his articles under the title *Anthropologie de la Grèce Antique* in 1968. Vernant himself, especially concerned with what he calls *psychologie historique*, "the history of the inner man," has given us a wealth of fresh and illuminating perspectives on Greek mythology, thought, religion, art, and literature, with a special emphasis on tragedy. Some of his many books have been works of collaboration: with Marcel Detienne, whose special field is religion and whose book *Les Jardins d'Adonis* is the only successful and rewarding application of the methods of Lévi-Strauss to Greek mythology; and with Vidal-Naquet, a historian who concerns himself with *formes de pensée, formes de société*, whose brilliant essays on ancient Greek politics, society, and literature draw strength and depth from his political engagement in the controversial issues of his own time—the war in Algeria, the Holocaust—and his sense of the vast perspectives, *la longue durée*, of history. (He recently served as editor of a remarkable *Atlas Historique*, a history of the human race from its prehistory to 1987 that makes inspired use of creative cartography and graphs.)

The problem posed by the rites of sacrifice is one of the principal concerns of these investigators; one of the many collaborative volumes issuing from their circle bears the evocative title *La Cuisine du Sacrifice Grec*. It is also the focus of an extraordinary book by Walter Burkert, a book that in its title has added to the already existing classifications of mankind—Homo erectus, Homo habilis, Homo sapiens, Homo sapiens sapiens, and so on—a new one: Homo necans, Man the Killer, Man the Sacrificer. Developing the theories of the Swiss folklorist Karl Meuli, Burkert traces the sacrificial ritual back to the preagricultural hunters, who, by their preservation of its hide, skull, and thigh bones, mimed a symbolic reconstitution of the slaughtered wild beast in a ceremony that absolved them from responsibility for its death—the "comedy of innocence"—and served as a magical deterrent to the extinction of the hunted animal's species. When, in the agricultural phase of human history, the victim was a domestic animal, the comedy of innocence, the pretense that the animal was a willing victim, became even more necessary. Burkert develops his probing analysis with immense learning, applying new insights drawn from his thesis to every aspect of Greek ritual and myth.

III.

One of the principal concerns of the Paris circle, the history of the inner man, was also the subject of an influential German book by Bruno Snell called *Die Entdeckung des Geistes* (translated as *The Discovery of the Mind*), which appeared originally in 1948. But unlike the theories of the Parisians, which are always impressive and suggestive even when they cannot be fully accepted, Snell's thesis about the early Greek mind, specifically about the mind of Homer, is fundamentally unsound. Snell's argument is that the discovery of the mind was an achievement of post-Homeric Greece, that in Homer's poems we are in a world that has not yet conceived the idea of the individual consciousness, of the personality.

As might have been expected from one of the editors of a lexicon of early Greek epic, one of the most useful tools for research in the Homeric texts, Snell's method is strictly philological. He points out that there is no word in the Homeric vocabulary for the spiritual or intellectual organ that we call "the soul" or "consciousness." There is, of course, the word *psyche*, but it is used only [for] whatever it is that leaves the body with the advent of death. For the emotional and intellectual functions of the living man, Homeric language offers a plurality of organs: the *thymos*, seat of violent passions, especially anger; the *phrenes*, seat of rational consideration and corresponding intention to act; *noos*, the organ of thought, of reflection, not connected with action or intention. And the word *phrenes*, which locates the rational faculty in the human body, does not mean, as we would expect, the brain; it means the diaphragm, the midriff.

Snell also claims that the Homeric language has no word for "body" either, except the word *soma*, which, as the ancient commentators pointed out, is used only of the dead body. The living body is thought of not as a unity, but as a collection of separate limbs—arms, legs, torso, head—just as the consciousness appears not as a central entity but as the separate realms of *thymos, phrenes*, and *noos*. All this, taken together with the frequency of expressions that attribute human action to divine intervention, seems to him to rule out for Homeric man the existence of a personal self in any sense we can understand. Snell's conclusion is disconcerting. "As a further consequence," he sums up,

> it appears that in the early period the "character" of an individual is not yet recognized. . . . There is no denying that the great heroes . . . are drawn in firm outline and yet the reactions of Achilles, however grand and magnificent, are not explicitly presented in their volitional or intellectual form as character, i.e., as individual intellect and individual soul.

Snell's case has an obvious weakness: it is an argument from silence, always a dangerous argument, especially when applied to two long poems that we know are only a fragment of what once existed in this epic genre. He is conscious of this weakness, though, and he tries to reinforce his position: "Through Homer, we have come to know early European thought in poems of such length that we need not hesitate to draw our conclusions, if necessary, *ex silentio*. If some things do not occur in Homer though our modern mentality would lead us to expect them, we are entitled to assume that he had no knowledge of them." But this, too, rests on a false assumption, on the assumption that the language of the epic poems is the language of Homeric society.

It was not, of course, the language of Homeric society (whatever that phrase may mean), nor of any society that ever existed. It was a language spoken neither by gods nor men, but one devised for epic song, full of ennobling archaisms, and every word and form amenable to the prosodic demands of the epic hexameter line. One scholar (an American this time) has gone so far as to argue that the Mycenean kings transmitted their mobilization orders in epic hexameter, and that pilots used the same medium to pass on sailing directions; but this picture of epic verse as a functional means of everyday communication (which Snell needs for his argument from silence to be taken seriously) is a fantasy. Suppose a soldier made some smart rejoinder to the mobilization order. The officer of the day would surely not have said to him what Homeric characters say to each other in such circumstances: *"poion se epos phugen herkos odonton"*—"What kind of word has escaped the stockade of your teeth?" There must have been some snappy Mycenean equivalent of "At ease, soldier!" And the chances are small that it would have fit the metrical pattern of the hexameter line.

In any case, the lexical method itself, with its assumption that the lack of a descriptive term argues the absence of the phenomenon for which there is no name, is a snare and a delusion. The English language—and I am not talking about 27,000 lines of early English verse, but about the whole range of spoken and written English from Chaucer to, say, Norman Mailer—has no word for that momentary self-congratulatory glow of satisfaction, immediately repressed, that is provoked by the news of the misfortunes of our friends, for the reaction "Better him than me" or "It's about time he learned the facts of life." When we want to describe this emotion, we have to fall back on a German word, *Schadenfreude.*

It is to be hoped that no future student of *Geistesgeschichte* will announce, on this basis, that this ignoble emotion was never experienced by people who grew up speaking English—or French, or Italian. Indeed, English propagandists in the First World War made much of this fact, and suggested that only the Huns had such base feelings. They were keeping silent about the fact that the classical

Greeks, whom they had all been taught to admire by Dr. Jowett of Balliol, had a very expressive word for it: *epichairekakia,* "rejoicing over calamities." (It is to be found in the *Nichomachean Ethics* of Aristotle, a text through which most Oxford men had been taken at a slow pace.)

Our researcher, however, had better look beyond the absence of such a word from the English and French dictionaries. In the first edition of his *Réflexions Morales,* published in 1665, La Rochefoucauld printed under the number 99 the following maxim:

Dans l'adversité de nos meilleurs amis nous trouvons toujours quelque chose qui ne nous déplaît pas. (In the adversities of our best friends we always find something which is not displeasing to us.)

La Rochefoucauld suppressed this scandalous thought in all succeeding editions of his famous maxims, but Dean Swift, in Dublin, had read the first edition and presented the idea, in his own fashion, to the English-speaking public:

Wise Rochefoucauld a maxim writ
Made up of malice, truth and wit . . .
He says: "Whenever Fortune sends
Disaster to our dearest friends
Although we outwardly may grieve
We oft are laughing in our sleeve."
 And when I think upon't this minute
I fancy there is something in it.

But the flaws in the argument from silence are even more serious than at first appears. The silence is far from perfect. There is, in fact, a Homeric word for the body as a unit, *demas,* a word that Snell dismisses hurriedly on quite inadmissible technical grounds. And there are many passages in the poems that suggest a Homeric conception of the unified individual personality. Above all, there is the hero's name, the name that he proudly bears and proclaims on all occasions, whether exulting over a fallen enemy or claiming his share of glory, the name that he conceals in the Cyclops's cave and later proudly, and as it turns out rashly, announces to his blinded enemy, the name by which later he proudly identifies himself at the court of the Phaeacians: "I am Odysseus, son of Laertes, known to all mankind for my crafty designs—my fame goes up to the heavens . . ."

This is the heroic self, the name, which in the case of Odysseus as in so many other cases is a speaking name, with more than a hint in it of the hero's

nature and destiny. But an individual personality is also suggested in those recurrent passages where a hero addresses some part of himself, his *thymos* or his *kradie,* his heart; the words used imply the central personality of the speaker, a personality to which the part addressed belongs. It might be added that Homer's reference to the diaphragm as the organ of the intelligence is no more surprising than our own frequent reference to the heart as the organ of the emotions or even of the intellect. Pascal knew all about the brain, but that didn't stop him from saying *le coeur a ses raisons,* and a famous American senator once ran for higher office with the slogan, "In your heart, you know he's right."

All this does not mean, of course, that Snell's careful analysis of Homer's language has to be rejected; his lexical approach has thrown light on many aspects of Homeric thought and feeling. What does not stand up to examination, however, is his claim that the language reveals the absence of a conception of individual personality, and that consequently a discussion of character as a base for speech and action is, in the case of the Homeric poems, irrelevant and misleading.

Many scholars who repudiate the extreme position still feel it necessary to warn against the use of the word "character." They give the impression that they think Snell is only half wrong: they claim that in Homer, and for that matter in Greek tragedy, we do not find the fully developed personalities with which we are familiar in modern literature. "However strong their impact as personalities"—I am quoting Albin Lesky, one of the most judicious scholars in this field—"they lack the wealth of individual features—often represented for their own sake—of their modern counterparts." He is obviously thinking of the novel—Emile Zola's gigantic creations, for example, or those of Thomas Mann; in *Buddenbrooks* the reader will find a myriad of "individual features . . . represented for their own sake." But the fact that Homer does not carry this extra baggage is something to be thankful for, not regretted. Shakespeare did not carry it either: he did not tell us what young Hamlet was studying at Wittenberg, or how many children Lady Macbeth had. Homer's characters, like Shakespeare's, like those of all great art, are the product of creative genius working in a rich tradition and equipped with an exquisite sense of artistic economy and balance. This poet knew what so many of his successors never learned, or else forgot: that (to quote Corinna's advice to Pindar) one should sow seeds with the hand, not the sack. Voltaire, many centuries later, put it another way: "The recipe for boredom is—completeness."

The proof of the pudding, in any case, is in the eating. Homer's characters are in fact among the most individually striking ever created. The later Greeks never tired of discussing, in prose and in poetry, the nature of Achilles' pride, the suicidal wrath of Ajax, the versatility of Odysseus; they re-created these figures in terms of their own time on the tragic stage. And subsequent ages have followed their example: Bloom, Dedalus, and Molly are only the most recent of a long series of re-embodiments of Homer's characters. Only Shakespeare can compete with Homer in this extraordinary power to impose his fictional personalities on the imagination of succeeding ages. Only scholars—and I speak of them with sympathy, since I am one of their number—could bring themselves to deny Homer the power to create literary character in the fullest sense of the words, in defiance of the brute fact that Homer's characters have fascinated and obsessed writers and readers for some 2,500 years, longer than any other such set of personalities except the characters of the Hebrew Old Testament.

IV.

The "inner man" is not the only precinct of ancient Greece to be explored with new insights and technologies. Attention has also been directed to two aspects of Greek, and especially Athenian, culture that the Victorians swept under the rug: slavery, and the inferior position, one might even say the subjection, of women. The Victorians were not alone in their indifference to the phenomenon of chattel and other kinds of slavery in Greece; as Moses Finley acidly pointed out, the very full index to *Paideia,* Werner Jaeger's three-volume work on the formation of the Athenian character, which appeared in 1933, contained no entry for "slaves" or "slavery." This despite the fact that, as Finley remarked elsewhere, "there was no action, no belief or institution in Greco-Roman antiquity that was

not, in one way or the other, affected by the possibility that someone involved might be a slave."

There were two things that the Greeks of the classical period prized above all others. One was *kleos* or fame, the admiration of his fellow men for his prowess as a soldier, an orator, or an athlete—particularly the last, for winners of events at Olympia and the other great games were so overwhelmed with honors and rewards that it was a commonplace in the odes that poets wrote, on commission, to celebrate their victories to remind them, in ways sometimes subtle and sometimes blunt, that they were not gods but only mortals. The other thing that the Greeks prized was *schole,* or leisure: freedom from the drudgery of work, time to stroll in the columned porticos of the city and discuss politics, points of law, or the latest tragedy, and to attend the law courts, where suits were under judgment, or the Assembly, where questions of policy, even of peace or war, were under discussion, and to frequent the gymnasium, where they could keep the body in shape and at the same time admire the beauty of the young men who might well be listening to a snubnosed, barefoot eccentric called Socrates.

Slaves rarely make an appearance in the dialogues of Plato (though there is an exception in the *Meno,* where a house-born slave boy is used for a demonstration that even the lowest form of human life has latent knowledge that can only have come from a previous existence). But without the slaves those long, leisurely conversations, in the gymnasia, the wrestling schools, the houses of the wealthy (Agathon, Callias, Polemarchus), and by the banks of the Ilissus, could not have taken place. Finley is only one of the historians (Vidal-Naquet is another) who have investigated the "peculiar institution" of the Greeks in all its complexity and its diversity—the chattel slaves of Athens, mostly of foreign origin, the native Helots of Sparta and Penestae of Thessaly, the various forms of debt bondage and the many other forms of dependence summarized in the ancient formula "between free and slave."

Slaves were not the only prerequisite, however, for those golden hours of leisure. Someone had to oversee the slaves. A man also needed a wife, whose excellence, according to one of Plato's characters, was "the duty of ordering the house well, looking after the property inside, and obeying her husband." What is

meant by "ordering the house well" is made clear in the *Oeconomicus,* another Socratic dialogue, this one by Xenophon. It introduces us to Ischomachus, a young gentleman who has just finished instructing his new bride, a girl of less than fifteen years, in her duties. He tells Socrates, proudly, what he prescribed: she is to train and to supervise a staff of domestic slaves, to organize the efficient storage of equipment and supplies, to store and to manage the distribution of grain, wine, and oil, to make and to meet the annual budget, and to see to the manufacture of household clothes from the raw fleece all the way to the finished garment. She is strongly urged not to use makeup of any kind and to avoid sitting by the fire; she is to be constantly on the move, checking, inspecting, helping. According to Ischomachus, she accepted the program with enthusiasm.

It is typical of the male Greek attitude that we are never told the wife's name. She is just "the wife of Ischomachus." This faceless anonymity was the norm for respectable Athenian women; even in legal cases, where their right or their claim to property may be the issue, they remain nameless. (A certain Neaera, an Athenian woman whose name does turn up in a court room speech, is, according to the speaker, not an Athenian citizen and has had a remarkable career as a prostitute.) When, at the end of the Funeral Speech that proclaimed the glory of the men who had fallen in battle, Pericles addressed a few cold words to their widows, telling them that *their* glory was "to be spoken about least," he was only expressing the firm conviction of the Athenian male.

Inside that house of which they were the managers and from which they rarely emerged, Athenian women must have been a formidable presence. Sometimes we get a glimpse of that aspect of the relations between the sexes, as in the *Lysistrata* of Aristophanes, where the play's heroine talks about wives asking husbands what they have been doing in the assembly today:

> Too many times as we sat in the house,
> we'd hear that you'd done it
> again—manhandled another affair of
>   state
> with your usual
> staggering incompetence. Then, masking
> our worry with a nervous laugh
> we'd ask you, brightly, "How was the
> Assembly today, dear? Anything
> in the minutes about Peace? . . ."

But since the books, the inscriptions, and the vase paintings on which we have to base our vision of Athenian home life were all made by men, who no doubt fully agreed with Pericles on the subject of women, such glimpses are rare.

Still, there was much more to be found and studied than previous generations had found (or wished to find), and modern scholars, women prominent among them, have combed, reinterpreted, and assembled the evidence to re-create the life of ancient Greek women, and especially Athenian women, from childhood through initiation rites of various kinds to marriage and motherhood in its legal, religious, and social context. Understandably, some of the female scholars who deal with this material strike a polemical note. One vigorous survey of the position of women in Athens at its political and artistic high point, the fifth century B.C.—a book remarkable for, among other things, its extraordinarily full coverage of the evidence from vase paintings—appeared under the title *The Reign of the Phallus.*

But there is one category of evidence that poses a problem: the picture of women that emerges not from the court speeches, vases, and inscriptions, but from poetry, the epic, and the drama. For classical Greek literature presents us with an astonishing wealth of imposing female characters, in this respect far surpassing the Roman literature that was formed on the Greek model, and rivaling any literature of the medieval or modern world.

Homer's *Odyssey,* which in its present form is probably a product of the late eighth century B.C., gives us not only Penelope, the faithful and resourceful wife, but also Helen, the wife whose adultery caused a ten-year war and who now presides in queenly fashion over the court of the husband whom she had abandoned. There is also Nausicaa, one of the most charming—and intelligent—young women in all literature, as well as Circe, the enchantress who turns men into swine, and Calypso, the importunate divine mistress.

And Athenian tragedy, at the high point of the reign of the phallus, presents us with a succession of female characters who play leading roles, from Clytemnestra, the wronged and vengeful wife who towers over the male figures of the *Oresteia,* to Antigone, the young woman who, invoking divine law against human

decrees, defies the power of the state; from Medea, the abandoned wife who makes her husband pay a terrible price for his ingratitude, to Electra, who, in Sophocles' play, never wavers from her resolve to avenge her father even when all hope seems lost; from Phaedra, wasting away from starvation as she tries, vainly, to resist the love for her stepson that Aphrodite has imposed on her, to Creusa and her passionate appeal to, and denunciation of, the god Apollo when she fears that he is not going to restore to her the child that she secretly bore him. Only one of the surviving tragedies has no female character, and the titles and fragments of the hundreds of lost plays tell the same story: women, on the tragic stage, play the active roles, as man's partner or more often antagonist, that real life, according to our other sources, denied them.

One proposed explanation of this surprising situation is that all the characters, men and women alike, belong to a far-off mythical past and so have little or no relevance to the passions and the concerns of the fifth-century audience. But this defies the realities of theatrical performance. Tragedy, Aristotle rightly says, should arouse pity and fear; it can only do so if it touches the deepest levels of its audience's hopes, wishes, and forebodings. And of course the Athenians did not think of the mythical heroes as far away and long ago; these figures were a forceful presence in the popular mind, as ideal models or awful warnings. When Socrates refuses to save his life by abandoning what he considers his god-given mission, he cites the example of Achilles, who refused to save his life by abandoning his resolve to avenge his friend Patroclus. And when the sentence of death is handed down, he tells the court he looks forward to meeting, in the lower world, such heroes as Palamedes and Ajax, who, like him, were unjustly condemned. In any case, Shakespeare's theater, too, presents characters and places far off or long ago. Not a single one of his plays is set in the late Elizabethan and early Jacobean context of his own time and country; and yet no one doubts that he lived up to Hamlet's prescription for the players and showed "the very age and body of the time his form and pressure."

It is true that with few exceptions, such as Aeschylus's Clytemnestra, the women in Greek tragedy act purely in

the domestic sphere, as virgins, wives, or mothers, or if beyond it as in the case of Electra, through men. Tragedy gives us a picture of a life on which our prose documents are silent, a picture of the inner life of the house, the intimacy of the relationships between husband and wife, mother and son, father and daughter. It shows the wife and mother in that confined space where she is both queen and prisoner—a picture that is very different from the one suggested by the bland eulogies of the funeral inscriptions. It suggests what one would have suspected, that in many cases the result of confining a wife to the house, the slaves, and the children was to create a potentially explosive, even dangerous, force.

Of course, Greek myth provided plenty of examples of women as dangerous, as the adversary, from the Amazons who engaged in open warfare against men to child-killers such as Medea and Procne, husband-killers such as Clytemnestra and Deianira, adulterous seducers such as Stheneboea or (in Euripides' lost first version) Phaedra. It even provided dangerous women in large groups, like the fifty daughters of Danaus, forty-nine of whom slaughtered their husbands on their wedding night, or the women of the island of Lemnos who went to the extreme limit of defiance of the male hierarchy by murdering their husbands and marrying their slaves. And tragedy eagerly embraced such themes.

The chorus in Aeschylus's *Suppliants* are the daughters of Danaus; by threatening to hang themselves on the statues of the city's gods, they force a reluctant king into fighting a battle for them in which he loses his own life, and although the last two plays of the trilogy are lost, we know that forty-nine of them duly murdered their husbands. In Sophocles' *Trachiniae,* Deianira (whose name means "husband-killer") is the unwitting and unwilling agent of the death of her husband, Heracles. In the seventeen tragedies of Euripides that have survived intact, Phaedra, Electra, and Agave kill or help kill a man, Medea kills a man and her male children, Hecuba blinds a man, and Creusa tries to kill one, while on the other hand Alcestis gives her life to save her husband's, and Iphigenia, Macaria, and Polyxena are sacrificed at the altar by men. Women's voices are so insistent on the Euripidean stage that Aristophanes can have him say, in the *Frogs,* that in his plays, "They all stepped up to speak their piece, the mistress spoke, the slave spoke too,/the master spoke, the daughter spoke, the grandma spoke."

Some feminist critics have developed the argument that such a concentration on women in the public performance of tragedy was simply a reinforcement of the dominant male ideology, a justification of the seclusion and the repression of women. The plays, written by men and acted by an all-male cast, were performed at an official festival of the male-dominated democracy; the decision to award first, second, and third prize was in the hands of male judges, and, even more important, the selection of the three playwrights who were to have their plays produced was also the prerogative of male officials. The plays, even those of Euripides, who has often been considered sympathetic to women, must have been a reaffirmation of the male values of Athenian society.

Interpretations along these lines have been advanced with greater or lesser degrees of subtlety. Still, even the most fair-minded and rewarding treatment of the role of women in tragedy, Froma Zeitlin's chapter called "Playing the Other" in *Nothing To Do with Dionysus?,* while it explores brilliantly the theme that "drama . . . tests masculine values only to find those alone inadequate to the complexities of the situation," also finds that "in the end tragedy arrives at closures that generally reassert male, often paternal, structures of authority."

It is true, of course, that women in tragedy, even in Euripides, are almost always agents of male destruction or willing sacrificial victims. The trouble is that Euripides loads the dice against any easy acceptance of these situations at face value. He does this by his presentation of the male characters involved. Iphigenia gives her life for Greece, but the men for whom she gives it—Agamemnon, Menelaus, Calchas, Odysseus, even Achilles—are unmasked as weaklings, braggarts, cowards, and base intriguers. In *Alcestis,* a wife surrenders her own life to save her husband's in ideal Athenian wifely fashion, but the lines that Euripides puts in the husband's mouth must have made the audience sit up.

After all, if your wife agrees to die instead of you (and in this age of organ transplants this play could be less of a fairy tale than it was for the Athenians),

you should know better than to react to her last dying wails with the customary formulas of the deathbed scene. You are the one husband in the world who cannot and must not say, as Admetus says, "In the name of the gods do not have the heart to abandon me—in the name of your children whom you will leave behind orphaned . . . raise your head up— be strong, endure—If you die I don't want to live." Above all, you don't say: "If I had the tongue and song of Orpheus, so that, enchanting Demeter's daughter or her husband by my music, I might have taken you from Hades, I would have gone below and neither Pluto's hound nor Charon the ferryman of souls would have prevented me from bringing you back to life and the light of the sun." He didn't have to go to such heroic lengths; he could just have died when his time came. And, as if this were not enough to set one's teeth on edge, Alcestis's death is followed by a quarrel between the husband and his father, who had declined, like his mother, to take his place in the grave. It is the most electric scene in the play, a sordid and bitter quarrel between two egotists, staged over the body of the woman whose self-sacrifice has made it possible for her husband to denounce his mother and father as cowards, and to disown them.

Jason, too, is condemned by his own words. Reminded by Medea that she saved his life in Colchis and left behind not only her family but also her status as a princess, he answers complacently that he owes his success at Colchis not to Medea, but to Aphrodite alone of gods and men; Medea was merely so madly in love with him that she couldn't help herself. In any case, he goes on to say, she has been amply repaid for what little she did do for him. "You left a savage country, to live in Greece; here you have known justice . . ." Medea will kill her sons, and Jason will lose not only them but also his bride and her father and his hope of a new kingdom; but after his speech it is hard to feel anything for him but contempt.

And the end of the play is no reassertion of "male . . . structures of authority." Jason is abandoned even by the gods to whom he appeals; they send down a magic chariot in which Medea escapes from Corinth. What is more, it is in this play that one of the fundamental male structures of authority is specifically repudiated: the ideal of martial glory, the

sanctification of male heroic death in battle that is so memorable a feature of Pericles' Funeral Speech. *"They say,"* Medea tells the chorus of Corinthian women, *"they* say we live a life free from danger in the house, while they fight, spear in hand. What fools! I'd be ready to take my stand in the shield line three times rather than give birth just once." That biological function that was for the Greek male chauvinist the only justification for woman's existence— "There ought to have been some other way," says Jason later on in the play, "for men to breed sons . . ."—that despised but necessary natural function is here given pride of place above the martial valor that was the highest virtue of the man and the citizen.

V.

The relocation of Attic tragedy in its social and religious context has added much to our understanding of it. And yet the attempt to cut it down to size, to make it a prisoner of its environment, limited in scope by the constraints of Athenian male ideology, is a waste of effort. The genie cannot be put back in the bottle. For great literature, though fashioned for and by its time and place, always reaches out beyond, speaking to later generations as well; it is, to use the terms of Jonson's eulogy of Shakespeare, not only of an age, but for all time. Many of the greatest poets are more fully appreciated by later ages than by their own. They foreshadow and help to create the sensibilities of the generations that come after them.

Euripides is a case in point. In the centuries that followed the end of Athen's great age, Aeschylus and Sophocles were revered as classics, but Euripides was performed. We have a vivid reminder of this fact in the shape of a broken piece of stone, part of an inscription of the fourth century B.C. that records the names of the nine tragedies offered by three poets at the Great Dionysia, together with the name of the author of the "old tragedy" regularly offered at this time in addition to the new ones. It covers the years 341, 340, and 339 B.C., and in each year the "old tragedy" was by Euripides.

Of course, he is not the only one to survive on the later stage. In recent years the plays of all three Greek tragic masters, in translation and in adaptation, have found fresh audiences on stage and screen, in theaters from Berlin to Edinburgh, from New York to San Diego; and they speak to us as if the centuries between our time and theirs had never been. In theaters all over the world, versions of Sophocles' *Antigone,* prominent among them those of Anouilh and Brecht, have faced modern audiences with the problem that Sophocles posed to his Athenian audience—the clash of loyalties, to the state and to older, higher obligations.

In Ireland, at Derry, the Irish poet Seamus Heaney recently produced his version of the *Philoctetes* of Sophocles, a play about a victim of injustice so embittered by suffering and by brooding on his wrongs that when salvation and a cure for his debilitating disease are offered by his enemies, for their own cynical purposes, he cannot bring himself to accept it; it takes a voice from the heavens to change his mind. Heaney wrote into what is for the most part a faithful as well as brilliant translation of the Sophoclean play a moral for his country and his times:

History says, *Don't hope*
On this side of the grave.
But then, once in a lifetime
The longed-for tidal wave
Of justice can rise up,
And hope and history rhyme.
So hope for a great sea-change
On the far side of revenge.
Believe that a further shore
Is reachable from here.
Believe in miracles
And cures and healing wells.

And we have seen, too, *Iphigenia in Aulis* played in New York as a protest against our war in Vietnam, and a French version of Euripides' *Trojan Women* produced in Paris as a protest against the French war in Algeria.

The Greeks are still very much with us. Even that strange ritual of sacrifice with which we started, that epitome of "otherness" so alien to our thought and our feeling, has its resonances in our world. We too might need some equivalent of the "comedy of innocence" if we had to kill a domestic animal with our own hands every time we ate meat. As it is, we leave the business of killing to others and try not to think about it. But in recent years many of us have indeed begun to think about it, to face the mechanical horrors of the stockyard slaughterhouse and worse, the refined cruelty of a system that raises animals confined and force-fed in narrow cages, so that even before its death the victim is deprived of any real life. Some of us have turned away altogether from eating meat, enough of us that public institutions and airlines make provisions for vegetarian meals. And in the ancient world, too, there were those—Pythagoreans and Orphics—who refused to take part in the sacrifice and the consumption of meat, even though it cut them off from the community and made them a people apart, and sometimes persecuted.

In fact, when one thinks again of that list of things that MacNeice, the Anglo-Irishman writing in Hampstead in 1938, found so unimaginably different, one can not help feeling that to an American, especially to an American living in or near the city of Washington, D.C., in the spring of 1992, they seem all too familiar. "When I should remember the paragons of Hellas," he wrote, "I think instead

Of the crooks, the adventurers, the
    opportunists,
The careless athletes and the fancy
    boys,
The hair-splitters, the pedants, the
    hard-boiled sceptics
And the Agora and the noise
Of the demagogues and the quacks;
    and the women pouring
Libations over graves
And the trimmers at Delphi and the
    dummies at Sparta and lastly
I think of the slaves.

The Agora was the marketplace, for which we have substituted the shopping mall. Women today may not pour libations on graves, but we have our macabre funeral parlors, where the late lamented, embalmed and touched up for the occasion, make a last appearance for relatives and friends. Our trimmers are not at Delphi, they are much closer to home. And our dummies are not at Sparta—but we have them all right. As for the slaves: Americans need no reminder that 150 years ago there were slaves and slaveowners on both sides of the Potomac.

Indeed, when we think of the two great flaws in Athenian democracy that recent scholarship has explored and emphasized, we ought to remember not only that slavery and male dominance were characteristic of all ancient societies, but also that we, of all people, have no right to cast the first stone. Pericles' proud claim for Athenian democracy—power in the hands of people, equality before the law—makes no mention of the slaves, but our Declaration of Independence, according to which "all men are created free and equal," does not mention them either, although the man who drafted it and many of those who signed it were owners of African slaves. That wrong was finally righted only by a bloody and destructive civil war, but we are still suffering the consequences of those many years of injustice. The wound in the commonweal is not healed yet, and we have to pray and to believe, like Heaney, that "a further shore/Is reachable from here," that "hope and history" may "rhyme."

As for the other flaw, the exclusion of women from Athenian public life, we should not forget that women in these United States had to struggle for more than half a century before the Nineteenth Amendment to the Constitution gave them full voting rights in 1920; that Great Britain reluctantly made the same concession in 1928; and that the French took the last word of the revolutionary slogan *liberté, egalité, fraternité*" so literally that French women were not given the right to vote until 1945.

All this does not entitle us, of course, to discard the results of the re-evaluation of Greek culture that has emphasized its "otherness," the attitudes and the institutions that resemble those of Egypt and Babylon, not to mention those of Lafitau's Algonquins, Hurons, and Iroquois. But we should not forget the astonishing originality that sets the Greeks apart, that makes them unique. They invented democracy more than 2,000 years before any modern Western nation took the first steps toward it. They invented not only philosophy and the theater, but also the model of a national literature, with its canon of great writers, its critics and commentators, its libraries. They invented organized, competitive athletics. They invented political theory, rhetoric, biology, zoology, the atomic theory. One could go on. Though we can no longer say, with Shelley, that we are all Greeks, nor can we claim, as the Victorians might have claimed, that GREEKS 'R' US, we must always acknowledge how greatly, how deeply, how irrevocably, we remain in their debt.

Greek Gifts?

Lesser breeds without the law? In a revealing new study of the Hellenistic world in the three centuries after Alexander carved out an empire in the East, Peter Green *argues that condescension and cultural arrogance rather than a mission to civilise marked Greek reaction to the population they ruled over.*

Peter Green

Peter Green is the Dougherty Centennial Professor of Classics in the University of Texas at Austin, and the author of Alexander to Actium: The Historical Evolution of the Hellenistic Age *published by the University of California Press and Thames and Hudson.*

Hellenisation, that primarily eastward diffusion of Greek language and culture, has been defined—ever since the German historian and nationalist J. G. Droysen proclaimed it in his *Geschichte der Diadochen* (1836)—as the essence of Hellenistic civilisation, the banner carried by Alexander the Great and his successors. Yet as a phenomenon it calls for very careful scrutiny. Its civilising and missionary aspects have been greatly exaggerated, not least by modern historians anxious to find some moral justification for aggressive imperialism. So has its universality. This trend has been matched by a persistent tendency to underplay both lure of conquest and commercial profits (which, with land-hunger, provided the main driving-force behind this Greek diaspora), as well as the stubborn refusal of allegedly inferior races to embrace the benefits of Greek enlightenment thus rudely thrust upon them.

Eponymous hero; Alexander the Great's thirteen spectacular years of conquest 336-323 BC left cities bearing his name throughout the East – this sandstone head comes from the Egyptian Alexandria.

Analysis of the evidence is revealing. The Greeks had long assumed in themselves, partly on environmental grounds, a cultural and ethnic superiority over all alien societies. This superiority even extended, in the visual arts, to idealising themselves (perfect bodies, nobly straight noses) while portraying outsiders with a realism often not far this side of caricature. Yet they never evinced any noticeable urge to convert or enlighten the 'barbarians', whom no less an intellectual than Aristotle regarded as slaves by nature, to be treated 'like animals or plants'. In classical drama, for example, Aristophanes' *Acharnians* (425) or *Thesmophoriazusae* (410), and Euripides' *Orestes* (408), the jabbering foreigner had always been good for a laugh. No one ever thought of *educating* him. Curiosity about the rest of the world undoubtedly existed, but was not, perhaps mercifully, accompanied by any desire to improve it.

Thus the dissemination of Hellenism, when it came, was incidental rather than conscious or deliberate. Further, those Macedonian soldiers and Greek businessmen who, in the wake of Alexander's conquests, exploited the indigenous populations of Ptolemaic Egypt or the Seleucid East could not, by any stretch of the imagination, be regarded as a cultural elite, much less as cultural missionaries. The stupid, bombastic, drunken, cowardly *miles gloriosus* who appears in literature from Menander's day onwards, with his toadying servant and chestfuls of Persian plunder, had all too real a basis in fact. Such men, like their counterparts in any age, were massively indifferent to the language and civilisation of any country they happened to be occupying, an attitude which their victims, for the most part, reciprocated.

Any Egyptian who wanted to get anywhere under the Ptolemies had to speak, and preferably also write, *koinē* Greek, that vernacular Attic which, from the fourth century BC on, became the *lingua franca* of the Mediterranean world. We have a letter of complaint (c.256/5) to an official from his (probably Egyptian) servant about the contemptuous ill-treatment he has received 'because I am a barbarian', and petitioning for regular pay in future 'so that I don't starve because I can't speak Greek'. Similarly an Egyptian priest is resentful of a Greek settler who 'despises me because I am an Egyptian'. Though later a certain degree of low-level acculturation took place, in the fourth and third centuries imperial

racism was rampant among the Greeks and Macedonians of Alexandria, and never really died out. No Macedonian of note before Cleopatra VII, and very few Greeks, ever bothered to learn Egyptian.

Borrowings and adaptations, then, we would expect to find in those areas which, first, required no linguistic skill, and, second, were commonly accessible without conscious intellectual effort: that is, the visual arts, architecture, and music. Apart from music, for which there is only the sketchiest of literary evidence (suggesting possible Oriental influence on Greek modes and instruments rather than vice versa), this is precisely the case. Yet even in the area of art and architecture what is often pointed to as evidence for cultural dissemination is, in the sense proposed, nothing of the sort. I am thinking particularly of the export of Greek building styles, pottery, statuary, mosaics, gymnasia, temples, theatres, and the rest of the civic impedimenta essential for any self-respecting *polis,* into regions as far afield as, say, Bactria. Ai Khanum on the Oxus is a good case in point. Like all Alexander's foundations, it was settled exclusively by Macedonian and Greek colonists.

Thus what we find in such cases, far from any real diffusion, is an alien enclave, an artificial island of Greek social and cultural amenities almost totally isolated from the indigenous population which it dominated. That much-touted respect for exotic 'alien wisdom' occasionally found in Greek literature—for example, Herodotus' astonishment, later shared by Plato and Aristotle, at the hoary, unchanging, Egyptian priestly tradition—depended in the main on unfamiliarity (because of the language barrier) with the actual literature in which such supposed wisdom was enshrined. Nor do we find any substantial evidence, in Ptolemaic Egypt, the Seleucid East, or India, for local interest in Greek literature or Greek ideas—the Hellenised Egyptian was not required to read, much less to enjoy, Greek poetry or philosophy, any more than his masters knew, or cared about, the age-old literary heritage of Egypt—but rather a great deal that suggests implacable hostility, with a religious and ideological no less than an ethnic basis.

Local acclimatisation tended, inevitably, to be restricted to two well-defined categories. On the one hand we find those still-independent rulers who 'went Greek' for their social and political ad-

vancement. Scions of Anatolian royal families (Ariarathes V of Cappadocia or Nicomedes IV of Bithynia) were sent west for their education, normally to sit at the feet of fashionable philosophers in Athens, as Indian princes under the Raj went through the privileged rigours of Harrow and Sandhurst. On the other, there were the intelligent and ambitious collaborators who set out to make a career in the administrative system of the occupying power: a tiny cadre—in the Seleucid empire, it has been calculated, not more than 2.5 per cent of the official class, and even that only after two generations—but of considerable significance. These were the men who became interpreters, scribes, tax-collectors, accountants, or other categories at subexecutive level in the bureaucracy. The whole Ptolemaic administration, for example—still, ironically, in essence Pharaonic—functioned at middle level through a corps of more or less bilingual native officials: competition for such posts, as in the earlier Pharaonic period, was intense.

Such men had an outside chance of clawing their way up the ladder of advancement to a position of real power as senior administrators or military (including police) officers. By so doing they committed themselves to the foreign regime they served in a social no less than a professional sense. Like Indians under the British Crown angling for the *entrée* to European club membership, they developed the taste for exercising naked, for worshipping strange gods, for patronising the theatre: they also courted municipal kudos by the lavish generosity of their benefactions. The prime motive in such cases was, clearly, social and professional ambition, even if a little genuine acculturation took place at the same time. Against this must be set that deep resentment and hostility felt by most of their fellow-countrymen towards an occupying power (not to mention the angry contempt, mixed with jealousy, that they themselves would attract), and, on the Graeco-Macedonian side, a powerful distaste for those who in any sense 'went native'.

When all these factors are taken into account, a radically modified picture of Hellenisation emerges. It is restricted, for the most part, to some curious instances of architectural and sculptural hybridisation; some limited social assimilations among non-Greek rulers and in the administrative sector of the major

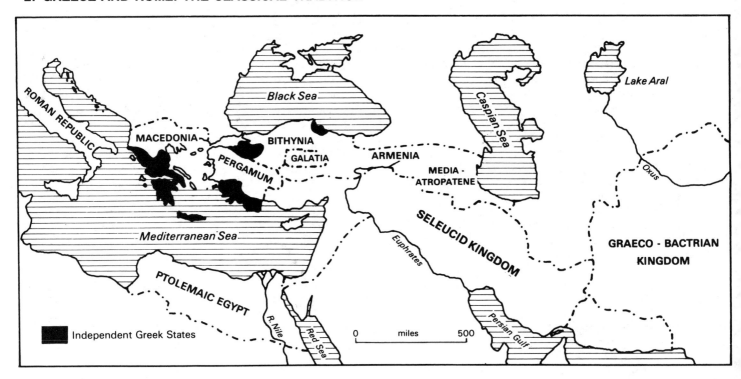

The Hellenistic world c.240 BC, showing how Alexander's great empire had been split into a number of successor kingdoms.

(particularly the Ptolemaic) kingdoms; a few religious syncretisations that transmuted their borrowings out of all recognition (Isis and Sarapis); and the establishment of the Attic *koinē* as a useful international language, primarily for administrative and commercial purposes, but also, later, for religious propaganda. The impact of the Greek and Macedonian colonists was, first and foremost, economic and demographic. It is hard to trace any conscious diffusion of Greek intellectual ideas in the Hellenistic East with any real confidence, and of genuine literary interpenetration between Greek and other cultures there is virtually no trace. For one thing, literary translations—as opposed to those of medical, mathematical, astronomical, or similar practical treatises—seem to have been non-existent, a sure sign of aesthetic indifference. Thus whatever the Greeks and, *a fortiori*, the Macedonians were up to (over and above financial exploitation) in the kingdoms ruled by Alexander's heirs, spreading cultural light formed a very small part of it. Itinerant sophists might peddle the latest philosophical clichés of Academy or Stoa at street corners, while the local-boy-made-good, with his Greek-style education, would have a small stock of well-worn quotations from Homer, Euripides

or Menander at his disposal. It does not add up to very much. To what extent the locals would ever patronise a Greek theatre (for example, that of Ai Khanum in Bactria), and what they absorbed, or even understood, if they did, remain highly problematical questions.

The failure of Hellenism to catch on among the indigenous inhabitants of the Ptolemaic and Seleucid kingdoms thus has nothing to do with its intrinsic intellectual or cultural merits as a system of ideas, a creative matrix, a way of life. It failed for several good and compelling reasons wholly unrelated to the criteria by which we would assess it: the bitter resentment of defeat, that found expression in passionate ethnocentrism; a theocratic temper that subordinated arts and sciences alike to the requirements of religion, and was chary of translating religious texts; a language barrier that no one cared to break except for the immediate requirements of commerce and administration. This general rejection throws into prominent relief the two striking exceptions for which we have evidence, and in both cases, as is at once apparent, special circumstances apply.

The first concerns the large and influential community of Jews in Alexandria, perhaps originating as prisoners of war settled there by Ptolemy I Soter. This

community, though ethnically debarred by its own religious laws from intermarriage, contained a high proportion of intellectuals, and, equally important, became bilingual in Greek. To a surprising extent, the external aspects of synagogue ritual were adapted to Greek custom. Even more important was the production, begun under Ptolemy II Philadelphos, but not completed until the second century, of the Septuagint, the Greek version of the Hebrew Bible. It is noteworthy that the prime motive for translation in this case was the increasing inability of the Greek-speaking Alexandrian Jews to understand either Hebrew or Aramaic. As a result, a considerable body of Helleno-Judaic literature passed into circulation.

Yet, once again, despite favourable conditions for direct mutual influence—they were all living in the same city, must often have passed one another in the street—the evidence reveals an almost total lack of contact, certainly in the third century BC and arguably for much longer, between this Jewish-Alexandrian literary movement and the contemporary tradition of Callimachus, Theocritus, Apollonius Rhodius and their successors. The *cognoscenti* of the Alexandria Museum reveal no interest in, or knowledge of, the prophetic mode of discourse so characteristic of Jewish thought, while the dominant influence on Jewish-Alexandrian literature is not Homer, much less Callimachus or Menander, but the Septuagint. The form and substance of those works that survive remain Jewish, prophetic, religious-inspired throughout. The nearest we come to classical influence are a couple of dull attempts at Jewish epic, and an extraordinary fragment of tragedy, in flat iambic trimeters, entitled *Exodus* and covering most of the life of Moses. This could hardly be described as an impressive cross-cultural record.

The one shining exception to all these predictable, if depressing, conclusions is, of course, provided by the greatest, and most historically significant, cultural confrontation of them all: that between Greece and Rome. Though the lack of a home-grown intellectual tradition has probably been exaggerated, Horace's familiar picture of 'captive Greece captivating her savage conqueror, and bringing the arts to rustic Latium' remains true enough in essence. The Roman attitude to Hellenism was highly ambivalent. On the one hand they swallowed Greek culture whole (a feast that gave the more old-fashioned among them severe indigestion), imitated Greek literature, rehashed Greek philosophy in ponderous, awkwardly abstract Latin, sedulously pastiched Greek art. On the other, perhaps not least because, as R. E. Smith once wrote, they 'had eaten of the apple of knowledge and knew themselves to be culturally naked'—a situation always liable to arouse resentment—they despised and mistrusted the Greeks themselves as slippery, unreliable, unwarlike, covetous mountebanks, confidence-tricksters with no moral principles and a quicksilver gift of the gab. Paradoxically, it was (as Horace notes) on the one occasion when the Greeks came as a defeated nation rather than as conquerors that their culture had most influence.

No accident, either, that it was the Romans—the most enthusiastic promoters of Hellenising standards, perhaps because they were so morbidly conscious of being cultural *parvenus* themselves—who were seriously worried about the real or fancied decline of those standards. Livy reports the consul Cn. Manlius as claiming that the latter-day Macedonians of Alexandria or Babylon had 'degenerated into Syrians and Parthians and Egyptians'. Juvenal in his notorious anti-Greek tirade makes pre-

In transit; this statue of Maitreya, the future Buddha, from first-century AD Grandhara, shows trappings of Greek influence.

cisely the same point. What proportion of the dregs washed across from Orontes to Tiber, he asks rhetorically, is really Greek anyway? In they all swarm, with their unintelligible native lingo and disgusting habits and weird musical instruments and gaudy prostitutes, to corrupt decent Romans. Long before the end of the first century AD Rome had taken over the Greek xenophobic attitude to *barbaroi*, and was applying it, with gusto, to the Greeks themselves.

This ingrained sense of superiority—whether masquerading as pan-hellenism to sanction the rape of the East, or, later, helping to keep Ptolemies and, to a lesser degree, Seleucids in cultural isolation, century after century, from the peoples

they ruled and exploited—is an extraordinarily constant factor in the history of the Hellenistic era. The Macedonians in particular began with a total indifference to, and contempt for, the cultures on which they imposed their rule. Yet in the interests of profit and efficiency they were more than willing to take over, virtually unchanged, not only existing modes of production, serf-labour, and land tenure (particularly throughout Asia), but also the various administrative systems, some more familiar than others, that they found *in situ*. Hence the indispensable corps of interpreters.

Alexandria was held—a nice distinction—to be *by* Egypt, but not *of* it. Alexander's attempts at racial fusion (whatever their motive) were abandoned immediately after his death. Seleucus, alone of his marshals, remained faithful to the 'Persian' (actually Bactrian) wife wished on him by Alexander at the time of the Susa mass-marriages. In all instances what the Successors set up were enclaves of Graeco-Macedonian culture in an alien world, government ghettos for a ruling elite. When we come to assess the ubiquitous Greek temples, Greek theatres, Greek gymnasia, Greek mosaics, and Greek-language inscriptions scattered throughout the Seleucid East, we should never forget that it was for the Hellenised Macedonian ruling minority and its Greek supporters, professional or commercial, that such home-from-home luxuries—not to mention the *polis* that housed them—were, in the first instance, provided.

In Egypt, for example, and probably elsewhere, the gymnasium resembled an exclusive club: entry was highly selective, by a scrutiny (*eiskrisis*) designed to keep out undesirables (that is, non-Greeks) and to foster Hellenism. There was a waiting-list, and children from suitable families were put down on it from a tender age. Only by the very end of the Ptolemaic period were wealthy local citizens sometimes admitted. Far from promoting Hellenisation, the gymnasium seems rather to have encouraged xenophobia and separatism. Again, the parallel of British India springs to mind, where the acceptance of English as a lingua franca, and the appetite of a minority of educated Indians for such plums of power as they could grab within the system as it stood (along with the social *mores* of club or cantonment) in no way mitigated the deep-abiding resentment of British rule, much less made any inroads

The temple of Apollo at Didyma – part of the network of Greek settlements along the coast of Asia Minor.

against India's own ancient cultural and religious traditions.

If it had not been for the Romans, whose strong obsession with Greek culture formed part of the overall imperial legacy that Rome disseminated throughout her far-flung provinces, the impact of Hellenism might well have been less fundamental, less widespread, and less enduring. Where Greek rulers lacked the authority of Rome to maintain and perpetuate their institutions, their impact tended to be minimal. As we have seen, the customary method of diffusion was by way of imposed rule, military settlements, commercial exploitation, by men who brought their own language and culture with them, and enforced their authority by means of a mercenary army. Exploitation exacerbated poverty, so that resistance was often felt at all social levels, with an abused peasantry rallying behind a dispossessed aristocracy or priesthood. The conquerors' artificial islands of culture were no more assimilable at first than a wrongly matched heart transplant.

The Ptolemies never cared about Egyptian civilisation, even when they went through the mummery of a pharaonic coronation (placating the powerful priesthood was another matter); the Egyptians still rebelled against them whenever they could. The extent and intensity of Iranian resistance—passive, militant, messianic or proselytic—to Alexander's conquest and occupation can be gauged from the considerable body of surviving literature (mostly prophetic and oracular) attacking it. Alexander is the 'Evil Invader'; above all, like the Ptolemies in Egypt, he is presented as a blasphemous disrupter of sacred tradition, while both he and his conquistadors figure as 'the demons with dishevelled hair of the race of wrath'. This was not the kind of atmosphere, to put it mildly, that encouraged acculturation across formidable religious and linguistic barriers. It could, indeed, be argued, with only minimal hyperbole, that the whole concept of Hellenisation as a beneficial spreading of light among the grateful heathen was a self-serving myth, propagated by power-hungry imperialists. Such a notion formed a useful reinforcement to panhellenism, and was later popularised by Plutarch. Bullying people for their own good has a long and depressing history.

Those who wore Greek dress (and removed it in the gymnasium), who aped Greek accents, attended Greek plays, and dropped their pinch of incense on Greek altars, had good and sufficient reasons for their behaviour, into which aesthetic or moral considerations seldom entered. Genuine cultural conversions did undoubtedly take place, but they seem to have been very much in the minority. What we find instead, more often than not, is a steely determination to get on in the world: the eagerness of some locals to assume Greek names should not necessarily be attributed to philhellenism. We know of no case where a Greek work was translated into an oriental language: hostility will have been at least as strong a reason for this as ignorance or mere indifference. The few intellectuals who did take the trouble to investigate Greek culture tended to borrow its style (as Ezekial from Euripides) or scholarly techniques and methodology (as Jewish historians from the Museum of Alexandria) or formal logic (as the Pharisees from the Stoa or Academy), husking out the theoretical insights and discarding the substance as irrelevant.

While all three Successor dynasties patronised scholarship and the arts for reasons of prestige, such activities remained exclusively a court function, pursued by Greeks for the benefit of Greeks. There is no hint of fusion or collaboration with the local culture. This omission is particularly striking in the case of Ptolemaic Egypt, since the (unwilling) host nation had a long and distinguished cultural history of its own. Prosopographical research shows something over two hundred literary figures in Ptolemaic Egypt: all are foreigners. Even in medicine and science, where we would expect a higher proportion of native practitioners, out of more than a hundred known names only about a dozen are

Egyptian (though it is of course true, and too seldom stressed, that an unknown proportion of these Greek names may in fact conceal Egyptian owners).

These statistics, fragmentary and uncertain though they are, nevertheless still tell their own story. The arrogance and xenophobia of Greek culture, at home or abroad, remains a constant factor. Not surprisingly, then, such assimilation as did take place (for example, among the urban poor of Alexandria in the second to first centuries BC) worked best at a low social level unaffected by intellectual prejudice: and on such occasions it was the Greeks who tended to pick up local habits rather than *vice versa*. The only cases of scholarly acculturation we know about are the compilations of Manetho on Egypt and Berossos on Babylonia, Greek-language digests of local science or history made by compliant bilingual priests for their new overlords. Neither in Egypt, Iran, nor India did Greek culture arguably leave any substantial trace—certainly not in the literature.

Antiochus IV (175-163 BC), the Seleucid king whose intolerance of Judaism provoked the national revolt of the Maccabees.

Copycats; the Romans absorbed Hellenistic culture voraciously into their empire – this mosaic from Pompeii of actors performing a scene from a Greek comedy is a copy of an original 3rd-century BC painting from Pergamum. Their enthusiasm for the Greeks themselves – or at least their Hellenistic descendents – was considerably more muted.

2. GREECE AND ROME: THE CLASSICAL TRADITION

The inscrutable East; the Greek rulers of the enclave at Bactria, though their coin portraits are classical—such as the fine profile above of Antimachus I (190-180 BC)—gradually embraced Indian ways, as in the case of Menander (155-130), a convert to Buddhism.

Perhaps the most extraordinary example of Greek enclave culture—finally, in this case, absorbed by something larger than itself—is that of the isolated Greek kingdoms in Bactria and India. For over two centuries, beginning with the renegade Seleucid satrap Diodotus about 250 BC, a series of more than forty Graeco-Macedonian kings ruled in the east, from Bactria to the Punjab. There are a few scattered literary references, but most of the story has been pieced together from these rulers' self-promoting and highly idiosyncratic coinage. Alexander had settled thousands of Greek colonists and time-expired Macedonian veterans and mercenaries in these frontier provinces, where they formed a handy buffer against the constant threat of invasion by northern nomads. Many of them (like white settlers in Rhodesia) gladly chose these fertile uplands rather than the unpredictable future of a retirement in Greece. When Diodotus broke away from the Seleucid empire, the large number of Greeks and Macedonians in Bactria gave his rule powerful support, and created an ethnic enclave of a most unusual sort: at once passionately Hellenic and cut off *in toto* from its Greek roots.

The recently excavated city of Ai Khanum, on the northern Afghan frontier with Soviet Russia, offers a marvellous example of persistent Hellenism in isolation. The Greek theatre, the great palatial complex with its peristyle court-

yard, the funerary cult-shrine *(herōon)* the lush Corinthian capitals of the hypo-style hall, a sophisticated sundial, fragments of what appears to be a post-Aristotelian philosophical treatise, the pottery, the bronze and terracotta figurines, perhaps above all the Delphic maxims inscribed, in Greek, on a base in the *herōon* (copied at Delphi, to be set up and paid for by a loyal globetrotting citizen), all reflect the inhabitants' determination to create a Hellenic oasis in this remote Bactrian wilderness beside the River Oxus. The gymnasium or palaestra covered an area of nearly a hundred square yards. There was a beautiful public fountain with carved gargoyles and waterspouts in the form of lions' and dolphins' heads.

Yet isolation exacted its price, and in more than one way. The large pebble-mosaic in the palace bathing-quarters is not only poor provincial work, but also, in its ignorance of cubes *(tesserae)* and the subtle modulations they made possible, over a century out of date. The mosaicists who went East clearly handed down their skills without any fresh infusion of outside talent. They will not have been the only ones to do so. Rootlessness also, in this special case, produced an unusual, but predictable, susceptibility to the *genius loci.* Just as a surprising number of Englishmen, despite their own caste system and xenophobic assumptions, were fatally seduced by the lure of

Eastern mysticism, so the Indo-Greeks, in a very similar situation, capitulated to some highly un-Greek local influences before they were done. Indian legends and Indian scripts invaded their coinage. Greek sculpture adapted itself to the lotus position, and—after a gap of four centuries—came up with a new and more enduring version of the mysterious 'archaic smile'.

For more than a hundred and fifty years these Graeco-Macedonian dynasts ruled in Bactria and western India, independent monarchs still long after Greece and Macedonia themselves had succumbed to the power of Rome. Yet Menander (ruled c. 155–130) was the only one of them to survive in Indian literature, under the name of Milinda—and not on account of his royal achievements, but because he was a convert to Buddhism (traditionally because of discussions with the Buddhist priest Nagasena). He may have set Pallas Athena on the reverse of his coins, but he also employed the Dharma-Chakra (Wheel of Law) symbol, and was associated with the building of stupas and the original iconography of the Buddha image. The ghost of Apollo still lurked behind the Buddha's features, but it was a losing battle. Far more important than Menander's prowess as a warrior was his status as a sage and thinker, who had embraced Eastern ways: when he died, he was revered as a saint, and his ashes were divided between the chief cities of his kingdom. Whatever impressed Menander's Indian subjects, it was not his superior Greek culture.

FOR FURTHER READING:

S. K. Eddy, *The King is Dead: studies in the Near Eastern Resistance to Hellenism 334–31 BC* (University of Nebraska-Lincoln Press, 1961); A. Momigliano, *Alien Wisdom: The Limits of Hellenisation* (Cambridge University Press, 1975); M. Avi-Yonali, *Hellenism and the East: Contacts and Interrelations from Alexander to the Roman Conquest* (Bell & Howell (UMI), 1978); J. W. Sedlar, *India and the Greek World: A Study in the Transmission of Culture* (Rowman, 1980); Amélie Kuhrt and Susan Sherwin-White (eds.), *Hellenism in the East: The Interaction of Greek and non-Greek Civilizations from Syria to Central Asia after Alexander* (University of California Press, 1987).

Why Brutus Stabbed Caesar

"The key to every man is his thought," wrote Emerson. But how should the historian approach that most characteristic of human activities? And what is the relationship of the history of ideas to the history of events? Elie Kedourie here ponders one of the central problems of the historian's craft.

Elie Kedourie

Elie Kedourie, a Wilson Center Fellow, died in Washington, D.C. on June 29, 1992, only days after completing this essay. Born in 1926 in Baghdad, Iraq, he was educated in England, where he lived and wrote for most of his life. Kedourie, who taught at the London School of Economics, was a well-known authority on the modern history of the Middle East, but his interests extended to the history of European political thought. The recipient of many honors, he was a Commander of the Order of the British Empire and a Fellow of the British Academy and of the Netherlands Institute for Advanced Study. Kedourie founded the journal Middle Eastern Studies *and was the author or editor of 19 books, among them* Nationalism *(1960),* The Chatham House Version *(1984), and* Politics in the Middle East *(1992).*

The study of history assumes time and place, without which a past event cannot be understood. Both are necessary, but are they sufficient? The question arises because there are often inquiries that are clearly not couched, as the physical sciences are, in terms of timeless causes and effects but that we do not consider to be history—inquiries relating to geology, botany, and zoology, in which it is necessary to specify time and place. Such inquiries have indeed been sometimes described as history. Thus the author of a book on ornithology dating from the end of the 18th century could title his book *A History of British Birds,* and French schoolchildren have long had to study a subject called *histoire naturelle.*

Natural history, however, is clearly not history, and we may distinguish between the two by saying that, unlike natural history, history proper is concerned with human activity, to understand which we must indeed see it as taking place at a particular time and in a specific place. But of human activity we also predicate that it is coherent and purposive, that it is not a sequence of (changeless) causes issuing in (uniform) effects, but rather that it is a complex of choices that are by definition unpredictable—and to say choice is necessarily to imply mind and will.

If choice, mind, and will are the hallmarks of human action, and if history proper is concerned with human activity, then a description of the historian's business such as that offered by the English philosopher R. G. Collingwood in *The Idea of History* (1946) would seem at first sight to be reasonable and convincing. "Historical knowledge," Collingwood says, "is the knowledge of what mind has done in the past." He says, further, that the "historian of politics or warfare, presented with an account of certain actions done by Julius Caesar; tries to understand these actions, that is to discover what thoughts in Caesar's mind determined him to do them." This implies the historian's envisaging for himself the situation in which Caesar stood and thinking for himself what Caesar thought about the situation and the possible ways of dealing with it. This activity Collingwood calls "the reenactment of past thought in the historian's mind." Can one speak in this way? Can one "reenact" past thought? The historian, after all, is someone who, having

present to him certain objects, documents, etc., which he comes to consider as "evidence," proceeds to compose a narrative that accounts satisfactorily for and is seen to remain within, the four corners of the "evidence." This is what distinguishes historical from fictional narrative.

Evidence, however is neither fixed nor univocal. New evidence is always cropping up; indeed, anything to a historian's eye can suddenly and unpredictably become evidence. Further all evidence is equivocal: The historian has to account satisfactorily for all the evidence, and there can be more than one way of doing so. Consider for instance what the historians reviewed in Pieter Geyl's *Napoleon For and Against* (1944) have done in their diverse ways with the evidence relating to Napoleon, or again how other historians have tried, each in his own particular way, to identify Shakespeare's Dark Lady of the Sonnets. If so many different accounts are offered, then there can be no question of the historian "reenacting" past politics or past warfare as conducted by Caesar or Napoleon or Churchill. Ten or 20 historians, each giving a different account of some past action or event, cannot possibly all be reenacting the same event. Again, to mention these examples, widely separated in time, is to make the point that the nearness or remoteness of the past does not affect their argument. Furthermore, the historian has the privilege—his only privilege—of hindsight. He knows more than Churchill or Napoleon can have known about their own situation. If nothing else, the existence of

From *The Wilson Quarterly,* Autumn 1992, 112-120. © 1992 by the Woodrow Wilson International Center for Scholars. Reprinted by permission.

this knowledge must forbid any talk of reenactment.

The way in which Collingwood envisages the historian's activity, as a reenactment of past thought, leads him to his well-known and striking definition of history: "All history," he asserts, "is the history of thought." If this means that all history exhibits the presence of purpose and choice, and therefore of mind, then no possible objection can be made. But Collingwood does mean something more by this definition. In order to illustrate his meaning, he goes on to describe the historian's activity in this way:

> The historian of philosophy, reading Plato, is trying to know what Plato thought when he expressed himself in certain words. The only way in which he can do this is by thinking it for himself. . . . So the historian of politics or warfare, presented with an account of certain actions done by Julius Caesar, that is, tries to discover what thoughts in Caesar's mind determined him to do them. This implies envisaging for himself what Caesar thought about the situation in which Caesar stood, and thinking for himself what Caesar thought about the situation and the possible ways of dealing with it.

Thinking for himself what Caesar thought? As is well-known, the novelist Flaubert said, *Madame Bovary c'est moi.* Madame Bovary is Flaubert simply because she is entirely his creation, but Martin Gilbert cannot say, *Churchill c'est moi,* John Morley cannot say, *Gladstone c'est moi.*

Collingwood's definition, again, leads him to put on the same footing an account of Caesar's wars and an account of Plato's philosophy, and thus to refuse to make a distinction between what may be called the history of events and what may be called the history of ideas. Is this distinction really superfluous? Let us again borrow a statement of Collingwood's: "When an historian asks, 'Why did Brutus stab Caesar?' he means, 'What did Brutus think, which made him decide to stab Caesar?'" History, we have said, is concerned with giving an account of past human activity, an account guided and delimited by the available evidence. When we hear that "Brutus" stabbed "Caesar" if we are to go beyond this bare, sterile, and meaningless record—and it is not always possible to do so, as the great number of unsolved murders testifies—we have to

provide a coherent account of the situation, an account that will make comprehensible the incident of Brutus's stabbing of Caesar. If we possess sufficient evidence, and if we have industry and imagination, we will proceed to exhibit Marcus Junius Brutus in his antecedents, his character, his associations, and his political activities. We will describe the political situation he confronted, what we may call the decay of the traditional republican institutions, and Caesar's roughly getting hold of power. We will show Caesar's political and military activities, we will trace his dealings with Brutus, and we will try to show if these dealings can have led to the stabbing. What we may possibly say goes something like this:

Marcus Junius Brutus was a descendant of Lucius Junius Brutus, the nephew of Tarquinus Superbus, the last king of Rome, against whom Lucius Junius Brutus is said to have led the uprising that ended kingship in Rome and established republican institutions. This Lucius Junius Brutus became one of the first two consuls under the Republic, and he is said to have put to death his own sons, who had attempted to restore the Tarquins. Marcus Junius Brutus was also the son of a half-sister of Cato of Utica and married to Porcia, Cato's daughter. This Cato of Utica was the great-grandson of Cato the Censor, who in his time preached a return to the simple virtues of the early Republic, and who was a man given to the uncompromising assertion of political principles. We will also say that in the civil war between Pompey and Caesar, Brutus was on Pompey's side but that after the battle of Pharsalus in which Pompey was defeated, he was pardoned by Caesar; who made him first governor of Cisalpine Gaul and then praetor. We will argue that a man of this character— an unbending character (the 48 percent interest he charged on money lent to Salamis in Cyprus, to collect which his agent shut several prominent Salaminians in the Senate House and kept them there without food until some of them died, may illustrate this aspect of his character)—also aware and proud of his ancestors and what he believed they stood for; mistrustful of Caesar and his appetite for power; fearful of betraying his principles and his ancestors out of gratitude to Caesar; determines—and Caesar's benefits make him all the more determined—to kill the usurper and save republican institutions.

This is a very short abridgement of what a historian would say in answer to Collingwood's question, Why did Brutus stab Caesar? The answer goes far beyond what could be an answer—if an answer were possible—to the question as Colgwood reformulates it, namely, What did Brutus think which made him decide to stab Caesar? The answer to this particular question understood literally and precisely is, in the absence of evidence about it, that God alone knows—the All-seeing and All-knowing, as Muslims describe him.

Brutus's stabbing of Caesar—or rather an account, having regard to the evidence, of how it could possibly have happened—it always being remembered that it need never have happened, either at all or in the way in which it did happen—is the kind of thing one means by a history of events. It is an account of men in the peculiarity, idiosyncrasy, and specificity of their personalities, outlooks, capacities, and positions, confronting or dealing with other men differently placed in respect to these things, and confronting or dealing with them in situations different from one another at least in respect of time and place, initiating, originating, taking measures, parrying, responding, reacting—the vocabulary we use to describe all this amply indicating that here are present an involved purpose and choice, mind and will.

We may then say that there are many objections to describing all history as the history of thought. Taken literally and precisely, it is not true, since history includes accidents, coincidences, and unpremeditated and unregarded happenings issuing in prodigious and unexpected events. We recall Pascal's observation that if Cleopatra's nose had been a shade longer the history of the world would have been different. We recall also the meteorological conditions in the Mediterranean in the year 1798 which facilitated Bonaparte's expedition to Egypt and his later escape to France which, had these conditions been different, would have put out of the question the 18th Brumaire and all that followed. Again, if after the first sustained bombardment of Gallipoli in March 1915, the British command could have known that the Ottoman troops had exhausted their ammunition, the Dardanelles expedition could have had quite a different outcome, with far-reaching consequences for Russia and the Middle East.

These are not a matter of thought in the literal and precise sense. Thought is, of course, involved in the decision to cope with the situation in this way rather than that, but it does not, all the same, make Collingwood's language any more satisfactory. Even taken figuratively, Collingwood's language is still not satisfactory. Whatever such figurative language is intended to convey, it does in fact obscure, indeed obliterate, differences between the historian's activity when he is elucidating the fortunes of a particular notion used and modified by successive generations, and when he is dealing with a statesman's character and career; or the ups and downs of a firm, or the course of a military campaign. There is a difference between having to cope with winds and tides, and having to examine, scrutinize, and bring out the implications of an idea or an argument. The aim in the criticism of ideas is to effect the utmost transparency of understanding, which no admiral could approach, desire, or comprehend.

A question, or an objection, may arise. History, it might be said, is a seamless robe. The past contains no obviously necessary boundary shutting off one event from another: For the All-knowing, history is a chain linking every happening to all the other happenings in the world. As Leibnitz put it: *Tout est conspirant,* all things work together; so that a division of history into "periods" or "areas" or "subjects" has always something arbitrary and temporary about it, and we could say that any event in the past implies in principle the whole past, that the historian is led by the very logic of his activity to look upon history as universal history.

However, even in the writing of universal history, the historian cannot treat events as an undifferentiated and uniform body of water flowing under the bridge. The evidence (by which he is bound) will seem to disclose highlights and obscurities, ups and downs. If only because of this, the historian will be led to enhance or emphasize here and pass over in silence there. But the record of historiography shows that "Dark Ages" can suddenly become illuminated and take on the strong hues of a distinctive character. This is the case of the Dark Ages of Europe, consigned for so long to darkness by a Renaissance periodization that considered nothing to be worthwhile in the interval between classical antiquity and its own day. It is only yesterday, in the last 150 years or so, that historians have begun to seek for and examine the evidence pertaining to the Dark Ages of Europe. Sometimes, again, dark ages can stay obstinately dark. Thus, the couple of centuries of British history following the Roman evacuation of the island have remained dark because, though there is a "past" there, no one has been able to describe its particular contours and specific anfractuosities.

If the historian does not, and cannot, look upon the past as placid and uniformly flowing water; he is not obliged to look upon it as a wild and romantic "English garden." He may even consider such a picture highly misleading. He would say: I do not see any Niagaras here, but I do see water slowly, imperceptibly flowing and meandering over the centuries. This is the picture called to mind by H. S. Maine's work on ancient law, or by Fustel de Coulanges's on the *polis* and the *civitas.* The picture is given a theoretical defense, indeed argued to be the only true likeness, by the school of history associated with the French journal *Annales.* The founders and leaders of this school distinguish between *histoire événementielle,* event-centered history, and *histoire structurale,* structural history. They believe that somehow the latter is deeper; more important, more fundamental than the former: that the study of "feudal society," to take the title of Marc Bloch's well-known work, is more important than the study of the Hundred Years' War, that the study of inflation in the 16th century should somehow take precedence over the study of the so-called wars of religion in that century. If it is taken seriously, the metaphor "structure" would mean the transformation of history into sociology, and "feudalism," "capitalism," etc., would become changeless ideal types. The distinction between structural and event-centered history is, however; fallacious, since so-called structures are also events continuously changing into other structures, that is, into other events, through the mediation of events. The change in the ties of feudal dependence may be so gradual as to be almost imperceptible, but it is change of the same character as something more spectacular—such as a change of dynasty or the outbreak of a war, or a nose job for Cleopatra. *Histoire structurale* is *histoire événementielle,* and feudalism is no more important or fundamental than the Hundred Years' War. It all depends on the question you ask, on the seam you decide to make in the seamless fabric of history.

Because it is incontrovertibly true that history is a seamless robe, it is no less true that the historian's activity seems to involve the making of seams—which are, however; highly provisional, being continuously made and unmade, and this not only when he is dealing with a "period," a "subject," or an "area," but also when he forswears such delimitation and proclaims the intention to write a universal history. Arnold Toynbee's *Study of History* (1946–61) is the most ambitious attempt so far to write a universal history. Toynbee articulates this history in terms of what he calls "civilizations," which he considers (arbitrarily) to be the only "intelligible" objects of historical study. In his first volume Toynbee thought he had identified 20 of the then "intelligible" civilizations. At the end of his life some four decades later; he increased these to 28.

If, then, the historian's activity is quite impracticable without the making of seams (even if they are made only to be unmade), if an historian is to distinguish and discriminate within the historical past, then the question will always arise concerning any particular distinction or delimitation whether it is at all, or more, or less appropriate. If so, we can examine whether the distinction between a history of ideas and a history of events is appropriate, and the manner in which it is appropriate.

Let us consider Brutus once again. The historian's account of Brutus's stabbing Caesar dwelt on his concern that the traditional republican institutions of Rome be defended against Caesar's ambition and restored to their original condition. When we speak of "republic" and "republican institutions," the expressions denote a cluster of ideas which we think the evidence warrants us in asserting that they were present to Brutus, that they constituted some of the ways in which Brutus articulated his objections to Caesar and justified the conspiracy and the assassination. We might be tempted to take this for a justification of Collingwood's assertion that all history is the history of thought. We would then be understanding the assertion in a way different from Collingwood's. We would be committing ourselves to the general proposition that "ideas govern events" or that "ideas move men": a proposition both current and popular; exemplified in, say, the conclusions of John Maynard Keynes's *General Theory of Employment, Interest and Money,* where he says that

Practical men, who believe themselves quite exempt from any intellectual influences, are usually the slaves of some defunct economist. Madmen in authority, who hear voices in the air; are distilling their frenzy from some academic scribbler of a few years back.

Whatever the exact significance of this general proposition, it is clearly incompatible with the historical mode of thought. In historical understanding, events have to be understood as mediated by other events, always in a context of time and place. In history, an event cannot be directly caused in the same way that pushing a button causes an engine to start.

If the historian refuses to commit himself to such a general proposition, he still has to elucidate what "republic" meant to Brutus and in his time. The historian's inquiry would be one into linguistic usage obtaining at a particular time and place. If he were to extend his inquiry into the meaning of the term from its first appearance in the evidence at his disposal, to follow and account for the changes in meaning which it underwent from *res publica* through to *res publica christiana,* and then from "republican virtue" and "republican legality" to "republic" as contrasted to "monarchy," he would then be doing a kind of history of ideas. The first thing to be said here is that the history of ideas arises because human thought is expressed, communicated, and handed down in words. As Genesis 2:20 puts it: "And Adam gave names to all cattle, and to the fowl of the air; and to every beast in the field."

"Adam gave names to all cattle": If that had remained the extent of the human vocabulary, the activity of the historian of ideas would have been extremely restricted, and its interest very small indeed. However; the ostensive function of language—the naming of cattle—is not its most significant one. In a celebrated essay on the origin of language, J. G. Herder argued that language can never have been, even at the origin, purely ostensive, because man as active mind never merely catalogues the things surrounding him but is always simultaneously expressing his attitude toward them.

If man, then, is a self-conscious creature, feeling a need to represent his experience in a fabulatory, symbolical, or ratiocinative manner; then words acquire from use in human intercourse a burden of nuances, associations, meanings, and overtones which are both implicit and continuously changing. This is why, as Francis Bacon said, words shoot back upon the understandings of the mightiest; the reason why, as the poet T. S. Eliot puts it,

Words strain,
Crack and sometimes break under the burden,
Under the tension, slip, slide, perish,
Decay with imprecision, will not stay in place,
Will not stay still.

The historian of ideas has, in a manner transcending lexicography, to exhibit the character and progression of this continuous change.

Take as an example the maxim of British foreign policy in the 19th century, that British interests required the maintenance of the independence and integrity of the Ottoman Empire. The maxim occurs in state papers, speeches, and official and unofficial discussions from about 1830. At its origin, it was a practical rule of thumb, formulated in the course of coping with a situation in which Britain was a powerful state with means such as to endow this maxim with more than academic significance; a state, moreover; which had substantial interests in regions whose safety would be affected by a change in the control of Ottoman territory, to the benefit of powerful European rivals tempted by Ottoman weakness into trying to annex some of that empire's domains. This state of affairs underlay the Near Eastern crisis of the 1830s involving Britain, France, and Russia. The maxim was formulated during this crisis and in the historian's eye is inseparable from it. To write the history of the Near Eastern crisis is to write a history of events, and this history will of course include this particular event, namely the formulation of the maxim concerning the independence and integrity of the Ottoman Empire, which is inseparable from these events.

Is it really inseparable? We have reason to think the contrary, for the maxim, once formulated, begins a life of its own which may have little connection with the circumstances of its coming to be. Such a maxim can have a life of its own because states are generally stable enti-

ties, as are, also generally, international alignments and rivalries; as are, similarly, the traditions of departments of state. Distinct from the history of the Eastern Question, which is a history of diplomatic and military transactions, there is the history of the maxim itself. This history may be elucidated under two distinct but related aspects. There is, first, the character of the maxim as a maxim, i.e. as a general rule, and its influence as such on the actions of statesmen at different points in the history of the Eastern Question or as a justification given for these actions. And there is, second, the elucidation of changes in what the maxim came to mean in the usage of successive statesmen, diplomats, and writers, according to their changing views about the Ottoman Empire and the possibility of its reform and also according to the states against whom it was directed, the earnestness with which it was accepted, and the manner in which it became, toward the end of its history, a meaningless and convenient cliche'. As it happens, just as it has a particular beginning, the history of this maxim also has an end, for in November 1914 Britain and the Ottoman Empire went to war. Ironically, for a year or so thereafter; the maxim carried on a kind of ghostly existence, for we see an official interdepartmental committee in 1915 laying it down that the independence and integrity of the Ottoman Empire remained a British interest. To write the history of this maxim is to do the history of ideas.

Alike in the life of mankind and in the development of the individual," writes the philosopher F. H. Bradley, "the deed comes first, and later the reflection." More gnomically, the poet Paul Valéry, echoing and emendating Descartes, wrote: "*Tantôt je pense et tantôt je suis*"—now I think and now I am. This is another way of making the distinction among events, ideas, and their respective history. If the deed comes first and the reflection afterward, yet the reflection, which takes one specific form of words, owing to its eloquence, to its evocative power; or to some other reason, may come to have significant connections with subsequent action. Consider Don Quixote, who immersed himself in romances of chivalry; Madame Bovary, who read too many sentimental novels; or Charles the Bold, Duke of Burgundy, of whom the chronicler Commines writes:

"Covetous he was of glory, which was the chief cause that made him move so many wars. For he desired to imitate those ancient Princes whose fame continueth till this present." For; says another chronicler; Charles "delighted only in romantic histories and the feats of Julius Caesar, Pompey, Hannibal, Alexander the Great and many other great and high men whom he wished to follow or imitate."

There is, thus, a continuous mutual influence of action upon reflection, and further action following the preceding reflection, giving rise to yet further reflection, in an endless gallery of (distorting) mirrors. From this is apparent the particular difficulty of doing the history of ideas—a difficulty further complicated by the fact that words over time acquire a miscellaneous burden of meanings that do not obviously or necessarily cohere with one another (e.g., Whig, Tory, Conservative, Liberal); or else that words used, to start with, in a technical sense, come to acquire a common currency: *enthusiasm* (which was once strictly part of the vocabulary of Christian theology), *establishment* (which had to do with the position of the Anglican Church within the state), *melancholy* (which formed part of the classification of "humors" in ancient Greek medicine), *traumatic* (which comes to us from the science of psychiatry). The difficulty is akin to what is involved in trying to use a gun whose bore is subject to continual and unpredictable change.

The maxim relating to the independence and integrity of the Ottoman Empire is an example of an idea whose history is intimately tied to the history of events, to wars, changes in alliances, in the balance of power, etc. There are ideas not so, or not so intimately, connected: the idea of the Trinity, or of happiness, or of natural law. These are really clusters of ideas more or less transparent, more or less coherent. If we were to do the history of these clusters of ideas, we would see that this means tracing how the "more or less" of transparency or coherence gives rise to successive objections, rejoinders, changes of emphasis and reformulations, such that through a process of continuous internal change a particular cluster of ideas ends by looking like an entirely different cluster. In his *European Thought in the 18th Century* (1954) Paul Hazard examines how, by this process of internal change, a cluster of ideas roughly described as classical becomes the cluster of ideas we loosely describe as romantic. This is how Hazard, in the first paragraph of the first chapter of his second volume, describes what he is doing:

We shall now look at another spectacle which will show us, in the coherent objectives which we have studied, the incoherency which will partially change them. We have, in fact, to examine how one of the transitions, which make the history of ideas a perpetual change, has taken place; how a doctrine was dissolved, not through the intervention of outside enemies, but from the inside; how obscurities subsisted in a theory which seemed most lucid, contradictions in a system which seemed most logical; how a proclaimed victory was yet premature; and how an immense effort to attain human happiness was once again to fail.

In the same chapter he poses questions which the book purports to answer:

Through what psychological necessities, through what subtle operations which, to start with, were almost invisible; not only through what estrangements, but rather through what help, through what compromises, through what misunderstandings did the *philosophe* set free the *antiphilosophe* and let loose the man of feeling?

To exhibit these transitions and their mediations is finicky and difficult work. It can be made even more difficult, not to say impossible, if we allow ourselves to fall prey to two prevalent and powerful temptations. The first I have mentioned earlier; namely the assumption that ideas govern events. John Milton in *Areopagitica* gives a striking example of this belief. "For Books," he says, "are not absolutely dead things, but doe contain a potencie of life in them to be as active as that soule whose progeny they are. . . . I know they are as lively, and as vigorously productive as those fabulous Dragons teeth; and being sown up and down, may chance to spring up armed men." Thomas Hobbes, too, in *Leviathan,* is extremely vehement about the subversion and disorder which the reading of classical literature and philosophy caused in his own day. The picture that Milton and Hobbes paint is of a special situation that frequently is taken to be generally true of all politics. The situation that both depict is one that obtains when an ideological style of politics, in which great importance is attached to general formulations and bookish knowledge, has taken hold. Milton and Hobbes of course lived through a period when this ideological style waxed very strong. Even so, contrary to their belief, it is not possible to establish a direct, causal connection between Lenin's *What Is To Be Done?* and the liquidation of the kulaks, between *Mein Kampf* and Auschwitz.

The second, even more prevalent temptation is to believe that ideas are "produced" by, are a "reflection" of, events, that they are a "superstructure" resting on some "substructure" somehow more fundamental, more real than the "superstructure." Such a view, held by Marxism, and more generally, by the sociology of knowledge, makes impossible the pursuit of the history of ideas. It is pointless to bother about the ideas in men's heads since we know that they are the reflection of their class interests or the time in which they live. This, however; is untenable, since contemporaries of the same class so-called, are found again and again to hold very different, not to say irreconcilable ideas: Consider Thomas Hobbes and Lord Clarendon, who belonged to the same intellectual set before the English Civil Wars, the second of whom vehemently attacked the political doctrine which the first was to set out in *Leviathan,* or Jean-Paul Marat and Joseph de Maistre, the one a revolutionary and the other a reactionary. The sociology of knowledge, further; finds itself in a vicious circle: The sociologist accounts for men's ideas by their social circumstances, and the cogency of these ideas, the pursuit of truth or coherence which they embody, cease to matter. If he is right, the sociologist finds himself in the same boat, obliging us to discount wholly what he says about the subjects of his study as being the mere reflection of his own circumstances and class interests: the biter bit.

NERO, Unmaligned

Remembered for his excesses and little else, the eccentric emperor was a discriminating patron of the arts, a keen judge of men, and—while Rome burned—an energetic fire fighter

Lionel Casson

Gnaeus Domitius Ahenobarbus was a human beast. He once slaughtered a servant merely for refusing to drink as much as he was told. Driving on the Appian Way, he deliberately whipped up his horses to run over a child. When someone criticized him in the Forum, he gouged out the man's eyes on the spot. In A.D. 37 he was brought before the emperor Tiberius on charges of treason, adultery, and incest; only Tiberius's unexpected death saved him. About the one respectable thing he did was to marry a princess of the royal blood, Agrippina, a great-granddaughter of Augustus himself. He had one child by her, a boy whom they named Lucius Domitius; history knows him as the emperor Nero.

Nero's mother was a match for his father in cruelty, but in her it was disciplined by a calculating intelligence and cloaked by ostentatious deportment as a proper Roman matron. Her husband died in A.D. 40. Agrippina played her cards with such consummate skill that within nine years she had become the fourth wife of the emperor Claudius, despite his sworn resolve never to marry again (he had executed his third for publicly cuckolding him). A few months after the wedding Agrippina talked her new husband into adopting Nero, even though he had a son and two daughters of his own by previous marriages. In the ensuing years she manipulated the emperor into giving Nero all the outward marks of preference, and in 53 she engineered the boy's marriage to Octavia, one of Claudius's daughters. Then, in 54, when her husband dropped dead—she had fed him a dish of poisonous mushrooms, so the rumors said—she got the troops of the palace guard to acclaim Nero as the successor.

And so a sixteen-year-old youth suddenly found himself heading an empire whose lands stretched from Gibraltar to the Syrian desert, from Britain to the Sahara, and whose subjects ran the gamut from primitive tribesmen to the highly civilized inhabitants of the ancient centers of Greece and the Near East. He was an absolute autocrat. His power rested, in the first place, on an army whose loyalty his predecessors had carefully secured, and, in the second, on the good will of Rome's multitudinous subjects to whom his predecessors had promised and furnished decent government. However, he was obliged to make it look as if he were but a partner in power, as if he shared the rule with the members of Rome's aristocracy who sat in the traditional governing body, the senate. This was a bit of theatre which, though it fooled nobody, for form's sake had to be maintained. Augustus, the founder of the Roman Empire, had devised the arrangement, and the elderly Tiberius and Claudius had kept it up, though with nowhere near his success, since they lacked his gift for public relations. In between was the brief reign of the young whippersnapper Caligula, who was clear-eyed enough to see that a Roman emperor was little short of a god on earth but not clear-headed enough to realize he dare not act like one; he treated the senate with contempt—and was assassinated within four years.

However, Nero was no Caligula. What is more, he had some of the best brains in the nation at his side to guide him during his apprenticeship. Since the age of eleven he had been the pupil of Seneca, the philosopher and moralist; Seneca was now promoted from tutor to confidential assistant in the administration of the empire. One of Agrippina's adroit moves in paving the way for her son's elevation to the purple had been to get in her own man, Sextus Afranius

Burrus, as head of the palace guard; he was made a high-level administrator and turned out to be a particularly able one. And then, at least in the beginning, there was Agrippina herself, the canniest politician in Rome, to keep the boy from any missteps.

The first five years or so of Nero's reign were, by all accounts, an unqualified success. His enemies—practically everything we hear about Nero comes in one way or another from his enemies—claimed that it was his advisers who were responsible for the operation of the government, and that the young emperor frittered away his time in frivolities and degeneracy. No doubt Seneca and Burrus did a great deal, but in many a key area Nero made his own contribution. He had a vast charm and an inborn sense of courtesy, gifts that helped him maintain harmonious relations with the stiff-necked senate, eternally resentful of their loss of power. He had a knack for selecting competent subordinates, and this resulted in the choice of a fine administrator for the city of Rome. His keen intelligence produced reforms in the law and the system of taxation (although a visionary proposal of his to abolish all indirect taxes and customs within the empire proved too heady for Rome's commercial interests).

Even in the quicksands of foreign policy he did well. He had inherited two troubling areas, Britain and the Near East, and he handled both with outstanding success, in good part because of the way he had of picking the right men for his jobs. Rome had invaded Britain in A.D. 43, during the reign of Claudius. A program of pacification followed, and this seemed to be going ahead without snags. Then, in 61, a revolt headed by a redoubtable native queen, Boudicca, exploded, the Roman forces that rushed to stop her were cut to pieces, her men massacred tens of thousands of Romans and other settlers, and the whole Roman position on the island hung by a thread. Nero's military appointee, however, kept his nerve and managed to save the day. At just the right moment Nero replaced him with a man whose talents lay in administration rather than leading troops, and Britain gave the emperors no further trouble for more than three centuries.

Beyond Rome's eastern border lay the only nation strong enough to be a political rival to Rome, Parthia. A century earlier Rome had tried war—and left the field licking her wounds. Augustus, astute and practical, settled for diplomacy, and that worked well enough for a time. However, when Nero ascended the throne, it had lost its effect; that year the Parthians invaded Armenia, which Rome up to then had carefully maintained as a buffer state. Nero's solution was to appoint as commander in chief of the forces in the area a certain Gnaeus Domitius Corbulo and leave it to him to rectify matters. Corbulo, a martinet of the old school, drilled and drilled his men into Rome's best fighting force, and by the year 60 he had the Parthians out and Armenia back in the hands of a local king.

No doubt about it, the young ruler was bright and able. Yet certain things about him gave people pause—his artistic and cultural interests, for example. Nero was a passionate devotee of literature and music: he composed verse, acted parts from Greek tragedy, and assiduously listened to the lyre-playing of the greatest virtuoso of the day. These were not qualities one looked for in a Roman, least of all a Roman chief of state. Even worse, Nero was distressingly cavalier about doing what was expected of an emperor, such as maintaining a grave demeanor, taking an interest in army matters, and watching gladiators spill each other's blood.

And there were disturbing indications that he was, after all, the son of his father. With a gang of kindred spirits, he used to roam the streets at night incognito, having a wild time housebreaking, looting, raping, and mugging passersby. During one of these escapades his career was all but cut short when he barely missed being clobbered to death by a resolute husband who stood his ground to defend his wife.

It was Nero's relations with his mother that revealed once and for all the Mr. Hyde that this charming, youthful Jekyll had within him. Agrippina, having won a crown for her son, settled down to enjoy pulling the strings from behind the throne. Nero quickly discovered how strong-willed a partner in power his mother could be, and equally quickly decided that there was no reason he had to put up with her. He neatly cut her out of all official business and removed one of her most useful tools, the minister of finance (replacing him with a man so able that four subsequent emperors retained him in office—yet another instance of his gift for picking subordinates). And when Octavia, the dutiful princess to whom Agrippina had married Nero, turned out to be unable to handle the imperial sexual appetite, he took on as mistress one of his servants, a freed slave, thus thumbing his nose at his mother and court propriety. Agrippina flew into a rage and let it be known that she was thinking of taking up the cause of her stepson, whose claims to the succession were as good as Nero's, maybe better. This was a serious blunder. In 55 the emperor eliminated this rival—the story given out was that the boy had died of an epileptic fit—stripped Agrippina of her bodyguard, and moved her out of the palace.

For three years she managed to steer clear of danger, until Nero met Poppaea, the *femme fatale* of the day. The new inamorata was no mere slave: she belonged to one of Rome's best and most wealthy families, and being Nero's mistress was not enough for her. But Nero was still married to Octavia, and Agrippina, though she willy-nilly had to stomach her son's liaisons, would under no circumstances swallow a divorce. In 59 Nero settled matters by committing his second bloody crime: he killed his mother. The murder, of course, had to look like an act of god, and the scheme he thought up reveals yet another facet of the man, his fascination with mechanical devices. He concerted with the admiral of the fleet to design a collapsible boat. While his mother was staying at her seaside villa on the Bay of Naples, he invited her to dinner at his own villa nearby and then sent her home in the death trap. The boat collapsed on schedule but, by a freak, Agrippina escaped and made it safely to shore. So Nero perforce sent assassins; the story goes that, as one raised his sword for the *coup de grâce,* she pointed to her womb and cried, "Strike here!"

Nero had consulted with Burrus and Seneca about the murder. If not before, certainly by this time they must have realized they had a tiger by the tail.

Somehow they managed to hold their charge in check for another two years, largely by encouraging his artistic interests and his appetite for grandiose public works. His passion for taking the stage to declaim or sing was stronger than ever, and he indulged it by giving ever more elaborate private performances; a special "emperor's claque" of five thousand young men carefully drilled in the art of rhythmic handclapping guaranteed adequate applause. He instituted a festival, to be held every four years, that featured Greeks events—contests in singing, dancing, and recitation, rather than gladiatorial fights, chariot races, and other typical Roman fare. He started the first of his great construction projects (and the only one he was ever to complete), a public gymnasium and bath in Rome not far from where the Pantheon stands. The building was vast and sumptuous, the forerunner of the celebrated edifices that Caracalla and Diocletian were to put up. "What was worse than Nero?" quipped the Roman wit Martial a half century later, "what better than his baths?"

Then, in 62, Burrus died, Seneca was allowed to resign his office and go into retirement, and Nero, just twenty-five, was on his own. In the first eight years of his reign he had committed but two murders, one a political execution and the other very likely inspired by tortured psychological drives. This year he added three more. Two of his victims were senators who had fallen under suspicion, the third was his unhappy wife. He had already divorced Octavia on the grounds of sterility and twelve days later had married Poppaea. Octavia was banished to a remote island, but somehow banishment was not enough for him, so the wretched woman was beheaded.

The year 64 was climactic. Nero's handling of its events graphically reveals the extraordinary mix of traits in his make-up—his sure hand in directing the affairs of his realm, his yearning to be recognized as a concert star, his feeling for art, his technological bent, and his brutal cruelty. The whole empire was at peace except for the old sore spot, Armenia. Two years earlier the country had slipped back into Parthian hands. Corbulo once again rescued it, and Nero then elected to try Augustus's method, diplomacy. He negotiated an agreement whereby the Parthians would put their man, Tiridates, on the Armenian throne but Nero would hand over the crown and scepter at Rome—in other words, give Parthia control of Armenia but make it look like Rome's free gift. When Tiridates arrived in Rome, Nero, with his flair for public relations and his taste for the theatrical, built up the ceremony into a stupendous spectacle. Backbiters griped at the fortune he spent on it; they had no way of knowing that the peace the money helped to buy was destined to last half a century.

While waiting for Tiridates to arrive, Nero finally satisfied a wish dear to his stage-struck heart—he made his public debut as a concert performer. Too nervous to open in Rome, he went to Naples; after all, the population there, being largely of Greek origin, could be counted on to appreciate the finer things more than a Rome audience with its taste for gladiators and chariot racing. We may be sure he was a *succès fou*.

And then came the event that was to make the name of Nero a household word. On the night of July 18, fire broke out in part of the Circus Maximus. For six days it raged unabated until a firebreak, by heroic efforts, was finally opened and the conflagration checked. Then it flared up again, though less intensely, in other parts of the city for three days more. By the time it was all over, only four of Rome's fourteen districts were intact; three had been wiped out, and seven nearly so.

Nero had been at his seaside villa at Anzio, some thirty miles away, when the fire started. He raced back to town and swung into action: he welcomed the homeless into his own gardens and all public buildings still standing, ordered additional emergency housing to be hastily erected, rushed in food from the waterfront and neighboring towns, and drastically cut the price of grain. His enemies rewarded him by putting about the story that, inspired by the spectacle, he had gone into his private theatre and sung "The Burning of Troy." In fact, he had been directing the fire fighting in his palace, which was near where the flames had first broken out, so careless of his own security that he came within a hair of being assassinated.

Once the crisis was over, Nero planned the resurrection of the city in a way that only one with a talent for technology could have devised. The ravaged areas were to be rebuilt with regular rows of streets and wide avenues, in place of the old narrow, crooked alleys, and with houses of a uniform height. The houses were to have adjoining yards in the back and continuous arcades along the front; the yards guaranteed light and air and served as a firebreak, and the arcades would be a blessing in the summer heat and the winter rains. He enacted ordinances requiring that a certain portion of every house be made of stone, with no wooden timbers or beams, that no house was to share a wall with its neighbor, and that the stone come from two specified quarries in the hills about Rome which furnished a particularly fire-resistant variety.

The populace, filled with helpless rage at the calamity, was ready to believe ugly rumors, assiduously spread by the many who had no love for Nero, that the emperor himself had started the blaze. Nero's defense was to supply a scapegoat. He picked out a small religious sect so un-Roman in its make-up and practices that the whole city, nobles as well as plebeians, viewed it with instinctive mistrust. Members of this sect were rounded up and given the full dose of Nero's cruelty: turning over his gardens for the spectacle, he had some torn to pieces by dogs, others made into human torches. It was Christianity's baptism of fire as a persecuted religion.

The devastation of Rome had included Nero's own palace. Its replacement, he decided, would be a totally new kind of imperial residence, a luxurious country home complete with farmland, woodland, flocks, game, and gardens, all in the very heart of the city. To accommodate all this he confiscated a vast piece of Rome's choicest real estate. The southern half of the Forum supplied one part of the grounds, the place where the Colosseum stands today was marked off for an ornamental pond, and the hill to the east of the Colosseum was cleared to take the main building, the Domus Aurea, or Golden House. After Nero's death, the emperor Trajan razed the structure and had a public bath put up on the site. Parts of the Golden House were incorporated in the foundations, and, by this quirk of fate, escaped total annihilation. These surviving remains lay hidden right till the end of the fifteenth century. Their sudden discovery brought a stream of artists and notables burrowing underground to visit them. Raphael sent a young assistant; he returned with sketches of the wall paintings he had seen, and Raphael was so impressed he included a number of motifs from them in his decorations for the Vatican loggias. The discoveries later inspired a school of painting.

Today art historians recognize that Nero's palace was strikingly avant-garde, that its murals represented a distinct new direction in painting and its architecture a veritable revolution. Its use of concrete rather than squared stone, its octagonal rooms and domed ceilings to provide novel interior spaces, and its other innovations made it a pioneer building, and prototype of such glories of Roman architecture as the Pantheon and Hadrian's vast villa at Tivoli. Quite possibly the radical departures were inspired by the art-minded emperor himself; at the very least he gets the credit for giving them his enthusiastic approval. There is no question that he had a hand in the ingenious mechanical gadgets the new palace boasted: overhead pipes in the dining rooms that sprayed perfume and overhead panels that opened to shower down flowers, a ceiling in the main banqueting hall that revolved in imitation of the heavens.

Rome's rank and file had nothing against Nero: his victims never came from their number, he was careful to see that their rations of bread and circuses were as regular as ever, and his cultural antics rather amused them. But the powerful aristocracy, the members of the senate, were not amused: on top of having to rubber-stamp whatever the young tyrant set his heart on, on top of having to pretend wild enthusiasm at his endless musicales, they now had to watch what they considered a pretentious and costly folly take over the very heart of their city. So, in the year 65, the eleventh year of Nero's reign, when the empire was still enjoying peace and a new Rome was rising from the ashes of the old, a powerful group formed a conspiracy to assassinate Nero. Its leader, a senator named Gaius Calpurnius Piso, was better known for degeneracy than political idealism, and most of the members were equally unsavory. The day before the murder was to take place, a freed slave got wind of the plot, and the affair was nipped in the bud.

The reaction was predictable: Nero became a killer for fair. Of the forty-odd people implicated in the attempt, sixteen who were undeniably guilty lost their lives (most were allowed to kill themselves), and a large number, including no doubt some who were innocent, were exiled and degraded. But it did not stop there: for the Roman aristocracy sudden accusation, conviction, and death became from that time on a routine part of daily life. Among the many who in these days received the order to do away with themselves was Petronius, Nero's "arbiter of taste" and the author of the unique and brilliant *Satyricon;* he went to his death in the elegant and unhurried style that had marked his life. Even old Seneca fell into disfavor and had to commit suicide.

With hate hanging heavy all about him, Nero serenely continued to pursue the passion of his life, his career as a concert artist. By now the Greek festival he had inaugurated was due again, and this time he did not hesitate to appear on the public stage in Rome. The senate, we are told, voted to award the prizes to him in advance, hoping to avoid the scandal of having the emperor appear in his own capital in a line-up of professional singers and actors, but Nero would have none of it. He insisted not only on being a contestant but on behaving exactly like the other competitors: he remained standing throughout, never let mucus from the nose or spittle from the mouth be visible, awaited the judges' decision on bended knee. We are further told that to ensure a full house spies informed on any who stayed away, and that spectators went home with their hands bruised from compulsory clapping.

All this acclaim still left Nero unsatisfied. He must needs reap laurels in the land of discriminating audiences—Greece. So, in September of 66, leaving the government in the hands of low-level subordinates, he set sail. The Greeks obligingly lumped together in 67 their four great festivals—the Olympian, Pythian, Isthmian, and Nemean games—which normally fall in different years, so he could attain what only the most renowned virtuosos had attained, victory in all four. He was applauded so wildly, carried off such a plethora of prizes, that, in an access of fellow feeling, he announced to the Greeks his decision to return to them their ancient freedom. It was a grand gesture which helped the Greek ego enormously, relieved them of the taxes they paid to Rome, and cost Nero very little, since the take from so poor a country was minimal. Also on behalf of his beloved Greeks, he launched the most ambitious public works project of his career, a canal through the Isthmus of Corinth, to spare ships the long and sometimes dangerous trip around the Peloponnese. At least three great rulers before him, including Julius Caesar, had gotten matters as far as the drawing

board; Nero actually got the work under way, personally carrying off the first basketful of earth. Like his other brainstorms, it was dropped when he died, but the little that was completed shows his customary technological expertise: the French engineers who tackled the canal again in 1881 followed the course he had mapped out and even used some of the cuttings his men had made.

By now danger signals were flying all over the empire. In Palestine there had erupted the bitter revolt that was to end with the razing of Jerusalem and the destruction of Solomon's temple. Another uprising was brewing in Gaul. And from Rome came frantic reports of unrest and cabals. Finally Nero tore himself away and early in 68 returned to the capital.

By March the revolt in Gaul was in the open, and Galba, the governor of Spain, had joined the dissidents. Though the trouble in Gaul was soon snuffed out, leaving mainly Galba to worry about, it was clear that something had happened to Nero. His cause was far from lost; all he had to do was issue appropriate orders, as he had so successfully done for years. But instead of taking action he talked, and so wildly or so grandiosely or so irrelevantly that he seemed mad. One day, for example, when the situation in Gaul was at its most critical, he convened a meeting of his key advisers and spent most of the time demonstrating a new type of water organ he planned to install in theatres.

In June the commanders of the palace guard, a pair of opportunists who figured it was time to desert a sinking ship, talked their men into switching allegiance to Galba, and the curtain was rung down on Nero's career. The senate scrambled to declare Galba emperor and Nero a public enemy. Only his freed slaves showed any loyalty. He fled to the house of one of them and there committed suicide. It is reported that during his last hours he ordered a grave to be prepared and then kept crying out, "To die! An artist like me!"

Christians, the victims of Nero's most hideous act, have made his name anathema. Yet, in a sense, they only picked up where the Romans themselves had left off: the two Roman authors who are the only sources we have for the facts of Nero's life had already destroyed his reputation. The first, Tacitus, wrote about half a century

after Nero died. A staunch member of the senatorial class, he purports to write history, but deliberately slants it to tell a tale of moral degradation: the decline that began with the subtle scheming of Augustus, was hastened by the hypocrisy of Tiberius, and reached its nadir with the mad and sinister antics of Nero. The second, Suetonius, who composed a short biography of Nero a few years later, gives us in effect a condensed version of Tacitus's account decked out with every lurid detail he could dig up. To judge Nero dispassionately is about as easy as judging Judas Iscariot.

As a leader of the state he deserves high marks, certainly for the first ten years of his fourteen on the throne. The bureaucracy of the empire functioned as efficiently and fairly as it ever had. The watchword of his reign was peace, and by and large he achieved it; his settlement of the Parthian problem, lasting as it did a full fifty years, was a masterstroke. He squandered money on spectacle and display, on public works that were often more showy than essential, but he avoided that most expensive luxury of all, wars of conquest. He was a murderer—but though he killed the innocent, he did not kill many; he was no Ivan the Terrible.

What made the opposition to Nero so intense was not his cruelty but his ever-burgeoning megalomania and the way it drove him to demean his high office. When he merely played at being a performing artist, he could be indulged, and, in any event, the spectacle was contained within the palace grounds. When he took himself seriously and paraded his talents publicly, he was not only being a fool but disgracing the office he held and by implication all who were associated with him in it, that is to say, the entire membership of the senate.

As for Nero's subjects in general, in their thinking the peace he maintained counted far more than the state of Rome's majesty. Indeed, among the masses of Greek-speaking peoples of the empire, his manifest partiality for all things Greek was a distinct asset. They mourned with true feeling when he died. Many even refused to believe he was dead. During the next half century at least two imposters arose who claimed to be Nero, and both immediately gained a following.

Nero may have gone awry about his talents as a performer, but that was the only lapse of his critical sense. No other Roman emperor was a man of arts and letters in the way he was. He was a poet, and his verse, as we can tell from the few surviving samples, was not at all bad. His artistic taste is reflected in the coins struck during his reign; aesthetically they are the finest ever to come out of a Roman mint. Where art was concerned he had, too, the admirable quality of being receptive to new currents—witness the avant-garde architecture of the Golden House and the novel paintings decorating its walls. He even managed to make a contribution in the world of music and song, though for the benefit of Rome's Tin Pan Alley rather than her concert halls: Suetonius reports that he used to act out comic ditties about the leaders of the revolts [i.e., in Gaul and Spain], which . . . have become popular favorites.

And then there is that dimension that is uniquely his: no other Roman emperor, in fact no other Greek or Roman writer or thinker we know of, possessed his avid interest in matters scientific and technological. The fiendish contraption for killing his mother is of a piece with the gadgetry in his new palace, with the down-to-earth specifics in his plans for a fireproof Rome, with the new type of water organ he was puttering over while the world was collapsing about him. He tackled the greatest public works project of ancient times, the Corinth canal; he did not complete it, but for other than technological reasons. He was responsible for a scientific voyage of exploration to the reaches of the upper Nile (his men came back with an exact measurement for the distance between Aswan on the First Cataract and Meroë just north of Khartoum). In Greece he took time off from his artistic endeavors to try to sound the bottom of a lake that, tradition had it, was bottomless. And what ruler or savant is there from any age who has earned renown in pharmacy? "A brimming tablespoon . . . of Nero's marvelous 'Quick Acting,' " states the author of a fourth-century treatise on medicines, "taken before meals . . . settles the stomach marvelously."

Nero deserves a better grade than history has assigned him. He was at times a monster, at times a fool, and he ended up a hopeless megalomaniac; but he was also a statesman, connoisseur, poet, songwriter and musician, mechanic, engineer, pharmacist—the closest equivalent to a "Renaissance man" to come out of the ancient world.

Everyday Life for the Roman Schoolboy

Keith Hopkins *takes us on a* tour de force *via original texts of the hopes, dreams, assumptions and frustrations of the Roman schoolboy.*

Keith Hopkins

Keith Hopkins is Professor of Ancient History at King's College, Cambridge and author of Death and Renewal *(Cambridge University Press, 1983).*

The term, 'everyday life', poses a problem: whose everyday life? One obvious temptation is to identify with the rich, the powerful and the beautiful. Reading a history journal is our best chance of becoming, if only for a moment, Empress of Rome or a victorious Roman general, riding in a chariot among cheering crowds, dressed like Jupiter in a purple cloak thrown over a toga sewn with golden stars. But does anyone imagine themselves to be a slave, a slaughtered prisoner or a child? And yet the Roman child's experience served as his or her introduction to the Roman world. Perhaps it can serve as our introduction too.

Needless to say, what we have on offer is not the child's view, but the adult's view of what the child ought to be experiencing. It is an ancient source composed by different ancient schoolteachers for instructing schoolchildren, both boys and girls, in Latin and Greek. These texts were repeatedly revised over several centuries from the third century BC to the fourth century AD. Let me cite some illustrative excerpts:

The teacher asks: 'What have you done today?' The pupil answer: 'I woke up early, got up and called my slave. I ordered him to open the window. He opened it fast. Once I was up, I sat on the frame of the bed. I asked for my shoes, and because it was cold, for my leggings. I took my linen undercloth; it was handed to me clean. Water was brought in a pitcher for my face. I

brushed my teeth and my gums. I spat out the detritus and wiped my nose. All this was poured away. I dried my hands, my arms and face, so that I would go out clean, because that is what a free boy ought to learn.'

The Roman schoolboy's account is a mixture of the strange and the familiar. It comes from a world which is both recognisable and recognisably different. Hence its appeal. When I learnt French at school, we too were asked to say in French what we had done that day. I gave, we all gave, highly conventional accounts, without being aware, I think, of the unconscious censorship at work

His master's voice: a Roman schoolboy reciting a poem before his teacher.

This article first appeared in *History Today,* October 1993, pp. 25-30. © 1993 by Keith Hopkins. Reprinted by permission of the author.

and the unselfconscious individualistic egoism: for example, '*Je me suis levé, je me suis lavé, je me suis babillé, j'ai pris le petit déjeuner, je suis allé à l'école.*' No natural functions, except eating, no thoughts, no fantasies, no parents, no feelings and of course, no slave. We talked out loud in the class room in a coded language, which omitted what mattered to us most.

These two accounts taken together, one ancient and one modern, the Roman schoolboy's and mine, encapsulate an intractable problem which we face in either writing or reading a history of everyday life. The ancient sources are usually both stylised and censored. In some sense, therefore, they are untrustworthy, not because they were written in order to deceive, but because they are unconsciously incomplete. For example, in the school books from which I have just quoted, the lessons were explicitly stated to be for both boys and girls. But specimen answers were written only for the boys. The slave appeared only as an impersonal appendage ('water was brought'; 'the detritus was poured away'). In other passages, the slave was cast as the faceless recipient of repeated orders: 'undress me, tidy everything up, hurry up, make my bed'. In a highly stratified society, pupils who learnt the languages of the cultured conquerors needed to know how to give orders. Masters barking commands, and waiting often impatiently for their execution, were tyrants, but they were also the dependents of their slaves. But what was the daily life of the slave like? On that

score, our sources are generally silent. And so, few modern historians give them much thought.

Roman schools began early in the day, around dawn. Boys and girls went to the same primary school from the ages of about seven to eleven, and some of them perhaps to the same secondary 'grammar' school. The school textbooks with which I began described a boy's day at school. They combined apparently acute observation of boy's behaviour and dialogue, with moralising prescriptions (understandably, since they were written by schoolteachers) about cleanliness, tidiness, quietness and politeness. Such texts combined idealism with realism, but in unknown proportions. They were designed as manuals to teach everyday language, not as mirrors of social practice. Their bias is visible but not measurable.

Even so, they project an image of a lost world which seems worth recapturing. The following quotations and subsequent examples are derived from several versions of the ancient texts (namely from this author's translations of the Latin and Greek of *Corpus Glossariorum Latinorum* vol. 3, G. Goetz, ed. Leipzig, 1892 and from new texts published by C. Dionisotti, from 'Ausonius Schooldays', *Journal of Roman Studies,* 72, 1982):

Setting Off: I go out of my bedroom with my tutor (*paidagogos*) and my nurse to greet my father and mother. I greet them both and kiss them both. . . . I go to find my writing kit and my

exercise book and give them to my slave. Then everything is ready. Followed by my tutor, I go out of the house and set off to school.

Arriving: I make my way through the portico which leads to school. My school fellows come to meet me. I greet them and they greet me back. I come to the staircase. I go up the stairs quietly; I raise the curtain, and greet the assistant teachers. I greet the master and he kisses me.

Settling Down: 'Let me have my place. Squeeze up a bit'. 'Sit here'. 'This is my place'. 'I got it first'. I sit down and set to work. My slave hands me my writing tablets, and my ink-stand and my ruler. I wipe the tablet clean and rule lines.

Praise and Punishment: I wrote my name and then stood, until those in front of me (gave in their versions), and I paid attention to the answers given by the teacher and my fellow pupils. For that is how we make progress, by paying attention to others, when something is being shown to them. That way confidence increases and we progress. And so, when my turn came, I went up, I sat down, I stretched out my right hand, I pressed my left hand to my clothes, and I began to render what I had been set to learn. Everybody reads the piece given to him, according to his ability. If anyone reads well, he is praised. If he reads badly, he is flogged.

Techniques of Writing: 'I do my copying. When I have finished, I show it to the master who corrects it and copies it out properly'. 'Do the up-strokes and down-strokes properly. Put a drop of water in your ink. You see now, it's all right. Let me see your pen, and your

Ivory tower education? A master sits between two scholars – with a slave in the background – in this second-century AD relief.

Education in Greece – from a 5th-century BC vase; the Hellenic model was very influential in Roman pedagogy, particularly in language, literature and grammar.

knife for sharpening your reed pen . . . It's not bad (or he may say) You deserved to be flogged. I'll let you off this time'.

Hurrying Home for Lunch: I have finished my lessons. I ask the master to let me go home for lunch. He lets me go. I say goodbye to him, and he returns my farewell. I go to my father's house. I take off my outdoor clothes and put on my everyday wear. I order, ask for, or myself get water to wash my hands. Because I am hungry, I say to my boy: 'lay the table and my napkin . . . Tell my mother I must go back to the schoolmaster's house. So hurry up and bring us a meal'. I have a good lunch and drink. The table is cleared. I get up, get my school things, books . . . I find the master reading. He says: 'Now to work again'.

Several points in these lively accounts of a Roman school deserve comment. First, the child of respectable and prosperous parents went to school followed by his own slave attendant or tutor, the *paidagogus,* and also by a second, younger slave boy who carried the young master's writing box. Both slaves stayed with the master throughout the school day. The tutor, a trusted slave, was ideally responsible for the boy's social and educational development. In all ancient handbooks of educational theory, he figures as a representative of the family within the school, a symptom at once of their complementary relationship and of the tension between them. Traditionally, Roman fathers had tutored their own children. Schools were a Greek innovation, admired but distrusted.

The tutor was the boy's guardian. His duties were far-ranging. He was expected to teach the boy table manners: not to grab for food, but to take it delicately, using thumb and one finger, and to be quiet and modest in his deportment. The tutor had the power to scold, to punish, rap knuckles, box ears, to beat. Some slave tutors ruled by fear, others by reason and persuasion. But whatever style the tutor adopted, the whole relationship must have been overshadowed, as the boy grew older, by his realisation that the tutor was only a slave, temporarily in charge of a young master.

Secondly, discipline. The boy, when he entered school, was kissed by the master. If he worked well, he was praised. If he worked badly, he was flogged, or a flogging was threatened. As so often in education, there were competing theories and divergent practices of humanity and harshness. On the one hand, some Roman educational theo-rists argued that parents and teachers should acknowledge that different children had different abilities, and that it was their task to help children along by praise and encouragement. On the other hand, according to the influential educationalist, Quintilian, there was the fear that children would be spoilt by kindness. 'We ruin our children's character . . . by petting, by soft upbringing, which distorts their character!' Beating the children in school seems to have been as common as beating slaves outside school. In one school exercise surviving from Roman Egypt, the teacher had written and the child had copied four times underneath: 'Work hard, boy, or you will be thrashed'. The Roman schoolboy's day fluctuated between the poles of kissing and beating.

Encouragement for severe corporal punishment, on hand, back or buttocks, with cane or rod, came from parents as well as teachers. One father in Roman Egypt wrote to his son's schoolmaster: 'Beat him; because ever since he left his father he has had no other beatings and he likes getting a few; his back has got accustomed to them and needs its daily dose'. St. Augustine in his *Confessions* recalled the brutality of his schooldays with horror; when he had complained to his parents, they had merely smiled. In due course, as we know now, the cycle of deprivation turned. Beaten sons became beating fathers. And so, St. Augustine advised fathers to be severe with their sons, in order to break their will, as though they were slaves. Nor did his sense of due punishment stop there. His idealisation of the severe father is clearly perceptible in his vision of the just God, who would punish wayward sons eternally, and without mercy, turning a deaf ear to the intercession of the saints. Oppressive schooling was the unwitting mould for cruelly repressive religious beliefs.

The main explicit objective of education at Roman schools for the élite was to cram pupils with Greek learning. Some theorists recommended even that Roman children in the highest social set should get a head start by having a Greek-speaking nurse; but others complained that this experience permanently ruined the child's Latin accent. Once children had learnt how to read and write in both languages, they began to study grammar and literature. Formal grammar was a Greek invention of the third century BC. It constituted a tremendous technical and intellectual breakthrough.

Some modern scholars criticise Roman élite education as derivative, imitative, intensely conservative and ritualistic. School, they allege, was not relevant to the real world. Roman schoolboys and university students, for example, practised rhetoric on completely unrealistic cases, chosen from textbooks or literature. For example, 'The law ordains that in a case of rape, the woman may demand *either* the death of her assailant *or* marriage without dowry. A man raped two women in one night. One woman demands his death; the other marriage'. Discuss. Their intellectual style is reminiscent of some question set in modern university examinations.

Ancient critics ridiculed the heavy diet of bombast which these rhetorical debates entailed. 'Young men are made into fools at school', was Petronius' jibe, 'people fed on this stuff can no more be sensible than kitchen workers can smell nice'. Of course, ancient rhetoricians and lawyers could muster a whole series of arguments in defence of declamation. Young men could sharpen their wits, improve their debating skills and gain in self-confidence before a crowd, just as easily, with more pleasure and less tedium, on fictional cases. Besides, these

fictional cases raised real points of Roman law. In law school and long afterwards, distinguished Roman lawyers argued serious points of law, from cases which probably had not occurred. The critics countered by claiming that declarations were aimed primarily at winning applause and at giving pleasure; hence the search for superficial brilliance or turgid bluster. In real law courts, at least by the middle of the first century AD, set pieces of declamation were no longer decisive, and in some courts impossible; opponents interrupted, the judge had to be persuaded, not just impressed with imagery, pathos and characterisation. Or so it was claimed.

The unrealism of Roman education is part of a broader issue. Roman élite intellectuals were simply not interested in the application of their knowledge and intelligence to practical problems of real life. Relevance had no kudos. Of course, there were exceptions, for example, in medicine, law, architecture, engineering and astronomy. But even medicine and law in Rome were surprisingly philosophical and unapplied. There was no lack of talent, application, inventiveness or theoretical sophistication. A quick glance, for example, at a Greek textbook of geometry or algebra confirms this. In the early third century, Eratosthenes had calculated the circumference of the earth, both brilliantly and accurately. Ptolemy in the second century AD calculated the latitude and longitude of all Roman towns, and made astronomical calculations on the basis of tables of observations compiled over the previous thousand years. Underwater archaeologists have discovered a delicate and complex machine, the so-called Anti-Cythera instrument, which simulates the trajectories of planets with a great number of brass differential gears, a formidable achievement both of calculation and metal-working. Similarly, in the first century AD, Heron devised, and Roman subjects apparently built, multiple pulleys to raise heavy theatre curtains, and devised dancing puppets driven by hot air, and a steam-powered dancing ball. But these were only charming toys. The Romans did not build effective steam-powered traction engines. Among the highly cultured, there was no burning interest in tinkering at the margins of technical efficiency, nothing apparently to match, for example, the sixteenth-century English gentlemanly interest in the manufacture of clocks. There was no demand among the upper

cultured for technical knowledge or efficiency. There was no Roman industrial revolution.

And so, Roman élite education could be, had to be, useless. Its prime function was to distinguish those who had mastered complex literary forms from those who had not. Its function was to create very special people, and to denote their difference from the ignorant mass. It did not matter much what the élite were special at. In the Roman empire as in traditional China, the élite was identified by its mastery of a complex literary style, written in a recondite language. Teachers of rhetoric and grammarians were the lesser priests of this upper-class culture, preaching to the young boys who wanted to maintain their father's social status or who wanted to climb the ladder of social success. They were also available for hire by the rich and powerful, who wanted to decorate their dinner tables with a few literate scholars, so that they could display learning vicariously.

Declamatory rhetoric on unreal issues provided Romans and their bourgeois subjects with a unifying cultural varnish and a common apolitical ideology. Their pointlessness was their point. To us, these Roman debating topics for schools and universities, with their themes of murder, torture, prostitution, disinheritance, brigands, love-potions, adultery, rape and incest, seem amazing in their stereotypical, Hollywood character. It is as though upper-class Roman education consisted of making 'B movies', with words but no pictures. The stock situations and characters are just the same as those we find in Graeco-Roman novels. School education (*ludi*) overlapped with entertainment; indeed, declamations given by the teachers were often public performances, a spectator sport, held in front of adult audiences. Declamations on these themes were secular sermons, without prescriptive morality, which allowed vicarious experience, storms at sea, swooning maidens, jealous stepmothers, as an escape from the everyday. The audience could hiss and cheer their favourite heroes and villains. Declamation was a long-winded morality play, with live actors and rapt audience attention, at least if we believe sophistical historians.

I began this article with a young boy waking up. The romantic or the forgetful might hope for a vision of innocence, or for an innocent's vision. Instead, a world of command and impatience: 'Slave, do it quickly. Why were you so slow?', a world of contrast between free and slave, between the washed, the dressed and those who dressed themselves, a world of parents to be kissed and of children walking, as perhaps many of us remember walking, to school, filled as mood and character dictated, with hope and fear, with a mixture of youthful vigour, excited expectation, and the fearful anticipation of oppression by fellow pupils and adult authority. The Roman world was a strange mixture of the familiar and the alien.

These school exercises for learning Latin and Greek show us the boy leaving home with his slave attendant walking behind him, carrying his books. Comportment was a guide to status. On the way to school, he greeted his friends, worshipped the gods and prayed that the day would turn out well. On entering the school, he was kissed by the schoolmaster, who asked him if he had brought along the school fees; he had not. One can imagine his embarrassment and shame. The texts show the boy asserting himself with his friends: 'move up, that's my place, I was sitting there', quarrelling with a fellow pupil over whose turn it was to do an exercise ('you're a liar'; and he said 'no, I'm not'), presenting his work to the schoolmaster, who praised him, but flogged others. Below the surface of hierarchy and achievement, ran violence.

After lunch, provided back at home by his mother, but served by a slave, the boy returned to school. The scene of the conversation lessons changed from school to public space. For example, there was a quarrel in the street between a free man and a slave:

'You are insulting me, I'll have you crucified. Curse you; I'm a free man, and you are a worthless slave'.

Elsewhere in the street, one man approaches another and asks for a loan, offers security, and inquires about the rate of interest. The lender politely refuses the proffered security (Heavens, No) and loftily leaves the poor debtor to fix his own rate of interest. But both parties are careful enough to record the transaction in writing—or so the schoolmaster insidiously tells them. In the fo-

rum, a guilty robber is flogged and tortured, 'as he deserves'. He denies his guilt, but is executed all the same. Then by contrast, another man is accused. He is defended by powerful and articulate patrons, and vouched for by respectable witnesses; and so he is freed, without torture or loss of reputation. In this status-dominated society, the moral is clear: it is better to be free than slave, but even if you are free, make sure that you too have powerful and educated friends.

The day ends with baths and an evening meal. In one scene, the father has got drunk and is trenchantly scolded by his wife. Her speech is particularly interesting, partly because the appearance of women is so rare in these texts, but also because it inverts the normal and expected power relations within the Roman family. The wife is temporarily on top.

How could you, a respectable master, drink so much? What will people say, when they see you in that state, as though you have never eaten out? Fancy, being that uncontrolled! Was that the way for the father of a decent family, a businessman who advises others, to conduct himself? . . . I'm ashamed of you . . . You don't want to vomit do you? . . . I'm shocked at the state you're in. I really don't know what to say . . .

And so she goes on. Perhaps, the schoolmaster, so near the bottom of the social pile of the educated and free, is subtly undermining the status hierarchy, and the powerful respectability of fathers, especially those who drink heavily and do not pay their school fees. Latin and Greek classes in my school were never like that. But in Rome, school and home were in opposition.

Not all dinners finish with drunken quarrels. One master at the end of a celebratory evening, has his bed laid, the mattress and the pillows comfortably plumped, and then reprimands his slaves for their poor service. He forbids any of them to visit friends or sleep out that night, threatens them with severe punishment if he hears anyone talking ('I shall not spare him'), and instructs them to wake him early, before cock's crow. He wants an early start. The slave's day goes on later and begins earlier than the mas-

ter's. In another version, the master feels that it is getting late, asks the time, tells the slave to bring the chamber pot and to send one of the boys to attend him to bed, but then changes his mind, no 'better yet, call one of the women'. Sexual access was a privilege or disadvantage of slavery, depending on your point of view. Schoolmasters considered that Roman boys soon would know, or already knew, about that.

Status, sexuality, conflict and violence permeate these school-texts, just as they probably permeated everyday life. But then schools are rehearsals for the life outside, just as the everyday both reflects and encapsulates the broader structures of society. What one learns in school is not only Latin and Greek, but who one is and how one should behave. The street scenes, involving the negotiation of a loan and a violent verbal brawl, were dramatic plays in the assertion of vertical status. The borrower humbly abased himself by asking publicly in the street, whether he could borrow. The lender affected to be indifferent, as a gentleman should be indifferent to crude details, such as the rate of interest payable and the written contract of loan. The reciprocal roles of patron and petitioner, lender-borrower in a steeply hierarchical society, permeated by debt and repeated crises of credit, must have reinforced in each pupil's mind, which role he would like, and would be likely to play.

Similarly with the verbal fracas: 'I'll knock his teeth out; I'll blind you; I'll send you to prison, where you deserve to rot'. This too revolved around a conflict of status. On the one side, a man who was both respectable and free born; on the other; his opponent, who was alleged to be a posturing slave: 'your master will hear of this; . . . I will not give you an explanation. Why? because you do not count . . . you are not my equal'. The words reveal how very thin the façade of respectability was, how easily it could be pierced, and therefore how very fiercely rank and status must be defended. These schoolroom conversations wittingly, or unwittingly, fixed on the borders of ambiguity, on the tensions which inevitably pervaded a society highly conscious of differences in status. Roman children acted out what we in our society affect to disguise, and so stimulated in some boys good at book-learning a fierce determination to rise socially.

School was even then, as it still is, a battle between competing values: home versus school, playground versus class-room, children versus authority. These are the arenas in which the young discover, are told, forget and then rediscover for themselves that their parents and their teachers are clay idols:

Questions	*Answers*
What is Man?	A short lived ghost
What are Riches?	Everyday Power
What are Words?	Blindness
What is Authority?	Poverty
What is Wealth?	A ridiculous page . . .
What is Women?	A daily Drudge
What is Law?	Necessity
What is Holiday?	Work
What is Death?	Freedom . . .
What is Loneliness?	Kingship

The morality contained within this list of questions and answers, from a Roman school text, is both explicit and unclear. What is clear is that by night-time, when our Roman school-boy was safely in bed, his conscious and unconscious mind was filled with a host of images, which mirrored, reinforced and eventually helped him to reproduce Roman social structure.

FURTHER READING:

William V. Harris, *Ancient Literacy* (Harvard UP, 1989) *Literacy in the Roman World, Journal of Roman Archaeology* Supplement 3 (Ann Arbor, Mich., 1991), S. F. Bonner, *Education in Ancient Rome* (London, 1977), H. I. Marrou, *A History of Education in Antiquity* (London, 1956).

Friends, Romans or Countrymen?
Barbarians in the Empire

Lead in the water, over-indulgent lifestyles, rampant inflation—the list of explanations for the fall of the Roman Empire in the west has been endless. But in a new study, **Stephen Williams** *and* **Gerard Friell** *turn the spotlight on the 'barbarians' who shored up Rome's armies and frontiers, and discuss if they were Rome's salvation or doom.*

Stephen Williams and Gerard Friell

Stephen Williams and Gerard Friell are the authors of Theodosius: the Empire at Bay, *Published by Batsford, priced £30.*

The importing of tribal 'barbarian' peoples (mainly Germanic) to the Roman Empire was a permanent imperial policy which expanded in scale over the centuries, and was continued by Byzantium after the Western empire had crumbled in the fifth century—supposedly destroyed by those same Germanic peoples. Like any strategy it had its risks and its critics 'The introduction of barbarians into the Roman armies,' intones Gibbon, 'became every day more universal, more necessary, and more fatal.'

It is a sombre observation that so many modern historians have split into anti- and pro-barbarian camps, like Roman writers themselves. To Gibbon, Bury, Piganiol, the Germans were a dangerous fifth column which undermined and eventually wrecked the empire. To German historians such as Otto Seeck (1923), W. Ensslin (1941, 1959) and Joseph Vogt (1964), they were an injection of new and vigorous blood which defended and then inherited an exhausted empire. This is not much of an advance on the rival polemics of the Greek rhetorician, Themistius, and the philosopher Synesius in the fourth century. It is surely

time to free ourselves from this Punch and Judy approach.

In the early first century, following the disastrous defeat of Varus' three legions in the German forests by Arminius the chief of the Cherusci, Augustus abandoned the earlier ambition of conquering Germany to the Elbe, and set limits to the empire. The Rhine and Danube were to be permanent frontiers. Henceforth, frontier policy involved not just roads, garrisons and fortified points, but an active diplomacy among the external tribes. Trade, protectorship, assistance, subsidies and influence in tribal politics played just as important a role as war or the threat of war.

The Roman aim was to encourage small, friendly client chieftainships who would both respect the Roman frontiers and protect them against other tribal threats, often in return for Roman help against their tribal enemies. Only in this indirect way, carefully conserving the strength of the legions, could the thousands of miles of frontier be policed and maintained. The clients would be formally recognised as 'allies and friends' of Rome (*socii et amici*), although the true relationship was not, of course, between equals. Chieftains would be honoured with Roman citizenship or, more palpably, money subsidies with which to impress and reward their followers. By the mid-first century there was a chain of clients from the lower Rhine to the middle

Danube: Frisii, Batavii, Hermunduri, Marcomanni, Quadi and Sarmatians.

The system did not always work smoothly, if only because the tribes were first and foremost warrior peoples to whom seasonal warfare was the normal mode of life. Nor could their nobles always control them, having no coercive apparatus in the manner of sophisticated kingdoms. But, like Highlanders, Pathans, Gurkhas, Zulus, the Germans were recognised not only as a potential threat, but also an enormous reservoir of warlike recruits. It was axiomatic that they would invariably fight each other in any case—let them do it in Roman interests. From the earliest, Germans had been recruited into the specialist auxiliaries in the Roman army, troops of lower pay and status than the legions, though not necessarily inferior in fighting skills. Arminius, who had massacred the three legions in Germany, had himself served as an auxiliary.

To the Germans, Rome represented boundless riches, magnificence and almost unlimited power, which might be plundered but was just as attractive as a high-paying employer of warriors. The German noble who was invited to cross the Rhine to meet Tiberius, said:

> I have today seen those gods, whom until now I had only hear tell of. . . . Our young warriors are foolish to try and defeat you, instead of gaining your trust.

A further move in the diplomatic repertoire was settling barbarians in Roman territory with their families and moveable wealth. As early as 38 BC. Agrippa allowed a German tribe, the Ubii, to settle west of the Rhine, and similar settlements continued intermittently throughout the first century. By the time of Marcus Aurelius in the second century, such transfers had become common practice: Marcus settled barbarians in Dacia (Romania), Pannonia (Western Hungary), Moesia (Romania-Bulgaria), the Rhineland and Italy itself, although the last-named settlement was not a success. Moves of this kind were presented to the Germans as concessions: in fact, they worked to Roman advantage. They dispersed and weakened the aggressive potential of the tribes, transferring part of this potential into Roman control instead. The barbarian youth were ever eager to fight—but now, within the framework and command structure of the Roman army, not their tribal warrior band.

The condition of immigration varied, as did the motive and the initiator. Sometimes it was a compulsory transfer by the Romans to defuse a situation, sometimes it was requested by the tribes who wanted land and security, and sometimes it was refused. Usually it was part of a peace treaty which reflected the degree of Roman ascendancy. After a crushing defeat, of course, prisoners of war who were considered to have no rights might be sold as slaves. Alternatively, captives and family groups would be assigned land as tenant farmers (*coloni*) tied to large landowners or imperial estates, where they would be liable to rent, tax and, later, military service. Increasingly, the defeated enemy was required to supply a specified quota of warriors who would be judiciously distributed among the Roman army.

Where the peace treaty was on more equal terms, different conditions operated. The tribes might supply whole units of troops on a contract basis, such as the 5,500 élite Sarmatian cavalry based at Ribchester (*Bremetennacum*) in the Ribble Valley: at the end of their service they naturally settled in Britain, where many of them had married and raised families, rather than return to their distant Hungarian homeland. Equally common was to allow specified numbers of a population land on which to settle, not as coloni but as the *Laeti:* a community of freehold farmers with all their

livestock and moveable wealth, their families and their tribal leaders. They would be disarmed, and subject to the overall authority of a Roman governor, the *Praefectus,* and encouraged to farm the land by subsidies, technical help, temporary tax exemption and whatever else was needed to promote a loyal, thriving community. In time, it was reasonably hoped, they would become Romanised as so many other provincials had done.

By the mid-third century the balance of power on the frontiers had shifted dramatically away from the empire. Great migration pressures were at work southward and eastward, down the Russian rivers, into the Donetz basin and the Hungarian plain, and the Vistula and Oder regions. Continuous tribal warfare, displacements and amalgamations had replaced the old familiar groupings with far larger tribal agglomerations—Visigoths, Ostrogoths, Vandals, Sarmatians, Burgundians, Alemanni, Franks, Saxons—who were a much more formidable threat to Rome. At the same time the Praetorian Guard and then the regional army groups themselves were setting up and murdering emperors in rapid succession. Between 235 and 284 there were fifteen 'legitimate' emperors and many more usurpers, almost every one of which died a violent death.

The military anarchy was both cause and effect of the heightened external threat. Continuous war on all frontiers simultaneously stretched the economic and military resources of the empire beyond their limits. Frontiers were breached, cities sacked and plundered, provinces temporarily overrun, communications disrupted. Continuous war demands and the shrinkage of productive land in the emergencies, drove up taxation and led to uncontrolled money inflation. Regional armies, continually fighting the invaders and demanding ever-higher pay and status, would support their own commanders' ambitions against a distant, ineffective emperor in Rome whose orders were increasingly irrelevant. This meant treason, and treason meant civil war, which denuded the frontiers yet further. Several main regions of the empire, including Gaul, Spain, Britain, Egypt and Syria, temporarily split off to form separate regional empires.

The empire was eventually bolted together again, most efficiently, by a series of tough soldier-emperors such as Aurelian, Diocletian and Constantine, be-

tween about 270 and 330: but it was now a different empire: autocratic, centralised and regimented, a fortress designed for indefinite siege. The armies were expanded, the various enemies defeated, the frontiers restored and greatly strengthened. Painfully but effectively, Roman superiority was everywhere reasserted.

In these circumstances, the need for military manpower was acute. General conscription was introduced, but it proved disappointing. As later empires were to discover, the very spread of civilisation and urbanisation made the populations less willing to become soldiers than their fathers had been. The idle Roman city plebs even cut off their thumbs to avoid the colours. As the fourth-century historian Ammianus observed, as the emperor negotiated a new immigration of Sarmatians from beyond the Danube:

> . . . now that foreign troubles were over and peace was made everywhere, he would gain more childbearing subjects and be able to raise a strong force of recruits: for the provincials would always rather pay tax in gold, to avoid offering their bodies.

It was always the more rustic peoples still with a strong warrior tradition, like today's rural Turks, who made the best and most willing soldiers. Roman recruitment had steadily run through the Gauls, the Spaniards, the Illyrians, and now had to look more and more to the Germanic peoples beyond the frontiers. Diocletian's army contained distinct units of almost every major tribe: Saxons, Franks, Alemanni, Vandals, Goths, Quadi, Sugambri and others.

So long as they were under clearly perceived Roman overlordship, laeti settlements made excellent sense, achieving three imperial policy aims simultaneously. They removed barbarian aggressive pressure by providing settlement land; they got vacant or deserted lands under cultivation again and yielding a tax: and they provided a steady flow of hardy recruits, which in time was converted into a system of conscription. Instead of money tax, the laeti were asked for men; and once a man had taken the military path, the obligation to serve was automatically passed on to his sons, in a way suggestive of later feudalism.

Laeti settlements were, of course, quite different from modern immigration into European nation-states that were originally ethnically and culturally homogeneous. The Roman Empire was al-

The Roman Empire and its Neighbours *c*. **AD 375 (before the Visigoth migration).**

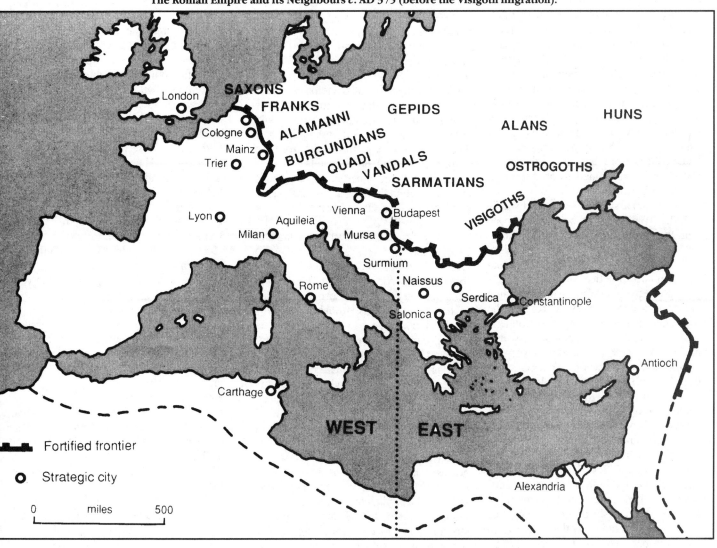

SAXONS
FRANKS
GEPIDS
HUNS
ALAMANNI
ALANS
BURGUNDIANS
OSTROGOTHS
QUADI
VANDALS
SARMATIANS
VISIGOTHS

London
Cologne
Mainz
Trier
Lyon
Aquileia
Milan
Vienna
Budapest
Mursa
Surmium
Rome
Naissus
Serdica
Constantinople
Salonica
Antioch
Carthage
Alexandria

WEST : **EAST**

■━ Fortified frontier

O Strategic city

0   miles   500

ways a multi-national conglomeration in which Greeks, Gauls, Copts, Britons, Dacians, Arabs co-existed but retained much of their national and cultural identity, including language and religion. It was reasonable to see the barbarian settlements as just one more component in this mosaic. After a generation, the difference between Roman and barbarian would blur. The great melting-pot was the army.

A veteran returning from his service would have been accepted by a military culture which honoured his prowess, but which was very different from the tribal war band and the mead-hall: he would be accepted in the powerful regimental traditions of those who served the great Caesar Augustus, and he would see remote parts of the world of which his

people knew nothing. He might gain honours and promotion as so many did, and he would automatically enjoy the respected social rank of *Honestior,* the right to wear the gold rings which was denied to a mere peasant or artisan. His attitudes would have changed by the time he returned to his community a prosperous and respected man, if indeed he returned at all. Like the Sarmatian cavalry, many Germanic soldiers would marry and settle far away from their original community.

The Illyrian soldier-emperors greatly expanded the laeti settlements: Vandals and Burgundians in Britain, Franks and Memanni in Gaul and Italy, Carpi in Pannonia, Visigoths in Moesia. Constantine settled some 300,000 Sarmatians in Italy, Macedonia, Thrace and

Syria. By about 350, perhaps 10 or 15 per cent of the empire's people, and certainly a majority of its army, were of barbarian origin. Constantine's reorganisation of the officer structure for the first time allowed officers of barbarian origin, who were very numerous, to reach the topmost commands. Generals such as Bauto, Arbogast and Richomer (Franks), Nevitta, Fravitta and Modares (Goths), Dagalaif (Alemanni), Victor (Sarmatian) proved superb commanders. They saw themselves not at all as mercenary tribal warriors but loyal Roman commanders and respected members of the ruling classes—which is just what they were.

Everyone recognised the basic distinction between these men, and the Germanic tribes beyond the frontiers. They, and the Germanic troops in the ranks and lower officer corps, would fight whoever the emperor commanded them to fight, including their own former kinsmen, without hesitation. There was no possibility for them to return to their former tribe—they would be killed on the spot if they did, as the Frank Silvanus discovered when, caught up in a treason plot, he thought of returning to his tribe, but was forcibly warned what would happen. Equally, their barbarian origins precluded them from aspiring to the imperial throne, and tended to hold them in check politically.

Diocletian and Constantine had stabilised the frontiers and the imperial throne with the establishment of a strong dynastic system (Constantine's house ruled, with colleagues, for seventy years) and the standard practice of collegial emperors of East and West, whose regional presence was necessary to control the thousands of miles of threatened frontiers.

But by the late fourth century new and unforseen external threats emerged, which altered the whole strategic situation. The seemingly irresistible pressure of the Huns into the Ukraine region subjugated or evicted the great nations of Goths and Alans, and completely disrupted the carefully balanced diplomatic-defensive system along much of the Danube frontier. The defeated Visigoths and Ostrogoths both desperately petitioned the Eastern emperor Valens to be admitted as laeti, in order to survive as independent peoples. Valens agreed to the first but refused the second. The immigrant numbers proved huge and unmanageable. They were neither properly disarmed, nor fed, nor dispersed, and their plight was shamefully exploited by the local Roman officials. A major revolt broke out, which was so dangerous that Valens had no alternative but to march against the Visigoths with the main Eastern field army. Their tribal kinsmen the Ostrogoths took advantage of the confused state of the Danube defences to cross also.

On the fateful day of August 9th, 378, the combined forces of the Goths met the Roman army outside Adrianople (modern Edirne), and owing to Valens' incompetent mistakes, the result was the most catastrophic Roman defeat for centuries. Over two-thirds of the army—perhaps 20,000 men—were slain, including Valens himself. The East was virtually defenceless as the Goths roamed unopposed, plundering Greece and the Balkans.

The Western emperor, Gratian, appointed the general, Theodosius, Emperor of the East, with the daunting task of restoring the situation. By ruthlessly scraping together a new army of dubious quality, by skilful use of the strategic fortified cities, by local victories, manoeuvre and by starving the Goths of supplies, the two coemperors were at last able to regain the military initiative. They could not expel the Goths from the empire (they had nowhere else to go), nor destroy them in battle. But they split their forces and their loyalties, and weakened them sufficiently to bring them to a peace treaty in 382.

This granted them settlement land in Moesia and Thrace as 'allies' (*Foederati*) with obligation to provide military forces for the emperor on demand. Despite contemporary—and modern—criticisms of this treaty, it was probably the very best that could be had in the desperate circumstances. Superficially, it was represented in imperial propaganda as 'business as usual', a continuation of earlier settlements. In reality, both the emperors and the Goths knew it was a distinct new departure. The clear pre-condition of all the earlier settlements—perceived, unambiguous Roman supremacy—was no longer there. The Visigoths were settled not as a disarmed community of laeti, subject to a Praefectus and supplying individual recruits or small units to be integrated into the Roman command structure. They were a semi-independent nation in arms, subject to their own tribal chieftains who had concluded an equal treaty with the emperor: they would fight *en masse* as a national allied army under their own leaders. It was open to them to see the treaty of 382 as a concession they had finally prized out of the Romans as a result of their victory at Adrianople. All the manoeuvres, shifts and bargainings of frontier diplomacy were now having to be enacted *within* Roman territory.

This step could not be reversed, but Theodosius tried hard to stop it becoming a precedent. He badly needed the Gothic manpower to rebuild his armies, and he probably hoped that given time, the Gothic state-within-a-state could be brought under firmer overlordship, like the conventional laeti. He followed a deliberate public policy of conciliation between Romans and barbarians, wooing their nobles with the benefits of 'Romanness' and co-operation, to the disgust of the senatorial aristocracy. His own niece was married to the loyal Vandal general, Stilicho.

Many responded. Some powerful Gothic leaders became enthusiastically pro-Roman, but now they knew there were far more favourable conditions of settlement than the old laeti: they saw themselves as allies, not subjects, and they husbanded their forces as the only ultimate safeguard against imperial bad faith. Still, the settlement worked acceptably during Theodosius' reign. The Visigoths kept their part of the bargain, helped him win two costly civil wars, and also made it possible for a fresh Ostrogoth invasion to be repulsed on the Danube in 386.

The situation might have stabilised at this point. But in 395 its architect, Theodosius, suddenly died, leaving the twin thrones of East and West to his two immature and inexperienced sons, Arcadius and Honorius. This was a gravely dangerous new situation. Inevitably, real power was wielded by ministers, generals, empresses, who could be no substitute for strong, militarily respected emperors. The traditional loyalty between the thrones of East and West was not only suspended, but turned into its opposite, as the two courts intrigued against each other like separate states. The Visigoths were not slow to occupy the power vacuum.

Their leader Alaric had wanted a full Roman generalship, which Theodosius had wisely refused. Alaric now had himself proclaimed king, and led his warriors on another grand plundering expedition, until the Eastern government, in desperation, granted him the top military command in Illyricum (Yugoslavia and the Balkans) which legitimised his plundering and gave him access to the Roman arms factories.

For the next fifteen years the volatile Alaric was a very destructive third force in the empire, who could be held in check and occasionally defeated, but not destroyed or tamed. To assemble the forces desperately needed against him, to crush a revolt in Africa and repel an Ostrogothic invasion of the Italian heartland, the Western generalissimo Stilicho was forced to buy barbarian troops on almost any terms: ad-hoc treaties ceding yet more territory to new Foederati. To defend Italy itself, he was forced to strip Britain and the Rhine defences below the danger level, and in 407 hordes of Vandals, Suevi, Alans and others poured across the frozen Rhine into Gaul, never to be dislodged again. This ultimately cost him his position and his life. In 408 his enemies procured his execution on a trumped-up treason charge. Half his soldiers deserted in disgust to Alaric.

Freed of the one military leader who could defeat him, Alaric went on to sack Rome in 410. Henceforth, the Roman military rulers in the West—Constantius, Aetius and others—not only had to rule through incompetent puppet emperors, but had to accept the military reality of new 'Foederati' in Pannonia, Gaul, Spain and then Africa, hoping to play off one against another. By now they dropped even the nominal pretence that these were Roman subjects, and officially recognised them as kings and allies. Alaric had set the dangerous precedent of uniting the two offices of Roman field-marshal (*Magister Militum*) and Gothic King. Henceforth other supreme warlords such as the Goth Ricimer could rule in reality, setting up and discarding imperial puppets at will, until eventually even these empty symbols were unneces-

sary, and in 476 were simply dropped. Insofar that a veneer of Roman legitimacy was needed, the kings looked to Constantinople, where there was still a real emperor. In the West, many Roman officers and civil servants made the best of things by serving the new kingdoms and hoping to civilise them.

There was no causal continuity between the earlier policies of controlled barbarian immigration, and the later carving out of large sections of the former Western empire into German proto-kingdoms. The nationalist picture of Germanic infiltration and subversion, and the opposing idealistic picture of heroic German saviours and newcomers, are both shallow and unhistorical. The Roman empire, perhaps more than any other on earth, disregarded ethnic origins and rewarded loyalty, skill and energies within its imperial system. Many of its greatest emperors were themselves Spaniards, Africans and above all, Illyrians. What happened in the Roman West in the fifth century had very little to

do with ethnic origins or even culture. It was a breakdown of crucial political parameters, beginning with the treaty of 382, which time and events did not allow to be re-established.

The Germanic allies did not initially seek to destroy or replace the Roman framework, provided they could find a strong, respected, federal place within it—which, in more favourable conditions, might well have been achieved. By 800 Charlemagne wanted nothing so much as the fictional crown of Holy Roman Emperor, equal to the emperor at Constantinople.

FOR FURTHER READING:

J. B. Bury, *The Later Roman Empire* (1923: Dover paperbacks, 1958); A. H. M. Jones, *The Later Roman Empire,* (Vol 1, Blackwell, 1964); J. M. O'Flynn, *Generalissimos of the Later Roman Empire* (Edmonton, 1983); P. J. Heather, *Goths and Romans,* (Clarendon, 1991).

The Judeo-Christian Heritage

Western civilization took root in the Graeco-Roman world but, notwithstanding all we owe to the classical ideal, we are no less indebted to the Judeo-Christian tradition. If we derive humanism and materialism, philosophy and science, from the former, we derive our God and our forms of worship from the latter. Of course, it is difficult (and perhaps misguided) to separate these traditions, for the Judeo-Christian heritage comes to us through a Hellenistic filter. "Jews and Christians in a Roman World" explores this angle.

On the political surface the history of the Jews seems similar to that of other small kingdoms of the Near East, situated as they were close by such powerful neighbors as the Babylonians, Assyrians, and Persians. Yet of all the peoples of that time and place, only the Jews have had a lasting influence. What appears to differentiate the Jews from all the rest, writes historian Crane Brinton, is "the will to persist, to be themselves, to be a people." The appearance of Israel on the map of the modern world 2,000 years after the Romans destroyed the Jewish client-state is a testimonial to the spirit described by Brinton.

The legacy of the Jews is a great one. It includes the rich literary traditions found in their sacred texts. Among the significant writings left by the ancient Jews are the Dead Sea Scrolls, which are reexamined here in the essay by Norman Golb. In addition to such materials, the Jews have bequeathed to Western civilization their unique view of history, which is at once linear and, based as it is on the Covenant idea, miraculous—God intervenes in history to guide, reward, or punish his Chosen People. They also gave birth to a messianic impulse that inspired Christianity and other cults, the elemental morality of the Ten Commandments, and the moral wisdom of the prophets. Their monotheism and their god, Yahweh, formed the model for Christian and Muslim notions of God.

A brief comparison of Yahweh and the Greek god Zeus illustrates the originality of the Jewish conception. Both gods began as warrior deities of tribal cultures. But, as Zeus evolved, he was concerned chiefly with Olympian rather than human affairs. Yahweh, on the other hand, was more purposeful and had few interests except his people. And unlike Zeus, who was in and of the universe, Yahweh was the creator of the universe. As Herbert Muller writes of Yahweh, "Once he had been endowed with benevolent purposes, and taught to concern himself with all mankind, he could become, as he did, the God of Judaism, Christianity, and Muhammadanism" (*The Uses of the Past,* Oxford University Press, 1957).

Certainly Christianity bears the stamp of Judaism. After all, Christ himself was a Jew. To his early followers, all of them Jews, he satisfied the powerful messianic impulse latent in Judaism. (Hartmut Stegemann's article explores this angle.) The New Testament recounts the growth and spread of Christianity from an obscure Jewish sect in Palestine to a new religion with wide appeal in the Roman world. Yet the central figure in this great drama remains shrouded in mystery, for there is a dearth of firsthand evidence. The Gospels, our greatest and most reliable source, contain wide gaps in their account of the life of Jesus. Nevertheless, they remain a profound record of early Christian faith. "Who Was Jesus?" confronts some of the problems we face in our quest for a historical Jesus. "Handmaid or Feminist?" deals with another problematical figure, Mary, mother of Jesus, and how her image has changed through the centuries. "Women and the Bible" assesses scholarly efforts to understand why ancient Jewish and early Christian writings ignored or downplayed the role of women.

As it split away from Judaism, Christianity took on new dimensions, including the promise of private salvation by sacramental means. From the start, its theology reflected the teachings of St. Paul, who was instrumental in spreading the faith to the Gentiles. Then, as it took hold in the Mediterranean, Christianity selectively absorbed Hellenistic elements. Among those trained in Greek learning, Stoicism and Platonism prepared the way for an amalgamation of classical philosophy and Christianity. The personal God of the Jews and Christians increasingly became the abstract god of the Greek philosophers. Biblical texts were given symbolic meanings that might have confounded an earlier, simpler generation of Christians. Christian views of sexuality, for instance, are fraught with multiple meanings and complexities.

Looking Ahead: Challenge Questions

Describe the relationship that existed among Jews, Christians, and pagans during the Roman era.

Who wrote the Dead Sea Scrolls? What light, if any, do these documents shed on early Christianity?

How do we know what we think we know about the life of Jesus? Why is the quest for the historical Jesus so difficult and so controversial?

How and why has the image of the Madonna changed over time? What functions has her image performed for Christians?

Why do ancient Jewish and early Christians ignore or downplay the domain of women?

Jews and Christians in a Roman World

New evidence strongly suggests that both in Roman Palestine and throughout the Diaspora, Judaism, Christianity, and paganism thrived side by side.

Eric M. Meyers and L. Michael White

More than a century ago, archaeologists began to rediscover the ancient world of the Mediterranean: the world of Homer and the Bible. Much of the early fieldwork in the classical world arose from a romantic quest to bring ancient literature to life. One thinks instinctively of Schliemann at Troy, a shovel in one hand and a copy of Homer in the other. In the Holy Land, the first biblical archaeologists were theologians and ministers who sought to identify and explore cities of the biblical world and to authenticate biblical stories and traditions; thus they arrived with preconceived ideas drawn from biblical texts and other literary sources. Because many were Old Testament scholars, New Testament archaeology in the Holy Land took a back seat. Outside the Holy Land, it remained for years in the shadow of classical archaeology.

Since World War II, and especially since the discovery of the Dead Sea scrolls in 1947, archaeology has been more attentive to the world of the New Testament. But the new archaeological knowledge has only slowly begun to have an impact because New Testament scholars have been slow to take archaeology seriously. Some scholars think archaeology is of peripheral concern to early Christian studies, concluding debatably that the "earthly" dimension of early Christianity is irrelevant. New Testament archaeology is also given low priority in Jewish studies, which traditionally have placed far greater emphasis on sacred texts. Many believe New Testament ar-

chaeology to be of limited value in the study of ancient Palestine, erroneously assuming that the archaeological time frame is restricted to only two generations, from the time of Jesus to the destruction of Jerusalem in the year 70. In fact, one cannot understand the development of either Judaism or Christianity without looking at the historical context over centuries, beginning with the introduction of Greek culture into the ancient Near East.

THE HOMELAND

Scholarly understanding of Judaism and Christianity in the Roman province of Palestine during the early Common Era (abbreviated C.E. and chronologically the same as A.D.) has long been burdened by some dubious suppositions. One is the belief that after the First Jewish Revolt against Rome in 66–70 C.E., the new Jewish-Christian community fled the Holy Land. Certainly there was significant emigration to other Mediterranean lands, but in light of archaeological evidence from the first two or three centuries C.E., a growing number of scholars have found the idea of wholesale Jewish-Christian migration untenable.

Actually, the first followers of Jesus were basically indistinguishable from their fellow Jews. Although they believed Jesus was the Messiah and professed a radical love ethic that had few parallels in Judaism—for example, love for one's enemies—the first Jewish-Christians observed most of the Jewish laws and revered the Temple in Jerusalem. They apparently got along well with their fellow Jews, contrary to the impression

created in the Gospels and other New Testament writings, where the Pharisees, the "mainstream" religious party of ancient Judaism, are presented in a negative light. The new Christians, in fact, were at odds mostly with the Sadducees, who were much more rigid in their religious outlook than the Pharisees, and far fewer in number. When the Apostles were persecuted by the Sadducean high priest, it was the Pharisee Rabbi Gamaliel who intervened to save them (Acts 5:17–42); when Paul was called before the Sanhedrin (the High Council) in Jerusalem, he obtained his release by appealing to the Pharisees (Acts 22:30–23:10); and according to the Jewish historian Josephus, when Jesus' brother James was put to death by order of the Sadducean high priest in 62 C.E., the Pharisees appealed to the king to depose the high priest. Jesus' natural constituency was the Pharisees, whose doctrine of love for one's fellow humans must surely have been the foundation for Jesus' ethical teaching.

The belief that all or most of the Jewish-Christians left Palestine after the First Revolt stems partly from the lack of clear material traces of the Christian community in the Holy Land from about 70 to 270 C.E. Early Christianity, however, vigorously sought to win converts both among gentiles and in the many Jewish communities throughout the Mediterranean. It is exceedingly hard to imagine these efforts bypassing the large Jewish community in Palestine.

Moreover, Jews from Jerusalem and the surrounding area fled in large numbers to Galilee after the revolt was crushed. Would the first Jewish-Christians have ignored Galilee, where Jesus spent his

 From *Archaeology*, March/April 1989, pp. 26-33. © 1989 by the Archaeological Institute of America. Reprinted by permission.

Surprise Findings From Early Synagogues

The synagogue provides a rare opportunity to study the Jewish people—and Jewish-Christians—as they forged a new religious way in Roman Palestine after the fall of Jerusalem. Even within a given region, we find a great variety of architectural forms and artistic motifs adorning the walls and halls of ancient synagogues. This great divergence of synagogue types suggests great variety within Talmudic Judaism, even though the members of different congregations belonged to a common culture.

Such diversity resulted in part from the catastrophe of 70 C.E., after which many sectarian groups were forced to fend for themselves in a new and often alien environment. Some groups settled in towns, others in urban centers; their choices reflected their understanding of how hospitable a setting their beliefs would find in either the sophisticated cities or the agrarian towns.

Synagogue excavations also attest to the primacy of Scripture in Jewish worship and provide a clearer view of the place held by the *bema,* or raised prayer platform, and the Ark of the Law. The Ark is the fixed repository for the biblical scrolls, which were stored in a central place in the synagogue by the third century C.E. Until recently, the dominant view was that the Ark remained portable throughout most of antiquity.

Some synagogue mosaics even suggest that Jewish art played an integral part in the composition of new poetry recited in the synagogue. In late Roman synagogue mosaics, themes based on the zodiac begin to appear. These mosaics are followed in the textual record by poems that name the actual constellations of the zodiac. The setting for reciting such poems, or *pzyyutim,* was undoubtedly the synagogue, where the intelligentsia would have gathered and included the poems in their worship.

Finally, survey and excavation of numerous synagogue sites in the Golan Heights have revealed an astonishingly lively and vigorous Jewish community in Palestine in late Roman, Byzantine, and early Islamic times. The supposed eclipse of Jewish life at the hands of early Christendom—especially after the conversion of Constantine and, later, the establishment of Christianity as the state religion in 383 C.E.—needs to be reexamined. In fact, one of the surprises of recent synagogue studies is the generally high level of Jewish culture in Palestine at the end of the Roman period (third and fourth centuries C.E.) and the continued though sporadic flourishing of synagogue sites in the Byzantine period (from the middle of the third century to 614 C.E., the year of the Persian conquest of Palestine). All the evidence points to a picture of a Judaism in Palestine that was very much alive until the dawn of the medieval period.

---

childhood and where he conducted his ministry? Later generations of Christians certainly did not, as evidenced by the numerous churches they built in Galilee. The presence of important Christian centers of worship makes it difficult to imagine a great Christian "repopulation" of Palestine between the third and fifth centuries. Rather, it seems there was a large community of Jewish-Christians in Palestine from the first century onward, a community later augmented by pilgrims in the age of Constantine.

Jerusalem is central in the study of early Christianity. It is there that the new religion received its most compelling moments of inspiration in the death and burial of Jesus; and it is from there that its followers took their message to the other cities and towns of the land. As long as the Temple stood, the first Christians continued to worship there and in private household meetings. With the destruction of the Temple, however, both Jews and Christians had to establish new patterns of worship. Thus the local synagogue, which was both a meeting place and a center of worship, became the focus of spiritual life for Jew and Jewish-Christian after 70 C.E.

Recent synagogue excavations have revealed that Jewish life enjoyed remarkable vitality in Palestine during the Roman period, and in some localities into the Byzantine period and beyond. In the pre-Constantinian era, the synagogue was quite possibly where Jewish-Christians worshiped as well. Although the archaeological record shows very little definitive evidence of Christianity until the end of the third century, the textual record is quite clear. In a reference that may go back to 100 or 120 C.E., the Jerusalem Talmud implies that Christians are a sect of *minim,* or heretics. Irenaeus, the first Christian theologian to systematize doctrine, speaks of Ebionites, who read only the Gospel of Matthew, reject Paul, and follow the Torah and the Jewish way of life. Epiphanius, another early Christian writer, speaks of Nazarenes, or Elkasaites, as Christians who insist on the validity of the Torah and laws of purity.

Whether one looks at early Christianity or rabbinic Judaism in Roman Palestine, it is clear that this was a period of great cultural and religious pluralism. One finds this pluralism in the Lower Galilee, at Sepphoris, and at the great site of Capernaum on the northwestern shore of the Sea of Galilee. The octagonal Church of St. Peter in Capernaum is built over what some excavators believe

is a Jewish-Christian "house-church" dating back to about the third century. The excavators have also found evidence of a first-century house below this church edifice that may have been Peter's residence. It is clear that by the fourth century, Christians venerated the site by erecting churches there. Next to these Christian structures are Jewish buildings, including a reconstructed synagogue. Archaeologists once thought the synagogue was from the first century C.E., the very building in which Jesus would have walked. Today there is universal agreement that it is a later structure, dating to the fourth or fifth century, that survived for hundreds of years into the early medieval period. Excavators have recently claimed finding another synagogue, from the first century, beneath this fourth- or fifth-century synagogue. If they are right, then in Capernaum a Jewish synagogue and a Jewish-Christian church existed side by side from the end of the first century on. The grander structures above both the early synagogue and the house of Peter in Capernaum suggest that Jewish and Christian communities lived in harmony until the seventh century. The continuous Christian presence for six centuries also casts serious doubts on the idea that the early

Christians fled Palestine after 70 C.E. Evidence like that found in Capernaum is plentiful in the Beth Shean Valley and in the Golan Heights, although the evidence there begins later, toward the end of the Roman period and into the Byzantine period.

In the middle of the fourth century, pluralism began to suffer as the Roman period in Palestine came to an end and the Byzantine period began. The transition from Roman to Byzantine culture as revealed by the archaeological and textual records was dramatic and coincides with either the so-called Gallus Revolt against Roman occupation in 352 or the great earthquake of 363. In the case of the revolt, the Byzantine emperor might have taken the opportunity to place the unruly province under his direct rule. In the case of the earthquake, the damage to Roman buildings would have presented the opportunity for a Byzantine architectural and cultural style to emerge as cities were rebuilt.

In either case, the revolt and the aftermath of the earthquake mark the beginning of a difficult period for Jews, in which they had little choice but to adjust to Christian rule. The Palestine of the Roman period, when Jewish sages spoke in Greek and when Rabbi Judah the Prince reputedly numbered the Roman emperor among his friends, became a land undergoing thorough and vigorous Christianization after the conversion of Constantine. Money poured into Palestine, and much of it went into building churches.

Nevertheless, archaeological evidence prompts us to exercise caution. Pockets of Judaism and Christianity remained in close contact during the Byzantine period. They may well have continued the harmonious relations established during the period of pluralism, even as Christianity became the dominant religion.

THE DIASPORA

Archaeology has also enriched our understanding of the New Testament world outside Palestine. It is significant to both Jewish and Christian history that the bulk of the New Testament is set outside the Jewish homeland. Jews and Christians alike called their communities outside Palestine the Diaspora, or "dispersion."

While the religious heritage of the New Testament may be Hebrew, its language is Greek. Its cultural heritage is not that of the ancient Near East but that of Greece and Rome. The world of the New Testament was fluid and pluralistic, with an extensive transportation network crisscrossing the Mediterranean. Christians and Jews traveled the highways and seaways, carrying their religion with them. This mobility is vividly reflected in the extensive journeys of Paul.

The work of archaeologists should not be used to prove New Testament stories about Paul. The remains of his day are simply too hard to find.

The New Testament record of Paul's travels provided early investigators with both an itinerary for their archaeological work as well as a "case" to be proved. From the 1880s to the 1920s, for example, the eminent Sir William Ramsay sought to corroborate the account given in the Acts of the Apostles of Paul's activities on his way to Rome, in Ephesus, Athens, Corinth, and Philippi. Shaping Ramsay's approach were attractive images of Paul, such as the one in chapter 17 of Acts, where he is depicted preaching to the philosophers on the Areopagus, or Mars Hill, below the entrance to the Acropolis. The story in Acts, and later Christian legends attributed to Paul's followers, are the only evidence we have for this. Paul left no footprints on the Areopagus for archaeologists to follow. It is also interesting that Paul, in his own letters, never once mentioned his activities or this episode in Athens. Still, this remains a popular tourist spot, and the legacy of early archaeologists like Ramsay lives on.

All over the eastern Mediterranean, tourists play out variations on this theme with local guides. (Though Paul was a tireless traveler, if he had visited every one of these places, he might have died of old age before he got to Rome.) Often the difficulties arise when local legends, which seem to grow like stratigraphic layers, become attached to a site. A prime example of this occurs at Paul's *bema* at Corinth.

Excavations at Corinth have revealed a fifth-century Christian church erected over what appears to be a bema, or speaking platform. The obvious assumption was that this was the site of Paul's defense before the Roman governor Gallio in Acts 18:12 ("But when Gallio was proconsul of Achaia, the Jews made a united attack upon Paul and brought him before their tribunal"). Indeed, the story is given further credence by the discovery of an inscription from Delphi that bears the name of Gallio as well as his title. This inscription has been very important in dating Paul's stay in Corinth to around the years 51 and 52 C.E. But it is most difficult to place Paul's trial on this particular bema, since the South Stoa of Corinth, where the bema is found, was expanded and rebuilt during the next two centuries. Other evidence found at Corinth does little to clear matters up. A pavement bearing the name of Erastus, the city treasurer named in Romans 16:23, identifies him as an *aedile,* a minor administrative official, not as treasurer ("Erastus, the city treasurer, and our brother Quartus greet you"). Is this a tangible record of a follower of Paul at Corinth? One cannot be sure. As at the Areopagus, the best advice may be *caveat* pilgrim.

Similar problems arise in trying to place Paul or John in Ephesus, since Byzantine and medieval accounts have been overlayed on the biblical stories. Current excavations at Ephesus have revealed an elaborate Roman city of the second to sixth centuries C.E., but evidence of the first-century city remains sparse. Extensive excavations at Philippi, in Macedonia, have uncovered a second-century forum and main roadway, but most of the remains come from churches and basilicas dating from the fourth to the seventh centuries. Once again, the remains of Paul's day are difficult to identify.

In some cases, the connection of a site with Paul is demonstrably wrong. For example, Christian pilgrimage and devotion in Philippi helped to equate a Hellenistic pagan crypt with Paul's "prison," as described in chapter 16 of Acts. In the late fifth century, a basilica was built around this site. In short, the work of archaeologists should not be used to prove such New Testament stories. Instead, archaeological work should be used more as a "backdrop" for the discussion of Paul's letters to Christian congregations living in these cities of the Roman world. The focus of archaeology should be placing the Christians and Jews in a cultural context.

Palestine's Sophisticated Cities

In recent decades, a number of important cities besides Jerusalem have undergone major excavation, yielding evidence of a sophisticated life-style in Palestine. These were Roman cities, built for the administrative infrastructure of imperial rule, but they also became conduits through which Greco-Roman culture was introduced into Palestine.

These cities dominated Palestine, except for the Upper Galilee and Golan regions in the North, but the level of sophistication dropped steeply when one moved away from these urban cores. In the surrounding areas, the older agrarian life-style was still very much dominant, and it was town more than city that ultimately encompassed most of Jewish, and Jewish-Christian, life in Palestine.

Nonetheless, there were some Hellenized centers of Jewish life, mostly along the major roadways, the Lower Galilee, the Rift Valley, and the coastal plain. The primary language here was Greek, and the surrounding Jewish population used Greek for trade and day-to-day discourse. In time, Greek eclipsed Hebrew as the common language, and many of Israel's most important sages buried their loved ones, or were themselves buried, in containers or sarcophagi that bore Greek epigraphs or Greco-Roman decorations. In striking contrast, virtually no Greek is found in the Upper Galilee or the Golan.

Such tombs are exceptionally instructive. For example, the Jewish catacombs of the sages in Beth Shearim, excavated in the late 1920s, attest to the high level of Greek spoken by the sages. They attest as well to the fact that the sages were comfortable with a style of decoration in their tombs that was thought by contemporary scholars to be incompatible with Jewish sensibilities and law, and with the proscription against representational and figural art contained in the Second Commandment. With the discovery in 1987 of the extraordinary Dionysos mosaic at Sepphoris, the heartland of the Jewish sages, an exciting new perspective was provided on the Hellenization of Roman Palestine.

It is not yet clear who commissioned the colorful mosaic stone carpet, found near both the Roman theater and Jewish buildings and homes, but the ramifications of the discovery are most significant. The mosaic dates to about 200 C.E., the time of Rabbi Judah the Prince, who was both a leader in the compilation of the Mishnah (Jewish traditional doctrine) and reputedly a close friend of the Roman emperor Caracalla. The central panel of the carpet shows Herakles/Dionysos in a drinking contest. The 15 panels that surround this scene depict the life and times of Dionysos, god of wine, the afterlife, revelry, fertility, and theater. What is so amazing is that they are all labeled in Greek, either to clarify the contents for those who didn't know Greek mythology—a gap in knowledge probably not uncommon in these eastern provinces—or to jog the memory of those who ate in the hall in which the stone carpet was located.

The implications of this discovery are many, but the three most important may be summarized as follows: the extent of Hellenization in Palestine by the third century C.E. is greater than was previously believed; Jews were more accepting of great pagan centers than was previously believed, and had more access to them; Jewish familiarity with Hellenistic culture in urban centers such as Sepphoris was a positive force affecting Jewish creativity. It hardly seems coincidental that the Mishnah was codified and published at Sepphoris during the very same period when a highly visible Hellenistic culture and presence flourished in Palestine.

More recent archaeological perspectives shed light on the development of Jewish and Christian institutions of the New Testament world. Originally, "church" (the Greek *ekklesia*) and "synagogue" (the Greek *synagoge*) were synonymous terms for assembly or congregation. Especially in the earliest days of the Diaspora, Christian groups, including gentile converts, were considered to be following a form of Jewish practice. Only in the second century would the terms "church" and "synagogue" begin to become specific to Christians and Jews. In fact, distinct architectural differences between them did not begin until the fourth century. In other words, if we were following Paul through Ephesus or Corinth, we would not be able to distinguish Christian or Jewish meeting places from the exteriors of the buildings.

Most of the congregations founded by Paul met in the houses of individual members. Significantly, Diaspora Jewish groups would have met in houses, too; but over time, more formal synagogue buildings appeared. If anything, house-synagogues were in use earlier in the Diaspora than in Palestine (as early as the first century B.C.E.). Of the six early Diaspora synagogues known from excavations—at Delos, Priene, Ostia, Dura-Europos, Stobi, and Sardis—five were originally houses that were renovated and adapted to special religious use. The earliest of these, from Delos, dates to the very beginning of the Common Era, or even slightly earlier.

There is evidence that Jews and Christians worshiped as neighbors in the Diaspora, as in Roman Palestine. One of the most impressive discoveries in this regard comes from Dura-Europos, a Roman garrison on the Euphrates River in what is now Iraq, dating to before 256 C.E. On one street was a house that had been renovated, in three stages, into a sanctuary of Mithras, a Persian god whose cult spread thoughout the Roman empire from the second half of the first century C.E. onward. Farther down the same street, another house had been converted, in two stages, into a synagogue. Its assembly hall contained one of the earliest datable Torah niches, and on its walls were elaborate frescoes depicting stories from the Hebrew Scriptures. Farther down the same street was a house that was renovated to become a Christian church, with a small assembly hall and a room set aside for baptism. The baptistry room in particular has attracted considerable attention, since it contains some of the earliest clearly datable Christian art, including representations of Jesus in scenes from the Gospels.

More evidence of religious pluralism in the Diaspora can be seen in Rome. Excavations beneath several basilicas, such as those of St. Clement and SS. John and Paul, reveal earlier buildings—houses or apartment complexes—that were being renovated for religious use as early as the first century. The house-church of St. Clement, for example, is generally identified with the first-century levels below St. Clement's Basilica. Interestingly, the second-century house adjacent to the house-church of St. Clement was used as a Mithraic cult sanctuary. Seven such Mithraic halls are known from Rome, and another 14 from the nearby port of Ostia. In addition, inscriptions from Jewish catacombs suggest at least 11 synagogues existed in Rome during imperial times.

The evidence suggests that Jews and Christians were able to live in much closer harmony with one another than has often been assumed.

The complex society that sustained such pluralism is now the focus of much research. A new group of biblical archaeologists, using what they refer to as a "social history" approach, are attempting to bring biblical texts and archaeological evidence into a more cohesive historical framework. The basis of their work is the use of archaeological evidence not merely as proof or illustration but as a key to the historical and social context of religion. In the Hellenized Roman cities of Palestine, such as Sepphoris, and in major urban centers of the Diaspora, such as Corinth, the activities of Jews and Christians must be seen as part of a complex culture and viewed over several centuries of development.

For example, textual evidence shows the existence of a Jewish community at Sardis in Roman Lydia (western Turkey) since the time of Julius Caesar; however, the first significant archaeological evidence of its activities comes hundreds of years later with the renovation of a public hall, part of the bath-gymnasium complex, to serve as a synagogue. Thus we know that Jews and Christians were both in Sardis for a long time, but apparently with no distinctions by which we can recognize their daily activities. The synagogue was in use from the third century to the sixth century, and its size and opulence attest to the vitality of Jewish life in Sardis. The synagogue was renovated by Jews at least twice after its initial adaptation, and these renovations were extensive and costly. Moreover, its inscriptions give evidence of the social standing and connections of the Jewish community: a total of 12 known donors to the renovations are titled "citizen" or "city councillor," and in some cases both. Other notables, including several Roman bureaucrats, are also named in the roster of donors. Here the archaeological record yields a picture of a Jewish community, over several centuries, that was politically favored and socially "at home" in the civic life of Sardis. To understand the life of the Jews of Sardis, however, one must place them not only in the context of their city but also ask how their local conditions compare to other Jewish groups from the Diaspora.

This same social history approach may be applied to Christian groups as well. At stake are a number of traditional assumptions about Judaism and Christianity in relation to their social and religious environment. It would seem that Jews and Christians were able to live in much closer harmony both with one another and with their pagan neighbors than has often been assumed. To an outsider, both church and synagogue might have resembled foreign social clubs or household cults.

The mobility within the Diaspora produced cultural as well as theological diversity, even within the Jewish and Christian traditions. We should not assume that the Diaspora synagogue communities conformed to Talmudic Judaism. A good case in point is seen in recent archaeological evidence, especially from inscriptions, for active participation and even leadership by women in Diaspora synagogues—something also seen in the homeland. This could eventually shed light on the significant role of women in Paul's churches. To date, however, the main information comes from the New Testament writings, which give evidence of women as house-church patrons, as in Romans 16:2–5.

There are numerous ways in which Jews and Christians of the Diaspora were influenced by their cultural environment. Especially noteworthy are conventions of letter writing drawn from the analysis of papyri, which can enhance our understanding of the letters of Paul. Likewise, conventions of building or donation inscriptions offer a means of understanding many synagogue inscriptions, such as those at Sardis. Still more common are Jewish and Christian burial inscriptions. Both in burial inscriptions and in funerary art one finds that the earliest Jews and Christians, when one can distinguish them at all, regularly used motifs and language common in the larger pagan environment.

Thus there is a wide array of new and old archaeological data available for students of Judaeo-Christian antiquity. Whether it comes from East or West, whether it is inscribed with letters or decorated with figural art, it constitutes the most significant body of evidence for reconstructing the cultural context in which Jews and early Christians lived.

Of all the human sciences, archaeology is best equipped to deal with such complex matters. When strongly tied to the literary and historical disciplines, it becomes the most reliable tool for reconstructing the ancient societies in which Judaism and Christianity, orphaned from Jerusalem, found new homes.

Who Wrote The Dead Sea Scrolls?

A New Answer Suggests a Vital Link Between Judaism and Christianity

Norman Golb

Norman Golb, professor of Hebrew and Judaeo-Arabic studies at the University of Chicago, and a member of the Société de l'Histoire de France, has written widely on historical themes and is well known for his manuscript discoveries. A student of the Qumrān scrolls for more than thirty years (his doctoral dissertation at Johns Hopkins dealt with the subject), he regularly leads graduate seminars on the texts at Chicago's Oriental Institute. He was awarded an honorary doctorate in History by the University of Rouen, in France.

Forty years ago this spring, on a desert cliff near the western shore of the Dead Sea, two bedouin shepherd boys ventured into a cave and, quite by accident, made one of the most important archaeological finds of the century. Hidden deep within the recess were seven parchment scrolls containing texts that had not been read since the first millennium. Over the next nine years, hundreds of such scrolls—some in small fragments, others fully intact, many surrounded by the remains of linen packets or pottery jars—would be discovered in this and other caves near the ancient settlement called Khirbet Qumrān. The findings would include a broad array of biblical and nonbiblical Hebrew writings and one scroll written on copper. But no one could have foreseen all this at the time. The chance recovery of such a wealth of cultural history from a single

cave in the Palestinian wilderness seemed a miracle.

When opened in Jerusalem, the parchment rolls were found to include two copies of the Book of Isaiah, as well as a number of previously unknown writings. One text, the so-called Genesis Apocryphon, or Abraham Romance, was an embellished version of events described in the Book of Genesis. Another, the War Scroll, contained visionary descriptions of an apocalyptic battle to take place between "sons of light" and "sons of darkness" at the end of days—a theme that pervades the Apocrypha, Jewish writings that appeared in Palestine during the centuries between the Old and New Testaments. A third text, often called the Hodayot, contained hymns in the style of the Book of Psalms. There was also a fragmentary text interpreting the Book of Habakkuk (Habakkuk was an Old Testament prophet) as a prediction of events of the interpreter's own time and the impending future, as well as a scroll describing the initiation ceremonies and ritual practices of an unnamed religious brotherhood.

The latter work, the Manual of Discipline, was particularly intriguing, for it strayed radically from what was thought to be mainstream Jewish thinking of the time, and even foreshadowed Christian doctrines later espoused in passages of the New Testament. Unlike the Hebrew Bible and known writings of the Apocrypha, the Manual of Discipline declared personal wealth spiritually defiling. It placed great emphasis on ritual purity—but, in a notable departure from the

Bible, dismissed ceremonial bathing as worthless unless accompanied by a similar cleansing of mind and spirit. The manual also described regular communal study sessions in which members of a hierarchical holy order were to explore the "secrets" and hidden meanings of scripture—a concept that stands in stark contrast to the type of personal wisdom extolled in the Book of Proverbs and the apocryphal Ecclesiasticus.

As investigators at the Hebrew University and at the American School of Oriental Research (both in Jerusalem) studied the seven newly discovered scrolls, they became convinced that the Manual of Discipline—and hence the other texts as well—must have been written by the Essenes, a small, four-thousand-member Jewish sect said to have inhabited parts of Palestine around the time of Christ. According to the contemporary Jewish writers Philo of Alexandria and Flavius Josephus, the Essenes had eschewed personal wealth, espoused ritual purity, and, like the sect described in the text, held communal study sessions to probe the secrets of the Torah. Moreover, Pliny the Elder, in his *Natural History,* had placed Essenes on the western shore of the Dead Sea, stating that "below" their settlement was the town of En-gedi, which is in fact only twenty miles south of the caves where the scrolls were found.

These coincidences were so striking that, by the mid-fifties, virtually every scholar studying the scrolls believed they were the work of Essene monks who had lived at Qumrān. Further, it became widely accepted that, because some of the texts found at Qumrān contain ideas that appear later, in the New Testament, the Essenic sect must have had a formative influence on Christianity. The American literary critic Edmund Wilson embraced the theory of Essenic authorship in his popular 1955 book, *The Scrolls from the Dead Sea,* and it has enjoyed virtually universal acceptance ever since. Today, encyclopedias, museum catalogues, textbooks, and even scholarly journals and doctoral dissertations all propagate the theory of Essene authorship. Readers of the current *Encyclopaedia Britannica* learn that the scrolls were "all part of a library belonging to a Jewish religious sect (Essenes) that flourished at Qumrān from the mid-2nd century BC to AD 68." And visitors to the Treasures of the Holy Land exhibition that opened at New York's Metropolitan Museum of Art last year, and is now at the Los Angeles County Museum of Art, read in the exhibition catalogue that Qumrān was "the center of the Jewish sect that had owned and used the scrolls." Those who see the scrolls displayed at the Israel Museum, in Jerusalem, are told the same story.

What they are not told is that the Qumrān–Essene theory, however widely accepted, is at odds with almost every shred of evidence that has surfaced during the past thirty-five years. In fact, the evidence makes demonstrably clear that the Dead Sea Scrolls originated not with an obscure monastic sect but with Palestinian Jews. And if the theory that Essene monks wrote the scrolls is dubious, so are the larger, historical beliefs it has inspired. That early Christian doctrines drew from the same sources as Essenism is now a tenet of conventional wisdom. "Such concepts in the New Testament as predestination, election, contradistinction of flesh and spirit, and the dualism of light and darkness and of truth and falsehood . . . are related to the theology of the Dead Sea sect," the Treasures of the Holy Land catalogue declares, expressing a view repeated endlessly over the past forty years with varying nuance. But what analysis of the scrolls actually reveals is that Judaism as a whole, not just one obscure sect, was the salient influence on the new religion.

There were signs almost from the outset that something was not quite right with the theory of Essenic authorship. The Essenes, as de-

scribed by Pliny the Elder, were insular, peace-loving, celibate monks; their order "has no women," he wrote, "and has renounced all sexual desire." Yet when archaeologists excavated a portion of the cemeteries at Khirbet Qumrān, they found the graves of women as well as of men. Moreover, the doctrine of unqualified sexual abstinence—which, according to Josephus, Philo, and Pliny, was a primary tenet of the Essene creed—could be found neither in the Manual of Discipline nor in any of the other original seven scrolls.

Rather than reconsider the fledgling theory, however, the authorities of the day—such eminent archaeologists and Hebrew scholars as Eleazar Sukenik and his son, Yigael Yadin, of Israel; André Dupont-Sommer and Father Roland de Vaux, of France; and many others in England, Germany, and the United States—clung to it, citing a statement by Josephus, in his *Jewish War,* to the effect that although most of the Essenes were celibate, some were not. The Qumrān area, the experts argued, must have had its share of noncelibate Essenes. It is possible, the Hebrew and Bible scholar Frank Moore Cross, of Harvard, wrote in *The Ancient Library of Qumrān and Modern Biblical Studies,* "that the older celibate community later became mixed, or we may suppose that within the environs of the desert of Qumrān was an order of married Essenes alongside a larger celibate community."

This explanation, unfortunately, does more to damage the Qumrān–Essene theory than to defend it, for the theory is based on Pliny's statement that there was a group of *celibate* Essenes living above En-gedi. Moreover, the theory holds that Qumrān was not just a remote Essene settlement but the nerve center of the Essene movement—the "laura," or "motherhouse," where many of its doctrines had been formulated and its books written. How could it be claimed that members of this very center did not practice celibacy, one of the sect's most conspicuous doctrines?

A more serious difficulty arose when the Qumrān settlement was excavated, during the early 1950s. Pliny had described the Essenic monks as having "only palm trees for company," implying that they had lived a rudimentary existence. Yet the ruins that archaeologists uncovered were far from rudimentary. The excavations showed a well-developed settlement, with cisterns, pools,

and reservoirs for water storage, and a complex of stone buildings that had included a dining hall and kitchen, stables, a pottery, and a tower adjoined by a building whose identity remains uncertain. To account for these troublesome findings, some archaeologists—Father de Vaux, for example, in his book *Archaeology and the Dead Sea Scrolls,* and Cross, in his *Ancient Library of Qumrān*—proposed that the Essenes must have lived in caves on the escarpment above the settlement or in nearby huts, and that the settlement buildings themselves served only as administrative headquarters. (The Treasures of the Holy Land catalogue treats this speculation as fact, explaining that the monks "lived in the neighboring caves . . . and most probably in tents and huts, of which nothing has remained.")

There *was* evidence of temporary habitation in some of the caves, but it is hard to believe that the Qumrān settlement was a mere commons for cave-dwelling monks. Besides being too elaborate, Khirbet Qumrān bears too many marks of a military fortress. Not only did excavations reveal fortifications and a siege wall, but the presence of large supplies of food and water, and of many signs of battle, indicated that the settlement had housed a troop of Jewish soldiers, who fought a protracted battle with the Romans around the time Jerusalem was overrun, in 70 A.D. Evidence of this fierce siege includes smashed walls, the remnants of a great fire, and a large number of arrowheads. The approximate date of the battle, and identity of the besiegers, was provided by dated Roman coins found amid the rubble.

Josephus did refer in *The Jewish War* to an Essene named John who had taken part in the war against the Romans. But Philo characterized the Essenes as the most peaceful of men, saying, "You would not find among them . . . anyone pursuing a war-involved project." And there is no written record that the Essenes defended a fortress or fought in pitched battles against Roman troops.

Had these inconsistencies been broached early on, the notion that Essene monks wrote the Dead Sea Scrolls might never have taken hold. But by the time Qumrān was fully excavated, in 1956, the theory had taken on a life of its own. Scrolls were by then being discovered in ever greater numbers in other caves on the escarpment.

And archaeologists working at the site, rather than considering new explanations, began to look for evidence that would connect the scrolls to the settlement.

When, for example, three plaster-covered tables and two small inkwells were found amid the ruined stone buildings at Qumrān, the room containing them was identified as a scriptorium, where, it was claimed, scribes had produced the manuscripts hidden in the caves. The room had constituted the second floor of the unidentified building near the watch-tower. Apparently at the time of the Roman attack, the second story had been destroyed, and its contents had fallen through to the floor below. Because those contents included the tables and inkwells, archaeologists inferred the existence of a scriptorium. When word of the impending Roman attack reached Qumrān, Father de Vaux and others theorized, the Essenes must have hastily gathered up the manuscripts being produced in this room, carried them to the caves above the settlement, and hidden them there in specially made pottery containers or in linen packets.

This assertion has at least two obvious problems. First, as numerous researchers have pointed out, ancient depictions of scribes do not show them sitting at tables while engaged in their art but rather seated on benches with their work propped up on their knees. Second, and more important: given that a large amount of rubble had formed a protective covering over the site until its excavation, the supposed scriptorium should have contained many inkwells—not just two—as well as other scribal tools, including reed pens, rolls of blank parchment, and instruments for indenting rules in it. But no scribal tools were found amid the debris, and not a single scrap of parchment.

All of this would suggest that the room served not as a scriptorium but as a chamber where several men held meetings, perhaps for civic or military purposes, and where some small amount of official (documentary, as opposed to literary) writing may have been done. To suggest that a military fortress contained such a room requires no elaboration or special pleading; the room was, after all, located near the watchtower, in the center of the complex of stone buildings. By contrast, the assumption that a chamber containing two inkwells and three tables was used by pious Essene scribes for the wholesale copying of literary manuscripts has never been convincingly documented. Despite the lack of evidence, however, the ruined chamber is still labeled Scriptorium by the conservators of the Qumrān site. And other authorities (including the authors of the Treasures of the Holy Land catalogue), while making no mention of the scriptorium theory, continue to assert that "the copying of sacred books" was among the activities carried out at Qumrān.

One detail that seemed, despite the weakness of the scriptorium theory, to bolster the claim that the manuscripts were created at Qumrān is that pottery fragments found near the scrolls in the caves were similar to shards excavated at the settlement. To the excavators of the site, this finding, and the fact that the pottery shards were roughly the same age as the manuscripts, favored the view that jars and manuscripts alike had originated at Qumrān and that the scrolls had been placed in the jars before they were hidden. This line of reasoning was proposed by Father de Vaux, in *Archaeology and the Dead Sea Scrolls,* and remains an article of faith among scroll scholars today.

It is entirely possible, of course, that the jars found in the caves were made at Qumrān, but that possibility hardly establishes that the scrolls were. In fact, the military character of the settlement, and the lack of evidence that the scrolls were produced there, weigh heavily against such an assumption. Leaving aside for now the question of where the scrolls did originate, we can say that the excavation of Khirbet Qumrān, far from confirming the theory of Essenic authorship, raised serious questions about it. And as the theory began to show weaknesses, its burden grew heavier, for more and more scrolls were being discovered in the caves.

By the spring of 1956, a total of eleven caves, spread over a distance of about two miles along the escarpment extending north from the Qumrān settlement, had been found to contain manuscripts. And a Jerusalem-based team of scholars, headed by Father de Vaux and the British archaeologist G. Lankester Harding, continued to study them. Some scrolls were found intact, others in thousands of fragments. This made an exact count impossible, but it was clear that the fragments came from at least five hundred manuscripts and perhaps as many as eight hundred. The painstaking work of reassembling, edi-ting, and publishing these texts—still far from finished—was divided among the eight members of the team, each taking responsibility for a number of fragments.

It was soon apparent that the scrolls embraced a wide variety of literary themes and genres. The texts were found to include hymns and liturgical compositions, commentaries on biblical books, and previously unknown apocryphal writings, including the Book of Mysteries and the Sayings of Moses. There were wisdom texts, messianic speculations, even horoscopes—in short, every type of literature one would expect to find among the Palestinian Jews of the first century A.D., and much more that was totally unexpected. Few of these new texts espoused the doctrines associated with Essenism, and many in fact contradicted the doctrines emphasized by Philo and Josephus. One such text—a fragment once evidently appended to the Manual of Discipline—defined an appropriate age for the beginning of sexual activity, and another, the so-called Psalms Scroll of Cave Eleven, expressed views that have been characterized as Hellenistic or even anti-Essenic.

The Qumrān–Essene theory, which was first proposed as an explanation for just seven scrolls, could not convincingly account for such an astoundingly large and heterogeneous body of literature. Still, its founders and their disciples stood by it; rather than concede that such diverse texts might have been written by diverse authors—and not by a small, isolated group of monks—they expanded their characterization of Essenism. The French scholar André Dupont-Sommer argued in his 1959 book, *The Essene Writings from Qumrān,* that the Essenes must have been numerous and widely dispersed, and that the sect's beliefs must have taken different forms over a long period of evolution. And even though both Josephus and Philo had stated that there were only four thousand Essenes in Palestine in the first century A.D.—and despite the lack of proof that the settlement at Qumrān was an Essene monastery—virtually no one dissented from that view. Instead, the Essenes were designated a large and important group, and Qumrān came to be seen as a major center of Hebrew literary production.

This facile pan-Essenism was no panacea, though, for it was not only the number and diversity of texts that strained the theory but also their *scribal character.* It does not normally occur to archaeologists, when unearthing ancient texts, to ask whether they are authors' originals or scribal copies, or to consider whether they are of a documentary or a literary character. Likewise, a Bible scholar has no particular reason to wonder whether a particular parchment manuscript was written in the hand of a prophet or in that of a scribe; he is interested primarily in content and has no hope of ever seeing the original. Manuscript specialists are quick to raise these questions, but the team assembled in Jerusalem included no scholar whose field was Hebrew manuscript studies. As a result, these distinctions—crucial ones, as it turns out—were missed.

Authors' originals (sometimes called autographs) are usually rugged specimens, full of insertions and deletions, whereas scribal copies are characterized by careful margins, graceful calligraphy, and few marks of interference. If, as the theory holds, the Qumrān settlement was the motherhouse of Essenism; and if the monks at Qumrān were not mere copyists but creative thinkers whose writings inspired people throughout Palestine; and if they had hastily hidden their work in caves as the Roman army approached, then surely the surviving manuscripts would show signs of work in progress. Yet, of the hundreds of scrolls recovered from the Qumrān caves and subsequently published, only one was an author's original. The rest were finished scribal copies of previously written texts.

That there were five hundred to eight hundred extremely diverse texts in the Qumrān caves, and that these included only one autograph, clearly suggest that the scrolls derived not from an authors' workshop (such as the scriptorium the Qumrān settlement is said to have contained) but from one or more large *libraries*. Apparently in response to this problem, some scholars have recently suggested that the monks at Qumrān must have had such a library in addition to the alleged scriptorium. And since no evidence of a library has ever been found at Khirbet Qumrān, they assert that the library, like the Essenes themselves, must have been based outside the settlement—in the caves where the scrolls were found. This view was reported as fact by *The Jerusalem Post Magazine* in June of 1985, in an article describing scholarly speculation about a group of scroll fragments found in Cave Four in

1952. "Cave Four had been the sect's library," the article declares, "unlike the other caves where scrolls had been hurriedly hidden."

This hypothesis seems to account neatly for the lack of original manuscripts among the texts found in the caves; libraries, after all, are normally devoted to finished works, not rough drafts. But it is hard to imagine that such a small, isolated desert community would contain so extensive a library. And it is harder still to believe that the purported Essenes of Qumrān, while maintaining a complex of fine stone buildings, would have climbed into cliffside caverns to engage in reading and scholarship. That such a notion could be seriously proposed only demonstrates what a small corner proponents of the original theory have painted themselves into. Forced to concede that the purported scriptorium should have contained original texts as well as copies, they propose the existence of a library. And faced with the troubling fact that the Qumrān settlement contained no library, they now place the library in a cave.

Even if the library-in-a-cave hypothesis made sense, however, it would not exonerate the larger theory. The next question would be: Why, if the Qumrān site was such an important religious center, did its occupants produce and save only *literary* texts? The study of other ancient settlements along the Dead Sea leaves no doubt that the Jews of Roman times preserved other kinds of documents. In 1952, when archaeologists excavated the caves in Wadi Murabba'at, a gorge just eleven miles south of Qumrān, they discovered not only letters dating to 132 A.D.—written in the hands of senders and containing many precise geographical and personal names—but a wealth of equally specific legal documents. If Qumrān was the administrative center of a large religious sect, one would expect to find the same sort of correspondence and archival records along with the sect's literary scrolls.

In the absence of any such documents, we can only assume that the imputed Essenes of Qumrān kept archival records strictly segregated from literary ones and that the ravages of time were highly selective; or that the Essenes, unlike their immediate neighbors, attached no importance to civil, personal, or administrative documents; or that something else prompted them to store hundreds of literary texts but not a single page of correspondence. Proponents of the

Qumrān–Essene hypothesis have yet to address any of these problems; so far, they have simply ignored them.

These grave and numerous contradictions would seem to render the Qumrān–Essene theory worthless. Yet scroll scholars continue not only to skirt serious questions about the theory but to ignore two discoveries that point directly to an alternative explanation. The first of these involves the artifact known as the Copper Scroll.

In 1952, when the Copper Scroll was unearthed in two pieces from Cave Three, it was so brittle that it could not be safely opened. But the investigators could see from the images that appeared in reverse on the scroll's outer surface that it contained descriptions of precious objects buried in various hiding places. Within four years, the scroll had been sawed into narrow strips at a laboratory in Manchester, England, and deciphered. But long before the text was made public, those in charge issued a statement to the world press casting doubt on its historical veracity. The scroll did contain inventories of buried treasures, the experts said, but the treasures were purely fictional. "It is difficult to understand why the Essenes of Qumrān were so concerned with these stories of hidden treasure," the statement reads, "and especially why they saw fit to engrave them on copper, which at that time was a costly metal. . . . At all events this guide to hidden treasure is the most ancient document of its kind to have been found, and is of interest to the historian of folk-lore."

But when the text of the Copper Scroll was finally published in the early sixties, it appeared to be anything but folkloric. In fact, unlike the vast majority of scrolls found near Qumrān, this one seemed to provide explicit clues about its own and the other scrolls' origins. The Copper Scroll had been executed not in a scribe's elegant book hand but in the relatively crude and haphazard style of lettering associated with documentary autographs. As for content, it was a terse, straightforward enumeration of various prized artifacts—*including written documents*—that had been sequestered at burial sites throughout the Judean wilderness.

The Copper Scroll even included a statement to the effect that "the duplicate of this writing" could be found "in a pit . . . to the north of Kohlat." This locality can no longer be identified, nor do we know which of the place-names in the Copper Scroll designated the Qumrān site. But many of the hiding places described in the text are, like Qumrān, located in the wadis, or dry desert riverbeds, that extend eastward and southward from Jerusalem. The text describes caches hidden near Jericho, for example—where books were indeed discovered during the third and ninth centuries (in the latter case, ironically, by Jews who were alerted by shepherds).

The use of so many place-names, the character of the handwriting, the manner of enumeration, and the reference to another copy of the same work—together with the fact that the entire text was inscribed on copper rather than parchment—all point to the scroll's authentic historical quality. It should finally have served as the point of departure for a new hypothesis concerning the origin of the Qumrān texts. What it describes, after all, is not the hiding of scrolls in a single group of caves (as the Qumrān-Essene theory requires) but the widespread sequestration of books and valuable artifacts at sites scattered throughout the Judean wilderness—in a pattern radiating not from Qumrān but from Jerusalem. That the scroll was officially dismissed as folklore—and that the dismissal came several years before its complete text had been published and thus long before conclusions about its significance were warranted—can be explained only as an attempt to protect the original theory from an obvious and devastating challenge.

The other discovery affecting the Qumrān-Essene theory also occurred in the early sixties, and it served to confirm the statements contained in the Copper Scroll. In two seasons of excavation at Masada, a Herodian fortress located thirty miles down the Dead Sea coast from Qumrān, archaeologists located the site at which the Jews of Palestine made their last stand against the Romans after the fall of Jerusalem, in 70 A.D. At that site, fragments of fourteen more scrolls, containing an assortment of biblical and apocryphal texts, were discovered. These scrolls were similar in age and scribal character to those at Qumrān; among them, in fact, were fragments of a work represented in the Qumrān finds—a liturgical text called the Songs of the Sabbath Sacrifices. When archaeologists found fragments of this poetic work at Qumrān, they attributed it (like all the other texts) to the

ostensible Essene monks. But the disposition of the fragments at Masada suggests quite a different origin.

No one has ever proposed that the scrolls found at Masada were written there; from their position in the ruins, it appears that they had been in the possession of the defenders of the site, who had fled there during the Roman invasion of 70 A.D. (The defenders occupied only one section of the settlement, and it was in that section, amid remnants of the siege, that all the scrolls were found.) Insofar as many of those defenders were refugees from Jerusalem, it would have been logical to infer that the scrolls were brought to Masada by such refugees, along with other items they managed to salvage when fleeing the capital. Jerusalem was, after all, the greatest metropolis of the Palestinian Jews and, until the Roman siege, the teeming center of their thought and culture. When the walls were finally breached, the line of flight moved southeastward, toward Masada.

The Qumrān-Essene theorists have never refuted this fact. Yet they have insisted that the Songs of the Sabbath Sacrifices, because it is also represented among the Qumrān texts, was brought to Masada not by refugees from Jerusalem but by Essenes from Qumrān. When the archaeologist Yigael Yadin advanced this hypothesis, in 1966, in *Masada: Herod's Fortress and the Zealots' Last Stand,* he bypassed the question of where the other thirteen scrolls might have come from—and proponents of the hypothesis have remained silent on that question ever since. In current books and articles, the Songs scroll is treated as if it had been found in pristine isolation—as if its similarity to a text found at Qumrān were the only clue to its origin.

One reason for this narrow focus on one out of fourteen scrolls may be that the mere mention of Jerusalem could have placed the whole Qumrān-Essene theory in danger. If one concedes that thirteen of the scrolls emanated from Jerusalem, it becomes difficult to argue that the fourteenth had a unique origin. And if all the Masada scrolls originated in Jerusalem, might not the Qumrān scrolls have originated there, too? The Masada scrolls are no different in scribal character from those found in the Qumrān caves; the handwriting styles are similar and all are of the same general age. Is it not therefore conceivable that the scrolls discovered at Qumrān—in caves a dozen miles downhill from

Jerusalem—were also carried into the wilderness by inhabitants of the capital before and during the siege?

This is exactly what the Copper Scroll intimates, and what the totality of evidence now clearly shows. The manuscript finds at Qumrān and Masada, as others of earlier centuries, testify that inhabitants of Jerusalem undertook a massive concealment of scrolls at Qumrān and elsewhere between 68 and 70 A.D., before or during the siege on Jerusalem, and that a small number of scrolls was carried to Masada by refugees fleeing the Roman invaders. This explanation not only accounts for all of the available evidence but is free of the strange anomalies that plague the Qumrān-Essene theory. It avoids the tortured assumption that marrying and celibate Essene monks lived together in caves. It requires no Essenic warriors; no dubious chamber where monkish scribes produced great numbers of Hebrew scrolls; no insistence that the one Qumrān scroll bearing the hallmarks of an autograph is a whimsical fantasy; no determined silence concerning the origin of thirteen of the Masada scrolls. And it is compatible with the absence of autograph texts among the scrolls found in the Qumrān caves.

According to this new theory, the Qumrān fortress was only a fortress, the chamber with two inkwells nothing more than an office or meeting room, and the Copper Scroll written on durable copper for good reason. And the hundreds of texts found at Qumrān depict not conflicts or developments within a single exotic sect but the surprising breadth of Jewish literary culture during the centuries between the Old and New Testaments. That many of the ideas contained in the scrolls seem uncharacteristic of early Judaism reflects only our lack of familiarity with certain strains in prerabbinic thought. Splinter groups or individuals were responsible for some of the writings found at Qumrān, but their ideas only add to the richness of the literary remains that were, by good fortune, preserved there.

The idea that the Essenic sect had a major influence on early Christianity—and, by implication, that mainstream Judaism did not—has no doubt affected the way people in many countries think about the relationship between the two faiths. A Catholic or a Presbyterian, thumbing through the catalogue of the

3. THE JUDEO-CHRISTIAN HERITAGE

Treasures of the Holy Land exhibition, might have felt a certain kinship with the obscure sect that supposedly created the texts at Qumrān. But if, as the evidence now compellingly suggests, the Christian ideas attributed to the Essenes—among others, predestination and election, and the dualities of flesh and spirit, darkness and light, falsehood and truth—evolved out of Judaism as a whole, then that sense of theological kinship should extend a good deal further. Judaism and Christianity cease to be distant theological cousins and become much closer relatives.

Had the Masada manuscripts and the Copper Scroll been discovered before the other texts, interpretation would surely have proceeded along these lines. But by the time those discoveries were made, scholarly opinion had ossified, and no amount of evidence now seems sufficient to reform it. To date, no adherent of the Qumrān-Essene theory—archaeologist, Bible scholar, or historian—has offered a point-by-point response to this critique. Meanwhile, doctoral theses, books, and articles continue to treat the Qumrān-Essene theory as fact while failing to address the crucial questions raised by the new configuration of evidence. May we not hope that in this, the fortieth anniversary year of the first discoveries, the reassessment will begin?

Who Was Jesus?

As Christians round the world gather to celebrate the birth of Jesus, once again they recite the story of a child born to a virgin. The details are familiar yet fabulous: harkening angels, adoring shepherds, a mysterious star. But is the story true? To the literal-minded, the infancy narratives of Matthew and Luke are the opening chapters in the official biography of Jesus. To scholars of the New Testament, however, they are not history at all but something infinitely more important: symbol-laden stories created to dramatize a deeper mystery—that the Jesus who was born 2,000 years ago was truly Christ, the Lord.

Since the nineteenth century, scholars have sought to isolate "the historical Jesus" from "the Christ of faith" proclaimed in the Gospels. But today, most Biblical scholars no longer make such a facile distinction. For one thing, there are no firsthand written accounts of Jesus' life from which a verbal or visual portrait could be fashioned. For another, while there were eyewitnesses to his public ministry, it is highly unlikely that any of them can be identified with the authors of the four Gospels, which were written 40 to 60 years after his death. Thus scholars agree that the real Jesus can no more be separated from the theology of the Gospel writers than the real Socrates can be separated from the dialogues of Plato.

ORAL TRADITIONS: In their quest for the real Jesus, scholars today emphasize the creative role of the four evangelists. Each of the four Gospels, they say, presents a different portrait of Jesus fashioned to meet the needs of the community for which it was written and to rebut views of Jesus with which they disagreed. By using the modern tools of historical criticism, linguistics and literary analysis, Biblical scholars try to distinguish the layers of oral traditions embedded within each Gospel and to confront the essential mind-set—if not

the actual words—of Jesus. "Primarily, the Gospels tell us how each evangelist conceived of and presented Jesus to a Christian community in the last third of the first century," says Father Raymond Brown, a leading expert on the Gospel of John and a professor at New York's Union Theological Seminary. "The Gospels offer only limited means for reconstructing the ministry and message of the historical Jesus."

Despite these limitations, New Testament scholars today know more about the Gospels themselves and the milieu in which they were formed than any previous generation of Biblical researchers. In the past decade alone, translations of several ancient texts from the period 200 B.C. to A.D. 200 have vastly enriched the Biblical trove. One is the Temple Scroll, longest of the Dead Sea Scrolls, which indicates that Jesus' strictures against divorce and other of his teachings were very similar to those held by the ascetic Essene sect at Qumran. Another is the recently translated Nag Hammadi codices, which contain gospels composed by second-century Gnostic rivals of orthodox Christians. And next year, Duke University professor James H. Charlesworth will publish the most complete edition of the Pseudepigrapha, a collection of some 53 texts by Jewish and early Christian scribes, many of which were regarded as sacred books by the Jews of Jesus' time.

MEANING OF TEXTS: In the effort to master all this new material, the burden of Biblical scholarship has shifted from Europe to the U.S. The 3,000 North American members of the Society of Biblical Literature now represent the largest group of Scripture scholars in the world, and their annual production of commentary and criticism outweighs that of all European countries combined. Moreover, modern Biblical research is thoroughly ecumenical; Roman Catholics teach the Bible at Protestant divinity schools, and Protestants publish books

for use by Catholic schools and parish study groups. Equally important, first-rate Scriptural scholars now occupy chairs of religious studies at secular universities. This trend, together with a new wave of popular handbooks on Biblical criticism, has made access to the Gospels available to millions of Americans, including those who prefer to discover Jesus without joining a church.

Most New Testament scholarship purposely focuses on what the texts meant to first-century Christians, but some of its implications call into question the authority sometimes claimed by Christian churches today. Roman Catholic analysts, for example, agree that the papacy in its developed form cannot be read back into the New Testament and that the words of Matthew's Gospel, "Thou art Peter and upon this rock I will build my church," were not necessarily uttered by Jesus during his ministry. Protestants, on the other hand, can find little support for the claim that Scripture alone is the basis for Christian authority; on the contrary, modern scholarship demonstrates not only that the church existed before the Gospels were written but also that the church shaped the New Testament writings. "It is much more difficult now for Protestants to speak naïvely about Biblical faith or Biblical religion," says professor Donald Juel of Northwestern Lutheran Theological Seminary in St. Paul, Minn. "The diversity of Scripture is a fact and it is something to which Christian tradition must now speak."

The Christians most threatened by contemporary scholarship are those conservative evangelicals who insist that every statement in the Bible—whether historical, scientific or religious—is literally true. Scholars who accept any form of modern Biblical research are under attack in several Protestant denominations, including the nation's largest—the Southern Baptist Convention. The issue of Biblical inerrancy has already created a schism in the Lutheran Church-Missouri Synod and now, with the editorial blessing of Christianity Today magazine, influential fundamentalists are pressing a new battle for the Bible at the risk of splitting the already wobbly evangelical movement. In Rome, meanwhile, the Vatican began a formal inquiry last week against Dutch Catholic theologian Edward Schillebeeckx on the widely disputed ground that his recent book, "Jesus: An Experiment in Christology," uses modern Biblical criticism to deny the divinity of Christ.

Virtually all Biblical scholars would vigorously deny that their work undercuts the central message of the Christian faith: that God was incarnate in human form and that He died and rose again from the dead to redeem mankind from sin. To call into question some of the historical assertions in the four Gospels is not to dispute their spiritual truth. "The truth of the Gospels is not simply historical and anyone who tries to identify their truth with historicity is misunderstanding them completely," says Jesuit Joseph Fitzmyer, a top Scripture scholar at the Catholic University of America. The problem, Fitzmyer complains, is that "in Scripture matters, education today is so retrograde that one cannot even pose a critical question without shocking people."

FOUR SHADOWY FIGURES: What is known about the historical Jesus is that he was born in the last years of Herod the Great and died during the reign of Tiberius Caesar when Pontius Pilate was Procurator of Judea. He was an itinerant rabbi—his thinking was close to the liberal school of Pharisees—who ate with sinners and publicans, was regarded by some as a prophet and religious visionary, aroused the antagonism of influential Jewish leaders, violated at least some Sabbath laws, entered Jerusalem during the Passover celebration, was interrogated by the Sanhedrin, tried before a Roman court and crucified as a common criminal.

Aside from this bare outline, not much is certain. The four Gospels contain individual sayings and stories based on memories of Jesus' earthly ministry, which were transmitted—and inevitably stylized in the process—by the oral traditions of the various Christian communities. The four evangelists themselves are extremely mysterious figures. Although there have been many guesses about their identities, Matthew, Mark, Luke, and John are simply names attributed to shadowy figures

who may even have been groups of people, not individual authors. Moreover, no one has yet pinpointed the Christian communities for which the Gospels were written, though several locations have been suggested.* What is known is that because of the Resurrection experience, followers of Jesus began to proclaim him as Christ, the Messiah, who would return shortly to judge the world.

PASSION: Most scholars now believe that the early Christians worked backward in developing their account of Jesus. At first, Christians focused on Jesus as the heavenly Messiah who would return soon in glory as the crucified redeemer who was raised from the dead. Only gradually did they incorporate into their preaching the earthly Jesus who had ministered to the people of Israel. The written Gospels, many scholars argue, also developed in reverse—from the Passion story to the earthly ministry (which is all there is in the earliest Gospel, Mark), to the infancy narratives (added by Matthew and Luke), to the pre-existence of Jesus as the eternal Word of God (unique to the last Gospel, John).

"Unfortunately, the majority of people carry around in their minds a composite picture of Jesus made up of whichever happens to be their favorite Gospel, plus some historical reminiscences about the first century and a whole lot of personal predilections which we all have," says Werner Kelber of Rice University, a specialist on Mark. "People do not take the trouble to read each Gospel separately or to recognize that each author gives us a different portrait of Jesus—and of all the other figures in the Gospel." Here, in brief, are the different slants of the four Gospels:

MARK: In this, the earliest and the shortest of the four, Jesus emerges as the long-awaited Messiah who redeems the world from Satan's grip by his own Passion and death. Mark signals his theological intent at the outset when John the Baptist announces the coming Messiah and is shortly "delivered up" to his enemies. This presages what will happen to Jesus and what Mark himself believes all followers of Christ must expect. "Mark is putting all of the early tradi-

---

*It has been thought that Mark wrote to a Roman audience; that Matthew and Luke both addressed themselves to people living at Antioch, in Syria, and that John's community was based at Ephesus, in Asia Minor.

tions about Jesus under the interpretive control of the Passion story," says New Testament scholar Paul Achtemeier of Union Theological Seminary in Virginia.

When Jesus begins his ministry, Mark presents him as a stereotypical miracle worker, a stock figure of Hellenic culture familiar to his gentile readers. His miracles win him little faith: Mark's Gospel is the only one in which those who should best understand him—his family, the scribes and especially his own disciples—all fail to recognize him as the Messiah, or misunderstand his mission. In the same episode in which Peter acknowledges Jesus as Messiah, for example, his Master repudiates him—"Get behind me, Satan"—for failing to accept that "the Son of Man" has not come to rule the world through personal power, but to redeem it by his death. Mark's crucifixion scene is exceedingly lonely. None of the disciples is present. Jesus dies with a cry of ultimate abandonment: "My God, My God, why hast thou forsaken me?" And it is left to a Roman centurion—a pagan who has watched Jesus die—to profess what the disciples could not: "Truly this man was the Son of God." In Mark's original conclusion, the disciples are never informed of the resurrection and thus are never reconciled with Christ.

This conclusion has created a major controversy among New Testament scholars. Some point out that verses later added to Mark by another author or authors do indicate a reconciliation in Galilee between the disciples and the risen Christ. Others believe that Mark's negative assessment of the disciples was intended to shift the focus of Christianity away from the church in Jerusalem, which was identified with the disciples, after that city was destroyed by Roman forces in A.D. 70. But the most radical conclusion is that of Professor Kelber, who believes Mark's disciples were the chief opponents of Jesus, repudiated by him and so not saved. Mark's point, says Kelber, is that readers of his Gospel were to look to the cross for salvation—a Lutheran position—and not rely solely on Jesus' miracles and message. Jesuit scholar John Donahue of Vanderbilt University does not go that far, but he concedes Mark is suggesting that knowledge of the historical Jesus is inadequate for salvation without faith in the crucified Christ.

MATTHEW: Here, Jesus is presented as a royal Messiah, the last King of Israel and the Son of God, sent to teach his people as well as to die for them. He is also a remarkably humble king, as Matthew's story of the Nativity makes clear. Though descended from the royal line of David, Jesus is born not in Jerusalem, but in Bethlehem, where foreign wise men come to worship him. This kingly image rivals that of Jesus as rabbi, which other scholars of Matthew emphasize. "In Matthew, Jesus' followers call him Lord and other royal titles," says New Testament specialist Jack Kingsbury of Union Theological Seminary in Virginia. "Only the Pharisees call him teacher and Judas alone calls him 'Rabbi'."

Matthew's Jesus is particularly antagonistic toward the Jewish establishment; he calls the scribes and Pharisees a "brood of vipers." In part, these passages seem to reflect Matthew's efforts to distinguish Christianity from rabbinical Judaism, which the Pharisees were developing in response to the catastrophic destruction of Jerusalem. Matthew's Jesus is presented as a new Moses when he delivers his Sermon on the Mount, one of five teaching discourses in the Gospel. But in Matthew's portrait, Jesus is not just an interpreter of the law; he is the lawgiver and personal fulfillment of Jewish prophecy. Christianity, Matthew wants to make clear, is a natural, long-expected development of Judaism. Time and again, the author follows an episode in Jesus' life with an Old Testament quotation introduced by a formula phrase such as, "This was done to fulfill what the Lord had spoken through the prophet."

Although Matthew incorporates a great deal of Mark's material, he bends it to his own theological purposes. Matthew's miracle stories, for example, are presented as demonstrations of Jesus' mercy and compassion, rather than as illustrations of his power. Where Mark's Jesus rebukes the disciples for failing to understand his power to walk on water, Matthew's Jesus helps the faltering Peter, whose hesitant faith nearly causes the disciple to drown.

LUKE: In this Gospel, Jesus is the innocent savior of the world, full of forgiveness and love, and the text follows the literary conventions of Hellenic culture. Written for a sophisticated gentile audience, Luke's portrait is the first effort to present a biography of Jesus. Gone is Mark's angst-ridden emphasis on the cross; in its place is a peaceful universality. Luke not only relates Jesus

to events of Roman, Palestinian and church history, he goes on to trace his genealogy all the way back to Adam. In this way, the evangelist locates the words and deeds of Jesus within a scheme of "salvation history," which describes what God is doing—and will continue to do—for man.

Despite this universal framework, Luke's Jesus is very much concerned with teaching Christians how they should spend their lives from moment to moment. For example, Luke amends The Lord's Prayer so that it asks the Father to "give us each [Matthew says "this"] day our daily bread"; elsewhere, his Jesus reminds Christians that they must bear their burdens "daily." In part, this concern with time reflects the fact that by A.D. 85 or thereabouts, when Luke wrote his Gospel, the Christians were beginning to realize the Second Coming might not be imminent and therefore were more concerned with the here and now. Moreover, says Father Fitzmyer, an international expert on Luke's writings, "Luke is the only evangelist who stresses that Christians have to live ordinary lives, and he has played the Christian message to fit this fact."

But the dominant theme in Luke's verbal portrait is Jesus' ready forgiveness of sinners. They love him and he loves them and other social outcasts. When Jesus works a miracle, the typical response from the crowd in Luke's Gospel is joy, rather than Mark's wonder at his power or Matthew's show of faith. Luke's Jesus is perhaps best understood in his crucifixion scenes, where the innocent savior manages to pray for his executioners: "Father, forgive them, for they know not what they do."

JOHN: There is no need for a nativity scene in John; he simply asserts in his Gospel's famous prologue that Jesus is "the Word of God" made flesh. Thus John's Gospel begins where the others leave off, with the recognition of Jesus as the Son of God. In John, the disciples immediately know who Jesus is.

John's Gospel differs from the three Synoptic Gospels in other ways as well. His Jesus works only seven miracles—none of them exorcisms—preaches no ethical exhortations and issues no apocalyptic warnings about the end of the world. On the contrary, the kingdom of God has already arrived in the person of John's Jesus, who comes "from above" and therefore speaks with God's authority. The implications of this sometimes

confuse his entourage. Nicodemus, a secret admirer, does not understand that disciples, too, must be "begotten from above"—a reference to Divine election that modern evangelists still sometimes interpret, instead, as requiring "born again" experiences.

Jesus' ultimate conflict with the Jews in the fourth Gospel reflects antipathies which were aroused when members of John's community were expelled from the synagogue for professing faith in Christ. "The key to current scholarly discussions about John is the extent to which conflicts in his own community are superimposed by the author on the struggles Jesus had in his ministry," observes Father Brown, author of the two-volume Anchor Bible commentary on John's Gospel. Both concerns are reflected in the controversy between John's Jesus and the Jews, who eventually condemn him for making himself equal to God.

Even in his passion and death, John's "Son of God" remains in full control. Unlike the other Gospels, John does not show Jesus suffering on his knees in Gethsemane. Instead, the Roman soldiers fall to their knees when they arrive to arrest him. And on the cross, Jesus is lucid enough to give John, his "beloved disciple," to Mary, a gesture symbolizing that he is leaving behind him a church. Then, satisfied that his work is done, he announces: "It is finished."

MIDDLE-CLASS ETHICS: At the very least, then, Biblical scholarship has shown that the Gospel writers all shaded the stories of Jesus' ministry according to their own interests and theological concerns. This is also true of the founders of modern Biblical criticism in the nineteenth century. In their various efforts to reconstruct a "naturalistic" life of Christ, they attempted to uncover the human Jesus before Christian doctrine had muddied the view. The result, with varying details, was a Jesus who looked very much like a nineteenth-century teacher of middle-class ethics. In his famous 1906 book, "The Quest of the Historical Jesus," Albert Schweitzer ended the life-of-Jesus movement by astutely observing that nineteenth-century scholars had looked into the well of the Bible and seen their own faces. In his patient dismantling of his predecessors' work, Schweitzer showed that Jesus was an apocalyptic Jew.

PARADOX: The temptation to see Jesus through contemporary eyes will

The Faces of Jesus

The Bible shows us Christ through a glass darkly; we see his figure, but not his face. None of the Gospels even hints at what Jesus might have looked like; there is no eyewitness account of his appearance. In painting him, therefore, artists have looked inward as often as heavenward. Picasso portrayed him as a bullfighter; Van Gogh, a redhead, gave him red hair. There have been black Jesuses and Oriental ones, and the American artist Richard West envisioned him as an Indian brave, praying on his knees in a tepee.

Historically, the most compelling vision of Christ has been that of the tortured martyr of the Cross, but this first appeared nearly a thousand years after his death. The vision that touched the earliest Christians was that of Christ as the Good Shepherd—a curly-haired, beardless youth rescuing his flock from the wolves, a familiar image in pagan art. From pagan sources also comes the "young philosopher" Chirst, which decorated sarcophagi of the third and fourth centuries. He was a cleanshaven figure in the tunic and mantle of an itinerant Cynic, two fingers raised in blessing, a scroll or book under his left arm.

With the conversion of Constantine, there occurred what H.W. Janson of New York University calls an "exchange of amenities" between the Emperor and Christ. Jesus acquired the imperial nimbus, now recognized as the halo; he is occasionally pictured on the Cross, but his eyes are open, his demeanor triumphant.

SECOND COMING: Only around the tenth century did artists begin to confront Christ's nature as both God and man who suffered and died. The reasons are obscure, but a new interest in death and resurrection took hold in philosophy about the same time, perhaps in anticipation of a Second Coming in the year 1000. Depictions of Christ suffering on the Cross appear first in Byzantine art and spread rapidly to the West, carrying with them the Eastern tradition that Christ was bearded. By the sixteenth century, artists had explored the macabre limits of the Passion: Grünewald's Isenheim altarpiece shows us a flayed and bloody Christ, his body studded with thorns, his livid lips drawn back in rictus. But that image was not universal. A late-medieval artist, flirting with the Gnostic belief that Christ was essentially a spiritual force, shows us an empty Cross with the centurion jabbing his spear into thin air—because the artist could not envision the Son of God made flesh.

The great artists of the Renaissance had no such mystical vision. The fifteenth century rediscovered God in the image of man. The Christ child changed from a solemn homunculus to Fra Angelico's plump-cheeked babe. Raphael's "Transfiguration" depicts an adult Christ of transcendent beauty—hair windblown, white robes trailing—but there are those who find the flame of his divinity obscured by the radiance of his physical perfection. The Christs of Rembrandt, drawn from models he found in Amsterdam's Jewish quarter, are masterpieces of portraiture, radiant yet unmistakably human.

By the nineteenth century, the decline of religion as a creative force was reflected in a devitalized Christian art. Those sentimental, effete images of Jesus—hands clasped in prayer, cow eyes turned deferentially heavenward—remain the mass-produced image of those who have seen Jesus only on calendars. In reaction to that saccharine vision, serious twentieth-century artists have given us "realistic" portraits, more or less. Diego Rivera has illustrated Christ's vaccination, an incident not recorded in the Bible. Max Ernst has shown us the Christ child on the Madonna's knee, receiving a spanking. For his Crucifixion painting, the American artist Rico Lebrun worked, in part, from concentration-camp photographs.

'FINAL VICTORY': Each generation adds its contribution to the understanding—or misunderstanding—of Jesus, each confronts in its own way the mystery of his nature. "You can't show an idealized Christ," says Father James Flanigan, chairman of the art department at Notre Dame. "But neither can you put too much emphasis on his death and suffering, or you miss the final victory." Flanigan points out that Michelangelo wrestled with the problem all his life. His early Pietà, the famous one in St. Peter's, tenderly evokes the death of a young man. But the Christ of his last Pietà, now in Milan, is stripped of human detail, little more than a trunk barely emerging from the stone. The flesh, Michelangelo realized at the end of his long life, is incapable of holding the divinity.

Jerry Adler

---

probably never cease. In our own century, German scholar Rudolph Bultmann sought to demythologize the Biblical Jesus and his message by translating the apocalyptic language into such modern, existential categories as angst and authenticity. Today, however, the search for Jesus is guided less by cultural or philosophical presuppositions than by the tentative assumption that scriptural analysis can yield more about him than old-fashioned rationalists ever imagined.

For example, after lengthy study of the miracle stories to determine whether they were purely literary inventions, Prof. Carl Holladay of the Yale Divinity School has concluded that Jesus was indeed a miracle worker and that the miracle stories are authentic. "Superimposing a post-Enlightenment view of such matters on the first century does injustice to what was truly going on," says Holladay. "But scholars must leave it up to believers to evaluate the claim that they were really the work of God."

What's more, most New Testament scholars believe that at least some sayings attributed to Jesus are authentically his, and a national conference is being planned in which scholars will try to reach a consensus on which passages qualify. Among the likeliest candidates are Luke's version of the Lord's Prayer, several proclamations that "the Kingdom of God is at hand," certain "aphorisms of reversal," such as Mark's "The first shall be last, the last first" and Jesus' familiar Aramaic word for God—"Abba," or Father—which many analysts believe captures the essence of Jesus' consciousness of his relationship to God.

Analysis of Jesus' parables has convinced other scholars that by understanding them as paradoxes readers can gain direct access to the mind of Jesus. This approach is based on the assumption that the deep structures of the human mind are universal, permitting twentieth-century readers to understand a first-century Jesus. For instance, they cite the famous parable of the good Samaritan, in which a Jewish traveler is robbed and left for dead. Both a priest and a Levite pass him by, but a Samaritan—a social and religious outcast—binds up his wounds and lodges him at the Samaritan's own expense. This story can be interpreted as a moral example of the neighborliness expected of Christians—as it often is in sermons—or as an allegory, as Saint Augustine did. But scholars see it as a paradox designed to transmit Jesus' special understanding of what God demands of everyone who would truly do his will.

WARY: "In this parable, Jesus is asking his Jewish audience to think the unthinkable by identifying goodness with the hated Samaritan," says theologian John Dominic Crossan, an expert in parable analysis at DePaul University in Chicago. In response, the listener either rejects the story or questions his deepest values and assumptions about life. When this happens consciousness changes, just as it does when a Buddhist solves a Zen koan. Mark takes this a step further. The crucified Jesus becomes Christ, the Messiah. And so the parable-teller becomes himself a parable told by the early church—the paradox of Christ crucified—which demands a conversion of consciousness.

Biblical scholars insist that better understanding of how the Gospels were written is a boon rather than an obstacle to faith. But defenders of traditional doctrine in all churches are wary of Biblical investigators. Catholic theologian Edward Schillebeeckx, for example, has tentatively argued from scriptural sources that Jesus' identity as Christ was evident even before the Cross—in the rejection he experienced during his life. Last week, during Schillebeeckx's secret hearing in Rome, Vatican inquisitors demanded to know instead whether he really believed that Jesus was divine. "Rome's inquisitorial behavior suggests they do not want Catholic understanding of the Bible enriched by contributions from the church's most gifted intellectuals," says one U.S. scholar.

Southern Baptists, meanwhile, are under increasing attack from Biblical fundamentalists who want to fire any teacher who does not agree that the Bible is literally true. At Baylor University, for instance, Prof. H. Jack Flanders has been criticized by fundamentalists for writing a book that questions the historicity of Adam and Eve and treats the story of Jonah in the whale as a parable. In Dallas, the administration of Dallas Baptist College has instructed all teachers to sign a statement of belief in Biblical inerrancy—a statement that Dr. Wallie Amos Criswell, the influential fundamentalist pastor of the nation's largest Southern Baptist church, wants the faculties of all Texas Baptist schools to affirm.

The fundamentalists' doctrine of inerrancy, says Professor Achtemeier, is rooted in the post-Reformation era, when Protestant scholastics countered the authority asserted by Rome with the authority of the Bible itself. The scholastics also came to regard the Bible as a sourcebook for systematic theology in which the verses were regarded as dogmatic propositions about scientific questions as well. When nineteenth-century scientists challenged the Christian world view, and historians discovered inconsistencies in the Bible, U.S. fundamentalists at Princeton University responded with a theory that fundamentalists still hold today: the Bible, they say, is inerrant in its original "autographs," or manuscripts, and even copies must be regarded as literally true.

TRUTH: To most Biblical scholars today, these demands for inerrancy are beside the point. The point is that the differences, even the contradictions, between the Gospel accounts do not detract at all from the spiritual truths that they contain. "God can reveal himself through inspired fiction, like the story of Jonah, just as well as through inspired history," says Father Brown.

Who was Jesus? Mark's Jesus dies alone, feeling forsaken but true to his Father's will. This Jesus will appeal to Christians who embrace life's tragedies with confidence. Matthew's Jesus dies only to return and promise his guidance to those who follow him. This Jesus will appeal to Christians who find assurance in the church. Luke's Jesus dies forgiving his enemies, knowing his Father awaits his spirit. This Jesus will attract Christians who have learned in life to trust God by imitating his mercy. John's Jesus dies in the confidence that he will return to the Father. This Jesus is for those Christians who have traveled the mystical way. All of these accounts express a truth; none of them is complete. All of these Jesuses are accessible only to those whose faith compels them on the search for "the way, the truth and the light."

KENNETH L. WOODWARD with RACHEL MARK and JERRY BUCKLEY in New York and bureau reports

Jesus and the Teacher of Righteousness

Similarities and Differences

Hartmut Stegemann

Hartmut Stegemann is professor of New Testament sciences, head of the Department of Studies in Ancient Judaism, and director of the Qumran Research Centre at Goettingen University in Germany. He received his Doctor of Divinity degree in Old Testament studies and his Ph.D. in oriental studies and history of religions. Since 1955, he has published more than 35 articles on the Dead Sea Scrolls and on the historical Jesus. He is the author of The Origins of the Qumran Community *(1971) and* The Essenes, Qumran, John the Baptist, and Jesus *(1993).*

The similarities between the Jewish Dead Sea Scroll community and early Christianity are sometimes striking. The public has been fascinated by these similarities, often forgetting the differences, which are in many ways greater.

In this article, I will compare the leaders, or founders, of these two religious organizations—the Teacher of Righteousness and Jesus. Their similarities—and differences—will, I believe, provide insights into the nature of both.

First, let us look at similarities. Both the Teacher of Righteousness and Jesus lived within the Judaism of the late Second Temple period, when there was no clearly defined and established Jewish "orthodoxy" and when Judaism was marked by a variety of different religious organizations or movements. Both the Teacher and Jesus functioned not in Egypt or in Babylonia, but in Palestine, close to Jerusalem and its Temple. Indeed, the *departure* of the Teacher of

Righteousness from Jerusalem led to the establishment of his separate community, while the circumstances of Jesus' last *arrival* in Jerusalem became basic to the creation of the Christian Church. Both religious leaders had a particular relationship to Jerusalem and to its religious institutions, establishing their specific leadership in altercations with other religious groups and institutions, such as the Pharisees or the Temple priesthood. But at the same time, both stood in a positive relationship to traditional Jewish authorities of the past—the Torah and the Prophets. And, finally, both regarded themselves as "teachers"; and both had "followers." These are at least the main similarities, if not all.

Access to the historical Teacher of Righteousness is much easier than it is to the historical Jesus, who has left us no written documents from his hand, so that we have recourse solely to third-, fourth- or fifth-hand information about him, mainly from the New Testament Gospels. These data and traditions come from many different informants who were more interested in telling of Jesus' significance for themselves and for the salvation of all humanity than in reporting the events of his life, his acts and his teachings for later historians or scholars.

On the other hand, we may assume that the Teacher of Righteousness was the immediate author of some of the hymns collected in the Thanksgiving Hymns Scroll from Cave 1 (1QH).*

He was probably also the author of the famous letter known as MMT,* which was addressed to the high priest at the Jerusalem Temple around the mid-second century B.C.E. Other characteristics and deeds of the Teacher of Righteousness were extolled by members of his community after his death. We find them mainly in the so-called Damascus Document (CD I–VIII/XIX– XX) and in two biblical commentaries from Qumran, 1Q Pesher Habakkuk (1QpHab) and 4Q Pesher Psalmsa,6[1] (4QpPsa,6[2]). These literary sources provide us with reliable information about the Teacher of Righteousness, though there are some slight differences between his self-evaluation as mirrored in his Thanksgiving Hymns and the appreciation of his function and significance expressed in texts written by others.

The Teacher of Righteousness was a priest. Not only is he referred to as *ha-cohen*, "the priest," in 1Q Pesher Habakkuk and in a fragmentary commentary on Psalm 37 from Cave 4 (4QpPsa,6[3]), but this is also consistent with his titles Teacher of Righteousness, Teacher of the Community and Interpreter of the Torah. For in this community, "to inquire of the Law" and "to teach" were restricted to the priests, who alone were invested with this authority.

Born to a Zadokite family and educated to function as a priest, the Teacher

---

*1Q stands for Qumran Cave 1, H for the *Hodayot* Scroll. *Hodayot* is the Hebrew word for psalms of thanksgiving.

---

*MMT stands for *Miqsat Ma'aseh ha-Torah* (literally, "Some Rulings Pertaining to the Torah"). See Lawrence H. Schiffman, "The Significance of the Scrolls," BR October 1990; and James C. VanderKam, The People of the Dead Sea Scrolls: Essenes or Sadducees?" **BR,** April 1991.

From *Bible Review*, February 1994, pp. 42-47, 63. © 1994 by the Biblical Archaeology Society, 3000 Connecticut Avenue, NW, Suite 300, Washington, DC 20008. Reprinted by permission.

of Righteousness was from his earliest years a member of a leading family. He was also destined by his lineage to become a mediator between the God of Israel and his people—the cultic role of priests during the Second Temple period. Thus, from his birth, the Teacher of Righteousness was a potential Jewish religious leader, independent of the concrete functions he assumed during his lifetime and of his priestly career at the Temple in Jerusalem.

Furthermore, the definite article "the" in his designations, *ha-cohen,* "the priest (of all)," or *moreh ha-sedeq,* "the most reliable (authoritative) teacher (of the Law)," characterizes him clearly as the high priest of his time. Historically, he was, in my opinion, the predecessor of the first Hasmonean high priest, Jonathan the Maccabee, who violently removed him from office in about 152 B.C.E. Before this event, the Teacher of Righteousness had served as the Jerusalem high priest during a short period (as reported by Josephus) when the office was otherwise vacant.[1] This period lasted a maximum of seven years. In his own view, however, the Teacher continued to be the unique high priest of all the people of Israel—even after his removal from office—to the end of his life.

Thus, the authority of the Teacher of Righteousness as a religious leader rested, on the one hand, on the traditional authority of a high priest; on the other hand, with his deposition from the Temple in Jerusalem, he also achieved the rank of an authoritative leader of a religious community.

In the fragmentary commentary on Psalm 37 already referred to (4QpPs a,6[2]), he is described as "the priest, the Teacher of [Righteousness] whom God called to arise, and whom He appointed to build up for Him a community of [holiness (?)] and guided him to His truth." According to this text, God himself granted the Teacher special authority, making him the founder of this community, and "guided him to His truth" in the sense that all further decisions of the Teacher proved to be right. This account was obviously formulated by members of the Teacher's community at a later date.

An additional aspect of the Teacher's special authority should be mentioned. In the Commentary (or *Pesher*) on Habakkuk (1QpHab), it is stated that God gave into (the Teacher's) heart the "insight to explain everything the prophets had

told."[2] This statement does not imply that the Teacher was regarded, or regarded himself, as a prophet. But by his priestly authority he discerned that what the biblical prophets had written related to their *future* and that his own days were the time of fulfillment of the prophets' predictions. His own days were regarded as "the last days" before the final judgment and the everlasting salvation of all Israel.

In contrast, Jesus was not a priest nor an educated religious leader. Nor is there a record that could be historically construed as his "call to office" in the tradition of the New Testament. The historian cannot detect the source of Jesus' authority. We only know that he began as a follower of John the Baptist. He later became independent of his early "master," but no information about why this happened or where his new orientations came from has been transmitted to us. The field remains open for speculation.

In my view, Jesus one day experienced "events" that he could not explain in any way other than to conclude that God had started to act on earth again, that is, that the eschatological end-of-days with the final extermination of all evil from the world had already set in. His basic experience may have been the "withdrawal of demons" from ill people and their sudden return to health without the application of any technical magical healing practices. No one except God could have done that. Jesus saw himself as integral to this process: "If I by the 'finger of God' [i.e., solely by God's own power] cast out the demons, the kingdom of God is already established amidst you" (Luke 11:20; cf. Matthew 12:28).

Later, his adherents, or the Christian communities, considered him to be a mediator of the kingdom of God, the royal Messiah, "the Son of God" and so on. To Jesus himself, however, such views were quite strange; he was witness to and involved in God's actions, but he did not feel that he alone had the leading role or function in this cosmic drama.

How can one describe the authority of Jesus within the framework of such indirect religious leadership? He was not like John the Baptist, who was born into a priestly family and, therefore, could become a mediator, who was "more than a prophet" (Matthew 11:9; Luke 7:26). By baptizing a penitent people, John could save them from their approaching punishment in the final judgment. Jesus, however, did not consider himself to be

such a priestly mediator. All his authority came from the acting God and from Jesus' own followers. He did not think of himself as possessing a specific personal authority. He became a "leader" only by extra-personal authority drawn from God from the people and, afterwards, from the belief of the Christian communities in his resurrection.

We have looked at the different authority of these two religious leaders. Now let us look at the relation of each to his followers.

From the Thanksgiving Hymns, we learn that the Teacher of Righteousness had a distinct group of individuals associated with him, whom he called *nismede sodi,* "servants of my council," or *'anshe 'asati,* "members of my Directory Board" (1QH 5.24). These close adherents of the Teacher were not identical with the common members of his community, whom he denotes in the previous line as *re'ai,* "my fellows," as *ba'e briti,* "they who entered my covenant," and as *no'adai,* "they who are appointed to me" (1QH 5.23). As a leader of his community, he had, therefore, a close inner circle of men of special confidence, perhaps his "followers" from the Temple, who became his counselors in problematic affairs afterwards in his community.

The organizational system of the Teacher's community was hierarchical, with strict obedience expected from the lower to the upper ranks. As long as the Teacher lived, all final decisions were his. He was their unique religious leader. This role did not derive from his personal authority or the persuasive power of his teaching. His leadership derived exclusively from his permanent function as a high priest of "all Israel," even if recognition of his role was now limited to the members of his community. This community, historically, included more than 4,000 Essenes—a very high number of members compared with more than 6,000 Pharisees and only a few hundreds of Sadducees and of Zealots—in the time of Jesus.

The Gospel of John reports that the first followers of Jesus were former "disciples" of John the Baptist, who sent them to Jesus (John 1:35ff.). The idea that John the Baptist "sent" them to Jesus may be a secondary tradition; but it may be true that some of Jesus' first adherents had formerly joined John the Baptist, but "followed" Jesus after the death of their master, or—more likely—after Jesus started his *own* "preaching."

Others of his followers may have been people whom he "healed" from their demons (see, e.g., Mark 5:18–20; Luke 8:2–3), or people impressed by his deeds or by his preaching (see, e.g., Luke 19:1–10).[3]

Contrary to the descriptions in the Gospels, Jesus did not want a circle of close adherents permanently accompanying him, either as "followers" or as "disciples." According to some New Testament traditions, most of which are gathered in Matthew 10, Jesus sent his disciples away to other places to tell their own experiences of the new "kingdom of God" on earth, to preach that kingdom and to drive out demons. Jesus never initiated a close circle of followers, nor anything resembling a "community" or a "church." During his lifetime there were only some devoted disciples who regarded him as their "master." The organizational framework of his followers actually developed only after his death. Jesus preferred to divert his followers' faith to the God acting in the world, not to his own person. He became a religious leader of sorts against his will, very much in contrast to the Teacher of Righteousness of the Essenes' community, a small group of whom—only about 50 members—settled at Qumran after the Teacher's death.

Despite Jesus' personal inclinations, his followers perceived his deeds and teachings as testifying to his personal qualifications as their "master" and "prophet." In their belief, Jesus was authorized by God to establish the final truth. In this indirect way, Jesus became a "religious leader," without ever having claimed this function or having assumed such a role.

Let us return now to the Teacher of Righteousness. It was impossible to have two high priests in Judaism at the same time. According to the personal claim of the Teacher of Righteousness, he had been and remained the unique leader of "all Israel," even if, due to circumstances, his authority was acknowledged temporarily only by one segment of a split community, the *synagogue Asidaion,* "association of pious people," of Maccabean times. The opposing leader of the other part of that community, later known as the Pharisees (i.e., "dissenters"), was condemned as "the liar who flouted the Law" (1QpHab 5.11–12). The Teacher of Righteousness believed that Jonathan, the Maccabean high priest who then officiated at the Temple, should resign from

office and follow the *halakhah,* the religious law, according to the interpretation of the Torah that he, the Teacher of Righteousness, offered. This claim is clearly demonstrated by the letter known as 4QMMT, in which the Teacher of Righteousness excoriates the lunar calendar used in the Temple and many laws of the reigning Jerusalem Temple authorities.

After the death of the Teacher of Righteousness—probably close to the end of the second century B.C.E.—no successor was acknowledged as the true high priest or the unique leader of the Essenes' community. This community continued to exist within Judaism, at least until the first Jewish revolt against the Romans (66–73 C.E.). After the death of its founder, this group was guided by a council of twelve (lay-)men and three priests (1QS 8.1 [Manual of Discipline]), who were at the same time under the leading authority of the Zadokite priests of this group as a collective responsibility.

Jesus, by contrast, did not achieve his uniqueness as a religious leader in opposition to some other Jewish leader. He became independent from John the Baptist, but never his opponent (see, e.g., Matthew 11:7–11//Luke 7:24–28). If indeed he was in conflict with the high priest of his time (see Mark 14:60–64; John 18:19–21), this was a last episode shortly before his death, and had no importance for his self-image during his lifetime.

During his lifetime Jesus believed that God had begun to establish his everlasting reign on earth. Jesus did not believe in the coming of a "messiah," or even conceive of himself as such. Neither Jesus nor anyone else could assume an "official" role where the almighty God himself was acting. The high priest in Jerusalem and his traditional function on the Day of Atonement were no longer necessary if a sinless "people of God" started to spread throughout the world. The religious leaders of the Sadducees, of the Essenes, of the Pharisees, of the Zealots and of all other Jewish groups or organizations were rendered totally unnecessary wherever God himself had taken over.

In accord with this concept, Jesus did not claim uniqueness, nor was such uniqueness attributed to him. Uniqueness was attributed exclusively to God and to the events of his present final coming, the inauguration of which Jesus experienced in his lifetime, an event never before experienced nor ever to be experienced again in the future.

But, quite independent of his self-understanding, some of Jesus' followers even during his lifetime began to regard him as their unique "master" or "religious teacher." After his death, they continued to believe in his function as their religious leader. Progressively, they included Jesus within the uniqueness of God's acting-in-history, and in this way Jesus finally was cast in the role of the unique savior of all humanity. This aspect of Christian belief cannot be traced back to the historical Jesus who attributed all uniqueness of leadership to God alone.

The Teacher of Righteousness and Jesus were both Jews, but they became religious leaders under rather different historical circumstances, and they represented quite different aspects and tendencies of Second Temple Judaism. They are similar, perhaps, in that their adherents' fervor made them unique leaders for all time, to a future end-of-days. Concomitantly their followers held that all other branches of Judaism were in error. But here the similarity ends. While the Teacher of Righteousness was indeed the unique religious leader of "all Israel" during his lifetime, Jesus, by contrast, attributed uniqueness to God alone. Jesus did not consider himself to be a religious "leader" or the royal "messiah." He was merely a witness to God's eschatological deeds, in which he was involved. He conveyed his observations to others, commented on them and argued against opponents who did not believe his view of the now-acting God. Jesus did not interpret the Torah or the Prophets better than others, nor did he perform miracles to convince others of his own religious power. But whatever he did or said, his followers felt themselves "guided" by his views—or by his deeds. In this indirect way, Jesus became a religious leader of his time, an everlasting "master" for his followers, and finally the founder of a new community, the Christian Church. Thus, after his death he gained a status that, in some respects, is similar to that which the Teacher of Righteousness enjoyed, at least within his community, already during his lifetime.

Although the Teacher of Righteousness and Jesus each arose as a result of circumstances that were perhaps typical for that time, each was a unique figure, and the types of religious leadership they exemplified were not similar—indeed they were both atypical for Judaism. Never again did Judaism—or Christianity—produce a religious leader like the Teacher of Righteousness or like Jesus.

In the centuries that followed, the typical religious leader in Judaism became the sage, or the rabbi. At first, he was a *doresh ha-torah,* an "interpreter of the Torah," and later also a *doresh dibre ha-hakhamim,* an "interpreter of the sayings of the sages." There was no longer any need for this kind of interpreter to be of priestly stock; laymen could exercise the same kind of authority. These rabbis were for the most part heads of schools in Mesopotamia or in Palestine.

Early Christianity, on the other hand, was marked by a rather diffuse plurality of religious leadership in its beginnings. Some types emerged from Judaism, others from Hellenistic patterns. At first, "the Twelve" existed in Jerusalem as representatives of the eschatological Israel; their true function, however, is as yet unknown. Afterwards, three *styloi,* "pillars," were the leaders of the Christian community in Jerusalem (Galatians 2:9), while other local communities were headed by an *apostolos,* "apostle," who had founded them, much as Paul had founded such local communities in Asia Minor and in Greece. Other Christian communities were guided—like synagogues—by a collective group of (seven) *presbyteroi,* "elders."

Only after a century of pluralistic Christianity did a special type of *episkopos,* "bishop," begin to attain religious leadership, at first as the head of a local community and later as a representative of a broader segment of the church. This specific Christian type of religious leader put its stamp on the church during the centuries when the sages were active in rabbinic Judaism. The roots of the office of the bishop are still debated. Perhaps it first developed from an organizing function in Hellenistic associations and only later received its religious connotation; alternatively, perhaps the bishop continues the function of the Essenes' *mebaqqer,* "overseer." But whatever its origins, the Christian bishop and the Jewish rabbi exemplified quite different types of religious leadership—and their leadership also differed from the kind of religious leadership exemplified by the Teacher of Righteousness and Jesus.

Thanks to the Dead Sea Scrolls, we know the different, uniqueness of the Teacher of Righteousness and of Jesus, their different relationship to God and to their followers, and also some differences in their teaching and behavior. Without the Qumran scrolls, much of the Jewish background of Jesus would still be unknown to us. Now the light from Qumran illuminates as well some of the darkness of Judaism in the late Second Temple period, which forms the true background of the beginnings of Christianity.

[1] Josephus. *The Antiquities of the Jews* 13.46.

[2] 1Q2 Pesher Habakkuk 2.8–10; cf. 7.3–5.

[3] According to the Gospels of Mark and Matthew, Jesus "called" to his disciples in a godlike fashion, bidding them "Follow me!" They followed him immediately without being motivated by a miracle or by any kind of persuasive preaching (see, e.g., Mark 1:16–20; 2:14; Matthew 4:18–22; 9:9). The psychologist Luke noticed this curious manner of enlisting followers, and he replaced it with a more plausible version: Simon Peter and the two sons of Zebedee are driven to become followers of Jesus by an impressive miracle (Luke 5:1–11). All traditions of this kind are secondary and cannot be traced back to the historical Jesus. Jesus' call of "the Twelve" (Mark 3:13–19//Matthew 10:14; cf. 1 Corinthians 15:5) was similarly modified by Luke to the call of the "twelve apostles" (Luke 6:12–18; cf. Acts 1:13). These 12 were clearly considered the representatives of the 12 tribes of Israel in the "new age," which started with Christ's resurrection, or with his initial epiphanies (1 Corinthians 15:58).

Women and the Bible

*Motivated variously by historical, theological, and personal concerns,
a rapidly growing cadre of scholars, most of them women, is exploring
one of the great overlooked subjects in scholarship: the domain of Jewish
and Christian women in ancient times*

Cullen Murphy

Cullen Murphy is the managing editor of The Atlantic Monthly. *He writes the comic strip* Prince Valiant *and is the author, with William Rathje, of* Rubbish!: The Archaeology of Garbage *(1992). Murphy's article "Who Do Men Say That I Am?", about research on Jesus, was* The Atlantic*'s cover story in December of 1986.*

Perhaps a rumor of impending persecution lay behind it, as several scholars have speculated. Perhaps the reason for concealment was something else entirely. We can never know why twelve ancient codices and a fragment of a thirteenth came to rest where they were found. The place was a rugged curtain of cliffs rising above the valley of the Nile River, near where today there is a village called Nag Hammadi. The time was the late fourth century or early fifth century A.D. For whatever reason, someone, perhaps a monk from the local monastery of St. Pachomius, took steps to preserve some holy books—Coptic translations of works that had originally been written in Greek, works of the kind that had been denounced as heretical by Athanasius, the archbishop of Alexandria. The words of the prophet Jeremiah may have played through the mind of the person hiding the codices: "Put them in an earthenware jar, that they may last for a long time." For it was in an earthen jar, hidden in a cavity under a rock at the base of the cliffs, that the papyrus manuscripts were eventually discovered.

The Nag Hammadi library, as these texts have come to be called, was brought to light in 1945. By the early 1950s, after feuds and transactions of Levantine complexity, almost all of the Nag Hammadi collection was in the safe but jealous hands of the Coptic Museum, in Cairo, which for many years proved exceedingly particular about whom it would allow to study the documents. It was clear very early, however, that the codices, which contained forty previously unknown works, would offer unprecedented access to the world of the Gnostics, a variegated group of Christian communities, active as early as a century after the time of Jesus, that diverged sharply from the emerging Christian orthodoxy in many ways—one of them frequently being the prominence, both in theology and in community life, of women.

Elaine Pagels was a doctoral student in religion at Harvard University during the late 1960s, when mimeographed transcriptions of the Nag Hammadi library were circulating among American and European scholars. Her area of interest was the history of early Christianity. There were no women then on the faculty of Harvard's program in religion, and the dean who accepted Pagels as a doctoral candidate had turned her down the first time she applied. In this field, he explained in a letter, women didn't last. But now, after applying again, here she was, with the working knowledge of Latin and Greek that anyone dealing with early Christian texts requires, and the Nag Hammadi mimeographs caught her attention. Because the transcriptions were in Coptic, which is Egyptian written with the Greek alphabet and a few other characters, Pagels added Coptic to her repertoire (and also Hebrew) and got to work.

Sitting one afternoon recently in her office at the Institute for Advanced Study, in Princeton, I spoke with Pagels about her Harvard years and other matters. Pagels, who is a professor in the religion department at Princeton University, works at certain times at the institute, which offers scholars a chance to pursue research without the distraction of teaching. It is a modern and spacious place, set impersonally among vast lawns. In Pagels's office a photograph of her late husband sat upon the sill. A girl's bicycle was propped against a wall. Pagels has two young children, and a demeanor that somehow manages to be calmer than her circumstances are.

"I discovered," Pagels said, thinking back to her initial encounter with the Nag Hammadi materials, "as did the other graduate students, that our professors had file folders full of Gnostic texts of secret Gospels that many of them told us were absurd and blasphemous and heretical—but interesting. And I *did* find these texts interesting. And exciting. I think that perhaps my empathy for them had something to do with being a woman in an environment that was almost exclusively male. I found things among the heretics that were startlingly congenial." Pagels became part of the team that would translate the Nag Hammadi texts into English and provide a critical apparatus for them.

Not until 1975, five years after completing a doctoral dissertation on certain aspects of the Nag Hammadi library, did Pagels have an opportunity to inspect the documents themselves. At various times during a stay in Egypt, Pagels would visit the small, unprepossessing room in the Coptic Museum where the Nag Hammadi library is kept, one day perhaps to examine The Interpretation of Knowledge, another to examine A Valentinian Exposition or The Gospel of Mary. The documents looked, she remembers thinking, like tobacco leaves. Each fragile page, each fragment, lies flat between sheets of hard plastic, the black lettering stark against a mottled golden background, the underlying weave of the crushed papyrus fronds plainly visible. The Coptic Museum was a place of columns and courtyards and quiet. The only interruption was caused by the cleaning woman, and Pagels and any other scholars present would continue working at their desks when she came in, lifting their legs as soapy water was spilled and spread beneath them over the stone floors.

In a book called *The Gnostic Gospels* (1979), which received wide attention when it was published and occasioned a sometimes bitter scholarly debate, Pagels took some of those fragments that lie flat between plastic and sought to give them dimension, set them in history, bring ancient sensibilities back to life. She described Gnostic groups who saw God as a "dyad" embodying both masculine and feminine aspects, and who explicitly invoked the feminine aspect in their prayers: "May She who is before all things, the incomprehensible and indescribable Grace, fill you within, and increase in you her own knowledge." Some groups conceived of the third person in Christianity's trinitarian God—a God consisting of Father, Son, and Holy Spirit—to be female, and so rendered the Trinity, logically enough, as Father, Son, and Mother. Powerful feminine imagery and ideology suffuse many Gnostic texts, and this found parallels in the practice of a number of Gnostic groups, which permitted women to hold priestly office. Gnostic thought was disorderly and fantastical, and for a variety of reasons was spurned by Christian polemicists (although some elements seem to find echoes in the Gospel of John). But it preserves some early Christian traditions, and is valuable for its reflection of currents in popular religion that are only dimly reflected in the canon of sanctioned Christian works—currents important to an understanding of Christianity's unruly beginnings.

Some of the Gnostics were much intrigued by the Creation stories in the Book of Genesis. Pagels, too, became intrigued, and in 1988 she produced *Adam, Eve, and the Serpent* a book more ambitious than *The Gnostic Gospels*. The Bible's Creation stories—or, perhaps more precisely, the interpretation of the Cre-

ation stories that came to be accepted—form the basis for a view of humanity as existing in a fallen state, of woman as having led humanity astray, of man as being ordained to be the master of woman, and of sexuality as a corrupting aspect of human nature. And yet, as Pagels shows, this is not how the Creation stories were interpreted by many Jews and early Christians, and it is sometimes difficult to see how such conclusions came to be drawn. Pagels points to other traditions in Jewish and Christian thought: of the Creation stories as parables of human equality, men and women both being formed in the image and likeness of God of the stories as evocations of God's gift of moral freedom. *Adam, Eve, and the Serpent* traces the clashes of interpretation in the early Church, which culminated in the triumph of Augustine, whose harsh views on the subject would become those of much of the Western world—would help define Western consciousness—for a millennium and a half.

The Creation stories form the basis for a view of humanity as existing in a fallen state, of woman as having led humanity astray, of man as being ordained to be the master of woman.

The point is, Pagels told me, early Christianity was a remarkably diverse and fractious religious movement. There were traditions within it that the evolution of a stronger, more institutionalized tradition would largely destroy. Acknowledging this fact has implications for our own time and for people who have often felt excluded or even oppressed by the dominant tradition. It has implications in particular for women. "The history of Christianity has been told from a single point of view," Pagels said. "If that point of view is no longer tenable historically then it enables people to develop other perceptions."

The work of Elaine Pagels is but one manifestation of a larger phenomenon: the rapidly expanding influence of feminist scholars in the study of Jewish and Christian history, and the reassessment of certain issues

that has ensued as a result. The body of work that these scholars have produced is by now substantial. Virtually all of it has been published within the past fifteen years. Most has been published within the past ten. While the writing can at times be difficult—some scholars don methodology like chain mail—a strikingly large proportion, whether in specialized journals or in books, is written so as to be broadly accessible to readers outside academe.

The motivations, besides simple intellectual curiosity, that lie behind this work are not difficult to discern. There is the perception that the Hebrew Bible and the New Testament deal with women unfairly in many spheres; the need to understand why they do; the suspicion that an alternative past awaits recovery. Among some scholars there is a conviction, too, that recovering the past could help change the present—for example, could help make the case for giving women access to positions in religious ministry and religious leadership from which they are now barred. Although half of all Christian denominations permit the ordination of women, as do Reform and Conservative Judaism, the issue remains a matter of strongly felt conflict. The work of feminist scholars, both individually and collectively, has been greeted in some quarters with impatience, irritation, dismissiveness, even contempt. But it has also established women's issues as a permanent focus of biblical studies. That it has done so is one important element of the broader engagement of feminism with every aspect of organized religion.

A few years ago I set out to explore this branch of scholarship—to meet some of its practitioners and become familiar with some of their work. My focus was not on politics but on research. The people whose work is touched on here are drawn not from the sometimes airy or angry outskirts of the feminist biblical enterprise but from its solid scholarly core. They come from several religious backgrounds, represent several scholarly disciplines, and, as feminists, display a range of stances toward religion in general and the Bible in particular. Their work thus defies easy summary. My intention is to let it speak for itself.

THE PATRIARCHY PROBLEM

The women's movement has as yet had meager impact on some academic realms, but the realm of religion is not among the scarcely affected. Even if the convergence of feminism and religion has prompted developments on the fringes of popular culture which would strike some as bizarre (the proliferation of neo-pagan "goddess" movements comes to mind), the truly significant consequences have occurred closer to the mainstream of ministry and scholarship. Walk into the department of religion or the divinity school at any major university today and the bulletin board will paint the same picture: seminar after workshop after lecture on almost any conceivable matter involving women and religion. The influx of women into divinity-school programs has by now received considerable attention. So has the movement to adopt "inclusive" language, when appropriate, in translations of Scripture, and to correct mistranslations of Scripture that have served to obscure feminine references and imagery. This movement saw its most important victory in 1990, with the publication by the National Council of Churches of the New Revised Standard version of the Bible. But much of the work being done by women in biblical scholarship and related fields—work that demands immense erudition—remains far less well known.

The Bible has always been a compelling object of study, both because questions of religious faith are inextricably involved and because it is a window—albeit one whose refractions may distort and occlude—onto much of human history. With respect to issues of gender the Bible is also, of course, highly problematic, to use a word that no feminist scholar I've spoken with can help uttering in a tone of ironic politeness. It is a central tenet of contemporary feminism that a patriarchal template governs the way people have come to think and behave as individuals and as societies. The Bible is no stranger to patriarchy. It is an androcentric document in the extreme. It was written mostly if not entirely by men. It was edited by men. It describes a succession of societies over a period of roughly 1,200 years whose public life was dominated by men. And because the Bible's focus is predominantly on public rather than private life, it talks almost only about men. In the Hebrew Bible as a whole, only 111 of the 1,426 people who are given names are women. The proportion of women in the New Testament is about twice as great, which still leaves them a small minority.

As a prescriptive text, moreover, the Bible has been interpreted as justifying the subordination of women to men: "In pain you shall bring forth children, yet your desire shall be for your husband, and he shall rule over you." "Wives, be subject to your husbands as you are to the Lord." "Indeed, man was not made from woman, but woman from man. Neither was man created for the sake of woman, but woman for the sake of man." As a text that has been presumed by hundreds of millions of people to speak with authority, moreover, the Bible has helped enforce what it prescribes. There is no getting around the disturbing character, for women, of much of the Bible, short of an interpretive reading (a "hermeneutic," to use the term of art) that may represent something of a stretch—short of what one biblical scholar has called an act of "hermeneutical ventriloquism."

The subjection of the Bible to historical and critical scrutiny, a revolution in scholarship that began during the latter half of the nineteenth century, was undertaken almost entirely by men. It did not occur to these men that the way the Bible treats women—or, just as important, fails to treat women—might be a fit matter for study. The Society of Biblical Literature, which remains to this day the leading professional group in the field, was founded in 1880, and inducted its first woman member in 1894. But the relative handful of women who embarked on careers in biblical studies in the nineteenth century and the first half of the twentieth showed virtually no interest in women's issues. As the historian Dorothy Bass, of the Chicago Theological Seminary, has shown, it was women outside academe who first pursued the matter: women like the abolitionist Sarah Grimké, in the 1830s, and, later, Frances Willard, of the Women's Christian Temperance Union.

Their aims, initially, were two. The first was to identify and critically confront passages and stories about women which they deemed objectionable—the stories, for example, of Delilah, in the Book of Judges, and of Jezebel, in I Kings. The second aim was to seek out and elevate to greater prominence passages and stories about women which are positive and ennobling—for example, the remarkable image of Wisdom personified as a woman, in Proverbs, and the stories of Deborah, in Judges, and of the prophetess Huldah, in II Kings. Both these strands of the early feminist re-

sponse to the Bible have survived, in increasingly sophisticated forms, down to the present.

The suffragist leader Elizabeth Cady Stanton made a contribution by means of that remarkable fin-de-siècle document *The Woman's Bible,* the first volume of which was published in 1895. Though well into her eighties, Stanton oversaw a committee of female editors who scrutinized and critically glossed every passage in the Bible having to do with women. She came to the conclusion that little could be salvaged from Scripture which was fully compatible with the belief system of a rational modern feminist. None of the women who worked on *The Woman's Bible* was a biblical scholar. Female biblical scholars refused to participate in the project, afraid, Stanton believed, "that their high reputation and scholarly attainments might be compromised by taking part in an enterprise that for a time may prove very unpopular."

Female biblical scholars did not face up to issues of gender—did not, as Frances Willard had urged, "make a specialty of Hebrew and New Testament Greek in the interest of their sex"—in any significant way until the 1960s. One call to action came from a professor of biblical literature at Smith College, Margaret Brackenbury Crook, who in a book called *Women and Religion* (1964) took aim at the "masculine monopoly" on all important matters in all the world's great faiths. She repeated the plaintive question of the biblical figure Miriam: "Has the Lord spoken only through Moses?" By the 1970s, of course, a generalized version of that question could be sensed almost everywhere in the culture. Departments of religion and divinity schools were merely two among the crowd of institutions that saw more and more women seeking access, bringing with them unfamiliar questions and ways of thinking.

Biblical scholarship is still a predominantly male endeavor, but inroads by women have been substantial. The female membership of the Society of Biblical Literature amounted to three percent of the total in 1970. It now exceeds 16 percent. The share of the student membership that is female—a harbinger, surely—is 30 percent. In 1987 the society elected its first woman president, Elisabeth Schüssler Fiorenza, a theologian who at the time was a professor at Episcopal Divinity School, and who now teaches at Harvard. The joint annual meeting of the SBL and the American Academy of Religion today features a large number of sessions on women's issues, chiefly by women but sometimes by men. "Prostitutes and Penitents in the Early Christian Church." "Redeeming the Unredeemable: Genesis 22—A Jewish Feminist Perspective." "Rape as a Military Metaphor in the Hebrew Bible." The opening address at the AAR portion of last year's joint meeting was given by Mary Daly, whose first two books, *The Church and the Second Sex* (1968) and *Beyond God the Father* (1973), were a source of inspiration to many women with an interest in religion. (Daly herself has ventured not only beyond God the Father but also beyond Christianity, and is by now well off the beaten track; she maintains an uneasy professorship in the department of theology at Boston College, a school run by Jesuit priests.) At the next joint meeting, this coming November, the SBL will install its second woman president: Phyllis Trible, of Union Theological Seminary.

It was Schüssler Fiorenza's work—most notably her book *In Memory of Her* (1983), to which I was introduced almost a decade ago in the course of research on a related subject—that drew me into the world of women whose academic lives revolve, one way or another, around the central texts of the Jewish and Christian traditions. Schüssler Fiorenza, a soft-spoken native of Germany, is the Krister Stendahl Professor of Divinity at the Harvard Divinity School. She is also a founder and a coeditor of the *Journal of Feminist Studies in Religion,* one of several academic journals in the field with a focus on women. Schüssler Fiorenza is quick to acknowledge that coming to the United States, as she did in 1970, with a fresh doctorate in New Testament studies from the University of Münster, marked a turning point in her interests. The United States offered what Germany at the time did not: a strong and active feminist movement and a university system whose faculties—crucially, whose theology-department faculties—were open to women. Schüssler Fiorenza, in her own words, "began doing theology as a woman and for women." Her writing has focused primarily on the role played by women during the conception, birth, and infancy of Christianity.

Historical reconstruction of the Jesus movement is risky and fraught. Among other things, as Schüssler Fiorenza reminded me during a conversation one afternoon, "within both Judaism and Christianity the patriarchal side won"—thus determining the lens through which interpretation would look. One must approach the texts with a "hermeneutic of suspicion," to use a phrase that is by now a cliché in feminist biblical circles. The references to women that do exist in Christian works, Schüssler Fiorenza said, surely represent the tip of the iceberg, though unfortunately much of the part that is submerged now is likely to remain submerged forever.

And yet, she went on, there is some significant material about women to work with, if only we are not blind to it. The Gospels, she noted, are unequivocal in placing women prominently among the marginalized people who made up so much of Jesus' circle. Women are shown as having been instrumental in opening up the Jesus community to non-Jews. After the Crucifixion it was the women of Galilee who helped hold together the Jesus movement in Jerusalem as other disciples fled. Women were the first to discover the empty tomb and the first to experience a vision of a resurrected Jesus. Jesus' message was in part a radical attack on the traditional social structures of the Greco-Roman world—structures that limited the participation of women in the public sphere, and that the Jesus movement sought to replace with what Schüssler Fiorenza calls "a discipleship of equals."

After the crucifixion it was women who helped hold together the Jesus movement. Women were the first to discover the empty tomb, the first to experience a vision of a resurrected Jesus.

And after Jesus was gone? Christianity's penumbral first centuries can be difficult to apprehend. The texts that would make up the New Testament—not to mention the many other texts that survive from Christian communities—were at this time being written, edited, and re-edited, each text created in the context of certain communities and to fulfill certain purposes. What emerges from Schüssler Fiorenza's reading is a Christian missionary movement that in its initial stages "allowed for the full participation and leadership of women." She notes in *In Memory of Her* that in the authentic letters of Paul, women are singled out by name and given titles the same as or comparable to those held by male leaders. Prisca, a traveling missionary, is described by Paul as a peer, a "co-worker." Phoebe, in Cenchreae, is called a *diakonos,* a title Paul also gives himself.

Some scholars have in the past tried to explain away evidence like this, Schüssler Fiorenza writes, by arguing that when held by women such titles must have been mere honorifics. Or they have translated the titles differently. *Diakonos,* for example, which is usually translated as "minister," "missionary," or "deacon" when associated with men, has usually been downplayed as "deaconess" or even "helper" when associated with women. Scholars have also argued that people whose names are apparently female must actually have been men. Schüssler Fiorenza observes that the social mores of the time left ample room for women to wield authority in early Christianity. For one thing, the rituals of Christianity evolved in a network of churches based in homes, and within the home, women could claim important rights and responsibilities. Schüssler Fiorenza argues, finally, that early Christianity was built around a theology of equality; that Paul's famous reiteration in Galatians 3:28 of the ancient baptismal formula—"There is no longer Jew or Greek, there is no longer slave or free, there is no longer male and female; for all of you are one in Christ Jesus"—represents not a radical and temporary breakthrough in Paul's thinking but an expression of broad and ordinary Christian belief. In Schüssler Fiorenza's view, Galatians 3:28 is "the magna carta of Christian feminism."

Schüssler Fiorenza is a theologian, and she has an explicitly theological agenda. In her approach to Scripture she aims to highlight themes of unfolding liberation and emancipation. But large portions of her work exemplify a strategy pursued by non-theologians as well: the attempt to pierce the veil of the sources, to discern what was social and religious reality in a distant time. This may involve textual scholarship—training attention on vocabulary, on rhetorical style, on whatever can be inferred about the editing process. It may involve the disciplines of archaeology and anthropology—coming at early Jewish and Christian life from the outside, and looking at what the physical record has to say. All this work presupposes a broad grounding in some very obscure aspects of history. The work can be frustrating in the extreme. The materials available are often meager, and the conclusions drawn sometimes precarious and insubstantial.

Elaine Pagels spoke about some of the endeavor's hazards and intricacies and opportunities in one of our conversations. We had been talking about the issue of an author's point of view. Pagels observed that in some instances the documentary record of certain suppressed opinions consists only of the surviving criticisms of those opinions. Before the discovery of the Nag Hammadi library, Gnostic thinking was a prime example: many Gnostic beliefs had been scathingly summarized in the writings of Irenaeus of Lyons, a second-century theologian and foe of heretics. Images of women can sometimes be made out in the same way. "We have to read the texts aware that the point of view may not reflect the whole social reality," Pagels told me. "It will reflect the point of view of the people writing the texts, and the groups they represent. And generally women were not doing the writing. So we have to make a lot out of the few clues that are found."

She reached for a comparison to bring home the nature of this situation. "Imagine," she said after a moment's reflection, "having to re-create the thinking of Karl Marx on the basis of a handful of anti-communist tracts from the 1950s."

SALVAGE OPERATIONS

Union Theological Seminary, in New York, occupies two city blocks along Broadway, in a neighborhood that might be thought of as upper Manhattan's religion district. The Jewish Theological Seminary of America lies across the street to the northeast, taking up much of a third city block. Across the street to the southwest, taking up a fourth city block, lies The Interchurch Center, which houses scores of religious organizations: groups devoted to social work, missionary work, publishing, broadcasting. (The square, clunky structure is known as

"the God box.") And across the street directly to the west, occupying a fifth city block, is Riverside Church, long a bulwark of social activism with a mildly hallowed cast. Union is an example of the kind of liberal, nondenominational seminary whose student body in recent years has become increasingly female: almost 55 percent of its more than 300 students are women. It is a comfortable, reassuring place. The architecture is monastic, preserving outwardly in cool stone a way of life that no longer prevails inside. In the library's reading room, whose shelves hold the leather-bound classics required for exegetic work, and from around whose perimeter gleam the marbled pates of learned men, it is perhaps possible to believe that this is still the Union Seminary of Paul Tillich and Reinhold Niebuhr. But in the hallways of the living quarters the tricycles and toys betray a changed demography. The omnipresent flyers announcing meetings also tell a story. "Hunger Strike Demanding Action for Peace and Reunification in Korea." "Feminists for Animal Rights." "Lesbian-Gay Caucus Sez Howdy." These people, one senses, are busy, committed. They do not lack up-to-date agendas.

Phyllis Trible is the Baldwin Professor of Sacred Literature. Her office at Union sits high above the quadrangle, under the eaves, and in it one can occupy a certain chair at a certain angle and almost be persuaded that the world outside the window is the world of Oxford or Cambridge. On a wall of Trible's office hangs a photograph of a white-haired man in a dark suit and tie—James Muilenburg, who was a professor at Union when Trible was a student here, in the late 1950s and early 1960s, and who taught the first class she attended at the seminary. "I'll never forget that class," Trible recalled one day. She speaks with precision in an accent shaped by her native Virginia. "He walked in with a stack of syllabi under his arm and he put them down on the table and started quoting Hebrew poetry: the 'Sword of Lamech,' in Genesis. And he dramatized the whole thing—took the sword and plunged it in. He asked us where that sword reappeared, and jumped to Peter in the New Testament. I was utterly captivated, and have never gotten over it to this day." Trible is but one of several female biblical scholars I've met who, whatever problems being a woman may have caused them in academe, warmly ac-

knowledge a close intellectual relationship with a male mentor.

Trible believes that the Bible can be "reclaimed" as a spiritual resource for women. The Bible, she said, is sometimes not as patriarchal as translations would make it seem.

Trible is the author of two books, *God and the Rhetoric of Sexuality* (1978) and *Texts of Terror: Literary–Feminist Readings of Biblical Narratives* (1984), that would appear in anyone's canon of feminist biblical studies. Even colleagues who have no affinity with Trible's work—who differ radically in outlook—may acknowledge a debt. Ask graduate students in their twenties or established scholars in their thirties or forties how an interest was awakened in women's issues and biblical studies, and the answer will often turn out to involve an article or a book by Trible.

It is important to recognize where Trible stands in a spectrum that ranges, as she explained to me, "from some fundamentalists who claim that they are feminists but say they have no problem with the Bible to those at the other extreme who are unwilling to concede the Bible any authority at all." Trible is in the middle. She doesn't forget for a minute, she said, that the Bible is a thoroughly patriarchal text. But she is hardly a member of the rejectionist camp. She believes that the Bible can be "reclaimed" as a spiritual resource for women. And in all fairness, she said, it must be pointed out that the Bible is sometimes not as patriarchal as translations would make it seem. This is not just a matter of exclusive language. Trible pulled down a copy of the Revised Standard Version of the Bible, opened it to Deuteronomy 32:18, and read this passage: "You were unmindful of the Rock that begot you, and you forgot the God who gave you birth." She said, "Those words 'gave you birth' are from a Hebrew term for 'writhing in labor,' so the translation, if accurate, is tame. But here is how the Jerusalem Bible translates it: 'fathered you.'"

The work that initially brought Trible to prominence was a pair of journal articles in the 1970s on the two Creation stories in the Book of Genesis. These articles—the first ones written on the subject from a feminist perspective—were an attempt at reclamation. Trible argued that properly understood, the Creation stories, including the story of Adam and Eve, did not actually say what centuries of interpretation have made them say. For example, is woman to be considered subordinate to man, as some traditional interpretations would have it, simply because she was created after he was? If that is the case, Trible argued, then why are human beings not regarded as subordinate to animals, since Genesis 1:27 plainly declares that human beings were created after the animals were?

But that is almost beside the point, because it is a mistake, in Trible's view, to think of the first human being, Adam, as male. She points out that the Hebrew word 'adham, from which "Adam" derives, is a generic term for humankind—it denotes a being created from the earth—and is used to describe a creature of undifferentiated sex. Only when the Lord takes a rib from 'adham to make a companion are the sexes differentiated, and the change is signaled by the terminology. The creature from whom the rib was taken is now referred to not as 'adham but as 'ish ("man"), and the creature fashioned from the rib is called 'ishshah ("woman"). In Trible's reading, the sexes begin in equality. It is only after the act of disobedience occasioned by the serpent's temptation, and the departure of 'ish and 'ishshah from their initial and intended condition, that the sexes fall out of equality. It is only then, in this disobedient state, that the man establishes his dominance. Oppression of women by men, then, is not what was meant for humanity, even if it is what we have come to. "Rather than legitimating the patriarchal culture from which it comes," Trible concluded, "the myth places that culture under judgment."

Much as one hears the polite word "problematic" applied to material in the Bible which some feminist scholars deem to be negative, so also one hears the polite word "optimistic" applied to interpretations that some feminist scholars deem to be too positive. Trible is not unfamiliar with the latter charge. Her response would be that "optimistic" is a term that makes sense only if one assumes that the relationship people have

with the Bible is as with something dead. She thinks of the Bible differently—as if it were a pilgrim forging new relationships over time. There are ways, she believes, of articulating a conversation between feminism and the Bible in which each critiques the other.

I was familiar, of course, with how feminism might critique the Bible. I asked Trible what critique the Bible offers of feminism. She replied that there was sometimes a tendency to make too 'much of feminism, to put it on a pedestal, and that the Bible calls attention to that kind of propensity. "It warns," she said, "against idolatry."

Trible's specialty is a form of criticism known as rhetorical criticism, which pays particular attention to a document's literary architecture. During one conversation Trible walked me through some passages that, together, may offer an instance of a biblical woman's falling victim to editorial manhandling. The passages tell the story of Miriam—the sister of Moses and Aaron, a woman who was perhaps considered by the Israelites to be the equal of her brothers, but of whom few traces survive in the Bible as it has finally come down to us.

We meet Miriam in the Book of Exodus. It is she who persuades Pharaoh's daughter to raise the infant Moses—left in a basket among the rushes on the banks of the Nile—as her own, and to bring along Moses' mother as nurse. Miriam is not at this point given a name; the woman who saves the infant's life is identified only as his sister. And as the story of Moses proceeds, Miriam disappears—until the crossing of the Red Sea. Then, when the Israelites reach the far shore, Pharaoh's armies having been destroyed, there is a song of rejoicing: the poetic Song at the Sea, sung by Moses and the people of Israel. It begins, "I will sing to the Lord, for he has triumphed gloriously; / horse and rider he has thrown into the sea." No sooner has Moses finished than there comes a small fragment of text that appears out of place. The fate of Pharaoh's armies is for some reason quickly retold, and then, with the Israelites once again safely on shore, we learn that "the prophet Miriam, Aaron's sister," begins to sing the very same Song at the Sea. She sings the first two lines. The text then moves on to other business.

Trible paused. There are several interesting things here, she said. One is that we learn for the first time that the sister of Aaron, who must also be the sister of Moses, has a name, and that it is Miriam. We also see that she is called a prophet and that this occurs at a place in the text well before the place where Moses is first called a prophet, though the precise meaning of "prophet" in the context of Exodus remains unclear. What this piece of text about Miriam represents, Trible said, is the dogged survival of an earlier version of the Exodus story. Indeed, she pointed out, scholars have argued that in the most ancient Israelite traditions the singing of the Song at the Sea was ascribed not to Moses but to Miriam. The role was only later shifted away from Miriam. (As an aside, Trible observed that the first work on the attribution of the Song at the Sea to Miriam dates back to the mid-1950s—and was done by men. She added pointedly, "I'm not one to say that you can't use the previous generation of scholarship—not at all.")

Miriam moves with the people of Israel into the desert, whereupon she disappears from the Book of Exodus. But she reappears later in the Bible, in connection with what seems to be a severe clash within the leadership, one from which Miriam emerges the loser—accounting, perhaps, for her diminished prominence. The reappearance occurs amid the jumble of the Book of Numbers, wherein Miriam and Aaron are heard to question the authority of their brother, asking the question that Trible and others ask more broadly: "Has the Lord spoken only through Moses?" The Lord does not punish Aaron, but Miriam is struck down with a skin affliction, possibly leprosy, for her rebelliousness, and later dies in the wilderness of Zin.

And yet there are signs that the memory of Miriam in the Israelite consciousness remains an active and uplifting one. Miriam has always been associated with water, Trible noted—remember the basket among the rushes? remember the Song at the Sea?—and the text immediately following the notice of Miriam's death again brings up the subject of water. It reads, "Now there was no water for the congregation." In standard editions of the Bible that sentence starts a new paragraph, as if the subject is suddenly being changed. Trible said, "Written Hebrew doesn't have such breaks. The paragraph marking after the end of the Miriam story is artificial. It makes you miss the idea that what is happening is connected to Miriam's death. Nature is mourning the loss of Miriam." Henceforward in the Bible, Miriam reappears only in hints and fragments, as in this passage from Deuteronomy: "Remember what the Lord your God did to Miriam on your journey out of Egypt." But she survives in real life—in the form of the continuing popularity of the name Miriam. The New Testament, compiled more than a millennium after Miriam's death, is populated with a multitude of women named Mary—the Hellenized version of the Hebrew Miriam. It is no coincidence, Trible has argued, that the Magnificat, the great canticle of Mary the mother of Jesus, borrows imagery directly from the Song at the Sea.

Miriam, Trible said, is only one of a number of apparently powerful women in the Bible who are alluded to almost in passing, the modesty of the references at odds with the importance of the roles these women seem to play. The references hint, perhaps, at the existence of a class of women in Israel whose history has in essence been lost, or can today be recovered only by means of the most delicate salvage, even then yielding mere wisps of insight. But that the references survive at all—that the editors believed some mention of these women had to be made—is itself suggestive.

Miriam is only one of a number of apparently powerful women in the Bible who are alluded to almost in passing, the modesty of the references at odds with the roles these women seem to play.

"It shows," Trible said, "that the stories just couldn't be squelched."

THE EARLIEST ISRAELITES

During part of almost every year for thirty years Carol Meyers, a professor of religion at Duke University, has left behind the comforts of university life for the rigors of archaeological excavations in the Middle East. For the past five summers she and her husband, Eric, have led excavations at a place called Sepphoris, in Israel, a site with remains as recent as the Crusades and as ancient as the Iron Age. Sepphoris, near Nazareth, in Galilee, is said in Christian tradition to be the birthplace of Mary. This summer Carol and Eric Meyers are excavating an Iron Age site at Sepphoris, one that dates to the earliest years of the Israelite people.

I visited Carol Meyers not long before her latest tour of duty in the Middle East, and she began describing the conditions under which she and her colleagues worked there. We were in her Gothic office at Duke, and the crowded shelves around us held books like *L'architecture domestique du Levant* and *Catalogue of Ancient Near-Eastern Seals in the Ashmolean Museum*—the sort of books that elicit in me a vague yearning for baked earth and native porters. When you step off the plane in Israel, Meyers said, it is always a visual shock. Even with the achievements of modern irrigation—even in the rainy season—much of the landscape is forbidding: barren, rocky, thorny. And in the summer it is *hot*. And in the winter, as people abroad often do not realize, it is *cold*. There is wind and hail and sleet.

These conditions are at their most extreme in the hill country of Judea and Samaria and Galilee, where the Israelites first emerged, inhabiting the unforgiving uplands because the Canaanite city-states controlled the fertile bottomlands. In this marginal ecological niche, where water was scarce and soils were bad, the tribes of Israel clung to a tenuous subsistence. They terraced the hills to make fields. They built cisterns lined with slaked-lime plaster to hold water.

Precisely who the Israelites were and where they came from remain matters of debate, but their appearance in the Land of Canaan can be dated to roughly 1250 B.C. The period of the Israelite monarchy, the kingdom of Saul and David and Solomon and their successors, was two centuries away, and the demands of social organization fell almost entirely upon the family—or, more precisely, upon clusters of related families. There was no central government, no structured politics, no sense of a public domain.

In this inhospitable and tribalized world, Carol Meyers believes, men and women functioned in social parity. The books of the Bible that describe this period of Israel's history—Judges and Joshua, primarily—do not necessarily show this to be the case, of course. Having achieved final form centuries later, they depict a society in which most of the important roles were played by men. But, as Meyers observed, there is frequently a big disjunction between a society's public stance and the everyday social reality; and everyday social reality in ancient Israel has only recently become an object of scrutiny. In biblical studies as in many other kinds of scholarship, social history has been a latecomer, and it is in social rather than political history that women tend at last to emerge from the background.

That Carol Meyers developed an interest in biblical studies at all is an accident of history. When she was an undergraduate at Wellesley, in the mid-1960s, a course in the Old Testament and the New Testament was required for graduation. Wellesley's insistence on biblical education, now long since dropped, had deep historical roots: Wellesley was a college where female biblical scholars had since the late nineteenth century found a congenial home. The first woman to present a paper at a meeting of the Society of Biblical Literature (1913) was a Wellesley professor, as was the first woman to publish a paper in the society's *Journal of Biblical Literature* (1917). Meyers found herself drawn to the world of the Bible and after a summer spent on an archaeological excavation in Wyoming, run by Harvard University, she knew that she wanted to combine biblical studies and archaeology. She began studying biblical Hebrew and then took up Akkadian, a Semitic language with many Hebrew cognates. In graduate school at Brandeis she was the only woman in most of her classes, and she had no female professors.

Needless to say, there was no such thing as feminist biblical studies. Nor did Meyers feel an inner tug in that direction. "It really was only once I began teaching at Duke," she recalled when we spoke, "that I became aware of the need and of the potential for gender studies with respect to Scripture. It really wasn't even at my own initiative—and I'm not embarrassed to say that. When I started teaching here, my colleagues said, 'Listen, you have to put a couple of courses on our curriculum that are of your own design. Why don't you think about doing some course on women and the Bible, or something like that?' This was in the mid-seventies, and I was the only woman in the department. Of course I said yes. When I started trying to put such a course together, I found out that there was no material. No one had done any research on it; no one had written about it. And that's when I started doing work myself."

Much of that work is embodied in *Discovering Eve: Ancient Israelite Women in Context* (1988), a book that draws on biblical sources and, more important, the insights offered by archaeology and social anthropology to reconstruct aspects of life in Israel before the dawn of monarchy and complex political institutions.

The economic functions of men and women at that time would have been separate and distinct, Meyers writes, with the men disproportionately responsible for tasks involving brute strength and the women responsible for tasks requiring technology or specialized skills or social sophistication: shearing wool and weaving cloth, processing and preserving food, teaching children, and managing a complex household whose membership, excavated floor plans suggest, usually went far beyond the nuclear family. In pre-monarchic Israel, as in primitive societies today where the household is the basic political and economic unit, women would have been central and authoritative figures.

Meyers observes further that the God of Israel, in sharp contrast to the gods of all other contemporaneous religions, was perceived at this time as asexual. Moreover, when God had to be described metaphorically, both male and female imagery was used. The prominence of God as father is a very late development in Israelite religion, Meyers argues, and makes only rare appearances in the Hebrew Bible itself (the term "father" is used in association with God just ten times).

The editors of the Bible have preserved traces of what Meyers believes was a relatively egalitarian regime. The Book of Judges, which reached its final form around the time of the Babylonian Captivity (586–538 B.C.), depicts life in Israel half a millennium earlier, and contains material that is very old. It brings to our attention an unusually large number of self-assured and powerful women. One of these, Deborah, is referred to as both a prophet and a judge. The "judges" in these earliest times were not magistrates but rather those few individuals among the Israelites whose authority extended beyond household and tribe and might be thought of as somehow national. Some scholars have even speculated that one portion of the Book of Judges, the so-called Song of Deborah, may have been composed by a woman. (Resolving such matters of authorship is at this point impossible. It should be noted that the recent and widely publicized *Book of J,* in which the literary critic Harold Bloom entertains the conceit that one of the authors of the Pentateuch, the so-called J source, was a woman, is not held in high regard by biblical scholars, whatever the truth about J's identity may be. An earlier and more reliable book that speculates briefly on the same question is *Who Wrote the Bible?* by Richard Elliott Friedman.)

To Israelite women's economic productivity—at least equal in importance to that of men—must be added the essential element of reproductivity. Meyers reads the Bible mindful of the precarious demographic circumstances confronting the early Israelites. "It's wrong," she said, "to impose our idea of the individual on a society in which that may not have been a driving force in human development. The 'me-ness' or the 'I-ness' of our own contemporary life cannot be superimposed upon another era. The demands of community survival meant cooperation and a sense that what people were doing was in order for the group to survive. I get annoyed at some feminist critics who don't consider the social-history perspective. They see things like 'Be fruitful and multiply, and fill the earth' as meaning that the sole purpose of a woman is to conceive children. And all her interactions with God or with her husband seem to be to bring that fact about. They say, 'Well, a woman is just giving up her body for her husband.' I would counter by saying that in an agrarian society large families are essential. And that the Israelites were settling into marginal lands that had never been developed before. And whether they would make it or not depended on a certain population base. So the injunctions for fertility—and remember, they are addressed to both men and women—can be seen as a way of encouraging something that was beneficial if not essential for community survival."

It was a hard life. Infant mortality approached 50 percent. Excavations of burials show that female life expectancy, owing in part to the risks involved in repeated pregnancies, was perhaps thirty years, ten years less than life expectancy for men. Meyers told me that whenever she is on an archaeological dig in the Middle East, she inevitably begins to imagine herself as one of those women of ancient Israel. During an excavation Meyers is working the same remorseless terrain as did the Israelites 3,000 years ago, the two sexes side by side. The toil is unremitting and tedious, the environment dry and dusty. The days when scores of local laborers were supervised by aristocrats in pith helmets are long over. Archaeology is a complex enterprise, group-oriented in the extreme. Being a mother, Meyers for years had other responsibilities as well: young children for whom she had to care, on the site, even as the excavations proceeded.

Meyers's research has now moved beyond the formative centuries of Israel to the Israelite monarchy, which was instituted under Saul around 1020 B.C. This is the Israel of the two books of Samuel and the two books of Kings, a unified monarchy until, after the death of Solomon, around 920 B.C., the country was partitioned into northern and southern kingdoms. Under its kings, political structures in Israel became increasingly centralized and urban centers became increasingly important. A market economy grew up alongside the subsistence one. During this period, too, at least in urban settings, the position of women relative to men became more unequal—came more to resemble the kind of society we see in the Bible. It is hard to know how closely the situation in, say, Jerusalem reflected life elsewhere. Jerusalem, Meyers explained to me, was always an anomaly. After the Assyrians overran the Northern Kingdom, in 721 B.C., the population of Jerusalem the capital of the Southern Kingdom, was swollen by refugees. The city grew to be ten times as large as the next largest city in Israel. Its inhabitants no longer had ties to the land, and women no longer had a central role in economic life. There was poverty and chaos and great social stratification. There were large numbers of foreigners. There was something called public life, and it was in the hands of men. This is the time and the place in which much of the Hebrew Bible was fashioned. No wonder, Meyers said, that it is androcentric.

And yet, Meyers went on, some 90 percent of the people of Israel continued to live in agricultural villages in the countryside. She is cautious about applying the label "patriarchal" either too broadly or too loosely. Often the social patterns that prevail in the city are quite different from those that survive in the country. The term "patriarchy" may be legitimate in some places and times and not in others. Who knows what this nineteenth-century construct even means when applied to a pre-modern society like that of ancient Israel? "It does a disservice," Meyers said, "to a complex piece of literature, the Bible, and to a society that existed for a thousand years, and changed and grew."

Meyers is cautious about applying the label "patriarchal" too broadly. Who knows what this nineteenth-century construct even means when applied to ancient Israel?

Our gaze is deflected, too, Meyers said, by the very focus of the Bible on public life. On the relatively rare occasions when it affords a glimpse of private life, a patriarchal society is not always what we see. The Song of Songs offers such a glimpse. It contains much archaic material, and is especially noteworthy for the amount of text written in a woman's voice, and in the first person. Some of the terminology is suggestively feminine, and even hints at female authority. For example, whereas in most of the Bible the standard term for a household is *bet'ab,* or "father's house," the term used in the Song of Songs is *bet'em,* or "mother's house." Indeed, there has been speculation that the Song of Songs was written by a woman.

> My beloved is mine and I am his;
> he pastures his flock among the lilies.
> Until the day breathes and the shadows flee,
> turn, my beloved, be like a gazelle
> or a young stag on the cleft mountains.

Regardless of the author's sex, the love poetry in the Song of Songs expresses an emotional bond not between a master and a subordinate but between equals.

PATRONS AND PRESBYTERS

"Do you know what a 'squeeze' is?" Under other circumstances I might have confidently given a reply, but after several hours of conversation with Ross S. Kraemer, a fellow at the University of Pennsylvania's Center for Judaic Studies, I had a feeling that the answer would be unexpected. We had met in Philadelphia, where Kraemer lives, and we talked over lunch and during a drive through town (interrupted by calls to a housekeeper on the car phone). Kraemer spoke about the Greek cult of Dionysus, which, though little attention has been paid to the fact, was in its ecstatic rites the province of women. (A study of the cult of Dionysus had been the nucleus of her doctoral dissertation at Princeton.) She spoke about Mary Magdalene, one of the women who figured most prominently in the circle around Jesus, and noted that, commonplace public assumptions notwithstanding, nowhere do the New Testament writings identify her as a prostitute. (The tradition may have been developed deliberately as part of an attempt to diminish Mary's stature, particularly in comparison with that of the Apostle Peter.) She spoke about the ancient "purple trade"—the trade in expensive purple-dyed fabric, the participants in which could be presumed to enjoy a certain affluence. This information bears on a woman named Lydia, a "dealer in purple cloth" from the city of Thyatira, who appears in the Acts of the Apostles and is an example of the kind of independent woman of means who seems to have played an especially active role in early Christianity.

Kraemer noted that, commonplace assumptions notwithstanding, nowhere do the New Testament writings identify Mary Magdalene, who was prominent in Jesus' circle, as a prostitute.

A squeeze is a mold of an ancient inscription carved in marble or other stone, obtained by coating the hard surface with a pliable substance—latex has supplanted papier-mâché as the medium most commonly used—and then peeling it off. Epigraphers, as those who study inscriptions are called, typically have a selection of them in their possession, along with files of photographs and transcriptions. The subject of squeezes had come up when Kraemer began describing the types of sources auxiliary to the Bible on which scholars can rely in the study of women and ancient religion. As time moves forward from primitive epochs, the sources become more plentiful. They include works of art and works of history and literature. They include a diverse array of documents involving women: for example, letters, tax receipts, wet-nurse contracts. And they include large numbers of inscriptions and fragments of inscriptions from buildings and monuments. Kraemer pointed to the work of one colleague whose analysis of Greek and Latin epigraphical evidence led her to conclude, contrary to the prevailing scholarly consensus, that at least sometimes Jewish women occupied prominent leadership roles in the ancient synagogue.

That the sources become more plentiful suggests a Mediterranean world that was becoming more complex. By the end of the sixth century B.C. the monarchic period in Israel had drawn to a close. The Israelites had endured a half century of exile in Babylon and then been allowed to return to their homeland. During the several hundred years that elapsed before the birth of Jesus, this homeland would be ruled by Persians, by Greeks, by Romans. The entire region would feel the influence of new economic and cultural systems. This is also the period when, in the Temple precincts of Jerusalem, the Hebrew Bible gradually cohered into the form in which we have it now, a collection of thirty-nine canonical texts, some of them incorporating material of great antiquity passed down through the ages more or less verbatim. (I remember Carol Meyers's once pointing out that the enormous stylistic variety of the Bible's Hebrew is one characteristic that eludes translation.) The canon of the Hebrew Bible was closed—no books would subsequently be added—toward the end of the first century A.D. By then the Romans had razed the Temple in Jerusalem, and the sacred texts of a new religious force, Christianity, were in the process of being compiled.

How egalitarian was that new religious force? More important (and borrowing the title of an influential and controversial 1971 article by Leonard Swidler, a professor at Temple), was Jesus a feminist? Such questions unfailingly stir up a range of scholarly responses. I asked Ross Kraemer to talk about those questions, and the conversation gravitated naturally to the work of Elisabeth Schüssler Fiorenza. Kraemer acknowledged the enormous debt that everyone owed Schüssler Fiorenza, acknowledged that her work had been groundbreaking in providing a new but also comprehensive and coherent way of viewing the Jesus movement and its context. But she added that she was less, well, optimistic than Schüssler Fiorenza. "I'm not as optimistic not so much in terms of her recovery of what she thinks women in early Christianity did, what roles they played—I think she's likely to be right about a lot of that. Where I would part company is with her argument that the earliest theology of Christianity is *intentionally* egalitarian and feminist. I'm really not persuaded of that, though I think that Christianity in many communities may have had egalitarian consequences. Elisabeth wants to locate the intent in Jesus himself. It's not so much that I think she's wrong as that I'm simply not convinced we can know that she's right. It's very hard to argue that we know *anything* about what Jesus really thought, and the few things that any scholar would be willing to attribute to Jesus himself with any confidence don't address this particular issue."

The difficulty is that the Gospels and other early texts are encrusted documents, layered accretions formed out of a mixture of sources and motivations. On women's issues as on other matters, they may be surer guides to the communities in which they were formed than to the community around Jesus that they ostensibly describe. Kraemer used the various Resurrection stories and the part played by women in those stories to illustrate the pitfalls. All four Gospels depict women as having been the first to discover the empty tomb of Jesus, and in two of the Gospels, Jesus first appears after the Resurrection to Mary Magdalene. This would certainly seem to make a point about the position of women in the Jesus movement, some scholars say, and would also bolster a claim to female authority in Christian affairs—at the time of Jesus or later. Others note, however, that the account of the Resurrection in Paul's first letter to the Corinthians, which was written at least twenty years before the Gospels existed in written form, makes no mention of Mary Magdalene or indeed of any women, and it makes no mention of the empty-tomb tradition.

What is going on? One possibility, of course, is that in his account Paul is deliberately ignoring a tradition he is fully aware of—perhaps so as not to deflect emphasis from the authority of men (and himself). This could suggest that the process of diminishing the authority of women in Christianity began at a very early date. If that is the case, the survival of the women-at-the-empty-tomb tradition in the Gospels—decades after Paul—suggests its sheer durability. Thus we should perhaps take at face value, after all, what the Gospels have to say about the prominent position of women in the Jesus movement.

But wait: What if Paul was unaware of the empty-tomb tradition? What if, indeed, it arose *after* Paul—arose, as some have ventured, in conjunction with a growing belief among Christians in the prospect of a physical resurrection of an uncorrupted body after death, a belief that Paul himself would have regarded as crudely simplistic, whether applied to Jesus' Resurrection or to a more general resurrection of the dead? If the tradition did arise after Paul, Kraemer argues, then casting women as the first to see the empty tomb might have subtly helped to explain why it took so long for the good news about the physical Resurrection of Jesus to spread: because they were women, the original witnesses had been afraid to divulge what they knew, or had been widely disbelieved. In either case, of course, the result is an implicit denigration of women.

The situation is something of a mess. As Kraemer points out in her book *Her Share of the Blessings,* the basic problem is that "early Christian communities, especially after the death of Jesus, experienced considerable conflict over the appropriate roles of women, and tended to retroject their positions about this conflict back onto the stories they told about the women who encountered the earthly Jesus."

Her Share of the Blessings is a wide-ranging exploration of the role of women in Greco-Roman religions—pagan, Jewish, Christian—from about the fourth century B.C. to the fifth century A.D. The comparative approach Kraemer takes has great advantages, allowing her to see how structures in one realm may have influenced those in another. If she believes that, for whatever reason, early Christianity was more egalitarian in terms of gender than it later became—and she does—it is not only because of the interpretation she accepts of early Christian writings. She knows also from looking at the larger context that it was not unusual for women to hold cultic office in pagan religion, not unusual for them to play the role of patron. In light of the social mores of the time, the emphasis in much of early Christianity on sexual asceticism would also have served to enhance female independence: it offered free women a radical new option, a door to open other than the traditional one of marriage and child bearing and domesticity. Another force conducive to egalitarianism was the expectation among many early Christians that the present earthly order would soon pass— that the Lord was about to return in glory. In such a climate attachment to social structures that were plainly "of the world" was considerably lessened. Did women serve as priests? The formal establishment of a priesthood in Christianity came very late, Kraemer writes, but a diverse body of evidence shows that women in early Christianity held the title *presbytera,* and that people who held this title performed all priestly functions: they taught, they baptized, they blessed the Eucharist.

There are, of course, tensions. One cannot read very far into the writings of Paul without becoming aware of his inner conflict when it came to questions of gender and sexuality. George Bernard Shaw once characterized Paul as the "eternal enemy of woman." In the epistle to the Galatians, Paul embraced an egalitarian formula, but in I Corinthians he showed himself to be clearly disturbed by the powerful and independent women in the Christian community at Corinth. He did not forbid the Corinthian women from prophesying, but he demanded that they cover their heads when they prayed in public, and he added a statement that defines women as subordinate to men. Is this last statement (along with some other problematic passages) a later interpolation, as some scholars believe? Perhaps. But tensions exist nonetheless, Kraemer writes, and they become deeper and more intolerable as Christianity moves further away in time from its origins, and moves closer to the contemporaneous social establishment.

Conflicting perspectives on women are apparent in later writings. One perspective is embodied in the apocryphal Acts of Thecla, probably written in the second century A.D., which celebrates the life of an ascetic female missionary supposedly sent out by Paul himself to teach and spread the word of the Lord. The Acts of Thecla, it must be said, has many decidedly odd elements (for example, Thecla is described as baptizing herself by jumping into a pool of hungry seals), but this text and many others like it enjoyed wide popularity. The other perspective is embodied, for example, in the epistles to Timothy, written in the second century, which contain some of the most stringent passages about women in the New Testament, passages that were then ascribed to Paul:

Let a woman learn in silence with full submission. I permit no woman to teach or to have authority over a man; she is to keep silent. For Adam was formed first, then Eve; and Adam was not deceived, but the woman was deceived and became a transgressor.

This is the perspective that hardened when Christianity became the religion of the Roman state.

WOMEN WHO LEAD

Was Junia, whom Paul, in his epistle to the Romans, called "prominent among the apostles," a man or a woman? What about the person named Jael, who is referred to in an inscription from Aphrodisias, in Asia Minor, as being the presiding officer or patron of a Jewish community there? These questions are not academic. They speak to issues of gender, status, and leadership.

Some would argue that Junia and Jael had to have been men. How, after all, could a woman be a Christian apostle or the presiding officer of a Jewish community, when we know that women were barred from such honors? This is the kind of reasoning that brings a note of both excitement and exasperation to Bernadette Brooten's voice. Brooten is a professor of Scripture and interpretation at the Harvard Divinity School and the woman who made the study of Greek and Latin inscriptions which Ross Kraemer referred to. This fall she will join the faculty at Brandeis University. It is bad enough, Brooten said during a conversation one day, for women to be invisible in ancient Judaism and Christianity because men didn't think to mention them or because they weren't in a position to be mentioned. Must we also argue away the few women in plain sight?

Junia was a common female name in the ancient world, Brooten said. Several ancient religious commentators, such as Origen of Alexandria and John Chrysostom, assumed as a matter of course that the Junia mentioned in Romans was a woman. This assumption prevailed until the Middle Ages. Then a reaction set in. Paul reserved the title "apostle" for persons of great authority—people who had served as missionaries and founded churches. To a medieval mind, such people had to have been men. Junia underwent a change of sex. Later Martin Luther popularized a reinterpretation of Junia as *Junias,* an apparently masculine name—the diminutive, perhaps, as scholars would later speculate, of Junianius or Junilius. There is only one problem, Brooten said. The name Junias cannot be found in antiquity: not on documents, not in inscriptions. It does not exist as a name, diminutive or otherwise. All that we have is Junia, a common name for a woman—in this case, the name of a woman "prominent among the apostles."

As for the name Jael, Brooten said, the only reason the question of gender has come up at all is that there is an important title attached to the name, and the name sits at the top of a list of other names, all of which are male. In less politically charged circumstances, this Jael would simply have been assumed to be a woman. Jael was—is—a well-known woman's name. A woman named Jael is prominent in Judges. But scholars have hunted through Scripture and other ancient sources to see if they can find precedent for a Jael who is a man, because it seems to them so unlikely that this Jael could have been a woman. In some manuscripts of the Book of Ezra, as it appears in the Septuagint, they have found such a Jael. The name is in a list of male exiles who had married foreign women and were now repudiating them upon their return to Israel. The identification is highly tentative, however. The Septuagint is the Hebrew Bible as translated into Greek, and the transliteration of Semitic names from Hebrew into Greek is haphazard and inconsistent. What this means, Brooten went on, is that to take Jael as a man's name one has to accept an instance that may be nothing more than an artifact of transliteration. One has to prefer this to the attestation of Jael as female in a major book of the Bible, the name being that of a well-known figure whose story was probably a staple of synagogue readings.

"All of which," Brooten said, "raises several questions for me. How many women do there have to have been for there to have been any? And if it's part of the marginalization of women that women are very rarely leaders to begin with, then even in those circumstances in which women do occur as leaders, they may be either perceived as not being women or perceived as not being leaders." The note of frustration in Brooten's voice gave way to something slyer as she summoned up an image of scholars one day confronting a document that referred to Prime Minister Margaret Thatcher and the members of one of her all-male Cabinets. It would be only a matter of time, Brooten said, before some scholar came along and pronounced Thatcher a man.

Harvard Divinity School is one of the many divinity schools to whose revival an influx of women has contributed greatly. Applicants are plentiful, with women accounting for well over half the enrollment in the school's various programs. Whatever this portends for the future, women as yet remain distinctly underrepresented among the school's senior faculty.

Brooten joined the Harvard faculty in 1985. She had received her doctorate from Harvard a few years earlier, and in the intervening period had taught at Claremont. Part of her academic training took place in Tübingen, the cobbled and timbered university town in Germany whose name has long been associated with new departures in theology. She describes the German academic environment for women in much the same way Schüssler Fiorenza does. "German theologians," Brooten told me, "will just say outright that they don't want women." Oddly, though, Tübingen is where Brooten took her first women's-studies course: Leonard Swidler, on leave from Temple, happened to be a visiting professor there for a year, and offered a seminar on women and the Church. Brooten was one of two students who signed up for it. "In the university as a whole," she recalled, "there was no interest in such things at all."

Brooten's office at Harvard has the dusky flavor of a Dickensian garret. Narrow pathways thread among tumuli of tables and books. Some of the books are old, spines worn to a dull sheen by centuries of palms. There is not even a computer to suggest the late twentieth century, though Brooten does use one at home. It is now standard in the field to have computer software that can print in Greek, Hebrew, and Coptic fonts. Computers have also made some kinds of research much easier for biblical scholars. For example, the great bulk of the writing that survives from antiquity in Greek, Latin, and Hebrew—not just works of literature but also snippets from tens of thousands of papyrus fragments and stone inscriptions—is now available on CD-ROM.

A capsule summary of the implications of Brooten's earliest research might read like this: with respect to roles played by women, there was more differentiation within Judaism in the Greco-Roman world than many scholars acknowledge. This touches on a highly sensitive issue. Some scholars, particularly among those who want a liberalization of Christian church policies concerning women, have argued that if early Christianity fell short of an egalitarian ideal, the cause lay in part in the nature of the Jewish world out of which Christianity emerged. Thus, one argument runs, there might have been more women leaders in Christianity if only there had been more in Judaism. Looking at the matter another way, to the degree that egalitarianism did exist in early Christianity, it is sometimes presented as a sharp break from Jewish tradition. Often implicit, this kind of thinking amounts, in the view of some, to locating the origins of patriarchal misogyny in the Hebrew Bible and those who inhabited its shadow. That is perhaps stating the problem too unsubtly, but it exposes a place where the nerve is raw. Brooten's view is that the spectrum of tolerable practice among Jews in ancient times was broad—just as it is in modern Judaism, just as it was and is in Christianity.

The work of feminist scholars has been greeted by some with impatience, irritation, even contempt. It has also established women's issues as a permanent focus of biblical studies.

In her doctoral dissertation, later published in book form as *Women Leaders in the Ancient Synagogue,* Brooten considered nineteen carved inscriptions dating from as early as 27 B.C. to as late as the sixth century A.D., in which Jewish women are accorded official titles relating to the communal life of a synagogue—titles such as "head of the synagogue," "leader," "elder." Titles like these, when applied to women, had long been interpreted as honorific rather than functional. "Rufina, a Jewess, head of the synagogue, built this tomb for her freed slaves and the slaves raised in her house"—these words come from a marble plaque, inscribed in the second century A.D., that was found in Smyrna. The traditional view has been that Rufina, the "head of the synagogue," the *archisynagogos,* had no real functional authority and was in all likelihood merely the wife of the true *archisynagogos.* Rufina is seen to have the title, as Brooten wryly notes, "*honoris causa.*" In dense, meticulous arguments that cannot be reviewed here, Brooten mounts an assault on that view. She takes up the cases of Rufina and the eighteen other women, and exposes what she deems to be the flawed presuppositions and tortured reasoning necessary to conclude that their titles were not functional. Women leaders of the synagogue were, of course, never the norm and were perhaps always the great exception. But, Brooten states, it is wrong to see the emergence of women leaders in Christianity as unprecedented.

Brooten's more recent work involves the writings of Paul, in particular his views on the proper place of women in society and where those views came from. One clue lies in Paul's condemnations of same-sex love. As Brooten explains, in a discussion that draws not only on religious texts but also on ancient materials as diverse as medical and astrological writings, Paul was in this regard no more than a man of his time. Whatever the exceptions in practice, on the normative gender map of the Roman world some behavior is appropriately masculine and some appropriately feminine, and the line is not supposed to be crossed. In sexual relations between members of the same sex this distinction is violated. One man becomes "like a woman"; one woman becomes "like a man." Underlying all this was a world view that, Brooten argues, saw the distinction between "active" and "passive" as more fundamental even than distinctions of sex. It was the basis of social order and social hierarchy. It was the

origin of the tension in Paul. Forward-looking in many ways, Paul could not let it go.

"Paul was happy to work with women as colleagues, and encouraged them," Brooten said. "So, for example, he mentions Junia, and he acknowledges Prisca and Tryphaena and Tryphosa and Persis and other women. He teaches with them, and he recognizes their prophecy, and he works with them as missionaries in the Roman world. On the other hand, while he was very willing to make a religious and societal break with Jewish tradition on points that were considered very central to Judaism, such as the issue of dietary laws and the circumcision of men, in order to permit Jew and Gentile to come together alike to accept Jesus as the Christ, with some customs concerning women he's not willing to make that kind of break. For example, the issue of the hairstyling and veiling of women. And, indeed, at that very point in the text he describes Christ as the head of man, and man as the head of woman, which goes beyond tolerating a custom and gives a theological underpinning to gender differentiation. I see his position as essentially ambivalent. On certain issues—gender, slavery, Roman power—he is very much interested in maintaining social order. But what's fascinating about Paul is that he experiments."

Toward the end of a long conversation we lingered for a moment on the nature of that first-century world of which Paul was a part: a world that those who know it well describe as more alien from our own in its psychology and belief systems and outlook than we imagine. How confident do you feel, I asked Brooten, that we can span the gulf between these two cultures, ours and theirs—can reconstruct something trustworthy about the dynamics of *then*?

"That's something I ask myself about all the time," Brooten said. And then she laughed. "I've often had this thought: that I'll die, and go to heaven, and Rufina will meet me, and I'll greet her as *archisynagogos.* And she'll say, '*Archisynagogos*? Nah. That was just my husband's title.' "

THE WRITING ON THE WALL

To focus on the work of a handful of scholars is necessarily to leave aside the work of scores of others. And there are, literally, scores. Their research by now covers just about every conceivable aspect of the Hebrew Bible and the New Testament. It has spread deeply into the fields of history and theology and literary criticism. I once asked David Tracy, the prominent Catholic theologian, what he thought would be the result of feminism's encounter with religion, and he said simply, "The next intellectual revolution." That assessment may sound overblown, but it isn't. Phyllis Trible used the metaphor of a conversation between feminism and the Bible. Feminism's larger conversation with religion touches every aspect of it, leaves no subject off the table. It engages doctrine, liturgy, ministry, and leadership, and it engages them all at once.

Scholarly work on women and the Bible faces certain inherent problems, certain inherent risks. In my talks with people in the field, the same worries were voiced by one scholar after another. A fundamental one has to do with the distinction between deriving an interpretation *from* a text and reading an interpretation *into* a text. It is one thing for a contemporary personal agenda—a desire, say, to see women enjoy a position of full equality in religious institutions—to direct one's research focus. Agendas of one sort or another frequently drive scholarship. But can't they also get out of hand? Another concern is an issue raised by Bernadette Brooten: the sometimes facile comparisons made between Christianity and Judaism. This has already begun to stir animosity outside the field of biblical studies, as evidenced by an eloquent recent essay in the Jewish bimonthly *Tikkun*.

The range of scholarly output on matters involving women and the Bible has been enormously diverse. As in any academic endeavor, the work has been of uneven quality. Much of the research remains tentative and preliminary, and there are severe limits, given the sparseness of what is likely to be the available evidence, to what can ever be known with certainty. The most we can hope for, Bernadette Brooten has written, is "a quick glimpse through a crack in the door." What has been accomplished thus far? One achievement is simply the staking out of ground. Several decades ago no one was particularly concerned—indeed, the thought rarely occurred to anyone—that the entire academic biblical enterprise was based on what was known about men's lives, was one that generalized from men to all humanity. Those days are gone. Another achievement has been a new emphasis on the sheer variety of thought and practice which sometimes existed within ancient religious groups. Scholars who perhaps went searching after some lost Golden Age—driven by the "earlier-is-better" bias that seems to be a characteristic of human thought—have stumbled into worlds that are more confused and complex than they may have anticipated, worlds that are in that sense not unlike our own. Yet another achievement is simply this: leaving aside the specific details, scholars have gone a long way toward bringing women in biblical and early Christian times into sharper relief. They have also shown how meaning has been shaded by the lacquer of interpretation. A good distillation of much of the research on women can be found in *The Women's Bible Commentary,* edited by Carol A. Newsom and Sharon H. Ringe.

Perhaps the most important lesson offered by the work of feminist biblical scholars comes in the form of a reminder: that in religion, as in other spheres, circumstances have not always been as we see them now. Evolution occurs. Some things, it turns out, are *not* sacred. This point may be obvious, but with respect to religion, especially, it is frequently overlooked—and, in fact, sometimes hotly denied. Whatever one believes about the nature of their origin, the handful of immutable precepts at any religion's core are embedded in a vast pulp of tradition, interpretation, and practice. And that pulp bears an all-too-human character. It is variously diminished, augmented, scarred, sculpted, and otherwise shaped by powerful human forces in every society and every time period through which it passes. Sometimes the change occurs slowly and almost invisibly. Sometimes it happens quickly and right before one's eyes, as I believe it is happening now—the proliferation of feminist scholarship on the Bible being both consequence and cause.

I write these last words on the day of my daughter's first communion in a denomination that still restricts the role of women, and I write them in the expectation that with respect to the position of women, matters will not remain—will simply not be able to remain—as in some places we see them now; in the expectation, to employ a biblical turn, that the present way's days are numbered.

Handmaid or Feminist?

*More and more people around the world are worshipping Mary—and it's led to a
holy struggle over what she really stands for*

Richard N. Ostling

When her womb was touched by eternity 2,000 years ago, the Virgin Mary of Nazareth uttered a prediction: "All generations will call me blessed." Among all the women who have ever lived, the mother of Jesus Christ is the most celebrated, the most venerated, the most portrayed, the most honored in the naming of girl babies and churches. Even the Koran praises her chastity and faith. Among Roman Catholics, the Madonna is recognized not only as the Mother of God but also, according to modern Popes, as the Queen of the Universe, Queen of Heaven, Seat of Wisdom and even the Spouse of the Holy Spirit.

Mary may also be history's most controversial woman. For centuries Protestants have vehemently opposed her exaltation; papal pronouncements concerning her status have driven a wedge between the Vatican and the Eastern Orthodox Church. Conflict surrounds the notions that she remained ever a virgin, that she as well as Jesus was born without sin and that her sufferings at the Crucifixion were so great that she participated with her son in the redemption of humanity.

Yet even though the Madonna's presence has permeated the West for hundreds of years, there is still room for wonder—now perhaps more than ever. In an era when scientists debate the causes of the birth of the universe, both the adoration and the conflict attending Mary have risen to extraordinary levels. A grass-roots revival of faith in the Virgin is taking place worldwide. Millions of worshippers are flocking to her shrines, many of them young people. Even more remarkable are the number of claimed sightings of the Virgin, from Yugoslavia to Colorado, in the past few years.

These apparitions frequently embarrass clerics who have downplayed her role since the Second Vatican Council of 1962-65. "It's all the fashion," sniffs Father Jacques Fournier of Paris, reflecting skepticism about the populist wave of sightings. The hierarchy is wary about most of the recent claims of miraculous appearances; only seven Marian sightings in this century have received official church blessing.

Church concern has served to highlight the most interesting aspect of the growing popular veneration: the theological tug-of-war taking place over Mary's image. Feminists, liberals and activists have stepped forward with new interpretations of the Virgin's life and works that challenge the notion of her as a passive handmaid of God's will and exemplar of some contested traditional family values. "Mary wants to get off the pedestal," says Kathy Denison, a former nun and current drug-and-alcohol counselor in San Francisco. "She wants to be a vital human being."

"The world will recognize in due time that the defeat of communism came at the intercession of the mother of Jesus."

Whether they hold to those views or not, people the world over are traveling enormous distances to demonstrate in person their veneration of the Madonna. The late 20th century has become the age of the Marian pilgrimage. Examples:

At Lourdes, the biggest of France's 937 pilgrimage shrines, annual attendance in the past two years has jumped 10%, to 5.5 million. Many new visitors are East Europeans, now free to express their beliefs and to travel. Despite the inevitable attraction of Lourdes for the ill and aged, one-tenth of the faithful these days are 25 or younger. "We also have new kinds of pilgrimages," reports Loïc Bondu, a spokesman at the site. "They dance, they sing, they praise out loud. They're more exuberant."

In Knock, Ireland, where 15 people saw the Virgin a century ago, the lines of the faithful lengthened dramatically after Pope John Paul II paid a visit to the shrine in 1979. Since then, attendance has doubled, to 1.5 million people each year. To handle the influx, a new international airport was opened at Knock in 1986.

At Fátima, Portugal, the shrine marking the appearance of Mary before three children in 1917 draws a steady 4.5 million pilgrims a year from an ever widening array of countries. One million devotees turned out last May when John Paul made his second visit.

In Czestochowa, Poland, attendance at the shrine of the Black Madonna has increased to 5 million a year, rivaling Fátima and Lourdes, since John Paul's visit in 1979. Last August the Pope spoke there to 1 million Catholic youths.

In Emmitsburg, Md., attendance has doubled in the past year, to 500,000, at one of the oldest of 43 major Marian sites in the U.S., the National Shrine Grotto of Our Lady of Lourdes.

The boom at such long-established sites is almost overshadowed by the cult of the Virgin that has developed through new reports of her personal appearances, most spectacularly at Medjugorje, Yugoslavia. Before Yugoslavia's civil war erupted and travel became much more difficult

---

last September, more than 10 million pilgrims had flocked to the mountain village since the apparitions began in 1981. Six young peasants there claim that the Virgin has been imparting messages each evening for 10 years. Hundreds of ailments have been reported cured during visits to the region where the visitations take place. None of them have been verified, however, by the meticulous rules applied at Lourdes.

Paradoxically enough, the Medjugorje apparitions are a headache for the local Roman Catholic bishop, Pavao Zanic. He flatly asserts that "the Madonna has never said anything at Medjugorje." Our Lady, he snaps, has been turned into "a tourist attraction" and "a bank teller." The Vatican has intervened to determine whether Medjugorje is a fraud. Rome is officially noncommital while the case remains open but advises bishops not to sponsor pilgrimages to the site.

Less spectacular appearances by the Virgin have attracted streams of the faithful in locales from Central America to the Slavic steppes. In Nicaragua, President Violeta Barrios de Chamorro is a strong believer in a series of visitations by the Madonna in the small town of Cuapa, where Mary was witnessed by a church caretaker several times from May through October of 1980. During a 1981 Mass celebrated at the spot by the Archbishop of Managua, with some 30,000 people in attendance, believers say the sun changed colors. In Hrushiw, Ukraine, tens of thousands of people gathered in 1987 after a 12-year-old claimed to see the Madonna hovering over a church that had been shut down by the ruling communists.

More recently, the Madonna has been seen in the U.S. Devotees by the thousands have been flocking to the Mother Cabrini shrine near Denver, where Theresa Lopez, 30, says the Virgin has appeared to her four times in the past seven weeks. Marian apparitions were reported by parish coordinator Ed Molloy at St. Dominic's Church in Colfax, Calif., for 13 weeks in a row last year, and there was a surprise reappearance six weeks ago. In Our Lady of the Pillar Church of Santa Ana, Calif., Mary's image has been seen by Mexican immigrant Irma Villegas on the mosaics each morning since October, boosting attendance at 7 a.m. Mass enormously. Says Villegas: "Mary told me to talk to people about it so I did."

This being the late 20th century, Americans participating in these epiphanies are doing something about it: networking. Says

Mimi Kelly of Louisiana's Mir [Peace] Group: "People come back with a burning desire to do something good for mankind." Some 300 groups of Medjugorje believers exist across the U.S., publishing at least 30 newsletters and holding a dozen conferences a year. There are 70 telephone hot lines that feature the Virgin's messages from Yugoslavia: in Alabama dial MOM-MARY. Over the past 16 months a Texas foundation has put up 6,500 billboards inspired by Medjugorje. The huge signs say the Virgin appeared "to tell you God loves you."

No one can take more satisfaction in the growth of faith in the Virgin—or feel more unease at some of the pathways it has taken—than John Paul II. Devotion to Mary was ingrained in the Pope in his Polish homeland, where over the centuries the Madonna has been hailed for turning back troops of the Muslim Turks, Swedish Lutherans and, in 1920, Soviet Bolsheviks. The precious Black Madonna icon was a mobilizing symbol for the country's efforts to throw off communism, and is still a unifying image for the entire nation.

When he was made a bishop in 1958, John Paul emblazoned a golden *M* on his coat of arms and chose as his Latin motto *"Totus Tuus"* (All Yours)—referring to Mary, not Christ. Once he put on St. Peter's ring, John Paul made Mary's unifying power a centerpiece of his papal arsenal. He has visited countless Marian shrines during his globe trotting, and invokes the Madonna's aid in nearly every discourse and prayer that he delivers. He firmly believes that her personal intercession spared his life when he was shot at St. Peter's Square in Rome in 1981; the assassination attempt occurred on May 13, the exact anniversary of the first Fátima apparition.

Moreover, John Paul is firmly convinced, as are many others, that Mary brought an end to communism throughout Europe. His faith is rooted in the famed prophecies of Mary at Fátima in 1917. According to Sister Lucia, one of the children who claimed to see her, the Virgin predicted the rise of Soviet totalitarianism before it happened. In a subsequent vision, she directed the Pope and his bishops to consecrate Russia to her Immaculate Heart in order to bring communism to an end.

According to Lucia, papal attempts to carry out that consecration failed in 1942, '52 and '82. John Paul finally carried out Mary's directive correctly in

1984—and the very next year Mikhail Gorbachev's rise to power inaugurated the Soviet collapse. Says Father Robert Fox of the Fátima Family Shrine in Alexandria, S. Dak.: "The world will recognize in due time that the defeat of communism came at the intercession of the mother of Jesus."

With such a powerful institutional presence behind the effort to revive Mary's influence, it was to be expected, at least to some degree, that her popularity would grow. What was far less predictable was the outpouring of new interpretations of the Virgin's message for believers. In his writings, the Pope has given a conservative tilt to the meaning of Mary's life. The Pontiff's 1988 apostolic letter *Mulieris Dignitatem* (On the Dignity and Vocation of Women), citing positions taken at Vatican II, declared that "the Blessed Virgin came first as an eminent and singular exemplar of both virginity and motherhood." He extolled both states as ways women could find their dignity.

John Paul's traditionalist leanings find their most pointed expression in the Pope's continued refusal to consider the ordination of women as priests. The Vatican's argument is that if Christ had wanted women priests or bishops, Mary above all would have become one. On the other hand, John Paul does not argue that women must shun careers just because Mary was a homebody. Although the Pope lauds Mary for her submissiveness, it is in relation to God, not to male-dominated society.

But a much more aggressive view of Mary is emerging from feminist circles within the church, emphasizing her autonomy, independence and earthiness. Old-fashioned views of the Virgin, complains Sister Elizabeth Johnson, a Fordham University professor of theology, "make her appear above the earth, remote and passive," with "no sex and no sass." She adds, "There's still a strong element of that in the present hierarchy."

The revisionist views of the Madonna claim her as an active heroine who was variously an earth mother and a crusader for social justice. Mary, says Sister Lavinia Byrne, who works with non-Catholic groups in Britain, stood by loyally during her son's crucifixion while all but one of his male disciples ran away. Her agreement to bear the Son of God, argues Ivone Leal of Portugal's Commission on the Status of Women, was the act of "a strong woman. She followed her son's adventurous life, which was known to be doomed to failure, and always sustained him." Says French writer Nicole Echivard: "The Mother of God is the one from whom women are created in their preference for love and for people, rather than for power or machinery. Mary is the most liberated, the most determined, the most responsible of all mothers."

Others emphasize the political dimension. "Mary stood up for the poor and oppressed," says Sister Mary O'Driscoll, a professor at the Dominican order's Angelicum university in Rome. She and others point out that in the Magnificat (Luke 1), the pregnant Mary declared that God "has put down the mighty from their thrones and exalted those of low degree; he has filled the hungry with good things, and the rich he has sent empty away."

The activist interpretations do not necessarily run counter to Vatican teaching. Back in 1974 Pope Paul VI portrayed Mary as a "woman of strength who experienced poverty and suffering, flight and exile." John Paul II has said much the same thing, referring to Mary's "self-offering totality of love; the strength that is capable of bearing the greatest sorrows; limitless fidelity and tireless devotion to work."

But some other views strike dangerously close to fundamental Catholic truths. Among them:

Virginal Conception. The Gospels of *Matthew* and *Luke* state that Mary was a virgin and that Jesus was conceived miraculously without a human father. This belief is also included in the ancient creeds, and traditional Christians insist upon it. Some liberal Catholic scholars, however, increasingly follow liberal Protestant thinkers and doubt that this was literally true. Father Raymond Brown, the leading U.S. Catholic authority on the Bible, has declared the issue "unresolved." Jane Schaberg, who chairs the religion department at the University of Detroit, goes further. She contends, to traditionalist scorn, that the unwed Mary was impregnated by a man other than fiancé Joseph and that she was a liberated woman who was "not identified or destroyed by her relationship with men."

Perpetual Virginity. A Catholic and Orthodox tradition 15 centuries old holds that Mary was ever virgin, meaning that she and Joseph never had sex and that the "brothers" of Jesus mentioned in the

Bible were cousins. This idea consolidated the tradition of celibacy for priests and nuns. Protestants reject the belief as antisexual and lacking in biblical support. Liberal Catholic theologian Uta Ranke-Heinemann of Germany contends that the notion of a celibate clergy demeaned women by robbing Mary of sexuality and normal motherhood. This is, Ranke-Heinemann declares, "a monstrous product of neurotic sexual fantasy." Responds a Vatican official: "The church doesn't have problems with sex. The world does."

Immaculate Conception. This tenet holds that Mary was conceived without original sin. The concept was popular for centuries but was not defined as Catholic dogma by the papacy until 1854, partly in response to popular pressure stirred up by Marian apparitions. Unofficial belief adds that Mary lived a perfect life. Protestants insist the Bible portrays Jesus as the only sinless person. Marina Warner, author of *Alone of All Her Sex: The Myth and Cult of the Virgin Mary,* contends that Rome's dogma artificially sets Mary apart from the rest of the human race.

There is yet another kind of rethinking of Mary going on. Protestants see no biblical basis for praying to her for favors, and they believe veneration of her can slide into worship that is due to God alone. They also reject the idea that human beings, Mary included, can contribute to humanity's salvation. Nonetheless, some Protestants are softening aspects of their hostility. Church of England theologian John Macquarrie has proposed revisions of such dogmas as the Assumption of Mary into heaven, which could then be seen as a symbol of the redemption that awaits all believers. Theologian Donald Bloesch of the University of Dubuque says fellow conservative Protestants "need to see Mary as the pre-eminent saint" and "the mother of the church." Similar convergences will receive a thorough airing in February, when U.S. Catholic and Lutheran negotiators issue an accord, years in the making, on Mary's role.

The shift in the debate over Mary represents a delayed backlash against the influence of the Second Vatican Council, which made Mary emphatically subordinate to her son in church teachings. Prior to Vatican II, Popes had proclaimed Mary the Co-Redeemer with Jesus. During the council, bishops were under pres-

sure from the faithful to ratify the Co-Redeemer doctrine; instead they issued no decree on Mary at all. Rather she was incorporated into the *Constitution on the Church,* a move that placed the Virgin among the community of believers in Christ rather than in anything resembling a co-equal position.

The effects of that downplaying have rippled through the observances of the church to the point that Mary's statues have been removed from some sanctuaries and Catholic parishes have gradually reduced the traditional novena devotions to the Virgin. John Paul clearly thinks the reconsideration went too far, and his fellow venerators of Mary agree. In Eastern Europe, says Warsaw priest Roman Indrzejczyk, enthusiasm for Mary is no less than "a reaction to the matter-of-fact religiousness of the West."

Behind Vatican II's reconsideration of the Virgin and some of the uneasiness expressed over her populist revival, say feminists, is a concern over making Mary into a competitive divinity, a tradition common to many of the pagan religions that Christianity superseded. Remarks Warner: "The great terror is that she will be worshipped above her son."

Even for feminists who have no desire to go that far, the idea of a return, however marginal, to that notion of supernatural feminine power is alluring. Says Sandra Schneiders, a professor at the Graduate Theological Union in Berkeley: "There has been a stupendous upsurge in goddess research and the feminine divinity as an antecedent to the male god. It's not unrelated that the Virgin Mary's popularity has also increased. Judeo-Christianity has been exclusively male, leaving a gap that cries out for feminine divinity."

It seems clear, though, that the world is crying out for many things from Mary, and in some fashion is receiving them. Devoted mother or militant, independent female or suffering parent, she remains one of the most compelling and evocative icons of Western civilization. Renewed expressions of her vitality and relevance are signs that millions of people are still moved by her mystery and comforted by the notion of her caring. Whatever aspect of Mary they choose to emphasize and embrace, those who seek her out surely find something only a holy mother can provide.

—With reporting by Hannah Bloch/ New York, Greg Burke/Medjugorje, Robert T. Zintl/Rome, and other bureaus

Muslims and Byzantines

Three orders emerged after Rome's fall. Germanic kingdoms filled the vacuum left by Rome in central and western Europe. In the Balkans and Asia Minor the eastern remnants of Rome evolved into the Byzantine empire. The Middle East, North Africa, and much of the Iberian Peninsula fell to an expanding Arab empire. Each area developed a unique civilization, based in each instance upon a distinctive form of religion—Roman Catholicism in much of Europe, Orthodox Christianity in the Byzantine sphere of influence, and Islam in the Arab world. Each placed its unique stamp upon the classical tradition to which all three fell heir. The articles in this unit, however, concentrate on the Byzantine and Muslim civilizations. The medieval culture of Europe is treated in the next unit.

Western perceptions of Islam and Arabic civilization have been clouded by ignorance and bias, as "The World of Islam" points out. To European observers during the medieval period, Islam seemed a misguided version of Christianity! In the wake of Arab conquests, Islam increasingly came to represent terror and devastation, a dangerous force loosed upon Christendom. Reacting out of fear and hostility, Christian authors were reluctant to acknowledge the learning and high culture of the Arabs.

Muslim commentators could be equally intolerant. Describing Europeans, one of them wrote: "They are most like beasts than like men. . . . Their temperaments are frigid, their humors raw, their bellies gross . . . they lack keenness of understanding . . . and are overcome by ignorance and apathy."

The stereotypes formed in early encounters between Christians and Muslims survived for generations. Centuries of hostility have tended to obscure the extent of cultural exchange between the Arab world and the West. Indeed, as historian William H. McNeill has observed, Muslims have been written out of European history.

However, the domain of Islam encroached upon Europe at too many points for the two cultures to remain mutually exclusive. In western Europe, Islam swept over Spain, crossed the Pyrenees, and penetrated France; in the central Mediterranean it leapt from Tunis to Sicily and then into Italy; in eastern Europe, Islam finally broke through Asia Minor and into the Balkans and the Caucasus. It is useful to recall, too, that early Islam was exposed to Jewish, Christian, and classical influences. History and geography determined that there would be much cross-fertilization between Islam and the West.

Yet there is no denying the originality and brilliance of Islamic civilization. For a start, there is the religion of Muhammad, unquestionably one of the world's most influential faiths. Additional evidence of Arabic creativity can be found in the visual arts, particularly in the design and decoration of the great mosques. The Arabs also made significant contributions to the philosophy and practice of history.

The medieval West borrowed extensively from the Arabs. The magnificent centers of Islamic culture—Baghdad, Cairo, Cordoba, and Damascus—outshone the cities of Christendom. As we learn from "The Rise of the Umayyad Dynasty in Spain," their administration of Andalusia was a model of successful governance. Islamic scholars surpassed their Christian counterparts in astronomy, mathematics, and medicine—perhaps because the Arab world was more familiar than medieval Europe with the achievements of classical Greece. (European scholars regained access to the Greek heritage at least partially through translations from the Arabic!)

As for the Byzantine Empire, it was for nearly 1,000 years a Christian bulwark against Persians, Arabs, and Turks. But it also made important cultural contributions. The distinctive icons of Byzantine artists set the pattern for subsequent visualizations of Christ in the West. Byzantine missionaries and statesmen spread Orthodox Christianity, with its unique tradition of Caesaro-Papism, to Russia. Byzantine scholars and lawmakers preserved much of the classical heritage. Even hostile Islam was subject to a constant flow of ideas from the Byzantines. Alexander Kazhdan discusses the strengths and weaknesses of Byzantine civilization in "Byzantium: The Emperor's New Clothes?" Michael Antonucci attributes the longevity of the Eastern Empire to its astute diplomacy in "War by Other Means: The Legacy of Byzantium."

Looking Ahead: Challenge Questions

How do medieval hostilities between the Arabs and the West color relations between the two in the modern world?

Do the articles in this unit betray any bias toward Islam and the Arabs? Describe any that you encounter.

How did the Arabs govern their holdings in Spain?

Was Byzantine civilization merely an extension of late Roman culture, or was it a new departure? Explain.

How did the Byzantines influence the development of Russia?

Byzantium: The Emperor's New Clothes?

Eastern Europe and Russian are the subject of intense scrutiny at present as questions of power, identity, and political structures are pursued at breath-taking speed. 'History Today' contributes a commentary on these events. . . . Alexander Kazhdan, senior research associate at Dumbarton Oaks, Washington D.C., considers the influence of totalitarianism and meritocracy in the Byzantine empire—and its relationship to the growth of the Russian and other successor states in the East.

Alexander Kazhdan

The state of Byzantium, the so-called Byzantine empire, has never existed; the term was invented in the sixteenth century to designate the empire the capital of which was Constantinople, the city on the Bosphorus, which was supposedly founded in 330 and destroyed by the Ottoman Turks in 1453. Byzantion (in the Latinised form Byzantium) was the name it held before being renamed by and in honour of the Emperor Constantine the Great (324–37), and throughout the Middle Ages the Byzantines were the citizens of Constantinople only, not the subjects of the emperor who reigned in Constantinople. These subjects did not even notice that they stopped being Romans and began being Byzantines—they continued to consider themselves Romans until they woke up under the rule of the sultans.

Thus the nomenclature itself is confused, and some purist scholars prefer to call the population of the Constantinopolitan empire Romans or Greeks, and terms such as 'the Eastern Roman empire' or 'Greco-Roman law' are still in use. But this is only the beginning of the problem, and we are in trouble when trying to define the date of birth of Byzantium. Was it 330, when Constantine celebrated the inauguration of his new residence on the Bosphorus? Was it 395, when the Emperor Theodosius I

died and bequeathed the empire to two different rulers, his sons Arkadios in Constantinople (395–408) and Honorius (395–423) in Milan and later Ravenna? Was it in 476, when the Herulian (or Hun) Odoacer deposed the last western emperor, Romulus Augustulus, and sent his regalia to Constantinople. Or was it in 554, when Justinian I (527–65), after having reconquered Italy, issued the Pragmatic Sanction and determined the status of this old-new province? None of these events had a lasting effect on the empire. All we can say is that Byzantium was not born in a day, and the changes were various and gradual.

The idea that radical ethnic changes gave birth to Byzantium was popular in the nineteenth century and still remains popular among some East European scholars; the Slavs are said to have invaded the Roman empire, settled in Greece and Asia Minor, rejuvenated the decrepit empire, become the backbone of the new victorious army and, even more, that of the Orthodox monarchy. Unquestionably, the Slavs invaded the Balkans in the first half of the seventh century. They left behind some traces in Balkan place-names. The Slavic influence on the administration, legal and fiscal systems, and military organisation is another matter—there is no data for such an assertion.

Territorial changes are more evident. In rough outline they coincided with the

Slavic invasion, and took place during the seventh century. The Mediterranean Roman empire disappeared, and was replaced by a new formation, concentrated around Greece and Asia Minor, the areas dominated by the Greek language and culture. But could not the empire retain its old character within a more restricted framework?

Religious changes seem to be attached to the activity of a single man, the Emperor Constantine. Tradition has it that he saw a vision of the cross and promulgated the Milan edict liberating the Christian church from discrimination. For medieval chroniclers this was a radical turning point, the creation of the Christian empire. We know now that the edict of tolerance was issued before Constantine, in 311, by the Emperor Galerius, whom Constantine's staunch flatterers depicted as a scoundrel. We also know that Constantine did not completely abandon pagan cults, particularly the worship of the solar deity (or deities), and that when Constantine, on his deathbed, formally accepted Christianity, he accepted the new religion in its heretical denomination, Arianism. Moreover, paganism regained momentum soon after Constantine, during the reign of Julian the Apostate (361–63). At the court of the Very Christian Emperor, Theodosius I, pagan politicians were influential, and the fifth century saw a revival of pagan culture represented by such men as the

philosopher Proklos and the historian Zosimos. Even in the sixth century, paganism was alive in the countryside, and the aristocratic intelligentsia, while paying lipservice to the official creed, stuck to the ancient philosophical and cultural traditions. Thus, the question arises: which phenomenon is more momentous: Constantine's cautious baptism or the seventh-century triumph of Christianity that had behind it the gigantic work of the church fathers who had elaborated the system of the new belief? The Trinitarian and Christological disputes, out of which this system emerged, came to halt only in the middle of the seventh century.

The changes in the administrative system are the most evasive, and some scholars place the roots of these changes in the reign of Justinian I, or even earlier. The search for these roots is a futile one—any important phenomenon has its roots in the past. What matters is not embryonic development but the critical mass. It is, however, very difficult to measure the critical masses of historical process, especially for the seventh century, notorious for its scarcity of available sources. Of course, Byzantium remained a monarchy in and after the seventh century, and was, at least in theory, administered from Constantinople, but it now seems sure that the new administrative system of districts, the so-called 'themes', appeared in the seventh century. The exarchates of Ravenna and of Carthage, organised by the end of the sixth century, were the direct predecessors of the themes; the themes were powerful organisations until the mid-ninth century and decided the destiny of the throne of Constantinople. Indeed, all major uprisings until the ninth century were based on themes.

In central government during the same seventh century, late Roman departments were replaced by new offices. The main functionaries such as praetorian prefect and *magister officiorum* disappeared, and the central bureaux worked under the supervision of the so-called *logothetai*. Some late Roman designations survived, although often in a changed sense. For example, the Byzantine hypatos-consul was worlds away from the magnificent consuls of the sixth century, and the Byzantine *magistros* was a title, rather than an office, like the late Roman *magister*. Some change of function must have occurred beneath the veneer of this terminological stability.

Power over God and Man; the Empress Irene, 752-803, whose achievements during a tumultuous career included the re-establishment of icon workship and the deposition of her own son Constantine as emperor in her bid for sole imperial power.

4. MUSLIMS AND BYZANTINES

And did society remain late Roman? We can divide the question into two sections: the urban and the rural. It seems that in the seventh century the Roman provincial city was in decline and that when it reappeared by around the tenth century, it had a new, medieval, character. Archaeological excavations are usually witness to the decline of cities, and the findings of coins from the second half of the seventh century become rare. In addition the setting of hagiographical literature shifts from the provincial city to either the capital or the countryside. The available data about the countryside between the seventh and late ninth centuries are scanty, and we are forced to build our conclusions more on the silence of our sources than on direct evidence. Silence, however, is fairly evocative. We hear little about large estates, slaves and *coloni* of this period; the most discussed case is that of St Philaretos who is said in his *Vita* to have possessed approximately fifty allotments (*proasteia*). Such figures are usually exaggerated, and we cannot take them for granted, the more so since Philaretos was the son of a peasant and could perfectly well manage his team of ploughing oxen. On the other hand, the so-called Farmers' Law, the Byzantine counterpart of the western *leges,* deals with free peasants. Certainly, the text is enigmatic, imprecisely dated and probably reflects some local conditions, but this is what we have—direct evidence about the free peasantry and very questionable data concerning large estates.

If we assume that the leading class of the ancient *polis,* the urban landowners, disappeared, or at least lost its former significance, a strange phenomenon coinciding with those changes becomes clearer: the disappearance of family names. Rare after the fourth century but still known in the sixth century, they are practically unknown between the seventh century and the end of the ninth century. Does this mean that the aristocracy or at least the concept of aristocracy ceased to exist? Certainly, we do not know of any powerful family from this period, and at the end of the tenth century Basil II (976–1025) wrote with astonishment and indignation about those families which had been pre-eminent for some seventy to one hundred years; so the phenomenon must have been a new one in his reign.

Thus all information converges on the seventh century; and although it is far from extensive or dependable, it allows us to hypothesise that in the seventh century some slow changes occurred and that establishing the seventh century as a watershed at least does not conflict with the available evidence.

But why should we bother our heads about Byzantium? Today we take for granted the impact of ancient cultural traditions—they are considered to be the foundation of western civilisation. In our perception of the past, Byzantium plays the role of a stepdaughter, a Cinderella; we allow it to store and transmit the *oeuvre* of great Greek minds. Byzantine culture is seen not as an achievement in its own right, but as an imitation and copy of the great classical paragon. The art has been looked at and the literature has been read with this presupposition in mind; as non-creative, repetitive, slavishly following ancient originals, disconnected from contemporary problems, concentrating on ridiculous theological niceties, and so forth. And since the purpose of their art, literature, philosophy, law and science was to imitate the great predecessors, Byzantine culture allegedly knew no development.

But was this really true? Bearing in mind the social and political changes of the seventh century already alluded to, can we see a cultural transformation taking place at the same time? Certainly building activity almost stopped, literary work contracted and even the most medieval genre, hagiography, was almost nonexistent in the eighth century. Manuscripts copied at that time are extremely few, and philosphical thought came to a halt. Thus, as in the West, the Byzantine Middle Ages began with a cultural gap that was followed by a revival around 800.

What is interesting in this revival is its social background: the vast majority of the known authors of this time belonged to the monastic world. But from the mid-ninth century onwards a different type of *literatus* came to the fore—the imperial or ecclesiastical functionary. In the twelfth century, again, a new type of writer emerges: the professional author, frequently called the 'beggar poet' since his existence depended upon the gifts and stipends from the emperor and others, and soliciting these gifts occupied a substantial part of his concerns and of his poetry.

The genres of literature were also in flux; in the twelfth century the saintly biography went through a crisis, very few contemporary biographies were produced, the writers preferring to revise old hagiographical texts, and Eustathios of Thessalonike, a rhetorician and commentator on Homer, issued a *vita* that was, in its core, a denial of traditional hagiographical virtues. This *vita* of a (fake?) saint, Philotheos of Opsikion, was a eulogy to a rich married man living in the world. However, while hagiography was fading a new genre appeared, or rather was revived, after a long absence: the romance. Poetic and prose panegyrics of secular leaders were of no significance before the eleventh century; the ethical ideal had remained either monastic or imperial. And the memoir did not come into being before Michael Psellos in the eleventh century.

The well-entrenched concept of Byzantine cultural uniformity does not stand up to examination, not only because Byzantium's cultural development was in a state of flux. A distinction can be drawn not only between difference generations but also between members of the same generation of different class and with different taste.

A classic example of such a distinction is a group of addresses to the emperor Alexios III Angelos (1195–1203) celebrating his victory over rebellious John Komnenos the Fat. Four orations survive; three of them are traditional, that is lacking in concrete detail, symbolic and full of propaganda. The fourth, by Nicholas Mesarites, is rich in details, dynamic and ironic. Mesarites does not strive to exclude realty in the interests of a higher moral truth; his aim is to make actual events vivid.

But if Byzantine culture was not a plain imitation of antiquity, then what was the difference between the two, and what was the former's contribution? Antiquity is a broad notion whatever characterisation we formulate, and what we now accept as essential may be perceived by other scholars in other times as incidental. There was clearly a considerable transitional period between the Roman and the Byzantine worlds. On the other hand, Byzantium is not 'linear', one-dimensional and simplistic; moreover, it was consciously orientated toward ancient culture. The Byzantines called themselves Romans, believed in this definition, and did not see a demarcation line between themselves and antiquity. Homer was their poet. Aristotle their philosopher, and Augustus their emperor. In their writings they followed ancient

Greek (although they spoke vernacular), and they filled their works with ancient quotations, proverbs and dead words. The cultural line between Rome and Constantinople is as indistinct as the chronological line between them.

There are, however, some points of difference which seem obvious. Byzantium was Christian, antiquity pagan; Byzantium was uniform, antiquity variegated; Byzantium was autocratic, antiquity republican. Unfortunately none of these statements is completely correct: Christianity was born in antiquity and inherited many ancient ideas; Byzantium's uniformity was relative; and both Hellenistic and Roman monarchies existed within the framework of ancient civilisation. But relative as they are, these oppositions reflect partial truth and highlight the direction of search.

Another set of obvious or half-obvious dichotomies refers to a different aspect of reality. Marxist theoreticians contrast ancient slave ownership with Byzantine feudalism. The word 'feudalism' is too questionable to be a useful tool of analysis, but it is plausible that the forms of exploitation differed between antiquity and Byzantium, even though slaves (and not only the household slaves but slaves in the fields, at the herds and in the workshops) were numerous in Byzantium. We can also say that the urban life so typical of antiquity lost its role in Byzantium and that the family not the *municipum* formed the main social unit and determined the structure of many other units.

Before we take the final step and attempt to define along very rough lines, the 'Byzantine particularity', let us shift from chronological to territorial distinctions, let us juxtapose not Byzantium and antiquity but Byzantium and the western medieval world. Of course, the western medieval world was diverse, nevertheless, some feeling of unity prevailed: the Byzantines, at least from the eleventh century onward, spoke of the 'Latins' as a specific group, differing from the Byzantines insofar as their beliefs, costumes and habits were concerned. For the westerners as well, the 'schismatic Greeks' formed a separate set of people; one could marry a Greek woman, trade in Greek ports, serve at the court of Constantinople, but the gap remained and even widened as time went on.

From the viewpoint of the westerners the Byzantines entertained a wrong theology, believing that the Holy Spirit pro-

ceeded from God the Father only; they were too bookish and bad soldiers; they adorned their churches with icons and not the sculptured crucifix, and their priests were married. But there was one point that usually dominated in the mutual contrasting of two societies.

In 1147 crusading armies arrived in Constantinople. The Greek historian, John Kinnamos, who was almost contemporaneous with the event, described them in great detail. Among other things, he noticed with a subdued surprise that:

> Their offices (or dignities) are peculiar and resemble distinctions descending from the height of the empire, since it is something most noble and surpasses all others. A duke outranks a count; a king a duke; and the emperor, a king. The inferior naturally yields to the superior, supports him in war, and obeys in such matters.

What struck Kinnamos was the hierarchical structure of western aristocracy, the system of vertical links.

In 1189 Isaac II (1185–95) sent an embassy to Frederick Barbarossa. The Byzantine historian, Niketas Choniates, relates that Frederick ordered the Greek ambassadors to be seated in his presence and had chairs placed in the hall even for their servants. By so doing, comments Choniates, the German ruler made fun of the Byzantines, who failed to take into consideration the virtue of nobility of different members of society and who appraised the whole population by the same measure, like a herdsman who drove all the hogs into the same pigsty.

Western society was perceived by both the Greeks and the Latins as one organised on the aristocratic and hierarchical foundation, Byzantine society as 'democratic', although in Byzantium the word *'demokratia'* had a pejorative tinge and was usually applied to the domination of the *demoi,* the unbridled mobs.

To sum up, Byzantium was an atomistic society with the family as its cornerstone. The man was primarily the member of the family and not of the *municipium* (as he was in Greco-Roman antiquity) or community or guild (as he was to be in the medieval West). Formal wedding ceremonies, prohibition of divorce, abolition of concubinage; all these contrasted with the 'free' late Roman family. Lineage played an insignificant role, and vertical (hierarchical) links remained practically unknown. Small family-like monasteries were common, and family-orientated terminology perme-

ated both political and ecclesiastical relations.

The aristocratic principle was underdeveloped. This does not mean that all the emperor's subjects were equal in rights and wealth, even though western observers kept repeating disparagingly that they were; in the tenth century, for instance, the German ambassador Liutprand asserted that all the participants in the imperial procession in Constantinople wore shabby and frayed costumes. The principle of inequality in Byzantium differed from that of the West; the Byzantines created a meritocracy based not on individual's 'blood' or origin but on his place in the bureaucratic machine. A system which, while less stable than nobility in the West, enabled more vertical mobility. This does not mean that they were less arrogant, but it does mean that, while less restricted by tradition, they were less defiant of the emperor's omnipotence.

The imperial power was both feeble and strong. It was strong since the emperor, in theory, was not restricted by law; he was the law itself. He combined in his hands legislative, administrative and judicial power, was the supreme army commander and claimed control of ideology. But he was poorly protected against schemes and plots, and half of all the Byzantine emperors ended their rule as victims of violence. Feeble as individuals (certainly some emperors had a strong personality) they were omnipotent as symbols of government; the emperors themselves might be criticised, but the principle of unlimited monarchical power was never questioned.

In practice, of course, everything was more complex, and many an emperor met social and religious resistence, even blunt bureaucratic intransigence. However, we can call the Byzantine empire a totalitarian state. And it was the only totalitarian state of the European Middle Ages. As such, Byzantium gives us material to observe a totalitarian state over a long period and to analyse its liabilities and assets, its roots and mechanism.

Several points are of importance. Was the totalitarian organisation of power interconnected with the atomistic structure of society? It seems quite plausible that western system of vertical and horizontal bonds created a better protection for the man, certainly for a nobleman, against the supreme power that condescended to respect the noble as the king's peer. I do not think that the western *villanus* was better protected than Byzantine *paroikos,* but probably western guilds gave more protection to their members than did Byzantine *somateia,* their counterpart. At any rate, atomistic feelings and fears, rejection of friendship and emphasis on individual way of salvation (rather than the role of sacraments) could contribute to the concept of the lonely man, a helpless slave in front of the powerful emperor, a toy of relentless doom. The political misfortunes of ever-shrinking Byzantium reinforced this concept; late Byzantine philosophers were unable to grasp why the most Christian, the 'chosen people' should be exposed to the crashing attacks of the Ottoman Turks.

How did the totalitarian state function? So much ink has been spilled to describe the unwieldy and rotten Byzantine governmental mechanism, and undoubtedly there is much truth in these two adjectives—based on the bitter words of contemporary critics. But there are some stubborn facts that cry out for explanation. How could the Eastern Roman empire, where centralised authority was more strongly developed than in the West, repel the same barbarian attacks that subdued Italy and Gaul? Why was it that, until the twelfth century, totalitarian Byzantium was economically and culturally ahead of the West? A century ago Russian Byzantinists developed a theory according to which the Byzantine emperors, especially in the tenth century, protected the peasantry and the village community against the so-called *dynatoi* ('powerful', i.e. the wealthy and influential members of the ruling class) and thus secured the existence of a strong army and of plentiful taxes. When, in the eleventh century, the emperors yielded to western feudalism, abandoned 'the minor brethren', and turned away from the principles of the Orthodox (and Slavic) monarchy, the decline of Byzantium began. This theory is political more than scholarly. The tenth-century state did not protect the peasantry either (it protected state taxes that were burdensome enough and the centralised power over the countryside), nor was the period of the eleventh and twelfth centuries that of decline. On the contrary, it was a period of economic growth and cultural upsurge. But in spite of all its weakness, totalitarian Byzantium managed to flourish during several centuries while the split-up ('federal') West suffered from shortages of food, dress and housing.

The problem is intensified by Byzantine ideological duplicity. A striking example is the fate of Roman law in Byzantium, the Roman law summarised and codified by Justinian I during the last stage of the late Roman empire. It was never abolished, although some attempts to make it simpler were made. Byzantine legal text-books adhered to Roman law, repeating, time and again, formulations that were in disaccord with reality. For instance, the official law-book of the ninth century, the *Basilika,* described administrative institutions that existed during the sixth century and had ceased to exist by the ninth. Furthermore, the agrarian terminology of the *Basilika,* translated from Latin into Greek, applied to no Byzantine reality, and often made no sense whatever. Whereas Roman law reflected the principles of the legal state, protecting individual rights and private ownership, the Byzantine empire did not give any legal protection to its subjects. Emperors could execute any citizen without trial and could confiscate any land without argument. Texts of the tenth century state that any land on which the emperor had put his foot could be taken from its owner. As more private documents have been published in recent decades, we can see more clearly that the Byzantine law of things and law of obligations deviated from Roman norms and that Byzantine tribunals acted on principles distinct from the Roman; but the words often remained the same, and private ownership of land was repeatedly affirmed in legal text-books.

This contrast between theory and practice had a strong impact on Byzantine mentality. I am not referring to the notorious Byzantine diplomacy or the lack of fealty, of which the Latin neighbours accused them; indeed I doubt that such accusations could be taken at face value. In fact they can be applied equally to many medieval leaders. Much more substantial was the Byzantine skill of allusion. Of course, their literature is in no way short of direct and open invectives against political and ideological enemies, but they loved, and knew how to say without saying, to evoke by an apparently occasional hint a broad gamut of emotions. They were much more attentive towards those details and nuances which usually escape modern understanding. One of the most drastic examples is the Byzantine insistence on the resemblance of their icons to sitter or subject, whereas modern art historians

are unable to perceive individual elements in Byzantine icons and are inclined to deny such resemblance. Equally, we are unable to catch allusions, political and personal, in their writings, particularly in their favourite game, the use of ancient and Biblical imagery.

Two conclusions can be drawn from this observation. In the first place, the Byzantines frequently cared more about nuances than general statements. Any totalitarian or uniform ideology possesses an established set of concepts which are above discussion; Byzantine ideology was no exception, with a set of political or religious formulae, perceived by everyone as final truth and rarely, if ever, discussed. But they certainly had discussions, and very vehement ones. These usually began over slight terminological differences, and it gradually becomes clear that behind such niceties loomed crucial dissentions. We are facing a paradox: an allegedly uniform ideology did not prevent the Byzantines from bitter disputes, only these disputes seemed to be limited to innocuous and insignificant problems: should the churches be adorned with images? Was the Holy Spirit proceeding from God the Father only or from the Son as well? How could Christ be at the same time the sacrifice offered to God, the priest offering the sacrifice, and God receiving it? Can one see the divine light, the divine energy with sensual eyes? And so on.

In the second place, we must reconsider the role of Byzantine intellectuals. Their indiscriminate eulogies addressed to those in power sound abominably grovelling to our ears. But as soon as we become acquainted with the nuances and methods of the rhetoric it is possible to strip them of the shroud of uniformity and flattery and understand the profound content concealed beneath the surface. Of course, most of their allusions have been lost in the passage of time and still remain incomprehensible to the modern reader, but even that little part of them that can be deciphered compels us to discard the traditional image of literary barrenness.

The Byzantine world was totalitarian; many will agree with such a statement. But it is hard to accept this heritage; we are more willing to reject it, to restrict the survival of the Byzantine 'axe and icon' to Eastern Europe, Slavic and/or Communist countries. The recent celebration of the millenium of the Russian Church sharpened this point yet more.

Totalitarian Russia seems to be as natural a successor of totalitarian Byzantium as the Russian icon is the heir of Byzantine images or Russian obscuring eloquence is the heir of Byzantine rhetorics.

The problem is once again, however, not that simple. Kievan Rus certainly had contacts with Byzantium. But did it experience Byzantium's direct impact beyond the ecclesiastical sphere? In fact Kievan temporal society absorbed very little of Byzantium: their weaponry came from the West, their glass producers followed western, not Byzantine recipes, their political structure was as distanced from the Byzantine one as possible. Political marriages of high rank between the two countries were almost unknown. Kievan Rus as a state did not travel the path the Byzantines had worn.

Only in the fifteenth century when Russian grand princes began to build up their centralised monarchy did they discover their Byzantine ancestry; Russia did not inherit Byzantine totalitarianism but used the model for their political ends. The process was not genetic or automatic—it was a part of the ideological programme, whether consciously or unconsciously applied.

It would be very tempting to assume that only those countries (Bulgaria, Serbia, Rumania, Russia) that were in direct contact with Byzantium developed a tendency to totalitarianism—but I am afraid that this is not true. Not only did Russia become totalitarian only after it had severed direct relations with Byzantium, (when it was separated from Byzantium by Mongolian seminomads and Italian trade republics which dominated the Black Sea coast), but there were also countries that for centuries had such contact and did not become totalitarian: Armenia, Georgia, Hungary, Italy. On the other hand, totalitarian governments could be traced in various European countries whose contacts with Byzantium were very slight, such as Spain and France, from the fifteenth century onwards. The French model of the Sun King followed the Byzantine paragon, and it is not sheer chance that sixteenth-century France contributed so much to the development of Byzantine studies.

Byzantium was an interesting historical experiment. It teaches us how totalitarian systems work, what a meritocracy ('nomenklatura') is, what the place of intellectuals in a totalitarian state is, and who owns the land and the means of production. It shows the advantages and disadvantages of the totalitarian system, and reveals under the surface of stagnation the suppressed class of political and ideological contrasts.

FOR FURTHER READING:

Romilly Jenkins, *Byzantium: the Imperial Centuries. A.D. 610–1071* (Weidenfeld & Nicolson, 1966); Cyril Mango, *Byzantium. The Empire of New Rome* (Weidenfeld & Nicolson, 1980); Arnold Toynbee, *Constantine Porphyrogenitus and his World* (Oxford University Press, 1973); Alexander Ḳazhdan and Ann Wharton Epstein, *Change in Byzantine Culture in the Eleventh and Twelfth Centuries* (University of Berkeley Press, Los Angeles, 1985); R. Browning, *The Byzantine Empire* (Charles Scribner's Sons, New York, 1980); N. G. Wilson, *Scholars of Byzantium* (The Johns Hopkins University Press, Baltimore, 1983).

War by Other Means: The Legacy of Byzantium

Michael Antonucci

Michael Antonucci is a freelance writer specialising in military and intelligence history.

The conventional view of diplomacy is one of negotiation and compromise leading to a settlement of differences. However, history often shatters this view. The conduct of international relations is also a struggle between competing national interests . . . and diplomacy can be as potent a weapon as any army. To alter Clausewitz's maxim, international relations can often be war conducted by other means. The Serbian government arms ethnic Serbs in Bosnia. The United States supports Kurds seeking the ousting of Saddam Hussein. The Soviets persuade Cubans to go to Angola while setting up nuclear freeze groups in Western Europe. The Chinese support the Khmer Rouge to nullify Vietnamese authority in Cambodia. Measures such as these are efforts to defeat an enemy's intentions without the risk and costs of overt military force. These international actions have become so commonplace they are considered legitimate tools in the foreign policy repertoire.

No nation-state did more to advance the cause of activist foreign policy than the Byzantine empire. For over 1,100 years it survived and expanded by skilfully manipulating opponents through its intricate diplomacy. Hundreds of years before Machiavelli, Byzantine historian, John Kinnamos, wrote: 'Since many and various matters lead toward one end, victory, it is a matter of indifference which one uses to reach it.' An examination of Byzantine diplomatic tactics could help today's diplomats understand the motivations of their counterparts at the negotiating table.

The Byzantines were the inheritors of the Roman empire. The Emperor Constantine founded a new capital on the site of the ancient city of Byzantium in AD 330, renaming it Constantinople. Strategically situated, the city stood at the crossroads of Europe and Asia, where commerce between the Black Sea and the Mediterranean could be regulated. By the year 395, the empire had been permanently divided into eastern and western halves, each ruled by a coequal emperor. When the last emperor of Rome was deposed in 476, the 'Roman' Emperor in Constantinople continued the imperial tradition.

As the years passed, the Byzantines were continuously beset by a flood of hostile peoples who coveted the lands and riches of the empire. Huns, Goths, Persians, Slavs, Arabs, Bulgars, Normans and others each had a turn at destroying the empire but all were turned away. With a military force that never numbered more than 140,000 soldiers, the Byzantines employed an activist foreign policy which enabled them to expand their influence throughout Central Europe and Italy while preserving the Graeco-Roman culture for posterity. Oddly enough, one of the strongest Byzantine influences was in the field of

The Bulgarian Khan Krum feasting after victory over the 9th-century Byzantine emperor Nicephorus – but more often than not the Byzantines got the better of 'barbarians' by guile and diplomacy.

Popegeld: Michael VIII (1261-81), who forestalled an Angevin attack on Byzantium by a large shipment of money to Pope Nicholas III.

diplomacy, as Venice, Russia, Ottoman Turkey and the Balkan countries all adopted Byzantine practices.

The Byzantine emperor established no permanent missions in foreign countries though he usually sent the same highly trusted nobles and clerics on his embassies. As a matter of practice, these ambassadors were familiar with the countries they visited, either through previous travels or through their ethnic backgrounds. Even so, they were thoroughly briefed before they set out. Not only were they drilled on the details of the goals to be achieved, but they were also apprised of current developments in the court they were visiting. Constant contact was maintained with Constantinople, and diplomatic missions could sometimes last up to a year. The Byzantines probably initiated the practice of sending regular diplomatic reports home to the government.

What separated Byzantium from other nations of the early Middle Ages was its active involvement in manipulating internal events in other countries. Today we take for granted the existence of government agencies which gather and interpret intelligence, cultivate support in foreign circles and perhaps even instigate rebel-

lion. To find such a sophisticated and centralised arrangement as early as the sixth century is truly remarkable.

To aid in dealing with other nations, the Byzantines established an organisation called the 'Bureau of Barbarians', which gathered information from every source imaginable (even priests) and kept files on who was influential who was susceptible to bribery, what a nation's historical roots were, what was likely to impress them, etc. In many cases, the information gathered by the Bureau was the first written record of these peoples, since barbarian tribes rarely had writing of their own. Armed with this knowledge, Byzantine emperors and diplomats had a complete understanding of the strengths of their allies and the weaknesses of their enemies.

The Byzantines employed a number of tactics, both overt and covert, to achieve their aims through diplomatic means rather than through force of arms: the use of ceremony was one such tactic. Imagine yourself as the chief of a nomadic tribe whose home is the steppes of central Asia. You are visited by representatives of the Byzantine emperor who shower you with fabulous gifts and invite you to the imperial palace in Constan-

tinople. Your entourage arrives in a city inhabited by almost half a million people—perhaps three times the size of your entire tribe. Its buildings are protected by huge walls, deep moats and well-armed soldiers. You see goods from all over the world in the bazaars. You view centuries-old cathedrals and are mystified by the Christian ritual.

You are led to a huge, ornate palace. On either side of you in the audience hall there are golden mechanical lions who open their mouths and roar. In golden trees are mechanical birds who sing. In front of you, seated upon a golden throne, is the emperor, attended by a chief minister. You approach the throne and prostrate yourself in front of it. You are bidden to rise and when you look up you discover that the emperor, throne and all, is suspended high above your head. Later, imperial officials give you rich presents and inform you that more wealth and support will be forthcoming if you will fight the emperor's enemies (pocketing any booty you may pick up along the way). It was a rare tribal chief who would turn down such an offer. This process was repeated time and time again throughout the history of Byzantium and it encouraged many to ally with the empire.

Another tactic was bribery. The bezant was the dollar of the Middle Ages and it purchased a lot of influence. Money was spread around freely, but bribery was actually very cost-effective. Often a well-placed bag of gold saved Byzantium from raising, supplying and deploying an army. No one was considered above targeting for bribery. In the late eleventh century, a Seljuq Sultan sent an ambassador to Constantinople to settle a border dispute. The Emperor Alexius I Comnenus struck a secret deal with the ambassador, 'buying' the fortress of Sinope from him. By the time the Sultan discovered what had happened, Byzantine troops had already occupied the city.

Some 200 years later, the empire's greatest enemy was Charles of Anjou, who controlled the island of Sicily and much of the Italian mainland. Charles had ambitions to take Constantinople and establish himself as emperor. Byzantine Emperor Michael VII Palaeologus prevented an Angevin attack in 1270 by sending a shipment of gold to Pope Nicholas III. In exchange, the pope forbade Charles to attack Constantinople and diverted his efforts to a crusade in Tunisia.

Shuttle diplomacy: Manuel II (1391-1425), whose round Europe trip of 1399-1403 was aimed at enlisting Catholic Christendom's support against the Ottoman Turks.

A further diplomatic ploy was the use of surrogates. The Byzantines hated the expense of war and could hardly afford the cost in human life. Often they would get others to fight for them. If the Bulgars were troublesome, the Russians were called in. If the Russians were troublesome the Patzinaks (a central Asian tribe) were summoned. The Cumans and Uzes acted as checks on the Patzinaks and so on. The Byzantines almost always had an ally to the geographic rear of a potential enemy.

The Byzantine emperor maintained a 'stable' of pretenders to almost every foreign throne in the known world. For instance, if the Turkish sultan seemed poised to attack, the Byzantine emperor could release a pretender, perhaps a younger brother of the Sultan. With Byzantine gold in his pockets and some armed supporters, the pretender could be counted on to wreak havoc in Turkish territory, spoiling the Sultan's attack.

In 1282, faced once again by the threat posed by Charles of Anjou, Michael VIII helped instigate the War of the Sicilian Vespers, in which native Sicilians rose up against Angevin rule. The rebellion ended Charles' dream of ruling in Constantinople. Michael VIII himself wrote: 'should I dare to claim that I was God's instrument to bring freedom to the Sicilians, then I should only be stating the truth'.

The word 'byzantine' has come to mean 'devious or characterised by intrigue'. This is due to some of the plots of questionable morality (but indisputable utility) that Byzantine emperors concocted. The Byzantines were of the opinion that anything done in the name of the Sacred Empire could not be judged treachery. Though they were diligent in adhering to the letter of their international agreements, they often violated the spirit of them. Strategic advantage was sought with fervour in every situation.

The Emperor Heraclius once intercepted a message from the Persian King Chosroes which ordered the execution of one of his generals, Shahr-Baraz. Heraclius added the names of 400 other Persian officers to the list and diverted the message to Shahr-Baraz. Heraclius' strategem was deviously brilliant. Had the executions been carried out, the Persian military would have been decapitated. Instead, Shahr-Baraz and the other officers rose in rebellion against Chosroes and overthrew him, subsequently making peace with Byzantium.

In another episode, a hostile Venetian fleet wintered at the island of Chios, directly threatening Byzantine territory. The Venetians sent ambassadors to Constantinople to negotiate an agreement. The Emperor Manuel I Comnenus refused to see them. The ambassadors returned to Chios with a Byzantine official, who suggested another embassy. The Venetian Doge commanding the fleet agreed to do so. After the second embassy had departed, illness swept through the Venetian camp. More than 1,000 soldiers and sailors died within a few days. The second embassy returned without having met with the emperor.

Sick from the plague (rumours spread that the Byzantines had poisoned the water), the Venetians sent a third embassy to Constantinople. By now well-informed of conditions in the Venetian camp, Manuel realised he need make no concessions. He stretched out negotiations for so long that the Doge was obliged to withdraw the fleet or face a mutiny among his ailing sailors. As the fleet limped back to Venice, a Byzantine naval force attacked without warning and decimated the Venetians. Soon afterward, Manuel sent a message to the Doge which literally added insult to injury: 'Your nation has for a long time behaved with great stupidity'.

It is important to resist the temptation to dismiss all these tactics as self-serving, self-justifying and Machiavellian. Had the Byzantines been less so, European history might have been greatly changed. Byzantine diplomacy was crucial not only in preserving the Byzantine Empire, but in preventing the Islamisation of Europe. Without this outpost of Christendom deflecting the Muslim tide from the seventh century to the fifteenth, it is unlikely that Western civilisation as we now know it would have endured. By the time the Ottoman Sultan Mehmet II took the city of Constantinople by assault in 1453 and renamed it Istanbul, the states of Eastern Europe had absorbed enough Byzantine culture (and diplomatic technique) to stand on their own. The walls of Constantinople and the imperial diplomats gave the fledgling Christian religion 700 years to grow and prosper.

Many historians have vilified the Byzantines for their tactics, often justifiably. Still, one does not have to approve of Byzantium's tactics to learn from them. Even today, diplomats frequently complain that the other side 'did not negotiate in good faith' or 'cheated'. The European Community negotiators and the United Nations teams spent countless hours thrashing out ceasefire agreements in Yugoslavia, only to see the best-crafted of them broken the next day. Like it or not, just because a nation cannot summon overwhelming military or economic strength does not mean it lacks the machinery to work its will. Though diplomatic practices today are much more civilised (or are they?), we should recognise in advance a country's tendency to use diplomacy the way the Byzantines did—as a low-cost, low-risk, manoeuvrable and effective weapon.

The World of Islam

THE MESSENGER OF ALLAH

In a cave at the foot of Mount Hira near Mecca, where he had spent six months in solitary meditation, the vision came to Muhammad. The Angel Gabriel roused him from his bed with the stern command: "Proclaim!" Rubbing his eyes, the startled Muhammad gasped, "But what shall I proclaim?" Suddenly his throat tightened as though the angel were choking him. Again came the command: "Proclaim!" And again the terrified Muhammad felt the choking grip. "Proclaim!" ordered the angel for a third time. "Proclaim in the name of the Lord, the Creator who created man from a clot of blood! Proclaim! Your Lord is most gracious. It is he who has taught man by the pen that which he does not know."

Thus it was, according to Islamic tradition, that an unremarkable Arab trader from Mecca was inspired to preach God's word in the year A.D. 610. Compared with Jesus or the Buddha, information about the life of the man who became known as the Messenger of Allah is relatively abundant, although the facts have been embellished with pious folklore. Some have claimed that at Muhammad's birth the palace of the Persian emperor trembled, or that a mysterious light ignited at his mother's breast, shining all the way to Syria, 800 miles away. It was said that his body cast no shadow and that when his hair fell into a fire it would not burn. Muhammad himself disdained any miraculous claims, insisting that he was merely the all-too-human conduit through which God had revealed himself.

It is known that the Prophet was born about A.D. 570 to a member of the respected Meccan clan of Hashim. His father died shortly before Muhammad was born, and his mother when the boy was only six. Two years later, his doting grandfather Abd al-Muttalib died, leaving the orphan in the care of a poor uncle, Abu Talib. As a youth, Muhammad was set to work tending his uncle's herds; he later recalled that task as a mark of divine favor. "God sent no prophet who was not a herdsman," he told his disciples. "Moses was a herdsman. David was a herdsman. I, too, was commissioned for prophethood while I grazed my family's cattle.

As a young man, Muhammad was exposed to the currents of religious debate then swirling through the Middle East. He would listen avidly as Jews and Christians argued over their faiths. Those discussions may have fed his dissatisfaction with the traditional polytheistic religion of the Arabs, who believed in a panoply of tribal gods and jinn, headed by a deity known as Allah. Says Muhammad's French biographer, Maxime Rodinson: "Both Jews and Christians despised the Arabs, regarding them as savages who did not even possess an organized church."

At 25, Muhammad accepted a marriage proposal from Khadijah, a rich Meccan widow 15 years his senior, for whom he had led a successful caravan. With his financial security assured by Khadijah's wealth and business, he began to venture into the desert, to contemplate and pray, as had other Arab holy men before him.

According to legend, Muhammad had earned a reputation as a wise and saintly man even before his first revelation from the angel on Mount Hira. Looking out from the balcony of his Mecca home one day, he saw the members of four clans arguing over which of them should be allowed to carry the Black Stone, a huge meteorite that the Arabs regarded as sacred, to its new resting place in a rebuilt shrine called the Ka'ba. Unknown to Muhammad, they had resolved to let the first man who walked into the sanctuary decide the matter. Entering the holy place, Muhammad proposed a satisfactory compromise: placing the Black Stone on a blanket, he instructed each tribe to lift one corner. Then he personally laid the meteorite in its new niche.

At 40, Muhammad began to preach the new faith of Islam, which was gradually being revealed to him on his sojourns in the desert. Some of this religion was familiar to Arabs who knew about the monotheistic teachings of Jews and Christians. His countrymen, for example, could readily accept Muhammad's assertion that Allah, long regarded as the highest of the desert gods, was the same God worshiped by Jews and Christians. But Meccan traders felt threatened by Muhammad's growing power. Both Jews and Christians questioned his claim that he was revealing the true word of God to the Arabs, in effect joining them as "People of the Book." In 622, after being harassed by his opponents, Muhammad and his followers escaped to Medina in a migration known as the hegira.

To a growing body of converts, Muhammad began to elaborate on his new religion. Revelations came to him in trances; his descriptions of those encounters, memorized and recorded by his adherents, were later collected as the Koran. As his followers grew in strength and numbers, Muhammad began a series of raids on Meccan caravans, which led to several indecisive battles with their avenging war parties. In 628 the Meccans agreed to let Muhammad's followers make their pilgrimage to the Ka'ba, which the new faith continued to regard as a sacred shrine. Muslims believe it is the spot where Abraham prepared to sacrifice his son Ishmael at God's command. Two years later the prophet led an army of 10,000 into his former city, taking control in a bloodless victory.

For all the pious legends that grew up even in his lifetime, Muhammad remained a humble and, in some ways, unfulfilled man. He occasionally incurred the wrath of his wives and concubines. All of his sons died in childhood, leaving him with no male heir. In 632 he led a pilgrimage to Mecca, where he declared, "I have perfected your religion and completed my favors for you." Three months later he fell ill in Medina and died. To his zealous followers went the task of spreading the word of Allah, not only throughout Arabia but far beyond it as well.

A FAITH OF LAW AND SUBMISSION

God's grandeur, and a path to follow

Eight words in Arabic sum up the central belief of the world's 750 million Muslims: "There is no god but God, and Muhammad is the Messenger of God." Five times a day, from Djakarta to Samarkand to Lagos, this *shahada* (confession of faith) is recited by the devout as meuzzins (callers to prayer) summon them to worship God.

In the prescribed daily prayers, a pious Muslim does not beseech God for favors, either material or spiritual, so much as for guidance and mercy. The word Islam means submission, and the true Muslim submits his life to the divine will of a deity who is the Compassionate, the All Knowing, the Strong, the Protector, the All Powerful—to cite only a few of the traditional 99 "most Beautiful Names" of God.

Muslims believe that God decrees everything that happens in the cosmos. Some critical Western scholars contend that this doctrine leads to a kind of passive fatalism, but Islamic theologians strongly deny that *qadar* (divine will) negates a person's freedom to act. It merely means, says Muhammad Abdul Rauf, director of the Islamic Center in Washington, that "when some misfortune befalls us, we resign ourselves to it as something coming from God, instead of despairing."

Islam stresses the uniqueness of the Creator, and strictly forbids *shirk*—that is, the association of anyone or anything with God's divinity. Along with Moses and Abraham, Jesus is revered by Muslims as one of the 25 scriptural prophets of God, and Islam accepts both his virgin birth and his miracles. But Muslims believe that Christian faith in the divinity of Jesus is polytheism. They resent being called "Muhammadans," which suggests that Muhammad's role in Islam is similar to that of Jesus in Christianity. The Prophet is revered as God's final Messenger to mankind, but is not worshiped as a divine being.

Because they accept the Bible, Jews and Christians have a special status in Islam as "People of the Book." Muslims also believe that the Bible in its present form is corrupt and that the true faith was revealed only to Muhammad. Those revelations are contained in the Koran, the Arabic word for recitation. Slightly shorter than the New Testament, the Koran has little narrative. There are evocations of divine grandeur in rhymed prose, florid descriptions of the harsh fate that awaits those who knowingly ignore God's will, and detailed instructions on specific ways that man must submit to his maker.

The basic spiritual duties of Islam are summed up in the so-called five pillars of faith. They are: 1) accepting the *shahada;* 2) the daily prayers to God while facing Mecca; 3) charitable giving; 4) fasting during the daylight hours of Ramadan, a 29- or 30-day month in Islam's lunar calendar* and 5) making the hajj, or pilgrimage, to Mecca at least once in an individual's lifetime—if he or she is financially and physically able. Some Muslims argue that there is a sixth pillar of the faith, namely jihad. The word is frequently translated as "holy war", in fact, it can refer to many forms of striving for the faith, such as an inner struggle for purification or spreading Islamic observance and justice by whatever means.

During the hajj, pilgrims throng Mecca, the men clad in two seamless white garments and sandals, the women in white head-to-toe covering. The pilgrims walk seven times around the Ka'ba, a cubical stone building covered by a gold-embroidered black canopy, in the exterior wall of which is set the Black Stone. The interior, now empty, once housed pagan idols, which Muhammad destroyed. The pilgrims also visit other holy sites, act out the search for water by Hagar, the mother of the Arab nation, perform a vigil on Mount 'Arafat (site of the Prophet's last sermon) and conduct a ritual sacrifice of goats, sheep and camels.

---

*By the Islamic calendar, this is the year 1399, dated from Muhammad's Hegira to Medina.

The devout Muslim is also expected to observe the Shari'a, which means "the path to follow." Based on the Koran, the deeds and sayings of Muhammad and the consensus of Islamic scholars, the Shari'a is not just a compilation of criminal and civil law, but a complex, all embracing code of ethics, morality and religious duties. It is a sophisticated system of jurisprudence that summarizes 1,400 years of experience and constantly adapts, in subtle ways, to new circumstances.

In Western eyes, however, the Shari'a all too often is denigrated as a relic of the Dark Ages. Some of its provisions do seem awesomely harsh: habitual thieves are punished by having a hand cut off; adulterers are either scourged or stoned to death; falsely accusing a woman of adultery calls for 80 lashes—the same penalty imposed on a Muslim caught drinking alcohol. The equivalence of the two punishments exemplifies the time-honored logic of the Shari'a. The Koran forbade the drinking of wine, but did not specify a punishment; 80 lashes, however, was decreed for those who bore false witness. Making the analogy that drink leads to hallucination and to telling untruths, Islamic sages decided that the punishment for the two sins should be the same.

Muslim jurists contend that stoning is no more typical of Islamic justice than extra-tough state laws against the possession of drugs are representative of the American legal tradition. Beyond that, the threat of the Shari'a is usually more severe than the reality. As in Western common law, defendants are presumed innocent until proved guilty. To convict adulterers, four witnesses must be found to testify that they saw the illicit act performed. Moreover, there are loopholes in the law and liberal as well as strict interpretations of it. For example, a thief can lose his hand only if he steals "in a just society"; the provision has been used by Islamic courts to spare men who steal because they are poor and have no other means to feed their families.

In Iran particularly, the reintroduction of the Shari'a under an Islamic republic is seen as a threat to rights that women won under the monarchy. Feminists do have reason to complain. Islamic law tolerates polygamy, so long as a husband treats his wives equally, and he can end a marriage simply by saying "I divorce thee" three times in front of witnesses. A woman may request a divorce under certain circumstances—for example, if she is mistreated or her husband is impotent. Women must dress modestly, and their inheritance is limited to a fraction of that of men. In defense of these sexist inequities, scholars of the Shari'a note that Islamic law was advanced for its time. Before Muhammad, women in Arabia were mere chattel. The Koran emphatically asserts a husband's duty to support his wife (or wives), who are allowed to keep their dowries and to own property—rights that did not emerge until much later in Western countries.

All Muslims accept the Koran as God's eternal word, but Islam to some extent is a house divided, although its divisions are not as extensive as those in Christianity. About 90% of all Muslims are Sunnis (from *sunna,* "the tradition of the Prophet"), who consider themselves Islam's orthodoxy. In Iran and Iraq, the majority of Muslims are Shi'ites ("partisans" of 'Ali), who differ from the Sunnis in some of their interpretations of the Shari'a and in their understanding of Muhammad's succession. The Prophet left no generally recognized instructions on how the leadership of Islam would be settled after his death. The Sunnis believe that its leader should be nominated by representatives of the community and confirmed by a general oath of allegiance. Shi'ites contend that Muhammad's spiritual authority was passed on to his cousin and son-in-law, 'Ali, and certain of his direct descendants who were known as Imams. Most Iranian Shi'ites believe that 'Ali's twelfth successor, who disappeared mysteriously in 878, is still alive and will return some day as the Mahdi (the Divinely Appointed Guide), a Messiah-like leader who will establish God's kingdom on earth. Meanwhile, Shi'ite religious leaders, such as Iran's Ayatullah Khomeini, have wide powers to advise the faithful on the presumed will of the "Hidden Imam." Sunni religious scholars, the ulama, have less authority, though both branches of Islam consider their leaders to be teachers and sages rather than ordained clergymen in the Western sense.

Both Sunni and Shi'ite Islam include Sufism, a mystical movement whose adherents seek to serve God not simply through obedience to the law but by striving for union with him through meditation and ritual. Sufism is considered suspect by fundamentalist Muslims like the puritanical Wahhabis of Saudi Arabia, because it allows for the veneration of *awliya*—roughly the equivalent of Christianity's saints. Islam also has spawned a number of heretical offshoots. One is the Alawi sect, a Shi'ite minority group to which most of Syria's leaders belong. The Alawis believe in the transmigration of souls and a kind of trinity in which 'Ali is Allah incarnate. Another is the secretive Druze sect of Israel, Lebanon and Syria, which split away from Islam in the 11th century. America's so-called Black Muslims were once generally regarded by Sunni Muslims as followers of a new heresy. By adopting orthodox beliefs and discarding a rule that limited membership to black Americans, the World Community of Islam in the West, as the movement is now known, has been accepted as being part of the true faith.

Islam is not a collection of individual souls but a spiritual community; its sectarian divisions, as well as the man-made barriers of race and class that Islam opposes, dissolve dramatically at the hajj. Once a pilgrimage made mostly by Muslims of the Middle East and North Africa, the hajj has become a universal and unifying ritual. For those who have taken part in it, the hajj acts as a constant testament to Islam's vision of a divine power that transcends all human frailties.

SOME SAYINGS FROM A HOLY BOOK

The grandeur of the Koran is difficult to convey in English translation. Although Islam's Holy Book is considered God's precise word only in Arabic, a generally recognized English text is that of Abdullah Yusuf 'Ali.

THE OPENING PRAYER. In the name of God, Most Gracious, Most Merciful. Praise be to God, the Cherisher and Sustainer of the Worlds; Most Gracious, Most Merciful; Master of the Day of Judgment. Thee do we worship, and Thine aid we seek. Show us the straight way, the way of those on whom Thou hast bestowed Thy Grace, those whose (portion) is not wrath, and who go not astray.

THE NATURE OF GOD. God! There is no god but He—the Living, the Self-subsisting, Eternal. No slumber can seize Him, nor sleep. His are all things in the heavens and on earth. Who is there can intercede in His presence except as He permitteth? He knoweth what (appeareth to His creatures as) Before or After or Behind them. Nor shall they compass aught of His knowledge except as He willeth. His Throne doth extend over the heavens and the earth, and He feeleth no fatigue in guarding and preserving them.

DRINKING AND GAMBLING. They ask thee concerning wine and gambling. Say: "In them is great sin, and some profit, for men: but the sin is greater than the profit."

THEFT. Male or female, cut off his or her hands: a punishment by way of example, from God, for their crime: and God is Exalted in Power. But if the thief repent after his crime, and amend his conduct, God turneth to him in forgiveness; for God is Oft-forgiving, Most Merciful.

POLYGAMY. If ye fear that ye shall not be able to deal justly with the orphans, marry women of your choice, two, or three, or four; but if ye fear that ye shall not be able to deal justly (with them) then only one, or (a captive) that your right hands possess.

CHRISTIANS. They do blaspheme who say: "God is Christ the son of Mary." But said Christ: "O Children of Israel! Worship God, my Lord and your Lord." Whoever joins other gods with God—God will forbid him the Garden, and the Fire will be his abode.

THE DAY OF JUDGMENT. When the sun is folded up; when the stars fall, losing their lustre; when the mountains vanish; when the she-camels, ten months with young, are left untended; when the wild beasts are herded together; when the oceans boil over with a swell; . . . when the World on High is unveiled; when the Blazing Fire is kindled to fierce heat; and when the Garden is brought near;—(Then) shall each soul know what it has put forward.

PARADISE. (Here is) a Parable of the Garden which the righteous are promised: In it are rivers of water incorruptible; rivers of milk of which the taste never changes; rivers of wine, a joy to those who drink; and rivers of honey pure and clear. In it there are for them all kinds of fruit, and Grace from their Lord. (Can those in such bliss) be compared to such as shall dwell forever in the

Fire, and be given, to drink, boiling water, so that it cuts up their bowels?

ISLAM, ORIENTALISM AND THE WEST

An attack on learned ignorance

In an angry, provocative new book called Orientalism *(Pantheon; $15), Edward Said, 43, Parr Professor of English and Comparative Literature at Columbia University, argues that the West has tended to define Islam in terms of the alien categories imposed on it by Orientalist scholars. Professor Said is a member of the Palestine National Council, a broadly based, informal parliament of the Palestine Liberation Organization. He summarized the thesis of* Orientalism *in this article.*

One of the strangest, least examined and most persistent of human habits is the absolute division made between East and West, Orient and Occident. Almost entirely "Western" in origin, this imaginative geography that splits the world into two unequal, fundamentally opposite spheres has brought forth more myths, more detailed ignorance and more ambitions than any other perception of difference. For centuries Europeans and Americans have spellbound themselves with Oriental mysticism, Oriental passivity, Oriental mentalities. Translated into policy, displayed as knowledge, presented as entertainment in travelers' reports, novels, paintings, music or films, this "Orientalism" has existed virtually unchanged as a kind of daydream that could often justify Western colonial adventures or military conquest. On the "Marvels of the East" (as the Orient was known in the Middle Ages) a fantastic edifice was constructed, invested heavily with Western fear, desire, dreams of power and, of course, a very partial knowledge. And placed in this structure has been "Islam," a great religion and a culture certainly, but also an Occidental myth, part of what Disraeli once called "the great Asiatic mystery."

As represented for Europe by Muhammad and his followers, Islam appeared out of Arabia in the 7th century and rapidly spread in all directions. For almost a millennium Christian Europe felt itself challenged (as indeed it was) by this last monotheistic religion, which claimed to complete its two predecessors. Perplexingly grand and "Oriental," incorporating elements of Judeo-Christianity, Islam never fully submitted to the West's power. Its various states and empires always provided the West with formidable political and cultural contestants— and with opportunities to affirm a "superior" Occidental identity. Thus, for the West, to understand Islam has meant trying to convert its variety into a monolithic undeveloping essence, its originality into a debased copy of Christian culture, its people into fearsome caricatures.

Early Christian polemicists against Islam used the Prophet's human person as their butt, accusing him of whoring, sedition, charlatanry. As writing about Islam and the Orient burgeoned—60,000 books between 1800 and 1950—European powers occupied large swatches of "Islamic" territory, arguing that since Orientals knew nothing about democracy and were essentially passive, it was the "civilizing mission" of the Occident, expressed in the strict programs of despotic modernization, to finally transform the Orient into a nice replica of the West. Even Marx seems to have believed this.

There were, however, great Orientalist scholars; there were genuine attempts, like that of Richard Burton (British explorer who translated the *Arabian Nights*), at coming to terms with Islam. Still, gross ignorance persisted, as it will whenever fear of the different gets translated into attempts at domination. The U.S. inherited the Orientalist legacy, and uncritically employed it in its universities, mass media, popular culture, imperial policy. In films and cartoons, Muslim Arabs, for example, are represented either as bloodthirsty mobs, or as hook-nosed, lecherous sadists. Academic experts decreed that in Islam everything is Islamic, which amounted to the edifying notions that there was such a thing as an "Islamic mind," that to understand the politics of Algeria one had best consult the Koran, that "they" (the Muslims) had no understanding of democracy, only of repression and medieval obscurantism. Conversely, it was argued that so long as repression was in the U.S. interest, it was not Islamic but a form of modernization.

The worst misjudgments followed. As recently as 1967 the head of the Middle East Studies Association wrote a report for the Department of Health, Education and Welfare asserting that the region including the Middle East and North Africa was not a center of cultural achievement, nor was it likely to become one in the near future. The study of the region or its languages, therefore, did not constitute its own reward so far as modern culture is concerned. High school textbooks routinely produced descriptions of Islam like the following: "It was started by a wealthy businessman of Arabia called Muhammad. He claimed that he was a prophet. He found followers among other Arabs. He told them that they were picked to rule the world." Whether Palestinian Arabs lost their land and political rights to Zionism, or Iranian poets were tortured by the SAVAK, little time was spent in the West wondering if Muslims suffered pain, would resist oppression or experienced love and joy: to Westerners, "they" were different from "us" since Orientals did not feel about life as "we" did.

No one saw that Islam varied from place to place, subject to both history and geography. Islam was unhesitatingly considered to be an abstraction, never an experience. No one bothered to judge Muslims in political, social, anthropological terms that were vital and nuanced, rather than crude and provocative. Suddenly it appeared that "Islam" was back when Ayatullah Khomeini, who derives from a long tradition of opposition to an outrageous monarchy, stood on his national, religious and political legitimacy as an Islamic righteous man. Menachem Begin took himself to be speaking for the West when he said he feared this return to the Middle Ages, even as he covered Israeli occupation of Arab land with Old Testament authorizations. Western leaders worried about their oil, so little appreciated by the Islamic hordes who thronged the streets to topple the Light of the Aryans.

Were Orientalists at last beginning to wonder about their "Islam," which they said had taught the faithful never to resist unlawful tyranny, never to prize any values over sex and money, never to disturb fate? Did anyone stop to doubt that F-15 planes were the answer to all our worries about "Islam"? Was Islamic punishment, which tantalized the press, more irreducibly vicious than, say, napalming Asian peasants?

We need understanding to note that repression is not principally Islamic or Oriental but a reprehensible aspect of the human phenomenon. "Islam" cannot explain everything in Africa and Asia, just as "Christianity" cannot explain Chile or

South Africa. If Iranian workers, Egyptian students, Palestinian farmers resent the West or the U.S., it is a concrete response to a specific policy injuring them as human beings. Certainly a European or American would be entitled to feel that the Islamic multitudes are underdeveloped; but he would also have to concede that underdevelopment is a relative cultural and economic judgment and not mainly "Islamic" in nature.

Under the vast idea called Islam, which the faithful look to for spiritual nourishment in their numerous ways, an equally vast, rich life passes, as detailed and as complex as any. For comprehension of that life Westerners need what Orientalist Scholar Louis Massignon called a science of compassion, knowledge without domination, common sense not mythology. In Iran and elsewhere Islam has not simply "returned"; it has always been there, not as an abstraction or a war cry but as part of a way people believe, give thanks, have courage and so on. Will it not ease our fear to accept the fact that people do the same things inside as well as outside Islam, that Muslims live in history and in our common world, not simply in the Islamic context?

The Rise of the Umayyad Dynasty in Spain

*How an exiled prince and his successors created a unique meeting point
between Orient and Occident*

J Derek Latham

J Derek Latham, of the United Kingdom, Doctor of Letters in the University of Oxford, is professor emeritus of Arabic and Islamic Studies and former head of the Muir Institute in the University of Edinburgh. He has been joint general editor and contributor to The Cambridge History of Arabic Literature *and a contributor to* Encyclopaedia of Islam *(new edition). Notable among his other published works are* Isaac Judaeus: On Fevers *(Arabic text and English translation with notes, 1980), and* From Muslim Spain to Barbary: Studies in the History and Culture of the Muslim West *(1986).*

In the year 93 of the Islamic era—the Hijra—and 711 of the Christian era, the great Muslim Arab empire was ruled from Damascus in Syria by al-Walid I, sixth caliph of the House of Umayya. From Kairouan in the country now called Tunisia, al-Walid's governor, Musa ibn Nusayr, was pursuing a policy of westward expansion spearheaded by his Berber freedman Tariq, commander of some 7,000 Berbers from North Africa. Before the end of the spring of 93 Tariq was on the rock from which Gibraltar takes its name—Jabal Tariq, "Mount Tariq".

Tariq's landing was the first step on a long, hard road which led 200 years later to the establishment of the caliphate of Córdoba by a scion of the House of Umayya. The second step was the conquest of the lands beyond Gibraltar. With his Berber troops, greatly reinforced from North Africa, Tariq soon defeated the Visigothic King Rodrigo, already harassed in the north by the Basques. The

tottering, unpopular Visigothic regime was now doomed. The fall of its capital, Toledo, to the north was followed in October 711 by the capture of Córdoba in the south.

July 712 saw Musa himself in the Iberian peninsula. Grudging his freedman the glory of conquest, he had crossed the Straits of Gibraltar with some 18,000, mainly Arab, troops. His relationship with Tariq was strained, but this did not prevent them from pursuing their common objective of conquest. By 714 Musa and Tariq had conquered all but the most inaccessible parts of the peninsula and gained for the Umayyad crown in Damascus a jewel of impressive resplendence. To this new, rich province the Arabs gave the name "al-Andalus", which is thought to derive from "Vandalicia", the name the Vandals gave to the old Roman province of Baetica in southern Spain. In English, "al-Andalus" is often translated as "Andalusia", but in its strict sense it designates Muslim Spain.

Like Rome, the Córdoba of the Umayyad caliphate was not built in a day. The glitter of that golden city did not materialize like Aladdin's genie at the rub of a magic lamp. It was born of the Umayyad emirate, and behind its glitter there lay a long and complex history.

THE ESTABLISHMENT OF THE UMAYYAD EMIRATE IN SPAIN

In 750 the 'Abbasid revolution in the east swept away the Syrian Umayyad caliphate and savagely butchered its princes. Miraculously, one of the latter, 'Abd al-Rahman, grandson of the caliph Hisham,

cheated his hunters of their prey and embarked on a perilous odyssey that took him to Morocco, where he won the protection of his mother's Berber tribe. After careful thought he decided to go to Spain, banking on support from elements owing loyalty to the Umayyads. Once on Andalusian soil, he played his hand and won—despite some militant opposition to his cause. In May 756, his final battle won, he entered the provincial palace of Córdoba. There, in the city's mosque, he led the Friday prayer and was proclaimed emir of al-Andalus. A young man in his mid-twenties at the time, he was to reign for over thirty years as the first of five Umayyad rulers of Spain to bear the name 'Abd al-Rahman.

The establishment of the emirate was only the start of a gruelling climb to power whose complexity is explained by the pattern of Andalusian society at that time. Al-Andalus was a country in which Arab and Berber immigrants had, at different times and under differing conditions, settled among the great mass of the Hispano-Roman population. Many Hispano-Romans had converted to Islam and, as neo-Muslims (*muwalladun*), become completely Arabized. Yet there remained a large Christian Hispano-Roman community of Mozarabs—a term taken from the Spanish form of an Arabic word meaning "Arabizer". As well as their own language, the Mozarabs spoke Arabic and adopted many Arab customs. Finally, there were the native Iberian Jews.

The Mozarabs and Jews caused 'Abd al-Rahman no trouble. They were only too glad to be rid of Visigothic tyranny and to live in peace. The Arabs, however, were to turn any dreams of peace

Reprinted with permission from *The Unesco Courier,* December 1991, pp. 24-27.

he may have cherished into something of a nightmare born of tribal feuds, jealousies and grievances, which led to sedition, armed conflict and open rebellion. Moreover, the Berbers resented not being treated as equals by their Arab fellow-Muslims, whose traditions and culture were quite different from their own.

And so, the prospect of revolts and uprisings was very real. The emir perceived the risk of siding with any single group within al-Andalus. He could count on unselfish loyalty from no one, not even from his Umayyad relations and clients. And so he recruited a highly disciplined professional army of Berber mercenaries and slave troops from Europe north of the Pyrenees. This was the only answer to internal turmoil and external danger from the Christian north.

'Abd al-Rahman was a Syrian, and the administrative system he created in Muslim Spain was in the Syrian Umayyad tradition. At its centre he made his own office of emir a unifying symbol, and in the provinces he appointed loyal and capable governors.

When he died in 788, he could be said to have proved himself an extraordinarily able statesman, whose greatest achievement had been to pacify and defend his realm. Today we see him as the founder of a dynasty that lasted more than twice as long as that of his Syrian ancestors and became a light that far outshone the brightest lights in contemporary Europe.

AN EVENTFUL HISTORY

All his successors sought, with varying degrees of success, to consolidate their political and military strength in a situation that was fraught with danger.

In many areas of the Iberian peninsula communications and transport militated against firm central control. Local notables, appointed as governors to uphold Umayyad authority in regions far from Córdoba, acted as powerful overlords serving not their ruler's interests but their own, and often taking the opportunity to rebel. This was particularly the case in the "Marches", sprawling tracts of nomansland separating the Christian realms to the north from the emirate's Muslim lands in the south.

The attitudes of the neo-Muslims and Mozarabs also changed, leading to insurrection and disorder. Córdoba itself was the home of certain Muslim political and religious malcontents. At the same time, the emirate was saddled with the perennial need to protect its northern borders against Christian invaders.

During the reign of al-Hakam I (796–822) there was a spate of troubles: disaffection in Toledo, savagely crushed in 797 by the massacre of its mainly neo-Muslim notables; the mass uprising in 818 of the so-called Suburb ("Arraval") of Córdoba, encouraged by disgruntled Muslim religious leaders and ruthlessly put down; protracted campaigns in the Marches of Saragossa, Toledo and Mérida against recalcitrant leaders; and, finally, the permanent loss of Barcelona to the Christians.

The emirate faced two other thorny problems. First, the initially peaceful Mozarabs became involved in a serious religious protest begun by Christian fanatics seeking martyrdom through public denunciation of the Prophet Muhammad. The protest, starting late in the reign of the kind and tolerant ruler 'Abd al-Rahman II (822–852), led to tensions and conflicts which neither the prince nor many of his Christian subjects relished. Secondly and more importantly, the reign of Muhammad I (852–886), witnessed in 880 a determined attempt by Ibn Hafsun, a rebel of neo-Muslim descent and later an apostate, to make himself ruler of al-Andalus from his centre of power, Bobastro, in the south of Spain. His insurrection, which commanded wide non-Arab support, dragged on for almost fifty years.

Largely because of al-Hakam I's draconian measures to enforce peace, his son 'Abd al-Rahman II, a very able monarch, enjoyed some thirty years of relative calm and prosperity, marked by significant improvements in the administrative system and a sharp rise in standards of culture and civilization. The emir's enthusiastic patronage of music and the arts was matched only by his zealous preoccupation with the creation of a strong navy capable of outclassing Norse squadrons that had found his shores a gateway to rich pickings.

AN EXCEPTIONAL RULER

The most disastrous period in the emirate's history came with the reign of 'Abd Allah (888–912), whose legacy to his grandson and successor 'Abd al-Rahman III (912–961) was nothing but an empty treasury and the general disintegration of Umayyad Spain. This legacy of leaden metal was to be miraculously transmuted into gold by the alchemy of a ruler who at the time of his accession was barely in his twenties. Endowed with patience, emotional stability and maturity of judgement beyond his years, the young 'Abd al-Rahman combined the energy and stamina of youth with political acumen and unswerving devotion to duty. As much European as Arab—his mother and paternal grandmother were of Christian stock—he was an observant Muslim but no fanatic. Throughout his reign he adopted, whenever possible, a generally tolerant policy towards Mozarabs and Jews.

Upon his succession, 'Abd al-Rahman brooked no opposition to his authority. Governors who refused or ignored his request for allegiance had to yield either to diplomatic persuasion or to force. In 913 he imposed his rule on the important city of Seville. The next year saw the start of a long war of attrition against Ibn Hafsun of Bobastro, the master of much of southern Spain. The struggle, continued by his sons after his death in 917, ended only in 928. It was not until 932 that the pacification of al-Andalus was complete, with the submission of the Algarve, eastern Spain, Toledo, Saragossa and other important strongholds.

THE APOGEE OF THE CALIPHATE

The most memorable event in Spanish Umayyad history took place in 929: the establishment of the caliphate. In proclaiming himself caliph, 'Abd al-Rahman III assumed, in addition to the caliphal title "Commander of the Faithful", the throne-name "Defender (al-Nasir) of God's Religion". The decision to revive the caliphate, lost by the Syrian Umayyads in 750, was largely his response to the growing power and prestige of the Shi'ite Fatimids, who had proclaimed their own caliphate in North Africa and were coming dangerously near to al-Andalus.

When he died in 961, al-Nasir had enforced respect for the frontiers of a country united under a strong central government. He had made al-Andalus second to none in the Western world, prospering thanks to a thriving domestic economy and a lucrative network of pan-Mediterranean trade. Córdoba, with about ten times the population of Paris, far outshone any other capital in Europe. In reputation and prestige, it surpassed Baghdad and rivalled Byzantine Constantinople, through diplomatic exchanges with which the caliph had ensured that his realm was seen as its equal. European envoys from France, Germany, Italy and elsewhere had eagerly made their way to his court. In addition to missions from North Africa, part of which he actually ruled, he had received delegations from Christian Spain, some of whose rulers he had made his tributaries.

His successor, al-Hakam II (961–976), was able to preserve his father's heritage of peace and prosperity. One of the biggest and best libraries of Islam was born of his passion for books and learning—a passion which also compelled him to promote scholarship, both religious and secular (astronomy and mathematics, for example), and to provide some education for the poor. In the Great Mosque of Córdoba, which stands to this day as a lasting memorial to Umayyad glory, he expressed his deep piety and refined artistic taste by almost doubling its size through the addition of a most pleasing extension and enhancing its prayer niche with ornamentation so exquisite as to make it a masterpiece.

Al-Hakam's death was the death of true Umayyad rule. The reign of his son Hisham II (976–1013)—a mere boy at the time of his accession—led to the caliphate's slide into extinction in 1031.

The Medieval Period

In the aftermath of barbarian incursions, Western civilization faced several massive challenges: to integrate Roman and Germanic peoples and cultures, to reconcile Christian and pagan viewpoints, and to create new social, political, and economic institutions to fill the vacuum left by the disintegration of the Roman order—in sum, to shape a new unity out of the chaos and diversity of the post-Roman world. The next millennium (c. 500–c. 1500) saw the rise and demise of a distinctive phase of the Western experience—medieval civilization.

Medieval culture expressed a uniquely coherent view of life and the world, summarized here by literary scholar C. S. Lewis:

> Characteristically, medieval man was not a dreamer nor a spiritual adventurer; he was an organizer, a codifier, a man of system. . . . Three things are typical of him. First, that small minority of his cathedrals in which the design of the architect was actually achieved (usually, of course, it was overtaken in the next wave of architectural fashion long before it was finished). . . . Secondly, the Summa of Thomas Aquinas. And thirdly, the Divine Comedy of Dante. In all these alike we see the tranquil, indefatigable, exultant energy of a passionately logical mind ordering a huge mass of heterogeneous details into unity. They desire unity and proportion, all the classical virtues, just as keenly as the Greeks did. But they have a more varied collection of things to fit in. And they delight to do it. (*Studies in Medieval and Renaissance Literature*, Cambridge University Press, 1966)

This outlook also expressed itself in a distinctly medieval social ideal. In theory medieval society provided a well-ordered and satisfying life. The Church looked after people's souls, the nobility maintained civil order, and a devoted peasantry performed the work of the world. Ideally, as historian Crane Brinton explains, "a beautifully ordered nexus of rights and duties bound each man to each, from swineherd to emperor and pope."

Of course, medieval society often fell short of this ideal. Feudal barons warred among themselves. Often the clergy was ignorant and corrupt. Peasants were not always content and passive. And medieval civilization had other shortcomings. During much of the Middle Ages there was little interest in nature and how it worked. While experimentation and observation were not unknown, science (or "natural philosophy") was subordinate to theology, which generally attracted the best minds of the day. An economy based on agriculture and a society based on inherited status had little use for innovation. Aspects of medieval politics and society are treated in "Studying the Lives of Medieval Women," and "Margery Kempe and the Meaning of Madness." Articles on the Fourth Crusade, El Cid, and the Mongol invasion explore facets of medieval warfare.

All this is not to suggest that the medieval period was static and sterile. Crusaders, pilgrims, and merchants enlarged Europe's view of the world. And there were noteworthy mechanical innovations: the horse collar, which enabled beasts of burden to pull heavier loads; the stirrup, which altered mounted combat; mechanical clocks, which made possible more exact measurement of time; the compass, which brought the age of exploration closer; and the paper-making process, which made feasible the print revolution, which in turn played key roles in the Reformation and the scientific revolution. "The Viking Saga" demonstrates that even during the so-called Dark Ages there existed possibilities for enterprise and progress. "The Golden Age of Andalusia under the Muslim Sultans" recounts the brilliant multicultural accomplishments made possible by Muslim rule in medieval Spain.

The medieval order broke down in the fourteenth and fifteenth centuries. Plague, wars, and famines produced a demographic catastrophe that severely strained the economic and political systems. Charles Mee's article explains how the Black Death affected many aspects of medieval life. During this period social discontent took the form of peasant uprisings and urban revolts. Dynastic and fiscal problems destabilized England and France. The Great Schism and new heresies divided the Church. "Jan Hus—Heretic or Patriot?" covers one of several challenges to the Church's authority, while "In France, An Ordeal by Fire and a Monster Weapon Called 'Bad Neighbor' " shows how the Church suppressed an earlier rebellion. Emergent capitalism gradually undermined an economy based on landed property. Yet these crises generated the creative forces that would give birth to the Renaissance and the modern era. The nation-state, the urban way of life, the class structure, and other aspects of modern life existed in embryonic form in the Middle Ages. And, as historian William McNeill has written, it was in medieval Europe that the West prepared itself for its modern role as "chief disturber and principal upsetter of other people's ways."

Looking Ahead: Challenge Questions

Explain how the collapse of a civilization constitutes an opportunity as well as a calamity.

On balance, were the Vikings destroyers or agents of progress? Explain.

Under what circumstances did the Inquisition begin?

Why was southern Spain a great center of culture during the Middle Ages?

Unit 5

The Viking saga

Magnus Magnusson

Magnus Magnusson, Icelandic-born author and journalist, is well-known in the UK as a TV and radio broadcaster specializing in archaeology and history. He wrote and presented in 1980 a major TV series on the Vikings which has been shown in many countries and has appeared in book form as Vikings! *(BBC Publications with Bodley Head). Among his many other published works are the award-winning* Introducing Archaeology *(1972),* Viking Expansion Westwards *(1973), and* Iceland *(1979).*

The term "Viking" has come to mean anyone who happened to be a Scandinavian in the Middle Ages, whether he was a seaman, a farmer, a merchant, a poet, an explorer, a warrior, a craftsman, a settler—or a pirate. And the term "Viking Age" has been applied by historians—somewhat indiscriminately, it must be said—to cover three centuries of dynamic Scandinavian expansion that took place from around 800 AD onwards.

It has become popularly associated with an age of terror and unbridled piracy, when Norse freebooters came swarming out of their northern homelands in their lean and predatory longships, to burn and rape and pillage their way across civilized Europe. They have always been portrayed as merciless barbarians, heedless of their own lives or of the lives of others, intent only on destruction. They were anti-Christ personified; their emblems were Thor's terrible Hammer and Odin's sinister Ravens, symbolizing the violence and black-hearted evil of their pagan gods.

This deep-rooted popular prejudice about the Vikings can be traced back directly to the lurid sensationalism of ecclesiastical writers who were the occasional victims of smash-and-grab Viking raids. In a turbulent age, when piracy and casual raiding were a commonplace of everyday life all over Europe the Vikings happened to be more successful at it than most other people; and they paid the price for it by getting an extremely bad reputation.

But, curiously enough, no one knows for certain what the word "Viking" actually means! It may be related to the Old Norse word *vik,* meaning "bay" or "creek", suggesting that a Viking was someone who lurked with his ship in a hidden bay. Some think it may come from the Old Norse verb *vikja,* meaning "to turn aside", so that a Viking was someone who made detours on his voyage—presumably to go raiding. A third school of scholarly opinion looks for a derivation in the Anglo-Saxon word *wic,* itself borrowed from the Latin *vicus,* meaning a fortified camp or trading-post, so that "Viking" might mean a raider or a trader, or both!

But not every Scandinavian was a professional warrior or Viking; and not every Viking was a pirate. Modern scholarship is now beginning to highlight the constructive, rather than the destructive, impact of the Viking Age. Spec-

Photos © L. A. East.
The British Museum, London

Coins struck by the Vikings attest to their receptiveness to the cultures with which they came into contact. Above, 10th-century silver pennies from the Viking kingdom of York. Left, coin inscribed ''Anlaf Cununc'' (King Olaf) is decorated with a raven, traditionally associated with Odin. Right, penny with the name of St. Peter shows a sword and also Thor's hammer, a symbol as potent to a Viking as a cross to a Christian.

Reprinted with permission from *The Unesco Courier,* December 1983, pp. 10-13.

To relieve the tedium of the long northern winters, the Vikings played various board games, including dice games and a game similar to chess. Pieces were made of bone, amber or glass. Left, 10th-century wooden Viking gaming board from Ireland.

Photo © National Museum of Ireland, Dublin

tacular archaeological excavations like Coppergate in York, which unearthed a whole street from the Viking Age, are revealing the ordinary Viking man-in-the-street as a diligent and skilled artisan—the Viking as man, not the Viking as myth.

If the origin of the word "Viking" is obscure, so too are the motive causes of the so-called Viking Age itself. There is no single, simple reason why the Scandinavians should suddenly have burst upon the European scene late in the eighth century (in the history books, at least—it probably wasn't as sudden as it has been made to appear). All major historical shifts have complex roots. We know that in the seventh century, the Scandinavians began developing new sources of iron, which had several consequences: improved iron production made for better weapons, and better farm implements; better farm implements led to agricultural improvements, which led in turn to better nutrition and a correspondingly lower mortality rate amongst infants. There is evidence about this time that land that had formerly been thought unsuitable for farming was being vigorously cleared of forest and scrub to make new farms for new generations of vigorous, well-nourished younger sons who wanted a place in the sun for themselves.

So an acute shortage of land was probably a major factor, which led to considerable settlement overseas; there is evidence of peaceful co-habitation between the Picts of northern Scotland and Norwegian emigrant farmers long before the outbreak of the Viking Age.

But there were other consequences, too. With its surplus iron production, Scandinavia had a new and much-prized product to sell to its neighbours; and the traders had sharp, well-tempered weapons with which to defend themselves from pirates that swarmed in the Baltic and along the shores of northern continental Europe. But in order to trade effectively, the Scandinavians needed good ships. They came in all shapes and sizes, from small six-oared boats for coastal waters to the enormous "dragon-ships" of royalty. In between came a versatile variety of cutters, ferries, pinnaces, plump-bellied cargo-boats, ocean-going ships and galleys.

But the pride of the fleet, the ship that has become the universal symbol of the Viking Age, was the lordly longship, undisputed master of the northern seas. These ships were the outcome of centuries of technological innovation and evolution which have been charted by chance archaeological discoveries, from flat-bottomed punts to the splendour and sophistication of the single-masted, square-

sailed longships. Without the ships, the Viking Age would never have happened at all.

The Viking Age was not a concerted effort at empire-building. The Vikings were never a single, homogeneous people imbued with the same aims and ambitions. The three countries of the Scandinavian peninsula, as they are now defined by political geography, were not really nations at all in the modern sense of the term. Norway, for instance, was a scatter of inhabited areas under independent tribal chieftains along the western seaboard; even the name Norway (*Norvegur*) simply meant "North Way"—not so much a nation as a trade-route. And the three countries had distinct if sometimes overlapping "spheres of influence"—the Swedes in the Baltic and Russia, the Danes on the Continent and in England, and the Norwegians in Scotland and Ireland and the North Atlantic islands.

The first recorded Viking raid took place in the year 793, with a seaborne assault by prowling Norwegian marauders on the Holy Island of Lindisfarne, just off the north-eastern shoulder of England. But long before that, the Swedes had been busy in the Baltic, growing rich on trade. At the outset of the Viking Age, Swedish entrepreneurs started to penetrate the hinterland of Russia (they called it "Greater Sweden") in pursuit of the rich fur trade and the exotic markets of Arabia and the Far East. Swedish pioneers made their way through Russia by way of the major rivers like the Volga and the Dnieper, dragging their ships in exhausting overland portages on the way to the Caspian Sea and the Black Sea.

By the ninth century they had reached the capital of the greatest power in the western world, the successor to Rome—the Byzantine Empire centred on Constantinople. There, Viking mercenaries formed the elite bodyguard of the Byzantine emperors, the feared and famous Varangian Guard, a kind of Scandinavian Foreign Legion. But the Swedes never conquered Russia, as such; they contented themselves with taking control of existing trading posts and creating new ones to protect the trade-routes, but within two or three generations they had become totally assimilated and Slavicized.

While the Swedes looked east, the Danes looked south-west along the northern coasts of Europe and towards England. Danish warriors were soon hammering at the cities of the crumbling Carolingian empire after the death of Charlemagne in 814 AD: Hamburg, Dorestad, Rouen, Paris, Nantes, Bordeaux—all river-cities, notice. The Viking longships, with their exceptionally shallow draught, could go much further up-river than had been thought possible before, and the effect was rather like that of dropping paratroops behind the enemy lines.

To start with, the Danish Vikings acted as pirates with official or unofficial royal backing. Later on, Danish designs on Europe, and especially England, became openly territorial; the flag followed the trade, just as trade had followed the piracy. But here, too, the Danes, just like the Swedes, became assimilated whenever they settled. In the year 911, one marauding army accepted by treaty huge

tracts of land in Northern France in what is now called Normandy—"Northmandy", the land of the Northmen; 150 years later, the descendants of these Norse-Frenchmen would conquer all England under William the Conqueror. Before then, but only briefly, under King Knut (Canute) in the eleventh century, there was a united Scandinavian empire of the North Sea, comprising England, Denmark and Norway; but it quickly fell apart.

Norwegian adventurers joined Danish Vikings in subjugating the whole of northern England (the Danelaw, as it was called) before settling there as farmers and traders, where they developed great mercantile cities like York. They also took over much of mainland Scotland, the Hebrides, and the Northern Isles of Shetland and the Orkneys. In Ireland they played a lusty part in the endless internecine squabbles of rival Irish clans, and founded Ireland's first trading posts: Waterford, Wexford, Wicklow, Limerick and, most especially, Dublin. They were insatiable explorers in search of new trade opportunities to exploit, new lands to settle, new horizons to cross. They discovered Spitzbergen and Jan Mayen Island; they discovered and colonized the Faroes, far out in the heaving Atlantic; they discovered and colonized Iceland, where they established Europe's first Parliamentary republic—a new nation that is still regarded as the oldest democracy in Europe, and which has left us the most enduring cultural monument of the Viking Age, the Icelandic Sagas.

From Iceland, they discovered and settled Greenland. And it was from Greenland, round about the millennial year of 1000, that the Vikings launched their last and most ambitious expeditions of all, the discovery and attempted settlement of the eastern seaboard of North America: "Vinland", the land of wild grapes, as it was called in the two Icelan-

dic Sagas that record the first undisputed European discovery of the New World.

The discovery of North America, and the abortive attempts at colonization which were thwarted by the indigenous Red Indians, used to be considered mere legend; but now archaeology has unearthed authenticated evidence of a Viking settlement at L'Anse aux Meadows, in northern Newfoundland. All other alleged Viking "finds", like the runic Kensington Stone, have long since been exposed as forgeries or hoaxes, or merely wishful thinking.

The impact of the Vikings was ultimately less lasting than might have been expected. Why was that? They had all the necessary energy, they had their own administrative systems of justice and royal authority, they had become converted to Christianity, they had their own coinage, they seemed to have everything. They had criss-crossed half the world in their open boats and vastly extended its known horizons. They had gone everywhere there was to go, and beyond. They had dared everything there was to dare. They had given Europe a new trading vigour, vigorous new art-forms, vigorous new settlers.

But they had neither the manpower nor the staying-power, neither the reserves of wealth nor the political experience, neither the cohesion at home nor the confidence abroad, to master effectively the older, richer, more stable States they tried to overrun. Instead, being rootless men of the sea, they put their roots down where they landed, and then blended into the landscape. Somehow or other, the dynamic simply petered out.

But they left in the annals of history, a heritage of heroic endeavour and courage, a legacy of robust audacity, that has won the grudging admiration even of those who would otherwise deplore their incidental depredations.

The Golden Age of Andalusia Under the Muslim Sultans

From the 8th to the 15th century, Islam ruled in Spain's rich southern region

Stanley Meisler

Stanley Meisler, former Madrid correspondent for the Los Angeles Times, *wrote on the Prado in January and on Berlin's Pergamon Museum in October 1991.*

On January 2 [1992], several thousand festive Spaniards crowded into the downtown streets of Granada to celebrate the 500th anniversary of the surrender of the last Islamic stronghold in Spain to King Ferdinand and Queen Isabella in 1492. That event, as every schoolchild in Spain knows, completed the Reconquest—the final defeat of the Muslims who had occupied much of the Iberian Peninsula for more than 700 years, the final victory of Christianity over Islam in Spain. For the anniversary ceremonies, priests celebrated a mass at the cathedral where Ferdinand and Isabella, known in Spain as the Catholic Monarchs, are buried, and dignitaries led a procession back to the city hall, where Mayor Jesús Quero shouted to a cheering crowd, "Granada! Granada! Granada! In the name of the illustrious Ferdinand of Aragon and Isabella of Castile, long live Spain! Long live the King! Long live Andalusia! Long live Granada!"

A half-mile away, however, in the Albaicín, the old Arabic quarter of narrow streets, mazelike alleys and whitewashed stucco homes that nestles opposite the great hill of the Alhambra, perhaps 50 Spaniards, some of them converts to Islam, gathered. They met by the monastery that now stands on the spot where, according to legend, the submissive and chastened Sultan Boabdil handed the keys of the city to the triumphant Catholic Monarchs.

Now, half a millennium later, the small group of Spaniards marked that surrender with a few moments of silence. Then their leader, Aberraman Medina, lamented, "The conquest of Granada in 1492 was a rehearsal for what would happen later in America—a liquidation of cultures, traditions and beliefs."

This conflict of moods in Granada reflects the excitement and anguish of history in today's Spain. Ever since the death of the dictator Francisco Franco in 1975 and the transformation of Spain into a democracy, Spaniards have felt the need to examine their past and their identity. It is an examination that often brings pain and confusion and controversy, but this does not halt the search.

The self-examination is intensifying in this 500th-anniversary year. The rest of the world knows 1492 as the year that Christopher Columbus discovered America. But Spaniards know it, as well, as the year Ferdinand and Isabella defeated the Arabs in Granada and then expelled the Jews from Spain. They also know that all these cataclysmic events are interrelated. Columbus, in fact, accompanied the Catholic Monarchs to Granada and could not get approval and funds for his voyage until Ferdinand and Isabella diverted their attention from the Arabs to his scheme. And the crusading victory over Islam nourished a Christianity in the Catholic Monarchs so fervent and exclusive that they refused to tolerate Jews in their kingdom.

Spaniards have been aided in their quest for the past by an extraordinary exhibition entitled "Al-Andalus: The Art of Islamic Spain." Earlier this year [1992], it was mounted within the walls of the renowned palaces of the Alhambra, which were built by the sultans of Granada in the dying years of their dynasty. It then moved [in the] summer to the Metropolitan Museum of Art in New York, where it remain[ed] on view until September 27. Displaying 97 pieces of Spanish Islamic art of every variety, from ceramics and carpets to swords and manuscripts, "Al-Andalus" gives Americans one of their first looks at the little-known but splendid Islamic side of Spain.

It is not easy to sort out history and identity in Spain. Too much has been cloaked for centuries by Spaniards trying to hide their antecedents from a society that discriminated against those who could not prove what was called "purity of blood"—a line of descent from old Spanish Christians and not from converted Arabs or Jews. One of Spain's most distinguished journalists José Antonio Martínez Soler, who grew up on the heavily Arab-influenced Almería coast, is now studying Arabic to understand his roots. He has an ironic line about the confusion over the search for self-identity these days. "I like to say," he told me recently, "that all of Spain now believes it is one-half Arabic, one-half Jewish and one-half Spanish."

AN OPULENT STAGE SET FOR THE LAST ACT

Even appearances sometimes get in the way of understanding history. The breathtaking palaces of the Alhambra are not what they seem, for their grand splendor represents defeat, not triumph. "The Alhambra is like a big stage set," says Jerrilynn D. Dodds, an associate professor of architectural history at the City University of New York and a special consultant to the Met. "It was cheaply done but in an opulent way. It was an incredibly defiant gesture. They were defying the Christian onslaught with their own sophisticated culture. But it's also a melancholy monument trying to ward off eventual demise."

The history needs to be sketched briefly, for not much is known outside Spain about the farthest reach of Islam into Europe. In the year 711, a Berber commander led 7,000 Arab and Berber troops from North Africa across the narrow Strait of Gibraltar into a weak and divided Visigothic Christian Spain. Within months, the Muslim invaders captured the Christian center of Toledo in central Spain. Continuing their northern march, they were finally turned back 20 years later in southern France. They then consolidated their hold on Spain, ruled most of it without challenge for three centuries, and then slowly retreated under Christian attack over the centuries until the final defeat in 1492.

The Muslims called Spain al-Andalus (a name that survives as "Andalusia," the southern region of Spain). Although the colonists were Arabs from the Middle East, and Berbers and mixed Arab-Berbers from North Africa, Spaniards tended not to make distinctions but usually called them all Moors (Moros, in Spanish) or sometimes all Arabs.

In less than two centuries, al-Andalus was transformed from a distant outpost to a center of Islam. Its capital of Córdoba, which grew to a population of one million, soon had few rivals in power and wealth anywhere in the world. As Desmond Stewart wrote in his book The Alhambra, by the mid-8th century Córdoba was regarded as the "first true metropolis in the West since the fall of Rome." Exporting lustrous ceramics, intricate textiles, wools, silks, felts, linens, carved ivory and European slaves throughout the Muslim world, the city was challenged as a market only by Constantinople and Baghdad. Its libraries and poets were celebrated. Sultan Abd al-Rahman I and his successors built the Great Mosque of Córdoba, an astounding work of architecture, to symbolize the political and religious power of al-Andalus. In 929, Abd al-Rahman III proclaimed himself a caliph, a successor to the Prophet Muhammad, thus assuming the same status as the rulers of Baghdad and Constantinople.

Within a century, however, the dynasty collapsed, and al-Andalus splintered into a cluster of petty kingdoms. Taking advantage of this weakness, the Spanish Christians in the north reconquered Toledo in 1085. The loss provoked the fearful kings into calling for help from a powerful and puritanical Muslim dynasty in North Africa. Two waves of Islamic zealots, the Almoravids and then the Almohads, ruled al-Andalus for 146 years, but their hold weakened under the pressure of the Christian armies in Spain and North African rivals in Morocco. When the Christians captured the Almohad capital of Seville in 1248, their chroniclers described the conquest as "one of the greatest and noblest that was ever . . . accomplished in the whole world."

Al-Andalus then found itself reduced to a mountainous domain in the southeastern corner of Spain, with 250 miles of coastline near North Africa. A succession of sultans from the Arab-descended Nasrid dynasty ruled this domain from Granada for 254 years. Perhaps because they were the last, perhaps because they built the Alhambra, the Nasrid sultans have been romanticized and celebrated by poets and novelists more than any other Islamic rulers of Spain.

For more than two centuries, the Nasrids staved off the Christians with a series of vassalage treaties continually signed and broken, and with a succession of skirmishes halted by truces. In fact, Boabdil, the last sultan, had received Christian help in his battles with his father and uncle for the throne, and had even sent congratulations to the Catholic Monarchs upon the defeat of his fellow Muslims at Málaga. But when the Christians began to devastate the farmlands that supplied Granada, Boabdil's forces attacked Christian fortresses. Ferdinand and Isabella then vowed to march onward without stopping until they placed a cross upon the towers of the Alhambra.

The Alhambra, which means "red citadel" in Arabic, takes its name from a fort that had been built from the red clay on the hill many years before. Looking for a stronghold in perilous times, the Nasrids had created a royal fortress city on this hill during the 14th century with palaces, enormous walls, formidable gates, military towers, a mosque, sumptuous gardens, and crowded residential and shopping streets for artisans and servants.

The Alhambra never fell in battle. Boabdil, facing certain defeat, negotiated a treaty of surrender with Ferdinand and Isabella, who pledged, falsely as it turned out, to allow his subjects to keep their Islamic faith and customs. According to legend, Boabdil, as he headed south into exile, looked back at Granada and the Alhambra and burst into tears. His mother, whose scheming had helped put Boabdil on the throne, told him with contempt, "You do well to weep like a woman for what you could not defend like a man."

It was a jubilant triumph for Christianity. The politically powerful Cardinal Mendoza of Spain carried the silver cross that Ferdinand had borne throughout the crusade and hoisted it upon the tower of the Alhambra fortress. An eyewitness wrote to the Bishop of León, "It was the most notable and blessed day that there ever was in Spain." In Rome, the bells of St. Peter's rang out as the pope and his cardinals led a solemn procession to celebrate high mass for the victory.

"A MOSLEM PILE IN A CHRISTIAN LAND"

Spain has no finer and more intact monument from the Islamic era than the Alhambra. Victor Hugo called it a "palace that the genies have gilded like a dream and filled with harmony." Washington Irving, who lived there for a few months, did more to popularize the Alhambra throughout the Western world than any other writer in the 19th century. He described it as a Moslem pile in the midst of a Christian land, an Oriental palace amidst the Gothic edifices of the West, an elegant memento of a brave, intelligent, and graceful people who conquered, ruled and passed away." A Spanish poet wrote of a blind beggar in Granada pleading with a woman leaving church, "Give me alms, my lady, for there is no worse affliction in life than to be blind in Granada."

Every year, 1.5 million people, half of them foreigners, visit the Alhambra. Of the six palaces, five of which perched on the escarpment overlooking Granada, two—the Palace of Comares and the Palace of the Lions—remain in almost pristine form. On walls and ceilings, swirls, strange geometric shapes, flowers, leaves, vines, acorns, shells and Arabic calligraphy twist in and out of one another. The patterns are sometimes symmetrical but, because of the calligraphy, often not. Most of the work has been done in stucco—plaster mixed from lime and earth—supplemented by ceramic tiles and carved cedar wood. Except for a few traces, mostly of blues, the once-polychrome stucco has lost its color, but the tiles bring color into every room.

Architecture and decoration are sometimes indistinguishable. Many of the rooms have ceilings fashioned with layers of hanging stucco stalactites; a visitor looking up has an illusion that the ceiling soars forever. Within the Palace of Comares' Hall of the Ambassadors, the sultan's reception room for envoys, every arched window frames a different view of Granada below. The magnificent Court of the Lions, with its famous fountain, is the inner patio of the Palace of the Lions that sultans used for relaxation and pleasure. Here, strolling among various arches and columns, one will see what seem like a dozen different patios.

The calligraphy on the walls of the Alhambra is so intricate that it is sometimes difficult to distinguish the Arabic script from the weaving vines and flowers. The motto of the Nasrid dynasty is repeated scores of times: "There is no conqueror but God." The simple prayers "Blessing" and "Happiness" can be found just as often. Nearby, at the library of the Renaissance palace that Charles V of Spain, the Holy Roman Emperor, built after the Reconquest, Emilia Jiménez is preparing her doctoral dissertation for the University of Granada. It is a study of the Arabic inscriptions of the Alhambra. Jiménez explained to me that several different subjects are treated. "You can find dynastic mottoes, brief prayers, quotations from the Koran, maxims, notes about the construction, instructive information, praises of the sultans, and poetry," she said.

"I AM THE GARDEN, I AWAKE ADORNED IN BEAUTY"

There are, in fact, 30 poems scattered throughout the palace and its grounds, poems often brimming with adulation for the Alhambra itself. "I am the garden, I awake adorned in beauty: Gaze on me well, know what I am like. . . . What a delight for the eyes! The patient man who looks here realizes his spiritual desires," sings 14th-century poet Ibn Zamrak in an inscription in one of the chambers surrounding the Court of the Lions.

It is surprising that so much of the Alhambra has been preserved for more than 600 years. When Washington Irving arrived in 1829, he reported that its

palaces had been filled only a few years earlier "with a loose and lawless population—contrabandistas who . . . [carried] on a wide and daring course of smuggling; and thieves and rogues of all sorts. . . . It is difficult to believe that so much has survived the wear and tear of centuries, the shocks of earthquakes, the violence of war, and the quiet, though no less baneful, pilferings of the tasteful traveller." Irving concluded that Granadians could be right when they insisted that the Alhambra was "protected by a magic charm."

Preservation, however, probably owes more to the interest of the Spanish kings. In awe of its beauty, the monarchs designated the Alhambra as their royal residence in Granada. Although few of them actually spent time there, the status ensured funds for maintenance. But by the 18th century this royal interest had slackened. When Napoleon occupied Spain, his troops used the Alhambra as their barracks in Granada. Irving commended the French for repairing and restoring the Alhambra, even though the troops tried to dynamite all its towers before fleeing Granada in 1812. A daring Spanish soldier managed to cut the main fuse leading to the dynamite, but he could not prevent all damage. Partly in response to pleas from Irving, whose book *Legends of the Alhambra* achieved worldwide popularity, the Spanish kings resumed the funding of repairs and upkeep. In 1870, the Alhambra was declared a national monument with its maintenance assured by an annual appropriation from the government.

"As a result of this, we have been restoring the Alhambra all the time for 120 years," says Mateo Revilla Uceda, the 43-year-old former professor of art history who has been director of the Alhambra for the past five years. "But deterioration is not a major problem. There is no contamination at the Alhambra. And the climate is dry." The Alhambra seems to have benefited as well from the choice of material. "The main material of the Alhambra—stucco—is very flexible, but it is also very resistant," says Revilla Uceda. "All the decoration gives the material an illusion of richness."

The idea for the exhibition came out of a chance conversation five years ago between the Metropolitan's assistant director, Mahrukh Tarapor, and Spain's Minister of Culture, Javier Solana. Solana had come to the Met to see an

exhibition of the paintings of Francisco de Zurbarán, which Tarapor had organized. After the opening, the minister asked her to take him through her favorite gallery in the museum. The Bombay-born Tarapor, a specialist in Islamic art, led Solana to the small Islamic rooms and told him there was so little space devoted to Islamic Spain because there still had not been enough study of this period. "Do you think the time is right for such study now?" Solana asked. "Would it be appropriate to prepare an exhibition on such art in Spain for 1992? Will you do it? Let's shake on it." Though somewhat surprised by this sudden proposal, Tarapor agreed to explore the idea.

The result is a rare look at the variety of the arts of al-Andalus. Newcomers to Islamic art sometimes feel that it all looks alike. There is an obvious reason for this. Islamic art tends not to strive for blatant novelty but to take familiar models and rework them with only subtle changes. Although it is not true, as many people believe, that the depiction of people and animals is forbidden in the Koran, much of Islamic art uses abstract patterns rather than realistic figures, and this tends to foster a mood of sameness. This seeming uniformity is reinforced as well by the heavy use of the Arabic script in design—a script that is familiar to most Muslims throughout the world. Yet, within this seeming uniformity, there are significant regional and epochal differences, which the Metropolitan exhibit makes clear.

Spain has a special place in Islamic art. The most striking features of the Great Mosque of Córdoba, for example, are the myriad double arches—one horseshoe arch perched on another—throughout its interior. This arrangement had been used before, but never to such startling effect. Spain's ceramic lusterware (plates and tall Alhambra vases that shone and glittered, often in green and manganese colors), intricate silk textiles, and elaborately carved ivory boxes were widely acclaimed and sought. Many of the artworks of al-Andalus were luxury goods, reflecting the wealth and power of the succession of sultanates in Spain.

The stellar pieces in the exhibition include a 10th-century Cordoban pyxis on loan from the Louvre in Paris. A pyxis is an ivory box fashioned from the natural cylindrical shape of a tusk and probably used to hold gifts of ambergris, musk and camphor—aromatics used as cosmetics and medicines. This one is carved with a host of elaborate scenes, including one showing two horsemen, accompanied by cheetahs and birds, picking dates off a tree.

The exhibition also feature[d] a 15th-century steel sword with a carved ivory hilt that once belonged to Sultan Boabdil, a sword that is usually on display in the Museum of the Army in Madrid. The pieces from the Met's own Islamic collection include a fragment of a 14th-century silk textile with designs that look like the stuccowork of the Alhambra. The Hermitage in St. Petersburg has contributed an enormous, lustrous, 14th-century earthenware vase, four feet high, known as an "Alhambra vase." It has wings like flying buttresses against its neck and Arabic inscriptions calling for "pleasure" and "health" and "blessing." It is believed that the Nasrids placed vases like this throughout the Alhambra for no other function than decoration. With this cachet of royal chic, Alhambra vases were to become some of the most cherished exports from al-Andalus.

A novice to Spain might be surprised that the Spanish Christians allowed so much art to remain from a civilization that had been defeated in a religious crusade. "Christians didn't look down on Islamic art," said Jerrilynn Dodds. "They treated it as the latest fashion. Muslim textiles were so prized that the Christians wrapped relics in them. When Christians expelled the Muslims, they turned the mosques into Christian churches."

At the Met, the exhibition include[d] a small part of the Alhambra itself—a part that has been missing from Granada for a century. In the 19th century, when governments were lackadaisical about their archaeological treasures, a German banker, Arthur Gwinner Dreiss, bought the Tower of the Ladies in one of the ramparts of the Alhambra. Before leaving Spain he sold the structure back, but he dismantled the wooden ceiling with its intricate geometric patterns and took it

with him to Germany. It now belongs to the Museum of Islamic Art in the Berlin suburb of Dahlem, which is loaning the ceiling to the Met. Ironically, the ceiling that visitors to the Alhambra see in the Tower of the Ladies is a reproduction put up years ago.

The fall of Granada in 1492 did not end the story of Islam in Spain. Ferdinand and Isabella promised that the Muslims could continue practicing Islam in peace, but the promise was soon broken. Cardinal Francisco Jiménez de Cisneros ordered a campaign of forced conversion and mass baptism under threat of torture and prison. By 1500 he could report back to the Catholic Monarchs that "there is now no one in the city who is not a Christian, and all the mosques are churches." The converts were known as Moriscos.

But most Moriscos knew little about Christianity and kept to their Muslim ways while going to churches that were once mosques. The Inquisition sent its agents to Granada to punish the new Christians who were backsliding into Islamic heresy. Royal edicts banned Arabic customs: Moriscos couldn't use the Arabic language, especially to name their children. Women had to drop their veils. Even the public Arab baths were closed as dens of sin. In vain, a Morisco leader protested that these baths were used only for cleanliness; men and women were never allowed in at the same time. If sinful women wanted to meet their lovers, he said, "they would manage this more readily by going on social calls, or visiting churches, or going to religious festivities and plays where men and women were mixed up together."

BUYING UP MORISCO LAND AT BARGAIN RATES

In 1568 the desperate Moriscos rose in rebellion in the Alpujarra Mountains between Granada and the Mediterranean

Sea. The Spaniards suppressed this uprising with great ferocity and brutality and, to make sure this would never happen again, forced most Moriscos to leave the Granada region and live elsewhere in Spain. Spaniards were invited to pour into Granada and buy up Morisco land at bargain rates. All this, however, did not solve what the Spaniards regarded as their "Morisco problem"—a large population of seemingly unchristian Christians. In 1609, Spain, claiming that this population might somehow become a fifth column for the Islamic Turks threatening Europe, decided to expel all its Moriscos, just as it had expelled all its Jews a little more than a century before. It is estimated that, within five years, 300,000 Moriscos were forced out of Spain. Perhaps 20,000, for one reason or another, managed to elude the expulsion order and remain.

They did not lose all their ways in a rural and provincial Spain that entered the modern age only a few decades ago. "When I grew up on the Almería coast, Martínez Soler told me, "there were women who wore veils and carried jugs of water on their heads. As late as 30 years ago, you could still see women with veils, even in church. Just a few years ago, I was the master of ceremonies at a music festival and was amazed at some of the songs of the people who came down from the Alpujarra Mountains. The words of their religious hymns were Catholic, but the music was Arabic."

Spaniards, in fact, are now proud that they did not wipe out all the traces of Islam. During a visit in 1986 to the unique cathedral that was created centuries ago out of the Great Mosque of Córdoba, King Juan Carlos, the successor to Ferdinand and Isabella in democratic Spain, said, "The light that shines upon us from the cathedral of Córdoba is neither moribund nor tremulous. It is intense, penetrating, illuminating the way. It represents the embrace of all the communities of the world."

Crusade's Strange Twist

They set out to rescue the Holy Land from the Muslims. Instead, they appeared at the walls of the greatest city in Christendom.

Richard McCaffery Robinson

Richard McCaffery Robinson, a writer for magazines and encyclopedias, once served as an officer aboard an amphibious LST. As further reading, he suggests John Godfrey's 1204: The Unholy Crusade, *which is "aimed at the general reader and provides more background"; and Donald E. Queller's* The Fourth Crusade.

Early in October 1202, a fleet of 200 ships set sail from the lagoon of Venice. Banners whipped from every masthead, some bearing the lion of Venice, others charged with the coats of arms of the noblest houses of France.

Leading the fleet was the state galley of Doge Enrico Dandolo, the elected "duke" of the Venetian Republic. He was more than 80 years old and nearly blind, but undimmed in vigor and ability. His galley was painted imperial vermilion, and a vermilion silk canopy covered the poop on which the doge sat in state. In front of him, four silver trumpets sounded, answered from the other ships by hundreds of trumpets, drums and tabors.

The goal of this expedition, this Fourth Crusade, was to win back the holy city of Jerusalem. Conquered by Islamic armies in the 7th century, it had been regained for Christendom by the First Crusade in 1099. In 1187, during the Second Crusade and just 15 years before the doge's fleet set sail, Jerusalem fell to the Muslim Saladin, who then stalemated a recovery attempt by the Third Crusade (1189–92). The Fourth Crusade was to follow a new strategy: strike at Egypt, the base of Muslim power. But it never reached its goal.

Instead, a bizarre twist of fate turned the latest crusaders in a totally unexpected direction—toward the greatest Christian city in the world—Constantinople, capital of the Byzantine (or Eastern Roman) Empire.

The Fourth Crusade was actually conceived in 1199 at a jousting tournament held by Thibaut, Count of Champagne, at Ecry-sur-Aisne in northern France. There, in a sudden wave of mass emotion, the assembled knights and barons fell to their knees weeping for the captive Holy Land. They swore solemn oaths to go as armed pilgrims to wrest it from the infidels. In the months that followed, the crusade took form in a series of feudal assemblies headed by Count Thibaut; Baldwin, Count of Flanders; and Louis, Count of Blois. Rather than wear out their army by a long land march through hostile territory, the leaders decided to reach Egypt by sea. A delegation of six trusted knights went to Venice, the leading seafaring city of Western Europe, to arrange for passage. One of those envoys, Geoffrey of Villehardouin, Marshal of Champagne, later wrote a chronicle of the expedition.

In Venice, Villehardouin and his fellow envoys hammered out an agreement with Doge Dandolo and his council. Venice would provide transport ships, crews and a year's provisions for 4,500 knights with their mounts, 9,000 squires and "sergeants" (feudal men-at-arms of less than knightly rank), and 20,000 ordinary footmen, for a total of 33,500 men and 4,500 horses.

The price for this armada would be 84,000 marks of silver. And the old doge made Venice not a mere supply contractor, but a full partner in the crusade. In return for a half-share of all conquests, Venice would provide an escort force of 50 fully manned war galleys. The great fleet was to sail in the summer of the next year, 1202.

About that time, a teenage boy escaped from captivity in Constantinople. He was Alexius Angelus, son of the deposed Byzantine Emperor Isaac II. Six years earlier, in 1195, Isaac's brother—also named Alexius—had overthrown and imprisoned him, taking the throne for himself as Emperor Alexius III. Isaac was blinded, the traditional Byzantine way of dealing with rivals, since by custom a blind man could not be emperor.

Alexius III's talents did not match his ambition. He made his brother-in-law admiral of the imperial navy. The brother-in-law stripped the fleet bare, selling off gear and entire ships to line his own pockets. The new emperor was also careless in guarding his captives. The blinded Isaac II was no threat, but his son Alexius was able-bodied enough to escape. Eventually he found his way to the court of German King Philip of Swabia, whose queen was the boy's sister Irene.

In the meantime, there was another fateful event—Thibaut of Champagne died before the crusade could set forth. To take his place as leader, his fellow barons chose a northern Italian nobleman, Count Boniface of Montferrat. Boniface had family ties to the nominal Christian king of Jerusalem, leader of the Christians who still held out in parts of the Holy Land. He also happened to be a vassal of King Philip of Swabia, the same with whom young Prince Alexius had taken refuge. Boniface and the young prince probably met when Boniface visited his liege lord's court late in 1201.

And now came the seeding of a new plan—the crusaders could stop at Constantinople on their way to Egypt, overthrow the usurper Alexius III and put the young Alexius on the imperial throne.

From *Military History*, August 1993, pp. 30–37. © 1993 by Cowles History Group, 741 Miller Drive, Suite D-2, Leesburg, VA 22075. Reprinted by permission.

NATIONAL ARCHIVES

A Venetian galley. The 60 fighting galleys that Venice committed to the Fourth Crusade were rowed by free, armed seamen rather than slaves or convicts.

For 500 years, it may be recalled, the Byzantine Empire had been Christendom's chief bulwark against the Islamic challenge. By 1201 the empire, though greatly shrunken and weakened, was still the most powerful and best organized of Christian states. But relations between Byzantines and Western Christians had deteriorated steadily through the century of the crusades, over which they were often at odds. From a Western viewpoint, an emperor who owed his throne to crusaders might be more cooperative.

During the late spring of 1202, the crusaders began to gather at Venice. By the intended departure date their host totaled some 10,000 men, far short of the 33,500 planned for—and too few to provide the agreed upon charter fee. The Venetians had suspended their regular commerce to build and equip an immense fleet. Now they demanded that the crusaders hold up their end of the deal: 84,000 marks, or no crusade.

The Fourth Crusade seemed on the point of collapse. Then Doge Dandolo made an offer. The Venetians would suspend the unpaid balance of the transport charge in return for a small consideration—the crusaders' assistance in conquering the city of Zara (later to become Zadar, Yugoslavia), a Hungarian-owned port on the Dalmatian coast of the Adriatic. To the more pious crusaders, this was a devil's bargain, an unholy act of war against fellow Christians. But others, including the leading barons, saw no choice if the crusade was to go forward. With some difficulty, they persuaded the dissidents to go along.

At last the fleet could set forth. It included three main ship types. About 40 vessels, called simply "ships," were standard Mediterranean heavy cargo ships, two-deckers for the most part, with high fore- and after-castles, twin steering oars and two masts on which triangular lateen sails were hung from long sloping yards. They were slow and unhandy, but their size and height made them effective in defense—or in attack against fixed objectives. Offering mobile support were 60 fighting galleys, rowed not by chained slaves or convicts, but by free and armed Venetian seamen.

The remaining 100 or so ships were "uissiers," horse transports. These resembled galleys, but were larger and heavier, with fewer oars. An uissier's hold was divided into stalls for horses, which were firmly strapped into place when the vessel was underway. A door-like hatch over an entry port in the hull aft could be lowered, drawbridge-fashion, to lead the horses in and out of the hold. These medieval counterparts to the LST (landing ship, tank) allowed knights to go ashore ready for immediate action.

On November 10, the fleet reached Zara, which surrendered after a 14-day siege. Many knights deserted rather than take part. (One was Simon de Montfort, whose son, also named Simon de Montfort, later won fame in England as the "father of Parliament." The elder Simon's moral scruples about crusading against Christians were short-lived, for it was he who later led the brutal "Albigensian crusade," which ravaged much of southern France in the name of stamping out heresy.) After Zara, meanwhile, Pope Innocent III excommunicated the Venetians and threatened to excommunicate the entire crusade.

The crusaders set up winter quarters at Zara, as it was too late in the season to go on. There, the leaders met with Prince Alexius and agreed to put him on the Byzantine throne in place of Alexius III. The usurper was hated in Constantinople, Prince Alexius assured them. In return for the crusaders' aid, he promised to pay off their debt to the Venetians and lead a Byzantine army in the proposed assault on Egypt.

In the spring of 1203, the crusade set out from Zara. And then an odd incident took place as the fleet rounded the southern tip of Greece. The crusaders passed two ships carrying knights and men-at-arms—who hid their faces in shame when the ships were hailed and boarded. They had never joined the main crusading force at Venice, but had sailed to the Holy Land on their own from another port. The errant knights had accomplished nothing and suffered heavily from the plague before giving up. According to Villehardouin, one now "deserted" in reverse.

"Do what you like with anything I've left behind," he told his comrades, "I'm going with these people, for it certainly seems to me they'll win some land for

Byzantines thought of their present emperor, they would not take a new one at the hands of foreigners.

Losing hope of a popular uprising, the crusaders then settled down to the serious matter at hand. The city of Constantinople (today's Istanbul, Turkey) was roughly triangular, set on a peninsula between the Sea of Marmara on the south and the Golden Horn, the city's great harbor, on the north. Only to the west could it be attacked by land—and the land walls were one of the world's greatest fortifications. Built 800 years earlier by the Roman Emperor Theodosius the Great, they consisted of a moat backed up by a parapet, and behind that a double wall. Less elaborate single walls protected the city along the Marmara shore and the Golden Horn harbor front. The Golden Horn was guarded by a chain across the harbor entrance, and the far end of the chain was covered in turn by a fortress called the Tower of Galata.

Armies far mightier than the crusaders had dashed themselves to ruin before those defenses. Constantinople withstood two epic sieges by the Muslim Arabs, from 673 to 678 and in 717, and other sieges by Avars, Bulgars and Russian Vikings. Manning its walls were the hard core of the Byzantine army, the feared ax-wielding Varangian Guard. First recruited from Vikings, the Varangian Guard became heavily Anglo-Saxon in the years after the Norman conquest of England. Aiding the defense were Pisans, bitter trading rivals of the Venetians.

The city's first line of defense normally would have been the dromons, Byzantium's great double-banked galleys. But the graft of the emperor's brother-in-law had reduced the fleet to 20 old and useless ships. The Byzantines could only take defensive positions and wait for the blow to land. It came on July 5. The crusaders crossed the Bosporus, landing near the Tower of Galata. A few dromons could have intervened with decisive effect at this point, but no Byzantine ships were fit for action.

Emperor Alexius III led a large field army out to oppose the landing. Crusader horse-transports ran onto the beach, supported by crossbow and archery fire, and dropped their entry-port covers as ramps. Down rode armored French knights, lances couched. A century earlier, the Byzantine princess and historian Anna Comnena had written that a French knight's charge "would make a

Jacopo Tintoretto's impression of the amphibious assault on Constantinople's walls across the Golden Horn. The Venetians ingeniously turned their ships into floating siege towers.

themselves!" And with that less-than-pious remark, he jumped into the boat with the departing boarding party and joined the fleet.

On June 24, 1203, the fleet passed in review beneath the walls of Constantinople. The crusaders landed on the Asian side of the Bosporus and—following a skirmish ashore—set up a base at the city of Scutari, just a mile across the Bosporus from Constantinople. On July 3, at Dandolo's suggestion, they tried to trigger a popular rising in young Alexius' favor. Alexius stood dressed in state robes on the poop of a galley that rowed back and forth under the walls of the city to display their rightful emperor to the people. The response was less than overwhelming. When the galley came close

to the walls it was met by a hail of arrows, not by the hoped-for cheers.

That episode was fair warning for the crusaders' leaders, who, especially wily old Dandolo, have been accused of cynically plotting the conquest of Constantinople for their own profit. If Dandolo and the other leaders sincerely believed in Prince Alexius as their vehicle, their belief was wrong. A Byzantine emperor was not a dynastic king like those of the feudal West. In the Roman imperial tradition, he was more a "president for life" with absolute authority. Whoever could take the throne and hold it was accepted as emperor. But young Alexius had no special right to the throne simply because he was the son of a deposed former emperor—and, whatever the

Baldwin of Flanders leads his Frenchmen over the walls. After Emperor Alexius IV was deposed, the crusaders eventually had to assault Constantinople a second time.

hole through the walls of Babylon." The Byzantines retreated, abandoning tents and booty to the crusaders.

The Tower of Galata was now open to attack. Its English, Danish and Pisan garrison mounted an active defense, making sallies against the invaders. In one such action the defenders were forced back and could not shut the gates of the tower before the advancing French. It fell by storm. A giant Venetian transport, *Aquila* ("Eagle"), charged the harbor chain under full sail and snapped it. Venetian galleys rowed into the harbor, quickly disposing of the weak Byzantine squadron drawn up behind the chain. The crusaders then took up quarters in the unwalled "suburbs" of Pera and Es-

tanor on the north side of the Golden Horn. Their leaders met to plan their attack on the city itself.

Doge Dandolo recommended an attack on the harbor wall. It was less formidable than the land walls, and the big transports could nudge close to serve as floating siege towers. The French, however, wanted to fight ashore, in their own element. The final decision was to mount a double attack, the Venetians against the harbor wall and the French against the north end of the land wall, adjacent to the Palace of Blachernae. This section of wall was a late addition and somewhat weaker than the original

Theodosian land walls. After crossing the Golden Horn, the French took up a position opposite the wall, near a fortified monastery they called Bohemond's Castle after a hero of the First Crusade.

The double assault was launched on July 17. The Venetian fleet formed up in line and advanced against the harbor wall. The big transports raised flying assault bridges, fashioned from spars and suspended from their foremasts, an arrangement that allowed men on the bridgeheads to fight, three abreast, from positions equal in height to the tops of the towers they were assaulting. Fire support was provided by mangonels and petraries, catapultlike mechanical artillery set up aboard the ships. Light and speedy by comparison, the maneuverable galleys were ready to throw reinforcements ashore where needed.

The attack hung in the balance until Doge Dandolo ordered his own galley to advance and set him ashore. The courage of the old doge fired up the Venetians, and they pressed home the attack. The Venetian banner was hoisted atop a wall tower. Soon 25 towers—about a mile of wall—were taken.

Behind the wall, however, the Varangian guardsmen held their ground. Unable to advance, the Venetians set fire to nearby buildings. Driven by the wind, the fire then burned much of the city. The Venetians also captured a few horses on the waterfront, and "with some irony," as one naval historian put it, sent them around to the French knights.

The French attack on the land wall did not go so well. Scaling ladders were less effective than the Venetians' floating siege towers, and the assault was thrown back. Emperor Alexius III took to the field in a counterattack, leading an imperial force of nine "battles," or massed formations, out the gates. The French met it with seven "battles" of their own.

As often happened with feudal armies, the logic of "command and control" conflicted with the chivalric impulse to be first in the attack. Count Baldwin, in command of the leading battle, at first held his ground, but other crusaders went brashly forward—forcing Baldwin to follow, to save face-until they all found themselves dangerously exposed to the Byzantine army and out of sight of most of their own force.

Word of the French peril reached Doge Dandolo. Saying he would live or die with the crusaders, he ordered his men to abandon their hard-won towers

The "Latin Empire" set up by the crusaders seemed as shaky as the Byzantine Empire. After ousting Boniface of Montferrat, Baldwin of Flanders was crowned Emperor Baldwin I.

and redeploy in support of their allies. And at the sight of Venetian galleys moving up the harbor to set more troops ashore, the emperor retreated into the city. He had achieved his tactical objective, holding off the French and forcing the Venetians to abandon their gains.

But Alexius III also had lost his nerve. That night he fled the city with his mistress and a favorite daughter—leaving his empress behind. Byzantine nobles hastily met and restored blinded old Isaac II, young Alexius' father, in disregard of the tradition that made blindness a bar to the throne. When the crusaders heard of this, they demanded that young Alexius be crowned alongside his father. They still had a powerful army and fleet, they had nearly taken the city, and there was no real leadership among the defenders. The demand was granted, and young Alexius was escorted into the city in state, along with the doge and the leading French counts and barons.

The crusaders' assault had failed tactically, but it had won its strategic objective. The late emperor, Alexius III, was a fugitive, and young Alexius now sat crowned beside his father as Emperor Alexius IV. And next? It was too late in the season to go on, but the crusaders looked forward to receiving supplies and Byzantine reinforcements. Come spring they could sail on to Egypt and restore the Holy Land to the Cross.

Alas, young Alexius could not keep the grand promises he had made. The imperial treasury was empty. Moreover, while the Byzantines and the crusaders were now allies in theory, their relationship was actually poor and grew steadily worse. The Byzantines detested the crudity of the French and the highhandedness of the Venetians. In turn, the Westerners despised the Byzantines as effete cowards.

After repeated riots, one of which led to a second disastrous fire, individual

crusaders no longer dared show themselves in the city. Moreover, Byzantine hatred of the "barbarians" extended beyond the crusaders to embrace all the Western Europeans who lived in the city—even the Pisans who had fought recently and well on the Byzantine side. Men, women and children were massacred. The survivors fled to the crusader camp, considerably reinforcing the invaders' army.

Young Alexius IV could not raise enough money to satisfy the crusaders, nor could he force them away. He fell under the influence of a noble adviser, Alexius Ducas, popularly known as Mourtzouphlos, a name that referred to his prominent, bushy eyebrows. Eventually, Mourtzouphlos did a typically Byzantine thing—he lured the young emperor into a trap, kidnapped and imprisoned him, and took the throne for himself.

Mourtzouphlos, now Emperor Alexius V (the third Emperor Alexius in one year!), was more of a leader than his recent predecessors. He slammed shut the gates of the city against the crusaders and put the defenses in order. Wooden superstructures were built atop the towers of the harbor wall, raising them two or three stories and reducing the effectiveness of the Venetian ships as floating siege towers. Gates in the wall were bricked up to eliminate weak spots in the defenses.

Mourtzouphlos also took active "outreach" measures. The crusader fleet was moored in the Golden Horn, directly across from the city. One December night when the wind blew from the south, he launched a fireship attack against the Venetian fleet. It was a textbook situation—in the confined anchorage, against a lee shore, the Venetians could not simply drop back and let the fireships burn out.

But they were not rattled. They manned their galleys, drove off boatloads of archers covering the fire attack, grappled the fireships and towed them clear of the fleet. According to Villehardouin, "No men ever defended themselves more gallantly on the sea than the Venetians did that night."

In January, Mourtzouphlos received word that a crusader foraging expedition was raiding the town of Philia, some miles northwest of Constantinople. He ambushed the returning crusaders, but the cornered and outnumbered French knights rallied to the counterattack. They drove off the Byzantines and captured the imperial standard and the holy icon that traditionally accompanied Byzantine emperors into battle.

Mourtzouphlos nonetheless returned to Constantinople and proclaimed a victory. Asked about the standard and icon, he claimed that they were put away in safekeeping. Word of this lie quickly reached the crusaders, who did the logical thing: they mounted standard and icon on a Venetian galley and paraded them back and forth under the harbor walls. That affair was fatal to the unfortunate prisoner Alexius IV. Mourtzouphlos, humiliated, feared a palace revolt in the young deposed emperor's name. After several efforts at poisoning failed, Mourtzouphlos had him strangled. Old Isaac II died about the same time, probably without need of assistance.

The crusaders saw they could not hope to have the cooperation of any Byzantine emperor. They resolved instead to conquer the city and take the entire Byzantine Empire for themselves. Six French and six Venetian nobles were to elect a new emperor, who would receive a quarter of the empire in his own name, the rest being divided between French feudal fiefs and Venetian holdings. Doge Dandolo—who had gradually emerged as the real leader of the crusade—saw to it that the Venetians owed no feudal duties for their "quarter and a half" (that is, three-eighths) of the Empire.

In the previous assault, the Venetians had succeeded against the harbor wall, so the French leaders were persuaded to join them in another amphibious attempt. Knights and horses embarked in the horse transports; others boarded the assault ships. As armor protection against Byzantine mechanical artillery, the ships were protected by wooden mantlets, which were covered with vines, to soften impacts, and vinegar-soaked leather as protection against incendiary Greek fire.

On the morning of April 9, 1204, the fleet moved forward against the harbor wall to the sound of trumpets, drums and tabors, with flags and pennants flying. But a south wind made it difficult to close with the shore, and only the largest ships carried structures high enough to match Mourtzouphlos' new defenses. Men on the bridges traded indecisive strokes with the ax-wielding Varangians in the towers. Other crusaders landed below the walls. Under cover of defensive shells called "turtles," they attempted to break through the bricked-up gates.

To no avail. After several hours and no success, the crusaders were forced back, and the fleet retired. They had lost about 100 dead, while Byzantine losses were few. According to Robert de Clari, a knight who wrote an eyewitness account, some defenders added insult to injury. They dropped their breechclouts and displayed bare buttocks to the retreating crusaders.

Mourtzouphlos had personally directed the defense from high ground behind the harbor wall, near the monastery of Christ Pantopoptes, the All-Seeing. Now he proclaimed success to his people. "Am I not a good Emperor?" he asked them, and answered his own question: "I am the best Emperor you have ever had. I will dishonor and hang them all."

A weary and dispirited group of crusading leaders met that evening to plan their next move. Some of the French suggested an attack on the Sea of Marmara side of the city, where the defenses had not been reinforced. Doge Dandolo explained that this was not practical, as the currents and prevailing winds would interfere with an assault there.

The final decision was for another attempt on the harbor wall, with one important innovation. The big transports were lashed together in pairs, allowing two ships' bridges and assault groups to concentrate against each tower.

The assault was planned for Monday, April 12. On Sunday, all the crusaders, including the excommunicated Venetians, celebrated Mass. To allow greater concentration on the task at hand, according to Robert de Clari, all the prostitutes accompanying the crusading army were bustled onto a ship and "sent far away."

On Monday the fleet attacked, aided this time by a favoring wind. But the previous setback had raised the defenders' spirits, and the walls and towers were heavily manned. For hours the fighting was indecisive. Then a gust of wind pushed two of the largest ships, *Peregrino* ("*Pilgrim*") and *Paradiso*, hard up against the foreshore.

An assault bridge made contact with the top level of a tower, and a Venetian scrambled onto it, only to be cut down. Then a French knight named André d'Ureboise made it across and stood his ground. (He must have been a man of exceptional skill and valor to be able to fight fully armored high above a swaying ship). Reinforcements joined d'Ureboise, and the Varangian defenders were forced out of the tower. Within minutes five towers fell to the attackers. The action now turned to the base of the wall. A group of men with picks broke through a bricked-up gate. A warlike priest—Robert de Clari's brother Aleaumes—crawled through the hole and drove back the defenders on the other side. A handful of knights climbed through after him.

That breakthrough took place right below Mourtzouphlos' command post. The emperor spurred forward to counterattack. The crusaders stood their ground, and he retreated. For him, and for Byzantium, it was a fatal loss of nerve. Other gates were broken open, and war horses swarmed out of the transports and into the city. The crusader knights formed up for a mounted charge. The Byzantine defensive formation broke, and the emperor himself fled into one of his palaces.

The corner had been turned, but the crusaders were worn out by the day's fighting and still outnumbered. They expected weeks of street-by-street fighting to come, and took up a defensive position along the wall, torched nearby buildings—the siege's third fire—to protect themselves against a counterattack in the night.

During the night, Alexius "Mourtzouphlos" Ducas fled, just as Alexius III had the previous fall. Resistance ceased.

For the next three days, this greatest of Christian cities suffered a thorough and ruthless sack. Priceless treasures of antiquity were smashed to pieces or melted down for their precious metals. While the French knights and men-at-arms went on a drunken rampage, the Venetians set to work like seasoned professional thieves, scooping up the best of the fallen city's treasures. The four great bronze horses that now grace the front of St. Mark's in Venice are only the most notable monuments to the thoroughness of their rapacity.

The Byzantine Empire never recovered. The "Latin Empire" that the crusaders set up in its place was a shaky affair that never gained control of much former Byzantine territory. Boniface of Montferrat, the crusade's nominal leader, was pushed aside, and Baldwin of Flanders became Emperor Baldwin I. The next year he was taken prisoner in an ill-advised battle. Soon the "Empire" was reduced to little more than the city of Constantinople, and in 1262 it was retaken by a Byzantine emperor-in-exile, Michael Paleologus. But the restored Byzantium never regained its former power and was finally and forever extinguished by the Turks in 1453.

As a military operation, the Fourth Crusade stands out as one of history's great amphibious assaults. Twice the harbor wall of Constantinople fell to direct assault from the ships of the Venetian fleet. In most land sieges, deploying just one siege tower was a major effort. The Venetian fleet had deployed an entire line of them!

During the later age of men-of-war armed with cannon, this newborn amphibious capability was lost. Successful amphibious assaults were rare during the age of fighting sail. Even in World War I, when the Allies unsuccessfully attacked Gallipoli (prelude to an intended assault on Constantinople), soldiers were condemned to flounder ashore in ships' boats ineffectually supported by warships. Not until World War II did amphibious warfare again reach the level of sophistication embodied in the Venetian fleet during the Fourth Crusade.

In France, an ordeal by fire and a monster weapon called 'Bad Neighbor'

David Roberts

A mountain climber and writer, David Roberts lives in Cambridge, Massachusetts, when not traveling. His most recent book is Iceland: Land of the Sagas.

On a sunny June morning, I sat atop a high wall on the ruined castle of Montségur in southern France, my feet dangling over the edge. Before me lay the narrow pentagon of the fortress' inner courtyard. Despite the summer warmth, it was easy to conjure up the gloom of medieval Decembers inside that claustrophobic keep. Floating in the sky at the apex of a pinnacle of gray limestone, Montségur seems to breathe adamantine inaccessibility.

On my left, 500 feet below, a group of schoolchildren had spread out their picnic on the edge of a field blazing with dandelions. The carefree music of their voices wafted up to me. It seemed unlikely that the youngsters knew much about that meadow, whose ancient name, Prat dels Crematz, means "Field of the Burned." There, one March day in A.D. 1244, knights of the French army built a huge pyre of brush and wood; then they led more than 200 chained prisoners from the castle down to the pyre and burned them alive. The victims were Cathars, nonviolent Christian heretics whose apostasy had convulsed Europe for half a century. They went to their deaths not so much in terror as with an eerie serenity.

To the average American, the Albigensian Crusade, if the term calls up anything at all, is but a musty vapor from some forgotten history lesson. To the inhabitants of Languedoc, the green and craggy winegrowing region that sprawls across southwestern France, the crusade forms a keystone of cultural identity. But for that bitter and protracted war—the only crusade ever declared by a pope against Europeans—Languedoc might today be an independent country. Its people might speak Occitan, not French, and troubadour poets might still sing of their love for unattainable ladies.

Like the Manichaes whom Saint Augustine combated at the end of the fourth century, the Cathars were dualists holding that all things on Earth were evil, the creation of the Devil who, in the strict version of the faith, was as eternal and powerful as God. Cathars rejected the Old Testament, whose wrathful Jehovah was actually Satan in disguise. They rejected the Catholic sacraments, including baptism at birth, marriage, confession and the Eucharist. Since all matter was evil, Cathars refused to believe that Christ had ever assumed a human body; his apparent incarnation was an illusion used by God to instruct the faithful. The only prayer Cathars said was the Lord's Prayer, which they recited as often as 40 times a day.

All men and women were composed of a corrupt body; a spirit, which alone could find heaven; and a soul that, "suspended between two abysses," sought to unite with the spirit while being sorely tempted by the flesh. The Cathars were divided into an elite, called *parfaits,* or "perfects," and a larger population of mere *croyants,* or "believers." To become a *parfait* required a novitiate in austerity lasting as long as three or four years, capped with a formal ceremony called the *consolamentum,* a kind of baptism by book and word rather than by water. *Parfaits* refused to eat meat or any other food, such as cheese or eggs, that was a byproduct of animal procreation. They could never touch women. (There were many *parfaites,* females who made equivalent vows, and who had equal status with the *parfaits.*) *Parfaits* resolved never to lie, and to face death without fear. "There is no more beautiful death than that of fire," they assured one another.

Until persecution made disguise essential, the *parfait* wore a long black robe under which he hung a parchment copy of the Gospel according to John from a leather belt. *Parfaits* were full-bearded and wore their hair long (women had to hide their hair). They traveled about the countryside in pairs, never alone, for safety but also to keep watch upon one another. Ordinary *croyants* could lead lives of normal sensuality, but near the end had to take the *consolamentum.* There sometimes followed a process called *endura,* in which the fresh convert deliberately starved to death.

The Cathars were drawn to southwestern France because of the region's tolerance for unorthodox ideas. By the 12th century, Languedoc had become, in the words of one scholar, "in many respects the most civilized part of western Europe." The city of Toulouse was more opulent and more intellectually advanced than Paris. Troubadour poets were engaged in the heady task of inventing the lyric poetry of the Renaissance. The Occitan language was regarded by literate Europeans as superior to French or Italian: Dante originally planned to write the *Divine Comedy* in that tongue. The rigid feudalism of the north did not hold sway in Languedoc, where peasants often owned their own land. In the 12th century, France was far from the unified country we know today: its king ruled a

From *Smithsonian* magazine, May 1991, pp. 40-48, 50-51. © 1991 by David Roberts. Reprinted by permission of the author.

territory only one-tenth the size of modern France. The count of Toulouse, as the most powerful lord in Languedoc, was virtually a king in his own right.

Alarmed by the rise of the Cathars, a series of 12th-century popes set out to stop them. Their remedy was to send the best Catholic orators to Languedoc to preach the truth. The first emissary was no less a figure than Saint Bernard, who packed the cathedral at Albi but failed to convert more than a handful. The preaching crusade gave way to a series of debates between Cathar and Catholic spokesmen. These wildly popular frays lasted as long as eight days. Led by such eloquent *parfaits* as Guilabert of Castres, the Cathars gave as good as they got.

FIGHTING THE HERETICS WITH THEIR OWN WEAPONS

One day in 1206, a pair of discouraged Spanish clerics paused for a rest in Montpellier, where they ran into some equally disheartened papal legates, veterans of these debates. It suddenly occurred to the Spaniards that the Cathars had won much of their following by the daunting example of their poverty and simplicity. Why not fight the heretics with their own weapons? The Spaniards set out barefoot, penniless, living on bread and water, to preach their way across Languedoc. The older priest quickly weakened and went home to die, but the younger made people sit up and take notice. Dominic de Guzman, soon to found an order of preaching friars now called the Dominicans, was regarded in Languedoc as an impressive madman. He slept by the roadside even in winter, and when crowds jeered him, he strode along singing.

Saint Dominic was a fierce debater, still full of energy on his eighth day of nonstop haggling. At least once he went head to head with his Cathar match, Guilabert of Castres. Yet even Dominic failed to dent the heresy. Unable to document mass conversions, his chroniclers cited instead the testimony of miracles. In a backcountry castle, they reported, Dominic and his opponent decided to let God settle the debate. Each committed his gospel to an envoy of the other side, who threw it into the fire. The Cathar book burned to ashes, but Dominic's leapt out of the flames and struck a rafter. In the church at Fanjeaux, the town where Dominic settled, you can

still see the rafter, scarred by the sparks that flew up with the book.

In 1198, Innocent III, who would come to be regarded as the greatest of medieval pontiffs, was elected pope. Relentless in his determination to wipe out the Albigensian heresy (named after the people, or *gens,* of Albi, a town rife with dualists), Innocent began snarling at the heels of the Languedocian nobility who sheltered Cathars. His main target was Raymond VI, count of Toulouse. A sensual, cultured man, Raymond would manage to steer his ship of state through a 20-year narrows of treacherous shoals.

Innocent's main outpost in Languedoc was the monastery of Fontfroide. From its cloister, the papal legate charged with exterminating heresy in Languedoc set forth for a meeting with Raymond VI. In January 1208 these two stubborn men locked horns at St.-Gilles. In a foul temper, Raymond refused to give in to the legate's demands, and uttered vague threats when the man announced his departure. The next morning, as the legate's party tried to ford the Rhône, a mysterious horseman charged the camp and killed the legate with a lance through the back.

Thus, in a single stroke, began what would become, in the words of Jonathan Sumption, whose *The Albigensian Crusade* is the best book in English about the subject, "one of the most savage of all mediaeval wars." Innocent declared the legate a martyr and launched the crusade. Monks roamed the northern roads, offering the papal indulgence of remission of all sins for 40 days' service in the holy war. An army of northerners more than 15,000 strong, swelled by German mercenaries, gathered in Lyon. As religious leader of the crusade, Innocent appointed the abbot Arnald-Amaury, an ambitious fanatic who had no qualms about killing heretics.

In July 1209 the army marched on the ill-prepared town of Béziers, in northeastern Languedoc. Led by a ragtag mob of camp followers and servants, the crusaders burst through the town gates and unleashed a riot of murder and looting. In the middle of the massacre, it was reported, Arnald-Amaury was asked how the soldiers could distinguish heretics from Catholics. "Kill them all," he replied; "God will recognize his own."

Terrified by the news from Béziers, other towns surrendered without a fight. Raymond VI dared not openly support the defenders, let alone ride at their head.

Already excommunicated by the pope, he was forced to undergo a humiliating public flogging in hopes of retaining his title as count of Toulouse. The defense of Languedoc fell instead to more-militant leaders, like Raymond-Roger Trencavel, the nephew of Raymond VI.

AT CARCASSONNE, A SAFE-CONDUCT BETRAYED

Only 24 at the time, Trencavel set up a garrison inside the walls of Carcassonne. The crusaders laid siege to the city. After 18 days, the defenders had repulsed the bravest attacks of the huge army, but the crowds that had taken refuge inside were beginning to perish from lack of food and water. Trencavel accepted a safe-conduct to negotiate with the crusaders, who immediately betrayed it, seizing the young viscount and clapping him in irons.

This time, however, the lives of the citizens were spared. Trencavel was thrown in prison, where he died three months later—perhaps from dysentery, though everyone in Languedoc today believes that the hero of the resistance was poisoned in his cell.

Far more than pitched battles, it was lengthy sieges that spelled the course of the Albigensian War. A radical new military technology was applied with a vengeance. The attackers built huge rock-throwing machines, called trebuchets and mangonels, on the spot. Defenders had their own trebuchets, as well as giant cross bows cranked up with winches, called ballistae, that were remarkably accurate. Incredibly daring sappers dug trenches up to the walls, where, in an age before explosives, under fire from the towers, they undermined the stones to make the walls collapse. The *tour roulante,* which could stand as tall as 150 feet and carry a hundred soldiers, was the ultimate war machine: pushed across wooden rollers up to a stone wall, it disgorged a horde of frenzied attackers who swarmed inside a fortified city.

Though the eradication of heresy was the pretext for the crusade, it quickly became a free-for-all of secular opportunism. The southerners recruited their own mercenaries, many of them from Spain. Petty lords of the north, languishing in bankrupt fiefdoms, saw the war as a chance to grow rich and powerful in Languedoc. At the siege of Carcassorine the most talented of these carpetbaggers emerged. Simon de Montfort, tall, athletic and fearless, was elected by his peers as head of the army, whose ranks were constantly depleted by crusaders returning home after serving their 40 days. In Sumption's words, Simon was "a model Christian of austere personal morals, and a military leader of genius."

The bloodiest period of the Albigensian War came in its first four years, from 1208 to 1212, as Simon swept brilliantly across the length and breadth of Languedoc. Victories were celebrated with atrocities. At Bram, Simon took a hundred hostages, cut off their noses and upper lips, and blinded all but one, who led the pitiful procession to the castle of Cabaret. Such spectacles were designed to terrify the populace and facilitate the conquest, but they revealed as well the self-righteous cruelty of fanaticism, second nature to men like Simon de Montfort and Arnald-Amaury. At Lavaur, Simon ordered 90 captured knights hung; when the gibbet broke under the weight of the first, he impatiently put his captives to death by sword. Giraude, sister of the commander at Lavaur and a noted Cathar, was thrown screaming down a well and stoned to death. Then some 300 to 400 heretics found hiding inside the walls were taken outside town where, as the crusade's historian, who was a participant, put it, we burned them alive with joy in our hearts."

The memory of these depredations is bitter and vivid in Languedoc today. But there were tortures and mutilations on the part of the southerners as well. They too cut off noses and lips, and sent victims back to their leaders as ghastly exemplars. At Toulouse, recorded the crusade's historian in tones of pious indignation, defenders blinded some of their prisoners, cut out the tongues of others and hacked still others to pieces, which they fired at the enemy with a trebuchet.

One of the bravest resistances took place at Minerve, an ancient town extraordinarily situated at the junction of two streams, guarded on three sides by vertical cliffs and linked to the surrounding plateau only by a tiny neck of land. The attackers set up trebuchets on three sides and battered the walls day and night. Their strategy was to assault the covered passageway that led to a well at the base of the cliff on the southeast, Minerve's only source of water. To do so, the crusaders built a giant trebuchet that they sardonically named Malevoisine (Bad Neighbor). After six weeks of

siege, a party of defenders made an intrepid sortie at night and managed to set Malevoisine on fire. But an engineer happened to leave his tent at that moment to relieve himself. He was quickly lanced, but the fire was put out and Malevoisine continued to hammer away at the covered passage.

At last the defenders capitulated. Arnald-Amaury agreed to spare the lives of Minerve's heroic garrison, including its 140 *parfaits,* if only they would abjure their heresy. But as the crusaders marched through the streets, the *parfaits* told them to save their breath: "Why preach at us? We care nothing for your faith, we deny the church of Rome." The *parfaites,* says the chronicler, were even more obdurate than the men. A pyre was prepared. The conquerors were spared the trouble of dragging their victims to their deaths: many Cathars threw themselves onto the flames.

By the end of 1212, Simon had conquered virtually all of Languedoc; yet the war would continue for another 17 years. In driving scores of local noblemen from their domains, the crusaders created a whole class of dispossessed outlaws hungry for revenge. The pride of Languedoc was its vineyards. In Roman times, the best wine in France came from Béziers. The loveliest ornament of the countryside today is its terraced vineyards, a blaze of light green in June, a rash of gold in the autumn harvest. Whenever he besieged a city. Simon de Montfort made it his practice to tear up all the vineyards. This has not been forgotten in Languedoc.

Roads dating from Roman times linked such major cities as Toulouse, Narbonne and Carcassonne. But the backcountry was a tortuous wilderness of dense forests, limestone gorges pocked with caves and mountains beetled with overhanging cliffs. It was all too easy for a displaced lord to bide his time and gather warriors in some remote fastness of the high Corbières or the Ariège. After the burnings of Lavaur and Minerve, the Cathars too fled to the forests and mountains. Their *parfaits* had long since stopped wearing black robes; now they shaved their beards and wore identifying cords secretly beneath their cloaks.

Gradually the Cathars and their adherents began to assemble in clifftop castles deep in the wilderness. The ruins of more than 50 of these sanctuaries stand today. *Citadelles du vertige,* they are called, "vertiginous fortresses," for in

their rude defensive isolation they remain the most spectacular medieval ruins in France.

To seek out these monuments to an extinguished faith is to make a Cathar pilgrimage. The astounding windowed curtain of Peyrepertuse, browing a long precipice: when the French army crested a pass to the north and first saw it, they were stupefied to a man. The cramped, mystic severity of Quéribus, last of all Cathar strongholds to succumb; Lordat, with its mottled, porous limestone lined with veins of black slate; spiky Aguilar, its mortar sprouting sprigs of rosemary and thyme; the four linked towers of Lastours, mirrored by towering cypresses; Termes, which withstood a grim four-month siege, only to be dismantled in the 17th century by a soulless governor; serene Roquefixade, never captured, from whose mount the Cathars signaled by fire to distant Montségur.

Last June, as I stood atop the walls of Puylaurens, to my mind the most graceful of all the *citadelles du vertige,* I pondered an oddity of the 13th century. For decades, a colony of hunted fugitives had led a precarious life inside the spartan precinct beneath my feet. Yet, as is true of most of the Cathar castles, almost no documents survive to attest to that ordeal. Puylaurens is barely mentioned by history.

The sun darted in and out of a morning mist that hung upon the surrounding peaks, and birds sang from the dark woods. In its precipitous, rugged grandeur, Puylaurens set my heart soaring. I found it all but unfathomable to imagine such beauty commanded by men and women to whom all created things were evil, for whom the very grass on which they lay at night was, in the words of a Cathar spokesman, "only corruption and confusion.

The war wound on, as Simon found it harder to keep his southern holdings than it had been to conquer them. One rebellion after another sprang up; the crusaders, who had perfected the art of siege, found themselves besieged. For nine months Raymond VI and Simon struggled over Toulouse, the most important town in Languedoc. Then one day in July 1218, a stone flung blind from a trebuchet hit Simon in the head, killing him. Languedocians still delight in the knowledge that the machine was loaded by women.

Simon's son took over the crusade, but he was not his father's equal. By 1224 the southerners had reclaimed nearly all of Languedoc and were close to winning the war. For years, Innocent III had beseeched the king of France to join the crusade; at last, in 1226, Louis VIII heeded the exhortation. Exhausted by two decades of warfare, which had turned much of their country into wasteland, the southerners gave up in 1229. With the Treaty of Meaux, Languedoc ceased forever to be an independent state. The conquerors tore down the walls of Toulouse and erected new churches. The grandiose cathedrals of Albi and Narbonne were built to proclaim to cowed citizens the eternal supremacy of the church of Rome.

Pope Innocent had died, but Pope Gregory IX knew there were still heretics hiding out all over the South of France. In 1233 he put the Dominicans in charge of a systematic effort to expunge them. Thus was born the Inquisition, whose sinister persecutions were to earn the church as much enmity in Languedoc as the crusade had. The burnings began again—210 at Moissac early on, perhaps 5,000 all told in the subsequent half-century. The inquisitors even convicted dead heretics, exhumed their bones and publicly burned them.

For the remaining Cathars, life became an incessant flight from one sanctuary to another. They ate scraps of leftover food for which they were too proud to beg, furtively announcing their arrival at a sympathetic house by tossing a pebble against the shutter, and guarded their speech, for anyone, even a shepherd in some high Pyrénées pasture, could be an informer. Yet they were heroes in their homeland: a peasant in Montaillou, for instance, kept for 22 years a few crumbs of bread that had been blessed by a *parfait*.

By the late 1230s, some 500 Cathars and supporters had taken refuge in the seemingly impregnable castle of Montségur, atop its steep plug of limestone. They included the brilliant debater Guilabert of Castres. Neither the church nor the royal army knew what to do about this bastion of heresy; for years it was left alone. Then in 1242, some knights from Montségur rode out and murdered a small band of inquisitors. Enraged, the church directed an army of several thousand troops to lay siege to Montségur.

It might have seemed an unequal struggle, but Montségur held out for nine months, through the bitter winter of

1243–44. The royal army had difficulty surrounding the peak's broad and convoluted base; the countryside was full of uncooperative villagers; and the garrison in the castle managed to reinforce itself with insulting ease.

The turning point came in January 1244. Under cover of night, several Basques, specialists at climbing, scaled the cliff on the southeast to attack the crucial east barbican of the castle. As chronicled by Guillaume de Puylaurens, their effort took them, they reported, "with the aid of God, up horrible precipices"; the next morning, "when they examined the terrifying route they had climbed during the night, they knew they would never have dared attempt it by day."

On my own visit to Montségur, I climbed the thousand-foot route that a French historian has identified as the Basque line. It begins in a frightening gully full of huge rocks that dislodge at a touch, and ends on a steep precipice, where there are good holds but immense exposure as well. Even in broad daylight, and in June rather than January, I found the ascent exciting. I was glad to have rock-climbing shoes on my feet, and even gladder not to have to knife any sentries on reaching the summit.

Having won the east barbican, the royal army was able to build a trebuchet that blasted the castle walls from close range. In early March, the garrison surrendered. For reasons that remain obscure, they were granted a grace period of 15 days before leaving the castle. One would think the less committed might have seized the chance to flee with their lives, but instead during that fortnight a steady stream of *croyants* received the *consolamentum*. On March 16, the army led more than 200 Cathars down the mountain and burned them in the meadow.

Unbeknownst to the attackers, the night before the holocaust four Cathar monks had slipped out of the castle, lowered themselves on ropes down the west face of Montségur and made their getaway. Their mission was to take the Cathar treasure, which had already been cached in the forest, and carry it to the caves of the Sabarthès, where it could be securely hidden. No one knows for sure what the Cathar treasure consisted of; before the Inquisition, one insider swore that it was "gold, silver, and a vast quantity of money." It has never been found.

From the late 19th century on, the lost Cathar treasure has inspired legions of

cultists who have prowled through the caves of the Sabarthès in search of esoteric revelations. The huge grotto of Lombrives, some say, became a secret Cathar cathedral. (This amazing cave, one of the largest underground chambers in Europe, did indeed harbor generations of outlaws from the Reformation, the French Revolution and the Napoleonic Wars, whose charcoal signatures scrawled on the walls can be seen today; but the place has never been firmly linked to the Cathars.) A German mystic deduced that the Cathar treasure was nothing less than the Holy Grail, and claimed to find the cave that had once housed it. Generations of Dutch, English and German Rosicrucians, anthroposophists, latter-day Druids, followers of Madame Blavatsky, and believers in extraterrestrial visitors have descended upon the Sabarthès, and continue to do so.

From the antique spa of Ussat-les-Bains, I was guided last June to Bethlehem Cave by a soft-spoken, black-bearded, intense young man named Christian Koenig. As we bushwhacked up a steep slope, he talked of telluric and cosmic currents in the valley; on a limestone wall where I saw only natural calcite drippings, he pointed out three lances entwined by a snake, the 13 intersections corresponding to the 13 lamentations of Sophia. I could take his Rosicrucian ravings with a grain of salt, but suddenly we stood inside the Bethlehem grotto.

Its main opening had been filled with a 25-foot-high wall and doorway, unmistakably Romanesque in style. On the right wall of the cave, incised to a depth of six inches, stood a near-perfect pentagon, large enough for a man to stand in and spread his limbs and head to fill the five points of a star. Was it a natural anomaly? If so, the carved steps leading up to it were certainly man-made. While Koenig talked confidently on about the stages of the Cathar initiation ceremony, I stared at the remarkable object in the middle of the floor. A huge stone slab, 8 feet by 5 feet by 3 feet thick, rested atop three smooth, round, stone pedestals. Was it a prehistoric dolmen? Similar tables are found all over France, dating back as far as the fifth millennium B.C. But I had never seen or read of a dolmen inside a cave.

THE LAST CATHAR IS BURNED AT THE STAKE

Had this amphitheater indeed sheltered heretics after Montségur? We know that through the last half of the 13th century, Cathars continued to meet clandestinely in forests and caves to hold their ceremonies, and the Sabarthès was one of their strongholds. The Inquisition continued to burn them when they caught them. The last enclave of heresy in Languedoc was the tiny upland village of Montaillou. Today the place is somnolent, ingrown. There I talked to an old-timer, who lamented that only two farmers still plowed the fields. I looked through the telephone book where, among only 16 names of residents, I found a "Baille" and several "Clergues"—the same names as those of leading villagers in 1308. But when I asked a local woman about the Cathars, she laughed and said in her country French: *"Ils sont tous dégénéres"*— "They have all disappeared." In 1308 the entire adult population of the town was arrested. Only one of the leading *parfaits* escaped. Guillaume Belibaste fled to

Catalonia, where he survived for more than a decade. But he made the mistake of trusting an old Montaillou neighbor, who had turned informer to the Inquisition. This man lured Belibaste into a trap. The *parfait* was burned at the stake in 1321. He is the last Occitan Cathar of whom we have record.

Wandering across the splendid landscape of Languedoc today, you are constantly nudged by inklings of the Cathar past. Millions of natives still speak Occitan; it is taught in many schools, and if you linger on a park bench in Toulouse or Albi, you can eavesdrop on oldsters conversing in their ancient patois. There are even indications of a new regional militancy, like that of Catalonia: spray-paint graffiti on highway signs that demand the indigenous tongue: *"En Oc!"*

Yet much about the Cathars remains mysterious. In its extirpating fury, the

church burned, along with the heretics, every piece of Cathar writing it could find. We know the Cathars wrote books, but we are left with mere fragments of their thought. What would a medieval scholar give to lay his hands on the meditations of Guilabert of Castres! Our grasp of the faith of the Cathars comes chiefly from confessions wrung from their lips by Catholic torturers who execrated everything they stood for.

An enigma, then—all the more so for the gulf that yawns between their bleak yet optimistic asceticism and modern notions of heaven and earth. Yet the Cathar presence haunts Languedoc still, nowhere more vividly than in the stern ruins that crown its startling peaks. There the wind whistles through gaping archways, the sun slants across broken towers, intimating a world of redeemed and perfect spirit that we shall never see.

Studying the Lives of Medieval Women

Emilie Amt

Emilie Amt is assistant professor of history at Washington College.

In 1322, the medical faculty of the University of Paris brought suit against a Parisian woman, Jacoba Felicie, for practicing medicine without the university's license. The transcript of Jacoba's trial gives us a detailed picture of her activities, of the ailments of her patients, both male and female, and of the medical practices and attitudes of the time. Jacoba herself, who was about thirty years old, argued that she was "experienced in the art of medicine and learned in the precepts of that art," and that "it is better and more suitable and proper that a woman wise and experienced in the art should visit sick women, and that she should examine them and inquire into the secrets of nature and its hidden things, than that a man should do so. . . ." Her patients testified that she had been able to cure them when other physicians had given them up for dead.

Readings like this trial transcript, written at the time of the events they describe, or by participants in those events, are what historians call "sources" or "primary sources." Whenever I teach a history course, I try to include this kind of material in the syllabus. Primary sources are the evidence upon which our picture of the past is built; from them, students learn how we know what we know about history. Sources also have an immediacy and vividness that no modern work can really provide. But when I started teaching a course on medieval women about six years ago, I found very little material of this kind in a format accessible to undergraduates.

The history of medieval women is a field that has exploded in the past ten to twenty years. Large numbers of books and articles have been published on the status, activities and conditions of women in the thousand years we call the Middle Ages (from the fifth to the fifteenth century), and new research continues to appear at a great rate.[1] Clearly there is abundant evidence available to scholars. But only a very limited range of primary sources, mainly the works of female mystics and poets, was available in print in English. To my surprise, no one had published a handy collection of translated historical sources by and about ordinary women in the Middle Ages.

So I decided to write the book that my students and I needed. Or, more accurately, to edit it.[2] This was to prove far more complicated than I imagined when I blithely announced my intentions. The biggest tasks were locating and selecting suitable translated sources (or in some cases translating them myself) and obtaining permission to reprint them from the copyright holders (including a mysteriously disappearing medical doctor; a scholar in Sweden who, fortunately, understood English; and Her Britannic Majesty's Stationery Office).

In the process I've become acquainted with a wonderful variety of individuals from all walks of medieval life. Their stories are revealed in personal narratives, laws, wills, legal instruments, court records, works of theology, manuals of advice, letters, liturgy, ecclesiastical documents, historical accounts, and even archaeological remains. The picture that emerges of life in medieval Europe is a much more complex one than we often imagine, and the attitudes expressed by medieval people can be both very alien to our way of thinking and startlingly familiar.

Take, for example, the area of marriage and family relations. The vast majority of medieval marriages (at least first marriages) were arranged by parents, and historians often speak of marriage as primarily a business arrangement. But behind such generalizations lie a wide variety of real human experiences. For example, Christina of Markyate, a twelfth-century English girl, vowed herself to celibacy and firmly rejected not only the husband her parents had chosen but marriage itself. According to her biographer, her parents "brought her gifts and made great promises: she brushed them aside. They cajoled her; they threatened her; but she would not yield. At last they persuaded one of her close friends and inseparable companions, named Helisen, to soothe her ears by a continuous stream of flattery, so that it would arouse in her, by its very persistence, a desire to become the mistress of a house." We might well expect churchmen, at least, to support Christina's determination to dedicate her life to God, but instead she found herself roundly rebuked by the local bishop for her disobedience to her parents and her implied disrespect for the sacrament of marriage. He also found her motives suspect: "Perhaps you are rejecting marriage with Burthred in order to enter a more wealthy one?"

Most women, of course, did marry, and their expectations of marriage were both pragmatic and optimistic. One thir-

teenth-century English writer summarized a typical young woman's attitude toward marriage as follows: " . . . a man's vigour is worth much, and I need his help for maintenance and food; of a woman's and man's copulation, worldly welfare arises, and a progeny of fair children, that give much joy to their parents. . . . [A] wife hath much comfort of her husband, when they are well consorted, and each is well content with the other." Even in arranged marriages the relations between husband and wife were expected to be close and tender. An anonymous author known as the Householder of Paris wrote to his young wife (she was fifteen when they married) that a hard-working man "is upheld by the hope which he has of the care which his wife will take of him on his return, and of the ease, the joys and the pleasures which she will do to him, . . . to be given good food and drink, to be well served and well looked after, well bedded in white sheets and night-caps, well covered with good furs, and assuaged with other joys and amusements, intimacies, loves and secrets whereof I am silent. And the next day fresh shirts and garments."

As for the "progeny of fair children," there is a common belief today that in pre-modern periods childhood was barely recognized as a distinct phase of life, and that parents could ill afford to lavish affection on their children, given the high infant mortality rate. But the sources show us (and medieval historians generally recognize) that it was utterly normal for parents to love their children deeply. We have a remarkable work written by a ninth-century noble-woman named Dhuoda for her son, from whom she had for some reason been separated by her husband: "I am well aware that most women rejoice that they are with their children in this world, but I, Dhuoda am far away from you, my son William. For this reason I am anxious and filled with longing to do something for you." The thirteenth-century writer quoted above tried to persuade women to remain celibate on the grounds that motherhood left them too vulnerable to worry and even tragedy: "As soon as [a child] appears in this life, it bringeth with it more care than joy, specially to its mother; for . . . if it is wellshapen and seemeth likely to live, a fear of the loss of it is instantly born along with it; for she is never without fear lest it go wrong, till one or other of the two lose the other."

And Guibert de Nogent, a twelfth-century French abbot, no doubt reflected a widely-held attitude in his memoirs, noting that when his widowed mother retired to a monastery, "there was none to give me the loving care a little child needs at such an age [and] that only a woman can provide."

Besides family members, medieval households at almost any level of society often included servants, and poorer women often found employment as maidservants. The household account books of Alice de Bryene, a widowed fifteenth-century gentlewoman, listed a "lady's maid and chamberlain, squires, chaplains, grooms, clerks of the chapel and boys" among her staff. Occasionally we find descriptions of the work and proper treatment of various kinds of maidservants in manuals of estate or household management. Among other duties, a thirteenth-century dairymaid was supposed to "receive milk, against a tally, by the number of gallons, and to make cheese and butter, and to take charge of the poultry, and frequently to render account and to answer to the bailiff and the reeve for the produce resulting therefrom. . . ." Younger servants, in particular, were the responsibility of the woman of the house. The Householder of Paris advised his wife "that if you have girls or chamber-maids of fifteen to twenty years, since they are foolish at that age and have seen nothing of the world, have them sleep near you, in a closet or chamber, where there is no dormer window or low window looking onto the road, and . . . if one of your servants falls ill, lay all your concerns aside, and take care of him yourself full lovingly and kindly, and visit him and think of him or her very carefully, seeking to bring about his cure." Not all employers treated servants so benignly. At the other extreme, Leonor López, a fifteenth-century Spanish noblewoman, mentions in her memoirs a dispute in which her aunt's servants became involved: " . . . maids of hers had turned her against me, so that she would not do [what I had asked], and I was so disconsolate I lost my patience, and the one who had most set my lady aunt against me died in my hands, swallowing her tongue."

Such detailed and personal information about medieval people is the exception rather than the rule, and for the lower ranks of society, in particular, we must rely on more fragmentary evidence. Some fascinating research on English peasant families has been based on legal records such as the coroners' rolls, which include detailed accounts of the circumstances surrounding unexpected deaths.[3] These brief narratives give us glimpses of home life, work and even recreational activities: "On 14 Jan. 1267 Sabillia, an old woman, went into Colmworth to beg bread. At twilight she wished to go to her house, fell into a stream and drowned by misadventure. The next day her son Henry searched for her [and] found her drowned. . . ." In estate surveys we find records of the landholdings and legal obligations of individual peasant women (usually widowed) who lived and farmed land on their own—under medieval law, widows enjoyed a high degree of independence.

In the commercial sphere, too, women often had more freedom of action than we might expect. Women worked not only as the partners of their merchant husbands but as employees and even businesswomen in their own right. Some crafts (especially in the textile and food industries) were dominated by female labor, and some of these were regulated by female guilds, whose regulations survive. While many guilds were restricted to men, some were open to both sexes, as the regulations of the Paris bathhouse-keepers make clear: "Be it known that no man or woman may cry or have cried their baths until it is day, because of the dangers which can threaten those who rise at the cry to go to the baths. No man or woman of the aforesaid trade may maintain in their houses or baths either prostitutes of the day or night, or lepers, or vagabonds, or other infamous people of the night. No man or woman may heat up their baths on Sunday, or on a feast day which the commune of the city keeps." Prostitution, incidentally, was legal in most parts of medieval Europe, but procuring was not, and municipal authorities often made efforts to regulate and contain prostitutes' activities.

Depending on the place and time, medieval women could make contracts, grant land, dispose of their personal belong-

ings by will, be prosecuted for infractions of commercial regulations, testify in court and sue or be sued; court records of all these activities exist. A London woman named Matilda La Megre brought charges against three moneylenders, two of them women, for "unjust detention" of cloth which Matilda had pawned for a sum of money; the husband-and-wife moneylending team ended up in the Tower of London because the other female moneylender's testimony proved Matilda's case.

When we think of medieval Europe we often think of the Christian church, which dominated so many aspects of life. Religious aspects of women's lives—or more accurately the lives of religious women—are well represented in the surviving sources. We have the monastic "rules" (sets of regulations) under which nuns lived; some of these are the same as rules for monks, while others were written specifically for nuns. Bishop Caesarius of Arles wrote the first rule for nuns in the sixth century; the first woman to write a monastic rule was St. Clare of Assisi in the mid-thirteenth century. It is in convents that we most often find women writers. Besides spiritual and theological works, nuns sometimes wrote about politics, history and medicine. Nor was a nun's life the only option for a woman who wished to dedicate herself to religion; anchoresses or recluses might live under less strict conditions, and Beguines lived communally without taking monastic vows.

While "rules" show us the ideals toward which nuns and other religious followers were supposed to be striving, it would be naive to assume that the rules were followed to the letter especially when so many nuns were selected for the religious life and placed in convents by their families. One type of source that balances the orderly picture created by the rules is the bishop's visitation, a record of the periodic inspection of religious houses. When Bishop Eudes of Rouen inspected the priory of Villarceaux in 1249, he found what was clearly a shocking state of affairs. No fewer than eleven of the twenty-three nuns are alleged in the records to have had affairs with various men, two of them had become pregnant as a result, and all the nuns "let their hair grow down to their chin, and put saffron on their veils." Moreover, "Ermengarde of Gisors and Joan of Hauteville came to blows. The prioress is drunk nearly every night. . . .

The prioress does not get up for Matins, does not eat in the refectory, and does not correct excesses." In other convents the offenses are less egregious: the nuns have pets or private possessions, the convent finances are in disarray, or the liturgy is sung too fast. Very seldom is the fastidious bishop able to write of some convent he has visited, "We found everything there to be in good condition."

For Christians dissatisfied with the orthodox beliefs and practices of the church, heretical sects offered an intense religious experience and, sometimes, a greater role for women in particular. We know this because Catholic churchmen wrote in consternation of women being allowed to preach in the heretical sects and even administer their sacraments. To espouse heresy was, of course, a dangerous alternative, for the church tried suspected heretics, and the secular government punished those who were convicted. The records of the Inquisition give us some particularly vivid accounts of the lives of heretics in the form of their confessions. In one long and rambling narrative from fourteenth-century France, the elderly Béatrice de Planissoles recounts the long process by which various heretical friends and neighbors persuaded her to become a heretic herself. Afterwards, "because she was very ill and in bed and her death was expected, [the Inquisitor] told her that if she had hidden anything concerning heresy in the confession that she had made above about herself or others, or if she had accused a person against truth and justice, she should admit it and reveal it, or she should exonerate the persons she had unjustly accused."

Finally, one should remember that although most of the population of medieval western Europe was Christian and of Germanic descent, there were also religious and ethnic minorities. Muslim communities in Spain, Sicily and southern Italy have left behind laws and personal narratives which show the place of women in medieval Islam. Jewish communities were found in towns throughout Europe, adhering to their own religious laws and standards of conduct while interacting with the Christian majority. Jewish wills include family history and customs, while Hebrew chronicles tell us of the persecutions that began in the late eleventh century. In the latter stories, women often took the lead in the acts of bravery with which the Jews faced attempts at forced conversion: "There was

a notable and pious woman [in Speyer] who slaughtered herself for the sanctification of the Divine Name. She was the first of those who slaughtered themselves in all the communities."

As I found in the course of my project, there is a wealth of material that reveals how women lived and worked in the Middle Ages. Of course this is just one part of the picture which, as historians, we are constantly enlarging and revising. From these sources which address women's lives we gain a deeper understanding not only of medieval women but of medieval society as a whole, in all its variety and richness.

NOTES

[1]Recommended basic books include Shulamith Shahar, *The Fourth Estate: A History of Women in the Middle Ages* (New York, 1983); Eileen Power, *Medieval Women* (Cambridge, 1975); Margaret Wade Labarge, *A Small Sound of the Trumpet: Women in Medieval Life* (Boston, 1986); Frances and Joseph Gies, *Women in the Middle Ages* (New York, 1978); Angela Lucas, *Women in the Middle Ages: Religion, Marriage and Letters* (New York, 1983).
[2]Emilie Amt, ed., *Women's Lives in Medieval Europe: A Sourcebook* (New York, 1993).
[3]Barbara Hanawalt, *The Ties That Bound: Peasant Families in Medieval England* (Bloomington, 1986).

Margery Kempe and the Meaning of Madness

The manuscript of Margery Kempe's autobiography written in the early 1400s.

'Living high above her bodily wits'—but was the 'madness' of a fifteenth-century English gentlewoman divine folly, marital stress or the stirrings of a self-conscious feminist?

Roy Porter

Roy Porter is senior lecturer in the social history of medicine at the Wellcome Institute, London, and author of A Social History of Madness: Stories of the Insane *(Weidenfeld & Nicolson, 1987).*

The history of madness must surely form part of the 'history of mentalities'. It poses, however, obvious problems of documentation. Amongst the most fascinating yet enigmatic kinds of historical sources are the autobiographical writings of 'mad people'. Hundreds of these are available in print, the bulk of course, deriving from the last two centuries. Using them presents certain grave problems to the historian; for the very fact that they were written by deluded, or supposedly deluded, people demands even greater scepticism than that required by autobiography in general, a genre itself always to be approached with the utmost caution.

Psychiatrists have often claimed that mad people's writings have nothing meaningful to say about external reality, being only the symptoms of sickness. But this is too dismissive: for they frequently afford privileged insights into the secret mental cultures of the past, the extreme fantasies and fears commonly shared, yet standardly censored by polite culture.

They sometimes also provide critical commentaries upon the official rationalities and moralities of past societies—perhaps paralleling the jibes of the Fool or court jester or the subversive 'world turned upside-down' parodies present in plebeian culture. And not least, they offer a unique record from inside of the experiences of derangement and alienation, and of the confrontations of madness with the all too often unreasonable world of the rational. Such writings have been little drawn upon by historians, but would amply repay further study.

The opening pages of what is in effect the earliest English autobiography present an account of a woman going mad. 'When this creature was twenty years of age, or somewhat more, wrote Margery Kempe—or rather 'dictated', since she, like most late medieval women, was illiterate—'she was married to a worshipful burgess and was with child within a short time, as nature would have it'. She was sick during pregnancy, and after childbirth, what we would call puerperal insanity set in. 'She despaired of her life and sent for her confessor', for 'she was continually hindered by her enemy—the devil'. She believed she was damned: 'Because of the dread she had of damnation on the one hand, and Satan's sharp reproving of her on the other, this creature went out of her mind and was amazingly disturbed and tormented with spirits for half a year, eight weeks and odd days'.

Margery Kempe's experience, recorded early in the fifteenth-century, commands attention as the story of a mad person; but it is doubly interesting as an account of a mad *woman,* for these are rare so many centuries ago. We have, it is true, been inundated over the last century with writing by disturbed and distracted women; indeed modern culture draws attention to the affinities between psychic disturbance, psychiatry, and women. Nowadays a significantly higher percent-

This 14th-century illustration of a Caesarian birth illustrates one of the many hazards of medieval childbirth - which Margery Kempe, as a mother of fourteen, was well aware of.

age of women than men end up under psychiatric care, in mental institutions, or simply taking tranquilisers. And this may be because our 'patriarchal' society places women under special strains, and allegedly uses psychiatry as a special tool for coping with the disorders thereby induced (prison for men, the mental hospital for women, it is often said).

Certainly, ever since Charcot's and Freud's studies of hysterical women, it has been the female unconscious, and, almost inevitably, the mystery of female sexuality, which have formed the grand arcanum of psychiatry (the great question, thought Freud, was 'what do women want?'). In some sense, somatic diseases have become 'male', and mental disorders 'female'. The problems of being a woman in a man's world have led a disproportionate number of women to break down, and in turn have disproportionately preoccupied psychiatry.

Yet what is intriguing is how few self-portraits we possess written by disturbed women before the last couple of centuries. Of course, women were never meant to speak for themselves ('Silence' was even a girl's Christian name in Stuart England); and in any case, their literacy rates were lower. All the same, the period between the Reformation and the emergence of Romanticism—when autobiography itself blossomed as a genre—is as relatively lacking in writing by women recording their own journeys into mental *terra incognita* as the last century and a half—the era of female emancipation—has been rich. Practically all the writings by disturbed people sur-

viving from early modern England are by men—James Carkesse, the Restoration poet, George Trosse, the Presbyterian minister, Goodwin Wharton, the Whig politician, and so forth. Only with the coming of the age of sensibility from the mid-eighteenth-century was disorder effectively 'feminised'.

This is certainly not, of course, because during the early modern centuries women were pictures of mental health. Michael MacDonald's exemplary study of Richard Napier, the early seventeenth-century Buckinghamshire doctor-parson, has shown that most of the clients attending him with 'psychiatric' problems—they called themselves 'distracted', 'disordered', 'melancholic', and so forth—were women. That is not surprising. They were crushed by the burdens of having to sustain multiple functions—productive labour, running households, raising families, coping with husbands. Moreover, the gynaecological consequences of repeated dangerous childbirths eroded their health, both physical and mental.

Thus medieval and early modern women commonly underwent mental trauma, yet infrequently left accounts of it. Therein lies the unique interest of Margery Kempe's life story. For not only did she record her experiences in great detail, but was able to make sense of them, during her mad bouts and in their aftermath—though not in terms of being a mad woman, but through the idiom of the Christian life of the spirit.

If what she got her scribe to write down for her in her 'book' (it is ex-

pressed in the third person) truly reflects what she felt and told people throughout her life, she never sought to conceal that she had indeed been through an episode of madness in her early twenties. Strange experiences beset her later as well, not least some extremely lurid sexual temptations. Some of her actions, she admitted, were not those of 'reason'. She envisaged herself running around 'like a mad woman' or like 'a drunk woman'; she could think of herself 'without reason', living 'high above her bodily wits'. And she was kept acutely aware that her expressions of religious devotion—such as her incessant weeping, often for many hours at a time—were liable to be censured as crazy, and believed to be the work either of the Devil or of disease.

Unlike certain other 'holy people', Margery never celebrated delirium as a positive, heaven-sent religious ecstasy. She regarded her chief bout of disturbance, following the birth of her first child, as a providential rap on the knuckles, with which she was visited essentially because she was then a vainglorious, thoughtless and proud young lady, susceptible first to the temptations and then to the threats of the Devil. While out of her mind, her conduct had been abominable; she had 'slandered' her husband and despaired of salvation. She did violence against herself and needed to be 'forcibly restrained both day and night'. She had forsaken God. By His infinite mercy, the Almighty had returned her to her 'right mind', rescued her from sin, and shown her His paths. Still she remained unregenerate, wedded to this world and its worldlings, and it took the business failure of the brewery she owned—her beer providentially all went flat—to humble her and turn her from this wicked world to true holiness.

God's first warning had merely affected her head; this second arrow penetrated to her heart. Though subsequently leading a life which to many contemporaries appeared perverse, Margery Kempe did not present her way of living through the idiom of exceptional divine madness. On the contrary, she was insistent that her own conduct was regular, and her faith orthodoxy itself. She had to be: she was living in an age when the religiously deviant were readily accused of being heretical Lollards, and Lollards were often tried and sometimes burnt.

Having undergone the twin crises of puerperal insanity and business failure, Margery experienced an overwhelming

On view at the 'Age of Chivalry' exhibition at the Royal Academy, Piccadilly.

The devil's snares; (above) at work among idle gossips in the 14th-century stained-glass from Stanford, Northamptonshire; (below) wooing a woman in a 15th-century woodcut by Ulvicus Molitorus—both temptations which Margery Kempe believed herself preyed upon in moments of weakness.

King's Lynn burgess (her father was successively mayor and Member of Parliament for the town). She had a husband to whom she was lastingly, if unconventionally, attached, and by whom she had a growing family—she gave birth, all told, to fourteen children. She was in no position simply to renounce the world by entering a nunnery: church dignitories would never have permitted it.

As she was forcibly reminded through the rest of her life, her attempts to follow what she saw as the divine signposts met enduring hostility. 'Woman, give up this life that you lead, and go and spin, and card wool, as other women do', the worldlings and the authorities told her. Wherever she went there was such 'evil talk about her' that the cleric who penned her life story was even afraid of recriminations against himself.

Sickened by the flesh, Margery strove to free herself from bondage to the world. She fasted; she did bodily penance; she clad herself in a hairshirt. And above all she sought to free herself from sexual slavery, knowing how the pleasures she and her husband once had taken in carnal delights were offensive to God, and now finding them 'abominable'

urge to sever herself from all the ways of the world, convinced that, by contrast to conditions on earth, it was 'merry in heaven' (how did she know? critics demanded). Breaking free meant a considerable wrench. She had been born around 1373 the daughter of a prosperous

to herself. She told her husband she now loved God alone; His body alone was what she wanted, sacramentally, in a mystical marriage. She begged him to accept a pact of mutual chastity; he agreed in principle, but, echoing St Augustine, said 'not yet', and for long insisted upon having his will. Eventually they came to an agreement by which he signed away his conjugal rights in return for Margery paying his debts.

Despite this apprentice mortification, she remained abysmally vainglorious. 'She thought that she loved God more than He loved her', she was to recall. In that state, she was easy prey to the Devil's snares. He laid for her a trap of lechery. A man made advances to her. Flattered, she willingly surrendered, only at the last moment to be spurned by him. Mortified, she craved Christ's forgiveness; it was granted, and, in return, her Saviour promised she could wear a hairshirt in her heart. As Christ had been persecuted, so should she be. Thereafter, tribulations were seen by Margery as secret tokens of holiness. Life best made sense to her when battling with the moils and toils which constitute the bulk of her wonderfully down-to-earth autobiography.

Her spiritual life began to blossom. She began seeing visions, and these were accompanied by the copious bouts of weeping which attended her to the end of her days. She started informally shriving penitents and acting as a mouthpiece for homely divine guidance. A 'miracle' secured her escape when a piece of falling masonry struck her, but did her no harm. And, not least, Christ mercifully intervened to kill off her husband's sexual appetite. She told him she would rather that he were slain than have to submit to his lusts, preferring to make herself 'freely available to God'. Her husband rebuked her: she was not a good wife. The general picture of their relationship given by the *Book of Margery Kempe* is, however, one of mutual understanding, support and charity.

Margery's increasingly conspicuous religious observances brought her public reproof. Her weeping bouts were despised; she was called 'false hypocrite', and her friends were advised to abandon her. Furthermore, she was accused of having the Devil in her and of being a 'false Lollard' ('and the people said, "Take her and burn her" '). But such trials merely fortified her sense of the Divine indwelling. When she heard mention of Christ's passion, she would swoon in ecstasy and experience divine music. The Lord called her his mother, his sister, his daughter, and she conversed—as in regular speech she insisted—with St Paul, St Peter and St Katherine.

Margery was initially perturbed. Were these voices and visions authentic? Or temptations of the Devil? Or simply sensory delusions? Seeking guidance, she consulted Dame Julian of Norwich, the contemplative mystic. From her she received reassurance: these were not fantasies of her own devising but truly signs from God. Margery must persevere: 'The more contempt, shame and reproof that you have in this world, the more is your merit in the sight of God'. Margery followed Dame Julian's words, which were reiterated by many 'honoured doctors of divinity, both religious men and others of secular habit'. Soon God was telling her that she would be the recipient of special revelations denied even to His own daughter Bridget, the Swedish mystic.

Reassured, Margery grew in confidence of her religious calling. Her holy circle expanded, and she attained a reputation as a woman with a divine vocation. Her practical advice was sought by people anguished over the great decisions of life; she relayed to them God's answers. She acquired minor powers of prophecy. One day, she predicted a great storm. It came about. Many remained suspicious, and she continued to entertain great fears of 'delusions and deceptions by her spiritual enemies'. But God comforted her by saying that though he would load her with tribulations on earth, when in heaven, she would be granted all her desires. At a later stage He told her that her earthly life would be the only purgatory she would ever suffer. Margery's conviction of divine love increased. God informed her: 'to me you are a love unlike any other', and, later, 'you do not know how much I love you'; for her part, she wished that it had been God that had taken her virginity. Eventually, being now on 'homely terms with God', she had a 'wedding ring to Jesus Christ' made at divine command, with *Jesus est Amor Meus* inscribed on it. The love of God proved the shame of the world.

Eventually, she set off on pilgrimage for the Holy Land. This was, ironically, her one visit to Bethlehem. So joyful was she at the holy sights that she nearly swooned and fell off her ass. And being so close to the scenes of Christ's Passion led her to weep and wail more than ever, and to 'wrestle with her body'. She was visited by a special vision of Christ's crucified corpse, and overwhelmed by irresistible impulses to weep. She could not stop it; it was the 'gift of the Holy Ghost'. Her roaring and crying riled her fellow pilgrims. Some thought she was just ill-behaved, puffed up with 'pretence and hypocrisy', or physically sick, suffering from epilepsy. Others accused her of drunkenness. Still others believed she had been possessed by evil spirits.

It was a dilemma which continually faced her when her tears poured out her passion. On a later occasion, she records:

Many said there was never saint in heaven that cried as she did, and from that they concluded that she had a devil within her which caused that crying. And this they said openly, and much more evil talk. She took everything patiently for our Lord's love, for she knew very well that the Jews said much worse of His own person than people did of her, and therefore she took it the more meekly.

As she later put it, if Christ's blood had had to flow, the least true believers should expect or want would be floods of their own lamentations. She asked God to grant her a 'well of tears'; and to one who tetchily asked her: 'why do you weep so, woman?', she responded, 'Sir, you shall wish some day that you had wept as sorely as I'. What other behaviour could be so appropriate in this vale of tears? She knew her Psalter which assured her that 'They that sow in tears shall reap in joy'.

Apart from a further pilgrimage late in life to shrines in North Germany, Margery passed the rest of her days in England. She had undergone a formal religious ceremony binding herself and her husband in mutual chastity, and thereafter they lived apart. When her husband became old and senile however, she returned to nurse him, against her own initial inclinations, but following God's advice. Meanwhile her religious reputation grew. She established good relations with numerous anchorites, contemplatives, scholars and other holy people; some evidently read to her out of the corpus of mystical writings. Clearly, many ordinary Christians accepted her special holiness, and were glad to have her weep for them.

Others were not so happy. Her fellow English pilgrims had found her a cross, with her continual wailing, her special dietary demands, and her moral and religious rebukes; sometimes they forced her to leave their party. Similar tribulations beset her in England. 'Evil talk' about her grew, and many said she had the Devil in her. Clerics and congregations deplored the way she constantly interrupted services and ceremonies with her weeping and wailing at the name of Jesus. A friar barred her from his sermons, claiming she was suffering from 'sickness'.

More seriously, she frequently ran the risk of ecclesiastical prosecution. Authorities both civil and religious looked with considerable suspicion upon this wife and mother wandering around the country in the guise of a holy woman, berating people for their hypocrisy and ungodly ways, and sometimes urging wives to leave their husbands and follow God (Who had informed her, that many women, if only they could abandon their husbands, would love him the way she did). Her insistence upon wearing white linked her in the eyes of some with dubious flagellant groups, while others, including the Abbot of Leicester, accused her of being a 'false heretic', ie, of involvement with Lollardy. 'She has the Devil in her', she reported such churchmen as saying, 'for she speaks of the Gospel'. Under examination however, her own faith proved triumphantly orthodox.

All the while, her love of God grew. She was privileged to overhear conversations about her between God the Father and the Son, and she records, in her homely way, that the Godhead informed her that he liked having her around to talk to. Her attention became fixed upon the 'manhood' of Christ; but it was the Godhead Himself who finally married her. The Father told her, 'I must be intimate with you and lie in your bed with you . . . take me to you as your wedded husband . . . Kiss my mouth, my head, and my feet as sweetly as you want'. The earlier sexual temptations which she had undergone were not, however, entirely a thing of the past; and in time she was visited by 'abominable visions', conjured up by the Devil, of being beset by threatening male genitals and being commanded to prostitute herself to them. Temporarily she felt forsaken by God, but recovered. At another point, she was overcome by a desire to kiss male lepers; her confessor prudently advised her to stick to women.

How are we to assess Margery Kempe's life? One type of interpretation simply confirms the truth of her visions. Katherine Cholmeley for example has argued that because Margery's experiences conform so closely to those of other well attested contemplatives and visionaries, they must literally be true, and should be accepted at face value as providential and miraculous. Other Christian historians, however, have taken a more jaundiced view, suggesting that Margery Kempe 'contaminated' the pure tradition of mystical contemplation with her emotional idiosyncrasies. All such interpretations are in danger of confusing history with hagiography, and begging the true historical questions.

The same stricture applies, *mutatis mutandis,* to interpretations advanced by psychoanalytical sleuths, who seem bent on proving her a 'sinner'. The truth about Margery Kempe, Trudy Drucker has thus argued, is that she constituted a 'case of religious hysteria', occasionally overlaid with 'overtly psychotic' episodes. In a similar way Dr Anthony Ryle has diagnosed her as a case of 'hysterical personality organisation with occasional "psychotic" episodes', during which she 'hallucinated about the sexuality of the males surrounding her'. Margery should best be treated, argues Drucker, as an 'unfortunate' who never recovered from puerperal fever, and who suffered from further organic or psychosomatic conditions such as epilepsy and migraine. She indulged, moreover, in 'psychotic behavior', in particular a propensity to 'self-inflicted pain', which, Drucker believes, resulted from 'pathologic distortion of the sexual impulse'. Her hysteria was unconsciously designed to serve the 'protective function' of keeping her 'agonized and distorted sexuality' at bay; this was not always successful, however, and her 'disguised sexual fantasies and guilts' sometimes thrust their way to the surface.

Margery was thus a 'victim of hysteria'; and some of its manifestations in her were 'repellant' and 'silly'. All the same, hysteria afforded her many 'secondary gains', bestowing upon her 'unique attention' (she took a 'child-like pride in her attacks'). That is why Kempe 'resists any suggestion that her spells are of natural origin'; had she accepted that view, she would have been reduced to just 'another uninteresting sick woman'. She was not, however, entirely to blame, Drucker continues, because such hysteria is inevitable in ages when female sexuality is repressed. In any case, behind her egoism, childhood events were responsible for her condition: 'probably the roots of her disease were buried deeply in childhood experiences thoroughly rejected by her adult recollection'. Alas, no Freudian couch was available to bring these to the surface and they remained 'past recall' and thus unrecorded.

Psychodynamic *post mortems* such as these seem trivial (for they do little more than fix fancy labels on the unknown): gratuitously dogmatic (in the absence of any shred of supportive evidence, there is no reason to attribute Margery's adult attitudes to childhood experiences); and, not least, harsh. They operate by identifying so-called 'psychological symptoms', and then turning them into moral verdicts which masquerade as medical diagnoses. Their blend of accusing and excusing isolates the individual and neglects the nexi of social, sexual and ideological pressures within which people's lives are led. It is easy to speak boldly of Margery's 'distorted sexuality' (eg, her wish to make her relationship with her husband chaste and to marry God); it is another to remember—as Drucker does not—that she bore her husband fourteen children, all but one apparently against her wishes. The absence of any substantial mention in her *Life* of her children surely indicates Margery's indifference to the motherhood thrust upon her. Likewise Drucker draws attention to Margery's rape anxieties, suggesting that they are further symptoms of her hysterically distorted sexuality. She might have remembered that crossing Europe as a pilgrim was perilous for a woman. Phrases like 'distorted sexuality' and 'hysteria' are inevitably stigmatising.

Both the devoutly Christian and the psycho-analytical approaches to understanding Margery Kempe's *Book* thus seem flawed. There is of course no single master-key to Margery's condition, or 'correct' way of reading her life. But the best way forward surely lies in attempting to understand her as a child of her times, religious, social and personal. Her mad behaviour expressed the conventions, beliefs and language of her day, though in extreme forms. For one thing, she was attempting to resolve the common dilemmas of true piety for a woman of the world. Though medieval society and medieval Christendom were both highly patriarchal, special institutions and roles were set aside for women in pursuit of the religious life within the Church—portals which were closed in later Protestant circles. Above all, it was possible for some women to escape the routine cares of marriage and the dangers of motherhood by entering a cloister, where they might make their devotions to the service of spiritual replicas of the life they had escaped: the cults of God the Father and God the Son.

For the more zealous this could lead to highly intense and deeply spiritual experiences, sometimes soaring into mysticism. Christianity itself encouraged—while also setting strict limits upon—ecstatic exercises such as mortification of the flesh and fasting. As Rudolph Bell has recently stressed, self-inflicted asceticism was occasionally carried to ambiguous extremes by holy women, who perhaps descended into a pathologically self-denying condition akin to today's *anorexia nervosa*. Outside the nunnery, traditions of mysticism and contemplation had emerged as suitable for married women. St Bridget of Sweden, with whose life Margery Kempe was familiar, had provided a model by arranging a pact of chastity with her husband and spending much of her life on pilgrimage; Dorothea of Mordau had similarly shown her holiness through a gift of tears, expressing by her compassion her affinity with the Passion. Such emotional piety extended the late medieval emphasis upon the 'humanity of Christ' and the Holy Family in ways especially fitting for women. Margery Kempe was clearly expresing her faith within these traditions, albeit in rather extreme forms. It would serve no purpose to label such exercise of spiritual discipline as a psychiatric disorder, not least because it was regulated by the conscious control both of the individual ascetic and of ecclesiastical superiors. Mystical flights and contemplations were highly programmed activities.

Thus the 'madness' of Margery Kempe is intelligible within the pietistic traditions of her time. It is also intelligible in terms of her own personal 'career', her attempt to take charge of and make sense of her own existence and place in society and under God. She knew that many people thought her voices and visions—indeed, her whole course of life—signified madness, to be attributed to illness or the Devil. She pondered that dilemma deeply, and sought advice. But the path to which she aspired—a closer walk, a spiritual communion, marriage even with God—was a path legitimate within the ideals of her times, though one exceptional and precarious. Margery wished, from early days, to free herself from a pattern of life (marriage, sex and childbirth), associated by her with madness and the Devil's temptations. The contemplative scenes into which she escaped of course reproduced in spiritual idiom the landscape of the mundane world: marriage to God replaced marriage to her husband. But they did so in ways which to her were benign and which allowed her a substantial element of control over her own destiny, otherwise essentially denied to her sex.

This is not to deny that Margery Kempe was—for a time at least—'mad'; but the madness had a 'method' in it, and provided a source of strength through which she came to terms with and helped resolve the key dilemmas facing all pious women in the late Middle Ages.

Saint Bridget setting down her revelations with visions of the Virgin and Child and Trinity overhead—she also like Margery Kempe, had set a pact of chastity with her husband.

This article is based on a recent talk given to the Past and Present Society in Oxford at a meeting sponsored by History Today, *and on a chapter in* A Social History of Madness: Stories of the Insane *just published by Weidenfeld and Nicolson at £14.95.*

FOR FURTHER READING

The Book of Margery Kempe, rendered into modern English, edited by Barry Windeatt (Penguin Classics, 1985); H. S. Bennett, *Six Medieval Men and Women* (Cambridge University Press, 1955); S. M. Stuard (ed.), *Women in Medieval Society* (University of Pennsylvania Press, 1976); Rudolph Bell, *Holy Anorexia* (University of Chicago Press, 1985); K. Cholmeley, *Margery Kempe: Genius and Mystic* (London, 1947); Clarissa W. Atkinson, *Mystic and Pilgrim. The Book and the World of Margery Kempe* (Cornell University Press, 1983).

The CID of History and The History of The CID

A myth for all seasons—the treatment through the centuries of Spain's medieval hero as a blend of Robin Hood and King Arthur provides revealing insights into the political needs of both his contemporary and more recent biographers.

Peter Linehan

The Cid—the individual who embodies Spain's medieval past for the casually curious just as securely as Robin Hood does England's—has provided successive generations of Spaniards with what they have needed to discover in him. More than this, he has also been permitted to appropriate the period of history through which he lived. 'The Cid's Spain' has a meaning and force that 'Robin Hood's England' lacks. For this Ramon Menéndez Pidal is principally responsible. Pidal's *La España del Cid* was first published in 1929. By the time its seventh and last edition appeared forty years later, in the year after the death of its author (1869-1968) the Spain of the Cid's lifetime had become The Cid's Spain and historians, critical though some of them may have been of particular features of Pidal's view of the period, had slipped into the habit of thinking and writing of it thus. Rodrigo Díaz de Vivar had upstaged his lord and king, Alfonso VI of Castile, something he had studiously refrained from doing in his own lifetime (?1043–99).

History has its great men, of course, but some historians need them and search harder for them than others. The effects of Pidal's enchantment with his hero (the only imaginable English equivalent of which would presuppose a bond between Sir John Neale and the Earl of Essex) are still strongly felt in 1987. While every aspect of the Cid and his Poem has been picked over, Alfonso VI, alone amongst Spain's medieval rulers of like stature, still awaits a serious study based upon the dispersed records of his achievements and failures.

It is perhaps not surprising that to Philip II in the sixteenth century the Cid should have appeared a figure of heroic sanctity worthy of canonisation, but that to Arabists of the nineteenth he was an unsavoury ruffian. What must seem remarkable is that as late as 1805 J. F. Masdeu the Jesuit who, it was said, 'believed in almost everything' would not believe in the Cid's very existence, and would admit it only to the extent of denouncing him as a traitor and criminal. Masdeu was a Catalan; hence his agnosticism or at best denunciation of the warrior reputed to have humiliated the Count of Barcelona. Three years later General Thibault, Napoleon's Governor of Old Castile, was similarly assured by J. A. Llorente, the historian of the Inquisition, that there never had been a Cid. To the fellow countryman of Corneille whose *Le Cid* (1637) had so enraged Cardinal Richelieu by glorifying the national hero of France's enemy, and who was currently wondering what to do with some bones in his possession said to be those of that hero, Llorente's assurance came as a blow. Dedicated as they were to subjecting Spain to the joys of enlightenment, Masdeu and Llorente identified the Cid with the obscurantism and pious frauds they so much abhorred. What was legendary had to be rejected.

It is for a proper understanding of what is legendary about the Cid's exploits that scholars continue to strive in their researches into the purpose and period of composition of the sources from which Pidal constructed the Cid's history. For if these sources are not, as Pidal held them to be, all more or less contemporary with their subject, but were composed fifty or a hundred years after his death then they are less instructive about the Cid than they are about the earliest use that later ages have made of him.

Most later ages have found a use for the Cid. At the beginning of the present century the loss of the last fragments of Spain's American empire prompted the architect of national regeneration, Joaquin Costa, to urge that a double lock be placed on the Cid's tomb so that he should never ride again or, at most, that only the civic Cid should be let out: the Cid of the legendary encounter with Alfonso VI at Santa Gadea—the Castilian Runnymede at which the monarch had been called to clear himself of murdering his brother; the Cid as statesman commissioned to root out the guilty men of 1898.

It was the military hero that Pidal offered to the public in the prologue to *La España del Cid*, however, the 'powerful influence on youth' in an age in which 'the military were not the most highly esteemed of the social virtues'. The year was 1929, and Primo de Rivera's dictatorship was on the point of collapse. Seven years later the military made their comeback and Francoist propaganda was quick to acclaim the *Caudillo*, installed as he was in the Cid's Burgos, as the new Cid. Conveniently forgetting the services rendered to the Christians' adversaries by the symbol of eleventh-century nationalism, and equally untroubled by Franco's introduction into the country of Moroccan legionaries, the author of an updated poem of the Cid—*Romancero de* la Reconquista (1937)—gloried in the almost unqualified support Franco was receiving from the leaders of the Spanish Church, just as Rodrigo Diaz had from the abbot of Cardeña.

In 1939 the fall of Valencia sealed Franco's victory: another Cid parallel for the paladins of the New Reconquest—though an unnerving one, it might have been thought, in view of the Moorish recovery of that city after the Cid's death. But history had served its turn, and 1939 was no time for pedantry. Ten years earlier Pidal had deplored the lack of a national public monument to the national hero. In 1943 the authorities made good this lapse, erecting the massive equestrian statue which stands, the present century's tribute to the Middle Ages, in the Cid's native Burgos. But history did not stop there. In 1963, soon after the filming of Samuel Bronston's epic had taught the public to think of the Cid and Jimena as Charlton Heston and Sophia Loren (and incidentally bringing some much needed hard currency to the Spanish economy), the New Cid was showing signs of wear, and a message (for which neither Pidal nor his critics could be cited in support) was chalked up on Seville Cathedral: 'El Cid era maricón' (The Cid was a fairy). It was soon rubbed out.

Incapable of being rubbed out because it is memorialised in the Burgos monument, in the form of the five massive tomes representing his life's work on the Cid, is the name of Menéndez Pidal. And justly so. It was Pidal who rescued the Cid from the scepticism of the nineteenth century and rendered him serviceable to the twentieth, he who gave the revisionists something to revise, and to whose work all who have come after have had to and continue to have to refer. What passes for our knowledge of the Cid's life and times is based on Pidal's reconstruction and his conviction that the sources from which that reconstruction was done were all nearly contemporary with the events they describe: the 129-line Latin verse Carmen Campidoctoris (circa 1090), the Latin Historia Roderici (1110), and the vernacular epic Cantar de Mio Cid—usually known as Poema de Mio Cid—(circa 1110, revised circa 1140).

Mio Cid's very title proclaims the hybrid nature of the society into which he was born probably in the early 1040s: a combination of the romance 'My' and the Arabic 'Lord' (sid, sayyid). (In the Latin History his other title—Campidoctor [Campeador: 'The Battler']—is invariably used.) Vivar, his birthplace, is a hamlet some ten kilometres north of Burgos. In the 1040s Vivar was a frontier place on a frontier not with the Moorish south but with the currently more hostile Christian kingdom of Navarre. As the epithet of the poem constantly states, The Cid was 'born in a good hour'. The 1040s and the following decades were all good years to be born in in a country which had everything to offer the resourceful and the adventurous. The authority of the Caliphate of Cordoba had collapsed in 1031 leaving al-Andalus fragmented and weak, easy prey to the fragmented and strong kingdoms of the north—Leon, Castile, Navarre, Aragon—and the county of Barcelona. Huge sums of gold was paid in tribute by the south to the north. Much of this was then re-routed beyond the peninsula, notably to the Abbey of Cluny of which Fernando I and Alfonso VI were massive benefactors.

Still vaster fortunes remained to be made from the sale of protection and military service by these proto-condottieri. Pidal held that term as it was applied to the Cid in the last century to be offensive. Yet that in essence was the function which he and others like him continued to perform until 1085. In that year Alfonso VI chose to reoccupy the dairy rather than continue milking the cow, and took possession of the old Visigothic capital, Toledo. The Cid was not involved in this, the major event of his lifetime. But for him, as for all Christian Spain, the consequences of it were profound. In response to the loss of Toledo the Muslim kings of the south called in Yūsuf, leader of the fanatical Almoravids from beyond the Straits of Gibraltar to provide protection of a kind different from that for which for half a century they had paid. At Sagrajas in 1086 Yūsuf inflicted a crushing defeat on Alfonso VI and inaugurated a century and a half of peninsular warfare which lasted until Seville was reconquered in 1248. During these years religious sentiments predominated as they had never done before. The Spanish Reconquest was presented as a branch of the crusade movement. For the beginnings of this development Alfonso VI's Cluniac advisors are held to have been partly responsible. By a strange coincidence Toledo surrendered to Alfonso VI on the very day that Gregory VII died.

In 1085 The Cid had lived three-quarters of his life. In only the last thirteen years of it was there a specifically religious content to the power struggle of the peninsula and since even during this period the Cid was prepared to do business with the followers of the Prophet it is not unreasonable to regard him as an entrepreneur by conviction—an entrepreneur of substance. His career, from his emergence in the late 1050s until his death, was bound up with the royal house of Castile-Leon. The Cid's story, in history as in legend, was a tale of successive exile and return determined by the state of his relationship with the king and the latter's attitude to him of wrath or favour, ire or benevolence. On this stretch of Europe's eleventh-century frontier reputations and fortunes were quickly made, and as soon lost. If only a fraction of what the record tells about the Cid's career is to be believed, the tittle-tattle of the envious had a lot to do with his ups and downs. Certainly there was no standing still—except for the rural labourer (and he was to that extent vulnerable). 'Whoever remains in one spot stands to lose.' Thus the poetic Cid to his followers after a triumphant skirmish—as the poetic Cid's skirmishes invariably were. The judgement held good too for peninsular society from 1086 until 1248. This was, as a recent historian of the period has described it, a society organised for war.

The poetic Cid reminds his followers at this point that they must prepare to move on. To move on necessitated a sturdy mount. Possession of a horse was an indicator of social status, and the quality of the creature an index of it. Not just mobility—the ability to pursue and attack—but upward social mobility too was a matter of horses. Upward social mobility indeed depended upon the ability to pursue and attack. The poetic Cid's horse, Babieca, was an unexampled beast. The Cid towards the end of the poem offered it to his king. But Alfonso would not accept it since only the Cid was fit to ride it. Babieca means 'chump'. The Cid's Babieca was so called, according to legend, because when as a lad Rodrigo was offered a colt by his godfather, the priest Peyre Pringos (Fat Pete), he plumped for a poor-looking specimen as the animals were shown to him. 'Chump', the bystanders said, meaning Rodrigo and not the horse, though fortunately for the Spanish epic it was to the horse that the name stuck. (If the Babieca of this interview was the same horse as the one later admired by the king it is a miracle that it had survived so long and no wonder that when in 1948 the Duke of Alba excavated for Babieca's remains at Cardeña there was no sign of them.)

Rodrigo Diaz was born into the lower nobility (*infanzones*), his father (it was later claimed) being descended from Lain Calvo, one of the founding fathers of Castilian independence from the tenth-century kingdom of Leon. He was knighted by the Infante Sancho during the latter years of the reign of Fernando I and after Fernando's death in 1065 remained attached to Sancho, Fernando's eldest son to whom Castile had been left as a kingdom, while his master contended with his two brothers but principally with the future Alfonso VI, whom he defeated, as it seemed decisively, at Golpejera in 1072. Later that year, however, Sancho was assassinated. Hence the Oath of Santa Gadea.

As the new reign began the Cid had old enemies. Yet the Cid received signal favours from Alfonso in these years, and not least his wife Jimena, the king's niece. Indeed all remained well until 1080–81 when the Cid, on a rent-collecting expedition to the King of Seville, became ensnared with Garcia Ordoñez, another Castilian nobleman who was similarly engaged in the direction of Granada. In the course of these events Garcia Ordoñez had his beard plucked by the Cid. This was serious. In the law codes of the time the penalties for beard-plucking were on a par with those for wilful castration. That, compounded by what was adjudged a further indiscretion committed in the king's absence, sufficed to secure the Cid's first exile.

In Pidal's words, life with the Moors was the inevitable fate of every exile. From 1081–86 the Cid earned his bread in the service of the Muslim rulers of Zaragoza. After a short-lived reconciliation with Alfonso he returned east where he was actively engaged south of Zaragoza towards the kingdom of Valencia. A second exile merged into a third: just two pages separate them in Pidal's 600-page history. During the last ten years of his life the Cid was occupied exclusively in the east of the Peninsula. After a siege lasting twenty months the city of Valencia fell to him in June 1094, an event which was followed by a settling of scores for which the Arab historians ensured that he would never be wholly exonerated. From 1094 until his death in

1099 the Cid ruled Valencia, and enjoyed the consolation of a Christian cathedral ruled by a French bishop in what had been the city's chief mosque. Three years after his death, in 1102, Alfonso VI evacuated the Cid's widow and what was left of the Christian garrison together with the hero's remains. According to the History, these were interred at Cardeña.

This is an extraordinary story of activity across the lines. Yet its extraordinariness depends upon assumptions about the nature of those lines which neither the Spanish observer of them centuries later nor any other observer is, for differing reasons, eager to contemplate. Clearly there are problems about regarding the Cid as a 'Christian hero'. Evidently he was a freebooter who offered what he had to offer wherever he could secure the best price for it.

For all this, the Cid's reputation survived him. In the late 1140s the author of the Chronicle of Alfonso VII, who was more certainly French than he was Castilian, represented him as the indomitable archetype whose victims had been the counts of Catalonia equally with the Muslim. In the same years the anonymous author of the *Historia Roderici* provided what to some must seem a one-eyed history of the subject which notices the Cid only when he is in the east of the peninsula and loses sight of him altogether whenever he strays into Castile, yet which provides what feeble framework there may be for the construction of his biography. And, to judge by appearances, the manuscript of the *Carmen*, whatever the date of its text may have been, can hardly have been much later than about 1160. By the end of the century the Cid had made the jump from the genre of biography into that of national history by earning inclusion in the *Chronica Najerensis*.

Exceptional as it was for any non-royal personage of the period in Spain to receive any biographical attention, however patchy, posterity's impression of Rodrigo Diaz would have remained a very two-dimensional one from the *Historia* alone. For the Cid as a human figure, and especially as a credible one, we are indebted to the Poem's powerful yet nuanced portrait. The intermittently tender Cid of the Poem, the loving husband and the fond father, belongs to the cultural world of the twelfth-century Renaissance as emphatically as the single-mindedly martial Cid of the History does not. How he acquired that personality—

whether by an invisible process of continuous renewal, as Pidal believed, according to which the Poem as we have it represents the latest stage of an oral tradition fostered by a succession of inevitably anonymous minstrels; or, alternatively, was the creation of the named scribe of the single surviving manuscript of work—is a question ultimately insoluble. Its traits, however, in comparison with that of the Cid of the History, and what the poet chose to emphasise and to omit can suggest some answers—though such a process obviously runs the risk of pursuing a circular argument.

By any reckoning the poetic Cid is a transformation. Nowhere in the poem is there any suggestion that he ever served a Moorish master, nowhere any sign of the Cid who had sold his services to Mohammed's cause as willingly as to Christ's. On the contrary it is the Cid's adversary the Count of Barcelona who has Moorish troops, and although the poem portrays one sympathetic Moor—the 'noble Moor' Avengalvón—as 'a fine brave fellow' and the Cid's *'amigo de paz'*, the Moors in the poem are the enemy. In battle 'the Moors called on Mohammed and the Christians on Santiago'. The lesson of Sagrajas has been learned, and a key figure in the process is the Bishop of Valencia, the Frenchman Jerome who had left home and joined the Cid, he says, 'for the desire I felt to kill a Moor or two'. Jerome claims a place in the front line of battle and accounts for more than just one or two of the enemy. Indeed he lost count. Jerome is an authentic man of the territorial reconquest which, in this literary creation, has become a religious crusade.

The second major shift in the Poem is geographical. While the History ignores Burgos and Castile, these are the Poem's points of reference, the city from which at its beginning the hero sets off into exile and the land to which at its end he returns in triumph to be vindicated at the Cortes of Toledo. Valencia and the eastern regions of the country provide the Cid with fame and fortune, yet they are 'strange lands'. Above all the Cid is now a Christian and a Castilian.

As such he was responding to the needs and developments of the late twelfth century, to the period between the new Sagrajas, the Almohad defeat of Alfonso VIII of Castile at Alarcos in 1195 and Alfonso's revenge at Las Navas de Tolosa in 1212, and of a peninsula which since the emergence in the 1170s of the independent kingdoms of Portugal and Aragon (the latter with Valencia assigned to its zone of endeavour) was becoming accustomed to partition along national lines while Alfonso VIII assumed on behalf of Castile the defence of Christendom.

The single manuscript of the 3735-line poem had already lost its first page when it was discovered at Vivar in the sixteenth century. Despite its truncated state, however, its opening could scarcely have been bettered for dramatic effect and affective appeal. 'Tears streamed from his eyes as he turned his head and stood looking at them', in Hamilton and Parry's sensitive translation. The weeping hero is about to leave for the exile his enemies have contrived and is gazing upon his abandoned house (here another translator renders the poet's inventory in the style of an auctioneer's catalogue) and the family he must leave behind. These—his wife Jimena and young daughters Elvira and Sol—he entrusts to the safe keeping of the Abbot of Cardeña. He dupes two Jews of Burgos into lending him money on the security of a pair of chests filled with sand (not a notably heroic act in itself but one which the poet's audience might have approved in the atmosphere prevailing after the loss of Jerusalem in 1187, as the Jews of York for example learned to their cost).

His campaigns in the east begin, invariably ending in success and enormously enriching his followers. He seeks to be restored to the king's favour, sending Alfonso lavish gifts. At the third approach a reconciliation is achieved. At Alfonso's behest, Elvira and Sol are married to the Infantes de Carrión. Poor types the Cid's new sons-in-law prove. Slighted, they take their revenge by assaulting their wives in a dark wood and leaving them for dead. The Cid of battle's reaction to this outrage is surprising and much has been made of it by the Poem's interpreters. Instead of pursuing the Infantes with fire and slaughter he resorts to the twelfth-century equivalent of appointing a sub-committee. He prosecutes in the courts, in Alfonso VI's Cortes at Toledo. The Cortes proceedings provide the Poem's culmination and occupy almost a quarter of the work. Victorious at law, the Cid through his champions defeats the Infantes through theirs. The rulers of Navarre and Aragon are granted his daughters in marriage; so 'today the kings of Spain are related to him and all gain lustre from the fame of the fortunate *Campeador'*. The poet had ended and his story concludes in Castile at Carrión, not far from where it had begun. The Cid has returned to Valencia but the poet does not follow him there. All we are told is that he died at Pentecost.

Who was this poet? And when was his poem written? The answers to these questions seem to be provided in its last lines: *'Per Abbat le escrivio en el mes de mayo / en era de mill e .cc xlv. años'* (Per Abbat wrote it down in May 1207 [= *era* 1245]). This seems clear enough. Yet over the years a plain reading of these words has been resisted. There is a gap in the date which Pidal believed once contained another C, giving the year 1307. *'Escrivio'* means wrote it down in the sense of copied it out rather than composed it, it has been argued, making Per Abbat a mere drudge of the early fourteenth century rather than a writer of genius a century before. (The manuscript is indeed of the fourteenth century, but that of course provides no clues as to the date of the Poem's *composition.*) The 'plain reading' is supported by all manner of internal evidence and is now quite widely accepted.

A Per Abbat (not an uncommon name) has been found with the right credentials and connections: a layman pleading before the king's court at Carrión in 1223. The knowledge of Roman Law displayed in the account of the Cortes scene has suggested to some that the poet himself was learned in that law, was one of the *'muchos sabidores'* from all over Castile whose presence on that occasion he mentions. The probability of this seems inescapable. Nor, at the turn of the twelfth and thirteenth centuries, would Per Abbat have needed to travel abroad to acquire whatever legal knowledge he possessed. He would not even have had to go so far as the university which Alfonso VIII founded at Palencia in these years, staffing it with scholars from Italy and France. (The presence there in the mid-1180s, recently established, of one such, Ugolino di Sesso, deserves especially to be mentioned: Ugolino's work was on precisely those procedural aspects of the law which the poetic Cid so skilfully deployed: appeals, recusation of judges, witnesses). He would not have needed a university at all, for the king's own household was staffed by Romanists. Pedro de Cardona who in the 1180s combined the office of royal chancellor with a teaching post at Montpellier was just one of those whose expertise was highly valued by a ruler coming to terms with the implications for Castile of the peninsula's new political configuration after the establishment of the flanking kingdoms of Portugal and (to the north of those 'strange lands') Aragon.

The Poem's emphases and supressions in comparison with the History could certainly support the view that it was composed in or not long before the year 1207 with a view to rallying Christian spirits before the coming encounter with the Almohads, at Las Navas in 1212. The Poem does indeed provide something for almost everyone: the prospect of social advancement of which the Cid is the incarnation, an example for the *infanzones,* reassurance for the hereditary nobility, with the whole social scene secure beneath the aegis of a king in whose *cort* right not might rules. It has even been suggested that the Poem was a work commissioned by the king and paid for by him, just as he had attracted the best scholars money could buy to Palencia. The poet exhibits great familiarity with the Burgos area. But the possibility deserves to be considered that he was also somehow associated with Toledo where he locates the denouement of his work.

The early years of the thirteenth century witnessed keen rivalry for national pre-eminence between Burgos, the capital of Castile, and Toledo, the capital of the Visigothic monarchy before the invasion of 711. So the poet's choice of Toledo as venue for Alfonso VI's third Cortes rather than the Cid's Burgos, for example—indeed after earlier assemblies at Burgos and Carrión, as the poet unnecessarily explains—would itself have been significant in May 1207. There may even actually have been a meeting of the Cortes at Toledo earlier in that year, as Francisco Hernández has recently argued, and unquestionably the cathedral chapter of Toledo numbered a Per Abbat in its ranks. Furthermore, the archbishop, Rodrigo Jiménez de Rada, as well as being actively engaged in recruiting warriors for Alfonso VIII's army was currently and no less energetically promoting the restoration of Toledo to its former greatness. The description of the 1211–12 muster at Toledo, as recorded in Rodrigo's national History (1243), bears interesting comparison with the poet's account of the Cid's preparations for the siege of Valencia. And finally. Pedro de Cardona, Alfonso VIII's Romanist chancellor, had also in 1180–82 been archbishop of Toledo—though he was also Catalan by birth.

Speculation on this level will surely continue. It would not be surprising if it were shown that the poet in 1207 was using the Cid for his own purposes, for Toledo's or whoever's. What would be surprising would be a claim that anything of the sort about the Cid and his Poem had been conclusively *proved*. What is unquestionable is the usefulness of the Cid to successive generations of Castilians and ultimately Spaniards from 1207 at latest to 1987 at least.

The earliest identifiable beneficiaries of the Cid connection were the monks of San Pedro de Cardeña. This was only fair since, as the History relates, he was buried there. By the 1270s the house had fallen on hard times. So equally had the king of Castile of the day, Alfonso X, the Learned rather than the Wise (another historian). Alfonso was currently at odds with his nobles, so the Cid, whose dealings with Alfonso VI had been so notably punctilious, could be useful to him—or, alternatively, damaging to them, in the less flattering account of the Cid by Ibn Alcama, as Dozy suggested and Pidal hotly denied. (Two years later, in the same spirit, the king translated from Pampliega—a Cardeña dependency as it happened—to Toledo the mortal remains of Wamba, the seventh-century ruler of

Spain to whom Toledo chiefly owed its claim to that distinction.) To suggest that a deal was struck between the king and the monastery would not be warranted. What resulted were new tombs for the Cid and his wife, provided at royal expense, and at the expense of historical truth an account of the Cid's career, lovingly embroidered over decades if not centuries, which *via* Alfonso X's History of Spain passed into the national record. It is in this version of history that the dead Cid leads his troops into battle, as in the Charlton Heston version, and sits embalmed at Cardeña for ten years until his nose falls off. (Why just ten years? In 1272 a hundred and a bit would have been unchallengable.)

It was this Cid—a Cid in the guise of a peninsular Charlemagne, visited on his deathbed by the Sultan of Persia (through emissaries) and St Peter (in person)—whom the Middle Ages bequeathed to the modern world. The publication of the History and the Poem in the eighteenth century came far too late to endanger him. As a Spanish Old King Cole he became an unshiftable element in the national story: the balladeer's revenge upon the credible.

To suggest then, as Costa suggested in 1898, that the Cid's tomb should be closed is preposterous. There will always be a bit of him or of the imagined him

capable of being transformed into a political platform. As long as there are two sides to an argument in Spain the Cid will serve his turn. For historians of that country the only pity is that Pidal's version of the past, battered though it is, still holds sway. Alfonso VI of Castile was portrayed in the film of the Cid as Hollywood's peninsular equivalent of Hollywood's bad King John, sneering and shifty. Neither the contemporary record nor indeed the Poem of the Cid warrants this. His is the tomb that needs to be reopened. It is high time.

FOR FURTHER READING:

There is an English translation, by H. Sutherland, of Menéndez Pidal's great work in abridged form, *The Cid and his Spain* (1934); the peninsular background is described in A. MacKay, *Spain in the Midle Ages. From frontier to empire, 1000–1500* (Macmillan, 1977); and in D. W. Lomax, *The Reconquest of Spain* (Longman, 1978); much interesting material is to be found in S. Clissold, *In Search of the Cid* (Hodder & Stoughton, 1965); of many modern translations of the *Poem,* probably the best is that of Rita Hamilton and Janet Parry, with introduction and notes by Ian Michael, *The Poem of the Cid* (Manchester University Press/Barnes & Noble, 1975), also in Penguin Classics; the most comprehensive survey of modern scholarship of the *Poem* and the fullest critique of Menéndez Pidal's theories is Colin Smith, *The Making of the 'Poema de mio Cid'* (Cambridge University Press, 1983).

Horsemen of Cruel Cunning

The Mongols had planned a campaign of two decades to subdue a quaking, 13th-century Europe, but in Hungary stiff opposition awaited the hordes from the East.

Peter A. Kiss

Peter A. Kiss studied economics in Hungary and America. Descendant of a long line of soldiers (one of his ancestors led a Hungarian cavalry unit in the battle of Mohi), he studied the more obscure aspects of military history. He considers Rene Grousett's The Empire of the Steppes *the essential work on Mongol history. James Chambers'* The Devil's Horsemen *is a readable, but more limited work.*

From a tree-shadowed hilltop in northeast Hungary, two nomad warriors gazed toward the enemy camp on the afternoon of April 10, 1241. The distance was great, but a hunter's keen eyes could make out some details, and an experienced campaigner's knowledge could supply the rest. They say, in the twilight, that the Hungarians had selected a good place for their camp: its rear was secure, its flanks protected by mountain and marshes. The camp was fortified by wagons chained together; its water supply was no problem, and deployment to the front would be easy. But the watchers also saw that the tents of King, nobles, and knights took up much of the space, which was too small, at any rate, for the 100,000 soldiers gathered there.

The watchers on the hillside, Batu Khan and Subedei Bahadur, were no ordinary nomads; they were commanders of the Mongol empire's campaign to conquer Europe, and in the past five years they had won many victories. Now, however, their army was much weakened. They had started with 150,000 horsemen, and they had pressed into service the fighting men of other, defeated nations. Such auxiliaries had limited

value—*their* heavy losses were not important. But the slow drain of trained, reliable Mongol soldiers and officers was keenly felt, since replacements from the Empire's heartlands seldom arrived. Large units had been detached to secure the flanks, and now the army was outnumbered by a tough, warlike enemy who did not seem eager to cooperate in his own defeat. It was going to be a severe test of Mongol fighting skill, of Mongol generalship.

The road to this Hungarian hillside had been long. It had begun 30 years before, when the nomad tribes of Central Asia elected Genghis Khan to lead them. They got more than they bargained for: in the following two decades the Great Khan had exterminated all who opposed his authority, whipped the warring tribes into a disciplined army, the likes of which the world had seldom seen, and created an empire that stretched from the Pacific Ocean to the Caspian Sea. When he died in 1227, his legacy to his heirs was an ambitious scheme of world conquest. By 1234 Ogedei Khan, the new emperor, had accomplished the immediate tasks left to him by his formidable father: Western Asia was occupied by 1231, the Kin Empire (northern China) conquered in 1234.

The Mongols then were ready for further conquests, and the Imperial Council (the Kuriltai) audaciously decided to start four wars at the same time. The army in the southern theater was already engaging the forces of the Sung Empire (southern China); a second army was dispatched to Korea to repress revolts instigated by the Korean King; the army in western Asia was advancing into Georgia and the Caucasus, and now a fourth army was assembled to invade Europe.

Europe was not entirely unknown to the Mongols: between 1221 and 1224, Subedei had led 30,000 horsemen on a raid to the borders of Hungary. These horsemen had ravaged Persia, crossed the Caucasus, and ranged over the Russian steppes as far as the foothills of the Carpathian Mountains, then returned to Central Asia. They had covered 4,000 miles, fought a number of victorious battles, and collected information on the civilized countries of Europe. The information promised rich plunder to those bold enough to reach for it—and plunder never failed to capture Mongol imagination. The aristocrats sent their best troops, and young warriors of noble birth volunteered to serve in the army.

To lend prestige to the enterprise, Genghis Khan's grandson Batu was selected to lead the campaign and rule the new territories. He had insufficient battlefield experience to command 150,000 men; Subedei, Genghis Khan's best student and faithful companion, was assigned as his mentor. The Chinese Mandarins who ran the Mongols' intelligence organization dusted off their files and prepared a detailed analysis of the countries beyond the western borders. On the basis of their report Subedei, who could think on a large scale, planned a campaign lasting 16 to 18 years and covering the western world from the Urals to the Atlantic.

The first operations took place in the winter of 1236–37. The kingdom of Bulgar was destroyed, and nomadic tribes east of the Volga River were defeated and exterminated. Their young men were pressed into the conquering Mongol army, and under Subedei's demanding supervision they were trained in Mongol methods of war during the summer and

From *Military History*, December 1986, pp. 34-41. © 1986 by Empire Press, Inc. Published by Cowles History Group, 741 Miller Drive, Suite D-2, Leesburg, VA 22075. Reprinted by permission.

fall of 1237. In the next year, the new troops acquired plenty of practical experience: the Mongol army, considerably strengthened by these recruits, crossed the Volga on the ice in December 1237.

The direct, easy route to western Europe, through the steppes between the Volga and the Carpathian Mountains, was open—the peasant levies of Russia promised to be no more than a momentary check in the march west. Still, Batu and Subedei advanced with caution. Were they to march directly west, the southern princes could withdraw into the forests of the north, where a cavalry army would operate at a disadvantage. Then, once the invasion of western Europe began in earnest, they could take the Mongol armies in flank and rear. To secure their vulnerable right flank, the Mongol generals destroyed the northern principalities first. They stormed Riazan and Kolomna, and occupied Moscow easily. In their wake, a chronicler noted, "no eyes remained open to weep for the dead." They next stormed Suzdal and Vladimir, and in a battle on the Siti River they destroyed the army of Prince Yuri, while flying columns sacked Yaroslav, Tver, and other cities. By March 1238, much of northern Russia was in smoking ruins, and Mongol units were only a hundred miles from the wealthy city of Novgorod, but on Subedei's advice, Batu ordered them back from the richest, most powerful Russian city.

The old general was well-acquainted with Russian weather conditions: he had recommended the winter campaign, when rivers were easy to cross on the ice, granaries were not yet empty, and only soldiers as tough and disciplined as the Mongols could fight effectively. He drove his troops mercilessly into blizzards, but withdrew them south before spring rains and melting snow could turn the country into a bottomless bog. Operations were resumed in the late fall of 1240, this time in southern Russia. The principalities of Chernigov, Kiev, and Galicia quickly were burned to the ground, and now the generals could make their final dispositions to invade central Europe.

While the Mongol army rested in the south and consolidated its brutal grip on the land east of the Don River, the largest nomad nation of the Russian steppes, the Cumans, sought refuge in Hungary. During Subedei's earlier raid they had fought against the Mongols, and their chieftain realized that east of the Carpathians no power was strong enough to resist the conquerors. He offered to accept Christianity on behalf of all Cumans in return for Hungarian King Bela IV's protection. The King welcomed him gladly: the conversion of 200,000 pagans would greatly increase Hungary's prestige in Rome, and the Cuman warriors would strengthen the power of the crown.

By the time Batu summoned a final council of war in Przemysl in December 1240, the West had received numerous warnings of impending danger. Dominican friars had brought the first reports of Mongol preparations (one dubbed them "Tartars"—the people from hell), and now Russian refugees had terrible tales to tell. But Europe was paralyzed by the political curse of the Middle Ages: lack of strong central authority, national dissension, petty feuds, and court intrigues. The Holy Roman Emperor, Frederick II, and Pope Gregory IX were locked in a struggle for earthly supremacy, and neither could spare troops to fight some obscure horsemen on a distant frontier. Italy was hopelessly fragmented, and the small principalities within Poland jealously guarded their independence. The Swedes, Lithuanians, and Teutonic Knights were ruthlessly attacking the already ravaged Russian cities, hoping to profit from that country's tragedy.

Some preparations were made to meet the Mongol threat, but these efforts came too late and were poorly coordinated. Through their spies, Batu and Subedei were well-acquainted with the situation in Europe, and deployed their forces accordingly. They would attack on three widely separated fronts, in a carefully coordinated sequence: the heaviest blow was to fall on Hungary, the most dangerous enemy, but only after flanking columns isolated that country from all possible support.

Even unsupported by allies, Hungary was a formidable enemy. The Hungarians were a warlike nation—they had been steppe-dwelling horse archers before they settled in the Danube Basin, and thus were well-accustomed to the tactics of mobile warfare. The aristocracy and their retainers had adopted western arms and the western style of horsemanship (they relied on the shock effect of lance and sword exclusively, and rode with straight knees), but most of the levies still used the short stirrup and fought with bow and saber. Their fire power, mobility, and endurance were somewhat inferior to the Mongols', but now they had been reinforced by the Cumans, a considerable advantage in cavalry.

The presence of the Cumans in Hungary irritated the Mongols. Batu, in an extraordinary letter to King Bela, warned in no uncertain terms what would happen to his country if Bela continued to shelter the Cumans. "Word has come to me," Batu wrote, "that you have taken the Cumans, our servants, under your protection. Cease harboring them, or you will make of me an enemy because of them. They, who have no houses and dwell in tents, will find it easy to escape. But you who dwell in houses within towns—how can you escape from me?" With the Mongols' devastation of Russia fresh in his mind, Bela was not inclined to take such a threat lightly.

The Hungarian army occupied the gorge of a natural bastion pointing east— it was formed by the Carpathian mountains and the Transylvanian Alps that surround Hungary from north to south in a large arc. The mountains were not impassable, but a vigorous defender could thwart an invasion attempt if he held the key passes in strength. Flat plains enclosed by the mountains facilitated the rapid movement of forces along interior lines, and the Danube served as a second line of defense, should the enemy penetrate the mountain barrier.

But the Hungarian nobles were no match for Subedei's generalship, and their King did not have the absolute authority of Batu Khan. A great national effort was needed to resist the invader; instead, a feud was brewing between Bela IV and the aristocrats (indeed, many nobles hoped for his defeat), and he was also threatened by the territorial ambitions of Frederick, Duke of Austria. When the bloody sword (traditional symbol of national emergency) was carried around the country, the nobles assembled readily enough, but then demanded concessions from the King before they would march to the borders. The meddling presence of Frederick was no help at all—he stayed in Hungary only long enough to damage Bela's cause, then returned west with his forces in time to stay out of the coming fight.

The Cumans were another problem. Their behavior was offensive to many Hungarians: their horses and cattle trampled the peasants' fields, and the nobles were uneasy to see their King suddenly acquire the loyal support of a large force over which they had no influence. Fights between Hungarians and Cumans be-

Incredible War Machine From the East

Mongol and Turkish horse archers raided China, Iran and eastern Europe for centuries. Feudal household troops and local peasant levies were no match for the mobility and firepower of thundering squadrons that covered immense distances in search of plunder and fought with great ferocity. The nomad youngsters learned to ride and fight from their earliest infancy; they were used to hardship, hunger, and harsh climate, and they grew up to be the world's finest light cavalrymen.

But the conditions of the steppes demanded self-reliance, and only Genghis Khan's forthright disciplinary measures could forge rugged individualists into an army. He punished the slightest disobedience or negligence, the slightest hint of cowardice, with death, but he richly rewarded valor and loyalty.

The Khan retained the decimal organization used by nomad armies for centuries: ten mounted archers formed a troop (*arban*); ten troops, a squadron (*jagun*); ten squadrons, a brigade (*minghan*); ten brigades, a division (*tumen*). Three or more *tumens,* with brigades of engineers, artillery or siege engines and other support units made up a Mongol field army (*ordu*).

Firepower and movement, combined with the ancient methods of the hunt, were the tactics of the Mongol army. Showers of arrows alternated with charges by heavy cavalry, feigned retreat, ambush and rapid dispersion to avoid an enemy charge. It was a method of war that proved all but irresistible. The principal weapon was a very powerful reflex bow; its range and rate of fire (upwards of 400 meters and 20 shots a minute) were not equalled until the invention of magazine rifles.

Fighting units were supported by a highly efficient supply system, which could replenish empty quivers, replace broken weapons, and bring up remounts even in the middle of a battle. In populated regions, food was obtained by ruthless foraging; horse milk was part of the daily ration, as was the meat of worn-out mounts. In uninhabited areas, the troops lived on rations they carried in their saddlebags: dried milk and powdered meat, mixed with water, provided simple, nourishing fare. They could also go without food for days, if necessary.

On campaigns, the army advanced in several parallel columns, screened by scouts; the columns maintained contact only through the courier service of "arrow messengers," who overcame all obstacles to deliver their dispatches. When an enemy force was located, the Mongols could concentrate their forces with amazing speed. Units were detached to cut the enemy's lines of communication; the main force engaged him, while a small body of picked troops made a wide detour to fall on his flank. Verbal commands were seldom needed: flags, gongs, trumpets, drums, and flaming arrows were used to transmit battle orders.

Such fast, reliable, and efficient communication made unit of command, coordination of maneuvers, and cooperation of units possible—once an order was issued, it was carried out. Ruthless discipline saw to that point.

No army ever equalled the Mongols in mobility: they could cover 60 to 80 miles a day, executing enveloping movements of several hundred miles and crossing regions believed impassable. Mobility gave Mongol generals the opportunity to plan campaigns on a scale never before (and very seldom later) contemplated, to seize and maintain the initiative. They could place a superior force into a decisive position at the critical time; they could select the time and place of battle, and they could engage or avoid the enemy as it suited them. They could concentrate faster than any opponent, and in case of defeat they could ride in retreat faster and farther than any pursuer.

Mongol leaders appreciated the psychological advantages of offensive action, and never fought on the defensive. Constant attack, even when the mission was defensive, was the hallmark of Mongol commanders; even when outnumbered, they would not fight a defensive engagement. Instead they would harass a superior force with long-range archery and sudden local attacks, or they would retire, trading space for time until they could engage the enemy on more advantageous terms.

Since they often were operating at a numerical disadvantage, Mongol generals had to apply economy of force with the utmost diligence—they relied on surprise and maneuver to achieve victory. Each unit had several tasks in order to utilize limited resources fully. Units in reserve were not idle: foraging and scouting was continuous; detachments far from the main force operated against the enemy's flanks and guarded against surprises.

Mongol armies were all but unbeatable, so long as the empire remained united under a single ruler, and there were no weapons to match the reflex bow's performance, no soldiers to match the Mongols' skill and discipline. The empire finally fell apart because of dynastic quarrels and religious strife—and because Chinese and Russian troops eventually proved a match for the Mongol soldiers, and their artillery a match for the Mongol bow.

came common, and the nobles did their best to encourage the peasants' hatred of the newcomers. At the worst possible time, when the Mongols were already invading Hungary, a rioting mob (probably incited by Frederick) killed the Cuman Khan, and threw his head out of a palace window. The outraged Cumans revolted and evacuated the country, not neglecting to pillage as they went.

While Bela IV, beset by internal and external problems, desperately was struggling to preserve his authority and organize the defense of his realm, Batu and Subedei unleashed their *tumens* (divisions). The coordination of their operations was amazing.

In February 1241 the flanking Mongol armies began to create a semicircle of destruction from Poland to Wallachia in order to isolate Hungary. In the north, Mongol princes Orda, Baidair, and Kadan crossed the Vistula with three *tumens,* burned Lublin, Zawichost and Sandomir, then divided in order to ravage a larger area. One *tumen* raided East Prussia, Pomerania, and Lithuania; Kadan rode northwest into Mazowia; and Baidar marched southwest, toward Cracow.

Meanwhile, the central Mongol army of six *tumens* was poised to force the Russian (Verecke) Pass into Hungary, while in the south another three *tumens* devastated Moldavia and Wallachia and then prepared to force the southern passes into Transylvania.

In March 1241, the long-dreaded invasion of Hungary began, as the flanking columns completed their work, insuring the country's isolation.

At Chmielnik, on March 18, Baidar lured the army of the Palatine Vladimir out of Cracow, decisively defeated him and burned Cracow. Then Baidar crossed the Oder River at Raciborz and marched on Breslau to rendezvous with Kadan. While waiting for Kadan he invested Breslau.

The central army forced the Russian Pass on March 12 and began to ravage eastern Hungary. A reconnaissance in force stormed Vac on March 17, only 20 miles from Pest, where the King's army was assembling. Mongol horsemen tried to lure the King into the open and cut down detachments of noblemen rash enough to take the bait.

The southern Mongol army crossed into Transylvania in three columns on March 31 and set about ravaging the province. One column defeated the army of the Transylvanian viceregent, while the others sought out the smaller Hungarian forces.

By the first of April, the flanking armies had destroyed almost all forces that could reinforce the Hungarian King, then prepared to tackle the Hungarian army itself.

On April 9, 1241, the battle of Liegnitz began. In the north, Baidar abandoned the siege of Breslau when he received intelligence that Henry the Pious, Duke of Silesia, had collected 30,000 troops in Liegnitz, and that the Bohemian King was marching to join him with a further 50,000. Baidar immediately sent word to Kadan, and the two Mongol generals set out alone for Liegnitz.

Henry did not know when to expect the Bohemian reinforcements, and, concerned that he would be unable to deploy his force if he allowed himself to be pinned down behind the walls of the city, he decided to engage. Organizing his army into three "battles" (brigades) of cavalry and one of infantry, he marched out alone to meet the Mongol invaders.

A few miles south of the city the two armies clashed on a wide plain. Henry's first cavalry brigade was immediately routed by a hail of arrows, and he rashly committed his remaining horsemen. In a short, murderous clash the Mongols first appeared to have the worst of it, and began yielding ground. The Silesian knights pursued them, only to learn a favorite Mongol maneuver the hard way: their disordered and extended lines caught in a well-laid ambush, the flower of Polish knighthood was soon destroyed. Meanwhile, a Mongol detachment raised a smokescreen behind Henry's knights; the rest of the army had no idea what was happening. Once the knights—and Henry, killed attempting to flee—were dealt with, the archers rode through the smoke and shot down the helpless infantry. Nine large sacks of victims' ears filled the Mongol war-wagons.

After the battle the Mongol *tumens* galloped west to lure Bohemian King Wenceslas farther away from Hungary, then dispersed and rode around his flanks, recalling the detached *tumen* from the Baltic and turning south to join Batu beyond the Carpathians. Their strategic mission thus was completed—they had removed all possible threat on the north flank.

Meanwhile, on the 5th or 6th of April, three or four days before the battle of Liegnitz, Batu struck camp and slowly withdrew to the east. The Hungarians ill-advisedly followed him the next day.

On the 10th, one day after the Battle of Liegnitz, the Mongols halted east of the Sajo River, ready to engage the Hungarian army. The stage was set to Mongol liking for the decisive battle of the campaign: both strategic flanks were secured; the main army was concentrated on the selected battlefield, and the enemy was completely isolated.

On the afternoon of the 10th, Subedei crossed the Sajo on the stone bridge near Mohi and halted his army some 10 miles farther east. Hoping to tempt Bela into a rash move, he left only a very weak detachment at the bridge. Bela reached the river later the same day, but disappointed Subedei by ignoring the bait of an unopposed crossing. Instead, he established a bridgehead on the east bank and occupied a strong position some distance west of the river.

Now Subedei had a problem: Bela had to be destroyed within a day or two, before he learned of his total isolation, in which case he would likely retire behind the Danube and garrison the strong fortresses of western Hungary. They would then have to be reduced one by one. But Bela at the moment occupied a well-

protected position, and he did not seem inclined to rush headlong into a trap. Subedei had no choice but to attack under very risky conditions. His two widely separated forces had to win or perish; they had no practical route of withdrawal once they were engaged. On the hill above the Hungarian camp, he and Batu finalized their strategy.

At dawn on April 11, the Hungarians beat back the first Mongol efforts to take the bridge. Confidently, they jeered at them across the river. The Mongols brought up seven siege engines—flat-trajectory *ballistae*—and bombarded the garrison of the bridge with firebombs until it withdrew to the west bank. Then the *ballistae* increased their range, and Mongol squadrons rode over the bridge, covered by a rolling barrage. They swept up Hungarian pickets on the riverbank and silently deployed, facing south.

The Hungarian commanders were surprised by the attack—they were used to more conservative methods of war—and only two contingents (one led by the King's brother Koloman, the other by one of the country's fighting bishops) were ready to engage the onrushing Mongols. They managed to hold until reinforcements came up from the camp, and after the first clashes the Mongols gave ground. The Hungarians, badly shaken by the swift attack, were just regaining their balance when another Mongol force materialized behind them. Subedei had crossed the river with three *tumens* during the night, and swept behind the Hungarians to take them in the rear.

In the spring the rivers of Hungary are in full flood; they are very deep and swift—formidable obstacles even to modern combat engineers. But the crafty Subedei had moved a large force across the Sajo at night, with a hostile army within easy striking distance. Now he attacked from the least likely direction: the small peninsula, enclosed by river and swamp, looked inaccessible from the east bank and was totally unsuitable for a sizeable force. Its outlet was barely two miles wide; no more than 2,500 horsemen could ride abreast in that space. A mixed detachment of 5,000 archers and heavy troops could have held the bottleneck—but all the Hungarian commanders were looking the other way.

The Hungarians did not panic, but they did lose the initiative. They still had superior numbers, but instead of charging through the Mongol center—much-thinned by the first clashes—they confusedly withdrew into their camp. The Mongols brought up their siege engines and bombarded the camp at leisure for several hours, then charged in three converging columns. Some Hungarian troops fled through a gap left by the Mongols for just such a purpose; soon individual desertions turned into a complete rout. Only a handful of Knights Templar stood their ground. Overwhelmed by the Mongols, they died to a man.

King Bela and the mortally wounded Koloman managed to escape; others were not so fortunate. For two days, as demoralized and exhausted Hungarians lurched toward the protection of the Danube River and the twin citadels of Buda and Pest, Mongol horsemen rode alongside, casually butchering the men as they came across them. Bodies littered the road to Pest "like stones in a quarry." Seventy thousand Hungarians died in the debacle.

News of the overwhelming Mongol triumph sent horrified shudders sweeping through Europe. The swift-striking invaders had appeared so suddenly, at so many different places, that Europeans now spoke of a mongol "horde," numberless and irresistible, bringing God's wrath down upon a sinful populace. Gruesome rumors, sparked by all-too-real Mongol atrocities, spread from city to city. The Mongols, some said, had the bodies of men but the heads of dogs, and fed on the bodies of their victims. Others said they were demon worshippers, and had been led across Hungary by evil spirits. In churches throughout Europe, white-faced congregations prayed, "From the fury of the Tartars, oh Lord, deliver us." Only a miracle, it seemed, could save them from the "horde."

King Bela, in the meantime, suffered considerable indignity at the hands of the Duke of Austria (not for nothing was that prince known as Frederick the Pugnacious), and finally established his court in his Adriatic province. A Mongol column was sent to capture him in early 1242, but he found sanctuary on Trogir Island in the Adriatic.

Batu and Subedei were now masters of eastern Hungary. They soon were formulating plans for the invasion of Germany, and their scouts were raiding near Vienna. The population of Hungary was subjected to unspeakable atrocities, but gradually Mongol cruelty abated; administration was established, coin was minted—all to encourage the peasants to come out of hiding and harvest the grain. Once the granaries were filled, though, another series of massacres took place.

As soon as the Danube froze the following winter, Subedei led the Mongol army across the ice, and only some of the fortified cities of Western Hungary could resist the assaults. Meanwhile the sovereigns of Europe, paralyzed with fear, simply waited for the descent of the barbarian hordes. They saw the devastation in the Mongols' wake between the Baltic and the Black Sea and knew that their undisciplined levies were no match for the terrible horsemen from the East.

A miracle of sorts then occurred to save Europe—in April 1242 the Mongols evacuated Hungary and returned east. Ogedei Khan's death was one reason for the unexpected withdrawal: according to Genghis Khan's law, Batu had to be in Karakorum for the election of the successor. But the decisive reason may have been strictly military—the Mongol forces were spread too thin, and in the devastated country the army would soon begin to suffer from lack of food. Hungary's strength was sapped—it could be reoccupied in a few years with ease. Several other Mongol conquests had been carried out thus, in two stages: in a whirlwind campaign a region's military force would be destroyed, its rulers killed, its inhabitants decimated, its wealth plundered. Then, in order to allow a measure of recovery, the conquerors would withdraw, only to return several years later, when the region was sufficiently recovered to allow orderly administration, but was still too weak to offer serious resistance.

Fortunately for western civilization, there was considerable dissension among Mongol aristocrats, and Ogedei's successor was not elected for some time. The defeated learn the lessons of a war more thoroughly than the victors: Bela had formidable castles built, invited the Cumans to return, and reorganized the army. The Mongols would attack Hungary again in 1285, but this generation of Mongol generals would not be cast in the mold of Subedei, and Bela's grandson would repulse them with little effort. The success of Mongol armies did not end then, but in following centuries Mongol energies were spent fighting among themselves. New conquerors emerged, but their conquests did not last long, and the once-great Mongol empire eventually fell apart.

Medieval annalists described the Mongols as half-human barbarians bent on rape and pillage, terrible apparitions with animal instincts for blood and plunder. Indeed, the horrors of a Mongol campaign are difficult to imagine—cities razed, provinces devastated, thousands enslaved, tens of thousands butchered. Their invasions caused fearsome destruction and led to the extinction of entire nations—medieval Hungary, for example, lost nearly 50 percent of its population.

But the chronicles do not explain the true reasons for Mongol successes. The history of their victories was written by their enemies, who understood but poorly the Mongol method of warfare and sought excuses for the shocking defeats of splendid armies by so-called barbarians. Mongol success was not due to superior numbers, acts of God, barbarous ferocity, or wonder weapons, but rather to brilliant generalship, careful planning, discipline, and organization. The Mongols were expert in mobile warfare, and the lessons of their campaigns are as important today as they were in the 13th century, when the Mongols were truly the masters of all they surveyed.

The Myths of Medieval Warfare

An absurd procession of chivalry or mad mass charges without tactics or reason?
Historical analysis of fighting in the Middle Ages has now become more subtle
than either of these scenarios, argues **Sean McGlynn.**

Sean McGlynn

Sean McGlynn is a research student at the London School of Economics.

The study of medieval warfare has suffered from an approach that concentrates on its social, governmental and economic factors to the detriment of military methods and practice. The nature of feudal society has been analysed in great depth, but its application to how wars were actually fought has largely been ignored and frequently misinterpreted. Despite recent important work these misinterpretations have been stubbornly persistent, perpetuating the long-held myth that the art of warfare reached its nadir in the Middle Ages. John Keegan's latest book, *A History of Warfare* (Hutchinson, 1993), reflects the view of some leading military historians in referring to 'the long interregnum between the disappearance of the disciplined armies of Rome and the appearance of state forces in the sixteenth century'. In

The Wars of the Roses (Cassell, 1993), Robin Neillands regards knightly warfare as involving no great skill, being simply a matter of bludgeoning one's opponent to the ground. Whereas these and other historians have assimilated a number of the more correct observations on medieval warfare, the complete picture has remained frustratingly obscure.

That this should be so is due in the main to the success of the pioneering work of historians in the nineteenth and early twentieth centuries, among whom were Henri Delpech, Hans Delbrück and Sir Charles Oman. Oman's influence has been particularly pervasive because of the continuing availability of a work considered a classic, *The Art of War in the Middle Ages* (the first edition was published by Blackwells in 1885, with a ninth printing by Cornell University Press in 1990; the final revised and improved edition in two volumes was published by Methuen in 1924, reprinted by

Greenhill in 1991). Although much of Oman's wide-ranging work was of value, his conclusions on 'feudal' warfare remained flawed. Ironically, both he and the distinguished historian, Ferdinand Lot, recognised the supreme importance of fortified places, but they concentrated instead on the appeal and drama of knights and battles.

Collectively, damaging myths of medieval warfare emerged from these historians. Battles were all important, fought by opposing armies of knights who would inadvertently encounter one another. The ensuing *mêlée* was a confusion of individual duels by glory-seeking knights set on establishing a martial reputation. The knight was ill-disciplined, too proud to fight on foot, adhered only to the most rudimentary tactics and was poorly led. No thought was given to logistics and ravaging was carried out for want of a coherent strategy. Infantry and archery, if present at all, were only mar-

Church militant: William the Conqueror's half-brother, Bishop Odo of Bayeux, (centre) wields a mean club (thus avoiding the injunction on shedding blood) in the Bayeux tapestry depiction of the battle of Hastings.

ginal and ineffective, insignificant until the revolutionary tactics of the fourteenth century. The early modern period saw a new age in warfare, marked by the greater efficiency and tactics of the standing armies and by the prevalence of sieges.

Unfortunately, the study of medieval warfare has been dominated by general historians (military and otherwise), soldiers and enthusiasts whose neglect or uncritical use of the available primary sources has led to judgements formulated through inappropriate modern and comparative interpretations. The growth in governmental records in the later Middle Ages has provided a wealth of quantitative information on military matters, and the period has accordingly received more research than the eleventh to thirteenth centuries; but the potential of chronicles from this earlier period has not been fully exploited.

Despite his contributions to the subject, John Beeler wrote that the only literate class of the day were the clergy and monks who understandably 'had little comprehension of military matters, and even less interest in . . . strategy and tactics' (*Warfare in Feudal Europe,* Cornell University Press, 1971). This overlooks the evidence: William of Pontiers, Villehardouin and Joinville were just a few of the fighting men who wrote detailed accounts of war. The monks and clergy, meanwhile, could show as keen an interest in war as their fathers, brothers and patrons were members of the fighting class, the *bellatores:* Suger, Abbot of St Denis, gives a vigorous account of King Louis VI at war in his *Life of Louis the Fat;* Bishop Hugues of Auxerre would gather knights about him to discuss military lessons from Vege-

tius' *De Re Militari,* a classical text valued as a handbook on war by medieval commanders. Many ecclesiastics took a more active involvement: the Bayeux Tapestry depicts Bishop Odo of Bayeux in battle at Hastings and Archbishop Turpin is given a heroic role in *The Song of Roland* ('Thousands of strokes the stout Archbishop strikes').

All writers, whether military or clerical, came from the first ranks of the social order. It is this social aspect that explains the relative omission of lowly foot-soldiers and archers in the sources: they were always present in war but were afforded little mention. This has mistakenly been taken as evidence for their very limited value before the end of the thirteenth century.

The more egregious errors concerning medieval warfare should have been dispelled by two important revisionist books, R. C. Smail's *Crusading Warfare 1097–1193* (Cambridge University Press, 1956) and J. F. Verbruggen's *The Art of Warfare in Western Europe During the Middle Ages* (North-Holland 1977; originally published in Brussels in 1954). Both authors discredited the excessive focus of their predecessors on battles, stressing that in fact medieval commanders would normally adopt a strategy of battle avoidance rather than risk the consequences of a pitched battle. King John II of France was taken prisoner at Poitiers (1356) and at Bosworth (1485) the death of Richard III meant the loss of both king and cause. Verbruggen observes that between 1071 and 1328 in Flanders, frequently invaded, there were only eleven battles of note.

Smail's study of crusading campaigns without battles shows that military activity on these occasions was nonetheless

intensive, with intelligence gathering, ravaging, logistical concerns and other actions. Battles were only one of the means available to attain the objects of war . . . 'the true end of military activity was the capture and defence of fortified places'. This meant that medieval warfare confined itself to the achievement of known and limited aims, a concept different to the twentieth century's one of engagement and destruction of the enemy's forces and the unconditional surrender of the defeated.

Verbruggen also recognised the role of the castle but, even more than Smail, he concentrated on armies in the field, successfully challenging the myth of the blundering knight who had no idea of tactics. He went further than Smail in emphasising the skill and the professionalism of the *milites,* the heavy cavalry of the Middle Ages. He contends that medieval warfare should not be judged according to the capability of the footsoldiers, as had been the case, 'but rather according to that of cavalry'. In reality, it should be evaluated on a number of important criteria—infantry, logistics, strategy, tactics, recruitment, and sieges for example—of which cavalry is only one, albeit very important, element.

Verbruggen dismisses the view of battles as involving little more than knights in a series of individual combats. This myth has arisen from a misuse of the sources:

historians have kept the name of the prominent nobleman who fought at the head of his unit, but in their account of the engagement they forget the words *cum suis, avec sa gent, cum sau acie* ['with his troops'], with the result that the fighting of entire formations is represented as a duel fought out by two champions.

Forage and pillage – as seen here in the Bayeux tapestry – were essential aspects of the logistics of medieval warfare as well as undermining the resources of the enemy.

5. THE MEDIEVAL PERIOD

These formations were made up of small tactical units (*conrois*) from which the larger *batailles* were formed. Knights trained for war in such units, especially at tournaments where manoeuvres and tactics were practised over a wide area through countryside and villages, formalised tilting at the lists coming only in the late thirteen century. Sources such as *The History of William the Marshall* confirm the level of skills necessary for combat; as the twelfth-century chronicler, Roger of Howen, wrote: 'without practice the art of war did not come naturally when it was needed'.

Training instilled discipline into the knight. The image of the impulsive knight charging headlong into the fray is largely a false one. An Arabian warrior in the Crusades, Usamah ibn Munqidh, complained of his enemies. 'Of all men, the Franks are the most cautious in warfare'. Discipline was vital to the success of the cavalry. The shock charge, the knight's greatest tactical weapon, depended on the serried ranks of the cavalry maintaining tight formation during the assault, thereby creating an irresistible force that could, according to the Byzantine, Anna Comnena, break through the walls of Babylon. The victory won by Simon de Montfort's greatly outnumbered French force at Muret in 1213 showed what it could achieve: the Crusaders burst through the enemy ranks to reach King Peter of Aragon, killing him and annihilating his army. Incidentally, this battle also offers a good example of a medieval commander directing his mounted tactical reserve in a decisive flank attack. Verbruggen also establishes that knights could be recalled from a charge and be reorganised for further assaults, rebutting a long-held belief to the contrary. A variation of this was the feigned flight, most famously employed at Hastings in 1066, a tactic devised to draw out the defences of the enemy, thereby rendering him more vulnerable to a renewed cavalry charge.

The knight, then, was a disciplined and well-trained professional soldier. Was he also chivalrous? The knight's code of honour should not be underestimated and was of great importance, but so was his quest for financial rewards. Capture of an opposing knight, whether in a tournament or on the battlefield, meant lucrative gains from ransom and booty (*preda*) in the form of expensive armour and warhorses. A knight was worth more alive than dead. Orderic

Vitalis, writing on the battle of Brémule in 1119, informs us that only three knights were killed, but 140 were taken prisoner. He attributes this to the protective efficacy of the armour and because the knights, as 'Christian warriors, had no desire to shed the blood of their brothers'. Indeed not: they desired instead to ransom their brothers for large sums of money. The belief that medieval warfare centred around knightly duels has fuelled the study of chivalry. However, in warfare, chivalry applied only to the knight, and it ignored other vital elements. Maurice Keen in *Chivalry* (Yale, 1984), the standard work on the subject, highlights this when discussing advances in cavalry tactics, judiciously noting that 'advances in castle building and in techniques of siege warfare were equally or even more important'.

The various strands of war are admirably drawn together in Philippe Contamine's classic, *War in the Middle Ages* (Blackwell, 1984; translated by Michael Jones). This authoritative overview stresses the interconnection of war with society as a whole, rightly holding that war is 'the product of a whole cultural, technical and economic environment'. He places war against the background of the commercial revolution and changes in government and administration in the twelfth and thirteenth centuries, the outcome of which was an increasing monetised society.

Perhaps the most obvious implication of a money economy for war was the emergence of the permanent armies identified with the early modern period. In this light the innovative indenture system of Edward I (1272–1307) is seen as instrumental in heralding the eventual decline of the feudal summons in favour of more professional, paid forces. This belief is countered in an important recent book edited by Matthew Strickland, *Anglo-Norman Warfare* (Boydell, 1992), which makes accessible to a wider audience a collection of eclectic academic articles by specialists, primarily written during the last fifteen years. Where recognition has been given to medieval warfare for proficient recruitment, the use of effective infantry, archery and dismounted knights, competent leadership and strategy, and the *chevauchée*, historians have tended to date these developments from the later Middle Ages, and especially from the revolution in tactics and organisation under Edward I. The contributors to *Anglo-Norman Warfare* trace these

developments to an earlier period, encouraging debate between early and late medievalists. Whereas some of these issues were raised by Smail, Verbruggen and Contamine, their conclusions were sometimes hesitant and not fully developed; more importantly, the degree of emphasis, repeatedly accentuated in these articles, recreates a much clearer and more authentic picture of the true nature of warfare throughout the Middle Ages.

J. O. Prestwich argues that feudalism has been overrated as a method of military organisation; money always formed the sinews of war and was a more consistent method of recruitment. As Richard FitzNeal wrote *c.* 1179, money was 'poured out in fortifying castles [and] in soldiers' wages'. The Treaty of Dover in 1101 is given as an example of an early indenture system. By the terms of this treaty, Henry I of England hired 1,000 Flemish knights from Count Robert of Flanders at the price of £500 per annum. Prestwich significantly remarks that at a time when the feudal levy of England did not produce more than 5,000 knights, Henry had 'been arranging for the service of 1,000 knights from one external source alone'. Elsewhere, he writes that the military household (*familia regis*) of the Norman kings 'supplied the standing professional element, capable of fighting independent actions and, for a major campaign, providing the framework into which other forces could be fitted'. This permanent force was prominent in battles and controlled an extensive network of castles; in structure and size it was comparable to the *familia regis* of Edward I. This degree of continuity in the military organisation of England in the Middle Ages reveals the long evolution to the standing armies of the early modern period.

In articles affirming the skill of medieval generalship as demonstrated by Richard the Lionheart, William the Conqueror and William the Marshal, John Gillingham addresses some of the routine activities in warfare. Ravaging (*terram depopulare, vastare*) and plundering were not matters of mindless destruction or the only means of obtaining food and supplies (the importance of logistics to military considerations is underlined); destroying the enemy's crops and livestock undermined his economic base and thereby deprived him of the revenues essential for the waging of war. It was a possible means of provoking an opponent into the field, but normally a strategy of battle avoidance prevailed. In 1054, Duke William defended Normandy by shadowing the invading forces, preventing them from ravaging and foraging his lands, all the while avoiding a full engagement. The effects of ravaging could be devastating, as commanders put into operation a cardinal lesson of Vegetius: 'the main and principal point in war is to secure plenty of provisions for oneself and to destroy the enemy by famine. Famine is more terrible than the sword'. In the Hundred Years' War ravaging is better known as the *chevauchée*.

According to Oman, the later Middle Ages lay claim to 'one of the first medieval generals who shows a complete appreciation of the value of time in war', referring to Edward IV on account of his 'accustomed celerity' in the Wars of the Roses. As Gillingham shows, *The History of William the Marshal* is just one source that makes repeated reference to rapid troop movements and the element of surprise: at Winchester in 1141 King Stephen's swift and unexpected arrival put the Empress Matilda to flight; and a night march by John Marshal in the same year was used to lay an ambush.

A royal act from France in 1188 stipulated that Tournai had to provide 300 heavy infantry (*pedites bene armatos*) when summoned by Philip II, a substantial number from one source, and one of many cases to rebut the view that medieval foot-soldiers only became a significant and effective force in the fourteenth century. Articles by Matthew Bennet, Jim Bradbury and John Gillingham reveal the 'vitally important' role of infantry by such telling examples as when the spears of Henry II's foot-soldiers saw off the French cavalry at Gisors in 1188 ('not the kind of thing that is supposed to happen in medieval warfare before the battle of Courtai in 1302') and the series of battles in England and Normandy between 1066 and 1141 which display the tactical combination of cavalry, dismounted knights, archers and infantry.

Medieval strategy cannot be understood outside the context of siege warfare and the castle's military role, areas that have been subject to oversight. Matthew Strickland's article on invasion and defence strategy builds on Smail's conclusions by analysing the Anglo-Scottish campaigns of 1138 and 1173–74. He details how some castles would be deliberately destroyed or left unprepared at the outbreak of war, with resources and manpower concentrated on a number of key strongholds. This was a common medieval practice, as implemented by Charles VI of France during the Hundred Years' War following a survey of his castles by his knights. Although this would not stop an invading army from ravaging the surrounding territories, 'the conquest of a disputed region could only be achieved by the occupation or the destruction of its castles'. Rather than giving battle and risk losing garrison manpower, a defending force was often better to remain in relative safety behind castle walls until the invading force withdrew. This was exactly the policy of Count Baldwin of Hainault in 1184 who, immured in his castle and watching enemies ravage his fields, remarked: 'They can't take the land with them'. Given that the most fundamental principle of medieval warfare was the rule of territory through occupying strongholds, much work remains to be done on castle strategy to improve our understanding of war in the Middle Ages. (A forthcoming companion volume to *Anglo-Norman Warfare*, focusing on castles and fortifications, will make more accessible some of this work.)

As the ultimate objective of medieval strategy was the control of fortifications, this meant sieges—and lots of them. As with ravaging, the chronicles are replete with references to sieges (*obsidiones*). Jim Bradbury's *The Medieval Siege* (Boydell, 1992) is a much needed comprehensive survey of this neglected field. The multitude of methods involved in taking a strongpoint—starving, mining, storming, bombardment, treachery, bribery, ruse and, most usually of all, negotiations—indicate how large a branch of conflict poliorcetics (siege warfare) is. It is also the most important part. Paradoxically, despite recognition of this, it has received relatively little attention; but nor has it been misrepresented. Sieges have occasionally been more closely identified with early modern warfare, but this should no longer be so as Geoffrey Parker has noted their key role in the Middle Ages in *the Military Revolution* (Cambridge University Press, 1988).

A major implication of sieges for armies in the field was their duration. A besieging army settling down for a long investiture was vulnerable to disease and being caught between the garrison and a

Falaise Castle, birthplace of William the Conqueror: the ability to fortify and provision effectively castles such as this was key to any defensive military strategy in the Middle Ages.

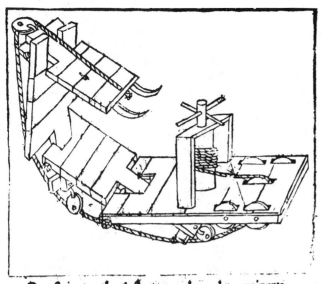

Q nefto e vno altro inftrumento de condure vno ponte

Mean machines: siege equipment depicted in a 1483 manual on military tactics. The development of gunnery and more powerful mechanisms for bombardment had already begun to influence the conduct of war significantly before the end of the Middle Ages.

relieving army. It is instructive that most battles arose from sieges and many involved relief forces: Tinchebrai (1106), Lincoln (1141), Formigny (1450). Primary strongholds generally required a lengthy blockade: Château-Gaillard (1203–4) and Rouen (1418–19) each lasted nearly six months; Calais (1346–47) took eleven months. Medieval warfare was clearly not a seasonal occupation restricted to the summer months.

A particularly contentious issue in medieval military debates concerns the longbow: was it a revolutionary or an evolutionary weapon? Jim Bradbury turns his attention to this question in *the Medieval Archer* (Boydell, 1985), convincingly challenging the conventional view that the longbow was a new and devastating weapon only fully adopted by the English after the experience of Edward I's armies against Welsh archers at the end of the thirteenth century. He notes that the term 'longbow' was not used by contemporaries, even during the Hundred Years' War. Of greater importance, he stresses the role of the archer throughout the Middle Ages, and not just from the fourteenth century. Although the 1181 Assize of Arms (Henry II's famous ordinance for the arming of his English subjects) makes no mention of the bow, the continental edict of the same time does (*arcum et sagittas*). Bradbury investigates the significant part played by archery at Hastings (1066), Bourgthéroulde (1124)

of the Standard (1138). Together with the specific mentions in Henry III's Assize of 1252, this brings the bow up to the eve of the Welsh Wars. The continuity is even more marked when one considers a successful summons by King John in 1213. Roger of Wendover reports that many men had to be dismissed from the expeditionary force; only the most important troops were retained, and these included the archers.

The archer's role is best recognised in the famous battles of the Hundred Years' War, most notably Crécy (1346) and Agincourt (1415), the startling result of Edward I's original tactics in his Scottish wars. But Bradbury clearly proves that the tactic of deploying archers with dismounted knights was a practice used in the twelfth century. Archers at Bourgthéroulde halted a cavalry charge before it reached the knights on foot. At the Battle of the Standard most of the English knights dismounted while others were kept for the cavalry reserve. Archer and spearmen were positioned in the front rank; dismounted knights were mixed in with the archers. In both battles archery was instrumental to the victory. Thus 'it is not easy to see anything novel in the use of dismounted men-at-arms and archers in the Hundred Years' War'. What was new and developed in the Scottish wars, however, was 'the sheer increase in the number of archers employed', and it was this that created such an impact in the fourteenth century.

Every period of history has its share of military blunders, inept leaders and poor organisation, but it is a mistake to consider them as the norm in medieval warfare rather than as exceptions to the rule. War in the Middle Ages was fought as competently as in any other period and the era does not represent a hiatus in the evolution of military history. In about 375 BC, Plato wrote in *The Republic* that it is 'of the greatest importance that the business of war should be efficiently run'. The Middle Ages channelled their best efforts to this end, and with appreciable success.

How a Mysterious Disease Laid Low Europe's Masses

In the 1300s, a third of the population died of plague brought by fleas, shocking the medieval world to its foundations.

Charles L. Mee Jr.

In all likelihood, a flea riding on the hide of a black rat entered the Italian port of Messina in 1347, perhaps down a hawser tying a ship up at the dock. The flea had a gut full of the bacillus *Yersinia pestis*. The flea itself was hardly bigger than the letter "o" on this page, but it could carry several hundred thousand bacilli in its intestine.

Scholars today cannot identify with certainty which species of flea (or rat) carried the plague. One candidate among the fleas is *Xenopsylla cheopis,* which looks like a deeply bent, bearded old man with six legs. It is slender and bristly, with almost no neck and no waist, so that it can slip easily through the forest of hair in which it lives. It is outfitted with a daggerlike proboscis for piercing the skin and sucking the blood of its host. And it is cunningly equipped to secrete a substance that prevents coagulation of the host's blood. Although *X. cheopis* can go for weeks without feeding, it will eat every day if it can, taking its blood warm.

One rat on which fleas feed, the black rat *(Rattus rattus),* also known as the house rat, roof rat or ship rat, is active mainly at night. A rat can fall 50 feet and land on its feet with no injury. It can scale a brick wall or climb up the inside of a pipe only an inch and a half in diameter. It can jump a distance of two feet straight up and four horizontally, and squeeze through a hole the size of a quarter. Black rats have been found still swimming days after their ship has sunk at sea.

A rat can gnaw its way through almost anything—paper, wood, bone, mortar, half-inch sheet metal. It gnaws constantly. Indeed, it *must* gnaw constantly. Its incisors grow four to five inches a year: if it were to stop gnawing, its lower incisors would eventually grow—as sometimes happens when a rat loses an opposing tooth—until the incisors push up into the rat's brain, killing it. It prefers grain, if possible, but also eats fish, eggs, fowl and meat—lambs, piglets and the flesh of helpless infants or adults. If nothing else is available, a rat will eat manure and drink urine.

Rats prefer to move no more than a hundred feet from their nests. But in severe drought or famine, rats can begin to move en masse for great distances, bringing with them any infections they happen to have picked up, infections that may be killing them but not killing them more rapidly than they breed.

Rats and mice harbor a number of infections that may cause diseases in human beings. A black rat can even tolerate a moderate amount of the ferocious *Yersinia pestis* bacillus in its system without noticeable ill effects. But bacilli breed even more extravagantly than fleas or rats, often in the millions. When a bacillus finally invades the rat's pulmonary or nervous system, it causes a horrible, often convulsive, death, passing on a lethal dose to the bloodsucking fleas that ride on the rat's hide.

THE ULTIMATE BACILLUS BREEDER

When an afflicted rat dies, its body cools, so that the flea, highly sensitive to changes in temperature, will find another host. The flea can, if need be, survive for weeks at a time without a rat host. It can take refuge anywhere, even in an abandoned rat's nest or a bale of cloth. A dying rat may liberate scores of rat fleas. More than that, a flea's intestine happens to provide ideal breeding conditions for the bacillus, which will eventually multiply so prodigiously as finally to block the gut of the flea entirely. Unable to feed or digest blood, the flea desperately seeks another host. But now, as it sucks blood, it spits some out at the same time. Each time the flea stops sucking for a moment, it is capable of pumping thousands of virulent bacilli back into its host. Thus bacilli are passed from rat to flea to rat, contained, ordinarily, within a closed community.

For millions of years, there has been a reservoir of *Yersinia pestis* living as a permanently settled parasite—passed back and forth among fleas and rodents in warm, moist nests—in the wild rodent colonies of China, India, the southern part of the Soviet Union and the western United States. Probably there will always be such reservoirs—ready to be stirred up by sudden climatic change or ecological disaster. Even last year, four authentic cases of bubonic plague were confirmed in New Mexico and Arizona. Limited outbreaks and some fatalities have occurred in the United States for years, in fact, but the disease doesn't spread, partly for reasons we don't understand, partly because patients can now be treated with antibiotics.

And at least from biblical times on, there have been sporadic allusions to plagues, as well as carefully recorded outbreaks. The emperor Justinian's Constantinople, for instance, capital of the Roman empire in the East, was ravaged by plague in 541 and 542, felling perhaps 40 percent of the city's population. But none of the biblical or Roman plagues seemed so emblematic of horror and devastation as the Black Death that struck Europe in 1347. Rumors of fearful pestilence in China and throughout the East had reached Europe by 1346. "India was depopulated," reported one chronicler, "Tartary, Mesopotamia, Syria, Armenia, were covered with dead bodies; the Kurds fled in vain to the mountains. In Caramania and Caesarea none were left alive."

Untold millions would die in China and the rest of the East before the plague subsided again. By September of 1345, the *Yersinia pestis* bacillus, probably carried by rats, reached the Crimea, on the northern coast of the Black Sea, where Italian merchants had a good number of trading colonies.

From the shores of the Black Sea, the bacillus seems to have entered a number of Italian ports. The most famous account has to do with a ship that docked in the Sicilian port of Messina in 1347. According to an Italian chronicler named Gabriele de Mussis, Christian merchants from Genoa and local Muslim residents in the town of Caffa on the Black Sea got into an argument; a serious fight ensued between the merchants and a local army led by a Tatar lord. In the course of an attack on the Christians, the Tatars were stricken by plague. From sheer spitefulness, their leader loaded his catapults with dead bodies and hurled them at the Christian enemy, in hopes of spreading disease among them. Infected with the plague, the Genoese sailed back to Italy, docking first at Messina.

Although de Mussis, who never traveled to the Crimea, may be a less-than-reliable source, his underlying assumption seems sound. The plague did spread along established trade routes. (Most likely, though, the pestilence in Caffa resulted from an infected population of local rats, not from the corpses lobbed over the besieged city's walls.)

In any case, given enough dying rats and enough engorged and frantic fleas, it will not be long before the fleas, in their search for new hosts, leap to a human being. When a rat flea senses the presence of an alternate host, it can jump very quickly and as much as 150 times its length. The average for such jumps is about six inches horizontally and four inches straight up in the air. Once on

human skin, the flea will not travel far before it begins to feed.

The first symptoms of bubonic plague often appear within several days: headache and a general feeling of weakness, followed by aches and chills in the upper leg and groin, a white coating on the tongue, rapid pulse, slurred speech, confusion, fatigue, apathy and a staggering gait. A blackish pustule usually will form at the point of the fleabite. By the third day, the lymph nodes begin to swell. Because the bite is commonly in the leg, it is the lymph nodes of the groin that swell, which is how the disease got its name. The Greek word for "groin" is *boubōn*—thus, bubonic plague. The swellings will be tender, perhaps as large as an egg. The heart begins to flutter rapidly as it tries to pump blood through swollen, suffocating tissues. Subcutaneous hemorrhaging occurs, causing purplish blotches on the skin. The victim's nervous system begins to collapse, causing dreadful pain and bizarre neurological disorders, from which the "Dance of Death" rituals that accompanied the plague may have taken their inspiration. By the fourth or fifth day, wild anxiety and terror overtake the sufferer—and then a sense of resignation, as the skin blackens and the rictus of death settles on the body.

In 1347, when the plague struck in Messina, townspeople realized that it must have come from the sick and dying crews of the ships at their dock. They turned on the sailors and drove them back out to sea—eventually to spread the plague in other ports. Messina panicked. People ran out into the fields and vineyards and neighboring villages, taking the rat fleas with them.

When the citizens of Messina, already ill or just becoming ill, reached the city of Catania, 55 miles to the south, they were at first taken in and given beds in the hospital. But as the plague began to infect Catania, the townspeople there cordoned off their town and refused—too late—to admit any outsiders. The sick, turning black, stumbling and delirious, were objects more of disgust than pity; everything about them gave off a terrible stench, it was said, their "sweat, excrement, spittle, breath, so foetid as to be overpowering; urine turbid, thick, black or red. . . ."

Wherever the plague appeared, the suddenness of death was terrifying. Today, even with hand-me-down memories of the great influenza epidemic of 1918 (SMITHSONIAN, January 1989) and the

advent of AIDS, it is hard to grasp the strain that the plague put on the physical and spiritual fabric of society. People went to bed perfectly healthy and were found dead in the morning. Priests and doctors who came to minister to the sick, so the wild stories ran, would contract the plague with a single touch and die sooner than the person they had come to help. In his preface to *The Decameron,* a collection of stories told while the plague was raging, Boccaccio reports that he saw two pigs rooting around in the clothes of a man who had just died, and after a few minutes of snuffling, the pigs began to run wildly around and around, then fell dead.

"Tedious were it to recount," Boccaccio thereafter laments, "brother was forsaken by brother, nephew by uncle, brother by sister and, oftentimes, husband by wife; nay what is more and scarcely to be believed, fathers and mothers were found to abandon their own children, untended, unvisited, to their fate, as if they had been strangers. . . ."

In Florence, everyone grew so frightened of the bodies stacked up in the streets that some men, called *becchini,* put themselves out for hire to fetch and carry the dead to mass graves. Having in this way stepped over the boundary into the land of the dead, and no doubt feeling doomed themselves, the *becchini* became an abandoned, brutal lot. Many roamed the streets, forcing their way into private homes and threatening to carry people away if they were not paid off in money or sexual favors.

VISITING MEN WITH PESTILENCE

Some people, shut up in their houses with the doors barred, would scratch a sign of the cross on the front door, sometimes with the inscription "Lord have mercy on us." In one place, two lovers were supposed to have bathed in urine every morning for protection. People hovered over latrines, breathing in the stench. Others swallowed pus from the boils of plague victims. In Avignon, Pope Clement was said to have sat for weeks between two roaring fires.

The plague spread from Sicily all up and down the Atlantic coast, and from the port cities of Venice, Genoa and Pisa as well as Marseilles, London and Bristol. A multitude of men and women, as Boccaccio writes, "negligent of all but themselves . . . migrated to the country, as if God, in visiting men with this pestilence in requital of their iniquities, would not pursue them with His wrath wherever they might be. . . ."

Some who were not yet ill but felt doomed indulged in debauchery. Others, seeking protection in lives of moderation, banded together in communities to live a separate and secluded life, walking abroad with flowers to their noses "to ward off the stench and, perhaps, the evil airs that afflicted them."

It was from a time of plague, some scholars speculate, that the nursery rhyme "Ring Around the Rosy" derives: the rose-colored "ring" being an early sign that a blotch was about to appear on the skin; "a pocket full of posies" being a device to ward off stench and (it was hoped) the attendant infection; "ashes, ashes" being a reference to "ashes to ashes, dust to dust" or perhaps to the sneezing "a-choo, a-choo" that afflicted those in whom the infection had invaded the lungs—ending, inevitably, in "all fall down."

In Pistoia, the city council enacted nine pages of regulations to keep the plague out—no Pistoian was allowed to leave town to visit any place where the plague was raging; if a citizen did visit a plague-infested area he was not allowed back in the city; no linen or woolen goods were allowed to be imported; no corpses could be brought home from outside the city; attendance at funerals was strictly limited to immediate family. None of these regulations helped.

In Siena, dogs dragged bodies from the shallow graves and left them half-devoured in the streets. Merchants closed their shops. The wool industry was shut down. Clergymen ceased administering last rites. On June 2, 1348, all the civil courts were recessed by the city council. Because so many of the laborers had died, construction of the nave for a great cathedral came to a halt. Work was never resumed: only the smaller cathedral we know today was completed.

In Venice, it was said that 600 were dying every day. In Florence, perhaps half the population died. By the time the plague swept through, as much as one-third of Italy's population had succumbed.

In Milan, when the plague struck, all the occupants of any victim's house, whether sick or well, were walled up inside together and left to die. Such draconian measures seemed to have been partially successful—mortality rates were lower in Milan than in other cities.

Medieval medicine was at a loss to explain all this, or to do anything about it. Although clinical observation did play some role in medical education, an extensive reliance on ancient and inadequate texts prevailed. Surgeons usually had a good deal of clinical experience but were considered mainly to be skilled craftsmen, not men of real learning, and their experience was not much incorporated into the body of medical knowledge. In 1300, Pope Boniface VIII had published a bull specifically inveighing against the mutilation of corpses. It was designed to cut down on the sale of miscellaneous bones as holy relics, but one of the effects was to discourage dissection.

Physicians, priests and others had theories about the cause of the plague. Earthquakes that released poisonous fumes, for instance. Severe changes in the Earth's temperature creating southerly winds that brought the plague. The notion that the plague was somehow the result of a corruption of the air was widely believed. It was this idea that led people to avoid foul odors by holding flowers to their noses or to try to drive out the infectious foul odors by inhaling the alternate foul odors of a latrine. Some thought that the plague came from the raining down of frogs, toads and reptiles. Some physicians believed one could catch the plague from "lust with old women."

Both the pope and the king of France sent urgent requests for help to the medical faculty at the University of Paris, then one of the most distinguished medical groups in the Western world. The faculty responded that the plague was the result of a conjunction of the planets Saturn, Mars and Jupiter at 1 P.M. on March 20, 1345, an event that caused the corruption of the surrounding atmosphere.

Ultimately, of course, most Christians believed the cause of the plague was God's wrath at sinful Man. And in those terms, to be sure, the best preventives were prayer, the wearing of crosses and participation in other religious activities. In Orvieto, the town fathers added 50 new religious observances to the municipal calendar. Even so, within five months of the appearance of the plague, Orvieto lost every second person in the town.

There was also some agreement about preventive measures one might take to avoid the wrath of God. Flight was best: away from lowlands, marshy areas, stagnant waters, southern exposures and coastal areas, toward high, dry, cool, mountainous places. It was thought wise to stay indoors all day, to stay cool and to cover any windows that admitted bright sunlight. In addition to keeping flowers nearby, one might burn such aromatic woods as juniper and ash.

The retreat to the mountains, where the density of the rat population was not as great as in urban areas, and where the weather was inimical to rats and fleas, was probably a good idea—as well as perhaps proof, of a kind, of the value of empirical observation. But any useful notion was always mixed in with such wild ideas that it got lost in a flurry of desperate (and often contrary) stratagems. One should avoid bathing because that opened the pores to attack from the corrupt atmosphere, but one should wash face and feet, and sprinkle them with rose water and vinegar. In the morning, one might eat a couple of figs with rue and filberts. One expert advised eating ten-year-old treacle mixed with several dozen items, including chopped-up snake. Rhubarb was recommended, too, along with onions, leeks and garlic. The best spices were myrrh, saffron and pepper, to be taken late in the day. Meat should be roasted, not boiled. Eggs should not be eaten hard-boiled. A certain Gentile di Foligno commended lettuce; the faculty of medicine at the University of Paris advised against it. Desserts were forbidden. One should not sleep during the day. One should sleep first on the right side, then on the left. Exercise was to be avoided because it introduced more air into the body; if one needed to move, one ought to move slowly.

By the fall of 1348, the plague began to abate. But then, just as hopes were rising that it had passed, the plague broke out again in the spring and summer of 1349 in different parts of Europe. This recurrence seemed to prove that the warm weather, and people bathing in warm weather, caused the pores of the skin to open and admit the corrupted air. In other respects, however, the plague remained inexplicable. Why did some people get it and recover, while others seemed not to have got it at all—or at least showed none of its symptoms—yet died suddenly anyway? Some people died in four or five days, others died at once. Some seemed to have contracted the plague from a friend or relative who had it, others had never been near a sick person. The sheer unpredictability of it was terrifying.

In fact, though no one would know for several centuries, there were three different forms of the plague, which ran three different courses. The first was simple bubonic plague, transmitted from rat to person by the bite of the rat flea. The second and likely most common form was pneumonic, which occurred when the bacillus invaded the lungs. After a two- or three-day incubation period, anyone with pneumonic plague would have a severe, bloody cough; the sputum cast into the air would contain *Yersinia pestis*. Transmitted through the air from person to person, pneumonic plague was fatal in 95 to 100 percent of all cases.

The third form of the plague was septocemic, and its precise etiology is not entirely understood even yet. In essence, however, it appears that in cases of septocemic plague the bacillus entered the bloodstream, perhaps at the moment of the fleabite. A rash formed and death occurred within a day, or even within hours, before any swellings appeared. Septocemic plague always turned out to be fatal.

Some people did imagine that the disease might be coming from some animal, and they killed dogs and cats—though never rats. But fleas were so much a part of everyday life that no one seems to have given them a second thought. Upright citizens also killed gravediggers, strangers from other countries, gypsies, drunks, beggars, cripples, lepers and Jews. The first persecution of the Jews seems to have taken place in the South of France in the spring of 1348. That September, at Chillon on Lake Geneva, a group of Jews were accused of poisoning the wells. They were tortured and they confessed, and their confessions were sent to neighboring towns. In Basel all the Jews were locked inside wooden buildings and burned alive. In November, Jews were burned in Solothurn, Zofingen and Stuttgart. Through the winter and into early spring they were burned in Landsberg, Burren, Memmingen, Lindau, Freiburg, Ulm, Speyer, Gotha, Eisenach, Dresden, Worms, Baden and Erfurt. Sixteen thousand were murdered in Strasbourg. In other cities Jews were walled up inside their houses to starve to death. That the Jews were also dying of the plague was not taken as proof that they were not causing it.

On the highways and byways, meanwhile, congregations of flagellants wandered about, whipping themselves twice a day and once during the night for weeks at a time. As they went on their way they attracted hordes of followers and helped spread the plague even farther abroad.

The recurrence of the plague after people thought the worst was over may have been the most devastating development of all. In short, Europe was swept not only by a bacillus but also by a widespread psychic breakdown—by abject terror, panic, rage, vengefulness, cringing remorse, selfishness, hysteria, and above all, by an overwhelming sense of utter powerlessness in the face of an inescapable horror.

After a decade's respite, just as Europeans began to recover their feeling of well-being, the plague struck again in 1361, and again in 1369, and at least once in each decade down to the end of the century. Why the plague faded away is still a mystery that, in the short run, apparently had little to do with improvements in medicine or cleanliness and more to do with some adjustment of equilibrium among the population of rats and fleas. In any case, as agents for Pope Clement estimated in 1351, perhaps 24 million people had died in the first onslaught of the plague; perhaps as many as another 20 million died by the end of the century—in all, it is estimated, one-third of the total population of Europe.

Very rarely does a single event change history by itself. Yet an event of the magnitude of the Black Death could not fail to have had an enormous impact. Ironically, some of the changes brought by the plague were for the good. Not surprisingly, medicine changed—since medicine had so signally failed to be of any help in the hour of greatest need for it. First of all, a great many doctors died—and some simply ran away. "It has pleased God," wrote one Venetian-born physician, "by this terrible mortality to leave our native place so destitute of upright and capable doctors that it may be said not one has been left." By 1349, at the University of Padua there were vacancies in every single chair of medicine and surgery. All this, of course, created room for new people with new ideas. Ordinary people began wanting to get their hands on medical guides and to take command of their own health. And gradually more medical texts began to appear in the vernacular instead of in Latin.

AN OLD ORDER WAS BESIEGED

Because of the death of so many people, the relationship between agricultural supply and demand changed radically, too. Agricultural prices dropped precipitously, endangering the fortunes and power of the aristocracy, whose wealth and dominance were based on land. At the same time, because of the deaths of so many people, wages rose dramatically, giving laborers some chance of improving their own conditions of employment. Increasing numbers of people had more money to buy what could be called luxury goods, which affected the nature of business and trade, and even of private well-being. As old relationships, usages and laws broke down, expanding secular concerns and intensifying the struggle between faith and reason, there was a rise in religious, social and political unrest. Religious reformer John Wycliffe, in England, and John Huss, in Bohemia, were among many leaders of sects that challenged church behavior and church doctrine all over Europe. Such complaints eventually led to the Protestant Reformation, and the assertion that Man stood in direct relation to God, without need to benefit from intercession by layers of clergy.

Indeed, the entire structure of feudal society, which had been under stress for many years, was undermined by the plague. The three orders of feudalism—clergy, nobility and peasantry—had been challenged for more than a century by the rise of the urban bourgeoisie, and by the enormous, slow changes in productivity and in the cultivation of arable land. But the plague, ravaging the weakened feudal system from so many diverse and unpredictable quarters, tore it apart.

By far the greatest change in Western civilization that the plague helped hasten was a change of mind. Once the immediate traumas of death, terror and flight had passed through a stricken town, the common lingering emotion was that of fear of God. The subsequent surge of religious fervor in art was in many ways nightmarish. Though medieval religion had dealt with death and dying, and naturally with sin and retribution, it was only after the Black Death that painters so wholeheartedly gave themselves over to pictures brimming with rotting corpses, corpses being consumed by snakes and toads, swooping birds of prey appearing with terrible suddenness, cripples gazing on the figure of death with longing for deliverance, open graves filled with blackened, worm-eaten bodies, devils slashing the faces and bodies of the damned.

Well before the plague struck Europe, the role of the Catholic Church in Western Europe had been changing. The Papacy had grown more secular in its concerns, vying with princes for wealth and power even while attempts at reform were increasing. "God gave us the Papacy," Pope Leo X declared. "Let us enjoy it." The church had suffered a series of damaging losses in the late 1200s—culminating in 1309 when the Papacy moved from Rome to Avignon. But then, the Black Death dealt the church a further blow, for along with renewed fear and the need for new religious zeal came the opposite feeling, that the church itself had failed. Historical changes rarely occur suddenly. The first indications of change from a powerful catalyst usually seem to be mere curiosities, exceptions or aberrations from the prevailing worldview. Only after a time, after the exceptions have accumulated and seem to cohere, do they take on the nature of a historical movement. And only when the exceptions have come to dominate, do they begin to seem typical of the civilization as a whole (and the vestiges of the old civilization to seem like curiosities). This, in any case, is how the great change of mind occurred that defines the modern Western world. While the Black Death alone did not cause these changes, the upheaval it brought about did help set the stage for the new world of Renaissance Europe and the Reformation.

As the Black Death waned in Europe, the power of religion waned with it, leaving behind a population that was gradually but certainly turning its attention to the physical realm in which it lived, to materialism and worldliness, to the terrible power of the world itself, and to the wonder of how it works.

Prophets Without Honour?

Jan Hus—Heretic or Patriot?

'Truth will conquer'—the Czech historian František Šmahel *traces the life and work of his fifteenth-century compatriot Jan Hus—whose uncompromising criticism of medieval Catholicism stirred national pride and acted as a forerunner of the Reformation.*

František Šmahel

František Šmahel is Senior Research Fellow at the Museum of the Hussite Movement, Tabor, Czechoslovakia.

Translated by Jitka Jenkins.

Even in the fifteenth century, in a case concerning a university professor and preacher, it was not usual to involve, successively, the leading lawyers and theologians, three archbishops, the judicial courts of two popes, and, last but not least, two kings (both bearers of the Holy Roman Crown). The singularity of this case extended beyond this fact. The Czech reformer Master John Hus, who was the person in question, was one of the first people to receive a personal invitation to attend the Council of Constance. Hus went voluntarily in order to defend his honour but he paid for his courage with his life. In premonition of his own end, he once wrote that 'He who dies, wins'. Until his last moment, he did not cease to believe in his biblical motto *Veritas vincit,* even though, at that time, truth was not prevailing against power.

A miniature from one of the famous Hussite hymn-books (graduals) recorded the development of the European Reformation thus: John Wycliffe struck the first spark, John Hus used it to ignite the candle, and Martin Luther raised the burning torch aloft; the blaze of the torch obliterated the glow of the candle and the spark in the general awareness of history. This encapsulation is not misleading; after an initial hesitation, Luther began to cite the heretic Hus, while Hus in turn regarded the Oxford apostate Wycliffe as his teacher.

Wycliffe's radical critique of traditional Catholic doctrine in the 1370s (in the course of which he had questioned its traditional hierarchy), putting forward a forerunner of the Reformation's priesthood of all believers, and his attack on the doctrine of transubstantiation had placed him in the forefront of heretical dissent which, without the patronage of Edward II's brother, John of Gaunt, could have led him to the stake rather than a peaceful death in 1384.

Moreover, the indictment against Hus at the Council of Constance was mostly related to the Wycliffian basis of his faith. The detailed dispute about Hus' intellectual ancestry has by no means ended; nevertheless, it is possible to assert, with the benefit of hindsight, that, without Wycliffe, Hus' doctrine would have lacked its reforming vehemence and, moreover, that it was only after Wycliffe's ideas had been transferred to Bohemia that they acquired their final European (Hussite) character.

The Reformation movement in the Kingdom of Bohemia only manifested itself significantly in the second half of the fourteenth century. It rapidly became popular and, thanks to both the University of Prague and the international contacts of the Luxembourg princely house which ruled Bohemia as part of the imperial domain, it readily incorporated additional stimuli of foreign origin. Apart from the Waldensian heresy of the German colonists (which was based on the principles of church poverty, preaching and teaching the scriptures in the vernacular and was driven deep underground after being deemed illegal by the Inquisition), most of the reforming efforts did not exceed the limits of tolerance of the clerics.

Hus' generation followed their native predecessors by returning to their traditions, independently reaching a set of nonconformist thoughts and demands. When the first writings of the Oxford Reformer John Wycliffe became known in Prague, by the end of the fourteenth century, the young John Hus added an almost prophetic remark to his own transcription of the writings in the form of a pun: 'Wycliffe, Wycliffe, many heads will become shaky.' (In Czech, *'Viklef, Viklef, nejednomu ty hlavu zvikleš''*, the name Wycliffe (Viklef) sounds similar to the word for shaking, making wobbly or loose.) The name of Wycliffe became a symbol for the other masters of the Czech faction in the university corporation who longed to be 'the head and not the tail' at the highest national educational institution. This was just provocative enough for the foreign professors there to launch an attack, and by the end of May 1403 they enforced, by a majority, a condemnation of forty-five heretic articles from Wycliffe's writings.

In April 1408 the Papal Curia forbade, under strict punishment, the spreading of Wycliffe's writings; those in possession were threatened by anathema, if they refused to give them up. Soon afterwards, the Prague Consistory also hardened its campaign against the Reformation group. The opponents of the Wycliffians, however, rejoiced prematurely. The spokesmen of the Czech nation made use of the favourable political situation and, with the help of influential adherents in the king's court, they pushed through a change in the university constitution in January 1409. According to a decree issued in Kutná Hora by Wenceslas IV, the native (Czech) university people were granted three votes against only one vote jointly for the three combined corporations of foreign masters and students. In the meantime, a pressure group of radical Wycliffians obtained the decisive influence in the Czech community, hence the university in Prague simultaneously embarked on the path of heresy. The victory on the domestic front, however, had an obverse side; before the Reformation movement could become a national social force, hundreds of former masters of Prague University started to sound an alarm against it, at home and abroad, after they had left Prague in protest against the Kutná Hora decree.

John Hus (born around 1370) attracted the attention of the foreign public for the first time in the stormy atmosphere of the years 1408–09. Up to that time he had been overshadowed by his senior colleagues. The situation required energetic leaders, who would not be frightened by the first threat. Hus was predestined for the leading role not only by his long-lasting teaching activities but by his increasing fame as a popular preacher in the Bethlehem Chapel. The governors of this spacious chapel, where only the Czech language was employed for preaching, had appointed him in 1402; he had obtained his clerical ordination shortly before, so he must have been about thirty years old at that time.

For Hus, a society divided into estates was a constituent part of the imaginary Church of Christ on Earth but it had little in common with the real Roman Catholic Church. Wycliffe's doctrine about the dual body of the Church had influenced him here. No-one, not even the pope, could say (according to Wycliffe) that he was predestined for salvation or damnation. Because of that, the terrestrial Church, as a sum of all the worshippers, must have included a dual community with totally different prospects in the next world. The basic conflict between the forces of good and evil, both within the individual and in the community, was thus fought between the chosen community of the followers of Christ and the equally imaginary throng belonging to the ruler of Hell.

Hus accepted this concept, which undermined the authority and power of the Church hierarchy, only with reservation. For instance, he continued to recognise the sacramental succession of the clerical office from the time of the Apostles and

thus the inequality between the clergy and the laity, and between a clergyman and a bishop. In principle, he also drew a sharp line through the whole social pyramid, thus dividing it into parallel communities obedient or disobedient to God's law, both structured into estates. On the one hand, he reprimanded the pride of the peasant *nouveaux-riches* and the minor swindles of the petty craftsmen; on the other hand, he did not exclude the God-fearing lords and patricians from the chosen community. He was seeking the support of the rich for his Reformation aims from the very beginning of his activities. Hus simply visualised an ideal, fair feudalism in which everyone would contribute by fraternal love to the prosperity of all.

It was this vision of the widely-opened arms of Hus' reforming programme that spread Czech opposition to the Church through all ranks of society—from king to journeyman. For this reason alone was the initially scanty handful of university Wycliffians able to survive the first hard trials. The more the movement gained adherents from the common people from town and country, the greater became the strains on the movement's social unity. The process began during Hus' life without being significantly reflected in his doctrine. The opponents of the Wycliffian-Hussite ideology realised much more acutely the danger of the appeal of the Reformation and of the growing potential revolt from below.

Hus was an immensely hard-working man. He preached almost every day in the Bethlehem Chapel, he fulfilled his duties in the Faculty of Arts in exemplary fashion, and he by no means neglected his own studies leading to the doctorate in theology. Hus was fortunate to be able to express his thoughts readily in both speech and writing and in a robust way, and more than once he let himself be carried away by personal invective. His preaching in the Bethlehem Chapel gained excitement from his comments on topical events. The majority of the forty Prague parsons cast a spiteful eye on the Bethlehem competition because Hus specifically castigated them. Some only grumbled, others went to the Bethlehem Chapel in disguise and wrote down every suspicious word, for immediate transmission to the Consistory.

The Archbishop of Prague, Zbyněk of Házmburk, had overlooked petty backbiting for a long time—in October 1407 he even rewarded Hus by giving him the

post of preacher at a clerical meeting (synod). But, when Hus dared to oppose the official standpoint just one year later, the Archbishop turned against him, and banned him instantly from preaching. Hus soon returned to the Bethlehem Chapel; however, he had acquired dangerous domestic opponents in Archbishop Zbyněk, his officials, and the Prague parsons. The majority of them were key members of Czech society. The unimpeachibility and uncompromising 'holiness' of the nation, which was a constant theme of the Czech nationalists of the reform circle, was thus significantly compromised. In spite of the mutual Czech-German malice, which later led to bloody conflict, Hus increasingly advocated the principle of true faith above the interests of the nation and the home country. For his mature codex of values, an appeal he made to his own followers is typical (October 1412):

Would you, please, at first consider God's business which has been injured. Secondly, you can pay attention to the dishonour of your country and your nation, and only then, thirdly, can you take account of the dishonour and wrong-doing which you personally innocently suffer.

Hus was not able to take over in his reforming practice all that Wycliffe had drafted at his peaceful desk in the form of pure theory. It is accepted that Hus brought Wycliffe's doctrine to life ideologically by his creative adaptation, but his attempts to develop independently of Wycliffe were not, as a rule, intellectual advances. Hus not only adapted Wycliffe's thoughts to his domestic situation but, simultaneously, he made them less sharply focused. Hus much more frequently referred to his Oxford teacher in the supreme works of the later period when, after his expulsion from Prague, he had time enough for literary activities. The programme of the Reformation party, described in his tract 'About the Church' (apart from some small alterations), he took from Wycliffe. The second part of this crucial document, which was written in the years 1412–13, consists of a masterly polemic against his opponents and a whole set of courageous thoughts concerning true and false obedience. Hus there generalised his experience with the religious courts at all levels and thus, indirectly, granted to his followers in subordinate posts the right to oppose all the authorities whose orders were in conflict with God's Law.

Therefore, if the Pope ordered me to blow a whistle, to build towers, to sew, to weave a cloth, or to stuff sausages, would not my common sense see that the Pope ordered a stupid thing? Why should I not prefer, in this matter, my own opinion to the Pope's order?

In Hus' statements of this sort we can already faintly hear the sound of the bugle announcing the beginning of the Hussite wars.

The very first of Hus' trials merged with the fight concerning the orthodoxy of Wycliffian doctrine. In accord with a decision of the papal court in April 1408, the Archbishop of Prague ordered everyone to hand over all copies of Wycliffe's works. Five students appealed against this edict to the Papal See. Since numerous reforming masters, including Hus, failed to obey the order within the designated time period, the archbishop put them into anathema.

Despite the university's protest, the archbishop again ordered (on June 16th, 1410) the surrender of Wycliffe's books. In addition, he banned all preaching in private places, in particular the Bethlehem Chapel. The edict provoked such strong indignation, even at the king's court, that Zbyněk promised to postpone the execution of the decree. In the meantime, the university protested again, and Hus published a brief statement in which he disproved the basis of the principle of destroying heretic books in the flames. The archbishop was even more irritated by an appeal which was submitted by Hus and several of his pupils on June 25th to the Papal Curia. In the middle of July, the archbishop ordered the burning of Wycliffe's works which had been found in his palace. For fear of street riots (which, indeed, occurred in Prague soon after), he fled to his castle in Roudnice, and from there proclaimed an anathema on Hus and those of his followers who had associated themselves with the appeal.

At the beginning of 1412 it might have seemed that the scales of papal justice would favour Hus. The decisive swing against Hus was again caused by his Prague opponents who managed to impose a court suit on Hus' dexterous advocate Master John of Jesenice. Even then, it might have been possible to influence the verdict if only Hus himself had not fanned the flames by his attitude to the selling of papal indulgencies. Trafficking in the trust of believers had provoked a mighty wave of protests at the

university and in Prague reforming circles, which was soon thwarted on the walls of the king's palace. For reasons which have not been truly understood, Wenceslas IV agreed to the sale of indulgences and accordingly ordered the Prague councillors to punish strictly all those who spoke against such sales.

At this critical moment, when one faction of the reformers began to turn their backs on their own Wycliffian beliefs, even Hus hesitated, and he temporarily shrank into the background. That happened after the execution of three journeymen, participants in the first big popular demonstration in Prague for the support of the reformation movement. Hus felt responsible not only for the executed, but for all his followers. After thirteen days, during which people in Prague whispered that halberdiers had shut Hus' mouth, he reassured his followers. In his sermon in the Bethlehem Chapel on July 24th, 1412, Hus condemned the massacre of the innocent martyrs of faith, and he appealed to the congregation not to be discouraged but to stand by the truth.

The news of Hus' invectives against the pope, which had eagerly been reported to the curia, accelerated the process of appeal. The verdict was brought to Prague by a papal legate, thus excluding the possibility of postponing its implicit consequences. At the synod on October 18th, 1412, the sentence of excommunication on Hus was reinforced. If he had not submitted within twenty days, an interdict would have been issued after a further twelve days on all the places in which he might have been found. A ban on all church services, including funerals, would have brought many difficulties for the 40,000 habitants of the city. The consequences could have turned people against the reformation movement. This led Hus to the decision to leave for the country. Still, before he left, he appealed to Christ against the verdict of the Papal See.

Hus' gesture of resignation was soon overshadowed by a hopeful counteraction by his solicitor John of Jesenice at the Lands court. The senior representatives of the lords proclaimed their right to demand a vote also in the matters concerning ideology of country-wide importance. In their edict of December 1412, they stated that a subpoena from a foreign court had no legal force. On the basis of this intervention, Wenceslas asked the archbishop, who was by this

time his trusted friend, Konrad of Vechta, to pacify the antagonistic domestic clergy.

The assiduous archbishop submitted the views of the opposing sides to the Crown council in February of the following year. The king then consigned the task of formulating a compromise agreement to a special commission; it ordered the Wycliffians and their opponents to commit themselves to accepting a verdict of arbitration under the penalty of paying 60,000 pieces of silver or of expulsion from the country. The four leading professors of theology found themselves trapped when they were ordered to pronounce that the country was freed from heresy. They preferred voluntary exile to loss of face. John Hus behaved with dignity, too, when he refused to accept the compromising proposals. With the words 'I do not want to sin any more', he eliminated any possibility of resolving the controversy on the domestic front.

The invitation to attend the Council of Constance presented a challenge which Hus could not decline. The initiative of the Holy Roman king, Sigismund, raised justified apprehension among the adherents of the reforms because the Czech public distrusted the character of this second son of the Emperor Charles IV. On the other hand, it was not possible to ignore the general merit of Sigismund's efforts to summon a council which would provide Hus with a platform from which to defend the Reformation programme at the most significant contemporary international forum.

Hus calmed his own apprehensions and doubts by drawing on limitless trust in the victory of the biblical truth. The reforming circle was resigned to the possibility of a court case, but only if the result of the public hearing was unfavourable to Hus. The risk to Hus could be mitigated only by a safe-conduct, which was actually promised to Hus by Sigismund, and which was granted after some delay. In the event of a public hearing, Hus was determined 'to profess the Lord Christ and, if necessary, to suffer death for His most truthful Law'. These words were not spoken to the winds. Before leaving for Constance, Hus left behind a sealed letter for his favourite pupil, with instructions that it should not be opened until after his death. In the letter, Hus revealed himself and the depth of his faith much more than in public proclamations. Simultaneously, the letter contained his last will, as far as his modest possessions were concerned.

In the remaining time, Hus hastily drafted three speeches for his public appearances. In the event, Hus was not able to deliver any of his intended speeches; he had instead to be grateful to be granted a public hearing during the court case. The safe-conduct granted by Sigismund did not protect Hus at all. By the end of November 1414, less than two weeks after Hus' arrival in Constance, Pope John XXIII capitulated to the pressure of the Czech accusers, and imposed provisional custody upon Hus. Disregarding the protests of Sigismund's courtiers, the pope refused to set Hus free, and on December 4th he entrusted the opening of the court case to a special investigating commission. Two days later, Hus was thrown into a stinking cell in the Dominican monastery, where he remained until the end of March 1415. Sigismund, after he arrived in Constance, showed goodwill in dealing with this Hus affair and, during his first encounter with the cardinals, he pressed for Hus' release. Some of the cardinals threatened to leave if the council could not make independent decisions in religious matters. Sigismund submitted; he insisted, however, on a public hearing and he secured Hus' transfer into an airy cell close to the monastery refectory. After that, Hus was able to resume his correspondence and occasionally receive visits from his companions and friends.

Sigismund was playing for high stakes against Pope John, and much politicking was involved, in the coils of which both the pope and his Czech critic became enmeshed. The pope fled from Constance on the night of March 21st, 1415; in the resulting confusion, no-one showed any interest in Hus. A word from the king would have been enough to release him from prison; it did not come because Hus' case was taken up, almost overnight, as the chief instrument by which Sigismund could continue the existence of the council. Hus was, by Sigismund's order, transported by ship to the castle of the Bishop of Constance in Gottlieben, where he stayed until the beginning of May. At that time, the two Johns exchanged places: the seized pope was interned in Gottlieben while Hus was taken back to Constance.

Hus' letters from prison sometimes take the form of a manifesto; at other times they constitute a deeply human testimony. In the struggle with his own doubts, and in fear for his own life, Hus demonstrated his internal strength. Sometimes it even seemed as though he had begun to see the uselessness of his defence at the council. The critical break occurred during the second public hearing on June 7th, 1415. Hus' stubbornness there provoked even King Sigismund, who took umbrage at Hus' statements regarding the moral disqualification of sovereigns, popes, and prelates in a state of mortal sin, exclaiming 'John Hus, no-one lives without sin!' The king's well-meant advice was unacceptable to Hus, and that provoked his judges even more. Face to face with his opponents and accusers he declared: 'I am standing in front of God's tribunal, which will justly pass judgement on both you and me according to our merits.' Sigismund waved away this threat from the next world and, as he left, instructed the cardinals to make short work of the case of Hus and also that of Master Jerome of Prague, who had come to Constance to support his friend.

The last public hearing in Constance Cathedral during the celebratory session of the council on July 6th, 1415, was merely a formal court ritual leading to the stake prepared on the embankment of the Rhine. The written statement submitted to the council by Hus on July 1st thwarted all the behind-the-stage efforts to save him. If he had perjured himself, or recanted, Hus would have betrayed his followers: 'for that, it would be proper', as he wrote to one of his friends, 'for me to have a millstone hung around my neck and be drowned in the depths of the sea.' The last attempt at a defence was muffled by the noise of curses and mockeries. Nevertheless, Hus' 'I do not recant' transcends place and time. His death in the flames accelerated the transformation of a peaceful reformation movement in Bohemia to an armed revolt against the worldly Roman Church and its profane protectors. The first phase of the victorious Reformation in Europe became generally known under Hus' name. Last but not least, Hus' courageous stance in Constance remains, for the present and the future, an inspiration in the fearless fight for the right to individual or collective truth.

FOR FURTHER READING:

Geoffrey Barraclough (ed.), *Eastern and Western Europe in the Middle Ages* (Thames and Hudson, 1970); Paul Roubiczek and Joseph Kalmer, *Warrior of God: The Life and Death of John Hus* (London, 1947); M. Spinka, *John Hus' Concept of the Church* (Princeton University Press, 1966); Gordon Leff, *Heresy in the Later Middle Ages* (Manchester University Press, 1966).

Renaissance and Reformation

The departure from medieval patterns of life was first evident in Renaissance Italy. There the growth of capital and the development of distinctly urban economic and social organizations promoted a new culture. This culture was dominated by townsmen whose tastes, abilities, and interests differed markedly from those of the medieval clergy and feudal nobility. "How Jacques Coeur Made His Fortune" shows how early capitalism functioned in France.

The emergent culture was limited to a minority—generally those who were well-to-do. But even in an increasingly materialistic culture, it was not enough just to be wealthy. It was necessary to excel in the arts, literature, and learning, and to demonstrate skill in some profession. The ideal Renaissance man, as Robert Lopez observes (in *The Three Ages of the Italian Renaissance*, University of Virginia Press, 1970), "came from a good old family, improved upon his status through his own efforts, and justified his status by his own intellectual accomplishments."

The new ideal owed much to the classical tradition. Renaissance man, wishing to break out of the otherworldly spirituality of the Middle Ages, turned back to the secular naturalism of the ancient world. Indeed, the Renaissance was, among other things, a heroic age of scholarship that restored classical learning to a place of honor. It was classical humanism in particular that caught the fancy of Renaissance man. In the new spirit of individualism, however, humanism was transformed. The classical version, "man is the measure of all things," became, in poet and scholar Leon Alberti's version, "A man can do all things, if he will." No one better illustrates Alberti's maxim than Leonardo da Vinci, Italian painter, sculptor, architect, and engineer.

Civic humanism was another Renaissance modification of the classical heritage. It involved a new philosophy of political engagement, a reinterpretation of political history from the vantage point of contemporary politics, and a recognition that one should not simply imitate the ancients but rival them. Of course, humans being what we are, Renaissance humanism had its darker side. And the Renaissance ideal did not fully extend to women, as J. H. Plumb's essay explains. That article should be read in conjunction with the piece by Israel Shenker, which shows how a shrewd, capable, ambitious woman of early-modern England managed to gain great wealth and influence despite the limitations generally imposed on women of that time and place.

Renaissance art and architecture reflected the new society and its attitudes. Successful businessmen were now as likely as saints to be the subjects of portraiture. Equestrian statues of warriors and statesmen glorified current heroes while evoking memories of the great days of ancient Rome. Renaissance painters rediscovered nature (which generally had been ignored by medieval artists), often depicting it as earthly paradise—the appropriate setting for humanity in its new image. And in contrast to the great medieval cathedrals, which glorified God, Renaissance structures enhanced humanity.

Some of these developments in art and architecture indicate changes in the role of Christianity and the influence of the Church, which no longer determined the goals of Western civilization as they had during the medieval period. Increasingly, civil authorities and their symbols competed with churchmen and their icons, while Machiavelli (treated in an article by Vincent Cronin) and other writers provided a secular rationale for a new political order. Nonetheless, most Europeans, including many humanists, retained a deep and abiding religious faith.

The Reformation, with its theological disputes and wars of religion, is a powerful reminder that secular concerns had not entirely replaced religious ones, especially in northern Europe. The great issues that divided Protestant and Catholic—the balance between individual piety and the authority of the Church, the true means of salvation, and so on—were essentially medieval in character. Indeed, in their perceptions of humanity, their preoccupation with salvation (and damnation), and their attacks

VS
COL·MACCHIAVE

upon the Church's conduct of its affairs, Luther, Calvin, Zwingli, and other Protestant leaders echoed the views of medieval reformers. Luther's lasting influence is examined in "Luther: Giant of His Time and Ours." The connections between Protestantism and German nationalism are set out in "The Forming of German Identity." As for Calvinism, see William J. Bouwsma's essay on John Calvin, in which the author attempts to correct modern misperceptions of the Swiss reformer.

Taken together, then, the Renaissance and Reformation constituted a new compound of traditional elements (classical and medieval, secular and religious) along with elements of modernity. The era was a time of transition, or as Lynn D. White describes it, "This was a time of torrential flux, of fearful doubt, marking the transition from the relative certainties of the Middle Ages to the new certainties of the eighteenth and nineteenth centuries." Such "fearful doubts" were expressed in the witch-hunts of the period. Other troubling facets of the era surfaced when Western civilization reached across the Atlantic. Many of these concerns have been revived in connection with the Columbus quincentenary. These matters are taken up in "Columbus—Hero or Villain?"

Looking Ahead: Challenge Questions

What does the career of Jacques Coeur tell us about the basic elements of early capitalism?

How did politics change at the beginning of the modern era? What part did the ideas of Machiavelli play in the shift from medieval to modern politics?

Did Renaissance humanism influence the place of women in European life?

How did Bess of Hardwick overcome the limitations placed on women in early-modern England?

How can we account for the conflicting images of Columbus, and by what standards can our age fairly judge the explorer?

Compare and contrast the ideas and accomplishments of Luther and Calvin.

How Jacques Coeur Made His Fortune

He made it none too scrupulously, and lost it at the whim of a much wilier scoundrel than himself

Marshall B. Davidson

One should visit Bourges to see the curious house that Jacques Coeur built, wrote Jules Michelet a century or so ago in his gigantic history of France. It was, he added, "a house full of mysteries, as was Coeur's life." Then, in one of the picturesque asides that make his history such a treasury of unexpected discoveries, he went on to describe that house and the man who built it—the self-made man who played banker to King Charles VII of France, and who bailed out that monarch when his kingdom was at stake; the intrepid man of the world who traded privileges with Moslem sultans, Christian popes, and European princes; the implausibly rich parvenu who, within less than twenty years, parlayed a few counterfeit coins into the largest private fortune in France.

By 1443, when construction of his house started, Coeur was quite possibly the wealthiest man in the world. His new dwelling was to be a monument to his worldly success, and according to one contemporary it was "so richly ornamented, so spacious, and yet, withal, so magnificent, that neither princes of the blood, nor the king himself, had any residence comparable to it." That last point was not lost on Charles VII, as, in the end, Coeur had bitter cause to know.

The house still stands in the cathedral town of Bourges, a short drive south of Paris. It is a unique survival, a memorial as much to a time in history as to the man who built it, for Coeur's life spanned a critical period in the destiny of France. In the last decade of his life the agonizing internecine strife and the bloody slaughter that accompanied the Hundred Years'

War were, with his substantial aid, finally brought to an end. The English were thrown back across the Channel, and the land was united as it had not been in living memory.

In the course of those protracted disorders the scrambled authority of feudalism gave way to the more orderly rule of national monarchy, the spirit of chivalry faded before the practical aims of an aspiring bourgeoisie, and the stultifying controls of medieval economy were turning into the growing pains of modern capitalism. To most contemporary eyes such vital changes appeared as a blurred image, like a dissolve in a movie. But Coeur's role in those transitions was so decisive, and he was so perfectly cast for the part he played, that he might well have written the script himself.

It could be said that in Coeur's time double-entry bookkeeping was proving mightier than the sword, for without that instrument of precision and convenience (apparently a fourteenth-century invention), he could hardly have managed his complex affairs. To him, and other businessmen, time and—timekeeping—took on new importance. For time was money made or lost. The easy rhythm of the canonical hours was being replaced by the stern measure of mechanical clocks that counted out the cost of fleeting opportunities, pointed the way to quicker profits, and ticked off interest on loans. And Coeur pressed every advantage. He even used carrier pigeons to bring him advance notice of approaching cargoes so that he could improve his position in the local markets.

From the very beginning Coeur's enterprise was, for better and for worse, closely associated with the interests of

his sovereign. Ironically, he first came to public notice in 1429, when, as an associate of the master of the Bourges mint, he was accused of striking coins of inferior alloy. Like so many other functions now considered the exclusive prerogative of government, minting money was then a private concession, albeit by privilege from the king, who took a substantial share of the milling toll as seigniorage, at rates fixed by law. Since no practical system of taxation was yet in force, this was one of the few ways the king could raise money. To meet the demands of the moment, debasing the coinage was approved practice, and the royal "take" could be enhanced by secretly altering the rate of seigniorage—that is, by still further debasing the coinage without advising the public. If the counterfeit was detected, the royal accomplice could disavow the scheme and leave his concessionaires to face the music. And this is what happened to Coeur and his associates in 1429.

Desperate necessities drove Charles VII to practice such duplicity. When he inherited the throne in 1422, the Hundred Years' War was in its eighth grim decade and the fortunes of France were at their lowest ebb. This ill-omened, youthful heir, the tenth child of a madman who disinherited him and of a mother of loose morals who disowned him (it was widely reported that he was a bastard, no matter of shame at the time, but a shadow on his claim to the throne), was holed up in Bourges. An English king reigned in Paris, and English forces occupied all the land from the Channel to the Loire. Philip the Good, the powerful and autonomous duke of Burgundy, tolerated the foreign invader and was allied with him.

And Brittany, ever mindful of its own independent traditions, wavered between allegiances.

The years that followed Charles's succession revolved in a murderous cycle of war and brigandage, pestilence and famine. The king could not afford a standing army, and his military leaders were independent contractors who, between battles with the enemy, roamed the land with their mercenaries, raping, stealing, burning, and killing. Under the circumstances, trade and commerce came to a standstill. Merchants took to the road only if they were armed to the teeth. The great international fairs of Champagne, once vital points of exchange for Europe's traffic, were abandoned as the north-south trade shifted to the sea routes between Flanders and the Mediterranean. France came close to ruin.

The winter of 1428–1429 brought a turning point, or at least a promise of deliverance. The English had laid seige to Orléans, the principal city remaining in Charles's rump of a kingdom. Had Orléans fallen there would have been pitifully little left of that kingdom. The city became a symbol of resistance, while the timid young monarch vacillated in his provincial retreat barely sixty miles away. His mocking enemies dubbed him the "king of Bourges" and anticipated the fall of his petty realm. His treasury was empty; it is said he even borrowed money from his laundress. Only by a miracle could he keep his tottering crown.

The miracle materialized when, as if in direct response to the widely whispered prophecy that an armed virgin would appear and drive the English from the land, Joan of Arc was brought before the king at the château of Chinon where he was then holding court. After grilling the maid for three weeks, the king's counselors decided that she was, as she claimed, divinely appointed by "voices" she had heard to save her king and her country. Somehow, Charles found money to provide her with troops, and the siege of Orléans was lifted. Joan then persuaded her wavering monarch to be crowned at Reims, where Clovis had been baptized. By that ritual the stain of bastardy was automatically removed, and Charles was indisputably the true king of France. It took him eight more years to win Paris from the English, but when he did ride triumphantly into that city, after its sixteen years of foreign occupation, he came as the rightful Christian king.

It was hardly a coincidence that Coeur and his associates were charged with counterfeiting almost immediately after the "miracle" at Orléans, or that Coeur was pardoned of the crime. Charles had most likely met the payroll for Joan's troops with funds provided by the mint's illegal operations, and as party to the crime he saw that Coeur got off easily. At least there is no better explanation.

In any case, soon after his pardon Coeur set out to make his fortune. He formed a new partnership with his old associates at the mint, this time to deal in "every class of merchandise, including that required by the King, Monseigneur the Dauphin, and other nobles, as well as other lines in which they [the partners] can make their profit."

For precedents in this new venture he looked abroad. The basis of Renaissance prosperity, already so conspicuous in Italy, was the carrying trade between East and West. For centuries Venice had fattened on this commerce, to the point where its successful and friendly business relations with Mongols and Moslems alike had encouraged those infidels to close in on the Christian world. Then, as European knighthood took the Cross to the Holy Land, Venetians supplied and equipped their fellow Christians and ferried them to the battle sites at exorbitant rates.

Venice also continued its flourishing trade in arms, armor, and diverse other goods with the Saracens of Egypt and Palestine. When Pope Benedict XII forbade unauthorized trade with the infidel, the merchants of Venice bought up papal authorizations wherever they could and used them as ordinary bills of exchange. With the Fourth Crusade, the "businessman's crusade," the merchants of Venice made a double killing. They dissuaded the debt-burdened knights from their proclaimed purpose of attacking Alexandria, one of Venice's richest markets, and persuaded them to sack the flourishing Christian capital of Constantinople.

Meanwhile, across the Apennines in Tuscany, enterprising merchants were swarming out of Florence into western Europe, collecting contributions to the Crusades as bankers to the Holy See, advancing money to land-poor feudal lords at fantastic interest rates, and with their ready cash buying up the privileges of the towns. During the Hundred Years' War the powerful Bardi and Peruzzi families equipped both French and English armies for the battlefields, prolonging the conflict and taking over the functions of state when it was necessary to secure their accounts. In return for helping Henry III of England with his running expenses, the Florentines asked for 120 per cent interest on advances and, when repayment was not prompt, added 60 per cent more. In such a company of greedy Christians, Shylock would have seemed hopelessly ingenuous.

During the most agonizing period of the Hundred Years' War, however, the Florentines had gradually abandoned their commercial colonies in France. Now that his time had come, Coeur moved to fill that vacuum with his own business and, with equal speed, to stake a claim among the markets of the East, so profitably exploited by Venice. His first try at emulating the Venetian merchants was a disaster. In 1432 he journeyed to Damascus, an awkward if not perilous place for Christians to be at the time, buying up spices and other exotic commodities for resale in the home markets of France. When his ship foundered off Corsica he lost literally everything but his shirt. He and his shipmates were stripped clean by the islanders.

He seems to have recovered promptly. He had centered his operations at Montpellier on the Mediterranean coast, the only French port authorized by the pope to deal with the infidel East. He threw himself with bounding determination into the development of the city's facilities, pressing the local authorities to improve its docks, dredge essential canals, construct adequate warehouses, and generally improve the advantages for commerce and navigation even spending his own money when he had to. As he later wrote the king, he had plans for developing a vast maritime empire under the lily banner of France.

Almost from the moment Charles returned to Paris, Coeur's affairs started to move in a steady counterpoint to the affairs of state. Within a year or two he was installed as *argentier,* receiver of the revenues used to maintain the royal establishment. Since in his capacity as merchant he was also the principal purveyor to that establishment, his position was doubly advantageous and ambiguous. And since for the most part the court could be accommodated only by long-term credit, both the advantage and the ambiguity were compounded. It must have been quite easy for Coeur to convince himself that what was good for Jacques Coeur was good for France.

A reciprocal rhythm of commissions and benefits, responsibilities and opportunities, honors and profits, increased in tempo for more than a decade. The king may already have been in debt to Coeur even before the royal entry into Paris, and this relationship became more or less chronic thereafter. The Paris campaign had again exhausted the royal treasury. In an effort to tighten the leaking economy of the state, Charles, possibly advised by his *argentier,* forbade the export of money from his realm except by a special license, which he then granted, apparently exclusively, to Coeur.

In 1440 Charles further recognized Coeur's services by according him patents of nobility. The following year he appointed him *conseilleur du roi,* in effect minister of finance and, as such, adviser in the revision of the nation's tax structure. Charged with assessing and collecting regional taxes, Coeur sometimes received not only his due commissions but gratuities from local representatives who both respected his influence at court and feared his power as a merchant banker. The "states" of Languedoc, for example, of which Montpellier was the principal port, paid him handsomely for his good offices in the interest of their maritime prosperity—canceling his share of their taxes as a matter of course.

The king, meanwhile, with an unprecedented income from the revenues he received, reorganized his military forces into a paid standing army. He was no longer a mere feudal lord but a monarch able to make policy and enforce it, if need be, with cannon—cannon, cast at the foundries of bourgeois manufacturers, that could reduce the proudest knight's castle to rubble. In 1444 Charles arranged a temporary peace with the English, who still held Normandy and Guyenne. It was at the gay spring *pourparlers* on the banks of the Loire by which the peace was negotiated that Charles first spied the indescribably beautiful Agnes Sorel, "the fairest of the fair," whom he shortly afterward made his mistress. As the king's bedmate, Agnes began to use her influence in matters of state, inaugurating a tradition in French history. As it later turned out, this was a fateful development in the life of Jacques Coeur. The immediate consequence of the truce arrangements, however, was that he could now move into

the English-held markets in Rouen and Bordeaux as well as across the Channel.

Coeur's influence was already recognized far beyond the shores of France. In 1446 he served as negotiator between the Knights of Rhodes and the sultan of Egypt. Two years later, through the intercession of Coeur's agents, the sultan was persuaded to restore trading privileges to the Venetians, who had for a time been banned from the Arab world. At the same time, Coeur consolidated his own position in the Mediterranean and put a cap on his immense commercial structure. Pope Eugenius IV issued a bull authorizing Coeur to trade for five years in his own right, beyond the privileges enjoyed by the port of Montpellier, with the non-Christian world. With this special authority in his pocket, Coeur shifted the base of his maritime enterprise to Marseilles.

One important matter still needed mending. For all Coeur's good offices and his wide reputation, official relations between France and the Arab world were less cordial than suited his interests. In 1447 he persuaded Charles to agree to a formal pact with Abu-Said-Djacmac-el Daher, sultan of Egypt. The French ambassadors, traveling in Coeur's ships and at his expense, arrived in Egypt "in great state" bearing lavish gifts provided by Coeur in the name of the king. The sultan, in turn, arranged an extravagant reception. Coeur's diplomacy triumphed. Peace between the two lands was agreed upon, and French traders received "most favored nation" privileges in Arab ports.

Aided by the gratitude of the Venetians and the Knights of Rhodes, the friendship of the sultan, the favor of the pope, and the indulgence of his king, Coeur secured unassailable advantages at every important point in the world of his day. "All the Levant he visited with his ships," wrote the duke of Burgundy's chronicler some years later, "and there was not in the waters of the Orient a mast which was not decorated with the *fleur-de-lis.*" The maritime empire he created remained for several centuries one of the principal bulwarks of French commerce. To carry on his far-flung, highly diversified operations—they had developed into a virtual monopoly of France's exclusive markets—Coeur employed some three hundred agents and maintained branch offices in Barcelona, Damascus, Beirut, Alexandria, and other strategic centers.

The inventories of his warehouses read like an exaggerated description of Ali Baba's caves. "All the perfumes of Arabia" were carried in stock, and spices and confections from the farthest shores; dyes and colors, cochineal and cinnabar, indigo and saffron—and henna to illuminate the king's manuscripts; materials of fabulous richness and variety, and gems supposedly from the navels of sacred Persian and Indian monkeys, which were mounted in precious metals and considered a universal antidote to human ills. He could provide for the court's most extraordinary or exquisite whim: a coat of mail covered with azure velvet for a Scottish archer of the king's bodyguard; a silver shoulder piece and Turkish buckler for Charles of Orléans; silks and sables for Margaret of Scotland; diamonds to set off the incomparable beauty of Agnes Sorel—they were all to be had, including cold cash for the queen of France herself, who offered up her "great pearl" for security.

In order to put his surplus money to work and to spread his risk, Coeur joined associations that profited from the licensing of fairs (reborn since the temporary truce with England), from speculation in salt, and from the exploitation of copper and silver mines of the Lyonnais and Beaujolais. He had interests in paper and silk factories in Florence. He even invested in three-quarters of two English prisoners of war, each worth a handsome ransom.

The list of his varied enterprises is almost endless. Cash was still in short supply among the nobility, the long war had brought ruin to many lordly tenants, and Charles's fiscal reforms were reducing their income from traditional feudal dues. So Coeur accommodated some of the greatest families of the realm by buying up their manor houses and properties until he held more than thirty estates, some including whole villages and parishes within their grounds. All told, the complex structure of his myriad affairs, his control of the production, transport, and distribution of goods, his private banking resources, and his secure grasp on essential markets all suggest something like the first vertical trust in history.

So far, nothing belied the motto Coeur was then having chiseled into the stones of his great town house at Bourges—*A vaillans cueurs riens inpossible,* nothing is impossible to the valiant. Coeur's star rose even higher in 1448 when he was

BOTH: ARCHIVES PHOTOGRAPHIQUES

Coeur's mansion is adorned both inside and out with whimsical vignettes of daily life.

The trompe l'oeil *couple may represent servants watching for their master's return.*

sent to Rome by Charles with a select group of ambassadors to help end the "pestilential and horrible" papal schism that for long years had been a great trial to the Church. The French ambassadors entered Rome in a procession of splendor—their cortege included three hundred richly caparisoned and harnessed Arabian horses—and Pope Nicholas V wrote Charles that not even the oldest inhabitants could remember anything so magnificent.

Coeur promptly took center stage. Through his efforts, the rival pope, Amadeo VIII, duke of Savoy, was finally persuaded to renounce his claim to the papal throne and accept a position in the church hierarchy second only to that of Pope Nicholas V. As a reward, Coeur's privilege of dealing with the non-Christian world was extended indefinitely. He was also given a franchise to carry Christian pilgrims to the Holy Land.

There were some who complained of the outrageous cost of that papal mission from which Coeur gained such honor and profit. Coeur had no doubt paid the bills, but whether from his own purse or from the king's treasury would have been difficult to determine. Coeur's wealth was by now beyond imagining. It was reported that his horses were shod with silver. His table service was of gold and silver. Each year, it was said, his income was greater than that of all the other merchants of France combined. "The king does what he can; Jacques Coeur does what he pleases" was a repeated observation. He might even be in league with the devil, they began to say.

Jacques Coeur had indeed reached a singular, and perilous, eminence.

How rich Coeur really was and what resources he could command came out in the years immediately following. The time had come, Charles decided, to break the truce with the English and to push them out of France altogether. To launch and maintain the campaign, however, Charles needed more money than he could find in the royal coffers, and he turned to Coeur for help. Coeur responded by dredging every sou he could manage from the resources available to him and by stretching his almost inexhaustible credit to the limit. By one means or another, he turned over to the king, at the very minimum, two hundred thousand ecus, a sum equal to more than one-fifth of the kingdom's annual tax revenues.

He also took to the field at the king's side. in the victorious procession that entered Rouen on November 10, 1449, Coeur rode in the company of Charles; mounted on a white charger, he was clothed in velvet and ermine and wore a sword embellished with gold and precious stones.

Coeur was now about fifty-five years old. For some twenty years he had enjoyed increasing wealth and prestige. Then, suddenly, the wheel of fortune changed direction. Three months after the ceremonies at Rouen, Agnes Sorel died in childbirth, after having been delivered of the king's fourth child. Rumors spread that she had been poisoned. Almost automatically, a cabal of debtors formed to point a finger at the king's *argentier,* "the money man" of almost

magical faculties, who was known to be one of the executors of Agnes's will. To convict Coeur of murder would serve to disembarrass the king and every important member of the court from the claims of their common creditor.

Charles was quick to play his part. One week in July, 1451, he expressed his gratitude to Coeur for his many services; the next week he issued an order for his arrest. Supported by his most recent favorites, the king confronted Coeur with a long list of indictments, starting with the poisoning charge and going back over the years to the counterfeiting charge of 1429, set aside so long ago by the pleasure and the convenience of Charles VII.

No sooner were the dungeon doors closed behind Coeur than "the vultures of the court" started picking away at the estate he could no longer protect. The nobility of France swarmed about the tottering house of Jacques Coeur to redeem their own fortunes from his disgrace. The trial that followed was a mockery. With his enemies as both prosecutors and judges he never had a chance. Even though his accusers confessed that the charge of poisoning Agnes Sorel was false, and the pope pleaded for clemency and justice in the case, Coeur was shunted for several years from prison to prison.

Finally, in May, 1453, at Poitiers, when he was threatened with torture, he issued a statement that led his judges to condemn him, banish him, and confiscate his properties. By a remarkable coincidence, on the day of Coeur's sentence the sorely tried city of Constantinople fell, this time once and for all, to the Turks. It was the end of an era. Less than a week later, the convicted man made an *amende honorable:* kneeling, bareheaded, before a large crowd and holding a ten-pound wax torch in his hands, he begged mercy of God, king, and the courts.

One more adventure remained. For almost a year and a half after his trial, Coeur was kept imprisoned in France, in spite of his banishment, while most of his holdings were seized and sold off. Then, in the autumn of 1454, he managed to escape. Aided by several of his faithful agents, he crossed the Rhone out of France and fled to Rome, where the pope received him with honor. He never returned to France, nor to the house that was his pride.

But he did take to the sea one last time. He arrived in Rome at a crucial moment in the history of the Church and of Western civilization. All Christendom had been shaken by the fall of Constantinople less than two years earlier and felt threatened by further advances of the Ottoman hordes. In the summer of 1456, Coeur, sixty years old and "toiled with works of war," set forth in command of a fleet dispatched by Pope Calixtus III to help retake Constantinople. On the twenty-fifth of November, on the island of Chios, his *vaillant coeur* was stopped, possibly by wounds he suffered in battle.

As he lay dying, Coeur sent one last appeal to Charles, begging the king to show consideration for his children. At this point Charles could afford to be indulgent. In an act of royal compassion he conceded that since "the said Coeur was in great authority with us and rich and abounding in this world's goods and ennobled in his posterity and line . . . it pleases us to have pity on [his children]," and ordained that what might be salvaged from their father's estate, including the house at Bourges, be returned to them.

It was, after all, little enough for him to do, and in the end Coeur had an ironic revenge. The thought of poisoning continued to haunt the king. Four years later, fearing he might be poisoned by his own son, he refused to eat, and died of starvation.

Machiavelli

Would you buy a used car from this man?

Vincent Cronin

Machiavelli—the most hated man who ever lived: charged, down the centuries, with being the sole poisonous source of political monkey business, of the mocking manipulation of men, of malfeasance, misanthropy, mendacity, murder, and massacre; the evil genius of tyrants and dictators, worse than Judas, for no salvation resulted from *his* betrayal; guilty of the sin against the Holy Ghost, knowing Christianity to be true, but resisting the truth; not a man at all, but Antichrist in apish flesh, the Devil incarnate, Old Nick, with the whiff of sulphur on his breath and a tail hidden under his scarlet Florentine gown.

Machiavelli is the one Italian of the Renaissance we all think we know, partly because his name has passed into our language as a synonym for unscrupulous schemer. But Niccolò Machiavelli of Florence was a more complex and fascinating figure than his namesake of the English dictionary, and unless we ourselves wish to earn the epithet Machiavellian, it is only fair to look at the historical Machiavelli in the context of his age.

He was born in 1469 of an impoverished noble family whose coat of arms featured four keys. Niccolò's father was a retired lawyer who owned two small farms and an inn, his mother a churchgoer who wrote hymns to the Blessed Virgin. Niccolò was one of four children; the younger son, Totto, became a priest, and the idea of a confessional occupied by a Father Machiavelli is one that has caused Niccolò's enemies some wry laughter.

Niccolò attended the Studio, Florence's university, where he studied the prestigious newly-discovered authors of Greece and Rome. Like all his generation, he idolized the Athenians and the Romans of the Republic, and was to make them his models in life. This was one important influence. The other was the fact that Florence was then enjoying, under the Medici, a period of peace. For centuries the city had been torn by war and faction; but now all was serene, and the Florentines were producing their greatest achievements in philosophy, poetry, history, and the fine arts.

This point is important, for too often we imagine the Italian Renaissance as a period of thug-like *condottieri* and cruel despots forever locked in war. We must not be deceived by the artists. Uccello and Michelangelo painted bloody battles, but they were battles that had taken place many years before. If we are to understand Machiavelli, we must picture his youth as a happy period of civilization and peace: for the first time in centuries swords rusted, muscles grew flabby, fortress walls became overgrown with ivy.

In 1494, when Machiavelli was twenty-five, this happiness was shattered. King Charles VIII of France invaded Italy to seize the kingdom of Naples; Florence lay on his route. In the Middle Ages the Florentines had fought bravely against aggressors, but now, grown slack and effete, they were afraid of Charles's veterans and his forty cannon. Instead of manning their walls, they and their leading citizen, Pietro de' Medici, meekly allowed the French king to march in; they even paid him gold not to harm their country.

This debacle led to internal wars, to economic decline, in which Niccolò's father went bankrupt, to much heart-searching, and to a puritanical revolution. Savonarola the Dominican came to rule from the pulpit. Thundering that the French invasion was punishment for a pagan way of life, he burned classical books and nude pictures and urged a regeneration of Florence through fasting and prayer. The French just laughed at Savonarola; he lost the confidence of his fellow citizens and was burned at the stake in 1498.

In that same year, Machiavelli became an employee of the Florentine Republic, which he was to serve ably as diplomat and administrator. Machiavelli scorned Savonarola's idea of political regeneration through Christianity; instead, he persuaded the Florentines to form a citizen militia, as was done in Republican Rome. In 1512 Florence's big test came. Spain had succeeded France as Italy's oppressor, and now, at the instigation of the Medici, who had been exiled from Florence in 1494 and wished to return, a Spanish army of five thousand marched against Tuscany. Four thousand of Machiavelli's militia were defending the strong Florentine town of Prato. The Spaniards, ill-fed and unpaid, launched a halfhearted attack. The Florentines, instead of resisting, took to their heels. Prato was sacked, and a few days later Florence surrendered without a fight. The Medici returned, the Republic came to an end, Machiavelli lost his job and was tortured and exiled to his farm. For the second time in eighteen years he had witnessed a defeat that was both traumatic and humiliating.

In the following year an out-of-work Machiavelli began to write his great book *The Prince*. It is an attempt to answer the question implicit in Florence's two terrible defeats: what had gone wrong? Machiavelli's answer is this: for all their classical buildings and pictures, for all the Ciceronian Latin and readings from Plato, the Florentines had never really revived the essence of classical life—that military vigor and patriotism unto death that distinguished the Greeks and Romans. What then is the remedy? Italy must be regenerated—not by Savonarola's brand of puritanism, but by a soldier-prince. This prince must subordinate every aim to military efficiency. He must personally command a citizen army and keep it disciplined by a reputation for cruelty.

But even this, Machiavelli fears, will not be enough to keep at bay the strong new nation-states, France and Spain. So, in a crescendo of patriotism, Machiavelli urges his prince to disregard the accepted rules of politics, to hit below the belt. Let him lie, if need be, let him violate treaties: "Men must be either pampered or crushed, because they can get revenge for small injuries but not for fatal ones"; "A prudent ruler cannot, and should not, honor his word when it places him at a disadvantage and when the reasons for which he made his promise no longer exist"; "If a prince wants to maintain his rule he must learn how not to be virtuous."

Machiavelli develops his concept of a soldier-prince with a couple of portraits. The first, that of the emperor Alexander Severus, is an example of how a prince should not behave. Alexander Severus, who reigned in the third century, was a man of such goodness it is said that during his fourteen years of power he never put anyone to death without a trial. Nevertheless, as he was thought effeminate, and a man who let himself be ruled by his mother, he came to be scorned, and the army conspired against him and killed him. Machiavelli scorns him also: "Whenever that class of men on which you believe your continued rule depends is corrupt, whether it be the populace, or soldiers, or nobles, you have to satisfy it by adopting the same disposition; and then *good deeds are your enemies."*

Machiavelli's second portrait is of Cesare Borgia, son of Pope Alexander VI, who carved out a dukedom for himself and then brought it to heel by appointing a tough governor, Ramiro. Later, says Machiavelli, Cesare discovered that "the recent harshness had aroused some hatred against him, and wishing to purge the minds of the people and win them over . . . he had this official (Ramiro) cut in two pieces one morning and exposed on the public square . . . This ferocious spectacle left the people at once *content and horrified."*

The words I have italicized show Machiavelli's peculiar cast of mind. He grows excited when goodness comes to a sticky end and when a dastardly deed is perpetrated under a cloak of justice. He seems to enjoy shocking traditional morality, and there can be little doubt that he is subconsciously revenging himself on

the Establishment responsible for those two profound military defeats.

Machiavelli wrote *The Prince* for Giuliano de' Medici. He hoped that by applying the lessons in his book, Giuliano would become tough enough to unite Italy and drive out the foreigner. But Giuliano, the youngest son of Lorenzo the Magnificent, was a tubercular young man with gentle blue eyes and long sensitive fingers, the friend of poets and himself a sonneteer. He was so soft that his brother Pope Leo had to relieve him of his post as ruler of Florence after less than a year. Preparations for war against France taxed his feeble constitution; at the age of thirty-seven he fell ill and died. Machiavelli's notion of turning Giuliano into a second Cesare Borgia was about as fantastic as trying to turn John Keats into a James Bond.

This fantastic element has been overlooked in most accounts of Machiavelli, but it seems to me important. Consider the *Life of Castruccio Castracani*, which Machiavelli wrote seven years after *The Prince*. It purports to be a straight biography of a famous fourteenth-century ruler of Lucca, but in fact only the outline of the book is historically true. Finding the real Castruccio insufficiently tough to embody his ideals. Machiavelli introduces wholly fictitious episodes borrowed from Diodorus Siculus's life of a tyrant who really was unscrupulous: Agathocles. As captain of the Syracusans, Agathocles had collected a great army, then summoned the heads of the Council of Six Hundred under the pretext of asking their advice, and put them all to death.

Machiavelli in his book has Castruccio perform a similar stratagem. Just as in *The Prince* the second-rate Cesare Borgia passes through the crucible of Machiavelli's imagination to emerge as a modern Julius Caesar, so here a mildly villainous lord is dressed up as the perfect amoral autocrat. In both books Machiavelli is so concerned to preach his doctrine of salvation through a strong soldier-prince that he leaves Italy as it really was for a world of fantasy.

Machiavelli had a second purpose in dedicating *The Prince* to Giuliano de' Medici (and when Giuliano died, to his almost equally effete nephew Lorenzo). He wished to regain favor with the Medici, notably with Pope Leo. This also was a fantastic plan. Machiavelli had plotted hand over fist against the Medici for no less than fourteen years and was known

to be a staunch republican, opposed to one-family rule in Florence. Pope Leo, moreover, was a gentle man who loved Raphael's smooth paintings and singing to the lute; he would not be interested in a book counseling cruelty and terror.

How could a man like Machiavelli, who spent his early life in the down-to-earth world of Italian politics, have yielded to such unrealistic, such fantastic hopes? The answer, I think, lies in the fact that he was also an imaginative artist—a playwright obsessed with extreme dramatic situations. Indeed, Machiavelli was best known in Florence as the author of *Mandragola*. In that brilliant comedy, a bold and tricky adventurer, aided by the profligacy of a parasite, and the avarice of a friar, achieves the triumph of making a gulled husband bring his own unwitting but too yielding wife to shame. It is an error to regard Machiavelli as primarily a political theorist, taking a cool look at facts. *The Prince* is, in one sense, the plot of a fantastic play for turning the tables on the French and Spaniards.

What, too, of Machiavelli's doctrine that it is sometimes wise for a prince to break his word and to violate treaties? It is usually said that this teaching originated with Machiavelli. If so, it would be very surprising, for the vast majority of so-called original inventions during the Italian Renaissance are now known to have been borrowed from classical texts. The Florentines valued wisdom as Edwardian English gentlemen valued port—the older the better.

In 1504 Machiavelli wrote a play, which has been lost, called *Masks*. It was in imitation of Aristophanes' *Clouds,* the subject of which is the Sophists, those men who claimed to teach "virtue" in a special sense, namely, efficiency in the conduct of life. The Sophists emphasized material success and the ability to argue from any point of view, irrespective of its truth. At worst, they encouraged a cynical disbelief in all moral restraints on the pursuit of selfish, personal ambition. Florentines during their golden age had paid little attention to the Sophists, preferring Plato, who accorded so well with Christianity and an aesthetic approach to life; but after the collapse in 1494 it would have been natural for a man like Machiavelli to dig out other, harderheaded philosophers.

The source for his doctrine of political unscrupulousness may well have been the Sophists as presented in Aristophanes' play. The following sentence from one of Machiavelli's letters in 1521 is close to many lines in *The Clouds:* "For that small matter of lies," writes Machiavelli, "I am a doctor and hold my degrees. Life has taught me to confound false and true, till no man knows either." In *The Prince* this personal confession becomes a general rule: "One must know how to color one's actions and to be a great liar and deceiver."

How was it that an undisputably civilized man like Machiavelli could advise a ruler to be cruel and deceitful and to strike terror? The answer lies in the last chapter of *The Prince,* entitled "Exhortation to liberate Italy from the barbarians." Often neglected, it is, in fact, the most deeply felt chapter of all and gives meaning to the rest. "See how Italy," Machiavelli writes, "beseeches God to send someone to save her from those barbarous cruelties and outrages"—he means the outrages perpetrated by foreign troops in Italy, a land, he goes on, that is "leaderless, lawless, crushed, despoiled, torn, overrun; she has had to endure every kind of desolation."

Machiavelli is a patriot writing in mental torment. He seldom mentions the deity, but in this chapter the name God occurs six times on one page, as an endorsement for this new kind of ruler. Machiavelli really believes that his deceitful prince will be as much an instrument of God as Moses was, and this for two reasons. First, Italy is an occupied country, and her survival is at stake; and just as moral theologians argued that theft becomes legitimate when committed by a starving man, so Machiavelli implies that deceit, cruelty, and so on become legitimate when they are the only means to national survival.

Secondly, Machiavelli had seen honest means tried and fail. Savonarola had hoped to silence cannon by singing hymns; Machiavelli himself had sent conscripts against the Spaniards. But the Italians had been then—and still were—bantams pitted against heavyweights. They could not win according to the rules, only with kidney punches. And since they had to win or cease to be themselves—that is, a civilized people as compared with foreign "barbarians"—Machiavelli argues that it is not only right but the will of God that they should use immoral means.

We must remember that *The Prince* is an extreme book that grew out of an extreme situation and that its maxims must be seen against the charred, smoking ruins of devastated Italy. The nearest modern parallel is occupied France. In the early 1940's cultivated men like Camus joined the Resistance, committing themselves to blowing up German posts by night and to other sinister techniques of *maquis* warfare. Like Machiavelli, they saw these as the only way to free their beloved country.

But the most original and neglected aspect of Machiavelli is his method. Before Machiavelli's time, historians had been the slaves of chronology. They started with the Creation, or the founding of their city, and worked forward, year by year, decade by decade, chronicling plague, war, and civil strife. Sometimes they detected a pattern, but even when they succeeded in doing so, the pattern was *sui generis,* not applicable elsewhere. Machiavelli was the first modern historian to pool historical facts from a variety of authors, not necessarily of the same period, and to use these facts to draw general conclusions or to answer pertinent questions.

He applies this method notably in his *Discourses on Livy,* and among the questions he answers are these: "What causes commonly give rise to wars between different powers?" "What kind of reputation or gossip or opinion causes the populace to begin to favor a particular citizen?" "Whether the safeguarding of liberty can be more safely entrusted to the populace or to the upper class; and which has the stronger reason for creating disturbances, the 'have-nots' or the 'haves'?"

Machiavelli does not wholly break free from a cyclical reading of history—the term Renaissance is itself a statement of the conviction that the golden age of Greece and Rome had returned. Nor did he break free from a belief in Fortune—what we would now call force of circumstance—and he calculated that men were at the mercy of Fortune five times out of ten. Nevertheless, he does mark an enormous advance over previous historical thinkers, since he discovered the method whereby man can learn from his past.

Having invented this method, Machiavelli proceeded to apply it imperfectly. He virtually ignored the Middle Ages, probably because medieval chronicles were deficient in those dramatic

human twists, reversals, and paradoxes that were what really interested him. This neglect of the Middle Ages marred his study of how to deal with foreign invaders. Over a period of a thousand years Italy had constantly suffered invasion from the north; the lessons implicit in these instances would have helped Machiavelli to resolve his main problem much better than the more remote happenings he chose to draw from Livy. For example, at the Battle of Legnano, near Milan, in 1176, a league of north Italian cities won a crushing victory over Frederick Barbarossa's crack German knights. The Italians didn't employ duplicity or dramatic acts of terrorism, just courage and a united command.

So much for Machiavelli's teaching and discoveries. It remains to consider his influence. In his own lifetime he was considered a failure. Certainly, no soldier-prince arose to liberate Italy. After his death, however, it was otherwise. In 1552 the Vatican placed Machiavelli's works on the Index of Prohibited Books, because they teach men "to appear good for their own advantage in this world—a doctrine worse than heresy." Despite this ban, Machiavelli's books were widely read and his political teaching became influential. It would probably have confirmed him in his pessimistic view of human nature had he known that most statesmen and thinkers would seize on the elements of repression and guile in his teachings to the exclusion of the civic sense and patriotism he equally taught.

In France several kings studied Machiavelli as a means of increasing their absolutism, though it cannot be said that he did them much good. Henry III and Henry IV were murdered, and in each case on their blood-soaked person was found a well-thumbed copy of *The Prince.* Louis XIII was following Machiavelli when he caused his most powerful subject, the Italian-born adventurer Concini, to be treacherously killed. Richelieu affirmed that France could not be governed without the right of arbitrary arrest and exile, and that in case of danger to the state it may be well that a hundred innocent men should perish. This was *raison d'état,* an exaggerated version of certain elements in *The Prince,* to which Machiavelli might well not have subscribed.

In England Machiavelli had little direct influence. England had never been defeated as Florence had been, and Englishmen could not understand the kind of desperate situation that demanded unscrupulous political methods. The political diseases Machiavelli had first studied scientifically were in England called after his name, rather as a physical disease—say Parkinson's—is called not after the man who is suffering from it but after the doctor who discovers it. Machiavelli thus became saddled with a lot of things he had never advocated, including atheism and any treacherous way of killing, generally by poison. Hence Flamineo in Webster's *White Devil:*

O the rare tricks of a Machivillian!
Hee doth not come like a grosse plodding slave
And buffet you to death: no, my quaint knave—
Hee tickles you to death; makes you die laughing,
As if you had swallow'd a pound of saffron.

The eighteenth century, with its strong belief in man's good nature and reason, tended to scoff at Machiavelli. Hume wrote: "There is scarcely any maxim in *The Prince* which subsequent experience has not entirely refuted. The errors of this politician proceed, in a great measure, from his having lived in too early an age of the world to be a good judge of political truth." With Hume's judgment Frederick the Great of Prussia would, in early life, have agreed. As a young man Frederick wrote an *Anti-Machiavel,* in which he stated that a ruler is the first servant of his people. He rejected the idea of breaking treaties, "for one has only to make one deception of this kind, and one loses the confidence of every ruler." But Frederick did follow Machiavelli's advice to rule personally, to act as his own commander in the field, and to despise flatterers.

Later, Frederick began to wonder whether honesty really was the best policy. "One sees oneself continually in danger of being betrayed by one's allies, forsaken by one's friends, brought low by envy and jealousy; and ultimately one finds oneself obliged to choose between the terrible alternative of sacrificing one's people or one's word of honor." In old age, Frederick became a confirmed

Machiavellian, writing in 1775: "Rulers must always be guided by the interests of the state. They are slaves of their resources, the interest of the state is their law, and this law may not be infringed."

During the nineteenth century Germany and Italy both sought to achieve national unity, with the result that writers now began to play up Machiavelli's other side, his call for regeneration. Young Hegel hails the author of *The Prince* for having "grasped with a cool circumspection the necessary idea that Italy should be saved by being combined into one state." He and Fichte go a stage further than Machiavelli: they assert that the conflict between the individual and the state no longer exists, since they consider liberty and law identical. The necessity of evil in political action becomes a superior ethics that has no connection with the morals of an individual. The state swallows up evil.

In Italy Machiavelli's ideal of a regenerated national state was not perverted in this way and proved an important influence on the *risorgimento.* In 1859 the provisional government of Tuscany, on the eve of national independence, published a decree stating that a complete edition of Machiavelli's works would be printed at government expense. It had taken more than three hundred years for "a man to arise to redeem Italy," and in the event the man turned out to be two men, Cavour and Garibaldi. Both, incidentally, were quite unlike the Prince: Cavour, peering through steel-rimmed spectacles, was a moderate statesman of the center, and Garibaldi a blunt, humane, rather quixotic soldier.

Bismarck was a close student of Machiavelli, but Marx and Engels did not pay much attention to him, and the Florentine's books have never exerted great influence in Russia. In contemporary history Machiavelli's main impact has been on Benito Mussolini. In 1924 Mussolini wrote a thesis on *The Prince,* which he described as the statesman's essential vade mecum. The Fascist leader deliberately set himself to implement Petrarch's call quoted on the last

page of *The Prince:*

*Che l'antico valore
Nell' italici cor non è ancor morto.*

Let Italians, as they did of old,
Prove that their courage has not grown cold.

After a course of muscle building, Mussolini sent the Italian army into Ethiopia to found a new Roman Empire. He joined Hitler's war in 1940, only to find that he had failed to impart to modern Italians the martial qualities of Caesar's legions. The final irony occurred in 1944, when the Nazis were obliged to occupy northern Italy as the only means of stopping an Allied walkover, and Italy again experienced the trauma of 1494 and 1512. Mussolini's failures discredit, at least for our generation, Machiavelli's theory that it is possible for one man to effect a heart transplant on a whole people.

What is Machiavelli's significance today? His policy of political duplicity has been found wanting in the past and is probably no longer practicable in an age of democracy and television. His policy of nationalism is also beginning to date as we move into an era of ideological blocs. His insistence on the need for military preparedness has proved of more durable value and is likely to remain one of the West's key beliefs. His technique for solving political problems through a study of the past is practiced to some extent by every self-respecting foreign minister of our time.

Was Machiavelli, finally, an evil man? He made an ethic of patriotism. In normal times that is a poisonous equation, but defensible, I believe, in the context of sixteenth-century Italy. Machiavelli wrote on the edge of an abyss: he could hear the thud of enemy boots, had seen pillage, profanation, and rape by foreign troops. Imaginative as he was, he could sense horrors ahead: the ending of political liberty and of freedom of the press, which put the lights out in Italy for 250 years. He taught that it is civilized man's first duty to save civilization—at all costs. Doubtless he was mistaken. But it is not, I think, the mistake of an evil man.

Women of the Renaissance

J. H. Plumb

François Villon, the vagabond poet of France, wondered, as he drifted through the gutters and attics of fifteenth-century Paris, where were the famous women of the days long past? Where Hélöise, for whom Abelard had endured such degradation? Where Thaïs, Alis, Haremburgis, where the Queen Blanche with her siren's voice, where were these fabled, love-haunted, noblewomen, of more than human beauty? Gone, he thought, gone forever. Even the rough Viking bards sang of their heroic women, of Aud the Deep-minded, who "hurt most whom she loved best." The lives of these fateful, tragic women, medieval heroines of love and sorrow became themes of epic and romance that were told in the courts of princes; yet even as Villon bewailed their loss, men were growing tired of them.

The age of heroes was dying. The unrequited love of Dante for Beatrice, the lyrical attachment of Petrarch for Laura, and, in a different mood, the agreeable pleasantries of Boccaccio, had domesticated love, making it more intimate. The dawn of a carefree, less fate-ridden attitude to woman was gentle, undramatic, and slow beginning way back with the wandering troubadours and the scholars who moved from castle to farm, from monastery to university, singing their lighthearted lyrics to earn their keep:

Down the broad way do I go,
Young and unregretting,
Wrap me in my vices up,
Virtue all forgetting,
Greedier for all delight
Than heaven to enter in:
Since the soul in me is dead,
Better save the skin.
Sit you down amid the fire,
Will the fire not burn you?
Come to Pavia, will you
Just as chaste return you?
Pavia, where Beauty draws
Youth with finger-tips,
Youth entangled in her eyes,
Ravished with her lips.

So sang the nameless Archpoet, young, consumptive, in love, as he wandered down to Salerno to read medicine. The time was the twelfth century—three hundred years before the haunting love poems of Lorenzo de' Medici were written. Yet the sentiments of both men were a part of the same process, part of the lifting tide of Southern Europe's prosperity, of its growing population, of the sophistication that wealth and leisure brought, for in leisure lies dalliance. The wandering scholars were few; their mistresses, chatelaines or girls of the town. Yet they were the naive harbingers of a world that was to reach its fullness in Italy in the fifteenth century.

It was the new prosperity that influenced the lives of women most profoundly. It brought them fresh opportunities for adornment; it increased their dowries and their value. It emancipated many from the drudgery of the household and from the relentless, time-consuming demands of children. Women entered more fully into the daily lives and pursuits of men. And, of course, the new delights of the Renaissance world—painting, music, literature—had their feminine expression. Much of the artistic world was concerned with the pursuit of love in all its guises. Women were a part of art.

Except for the very lowest ranks of society, women were inextricably entangled in the concept of prosperity, and their virtue was a marketable commodity. They were secluded from birth to marriage, taught by women and priests, kept constantly under the closest supervision in the home or in the convent. Marriage came early: twelve was not an uncommon age, thirteen usual, fifteen was getting late, and an unmarried girl of sixteen or seventeen was a catastrophe. Women conveyed property and could often secure a lift in the social scale for their families. Even more important was the use of women to seal alliances between families, whether princely, noble, or mercantile. The great Venetian merchants interlocked their adventures over-

seas with judicious marriages at home. The redoubtable Vittoria Colonna was betrothed at the age of four to the Marquis of Pescara to satisfy her family's political ambition. Lucrezia Borgia's early life was a grim enough reminder of the dynastic value of women. Her fiancé's were sent packing, her husbands murdered or declared impotent, so that Alexander VI could use her agáin and again in the furtherance of his policies.

In less exalted ranks of society women were still traded. It took Michelangelo years of horse trading to buy a young Ridolfi wife for his nephew and so push his family up a rank in Florentine society. Marriages so arranged were symbolic of power and social status as well as wealth, and their celebration, in consequence, demanded the utmost pomp and splendor that the contracting parties could afford. Important Venetian marriages were famed for an extravagance that not even the Council of Ten could curb.

The festivities began with an official proclamation in the Doge's Palace. The contracting parties and their supporters paraded the canals *en fete*. Gondoliers and servants were dressed in sumptuous livery; the facades of the palaces were adorned with rare Oriental carpets and tapestries; there were bonfires, fireworks, balls, masques, banquets, and everywhere and at all times—even the most intimate serenades by gorgeously dressed musicians. Of course, such profusion acted like a magnet for poets, dramatists, rhetoricians, painters, and artists of every variety. For a few ducats a wandering humanist would pour out a few thousand words, full of recondite references to gods and heroes; poets churned out epithalamiums before they could be asked; and painters immortalized the bride, her groom, or even, as Botticelli did, the wedding breakfast. And they were eager for more mundane tasks, not for one moment despising an offer to decorate the elaborate *cassoni* in which the bride took her clothes and linen to her new household. Indeed, the competitive spirit of both brides and painters in *cassoni* became so fierce that they ceased to be objects of utility and were transformed into extravagant works of art, becoming the heirlooms of future generations.

The artistic accompaniment of marriage became the height of fashion. When the Duke and Duchess of Urbino returned to their capital after their wedding, they were met on a hilltop outside their city by all the women and children of rank, exquisitely and expensively dressed, bearing olive branches in their hands. As the Duke and Duchess reached them, mounted choristers accompanied by nymphs à *la Grecque* burst into song—a special cantata that had been composed for the newlyweds. The Goddess of Mirth appeared in person with her court, and to make everyone realize that jollity and horseplay were never out of place at a wedding, hares were loosed in the crowd. This drove the dogs insane with excitement, to everyone's delight. No matter how solemn the occasion, marriage always involved coarse farce, usually at the climax of the wedding festivities, when the bride and the groom were publicly bedded. Although there was no romantic nonsense about Italian weddings—certainly few marriages for love—everyone knew that the right, true end of the contract was the bed. The dowager Duchess of Urbino, something of a bluestocking and a Platonist and a woman of acknowledged refinement, burst into her niece's bedroom on the morning after her marriage and shouted, "Isn't it a fine thing to sleep with the men?"

Marriage for the women of the Renaissance gave many their first taste of opulence, leisure, and freedom. They were very young; the atmosphere of their world was as reckless as it was ostentatious; and furthermore, they had not chosen their husbands, who frequently were a generation older than they. Their men, who often were soldiers or courtiers living close to the razor-edge of life, fully enjoyed intrigue, so the young wife became a quarry to be hunted. As she was often neglected, the chase could be brief. Even Castiglione, who was very fond of his wife, treated her somewhat casually. He saw her rarely and made up for his absence with affectionate, bantering letters. Of course, she was a generation younger than he and therefore hardly a companion. Such a situation was not unusual: a girl of thirteen might excite her mature husband, but she was unlikely

to entertain him for long. She fulfilled her tasks by bearing a few children and running a trouble-free household, and neither matter was too onerous for the rich. Nurses took over the children as soon as they were born; a regiment of servants relieved wives of their traditional housewifely duties. So the leisure that had previously been the lot of only a few women of very high birth became a commonplace of existence for a multitude of women.

The presence of these leisured women in society helped to transform it. It created the opportunity for personality to flourish, for women to indulge the whims of their temperaments—free from the constraining circumstances of childbirth, nursery, and kitchen. There were men enough to adorn their vacant hours. Italy was alive with priests, many of them urbane, cultured, and idle, whose habit acted as a passport, hinting a security for husbands that their actions all too frequently belied. Nevertheless, they were the natural courtiers of lonely wives, and they swarmed in the literary salons of such distinguished women as Elisabetta Gonzaga at Urbino, the Queen of Cyprus at Asolo, or Vittoria Colonna at Rome.

Soldiers as well as priests needed the sweetness of feminine compassion to soften their tough and dangerous lives. Fortunately, military campaigns in Renaissance Italy were short and usually confined to the summer months, and so the horseplay, the practical jokes, and the feats of arms that were as essential to the courtly life as literary conversations or dramatic performances were provided by the knights.

In addition to soldiers and priests, there were the husbands' pages, all in need of the finer points of amorous education. For a princess, further adornment of the salon was provided by an ambassador—often, true enough, a mere Italian, but at times French or Spanish, which gave an exotic touch that a woman of fashion could exploit to her rivals' disadvantage. Naturally, these courts became highly competitive: to have Pietro Bembo sitting at one's feet, reading his mellifluous but tedious essays on the beauties of Platonic love, was sure to enrage the hearts of other women. In fact, the popularity of Bembo illustrates admirably the style of sophisticated love that the extravagant and princely women of Italy demanded.

Pietro Bembo was a Venetian nobleman, the cultivated son of a rich and sophisticated father who had educated him in the height of humanist fashion at the University of Ferrara, where he acquired extreme agility in bandying about the high-flown concepts of that strange mixture of Platonism and Christianity that was the hallmark of the exquisite. Petrarch, of course, was Bembo's mentor, and like Petrarch he lived his life, as far as the pressures of nature would allow him, in literary terms. He fell verbosely and unhappily in love with a Venetian girl; his ardent longings and intolerable frustrations were committed elegantly to paper and circulated to his admiring friends.

This experience provided him with enough material for a long epistolary exchange with Ercole Strozzi, who was as addicted as Bembo to girls in literary dress. Enraptured by the elegance of his sentiments, Strozzi invited Bembo to his villa near Ferrara, doubtless to flaunt his latest capture, Lucrezia Borgia, as well as to indulge his insatiable literary appetite. However, the biter was quickly bitten, for Bembo was just Lucrezia's cup of tea. A mature woman of twenty-two, thoroughly versed in the language as well as the experience of love, she was already bored with her husband, Alfonso d'Este, and tired of Strozzi. Soon she and Bembo were exchanging charming Spanish love lyrics and far larger homilies on aesthetics. After a visit by Lucrezia to Bembo, sick with fever, the pace quickened. Enormous letters followed thick and fast. Bembo ransacked literature to do homage to Lucrezia; they were Aeneas and Dido, Tristan and Iseult, Lancelot and Guinevere—not, however, lover and mistress.

For a time they lived near each other in the country while Ferrara was plague-ridden. Proximity and the furor of literary passion began to kindle fires in Bembo that were not entirely Platonic, and, after all, Lucrezia was a Borgia. Her tolerant but watchful husband, however, had no intention of being cuckolded by an aesthete, and he rattled his sword. Bembo did not relish reliving the tragedy of Abelard; he might love Lucrezia to distraction, but he cherished himself as only an artist can, so he thought it discreet to return to Venice (he had excuse enough, as his brother was desperately sick). There he consoled himself by polishing his dialogue, *Gli Asolani*, which already enjoyed a high reputation among those to whom it had been circulated in manuscript. Resolving to give his love for Lucrezia its final, immortal form, he decided to publish it with a long dedication to her. To present her with his divine thoughts on love was a greater gift by far, of course, than his person. Doubtless both Lucrezia and her husband agreed; whether they read further than the dedication is more doubtful.

Bembo had written these highfalutin letters—informal, mannered, obscure, and so loaded with spiritual effusions on love, beauty, God, and women that they are almost unreadable—during a visit to that tragic and noblewoman Caterina Cornaro, Queen of Cyprus. The daughter of a Venetian aristocrat, she had been married as a girl to Giacomo II of Cyprus for reasons of state and declared with infinite pomp "daughter of the republic." Bereaved of both husband and son within three years, she had defied revolution and civil war and maintained her government for fourteen years until, to ease its political necessities, Venice had forced her abdication and set her up in a musical-comedy court at Asolo. There she consoled herself with the world of the spirit, about which Bembo was better informed than most, and he was drawn to her like a moth to a flame. Her court was elegant, fashionable, and intensely literary. *Gli Asolani,* published by Aldus in 1505, made Bembo the archpriest of love as the *Courtier* was to make Castiglione the archpriest of manners. Indeed, Bembo figures in the *Courtier,* and Castiglione adopted his literary techniques. These two subtle and scented bores were destined to turn up together, and nowhere was more likely than the court of Elisabetta Gonzaga at Urbino, for her insatiable appetite for discussion was equal to their eloquence; her stamina matched their verbosity; and night after night the dawn overtook their relentless arguments about the spiritual nature of love. Neither, of course, was so stupid as to think that even the high-minded Caterina or Elisabetta could live by words alone, and Bembo, at least, always interlarded the more ethereal descriptions of Platonic love with a warm eulogy of passion in its more prosaic and energetic aspects. Indeed, he was not above appearing (not entirely modestly disguised) as an ambassador of Venus, in order to declaim in favor of natural love. After six years of this excessively cultured refinement at Urbino, Bembo became papal secretary to Leo X in Rome. Ap-

propriately, at Rome the word became flesh, and Bembo settled into the comfortable arms of a girl called Morosina, who promptly provided him with three children. It is not surprising, therefore, that Bembo's interests became more mundane, turning from Platonic philosophy to the history of Venice. After the death of his mistress, the life of the spirit once more claimed him, and he entered the College of Cardinals in 1538. More than any other man of his time, he set the pattern of elegant courtship, so that the flattery of the mind, combined with poetic effusions on the supremacy of the spirit, became a well-trodden path for the courtier. It possessed the supreme advantage of passionate courtship without the necessity of proof—a happy situation, indeed, when the object was both a bluestocking and a queen.

Yet it would be wrong to think that the gilded lives of Renaissance princesses were merely elegant, sophisticated, and luxurious or that flirtation took place only in the most refined language. Few could concentrate their thoughts year in, year out, on the nobility of love like Vittoria Colonna. She, who inspired some of Michelangelo's most passionate poetry, even into old age, could and did live in an intense world of spiritual passion, in which the lusts of the flesh were exorcised by an ecstatic contemplation of the beauties of religion. She managed to retain her charm, avoid the pitfalls of hypocrisy, and secure without effort the devotion of Castiglione and Bembo as well as Michelangelo. Even the old rogue Aretino attempted to secure her patronage, but naturally she remained aloof. In her the Platonic ideals of love and beauty mingled with the Christian virtues to the exclusion of all else. Amazingly, no one found her a bore. However, few women could live like Vittoria: they sighed as they read Bembo, became enrapt as they listened to Castiglione, but from time to time they enjoyed a quiet reading of Boccaccio and, better still, Bandello.

Matteo Bandello had been received as a Dominican and spent many years of his life at the Convento delle Grazie, at Milan, which seems to have been a more exciting place for a short-story teller than might be imagined. He acted for a time as ambassador for the Bentivoglio and so came in contact with that remarkable woman Isabella d'Este Gonzaga, whose court at Mantua was as outstanding for its wit, elegance, and genius as any in Italy. There Bandello picked up a mis-

tress, which put him in no mind to hurry back to his brother monks. At Mantua, too, he laid the foundations of his reputation for being one of the best raconteurs of scandal in all Italy, Aretino not excepted. How true Bandello's stories are is still a matter of fierce warfare among scholars, but this they agree on: they did not seem incredible to those who read them. That being so, they give a hairraising picture of what was going on at courts, in monasteries, in nunneries, in merchant houses, in the palaces and the parsonages of Italy. The prime pursuit, in the vast majority of Bandello's stories, is the conquest of women, and to achieve success, any trick, any falsehood, any force, is justifiable. His heroes' attitude toward success in sex was like Machiavelli's toward politics—the end justified any means. The aim of all men was to ravish other men's wives and daughters and preserve their own women or revenge them if they failed to do so. Vendettas involving the most bloodcurdling punishments were a corollary to his major theme. In consequence, Bandello's stories, cast in a moral guise, nevertheless read like the chronicles of a pornographer. Here are the themes of a few that were thought to be proper entertainment for the lighter moments of court life or for quiet reading by a bored wife: the marriage of a man to a woman who was already his sister and to his daughter; the adultery of two ladies at court and the death of their paramours, which is a vivid record of sexual pleasure and horrifying punishment; the servant who was decapitated for sleeping with his mistress; the death through excessive sexual indulgence of Charles of Navarre; Gian Maria Visconti's burial of a live priest; the autocastration of Fra Filippo—and so one might go on and on, for Bandello wrote hundreds of short stories, and they were largely variations on a single theme. The women of the Renaissance loved them, and few storytellers were as popular as Bandello (such abilities did not go unmarked, and he finished his career as Bishop of Agen). Nor was Bandello exceptional: there were scores of writers like him. Malicious, distorted, exaggerated as these tales were, they were based on the realities of Italian life. Undoubtedly the increased leisure of men and women released their energies for a more riotous indulgence of their sexual appetites.

However daring the Italian males of the Renaissance were, the prudence of wives and the vigilance of husbands prevailed more often than not. The Emilia Pias, Elisabetta Gonzagas, Isabella d'Estes, Lucrezia Borgias, Costanza Amarettas, and Vittoria Colonnas were rare—particularly for cardinals and bishops ravenous for Platonic love. So in Rome, in Florence, in Venice, and in Milan there developed a class of grand courtesans, more akin to geisha girls than to prostitutes, to the extent that the *cortesane famose* of Venice despised the *cortesane de la minor sorte* and complained of their number, habits, and prices to the Senate (they felt they brought disrepute on an honorable profession). Grand as these Venetian girls were, they could not compete with the great courtesans of Rome, who not only lived in small palaces with retinues of maids and liveried servants but also practiced the literary graces and argued as learnedly as a Duchess of Urbino about the ideals of Platonic love.

Italy during the Renaissance was a country at war, plagued for decades with armies. A well-versed condottiere might battle with skill even in the wordy encounters of Platonic passion, but the majority wanted a quicker and cheaper victory. For months on end the captains of war had nothing to do and money to spend; they needed a metropolis of pleasure and vice. Venice, with its quick eye for a profit, provided it and plucked them clean. There, women were to be had for as little as one *scudo,* well within the means even of a musketeer. And it was natural that after Leo X's purge, the majority of the fallen from Rome should flow to Venice. That city, with its regattas, *feste,* and carnivals, with its gondolas built for seclusion and sin, became a harlot's paradise. The trade in women became more profitable and extensive than it had been since the days of Imperial Rome. The Renaissance recaptured the past in more exotic fields than literature or the arts.

Life, however, for the noblewomen of the Renaissance was not always cakes and ale; it could be harsh and furious: the male world of war, assassination, and the pursuit of power frequently broke in upon their gentle world of love and dalliance. Indeed, Caterina Sforza, the woman whom all Italy saluted as its *prima donna,* won her fame through her dour courage and savage temper. Castiglione tells the story of the time she invited a boorish condottiere to dinner and asked him first to dance and then to hear some music—both of which he declined on the grounds that they were not his business. "What is your business, then?" his hostess asked. "Fighting," the warrior replied. "Then," said the virago of Forlì, "since you are not at war and not needed to fight, it would be wise for you to have yourself well greased and put away in a cupboard with all your arms until you are wanted, so that you will not get more rusty than you are." Caterina was more a figure of a saga than a woman of the Renaissance. Three of her husbands were assassinated. At one time she defied the French, at another Cesare Borgia, who caught her and sent her like a captive lioness to the dungeons of Sant' Angelo. She told her frantic sons that she was habituated to grief and had no fear of it, and as they ought to have expected, she escaped. Yet tough and resourceful as she was, Caterina could be a fool in love—much more than the Duchess of Urbino or Vittoria Colonna. Time and time again her political troubles were due to her inability to check her strong sexual appetite, which fixed itself too readily on the more monstrous of the Renaissance adventurers. So eventful a life induced credulity, and like the rest of her family, Caterina believed in the magical side of nature, dabbled in alchemy and mysteries, and was constantly experimenting with magnets that would produce family harmony or universal salves or celestial water or any other improbable elixir that the wandering hucksters wished on her. At any age, at any time, Caterina would have been a remarkable woman, but the Renaissance allowed her wild temperament to riot.

Certainly the women of the Renaissance were portents. Elisabetta Gonzaga and Isabella d'Este are the founding sisters of the great literary salons that were to dominate the fashionable society of Western Europe for centuries. But the courts of Italy were few, the families that were rich enough to indulge the tastes and pleasures of sophisticated women never numerous. The lot of most women was harsh; they toiled in the home at their looms or in the fields alongside their men. They bred early and died young, untouched by the growing civility about them, save in their piety. In the churches where they sought ease for their sorrows, the Mother of God shone with a new radiance, a deeper compassion, and seemed in her person to immortalize their lost beauty. Even the majority of middle-class women knew little of luxury or literary elegance. Their lives were dedicated to their husbands and their children; their ambitions were limited to the provision of a proper social and domestic background for their husbands; and they were encouraged to exercise prudence, to indulge in piety, and to eschew vanities. Yet their lives possessed a civility, a modest elegance, that was in strong contrast to the harsher experiences and more laborious days of medieval women. Their new wealth permitted a greater, even if still modest, personal luxury. They could dress themselves more finely, acquire more jewels, provide a richer variety of food for their guests, entertain more lavishly, give more generously to charity. Although circumscribed, their lives were freer, their opportunities greater. It might still be unusual for a woman to be learned or to practice the arts, but it was neither rare nor exotic. And because they had more time, they were able to create a more active social life and to spread civility. After the Renaissance, the drawing room became an integral part of civilized living; indeed, the Renaissance education of a gentleman assumed that much of his life would be spent amusing women and moving them with words. As in so many aspects of life in Renaissance Italy, aristocratic attitudes of the High Middle Ages were adopted by the middle classes. Courtesy and civility spread downward, and the arts of chivalry became genteel.

Bess of Hardwick was a woman to be reckoned with

Like Monopoly, the game in Elizabethan days was to acquire land and build; the dice were in her favor—but she also knew how to play

Israel Shenker

The author is a frequent Smithsonian contributor.

Now that four centuries have passed, perhaps we can fully appreciate Bess of Hardwick, an awesome figure, ambitious and strategic in every aspect of her life. Outliving four husbands, she grew richer from each, amassing vast expanses of the English countryside and presiding over property and progeny with firm hand and ready tongue.

Bess has been called by her detractors a "termagant Countess," "an incorrigible intriguer with the tongue of an adder," "overbearing, selfish, proud, treacherous and unfeeling." In other words, not the model "lady" of her times. She loved grandeur, luxury and beauty. "A woman of masculine understanding and conduct, proud, furious, selfish and unfeeling," maintained a venerable history. "She was a builder, a buyer and seller of estates, a moneylender, a farmer and a merchant of lead, coals and timber; when disengaged from these employments, she intrigued alternately with [Queen] Elizabeth and Mary [Queen of Scots], always to the prejudice and terror of her husband." This woman sounds anything but boring. And the question does arise: If she caused men so much trouble, why did they keep marrying her?

In her later years, she had a powerful role model, to be sure, in Queen Elizabeth. Bess of Hardwick and Bess of England—flamboyant redheads both—were vigilant about their status and sta-

tion and privileges, their right to rule and be obeyed. This was England's golden age, a time of peace; on a green and rural half-island of four million, people kept sheep, tended cattle, sowed and reaped.

Queen Elizabeth's father, Henry VIII, had ruled with iron whim. Elizabeth, daughter of Henry and Anne Boleyn, was a benevolent despot who is today regarded as one of the greatest English monarchs. Her style of wielding power was characterized by charm—and the tendency to dissemble and procrastinate. This is how she handled the issue of matrimony. That a woman should rule was exceptional, and of course her duty would be to marry and have a man to guide her, to rule the kingdom and to produce a male heir. Her father had rid himself of more than one wife who failed to produce a son; female children were adornments but not the stuff of kinghood. But Queen Elizabeth saw things differently. For her, matrimonial prospects served diplomacy—her ability to make alliances and frustrate enemies, and to encourage loyalty and pacify Parliament. Courted and flattered, she remained the Virgin Queen, relishing independence too much to share sovereignty with a husband.

During the brief reign of her half-sister Mary, Elizabeth was suspected of designs on the throne and imprisoned in the Tower of London. As queen, she too used the Tower for those who plotted and conspired or in some other way posed a threat. One of those was Bess of Hardwick herself, twice sent to the Tower, twice returned to Her Majesty's favor. Like the queen, Bess regarded matrimony as a way to advance her aims; but while Elizabeth profited by resisting,

Bess profited by mastering the game. The turbulent currents of life and death brought opportunities to increase her wealth and distinction, and she converted every opportunity to advantage, every husband to coin of the realm. As author Vita Sackville-West put it, Bess "bullied and survived them all."

Horace Walpole, author and son of a Prime Minister, commemorated Bess' enterprise with these lines:

Four times the nuptial bed she warm'd,
And ev'ry time so well perform'd,
That when death spoiled each husband's billing,
He left the widow every shilling. . . .

As the late 16th century unfolded, England took an increasingly large role on the European stage in politics, culture and the arts. Quite naturally, on the home front, it was also a time when pounds, shillings and pence—as well as social position—were made visible in wood, stone and mortar. And so for Bess, in flourishing maturity and stalwart age, one obsession ruled: a passion for building. Repeatedly she drew up plans, collected workmen and launched a great new dwelling place. Chivying craftsmen to greater effort, subjecting each account to probing scrutiny, she saw her dreams take solid form in the grandeur that was home—time and again. Today, ivy and moss curtain the remnant stone, and the magnificent ruins of her labors litter the English countryside.

One masterpiece, however, has endured. In rural Derbyshire stands perhaps the greatest architectural survivor of the Elizabethan Age, a splendid structure popularly summarized as "Hardwick Hall—more glass than wall." It still houses tapestries, portraits and lavish furnishings that Bess inventoried in 1601. She ruled this glorious roost like a queen, with family, friends and attendants forming the image of a royal court.

In England, Bess of Hardwick and her last great monument have become legend. No other house in that country, writes historian Mark Girouard, is "so closely connected in popular imagination with one person." Nigel Nicolson called Hardwick Hall "one of the most beautiful buildings ever created," describing the exterior as "splendidly arrogant and adventurous," the interior as "cool and sedate as a convent." Sacheverell Sitwell thought Hardwick's High Great Chamber the most beautiful room in all Europe.

Bess began humbly enough, in about 1527, in a large farmhouse just a hundred yards from Hardwick Hall. Sent to seek her fortune in the household of a distant relative, she helped nurse young Robert Barlow. Child marriages were not unknown, and Robert, about 13, married Bess, about 15. When he died soon thereafter, she acquired a modest settlement, precocious widowhood and an eye for the main chance.

Her eye fell on William Cavendish. As a commissioner for Henry VIII, Cavendish had confiscated convents and monasteries. Not the last to profit, he had received extensive church property and been appointed Treasurer of the King's Chamber. Sir William drew a fortune from rent, still more from annuities, and increased the bounty by selling favors—a common practice in an age of widespread corruption.

Sir William was more than eligible; he found Bess more than eligible, too. They were married in 1547, when she was about 20. In his two earlier marriages he had fathered eight children, of whom three daughters survived; Bess gave birth to eight children, of whom six survived. Ensconced in gratifying splendor, she had fine silver and linen, 15 servants in blue livery, and at meals a harpist and two minstrels. In harmony—the property was registered in joint names—the Cavendishes did real estate deals, their negotiations smoothed by gifts of game and fish to government assessors. Among acquisitions was the estate of Chatsworth, including the old manor, and there the happy couple began building on a grand scale.

But suddenly a discrepancy was noted in government accounts. Sir William was charged with a shortage of £5,237, an enormous sum in Elizabethan days. He sought to defend himself: an underling had absconded with £1,231 in the "tyme of my sickness," previous sovereigns had promised money they'd never paid, and he'd spent a fortune raising soldiers for the defense of the monarchy. Pleading for mercy, he described his "poor wife" and "miserable and innocent children . . . kneeling and standing before me (not without sorrowful tears) presenting our misery."

But before the matter could be settled, Sir William died, leaving Bess with six of her own children, two stepdaughters (one had died) and her husband's debt to the Crown. Together they had undertaken the lifelong task of assuring a place in history for the Cavendish line. And now she was left to carry on alone.

Fortunately, when Elizabeth took the throne in 1559 she appointed Bess a lady-in-waiting. What Bess was waiting for was a third husband, and he was ready. Sir William St. Loe—a landowner with comfortable income, a favored courtier, himself twice married—was more than happy to join his fortunes and land to Bess'. In letters he addressed her as "My own good servant and chief overseer" and "My honest, sweet Chatsworth."

Beyond these qualities, Bess was also prepared to act as discreet confidante. She lent a ready ear when Catherine Grey, who was of royal blood, confessed that she had secretly married without asking the queen's permission. Elizabeth thought that she should have been informed and sent Bess to the Tower. There the Lady St. Loe was held 31 weeks in durance not exactly vile: she had a servant and spent lavishly for food.

Not even imprisonment frustrated Bess' dynastic designs. Just before her confinement, she had begun to arrange the marriage of her eldest daughter, 13, to a 15-year-old. She finished these negotiations from the Tower, then persuaded her husband to offer a dowry sufficient to buy a marriage for one of her stepdaughters. What was more, Queen Elizabeth agreed to reduce Bess' debt from £5,000 to £1,000, which St. Loe paid. Then (it seemed the fate of dutiful husbands) Sir William died.

Rich and eligible, Bess knew where *her* duty lay. She left Chatsworth and returned to court to try her luck again. There she found the excessively prosperous George Talbot, 6th Earl of Shrewsbury. He had a long, sorrowful face, a pointed beard and no excess of intelligence—his fortune had come through the family and from rewards for his extreme loyalty to Elizabeth. Though only four years younger than the earl, the queen called him her "old man." A widower with seven children, Shrewsbury was Lord Lieutenant of Yorkshire, Derbyshire and Nottinghamshire, and Chamberlain of the Receipt of the Exchequer. He had eight main houses—Sheffield Castle, Sheffield Manor, Rufford Abbey, South Wingfield Manor, Welbeck Abbey, Buxton Hall, Worksop Manor and Tutbury Castle (leased from the queen)—plus two more in London, one in nearby Chelsea, and a few lesser manors. Bess had at least four houses of her own, and her Derbyshire property adjoined some of his. This was a marriage made in heaven and cemented on earth. "I have been glad to see my Lady Saintlo, but now more desirous to see my Lady Shrewsbury," said the queen. "There is no Lady in this land that I better love and like."

In 1567 Bess became Countess of Shrewsbury, having artfully negotiated with the earl an agreement that would keep lands within the family: two of her children were to marry two of his. But cold arrangements did not impair their love. Shrewsbury to Bess: "As the pen writes so the heart thinks that of all earthly joys, that hath happened unto me I thank God chiefest for you: for with you I have all joy & contentation of mind & without you death is more pleasant to me than life if I thought I should be long from you."

Then, with the arrival of an unwelcome houseguest in 1569, joy went out the window. Mary, Queen of Scots and, as a cousin of Elizabeth's, a claimant to the English throne, had fled Scotland and sought refuge in England. Needing a loyal jailer for her royal prize, Elizabeth picked ever faithful Shrewsbury to receive Mary at Tutbury Castle. Bess wished she'd had more notice: "I have caused workmen to make forthwith in readiness all such things as is most needful to be done before her coming and God willing I shall cause forthwith three or four lodgings to be furnished with hangings and other necessaries. . . ."

THE PRISONER WAS HARD TO PLEASE

Required to provide endless wood, coal and hay for Mary's retinue, Shrewsbury complained that people at Tutbury were "marvelously molested." Mary, not content with a score of servants, including three cooks, a baker, a pastrymaker, two pantrymen, three lackeys, an embroiderer and a priest, wrote that she was living in an old hunting lodge "in a walled enclosure . . . exposed to all the winds and inclemencies of heaven . . . built of timber and plaster, cracked in all parts . . . so damp [on one side] that you cannot put any piece of furniture in that part . . . without its being in four days completely covered with mould." As hundreds of hangers-on gathered, Shrewsbury pleaded with Queen Elizabeth to increase the allowance for the care of Mary. "The Queen of Scots coming to my charge will make me soon greyheaded," he complained. But the Queen of England was herself short of the ready, and the prospect of a grayhaired courtier was not alarming.

To isolate Mary from conspirators, the queen issued severe orders to define her imprisonment. Even Bess was to see Mary "very rarely"—only if the Queen of Scots was ill or wished to speak with her. No other gentlewoman was to be admitted. But Bess and Mary shared a love of embroidery and spent long hours together. Mary gave Bess gifts of jewelry.

When reports circulated that Bess was overfriendly, the Shrewsburys protested that they were loyally discharging their responsibilities. There being no shortage of Shrewsbury homes in which to assure the prisoner's security, Mary was moved 46 times during her 16-year stay. She received her own royal pension, but much of it went to plots and intrigue that sought to arrange rescue, revolt or marriage—or all three. Letters were intercepted and deciphered. One of her fiancé's, the Duke of Norfolk, implicated in a plot against Queen Elizabeth, was executed in 1572. Shrewsbury presided over the trial and succeeded Norfolk as Earl Marshal.

At this point, Bess pulled out all the stops. In 1574 she secretly arranged for her daughter Elizabeth Cavendish, to marry Charles Stuart. This was a very tricky maneuver because Charles, a half-cousin and brother-in-law of Mary, Queen of Scots, was also a cousin of Queen Elizabeth's. "From Bess' point of view the marriage was a triumph," writes historian David Durant in his biography *Bess of Hardwick*. "Her daughter Elizabeth was now married into kinship with the Queen of England, and

her grandson, should there be one, could rule over England and Scotland."

Yet again Elizabeth had been kept in the dark. According to some accounts, Bess was sent to the Tower; at the very least, the queen was greatly displeased with her. Shrewsbury, too, was angered because Bess' actions jeopardized his relationship to the queen. This created a rift between Bess and her husband that would continue to grow.

MARRIAGE ARRANGEMENTS WERE SERIOUS BUSINESS

Arabella Stuart, only child of the marriage Bess had arranged, was born in 1575. As a potential claimant to the crown (she was third in the line of succession), she seems to have enjoyed royal favor for a few years. Bess became her guardian by the death of the child's parents. When Arabella was 8, Bess, inveterate matchmaker as well as match, arranged for her to be engaged to Lord Denbigh, age 4, son of the Earl of Leicester. But the prospective groom died before he was 5. With time, Arabella sought to escape from her grandmother's control. There was talk of marriage to France's Henry IV—and he was willing, provided Arabella was declared presumptive heir of Queen Elizabeth. But England's monarch was in no hurry to pronounce on the succession and showed her displeasure with Arabella, who never was bestowed the throne.

In the meantime, Bess continued building activities. She bought old Hardwick (the farmhouse in which she had been born) in 1583. She also engaged workmen for her husband's construction project at Worksop of a great house worthy of receiving England's queen, her erstwhile jailer. It was to be the grandest mansion in the Midlands, to include a gallery 224 feet long. As Bess—who spoke of her building enterprises as her "workes"—bought more and more land, Shrewsbury complained that she was driving him bankrupt. "The old song," he called her demands for money, and the marriage degenerated into open dissonance.

Shrewsbury wrote two of his sons who were returning from abroad "to be stout with the Countess." They didn't see Bess, but they were given a letter by the Earl of Leicester telling Shrewsbury to make up with Bess, for "she ys your wife

and a verrye wyse gentlewoman." Shrewsbury complained that she called him "knave, foole and beast," mocking him with words and gestures "from a heart replenished with deadly malice and hatred." He cut off her allowance, seized her revenues and turned up at Chatsworth with 40 mounted men. But he was refused admittance by Bess' son, William Cavendish, "with halberd in hand and pistol under his girdle."

Shrewsbury inveighed against this "insolent behaviour," and complained to the queen that Bess "deserveth no longer to have any part in my liberality. It were no reason that my wife and her servants should rule me and make me the wife and her husband." But the queen saw nothing wrong. To his brother-in-law, Shrewsbury wrote: "I try all I can to be rid of this troublesome burden." "How I have deserved your indignation," she wrote to him, "is invisible to me."

In 1584, Queen Elizabeth agreed to a commission of enquiry—the Lord Chancellor and two Chief Justices. Shrewsbury testified that Bess pestered him for money whenever he was ill and spent lavishly on land. Bess said little. The commission ordered Shrewsbury to take Bess back and refund rents he had seized. Shrewsbury said he would abide by the decision, then ignored every provision. He wrote Bess that he wanted a confession in writing "that you have offended me . . . and upon your knees (without either if or and)."

Then Queen Elizabeth ordered a reconciliation, but Shrewsbury merely went through the motions. Things got nasty—arguments ensued about the hangings, silver and furnishings Bess had taken to Hardwick. Bess claimed that she did not even have enough fuel for a decent fire. Meanwhile, Shrewsbury consoled himself with a lady of his household.

Rumors had spread earlier that Mary, Queen of Scots was consoling *herself* with Shrewsbury, even had had his child, perhaps even two children. Not true, said Shrewsbury, and he blamed Bess for the rumors. When the Scottish queen was found guilty of high treason in 1587, it was Shrewsbury as Earl Marshal who gave the signal to the executioner.

When Shrewsbury died, in 1590, there was a mammoth funeral, and then Bess could—with little contest—enjoy what came to her: Bolsover Castle with its coal pits, Wingfield Manor and its ironworks, land in Staffordshire, Derbyshire and Yorkshire, glassworks, smithies, pastures and timber. By fits and starts she had added to old Hardwick. Most of the materials came from her own property—lead and timber and sandstone, even alabaster and marble.

But what Bess really wanted was a new Hardwick. Late in 1590, when she was in her 60s, 20 workmen started on foundations and cellars 100 yards from the old building, which was to be reserved for the overflow of guests and servants. An astute mistress of the "workes," Bess noted, for example, that "because the walls rise and be not well nor all of one color, they must be whitened at the plasterers' charge." In Bess' accounts, 375 people who worked on the building are listed. Even after Hardwick Hall was finished, Bess acquired new holdings: desperate for money, the queen, for £12,750, sold vicarages and parsonages to her.

URGING ON WORKERS AT THE SITE

In 1607, two of Bess' children came to Hardwick to be reconciled with her. They were well received and reported that they found "a lady of great years, of great wealth, of great wit, which yet still remains." By this time, Bess' building activities had already become the stuff of legend, which widely celebrated her resourcefulness. In one account, learning that her workmen couldn't make mortar

at one of the sites—the water froze—she defied the cold and hurried to the building site. Bess urged the men on: Could they not heat ale to use instead of water? It was no use, construction had to wait; and Bess, at 80, was slowing down. There was a legend that Bess would not die so long as she was building, and now her days were plainly numbered. She succumbed on February 13, 1608, and, embalmed, lay in state for three months before entombment in a church in Derby.

Less squeamish than Elizabeth about her legacy, Bess left a detailed will. Elizabeth's death, without benefit of will, brought increased favor to Bess' family, and James I (James VI of Scotland) ennobled Bess' son William. But Arabella's secret marriage to another possible claimant to the throne led to her imprisonment and death in the Tower.

After their mother's death, William and Charles Cavendish surveyed their estates and concluded that each had 100,000 acres. Bess' descendants were illustrious—and some inherited the building gene. William's progeny became dukes of Devonshire, their family seat a new, even grander Chatsworth. From others descended the dukes of Newcastle, of Portland, of Kingston, of Norfolk; the earls Manvers, the earls of Pembroke, of Kent and of Arundel. Even from the son Bess called "Bad Henry" came the lords Waterpark. (Henry had no children from his marriage, but beyond the bounds of matrimony he was

remembered as "the common bull of Derbyshire and Staffordshire.") An old poem memorialized a few of the houses:

Hardwick for hugeness, Worksop for height,
Welbeck for use, and Bolser for sight. . . .
Worksop is wise, Welbeck is witty,
Hardwick is hard, Bolser is pretty.
Hardwick is rich, Welbeck is fine,
Worksop is stately, Bolser divine.

Scaffolding has been erected to preserve the ruins of Old Hardwick, where Thomas Hobbes, the illustrious philosopher, died; his ghost is believed to haunt a path beside the old hall. As part payment for death duties after World War II, "new" Hardwick went to the Treasury, which gave it to the National Trust. In an interior shrouded from damage by sunlight, a gallery 162 feet long and 26 feet high displays portraits of the age's monarchs as well as of Bess' last three husbands. The house boasts four portraits of Bess herself, stately and commanding.

It is not hard to imagine Bess as a living presence, seated at her embroidery, poring over accounts, eating in solitary splendor, receiving guests from the court, contentedly contemplating the view of Old Hardwick. She could recall that her life had begun in that great home when it was a simple farmhouse, and that—bending each occasion to her sovereign will—she had risen from obscurity to royal favor, the benefactor of a great and noble line.

Hungary's Philosopher King: Matthias Corvinus, 1458–90

Valery Rees *surveys the life and achievements of the ruler who put late fifteenth-century Hungary on the map, both culturally and geographically, but whose efforts may have put an intolerable strain on the body politic.*

Valery Rees

Valery Rees studied History at Newnham College, Cambridge. She teaches Latin at St James Independent School for Girls, London. Work on the Ficino Letters and travel in Eastern Europe have led her to research on the Renaissance in Hungary.

Let me invite you on a journey across Europe in the 1480s. Life in the rich cloth towns of Antwerp or Bruges is easy to picture. We can visualise the glories of Italy in Florence, Siena, Urbino, Rome. Recent restoration work in Rothenburg and Bamberg shows how life was lived in Germany. But what about further east? Let us journey on across the lands of the Holy Roman Empire, eastwards from Bamberg, through Austria, stopping at Linz and the great monastery of Melk, into Bohemia, Slovakia and finally into Hungary. As we follow the course of the Danube through the changing landscapes of hills and river plains, we notice the cultural unity. The cities still look German: the churches are built in the same style, the language of learning and religion is still Latin. The king and queen of this great country are in close personal correspondence with Italian states and are steeped in Italian culture. So we can abandon any idea that Europe in the fifteenth century ends at Vienna.

Hungary at this time is a large country, including not only the Danube basin and its great plains which supplied Europe with fine horses, and wheat and fruits in abundance, but also stretching from the Dalmatian coast in the west across the

wealthy mining towns of Slovakia from the vine-clad hills of upper Hungary over the Carpathian mountains of Transylvania to the Vlach (Wallachian) territories of Romania in the east, with a chain of border fortresses across the south, crossing Serbia and Croatia. We are at the edge of Christendom. Beyond Hungary are the Turks.

The Hungarian border fortresses were of immense importance to the whole of Europe as Turkish expansion began to change the face of the known world. In 1453 the fall of Constantinople had brought Greeks and Greek learning to Italy. The study of Greek texts that had been unknown in the West hitherto brought a rebirth of interest in the classical world and philosophy. This in turn served as inspiration for all that we call the Renaissance in Italy. There was, of course, no guarantee that Turkish expansion would stop at Constantinople and it is hard for us to appreciate now either the excitement caused by the rediscovery of Plato or the very real fear people felt towards an invader of such power, whose methods of warfare were so utterly destructive and whose culture was so alien. Not for nothing did Marsilio Ficino write to Pope Sixtus IV in 1478 of 'the ravening wolf threatening to devour the entire flock of Christendom'. In August 1480 the Turks sent a small naval detachment to Italy and burned Otranto. They put half the inhabitants to the sword and carried off the remainder into slavery.

It was the King of Hungary's troops, under Blaise Magyar, that recovered the fortress of Otranto for the Italians in September 1481. During the same year

King Matthias also won a series of important victories against the Turks on home ground, driving them out of Serbia. Hungary was quite literally the bulwark of Europe. Ficino called Matthias a second Messiah, a second Moses, the man who would save Europe from the Turks.

From the correspondence of Ficino with the court at Buda we can learn much about Hungary's status in Europe. Ficino was the leader of the Platonic Academy in Florence, a man of considerable authority and influence. He translated the newly rediscovered works of Plato and Plotinus into Latin, and his teachings and commentaries on them reconciled Christian thought and Greek philosophy. His letters, collected and widely circulated in his own lifetime, provide us with a rich source of material in many fields.

Matthias was not the only ruler Ficino wrote to in his efforts to bring peace to a troubled world, but in Matthias Ficino and his circle held the greatest hope of fulfilling Plato's ideal of a philosopher-king: a king who would establish the reign of peace and justice, so that truth and the love of God might find full expression in the world. It was obviously no use looking to the papacy for such leadership: in 1464 Pius II had tried to unite Europe, including Hungary, in a crusade against the Turks, travelling to Ancona to lead it in person, but he died there before setting sail, aware of how little support had actually materialised. After him successive popes cared less and less about crusade. Besides, as personal ambition eclipsed piety, St Peter's heirs were fast losing their spiritual authority. Nor had the Holy Roman Emperor sufficient authority or political will to fulfil the role of protector. So it was entirely natural that Ficino and his circle should turn to Matthias, who seemed to unite in one person the spiritual, intellectual and temporal forces needed for the task.

To what extent were these grand hopes justified? Hungary had already gained some notable successes against the Turks in the previous generation: under King Ulászló (1440–1444), János Hunyadi, Matthias' father, had risen rapidly to prominence as a gifted military commander. Then, as regent for the young László V, his popularity had risen even higher as he turned from successful defence to a daring offensive campaign against the Turks. Fighting continued throughout Hunyadi's life, culminating in the recapture of Belgrade in 1456. He died of fever shortly afterwards, but such was his prestige in the kingdom that his sons were considered candidates for the elective crown if the young King Lásló should die without an heir. Hunyadi's elder son inherited the command of Belgrade, but within eight months baronial intrigue had secured his execution and the imprisonment of his younger brother Matthias in Prague. Then suddenly László died of plague, in 1457.

Several European royal houses had claims to the Hungarian throne. Matthias Hunyadi was a mere youth, the son of an 'upstart' (though some said that János Hunyadi had been the natural son of Sigismund, King of Hungary 1387–1437, and Holy Roman Emperor). The Diet met in Buda to elect a new king. The townsfolk favoured Hunyadi's son. The nobles were largely opposed. But a show of strength by Matthias' uncle, marching a powerful army of mercenaries up the frozen Danube towards them, carried the election. Matthias returned from Prague in January 1458 as king elect, engaged to the daughter of his recent captor. He inherited from his father vast landholdings in Transylvania, qualities of courage and leadership and a deep-rooted faith in humanism. He found himself at the head of a rich and powerful country, but one dominated by factions of extremely powerful nobles. Moreover, the Emperor Frederick III was in possession of the holy crown of Hungary without which no coronation could be valid. From 1458 until his coronation in 1464, Matthias

had to make good his title against challenges from many quarters.

First he had to free himself from the influences of those who felt he owed his election to them. His mother, Elisabeth Szilágyi had paid his ransom, and, with her powerful brother Mihály, had entered an agreement with the Garai family to ensure Matthias' election in return for their continued influence. Matthias refused to feel bound by this, and proceeded to form working alliances with the lesser nobility within the Diet. Recognising his uncle's own ambitions, Matthias sent him off as soon as possible in command of an army against the Turks on an expedition in which he lost his life. The offended Garai barons transferred their support to the Habsburgs: five years of bitter troubles followed, resolved only by a compromise in 1463, whereby Frederick III allowed Matthias the crown in return for Habsburg rights of succession if he should die childless. Meanwhile Matthias valued his mother's support and she continued to guide him through the web of baronial politics, finally retiring to a convent not long after his second marriage in 1476.

In these early manoeuvres Matthias was also able to rely on the support of his Chancellor, János Vitéz, Bishop of Oradea. Vitéz had entered the chancellery under Sigismund and had remained at the centre of affairs through all the changes of regime since. He was by now immensely experienced in diplomacy and government. Indeed Vitéz had been Matthias' tutor through childhood, schooling him in Latin, history, mathematics and astronomy as well as the practical aspects of diplomacy. It was a thoroughly humanist education and Matthias was a willing and able pupil.

Matthias' favourite reading as a boy had been Quintus Curtius' *Life of Alexander* and Silus Italicus' epic of the Punic wars. He seems also to have developed a classical sense of his own destiny. In 1458 Pope Calixtus III had called him 'the man sent by God'. Matthias was certainly conscious of his providential role as defender of Christendom against the Turks, but he looked to the classics for his inspiration. As Italy was the acknowledged home of the new interest in the classics, a steady flow of books and visitors came to Hungary from Italy.

Yet, for all that, Matthias was thoroughly Hungarian. His great talent was to put what he learned from the classics to practical effect in the everyday affairs

of his kingdom. From his studies of the Greek philosophers, which he approached first through Vitéz and later through Ficino, he understood the essential unity of mankind under God and applied high standards of moral and ethical conduct to his everyday affairs. Devotion to his subjects' welfare earned for him an enduring presence in Hungarian folklore as Matthias the Just; stories of his wisdom, imagination and good deeds abound.

From his studies of the Roman historians, especially Caesar, he understood the need for a highly trained, disciplined army which could march in step and perform complex manoeuvres requiring skills of timing and co-operation between units. Most of these skills had been lost since classical times. As king, Matthias, with all the freshness and enthusiasm of youth, decided to reintroduce them to his own army. This could only be done with an army which stayed together long enough to practise. So among his earliest laws are a series of measures designed to improve the quality of the traditional threefold levy. After his conquest of Bohemia, he supplemented this with a standing army of Hussite and Polish mercenaries.

Keeping a standing army involved huge expense, so reforms of the tax system soon followed. By renaming the standard taxes, it was possible to remove many exemptions and immunities that had been granted. In addition, from the 1470s, the Diet granted an extraordinary tax for military purposes, renewed almost every year of Matthias' reign. These changes had two important side effects. The first was the centralising tendency we recognise as characteristic of the 'new' monarchies of the sixteenth century. The medieval tax system had operated on a local basis: both the funds for raising the militia and the command over it went to the count or castellan in each administrative area. The king had direct control of only a small proportion of the men at arms. Now, however, revenues were doubled; 20,000 men or more were maintained as mercenaries, and the king had increasing control over the remaining 100,000. Legislation enabling these changes had to be passed by the Estates, or parliament, which began to meet more regularly and to enjoy more power. Attracted by a share of this power, the lesser nobility were content to help the king reduce the might of the great barons by a series of modest but steady changes in the administration, not unlike Tudor reforms in England, designed to enforce the king's law and eliminate corruption.

The second side effect of the changes was a social one. During Matthias' reign, increasingly notable in the chancery lists are the names of young churchmen of peasant origin, who entered the church to receive an education and then rose on their own merits to positions previously reserved for the nobility. The majority of the nobility, both great and small, remained illiterate. This is not to say they were uncultured: there was a fine and rich oral culture based on Hungarian epics and religious ballads. But Matthias now took on the ambitious idea of making his nation a new home of classical learning. He was ready to promote any who showed talent in this direction.

The relative importance of the barons was also being eroded by the encouragement Matthias gave to towns and cities. Hungary was very much an agrarian society, but market towns and cities were growing: royal charters gave cities exemption from the jurisdiction of the landed aristocracy and their taxes were payable directly to the king. The king had an interest in fostering trade. When Matthias' war efforts began to turn away from the Turks and towards Vienna, it was partly in order to stem the outward flow of the profits of trade. Hungary's exports were channelled through foreign merchants in Vienna. Moreover the mines, the major industrial enterprise on Hungarian soil, were mostly in Italian or German ownership. Hungary's imports were mainly cloth and luxury goods, and although embroidery and metalwork were flourishing there, the idea of investing in manufacture seems not to have taken root. The cities were often German enclaves within a Hungarian rural hinterland. Some, including Buda, the capital, operated under German law and custom, answering only to their own elected elders and to the king's personal representative, the *magister tavernicarum.* The cultural unity with Germany and Bohemia that we noted earlier was thus perhaps only skin deep, a feature of city life and not valid for the great Hungarian plains. It certainly seems that the economic and social transformation brought about by the growth of cities in Western Europe was not matched by developments in Hungary.

The Hungarian church, while wholly Catholic, enjoyed some independence from Rome, especially in the matter of ecclesiastical appointments. Consequently the church was the king's dependable ally in government. Even so, when Matthias' military tax-raising ventures began to require sizeable contributions from church property, he met fierce opposition, led by the two bishops who had hitherto been his most loyal supporters: János Vitéz and his nephew, Janus Pannonius.

Matthias' situation was a difficult one: he realised that only Hungary was powerful enough to face the Turks. But he was acutely aware that even Hungary could not do this alone, despite increased revenues and the new, well-trained forces. Various attempts were made to raise cooperative ventures, in the hope that a combination of Italian and German wealth, Bohemian and Polish soldiers and Matthias' leadership might drive the Turks back into Asia. But negotiations bore little fruit. The Turkish threat remained as pressing as ever. Raids continued all along the border defence line and from 1468 Matthias turned his attentions increasingly to the lands north and west

of Hungary. If Italy could not join forces with him, then he must rely on his own strength and build up a strong Danube empire.

Imagine then the plight of the churchmen, asked to give church property for a war not against the Turks but against other parts of Christendom including the Holy Roman Empire. The conflict with Vitéz and Pannonius now became inevitable and open. Armed uprising in 1471 led to the imprisonment of the one and the flight and death of the other, and to disillusionment on Matthias' part for a time with all things Italian and humanist.

However this did not last long, and by 1476 Italian emissaries were again very much in favour at court. Matthias had for some time been contemplating an Italian marriage. After the death of his first wife in 1464 he had opened negotiations with the Sforza family, but in 1465 Ippolita Sforza was married to the Duke of Calabria, eldest son of the King of Naples. The kingdom of Naples offered a glorious example of Renaissance court life, and soon Matthias had resolved to marry the king's beautiful and accomplished second daughter, Princess Beatrix of Aragon. After some delay, caused by constant wars, the marriage was solemnised in 1476, and Beatrix arrived in Hungary to be crowned queen.

With Beatrix came Francesco Bandini. He had entered King Ferdinand's service after spending some years with Marsilio Ficino in Florence. In Hungary he rapidly became Matthias' friend and closest adviser. It was Bandini who advised the king in matters of taste and style. Another Italian, Antonio Bonfini, was commissioned in the 1480s to rewrite the chronicles of Hungary in a fitting, humanist style. During the late 1470s and the 1480s classical learning began to blossom in Hungary. The new queen took on enthusiastically the task of redecorating the palace at Buda and engaging the finest musicians in Europe. The ever increasing flow of visitors from Italy included not only Beatrix's personal guests, luxury goods, merchants and adventurers, but also Renaissance scholars, writers, artists, stone-masons and architects, all looking to Matthias for patronage and work.

The style of architecture he adopted was *all'antica,* a revival of the aesthetic principles of ancient Greece and Rome. The governing idea, elaborated from the works of Filarete, was that a prince may lawfully engage in works of public *mag-*

nificentia for the greater glory of his nation or of God, without incurring penalty for the sin of pride or lavish excess. Such a programme was enthusiastically undertaken by the king in person. The royal palace at Buda underwent extensive modifications at the hands of Italian craftsmen. That of Visegrad was renowned for its beauty and tranquility. Most remarkable of all was the conception and successful realisation of the great Corvina library, the largest library of its kind. It was filled with every known text of Latin and Greek, many of them beautifully copied out and illuminated at the great Italian manuscript houses. This was not only for the king's personal delight; he wished to encourage both nobility and church to take an active interest in intellectual pursuits and to make use of this wonderful collection. He also wished to establish Buda as a centre of European learning. The university he founded at Pozsony (Bratislava) had rather faded away after the death of Vitéz, but during the 1480s he tried to persuade Ficino to come in person and set up a Platonic Academy in Buda. A modest start was made under Bandini in the Dominican Cloisters next to the Coronation Church, with plans for an impressive expansion, but Ficino never came and Matthias died before the plan was fulfilled.

In 1485 Matthias had conquered much of Austria, and had made Vienna his capital, though keeping always great affection for Buda, the centre of his Hungarian realm. It was at Vienna that he died, on April 6th, 1490, probably of a stroke, though he had been in poor health for some months before. In many ways, Matthias behaved as a model Renaissance prince. Plato's philosopher king was the ideal held out to him by Ficino, and clearly it was a vision that appealed to him. Why then was there so little of his glory left in Hungary only a generation after his death?

There were two main reasons. First was the lack of a legitimate heir. Neither Matthias' first wife, Catherine Podiebrad, nor Beatrix gave him a child. He did have a natural son, János Corvinus, in between his two marriages and, when it began to be clear that Beatrix would produce no heir, Matthias determined to make János his successor, educating him appropriately to continue the work of a Renaissance prince. The unfortunate price of this was increasing conflict with Beatrix. Yet Matthias never gave up hope

that reason would prevail and he was still engaged in securing a princely marriage alliance for János when he died. However with Beatrix against him, and no shortage of foreign contenders, János was unable to command sufficient support in the assembly of nobles after his father's death.

The second factor was the very nature of the reforms Matthia's had implemented to bring the government of the realm under his own control. Resentment ran deep among the old baronial families. They now quickly seized upon the opportunity of rectifying matters by deliberately electing a weak king. Even the new nobles, those same faithful servants whom Matthias had used to control the old barons, and had rewarded with grants of land and power, deserted the Hunyadi claim. The very bishops Matthias had raised up from humble origins became the princely prelates of the Jagiellonian period. Besides, having made large grants of land, Matthias passed on a far smaller personal power base to his successor than he had inherited from his own father.

So it was that János Corvinus was voted King of Bosnia, and sent off to rule this troublesome border territory, while the crown of Hungary was given to Ladislas Jagiello of Poland. He soon earned the nickname *Dobje,* because he simply agreed to whatever was put before him. Matthias' mercenary army was sent off to face a relatively minor Turkish raid. Its pay was withheld, as the magnates had negotiated a promise from Ladislas that he would no longer exact the military tax. The army, understandably, fell to pillaging local villages for food and supplies, so Pál Kinizsi, Matthias' ablest commander, was sent against it to destroy it. Then, in 1514, when a large army of peasants started to assemble in response to fresh calls for a crusade against the Turks, they too were massacred by the ruling nobles, with devastating long-term social consequences.

Leaving no army capable of resisting Turkish advance, Hungary's nobles had sealed their own doom. The southern border fortresses were in a state of neglect. Belgrade fell in 1521, leaving the way open for the Turks to advance up the Danube. On August 2nd, 1526, they met a hastily assembled Hungarian force at Mohács and a pitched battle was fought. In spite of astonishing acts of bravery from individual sections of the Hungarian army, they were utterly annihilated, with the loss of king, bishops, many nobles and thousands of men.

What followed is well known. Hungary was divided into three parts. One fell to the Habsburg family, as yet again the slain king left no heir. One was ruled directly by the Turks under conditions inimical to the development of Hungarian culture. The third, Transylvania, continued a semi-independent life under Turkish suzerainty.

It is to Transylvania that we must look for the continued growth of Renaissance culture in Hungary after 1526. Little work has been done on this, but travel and research in the eastern part of old Hungary is now a possibility. What has already occurred since the fall of Communism in Eastern Europe is the opening up of archives and sites of archaeological interest in Western Hungary. They reveal a period of European history when the very idea of Europe was larger than we have usually considered. Furthermore, in the figures of Matthias and Beatrix, in the writings of their court advisers and all that has survived, we can look afresh at ideas of statecraft and kingship in early modern Europe.

FOR FURTHER READING:

P. Sugar *A History of Hungary* (London & New York, 1990); *The Letters of Marsilio Ficino,* are in English translation (Shepheard-Walwyn, 1975–1988 and further volumes in preparation); articles by E. Fügedi are reprinted in *Kings, Bisbops, Nobles & Burghers in Medieval Hungary,* (Variorum Reprints, 1986); Béla Király (ed), *War and Society in Medieval and Early Modern Hungary* (New York, 1982); C. Csapodi and K Csapodi-Gárdonyi, *Bibliotbeca Corviniana,* (Budapest 1969, reprinted in 1981), R Feuer-Toth, *Art and Humanism in Hungary in the Age of Matthias Corvinus,* (Budapest, 1990).

Columbus—Hero or Villain?

Felipe Fernández-Armesto *weighs up the case for and against the man of the hour and finds a Columbus for all seasons.*

Felipe Fernández-Armesto

Felipe Fernández-Armesto is a member of The Faculty of Modern History of Oxford University.

This year, his statue in Barcelona exchanged symbolic rings with the Statue of Liberty in New York; meanwhile, the descendants of slaves and peons will burn his effigy. In a dream-painting by Salvador Dali, Columbus takes a great step for mankind, toga-clad and cross-bearing—while a sail in the middle distance drips with blood. The Columbus of tradition shares a single canvas with the Columbus of fashion, the culture-hero of the western world with the bogey who exploited his fellow-man and despoiled his environment. Both versions are false and, if historians had their way, the quincentennial celebrations ought to stimulate enough educational work and research to destroy them. Instead, the polemical atmosphere seems to be reinforcing *à parti pris* positions.

It is commonly said that the traditional Columbus myth—which awards him personal credit for anything good that ever came out of America since 1492—originated in the War of Independence, when the founding fathers, in search of an American hero, pitched on the Genoese weaver as the improbable progenitor of all-American virtues. Joel Barlow's poem, *The Vision of Columbus,* appeared in

1787. Columbus remained a model for nineteenth-century Americans, engaged in a project for taming their own wilderness. Washington Irving's perniciously influential *History of the Life and Voyages of Christopher Columbus* of 1828—which spread a lot of nonsense including the ever-popular folly that Columbus was derided for claiming that the world was round—appealed unashamedly to Americans' self-image as promoters of civilisation.

Yet aspects of the myth are much older—traceable to Columbus' own times and, to a large extent, to his own efforts. He was a loquacious and indefatigable self-publicist, who bored adversaries into submission and acquired a proverbial reputation for using more paper than Ptolemy. The image he projected was that of a providential agent, the divinely-elected 'messenger of a new heaven', chosen to bear the light of the gospel to unevangelised recesses of the earth—the parts which other explorers could not reach. His plan for an Atlantic crossing 'God revealed to me by His manifest hand'. Playing on his christian name, he called himself 'Christo ferens' and compiled a book of what he said were biblical prophecies of his own discoveries. Enough contemporaries were convinced by his gigantic self-esteem for him to become literally a legend in his own lifetime. To a leading astrological guru at the court of Spain, he was 'like a new apostle'. To a humanist from Italy who taught the would-be Renaissance men of Castile, he

was 'the sort of whom the ancients made gods'.

From his last years, his reputation dipped: writers were obliged to belittle him in the service of monarchs who were locked in legal conflict with Columbus' family over the level of reward he had earned. Yet his own self-perception was passed on to posterity by influential early books. Bartolomé de Las Casas—Columbus' editor and historian—professed a major role for himself in the apostolate of the New World and heartily endorsed Columbus' self-evaluation as an agent of God's purpose. Almost as important was the *Historie dell'Ammiraglio,* which claimed to be a work of filial piety and therefore presented Columbus as an unblemished hero, with an imputed pedigree to match his noble soul.

Claims to having access to a divine hot-line are by their nature unverifiable. Demonstrably false was the second element in Columbus' self-made myth: his image of tenacity in adversity—a sort of *Mein Kampf* version of his life, in which he waged a long, lone and unremitting struggle against the ignorance and derision of contemporaries. This theme has echoed through the historical tradition. That 'they all laughed at Christopher Columbus' has been confirmed by modern doggerel. Vast books have been wasted in an attempt to explain his mythical perseverance by ascribing to him 'secret' foreknowledge of the existence of America. Yet almost all the evidence which underlies it comes straight out of Columbus' own propaganda, according to which he was isolated, ignored, victimised and persecuted, usually for the numinous span of 'seven' years; then, after fulfilling his destiny, to the great profit of his detractors he was returned to a wilderness of contumely and neglect, unrewarded by the standard of his deserts, in a renewed trial of faith.

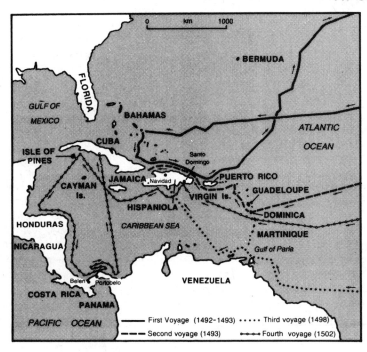

The image of Columbus-as-victim of the Spanish courts is explained by his relishing his own misfortunes as good copy and good theatre.

These passages of autobiography cannot be confirmed by the facts. The documented length of his quest for patronage was less than five years. Throughout that time he built up a powerful lobby of moral supporters at the Castilian court and financial backers in the business community of Seville. His own protestations of loneliness are usually qualified by an admission that he was unsupported 'save for' one or two individuals. When added together, these form an impressive cohort, which includes at least two archbishops, one court astrologer, two royal confessors, one royal treasurer and the queen herself. In his second supposed period of persecution, he was an honoured figure, loaded with titles, received at court, consulted by the crown and—depite his woebegone protestations of poverty—amply moneyed.

The explanation of the image of Columbus-as-victim must be sought in his character, not in his career. He was what would now be called a whinger, who relished his own misfortunes as good copy and good theatre. When he appeared at court in chains, or in a friar's habit, he was playing the role of victim for all it was worth. His written lamentations—which cover many folios of memoranda, supplications and personal letters—are thick with allusions to Jeremiah and Job. The notions of patience under suffering and of persecution for righteousness' sake fitted the hagiographical model on which much of his self-promotional writing was based: a flash of divine enlightenment; a life transformed; consecration to a cause; unwavering fidelity in adversity.

The images of Columbus-as-hero and Columbus-as-villain has a long historical and literary tradition.

The most successful promotional literature is believed by its own propagators. To judge from his consistency, Columbus believed in his own image of himself. It is not surprising that most readers of his works, from Las Casas onwards, have been equally convinced. Columbus seems to have been predisposed to self-persuasion by saturation in the right literary models: saints, prophets and heroes of romance. Despite his astonishing record of achievement, and his impressive accumulation of earthly rewards, he had an implacable temperament which could never be satisfied, and an unremitting ambition which could never be assuaged. Such men always think themselves hard done by. His extraordinary powers of persuasion—his communicator's skills which won backing for an impossible project in his lifetime—have continued to win followers of his legend ever since his death.

Like Columbus-the-hero, Columbus-the-villain is also an old character in a long literary tradition. Most of the denunciations of him written in his day have not survived but we can judge their tenor from surviving scraps. The usual complaints against servants of the Castilian crown in the period are made: he acted arbitrarily in the administration of justice; he exceeded his powers in enforcing his authority; he usurped royal rights by denying appeal to condemned rebels; he alienated crown property without authorisation; he deprived privileged colonists of offices or perquisites; he favoured his own family or friends; he lined his pockets at public expense. In the course of what seems to have been a general campaign against Genoese employees of the crown in the late 1490s, he was 'blamed as a foreigner' and accused of 'plotting to give the island of Hispaniola to the Genoese'.

Other allegations attacked his competence rather than his good faith, generally with justice. It was true, for instance, that he had selected an unhealthy and inconvenient site for the settlement of Hispaniola; that he had disastrously misjudged the natives' intentions in supposing them to be peaceful; and that his proceedings had so far alienated so many colonists that by the time of his removal in 1500 it was a missionary's opinion that the colony would never be at peace if he were allowed back. All these complaints reflect the priorities of Spaniards and the interests of the colonists and of the crown. There were, however, some charges against Columbus which anticipated the objections of modern detractors, who scrutinise his record from the natives' point of view, or who look at it from the perspective of fashionably ecological priorities.

First, there was the issue of Columbus' activities as a slaver. Coming from a Genoese background, Columbus never understood Spanish scruples about slavery, which had been characterised as an unnatural estate in the most influential medieval Spanish law-code, and which the monarchs distrusted as a form of intermediate lordship that reserved subjects from royal jurisdiction. Castilian practice was, perhaps, the most fastidious in Christendom. The propriety of slavery was acknowledged in the cases of captives of just war and offenders against natural law; but such cases were reviewed with rigour and in the royal courts, at least, decision-making tended to be biased in favour of the alleged slaves.

Shortly before the discovery of the New World, large numbers of Canary Islanders, enslaved by a conquistador on the pretext that they were 'rebels against their natural lord' had been pronounced free by a judicial inquiry commissioned by the crown, and liberated, in cases contested by their 'owners', in a series of trials. This does not seem, however, to have alerted Columbus to the risks of slap-happy slaving.

Although the ferocious Caribs of the Lesser Antilles were generally deemed to be lawful victims of enslavement (since the cannibalism imputed to them seemed an obvious offence against natural law) Columbus' trade was chiefly in Arawaks, who, by his own account, were rendered exempt by their amenability to evangelisation. By denying that the Arawaks were idolatrous, Columbus exonerated them of the one possible charge which might, in the terms of the time, be considered an 'unnatural' offence. Even when the monarchs reproved him and freed the Arawaks he sold, Columbus was astonishingly slow on the uptake. In a colony where the yield of other profitable products was disappointing, he traded slaves to allay the colony's grievous prob-

lems of supply. 'And although at present they die on shipment,' he continued, 'this will not always be the case, for the Negroes and Canary Islanders reacted in the same way at first'. In one respect, contemporary criticisms of the traffic differed from those made today. The friars and bureaucrats who denounced Columbus for it did so not because it was immoral, but because it was unlawful.

Slavery was only one among many ills which Columbus was said to have inflicted on the natives. The current myth incriminates him with 'genocide'. In the opinion of one *soi-disant* Native American spokesman, 'he makes Hitler look like a juvenile delinquent'. This sort of hype is doubly unhelpful: demonstrably false, it makes the horrors of the holocaust seem precedented and gives comfort to Nazi apologists by making 'genocide' an unshocking commonplace. Though he was often callous and usually incompetent in formulating indigenist policy, the destruction of the natives was as far removed from Columbus' thoughts as from his interests. The Indians, he acknowledged, were 'the wealth of this land'. Their conservation was an inescapable part of any rational policy for their exploitation. Without them the colony would have no labour resources. At a deeper level of Columbus' personal concerns, they were the great glory of his discovery: their evangelisation justified it and demonstrated its place in God's plans for the world, even if the material yield was disappointing to his patrons and backers. And Columbus had enough sense to realise that a large and contented native population was, as the monarchs said, their 'chief desire' for his colony. 'The principal thing which you must do,' he wrote to his first deputy,

is to take much care of the Indians, that no ill nor harm may be done them, nor anything taken from them against their will, but rather that they be honoured and feel secure and so should have no cause to rebel.

Though no contemporary was so foolish as to accuse Columbus of wilfully exterminating Indians, it was widely realised that his injunctions were often honoured in the breach and that his own administrative regulations sometimes caused the natives harm. The missionaries almost unanimously regarded him as an obstacle to their work, though the only specific crime against the natives to survive among their memoranda—that

'he took their women and all their property'—is otherwise undocumented. The imposition of forced labour and of unrealistic levels of tribute were disastrous policies, which diverted manpower from food-growing and intensified the 'culture-shock' under which indigenous society reeled and tottered, though Columbus claimed they were expedients to which he was driven by economic necessity.

Columbus was a man of extraordinary vision with a defiant attitude to what was possible; he could not anticipate the consequences of his discovery.

Some contemporaries also condemned the sanguinary excesses of his and his brother's punitive campaigns in the interior of Hispaniola in 1495–96. It should be said in Columbus' defence, however, that he claimed to see his own part as an almost bloodless pacification and that the 50,000 deaths ascribed to these campaigns in the earliest surviving account were caused, according to the same source, chiefly by the Indians' scorched-earth strategy. The outcome was horrible enough, but Columbus' treatment of the Indians inflicted catastrophe on them rather by mistakes than by crimes. In general, he was reluctant to chastise them—refusing, for instance, to take punitive measures over the massacre of the first garrison of Hispaniola; and he tried to take seriously the monarchs' rather impractical command to 'win them by love'.

It would be absurd to look for environmental sensitivity of a late twentieth-century kind in Columbus' earliest critics. Yet the accusation of over-exploitation of the New World environment, which is at the heart of the current, ecologically-conscious anti-Columbus mood, was also made before the fifteenth century was quite over. According to the first missionaries, members of Columbus' family were 'robbing and destroying the land' in their greed for gold. Though he declined to accept personal responsibility, Columbus detected a similar problem when he denounced his fellow-colonists' exploitative attitude: unmarried men, with no stake in the success of the colony and no intention of permanent residence, should be excluded, he thought. They merely mulcted the island for what they could get before rushing home to Castile.

The danger of deforestation from the demand for dyestuffs, building materials and fuel was quickly recognised. The diversion of labour from agriculture to gold-panning aroused friars' moral indignation. The usefulness of many products of the indigenous agronomy was praised by Columbus and documented by the earliest students of the pharmacopoeia and florilegium of the New World. The assumption that there was an ecological 'balance' to be disturbed at hazard was, of course, impossible. On the contrary, everyone who arrived from the Old World assumed that the natural resources had to be supplemented with imported products to provide a balanced diet, a civilised environment and resources for trade. The modifications made by Columbus and his successors were intended, from their point of view, to improve, not to destroy. They introduced sources of protein—like livestock; comforts of home—like wheat and grapes; and potential exports—like sugar, whether these changes were really disastrous is hard to judge dispassionately. The loss of population in the early colonial period was probably due to other causes. In the long run, colonial Hispaniola proved able to maintain a large population and a spectacular material culture.

Since it was first broached in Columbus' day, the debate about the morality of the colonisation of the New World has had three intense periods: in the sixteenth century, when the issues of the justice of the Spanish presence and the iniquity of maltreatment of the natives were raised by religious critics and foreign opportunists; in the late eighteenth century, when Rousseau and Dr Johnson agreed in preferring the uncorrupted wilderness which was thought to have preceded colonisation; and in our own day. Until recently, Columbus managed largely to avoid implication in the sins of his successors. Las Casas revered him, and pitied, rather than censured, the imperfections of his attitude to the natives. Eighteenth-century sentimentalists regretted the colonial experience as a whole, generally without blaming Columbus for it. This was fair enough. Columbus' own model of colonial soci-

ety seems to have derived from Genoese precedents: the trading factory, merchant quarter and family firm. The idea of a 'total' colony, with a population and environment revolutionised by the impact and image of the metropolis, seems to have been imposed on him by his Castilian masters. In making him personally responsible for everything which followed—*post hunc ergo propter hunc*—his modern critics have followed a convention inaugurated by admirers, who credited Columbus with much that [h]as nothing to do with him—including, most absurdly of all—the culture of the present United States. Columbus never touched what was to become US territory except in Puerto Rico and the Virgin Islands. The values which define the 'American ideal'—personal liberty, individualism, freedom of conscience, equality of opportunity and representative democracy—would have meant nothing to him.

Columbus deserves the credit or blame only for what he actually did: which was to discover a route that permanently linked the shores of the Atlantic and to contribute—more signally, perhaps, than any other individual—to the long process by which once sundered peoples of the world were brought together in a single network of communications, which exposed them to the perils and benefits of mutual contagion and exchange. Whether or not one regards this as meritorious achievement, there was a genuine touch of heroism in it—both in the scale of its effects and in the boldness which inspired it. There had been many attempts to cross the Atlantic in central latitudes, but all—as far as we know—failed because the explorers clung to the zone of westerly winds in an attempt to secure a passage home. Columbus was the first to succeed precisely because he had the courage to sail with the wind at his back.

Historians, it is often said, have no business making moral judgements at all. The philosophy of the nursery-school assembly, in which role-models and culprits are paraded for praise or reproof seems nowadays to belong to a hopelessly antiquated sort of history, for which the reality of the past mattered less than the lessons for the present and the future. A great part of the historian's art is now held to consist in what the examiners call 'empathy'—the ability to see the past with the eyes, and to re-construct the feelings, of those who took part in it. If value judgements are made at all, they

ought at least to be controlled by certain essential disciplines. First, they must be consistent with the facts: it is unhelpful to accuse of 'genocide', for instance, a colonial administrator who was anxious for the preservation of the native labour force. Secondly, they should be made in the context of the value-system of the society scrutinised, at the time concerned. It would be impertinent to expect Columbus to regard slavery as immoral, or to uphold the equality of all peoples. Conquistadors and colonists are as entitled to be judged from the perspective of moral relativism as are the cannibals and human-sacrificers of the indigenous past. Thirdly, moral judgements should be expressed in language tempered by respect for the proper meanings of words. Loose talk of 'genocide' twists a spiral to verbal hype. Useful distinctions are obliterated; our awareness of the real cases, when they occur, is dulled.

Finally, when we presume to judge someone from a long time ago, we should take into account the practical constraints under which they had to operate, and the limited mental horizons by which they were enclosed. Columbus was in some ways a man of extraordinary vision with a defiant attitude to the art of the possible. Yet he could not anticipate the consequences of his discovery or of the colonial enterprise confided to him. Five hundred years further on, with all our advantages of hindsight, we can only boast a handful of 'successful' colonial experiments—in the United States, Siberia, Australia and New Zealand—in all of which the indigenous populations have been exterminated or swamped. The Spanish empire founded by Columbus was strictly unprecedented and, in crucial respects, has never been paralleled. The problems of regulating such vast dominions, with so many inhabitants, so far away, and with so few resources, were unforeseeable and proved unmanageable. Never had so many people been conquered by culture-shock or their immune-systems invaded by irresistible disease. Never before had such a challenging environment been so suddenly transformed in an alien image. In these circumstances, it would be unreasonable to expect Columbus' creation to work well. Like Dr Johnson's dog, it deserves some applause for having performed at all.

So which was Columbus: hero or villain? The answer is that he *was* neither but has *become* both. The real Columbus was a mixture of virtues and vices like the rest of us, not conspicuously good or just, but generally well-intentioned, who grappled creditably with intractable problems. Heroism and villainy are not, however, objective qualities. They exist only in the eye of the beholder.

In images of Columbus, they are now firmly impressed on the retinas of the upholders of rival legends and will never be expunged. Myths are versions of the past which people believe in for irrational motives—usually because they feel good or find their prejudices confirmed. To liberal or ecologically conscious intellectuals, for instance, who treasure their feelings of superiority over their predecessors, moral indignation with Columbus is too precious to discard. Kinship with a culture-hero is too profound a part of many Americans' sense of identity to be easily excised.

Thus Columbus-the-hero and Columbus-the-villain live on, mutually sustained by the passion which continuing controversy imparts to their supporters. No argument can dispel them, however convincing; no evidence, however compelling. They have eclipsed the real Columbus and, judged by their effects, have outstripped him in importance. For one of the sad lessons historians learn is that history is influenced less by the facts as they happen than by the falsehoods men believe.

FOR FURTHER READING:

J. H. Elliott, *The Old World and the New* (Cambridge University Press, 1970); A. W. Crosby, *Columbian Exchange: Biological and Cultural Consequences of 1492* (Greenwood, 1972); J. Larner 'The Certainty of Columbus', *History,* lxxiii (1987); F. Fernández-Armesto, *Columbus* (Oxford University Press, 1991).

Luther: Giant of His Time and Ours

Half a millennium after his birth, the first Protestant is still a towering force

It was a back-room deal, little different from many others struck at the time, but it triggered an upheaval that altered irrevocably the history of the Western world. Albrecht of Brandenburg, a German nobleman who had previously acquired a dispensation from the Vatican to become a priest while underage and to head two dioceses at the same time, wanted yet another favor from the Pope: the powerful archbishop's chair in Mainz. Pope Leo X, a profligate spender who needed money to build St. Peter's Basilica, granted the appointment—for 24,000 gold pieces, roughly equal to the annual imperial revenues in Germany. It was worth it. Besides being a rich source of income, the Mainz post brought Albrecht a vote for the next Holy Roman Emperor, which could be sold to the highest bidder.

In return, Albrecht agreed to initiate the sale of indulgences in Mainz. Granted for good works, indulgences were papally controlled dispensations drawn from an eternal "treasury of merits" built up by Christ and the saints; the church taught that they would help pay the debt of "temporal punishment" due in purgatory for sins committed by either the penitent or any deceased person. The Pope received half the proceeds of the Mainz indulgence sale, while the other half went to repay the bankers who had lent the new archbishop gold.

Enter Martin Luther, a 33-year-old priest and professor at Wittenberg University. Disgusted not only with the traffic in indulgences but with its doctrinal underpinnings, he forcefully protested to Albrecht—never expecting that his action would provoke a sweeping uprising against a corrupt church. Luther's challenge culminated in the Protestant Reformation and the rending of Western Christendom, and made him a towering figure in European history. In this 500th anniversary year of his birth (Nov. 10, 1483), the rebel of Wittenberg remains the subject of persistent study. It is said that more books have been written about him than anyone else in history, save his own master, Jesus Christ. The renaissance in Luther scholarship surrounding this year's anniversary serves as a reminder that his impact on modern life is profound, even for those who know little about the doctrinal feuds that brought him unsought fame. From the distance of half a millennium, the man who, as Historian Hans Hillerbrand of Southern Methodist University in Dallas says, brought Christianity from lofty theological dogma to a clearer and more personal belief is still able to stimulate more heated debate than all but a handful of historical figures.

Indeed, as the reformer who fractured Christianity, Luther has latterly become a key to reuniting it. With the approval of the Vatican, and with Americans taking the lead, Roman Catholic theologians are working with Lutherans and other Protestants to sift through the 16th century disputes and see whether the Protestant-Catholic split can some day be overcome. In a remarkable turnabout, Catholic scholars today express growing appreciation of Luther as a "father in the faith" and are willing to play down his excesses. According to a growing consensus, the great division need never have happened at all.

Beyond his importance as a religious leader, Luther had a profound effect on Western culture. He is, paradoxically, the last medieval man and the first modern one, a political conservative and a spiritual revolutionary. His impact is most marked, of course, in Germany, where he laid the cultural foundations for what later became a united German nation.

When Luther attacked the indulgence business in 1517, he was not only the most popular teacher at Wittenberg but also vicar provincial in charge of eleven houses of the Hermits of St. Augustine. He was brilliant, tireless and a judicious administrator, though given to bouts of spiritual depression. To make his point on indulgences, Luther dashed off 95 theses condemning the system ("They preach human folly who pretend that as soon as money in the coffer rings, a soul from purgatory springs") and sent them to Archbishop Albrecht and a number of theologians.*

The response was harsh: the Pope eventually rejected Luther's protest and demanded capitulation. It was then that Luther began asking questions about other aspects of the church, including the papacy itself. In 1520 he charged in an open letter to the Pope, "The Roman Church, once the holiest of all, has become the most licentious den of thieves, the most shameless of brothels, the kingdom of sin, death and hell." Leo called Luther "the wild boar which has invaded the Lord's vineyard."

The following year Luther was summoned to recant his writings before the Diet of Worms, a council of princes

---

*Despite colorful legend, it is not certain he ever nailed them to the door of the Castle Church.

From *Time*, October 31, 1983, pp. 100-103. © 1983 by Time Inc. Magazine Company. Reprinted by permission.

convened by the young Holy Roman Emperor Charles V. In his closing defense, Luther proclaimed defiantly: "Unless I am convinced by testimony from Holy Scriptures and clear proofs based on reason—because, since it is notorious that they have erred and contradicted themselves, I cannot believe either the Pope or the council alone—I am bound by conscience and the Word of God. Therefore I can and will recant nothing, because to act against one's conscience is neither safe nor salutary. So help me God." (Experts today think that he did not actually speak the famous words, "Here I stand. I can do no other.")

This was hardly the cry of a skeptic, but it was ample grounds for the Emperor to put Luther under sentence of death as a heretic. Instead of being executed, Luther lived for another 25 years, became a major author and composer of hymns, father of a bustling household and a secular figure who opposed rebellion—in all, a commanding force in European affairs. In the years beyond, the abiding split in Western Christendom developed, including a large component of specifically "Lutheran" churches that today have 69 million adherents in 85 nations.

The enormous presence of the Wittenberg rebel, the sheer force of his personality, still broods over all Christendom, not just Lutheranism. Although Luther declared that the Roman Pontiffs were the "Antichrist," today's Pope, in an anniversary tip of the zucchetto, mildly speaks of Luther as "the reformer." Ecumenical-minded Catholic theologians have come to rank Luther in importance with Augustine and Aquinas. "No one who came after Luther could match him," says Father Peter Manns, a Catholic theologian in Mainz. "On the question of truth, Luther is a lifesaver for Christians." While Western Protestants still express embarrassment over Luther's anti-Jewish rantings or his skepticism about political clergy, Communist East Germany has turned him into a secular saint because of his influence on German culture. Party Boss Erich Honecker, head of the regime's *Lutherjahr* committee, is willing to downplay Luther's antirevolutionary ideas, using the giant figure to bolster national pride.

Said West German President Karl Carstens, as he opened one of the hundreds of events commemorating Luther this year: "Luther has become a symbol of the unity of all Germany. We are all Luther's heirs."

After five centuries, scholars still have difficulty coming to terms with the contradictions of a tempestuous man. He was often inexcusably vicious in his writings (he wrote, for instance, that one princely foe was a "faint-hearted wretch and fearful sissy" who should "do nothing but stand like a eunuch, that is, a harem guard, in a fool's cap with a fly swatter"). Yet he was kindly in person and so generous to the needy that his wife despaired of balancing the household budget. When the plague struck Wittenberg and others fled, he stayed behind to minister to the dying. He was a powerful spiritual author, yet his words on other occasions were so scatological that no Lutheran periodical would print them today. His writing was hardly systematic, and his output runs to more than 100 volumes. On the average, Luther wrote a major tract or treatise every two weeks throughout his life.

The scope of Luther's work has made him the subject of endless reinterpretation. The Enlightenment treated him as the father of free thought, conveniently omitting his belief in a sovereign God who inspired an authoritative Bible. During the era of Otto von Bismarck a century ago, Luther was fashioned into a nationalistic symbol; 70 years later, Nazi propagandists claimed him as one of their own by citing his anti-Jewish polemics.

All scholars agree on Luther's importance for German culture, surpassing even that of Shakespeare on the English-speaking world. Luther's masterpiece was his translation of the New Testament from Greek into German, largely completed in ten weeks while he was in hiding after the Worms confrontation, and of the Old Testament, published in 1534 with the assistance of Hebrew experts. The Luther Bible sold massively in his lifetime and remains today the authorized German Protestant version. Before Luther's Bible was published, there was no standard German, just a profusion of dialects. "It was Luther," said Johann Gottfried von Herder, one of Goethe's mentors, "who has awakened and let loose the giant: the German language."

Only a generation ago, Catholics were trained to consider Luther the arch-heretic. Now no less than the Vatican's specialist on Lutheranism, Monsignor Aloys Klein, says that "Martin Luther's action was beneficial to the Catholic Church."

Like many other Catholics, Klein thinks that if Luther were living today there would be no split. Klein's colleague in the Vatican's Secretariat for Promoting Christian Unity, Father Pierre Duprey, suggests that with the Second Vatican Council (1962–65) Luther "got the council he asked for, but 450 years too late." Vatican II accepted his contention, that in a sense, all believers are priests; while the council left the Roman church's hierarchy intact, it enhanced the role of the laity. More important, the council moved the Bible to the center of Catholic life, urged continual reform and instituted worship in local languages rather than Latin.

One of the key elements in the Reformation was the question of "justification," the role of faith in relation to good works in justifying a sinner in the eyes of God. Actually, Catholicism had never officially taught that salvation could be attained only through pious works, but the popular perception held otherwise. Luther recognized, as University of Chicago Historian Martin Marty explains, that everything "in the system of Catholic teaching seemed aimed toward appeasing God. Luther was led to the idea of God not as an angry judge but as a forgiving father. It is a position that gives the individual a great sense of freedom and security." In effect, says U.S. Historian Roland Bainton, Luther destroyed the implication that men could "bargain with God."

Father George Tavard, a French Catholic expert on Protestantism who teaches in Ohio and has this month published *Justification: An Ecumenical Study* (Paulist; $7.95), notes that "today many Catholic scholars think Luther was right and the 16th century Catholic polemicists did not understand what he meant. Both Lutherans and Catholics agree that good works by Christian believers are the result of their faith and the working of divine grace in them, not their personal contributions to their own salvation. Christ is the only Savior. One does not save oneself." An international Lutheran-Catholic commission, exploring the basis for possible reunion, made a joint statement along these lines in 1980. Last month a parallel panel in the U.S. issued a significant 21,000-word paper on justification that affirms much of Luther's thinking, though with some careful hedging from the Catholic theologians.

There is doubt, of course, about the degree to which Protestants and Catholics can, in the end, overcome their differences. Catholics may now be permitted to sing Luther's *A Mighty Fortress Is Our God* or worship in their native languages, but a wide gulf clearly remains on issues like the status of Protestant ministers and, most crucially, papal authority.

During the futile Protestant-Catholic reunion negotiations in 1530 at the Diet of Augsburg, the issue of priestly celibacy was as big an obstacle as the faith *vs.* good works controversy. Luther had married a nun, to the disgust of his Catholic contemporaries. From the start, the marriage of clergy was a sharply defined difference between Protestantism and Catholicism, and it remains a key barrier today. By discarding the concept of the moral superiority of celibacy, Luther established sexuality as a gift from God. In general, he was a lover of the simple pleasures, and would have had little patience with the later Puritans. He spoke offhandedly about sex, enjoyed good-natured joshing, beer drinking and food ("If our Lord is permitted to create nice large pike and good Rhine wine, presumably I may be allowed to eat and drink"). For his time, he also had an elevated opinion of women. He cherished his wife and enjoyed fatherhood, siring six children and rearing eleven orphaned nieces and nephews as well.

But if Luther's views on the Catholic Church have come to be accepted even by many Catholics, his anti-Semitic views remain a problem for even his most devoted supporters. Says New York City Rabbi Marc Tanenbaum: "The anniversary will be marred by the haunting specter of Luther's devil theory of the Jews."

Luther assailed the Jews on doctrinal grounds, just as he excoriated "papists" and Turkish "infidels." But his work titled *On the Jews and Their Lies* (1543) went so far as to advocate that their synagogues, schools and homes should be destroyed and their prayer books and Talmudic volumes taken away. Jews were to be relieved of their savings and put to work as agricultural laborers or expelled outright.

Fortunately, the Protestant princes ignored such savage recommendations, and the Lutheran Church quickly forgot about them. But the words were there to be gleefully picked up by the Nazis, who removed them from the fold of religious polemics and used them to buttress their 20th century racism. For a good Lu-

The room where Luther translated the New Testament; title page of his Bible

theran, of course, the Bible is the sole authority, not Luther's writings, and the thoroughly Lutheran Scandinavia vigorously opposed Hitler's racist madness. In the anniversary year, all sectors of Lutheranism have apologized for their founder's views.

Whatever the impact of Luther's anti-Jewish tracts, there is no doubt that his political philosophy, which tended to make church people submit to state authority, was crucial in weakening opposition by German Lutherans to the Nazis. Probably no aspect of Luther's teaching

is the subject of more agonizing Protestant scrutiny in West Germany today.

Luther sought to declericalize society and to free people from economic burdens imposed by the church. But he was soon forced, if reluctantly, to deliver considerable control of the new Protestant church into the hands of secular rulers who alone could ensure the survival of the Reformation. Luther spoke of "two kingdoms," the spiritual and the secular, and his writings provided strong theological support for authoritarian government and Christian docility.

The Lutheran wing of the Reformation was democratic, but only in terms of the church itself, teaching that a plowman did God's work as much as a priest, encouraging lay leadership and seeking to educate one and all. But it was Calvin, not Luther, who created a theology for the democratic state. A related aspect of Luther's politics, controversial then and now, was his opposition to the bloody Peasants' War of 1525. The insurgents thought they were applying Luther's ideas, but he urged rulers to crush the revolt: "Let whoever can, stab, strike, kill." Support of the rulers was vital for the Reformation, but Luther loathed violent rebellion and anarchy in any case.

Today Luther's law-and-order approach is at odds with the revolutionary romanticism and liberation theology that are popular in some theology schools. In contrast with modern European Protestantism's social gospel, Munich Historian Thomas Nipperdey says, Luther "would not accept modern attempts to build a utopia and would argue, on the contrary, that we as mortal sinners are incapable of developing a paradise on earth."

Meanwhile, the internal state of the Lutheran Church raises other questions about the lasting power of Luther's vision. Lutheranism in the U.S., with 8.5 million adherents, is stable and healthy. The church is also growing in Third World strongholds like racially torn Namibia, where black Lutherans predominate. But in Lutheranism's historic heartland, the two Germanys and Scandinavia, there are deep problems. In East Germany, Lutherans are under pressure from the Communist regime. In West Germany, the Evangelical Church in Germany (E.K.D.), a church federation that includes some non-Lutherans, is wealthy (annual income: $3 billion), but membership is shrinking and attendance at Sunday services is feeble indeed. Only 6% of West Germans—or, for that matter, Scandinavians—worship regularly.

What seems to be lacking in the old European churches is the passion for God and his truth that so characterizes Luther. He retains the potential to shake people out of religious complacency. Given Christianity's need, on all sides, for a good jolt, eminent Historian Heiko Oberman muses, "I wonder if the time of Luther isn't ahead of us."

The boldest assertion about Luther for modern believers is made by Protestants who claim that the reformer did nothing less than enable Christianity to survive. In the Middle Ages, too many Popes and bishops were little more than corrupt, luxury-loving politicians, neglecting the teaching of the love of God and using the fear of God to enhance their power and wealth. George Lindbeck, the Lutheran co-chairman of the international Lutheran-Catholic commission, believes that without Luther "religion would have been much less important during the next 400 to 500 years. And since medieval religion was falling apart, secularization would have marched on, unimpeded."

A provocative thesis, and a debatable one. But with secularization still marching on, almost unimpeded, Protestants and Catholics have much to reflect upon as they scan the five centuries after Luther and the shared future of their still divided churches.

—By Richard N. Ostling.
Reported by Roland Flamini and
Wanda Menke-Glückert/Bonn, with
other bureaus.

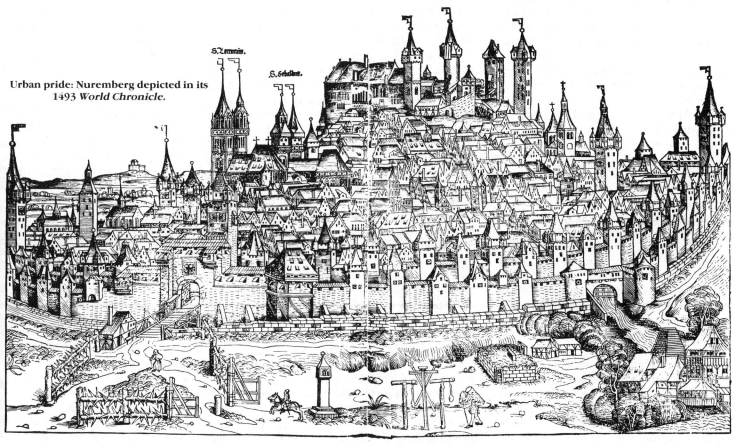

Urban pride: Nuremberg depicted in its 1493 *World Chronicle.*

The Forming of German Identity

Robin Du Boulay *looks at the social and cultural context in the 'jigsaw of lordships' which nevertheless produced a distinctive identity of 'speech and spirit' by the time of Luther's Reformation.*

Robin Du Boulay

Robin Du Boulay is Emeritus Professor of Medieval History in the University of London. His new book, The England of 'Piers Plowman', *was published in 1991.*

In the course of time nations are forged together, and sometimes they fall apart again, but a society's identity is first formed at a deeper level than that of political obedience. A dominant common language seems to be an early condition of a people's character. Only through language can a people come to rule and express themselves in ways less changeable than administrations.

'Through language a society enters history', wrote Jacob Grimm (d. 1863), collector of German folk-tales and pioneer of German lexicography. Writing before his own people had fully set up a nation-state, he invites us to discover German identity in a remoter past, unjustly neglected today, when Germans were growing rich in the arts of communication despite their fragmented and makeshift government.

Between about 1300 and 1530 the main languages of the European West emerged into a more standardised form. English took over in our own government. Chaucer expected to be understood all over the land, and the rhythms of Cranmer still have some power over us. So too in Germany, Luther (1483–1546), made hugely popular the German language which he found, but did not create. 'I use the common German language', he wrote from Saxon Wittenberg in about 1530, 'so that both High and Low Germans may understand me equally well.

In speech I follow the Saxon chancellery, which is imitated by all the princes and kings in Germany'. As a man of the people, though, Luther did not use official or courtly vocabulary, but said plainly that he looked to the mother in the house, the children on the streets, and the common man in the marketplace, watching their mouths as they spoke, and making his Bible translation accordingly.

This bond of language was fundamental in a vast society divided up into a jigsaw of lordships and united only weakly under the Holy Roman Emperor. In the fifteenth century there were about 120 principalities nominally held of the emperor, many of them bishoprics or abbeys, over 100 countships of very unequal size and importance, and a mass of lesser lordships. These German lands were studded with towns, ranging in size from a dozen great cities, comparable in English terms only with London, down to perhaps 3,000 settlements which could call themselves urban.

These communities were often at daggers drawn, individually or in alliances or leagues. Large-scale warfare was rare, but feuds were constant and were waged because no king had power to forbid private war, nor courts to adjudicate its causes. Great lords sometimes fought each other, cities strove against lords, the Teutonic Knights fought colonial wars in the north-east, knights were glad to fight as mercenaries, and cities themselves were sometimes riven with violent affrays between social and economic groups.

But, paradoxically, this state of brotherly hate had its positive side, since it helped in many ways to stimulate vernacular communication. Since law-courts were rarely able to settle disputes and outrages between strong parties, often in different jurisdictions, communities which felt wronged took matters into their own hands. Yet even this needed writing. Whether on a large scale or small, there were alliances to be arranged, fighting-men to be hired, and supplies procured for campaigns.

Towns which required their fortifications to be worked on had to finance them through taxation-lists. As crises developed, warnings had to be sent to threatening enemies and reports sent by captains to city councils. After the fighting there were arbitrations to be set up, ransoms demanded and paid and, in a proud, resentful and literate society, feud-books to be kept as a city's record

of wrongs suffered and sometimes victories written up as special reports or celebrated in a town's chronicle. All this was done in German.

At the heart of political life was the feud, or private war. There were agreed rules about its conduct, which included formal stages of notification, and about its termination, by written compromise, surrender or third-party arbitration. To take a single example, the city of Frankfurt on the Main recorded 229 feuds between 1380 and 1453: over three new ones every year. Very often these were started by neighbouring members of the lesser nobility who in parts of western Germany formed a numerous class of professional quarrellers available for hire. A hundred years later a friend of Götz von Berlichingen, one of their kind, who in old age wrote his own memoirs, described the lives of these thugs who slept until midday and then slopped idly about, wenching, playing with the dogs, boozing half the night and chattering about the latest fashions. Often quite poor and under-employed, men like this were ready for hire as mercenaries or to fall on travellers for ransoms.

Most feuds were about damage to property, theft of cattle, robbery of merchants or disputed inheritances. Sometimes villages were burned, but even with Frankfurt's vulnerability from its twice-yearly fair the city often exaggerated the wrongs it had suffered. To take a single example of a routine feud, a knight called Philip von Reifenberg, in 1413 seized two citizens as hostages and in reprisal Frankfurt soldiers rounded up seventy-eight cows and thirty-one goats from Philip's property. An exchange was quickly arranged.

Germany experienced some larger-scale feuds, but even when princely forces were involved, hostilities often petered out without result, perhaps for lack of pay or because mercenary captains did not want to hurt friends or kinsmen hired by the other side. Even where armed forces were better disciplined and organised, like those of the Count of Württemberg, they were quite small.

Central and western Germany was a land of many small lordships and uncertain frontiers. The sharing of territories between heirs or pledging bits to raise cash kept the kaleidoscope turning. It was not in the interests of towns or princes to start fighting, and it is not surprising that arbitrations were an ev-

eryday occurrence, placed by agreement in the hands of reputable assessors. On a larger scale pacts were periodically drawn up by groups of magnates to keep the public peace and suppress certain categories of violence over whole provinces. For defined periods these treaties of 'provincial peace' might safeguard families in villages and folk going about their lawful business.

There were many little mechanisms to control anarchy. If merchants grumbled at tolls, they were also protected by armed escorts on the move and by fortifications around their towns and markets. At Rothenburg-ob-der-Tauber the tourist on the ramparts can still see how the Shepherds' church formed part of the outworks. Round Nuremberg too, the weir-houses on the river made famous in Dürer's pictures could serve as holiday homes for rich burghers who had nonetheless to keep them in good order as garrison points.

It is easy to be patronising about a country so deficient in central government in an age when the judges of Valois, Plantagenet and Tudor were serving their monarchies well enough. But in the German lands too, writing and discussion helped to control and record violence. Without this skill and will the contents of houses and churches could not have survived, and the incessant journeys of civilised men could not have taken place.

Written German was not merely a means of handling conflict. It was a basic medium in creating German identity, from the government of the great dynasts down to village regulation and the contracts between patrons and artists.

At the summit of political life the Emperor Charles IV (1347–78) must be remembered for his leadership in the arts of peaceful government. He saw it as a family concern—he was a member of the House of Luxemburg, brought up in France but ruling later from Prague in Bohemia (acquired by marriage)—yet it was pre-eminently Germany he helped to shape. He employed a brilliant German Chancellor, Johann von Neumarkt—and a highly literate staff recruited mainly from western Germany, who set the standard for government in the German language. Lower down the scale we see ordinary local officers reporting to their princely masters in the German language even while they continued to write the address formally in Latin. In the same epoch many towns were developing writing-offices where literate laymen ran their administrations in German, worked sometimes on a local chronicle in their spare time, were able to move jobs to another town, and always taught their juniors good German.

A mass of German writing therefore survives from the late Middle Ages, from the worlds of work and recreation, and it opens to us a much wider vista than that of aristocratic courts with their chivalric literature. We are aware of Germans talking and writing to each other in deep countrysides and crowded towns. In rural areas landlords were sending out agents armed with pens to question and argue with villagers about their customary conditions of work and rent, and they wrote down what they thought was agreed. There are thousands of these documents (the Germans called them *Weistümer*). Peasants did not much like educated men writing down their 'good, old customs': to define a right is often to limit freedom. But the German countryman was not easily cowed, and his freedoms of hunting and woodcutting remained embedded in his mind as a natural right.

Germany was also a merchant society. A network of routes spread over the homelands and far beyond their frontiers of land and sea. Fleets of cargo ships like the *Jesus of Lübeck* and hundreds of pack-convoys were despatched by the city entrepreneurs and manned by their young employees. The best-known of these networks is the Hanseatic League. It was an ever-renewed business partnership between a line of Baltic ports: Danzig, Rostock, Lübeck and Hamburg lay at the centre of the axis, but sea and land routes connected them deeply into Russia as far as Novgorod and Smolensk, southward over central Germany, and far westward, especially to the cloth-sellers in England. One of their warehouses can still be seen in King's Lynn, although it was not as important as the 'Steelyard' (under modern Cannon Street) where Holbein painted the rich Danzig merchant Georg Gisze (1532) in the act of opening a letter and surrounded with office equipment.

Men like this had wide horizons. Sent in their youth from their native German cities they could become good mixers and good learners abroad. In London they liked to have a German priest who could hear confessions, yet it was also possible for a Hanseatic German to become a naturalised Englishman and a dignified Londoner. There were also the south European networks, with Venice as an even more notable depot than London. German companies were active in Hungary, Poland and beyond, up the Danube westward or spreading outward from Augsburg. The immigrant clothier family of Fugger became, as everyone knows, financiers to emperors.

In a different way, we can come close to people by knowing what they liked to read for pleasure. Chivalric epic appealed to some—schoolmasters as well as fine ladies—but there was a wide market for fantastic romances, mostly derived from French or German sources, which were multiplied with the advent of printing. These are sometimes called 'people's books' *(Volksbücher)* and appealed to the imagination. One of them, *The Beautiful Melusina,* was about a mermaid who told her love-lorn husband not to seek her out on Saturdays, but he did so, and found her swishing her fish's tail in the bath, whereupon she vanished again forever into the sea. There is a much-used paper manuscript of this tale, illustrated with lively ink drawings of daily life about 1456, now in the German National Museum at Nuremberg.

Germans also liked more serious books about the ups and downs of human fortune. *The Mirror of Human Life* reviewed different trades and callings in both joyful and gloomy light, illustrating them with woodcuts connected by a short running text. Heaven and Hell were popular with readers too, and the secular books were matched by *The Mirror of Human Salvation* and by so-called Poor Men's Bibles *(Biblia Pauperum)* in which scenes from the New Testament were printed against parallel stories from the Old Testament, rounded off by depictions of the last Judgment. Intended as aids to poor clergy in their preaching, they strike a modern reader as heavy with a moral teaching inspired by fear rather than joy.

Books are the product of towns, and it was the towns that impressed upon Germany her lasting identity. They did this especially by stimulating the writing of their own chronicles. Far more often than in England and France, townsmen in Germany were moved to describe and glorify their own communities, to express horror at an outside world which seemed full of enemies, and above all to commemorate their leading families.

One of the best-known is the *Nuremberg World Chronicle* by Hartman Schedel, printed in both Latin and German in 1493 and embellished with woodcuts 'for the common delight'. It presents the reader with scenes of towers and roofs, regarded as the centre of the world: it was the world in which Dürer grew up. In fact the literate German world extended all over central Europe. There are scores of earlier, manuscript annals, some illustrated with painted scenes, from Cologne in the west to Magdeburg in the east, Lübeck in the north and Switzerland (still part of the 'German lands') in the south. Their compilers were mostly laymen employed in writing offices, and they display an intense love of their own territory but often the vaguest of notions about the world beyond their own horizons and before their own time.

Within these towns life was ruled by the great burgher families who grew rich by trading and manufacturing. We might call them patricians, but they actually called themselves the Families (*Geschlechter* or *Dynasten*) and habitually described themselves as the 'best' and the 'wisest' among their large working populations. It was for them that chronicles were written. The 'common delight' meant theirs. Their intense self-preoccupation is shown well by the earliest Nuremberg history-book. It was begun in 1360 by Ulman Stromer who called it his 'little book of my family and of adventures', and as he wrote down what he had heard and experienced he was clearly thinking of his ancestors and their successful descendants down to his own day.

Stromer's knowledge went back to a thirteenth-century knight, Gerhard von Reichenbach, whose castle was not far from Nuremberg and whose son, Conrad, married a Nuremberg girl. Her father was an official in the imperial forests which encircled Nuremberg. But like so many mothers she died young, and Conrad made two subsequent marriages and fathered thirty-three children. In this way Ulman Stromer had a ready-made audience for his family memoirs. There were other families like this, such as the Tuchers of Nuremberg, and they formed the nuclei of the industrious and increasingly articulate country which was beginning to consolidate in description from *deutsche lande* into *Deutschland*.

A different aspect of German imagination is shown in the carnivals that were mounted at the beginning of Lent. They took place in various big cities, but texts and drawings of the proceedings from Nuremberg have been specially studied.

To this day the Carnival is an occasion when otherwise solemn citizens may feel able to let themselves go in displays of public humour. But it could also be a release for the fears and jokes of the day. If we look closely at the programme—but with caution about making easy generalisations—we may see things which worried the people of Nuremberg.

The day began with a wild run through the city by young men in masks and bright costumes, who capered about collecting 'donations' from Jews and brothel-keepers. During the day special carnival plays were acted in various inns, and festivities ended with the burning of a huge float, symbolising Hell, in the market-place. The fire was a sort of catharsis, clearing away the evil anxieties; the nature of these anxieties is described in detail in the texts of the plays.

One of the more popular of these plays in the late fifteenth century was *The Grand Turk* which referred to the Turkish advance and the fall of Constantinople in 1453. The Sultan meets city councillors who address him with respect and complain that the Christian princes cannot keep order and protect merchants and peasants. The townsmen saw this Muslim as a possible peace-keeper, even though the German nobles object to this role in the hands of a 'pagan'. But the Sultan is allowed to speak of the evil-living Christian lands. It is not really an ecumenical play at all, as the town chronicles show well enough how little was understood about the religion and geography of the east. Rather it is a bitter commentary on the social divisions in Germany, especially between towns and nobles.

Other carnival plays tell similar hostile stories about peasants, Jews and the papal court. Peasants are depicted as lustful and gluttonous: townsmen were becoming alarmed about immigration from the countryside. The Jews were given the more dignified medium in the carnival of a dispute between a rabbi and a priest, which of course the priest was made to win. But again, the theology seems a cloak for economic and social tensions. It is interesting that the Jews flourished best on German land where their skills were gladly employed by princes like the Duke of Cleves and the Prince-Archbishop of Trier.

Then there was the carnival play of *The Pope, Cardinals and Bishops,* and once again this is less about religion than about the financial fleecing of decent Germans,—the 'true poor'. We are reminded that the German church hierarchy was extremely aristocratic: a great proportion of bishops and abbots were noblemen and acted as such. It is hard not to see some connection between the Lutheran Christ who alone pays the debts which men cannot pay and a people who had been led to confuse their temporal and spiritual obligations.

In this 'town mentality' which was shaping German identity it is easy enough to point to the fears and hatreds which nourished the patricians' sense of solidarity, but it is also easy to overlook the obvious truth that it was a woman's world too. Not that women formed a coherent group, for they were just as divided as their brothers according to wealth and status. But the activities that were recorded were mostly men's activities. To perceive the feminine vitality of the times we must use our imaginations aided by the many images of women drawn by Dürer and carved by his contemporaries, and the sermons of great preachers like Eckhardt, who attracted many women to their congregations.

Writing about a man's world the historian has perforce to pay attention to the work of men like the leading merchants and artists. The records are there and teach the central lesson; that the German world was a city and inter-city network of entrepreneurial families. The Stromers of Nuremberg were early industrialists as well as merchants and citizens. When he began his chronicle, Ulman was busy buying coal and iron in western Germany and running metal works in his own city where the machinery was powered by the River Pegnitz. At the same time his family firm was doing business in Spain, Italy, Poland and even Russia. They were well placed to take advantage of both war and peace.

The wars and feuds in which both Nuremberg and her friendly emperor were involved called urgently for organisation, and this meant good communications and administration, in a word, paper-work, and this is exactly what the Stromers and their partners did. Parchment was clumsy and expensive, but paper had to be imported, especially from Italy. At royal request the firm of Stromer stole technical secrets from northern Italy, and as a consequence the first German paper-mill was set going in about 1390 on the river outside Nuremberg where sword-blades were already being forged by water-power. Other paper works soon followed in central and western Germany.

Technical and commercial skills and family connections all flourished together, and although individual cities were intensely proud of themselves, their leading families were often in business touch with friends who lived in other German towns. For example, Strassburg also became a paper-making town, and it was there that John Gütenberg's early work on printing with movable type may have begun, at a time when he lived there as a refugee from the problems in Mainz. Back in Mainz, however, he set up presses and installed them in the house of a family called Zum Jungen. These were friends of the Stromers. In due course (1455) Gütenberg went bankrupt and some of his stock after he was sold up found its way to Bamberg, just north of Nuremberg; and it was at Bamberg that Albert Pfister was working as the first printer to illustrate his books with pictures. In such ways the German world of communications developed and revolved round important civic families,—manufacturers, inventors, merchants, financiers and writers of their own histories.

The often despised late Middle Ages was an epoch of great vitality in the German-speaking lands, but despite fears and ignorance about much of the outside world shown in the town chronicles, the German merchants were neither isolationist nor self-satisfied. They had the courage and the curiosity to travel and learn, in France and the Netherlands of course, but above all in Italy. That world beyond the Alps which had lured German armies to their downfall for centuries now yielded treasures of the hand and spirit to make Germany an Aladdin's cave of civilisation.

We may end by glancing at some creators of these treasures in the visual arts. Their achievements were built on older skills, sometimes from abroad, and nourished by church patronage, but they attain heights of genius from the later fifteenth century, as independent masters in their workshops catered more for individual lay patrons and developed a more specifically German style. Their work is often to be seen in the great city churches like St Lawrence, Nuremberg, but independently of the enclosing structure and clearly ascribed to the funding patron.

One such artist was Veit Stoss who worked for a time in the great ecclesiastical and artistic city of Cracow in Poland, but who will be unforgettably known to Nuremberg visitors for his painted carving of the Annunciation of the Rosary that hangs high over the nave of St Lawrence's. It commemorates the patrician Tucher, who in 1517 ordered a special lime tree to be felled in the nearby forest for its carving.

The artists were travellers. On one visit to the Whitsun fair at Nördlingen Stoss was told to move his pitch from one church porch to another. Tilman Riemenschneider also journeyed within German-speaking lands although his prosperity flourished especially in Würzburg, rich in his stone and limewood carving. One of his sons was a pupil of Dürer in painting. In the work of both Stoss and Riemenschneider there is a mixture of sweetness and luxuriance as the wooden draperies fold and fall and the intense or hooded eyes are set amidst ringlets and great beards.

Adam Kraft worked only in stone, and he too dominates the Lorenzkirche in Nuremberg with his painted sandstone tabernacle on which he carved himself and his assistants supporting the structure on their shoulders and holding the tools of their trade. Made during the 1490s it was given by the prominent councillor, Hans Imhoff the Elder.

Hans Leinberger, another professional south German wood-carver, impresses the viewer by his combination of delicate skill and brutal realism. His scenes from the martyrdom of St Castulus by Diocletian are created with fine formal composition of figures against subtly chisel-textured backgrounds, and display meticulously thought-out torments, down to the rope thongs carved in limewood holding the crucified body. Once they hung in the Bavarian church of Moosburg to be seen by pilgrims. But by 1600 they had fallen out of favour with both Protestants and Catholics.

In the end, the admirer of the German Renaissance, age of creation and not just re-birth, must come back to Albrecht Dürer (1471–1528), for his prolific versatility in cutting, etching, drawing and painting, and for his ability to revivify his Gothic genius with graces inspired by Bellini and Mantegna. It is worth comparing his Nuremberg and Venetian girls. But in the present context Dürer is special because he brings to the German scene some of the same experiences and gifts as Martin Luther, with whom this article began. Both visited Italy with transforming, though different, effects. Both used a common language of German people with tongue and hand. Friendly with the great who protected and paid them, they were able to observe the poor with love. Luther watched them as they spoke, and Dürer drew peasants, and especially his mother in old age, with a penetrating understanding.

Dürer did not follow Luther out of the Catholic Church but they shared a melancholy and also an ability to solace it through artistic expression. For Luther wrote of music as the only art other than theology which could give a quiet and happy mind, and Dürer said in 1520 that Luther had saved him from 'those terrible fits of depression' which he had sometime sought to purge in the features of suffering faces.

Nuremberg has occupied a leading place in this article because it lay at the heart of Germany, both in its geographical position and in the achievements of its citizens. Its artists or merchants who set off for the Netherlands or Lübeck, Cracow or Italy, had roughly similar distances to travel. It was a centre, and knew itself to be such. One of the earliest printed maps on which roads are marked was made in Nuremberg in about 1492 and shows the whole of central Europe with South at the top of the sheet and Nuremberg in the middle. It was a guidemap for pilgrims to Rome and is labelled, in the German of the day, 'This is the Rome route, mile by mile with the points indicated from one town to another through German land'. There is a copy in the British Museum and another in the American National Gallery of Art in Washington.

German identity was deeply affected by the Roman connection, both through attraction and repulsion. The indulgences of the Holy Year 1500 (for which the maps may have been produced), could be earned by those unable to travel, in Nuremberg churches. The journey made by some with piety gave shattering scandal to others, as the world knows. So the German lands were divided and have remained so, in religion and style, over the centuries. Yet their diversity may now more happily be called pluralism, and exists within a broad identity of speech and spirit over the geographical space already indicated in the map of 1492.

FOR FURTHER READING:

Michael Baxandall, *The Limewood Sculptors of Renaissance Germany,* (New Haven and London, 1980); Marcel Brion, *Dürer, his life and work,* Engl. transl. (London 1960); A. G. Dickens, *The German Nation and Martin Luther,* (London 1974); F. R. H. Du Boulay, *Germany in the Later Middle Ages,* (London 1983); E. G. Rupp and B. Drewery, *Martin Luther,* Open University Set Book, (London 1970); Gerald Strauss, *Nuremberg in the Sixteenth Century,* (New York 1966).

Explaining John Calvin

John Calvin (1509–64) has been credited, or blamed, for much that defines the modern Western world: capitalism and the work ethic, individualism and utilitarianism, modern science, and, at least among some devout Christians, a lingering suspicion of earthly pleasures. During the most recent American presidential campaign, the two candidates appealed to "values" that recall the teachings of the 16th-century churchman, indicating that what William Pitt once said of England—"We have a Calvinist creed"—still may hold partly true for the United States. But the legend of the joyless tyrant of Geneva obscures both the real man, a humanist as much as a religious reformer, and the subtlety of his thought. Here his biographer discusses both.

William J. Bouwsma

William J. Bouwsma, 65, is Sather Professor of History at the University of California, Berkeley. Born in Ann Arbor, Michigan, he received an A.B. (1943), an M.A. (1947), and a Ph.D. (1950) from Harvard. He is the author of, among other books, Venice and the Defense of Republican Liberty *(1968) and* John Calvin: A Sixteenth-Century Portrait *(1988).*

Our image of John Calvin is largely the creation of austere Protestant churchmen who lived during the 17th century, the century following that of the great reformer's life. The image is most accurately evoked by the huge icon of Calvin, familiar to many a tourist, that stands behind the University of Geneva. There looms Calvin, twice as large as life, stylized beyond recognition, stony, rigid, immobile, and—except for his slightly abstracted disapproval of whatever we might imagine him to be contemplating—impassive.

Happily, the historical record provides good evidence for a Calvin very different from the figure invoked by his 17th-century followers. This Calvin is very much a man of the 16th century, a time of religious strife and social upheaval. His life and work reflect the ambiguities, contradictions, and agonies of that troubled time. Sixteenth-century thinkers, especially in Northern Europe, were still grappling with the rich but incoherent legacy of the Renaissance, and their characteristic intellectual constructions were less successful in reconciling its contradictory impulses than in balancing among them. This is why it has proved so difficult to pigeon-hole such figures as Erasmus and Machiavelli or Montaigne and Shakespeare, and why they continue to stimulate reflection. Calvin, who can be quoted on both sides of most questions, belongs in this great company.

Born in 1509 in Noyon, Calvin was brought up to be a devout French Catholic. Indeed, his father, a lay administrator in the service of the local bishop, sent him to the University of Paris in 1523 to study for the priesthood. Later he decided that young John should be a lawyer. Accordingly, from 1528 to 1533, Calvin studied law. During these years he was also exposed to the evangelical humanism of Erasmus and Jacques Lefèvre d'Étaples that nourished the radical student movement of the time. The students called for salvation by grace rather than by good works and ceremonies—a position fully compatible with Catholic orthodoxy—as the foundation for a general reform of church and society on the model of antiquity.

To accomplish this end, the radical students advocated a return to the Bible, studied in its original languages. Calvin himself studied Greek and Hebrew as well as Latin, the "three languages" of ancient Christian discourse. His growing interest in the classics led, moreover, to his first publication, a moralizing commentary on Seneca's essay on clemency.

Late in 1533, the French government of Francis I became less tolerant of the Paris student radicals, whom it saw as a threat to the peace. After helping to prepare a statement of the theological implications of the movement in a public address delivered by Nicolas Cop, rector of the University, Calvin found it prudent to leave Paris. Eventually he made his way to Basel, a Protestant town tolerant of religious variety.

Up to this point, there is little evidence of Calvin's "conversion" to Protestantism. Before Basel, of course, he had been fully aware of the challenge Martin Luther posed to the Catholic Church. The 95 Theses that the German reformer posted in Wittenberg in 1517 attacked what Luther believed were corruptions of true Christianity and, by implication, the authors of those errors, the Renaissance popes. Luther, above all, rejected the idea of salvation through indulgences or the sacrament of penance. Excommunicated by Pope Leo X, he encouraged the formation of non-Roman churches.

In Basel, Calvin found himself drawing closer to Luther. Probably in part to clarify his own beliefs, he began to write, first a preface to his cousin Pierre Olivétan's French translation of the Bible, and then what became the first edition of the *Institutes,* his masterwork, which in its successive revisions became the single most important statement of Protestant belief. Although he did not substantially change his views thereafter, he elaborated them in later editions, published in both Latin and French, in which he also replied to his critics; the final versions appeared in 1559 and 1560.

The 1536 *Institutes* had brought him some renown among Protestant leaders, among them Guillaume Farel. A French Reformer struggling to plant Protestantism in Geneva, Farel persuaded Calvin to settle there in late 1536. The Reformation was in trouble in Geneva. Indeed, the limited enthusiasm of Geneva for Protestantism—and for religious and moral reform—continued almost until Calvin's death. The resistance was all the more serious because the town council in Geneva, as in other Protestant towns in Switzerland and southern Germany, exercised ultimate control over the church and the ministers.

The main issue was the right of excommunication, which the ministers regarded as essential to their authority but which the town council refused to concede. The uncompromising attitudes of Calvin and Farel finally resulted in their expulsion from Geneva in May of 1538.

Calvin found refuge for the next three years in Protestant Strasbourg, where he was pastor of a church for French-speaking refugees. Here he married Idelette de Bure, a widow in his congregation. Theirs proved to be an extremely warm relationship, although none of their children survived infancy.

During his Strasbourg years, Calvin learned much about church administration from Martin Bucer, chief pastor there. Attending European religious conferences, he soon became a major figure in the international Protestant movement.

Meanwhile, without strong leadership, the Protestant revolution in Geneva foundered. In September of 1541, Calvin was invited back, and there he remained until his death in 1564. He was now in a stronger position. In November the town council enacted his *Ecclesiastical Ordinances,* which provided for the religious education of the townspeople, especially children, and instituted his conception of church order. It established four groups of church officers and a "consistory" of pastors and elders to bring every aspect of Genevan life under the precepts of God's law.

The activities of the consistory gave substance to the legend of Geneva as a joyless theocracy, intolerant of looseness or pleasure. Under Calvin's leadership, it undertook a range of disciplinary actions covering everything from the abolition of Catholic "superstition" to the enforcement of sexual morality, the regulation of taverns, and measures against dancing, gambling, and swearing. These "Calvinist" measures were resented by many townsfolk, as was the arrival of increasing numbers of French Protestant refugees.

The resulting tensions, as well as the persecution of Calvin's followers in France, help to explain the trial and burning of one of Calvin's leading opponents, Michael Servetus. Calvin felt the need to show that his zeal for orthodoxy was no less than that of his foes. The confrontation between Calvin and his enemies in Geneva was finally resolved in May of 1555, when Calvin's opponents overreached themselves and the tide turned in his favor. His position in Geneva was henceforth reasonably secure.

But Calvin was no less occupied. He had to watch the European scene and keep his Protestant allies united. At the same time, Calvin never stopped promoting his kind of Protestantism. He welcomed the religious refugees who poured into Geneva, especially during the 1550s, from France, but also from England and Scotland, from Italy, Germany, and the Netherlands, and even from Eastern Europe. He trained many of them as ministers, sent them back to their homelands, and then supported them with letters of encouragement and advice. Geneva thus became the center of an international movement and a model for churches elsewhere. John Knox, the Calvinist leader of Scotland, described Geneva as "the most perfect school of Christ that ever was on the Earth since the days of the Apostles." So while Lutheranism was confined to parts of Germany and Scandinavia, Calvinism spread into Britain, the English-speaking colonies of North America, and many parts of Europe.

Academic efforts to explain the appeal of Calvinism in terms of social class have had only limited success. In France, his theology was attractive mainly to a minority among the nobility and the urban upper classes, but in Germany it found adherents among both townsmen and princes. In England and the Netherlands, it made converts in every social group. Calvinism's appeal lay in its ability to explain disorders of the age afflicting all classes and in the remedies and comfort it provided, as much by its activism as by its doctrine. Both depended on the personality, preoccupations, and talents of Calvin himself.

Unlike Martin Luther, Calvin was a reticent man. He rarely expressed himself in the first person singular. This reticence has contributed to his reputation as cold and unapproachable. Those who knew him, however, noted his talent for friendship as well as his hot temper. The intensity of his grief on the death of his wife in 1549 revealed a large capacity for feeling, as did his empathetic reading of many passages in Scripture.

In fact, the impersonality of Calvin's teachings concealed an anxiety, unusually intense even in an anxious age. He saw anxiety everywhere, in himself, in the narratives of the Bible, and in his contemporaries. This feeling found expression in two of his favorite images for spiritual discomfort: the abyss and the labyrinth. The abyss represented all the nameless terrors of disorientation and the absence of familiar boundaries. The labyrinth expressed the anxiety of entrapment: in religious terms, the inability of human beings alienated from God to escape from the imprisonment of self-concern.

One side of Calvin sought to relieve his terror of the abyss with cultural constructions and patterns of control that might help him recover his sense of direction. This side of Calvin was attracted to classical philosophy, which nevertheless conjured up for him fears of entrapment in a labyrinth. Escape from this, however, exposed him to terrible uncertainties and, once again, to the horrors of the abyss. Calvin's ideas thus tended to oscillate between those of freedom and order. His problem was to strike a balance between the two.

He did so primarily with the resources of Renaissance humanism, applying its philological approach to recover a biblical understanding of Christianity. But humanism was not only, or even fundamentally, a scholarly movement. Its scholarship was instrumental to the recovery of the communicative skills of classical rhetoric. Humanists such as Lorenzo Valla and Erasmus held that an effective rhetoric would appeal to a deeper level of the personality than would a mere rational demonstration. By moving the heart, Christian rhetoric would stimulate human beings to the active reform of both themselves and the world.

Theological system-building, Calvin believed, was futile and inappropriate. He faulted the medieval Scholastic theologians for relying more on human reason than on the Bible, which spoke uniquely to the heart. The teachings of Thomas Aquinas, and like-minded theologians, appealed only to the intellect, and so were lifeless and irrelevant to a world in desperate need.

As a humanist, Calvin was a *biblical* theologian, prepared to follow Scripture even when it surpassed the limits of human understanding. And its message, for him, could not be presented as a set of timeless abstractions; it had to be adapted to the understanding of contemporaries according to the rhetorical principle of decorum—i.e. suitability to time, place, and audience.

Calvin shared with earlier humanists an essentially biblical conception of the human personality, not as a hierarchy of faculties ruled by reason but as a mysterious unity. This concept made the feelings and will even more important aspects of the personality than the intellect, and it also gave the body new dignity.

Indeed, Calvin largely rejected the traditional belief in hierarchy as the general principle of all order. For it he substituted the practical (rather than the metaphysical) principle of *utility*. This position found expression in his preference, among the possible forms of government, for republics. It also undermined, for him, the traditional subordination of women to men. Calvin's Geneva accordingly insisted on a single standard of sexual morality—a radical departure from custom.

Calvin's utilitarianism was also reflected in deep reservations about the capacity of human beings to attain anything but practical knowledge. The notion that they can know anything absolutely, as God knows it, so to speak, seemed to him deeply presumptuous. This helps to explain his reliance on the Bible: Human beings have access to the saving truths of religion only insofar as God has revealed them in Scripture. But revealed truth, for Calvin, was not revealed to satisfy human curiosity; it too was limited to meeting the most urgent and practical needs, above all for individual salvation. This practicality also reflects a basic conviction of Renaissance thinkers: the superiority of an active life to one of contemplation. Calvin's conviction that every occupation in society is a "calling" on the part of God himself sanctified this conception.

But Calvin was not only a Renaissance humanist. The culture of 16th-century Europe was peculiarly eclectic. Like other thinkers of his time, Calvin had inherited a set of quite contrary tendencies that he uneasily combined with his humanism. Thus, even as he emphasized the heart, Calvin continued to conceive of the human personality as a hierarchy of faculties ruled by reason; from time to time he tried uneasily, with little success, to reconcile the two conceptions. This is why he sometimes emphasized the importance of rational control over the passions—an emphasis that has been reassuring to conservatives.

Calvin's theology has often been seen as little more than a systematization of the more creative insights of Luther. He followed Luther, indeed, on many points: on original sin, on Scripture, on the absolute dependence of human beings on divine grace, and on justification by faith alone. Other differences between Calvin and Luther are largely matters of emphasis. His understanding of predestination, contrary to a general impression, was virtually identical to Luther's; it was not of central importance to his theology. He believed that it meant that the salvation of believers by a loving God was absolutely certain.

In major respects, however, Calvin departed from Luther. In some ways he was more radical, but most of his differences suggest that he was closer to Catholicism than Luther, as in his insistence on the importance of the historical church. He was also more traditional in his belief in the authority of clergy over laity, perhaps as a result of his difficulties with the Geneva town council. Even more significant, especially for Calvinism as a historical force, was Calvin's attitude toward the everyday world. Luther had regarded this world and its institutions as incorrigible, and was prepared to leave them to the devil. But for Calvin this world, created by God, still belonged to Him; it remained potentially His kingdom; and every Christian was obliged to devote his life to make it so in reality by reforming and bringing it under God's law.

Calvin's thought was less a theology to be comprehended by the mind than a set of principles for the Christian life: in short, spirituality. He was more concerned with the experience and application of Christianity than with mere reflection about it. His true successors were Calvinist pastors rather than Calvinist theologians. Significantly, in addition to devoting much of his energy to the training of other pastors, Calvin was himself a pastor. He preached regularly: some 4,000 sermons in the 13 years after his return to Geneva.

Calvin's spirituality begins with the conviction that we do not so much "know" God as "experience" him indirectly, through his mighty acts and works in the world, as we experience but can hardly be said to know thunder, one of Calvin's favorite metaphors for religious experience. Calvin also believed that human beings can understand something of what God is like in the love of a father for his children, but also—surprisingly in one often identified with patriarchy—in the love of a mother. He denounced those who represented God as dreadful; God for him is "mild, kind, gentle, and compassionate."

Nevertheless, in spite of this attention to God's love for mankind, Calvin gave particular emphasis to God's power because it was this that finally made his love effective in the work of redemption from sin. God, for Calvin, represented supremely all the ways in which human beings experience power: as energy, as warmth, as vitality, and, so, as life itself.

Sin, by contrast, is manifested precisely in the negation of every kind of power and ultimately of the life force given by God. Sin *deadens* and, above all, deadens the feelings. Saving grace, then, must be conceived as the transfusion of God's power—his warmth, passion, strength, vitality—to human beings. It was also essential to Calvin's spirituality, and a reflection of his realism, that this "transfusion" be not instantaneous but gradual.

Calvin's traditional metaphor for the good Christian life implied activity: "Our life is like a journey," he asserted, but "it is not God's will that we should march along casually as we please, but he sets the goal before us, and also directs us on the right way to it." This way is also a struggle.

Complex as his ideas were, it is easy to see how the later history of Calvinism has often been obscured by scholars' failure to distinguish among (1) Calvinism as the beliefs of Calvin himself, (2) the beliefs of his followers, who, though striving to be faithful to Calvin, modified his teachings to meet their own needs, and (3) more loosely, the beliefs of the Reformed tradition of Protestant Christianity, in which Calvinism proper was only one, albeit the most prominent, strand.

The Reformed churches in the 16th century were referred to in the plural to indicate, along with what they had in common, their individual autonomy and variety. They consisted originally of a group of non-Lutheran Protestant churches based in towns in Switzerland and southern Germany. These churches were jealous of their autonomy; and Geneva was not alone among them in having distinguished theological leadership. Ulrich Zwingli and Heinrich Bullinger in Zurich and Martin Bucer in Strasbourg also had a European influence that combined with that of Calvin, especially in England, to shape what came to be called "Calvinism."

Long after Calvin's death in 1564, the churchmen in Geneva continued to venerate him and aimed at being faithful to his teaching under his successors, first among them Theodore de Bèze. But during what can be appropriately described as a Protestant "Counter Reformation," the later Calvinism of Geneva, abandoning Calvin's more humanistic tendencies and drawing more on other, sterner aspects of his thought, was increasingly intellectualized. Indeed, it grew to resemble the medieval Scholasticism that Calvin had abhorred.

Predestination now began to assume an importance that had not been attributed to it before. Whereas Calvin had been led by personal faith to an awed belief in predestination as a benign manifestation of divine providence, predestination now became a threatening doctrine: God's decree determined in advance an individual's salvation or dam-

nation. What good, one might wonder, were one's own best efforts if God had already ruled? In 1619 these tendencies reached a climax at the Synod of Dort in the Netherlands, which spelled out various corollaries of predestination, as Calvin had never done, and made the doctrine central to Calvinism.

Calvinist theologians, meanwhile, apparently finding Calvin's loose rhetorical style of expression unsatisfactory, began deliberately to write like Scholastic theologians, in Latin, and even appealed to medieval Scholastic authorities. The major Calvinist theological statement of the 17th century was the *Institutio Theologiae Elencticae* (3 vols., Geneva, 1688) of François Turretin, chief pastor of Geneva. Although the title of this work recalled Calvin's masterpiece, it was published in Latin, its dialectical structure followed the model of the great *Summas* of Thomas Aquinas, and it suggested at least as much confidence as Thomas in the value of human reason. The lasting effect of this shift is suggested by the fact that "Turretin," in Latin, was the basic theology textbook at the Princeton Seminary in New Jersey, the most distinguished intellectual center of American Calvinism until the middle of the 19th century.

Historians have continued to debate whether these developments were essentially faithful to Calvin or deviations from him. In some sense they were both. Later Calvinist theologians, as they abandoned Calvin's more humanistic tendencies and emphasized his more austere and dogmatic side, found precedents for these changes in the contrary aspects of his thought. They were untrue to Calvin, of course, in rejecting his typically Renaissance concern with balancing contrary impulses. One must remember, however, that these changes in Calvinism occurred during a period of singular disorder in Europe, caused by, among other things, a century of religious warfare. As a result, there was a widespread longing for certainty, security, and peace.

One or another aspect of Calvin's influence has persisted not only in the Reformed churches of France, Germany, Scotland, the Netherlands, and Hungary but also in the Church of England, where he was long as highly regarded as he was by Puritans who had separated from the Anglican establishment. The latter organized their own churches, Presbyterian

or Congregational, and brought Calvinism to North America 300 years ago.

Even today these churches, along with the originally German Evangelical and Reformed Church, remember Calvin—that is, the strict Calvin of Geneva—as their founding father. Eventually Calvinist theology was also widely accepted by major groups of American Baptists; and even Unitarianism, which broke away from the Calvinist churches of New England during the 18th century, reflected the more rational impulses in Calvin's theology. More recently, Protestant interest in the social implications of the Gospel and Protestant Neo-Orthodoxy, as represented by Karl Barth and Reinhold Niebuhr, reflect the continuing influence of John Calvin.

Calvin's larger influence over the development of modern Western civilization has been variously assessed. The controversial "Weber thesis" attributed the rise of modern capitalism largely to habits encouraged by Puritanism, but Max Weber (1864–1920) avoided implicating Calvin himself. Much the same can be said about efforts to link Calvinism to the rise of early modern science; Puritans were prominent in the scientific movement of 17th-century England, but Calvin himself was indifferent to the science of his own day.

A somewhat better case can be made for Calvin's influence on political theory. His own political instincts were highly conservative, and he preached the submission of private persons to all legitimate authority. But, like Italian humanists of the 15th and 16th centuries, he personally preferred a republic to a monarchy; and in confronting the problem posed by rulers who actively opposed the spread of the Gospel, he advanced a theory of resistance, kept alive by his followers, according to which lesser magistrates might legitimately rebel against kings. And, unlike most of his contemporaries, Calvin included among the proper responsibilities of states not only the maintenance of public order but also a positive concern for the general welfare of society. Calvinism has a place, therefore, in the evolution of liberal political thought. His most durable influence, nevertheless, has been religious. From Calvin's time to the present, Calvinism has meant a peculiar seriousness about Christianity and its ethical implications.

That Others Might Read

Development of the first English-language Bibles was not merely a matter of translating from one tongue to another. Brave and yet controversial faith had to lead the way.

Joseph H. Hall

Few of the Christianity's earliest martyrs could have told a more harrowing tale of persecution than that of a young translator from 16th-century England. Finding a cold reception for his proposed work at home, he betook himself to Germany in hope of finding a more friendly environment. His printer in Cologne had only reached the tenth sheet of William Tyndale's great opus, however, when a powerful German enemy discovered what they were doing.

Tyndale and his assistant, William Roye, hurriedly gathered some of the printed sheets and fled up the Rhine River, to Worms. More of the work was printed there, but various authorities did their best to suppress the printings. Some were smuggled into England, like contraband. Tyndale, in the meantime, lost a significant part of his further translation in a shipwreck off the coast of Holland.

Still, he perservered; he would not give up his life's work. Settling for the moment at Antwerp, he remained in exile from his homeland. The King of England (Henry VIII), in fact, was demanding his forcible return. Tyndale allegedly was spreading sedition in England. Tyndale left Antwerp for two years.

Upon his return, however, he was arrested. He was imprisoned in a castle, and while there may have done his last translating work. He was tried for heresy and condemned. On October 6, 1536, he was bound to a stake, and strangled. His body was then burned.

And the controversial work for which William Tyndale gave his life? It was his translation of the Bible into his native tongue—English.

The fact is, the Bible had not—until Tyndale—been accessible to the ordinary English-speaking Christian. For centuries, churches in England and the Scottish Lowlands—or churches anywhere in Western Europe, for that matter—had echoed the fifth-century Latin of Jerome's Vulgate, the official Bible of the Western Church. Even though few Christians knew Latin, the situation wasn't considered strange or needing remedy. If the laity wanted to know what was in the Bible, simplified rhyming Bibles or story Bibles retold the more famous tales from the Old Testament, New Testament and Apocrypha. Even when some of the languages of Europe began developing their own vernacular literature, Bible translations into French, German or Dutch did not supplant the Latin Vulgate in the churches of those lands. At best, these pre-Reformation translations were for the private edification of a few literate laymen.

Reforming movements of the late Middle Ages and the Reformation itself gave impetus to the spread of the translated Bible. Indeed, the Bible in the vernacular languages—to be read and applied by ordinary Christians and to be used in the public worship of the churches—became one of the major weapons and hallmarks of the Protestant Reformation. This was true in the Germany of Martin Luther, the Switzerland of Ulrich Zwingli and the Geneva of John Calvin. Within 50 years of Luther's death in 1546, most of the languages of Western Europe would possess complete translations of the Bible.

In England, interest in religious reform also manifested itself in demands for an English-language Bible, not only in the 16th century, but even earlier.

The Englishmen John Wycliffe (1330–1384) and William Tyndale (1494–1536) saw that it simply was not enough to have Scripture in Latin, Greek or Hebrew available only to priests and scholars. To these two men, the absence of good preaching could be blamed upon illiterate priests, while the use of Latin in the church was further indication that the common people needed to be able to read the Word of God themselves. They believed that all Christian laymen, like the early Berean Christians mentioned in the Book of Acts, should be able to search the Scriptures to see for themselves if their clergy—including the Pope himself—were teaching in accordance with Biblical teaching. Both Wycliffe and Tyndale believed that each man, woman and child was individually responsible before God and therefore should have the Bible available in a language readily understood. These of course, were controversial stands to take.

Nonetheless, Wycliffe persisted in declaring that all persons, whether priest, knight or peasant, must "carefully study the gospel in that tongue in which the meaning of the gospel [is] clearest to them . . ." Tyndale, in speaking to a dogmatic priest opposed to Tyndale's translation work, clearly borrowed the words of the great Erasmus by declaring, "If God spare my life, I will cause a boy that driveth the plough shall know more of the Scripture than thou dost." These two were determined men, driven by what they considered man's greatest need—to have God's word as the only absolute and complete authority to rule over them.

Before England entered the 14th century, English was the tongue used primarily by commoners, while the nobility preferred French, and scholars used Latin. Only some priests read and wrote in English. The poet and courtier Geoffrey Chaucer, however, broke the clergy's virtual monopoly on English writing and made it available to the nobility and common people. Chaucer provided a standard English into which the Bible could be translated and read by all three estates of traditional society—clergy, nobility and commoners. For the first time since the Norman conquest in 1066, English became the dominant language in England, a vehicle not only for a vigorous young literature, but for a reawakened national pride as well.

Into this milieu stepped an Oxford don whose revolutionary ideas were destined to find root, grow and finally flower as part of the Protestant Reformation. Indeed, he is called the "morningstar of the Reformation." Although John Wycliffe sought to reform the church in many areas, none of his contributions was more far-reaching than his teaching that the Bible is man's final authority and that it must be available to all Englishmen in the language they habitually spoke.

Of Wycliffe's early life we know very little. He was born around 1330 in Yorkshire, a district that came under the lordship of John of Gaunt, Duke of Lancaster, second son of King Edward III. Providentially, the circumstance of John of Gaunt's powerful patronage gave Wycliffe the protection he needed to promulgate his views on Bible-based religious reforms.

Wycliff followed an academic career, first as a philosophy teacher at Oxford. Later he pursued theological studies, becoming a doctor in 1372. He remained at Oxford until 1382, when he was expelled for teaching that "God's law"—the Bible—was to be preached, read and believed if one were to exist in a state of grace.

From Wycliffe's burning desire to see the Bible translated into English, the Wycliffe Bible developed. But was it John Wycliffe's own translation? Some of his contemporaries did ascribe it to him. For example, Archbishop Thomas Arundel, writing to Pope John XXIII in 1411, spoke of Wycliffe's "devising . . . the expedient of a new translation of the Scriptures into the mother tongue." The Bohemian reformer John Huss also considered Wycliffe as the translator. But did he, in fact, translate it? Apparently not, since there were two different translations of the Wycliffe Bible reflecting the work of different translators, neither agreeing with the translations of Biblical texts made in connection with Wycliffe's own sermons. Therefore, we must conclude that Wycliffe was not himself responsible for the actual translation.

At the same time, however, had Wycliffe not vociferously expressed his new idea that the common person must have the Bible in English as his final authority, the medieval Bible version that bears Wycliffe's name would not have been translated. Wycliffe's influence was paramount in motivating the two men largely responsible for the production of the two translations, Nicholas of Hereford and John Purvey.

Nicholas of Hereford, regent master in theology, began to advocate Wycliffite doctrines while a fellow at Queen's College, Oxford. In 1382, however, he preached that an archbishop had been righteously slain in the Peasants' Revolt of the previous year. Excommunicated and condemned by the archbishop of Canterbury, he then journeyed to Rome to petition against the sentence. In 1385, he made his way back to England, where he continued to lead the Lollards—Wycliffe's supporters—until 1391, when he was captured and recanted, becoming as vociferous an enemy of the Lollards as he had been a Wycliffite preacher earlier.

John Purvey (1353–1428) was ordained a priest in 1377 and served Wycliffe as his secretary at Lutterworth, near Oxford. Both fellow Lollards and opponents spoke of Purvey as "doctor." Even the Carmelite Friar Walden, persecutor of the Wycliffites, spoke of Purvey with respect. Like Nicholas, Purvey recanted of his heresy after a period of imprisonment in 1401—during which time the burning of William Sawtrey, another Lollard, might have helped convince him. The last we hear of Purvey is that he was imprisoned once again for Lollard opinions in 1421, and was still alive in 1427. Perhaps he continued as a Lollard for the remainder of his life. In any event, Purvey was widely known as a Bible translator and disseminator of Wycliffe's writings.

Nicholas and Purvey both used as their source a copy of Jerome's Latin Vulgate, the text accepted by the church. While the style of Nicholas is word-for-word and very literal, Purvey's style is both faithful to the original words and more flowing, even conversational.

Nicholas' literal method was intended more for scholars and the learned, whereas Purvey's translation was more popular and became the Bible for the Lollard movement. Originally an educated reforming movement, the Lollards became, after 1410, a lay movement emphasizing Bible reading and a simple Christian lifestyle.

Many Lollard beliefs anticipated later Protestantism. Lollards spoke against the hierarchical system of the church, in which power came to be vested in a handful of bishops. They also criticized the celibacy requirement imposed on clergyman and the church's claim to temporal as well as spiritual power. They disavowed the doctrine of transubstantiation—the belief that the priest changes the bread and wine of the Mass into the actual body and blood of Christ—and the veneration of images. A similar movement, the Waldensians, appeared during the 13th century in southern France and northern Italy, while the Hussite movement in Bohemia appeared shortly after Wycliffe launched the Lollards. The Hussites may even have been a direct offshoot from the Lollards, for numerous Czech students were at Oxford during the years when Wycliffe's movement flourished.

The Lollards suffered numerous shocks and setbacks, especially after John Wycliffe, its founder, died in 1384, and Parliament decreed in 1401 that unrepentant Lollards were liable to death by burning. Nonetheless, they did not completely die out, for there is much evidence of their activities from the 15th century. Early in the 16th century, small groups of Lollards were found in parts of rural England and in the Lowlands of Scotland. These quickly made common cause with Protestantism and were absorbed into the mainstream of British religious life after England and Scotland officially became Protestant. Intended or not, Wycliffe and his cohorts, like Chaucer, had provided stimulating boost to the development of the English language as it is known today.

In the meantime, however, translating the Bible, or even owning a Wycliffe Bible, had become very dangerous. Particularly risky was the ownership of a Bible having marginal explanatory notes that countered the official teaching of the church. Even so the Lollards had continued to own, read and memorize the Wycliffe Bibles, especially those without notes. Since printing had not yet begun in the West, all manuscripts were handwritten and it was not uncommon to find reproduced portions of the Scripture, rather than completely copied Bibles.

More than 100 years would pass before the next English Bible would appear—William Tyndale's New Testament. These intervening years were exciting ones that ushered in printing around 1450, a development eliminating the laborious hand-copying of manuscripts. Less spectacular, but no less important, was the availability of Greek and Hebrew Biblical texts which would demand new vernacular translations. Finally, the Reformation itself climaxed the excitement and brought an unparalleled demand for translations, both on the Continent and in England and Scotland.

During this fresh ferment a man came to the forefront who not only would permanently standardize modern English, as did Luther modern German, but also become the catalyst for the English Reformation. Tyndale, the man whom Sir Thomas More called the "captain of our English hereticks," was born around 1495 in Gloucestershire of hardy yeoman stock. Young William was a precocious child quite able to attend Oxford University, which by that time was already one of the best-known and respected Universities in all of Western Europe. Tyndale entered the University as a teenager, studying there from 1510–1515. Tyndale studied further at Cambridge during this period of great excitement. It is probable he met the great humanist Erasmus who taught briefly at Cambridge. Without doubt, Erasmus's great love of languages, and even his skepticism about certain traditions in the established church, greatly influenced the young Tyndale.

A still greater influence permeated certain quarters around Cambridge—that of Martin Luther. After 1517, materials in the German language were smuggled up the Thames River by the steel merchants and were made available especially to university students. Cambridge became a hotbed of Luther's adherents. Though small in number, a group of Cambridge students meeting at the White-Horse Inn near the university were called "White-Horse Germans." While Tyndale cannot be traced to this group, it is fairly certain that he, too, was affected by the new, "Lutheran heresy."

Leaving the university scene, Tyndale became a tutor in the household of Sir John Walsh at Little Sudbury, near his own home. While preaching nearby, he ran afoul of a local priest whose ignorance Tyndale despised. He resolved at all costs to translate the New Testament, because he had "perceived by experience how that it was impossible to establish the lay people in any truth except the Scripture were plainly laid before their eyes in their mother tongue . . ."

Tyndale moved quickly to legitimize his translation and requested support from the Bishop of London, Cuthbert Tunstall. The Bishop, perhaps recognizing the danger of personal involvement, rejected the plan and advised Tyndale to go elsewhere. The young translator next lodged with a rich cloth merchant, Humphrey Monmouth, member of a group called "Christian Brethren," and trans-

A Royal Commission Produces a Bible

When James VI of Scotland became King of England following the death of Queen Elizabeth in 1603, two translations of the Bible competed in England. One was the Bishops' Bible, used by the clergy of the established church. The other was the Geneva Bible, so named for its publication in Geneva, where many English Protestants had fled during the reign of the Roman Catholic Queen Mary. The Geneva Bible was the version most widely read by the common people of Britain.

The Church of England might have found a way to live with two Bible translations had it not been for the Geneva Bible's association with Puritan demands for a more thorough reform of both church and state. The Geneva Bible also had numerous marginal notes supporting Puritan interpretations, one of which was especially displeasing to King James: At Exodus 1:19, a note suggested that the Hebrew midwives who disobeyed the Pharaoh's command to kill all male Hebrew children at birth were right to disregard and mislead their sovereign.

James, who while King of Scotland had been called "God's silly vassal" to his face, had had enough of Puritan suggestions that rulers could not claim absolute power! As King of both England and Scotland, furthermore, he set in motion the creation of a common version of the English Bible for the whole realm.

By June 1604, the translators of the new version had been selected from the universities and churches of England. Their number included the moderate Puritan John Rainolds, President of Corpus Christi College at Oxford, and the learned Dean of Westminster Cathedral, Lancelot Andrewes, skilled in 15 languages. Another was John Bois, who had read the entire Hebrew Bible by the time he was six years old.

The translators broke up into six companies, each company working on an assigned portion of the Scriptures. The translators' task was to strive for fidelity to the original languages, keep the new translation as much in harmony with previous translations as possible and to avoid all marginal notes save explanations of certain difficult Hebrew and Greek words and cross-references. Each man in a given company would translate the same portion, and then compare his results with the others, after which the company would agree on the best translation for a given text. The actual translation was completed by 1609, but the editing and printing process required another two years.

In the end, the translators produced the Bible translation that has long been recognized as one of the noblest works in English prose ever written. Although all of its translators were in fellowship with the established Church of England, its accuracy caused it to supplant the Geneva Bible among even Presbyterians and Congregationalists by the 1640s. Its place among English-speaking Protestants was secure.

The King James Version was not challenged by a new translation until 1876, when the English Revised Version of the New Testament was published.

Even now, when there are literally hundreds of more modern translations on the market—some of which are on the whole more accurate and all of which are backed by better promotion and advertising—the version authorized by King James VI and I of Scotland and England is still the most widely used English translation.

lated into English *The Handbook of the Christian Soldier* by Erasmus. Generally exposed to the life around London, Tyndale again saw the need for a translation of the Bible into English. But he further saw that London would not be the place to do the work and went abroad.

Leaving England in 1524, Tyndale went first to Hamburg, then most probably traveled up the Elbe River to Wittenberg. He seems to have registered at the University of Wittenberg under a pseudonym, Guillelmus Daltici. Doubtless Tyndale met Martin Luther, professor at Wittenberg, although the translator later vowed to Sir Thomas More that he never became a "confederate of Luther."

At the university library Tyndale had access to all the necessary tools for translating, as well as an excellent facility for acquiring proficiency in German and Hebrew. By the time he left Wittenberg, returning to Hamburg in the spring of 1525, Tyndale must have completed most of his New Testament translation. By August of that year he was ready to publish his work, and he departed for Cologne, believing it to be a good place for publication. No sooner had the printing begun, however, than Tyndale received word that John Cochlaeus, anti-Reformation dean of Frankfurt, was asking the city government to stop the printing. Tyndale hastily secured the few sheets already printed and fled up the Rhine to Worms.

There, his work indeed would be printed—it is altogether fitting that the first printed English New Testament should first appear at Worms, the famous city on the Rhine. There, five years earlier, Martin Luther had made his famous "Here I stand" speech, in which he declared that his conscience was captive only to the Word of God. Unfortunately, of the 3,000 copies of this historic edition of the English Bible printed, only two are known to survive today.

The 1526 Worms edition has both marginal cross references and explanatory comments, many of which were taken from Luther's 1522 German New Testament. The order of the New Testament books also shows Luther's influence. The books of Hebrews, James, Jude and Revelation are placed at the end, completely separated. It is doubtful that Tyndale completely shared Luther's lower view of these four books because in the final, 1534 edition of Tyndale's

translation, he placed these books in line with the other 23.

While Luther's German New Testament of 1522 did influence Tyndale's English translation, as did the Latin Vulgate, the primary source Tyndale used was the third printed edition of Erasmus' Greek New Testament. Unlike Wycliffe before him, interestingly, Tyndale did his own translation rather than use assistants.

Copies of the Worms edition were smuggled into England by merchants interested in reforming the church. Alarmed at their introduction and declaring that he found 3,000 errors in the translation, Tunstall—the very bishop from whom Tyndale earlier requested support—sought to destroy the work. He first burned those he could find in England. He also began a campaign to purchase and destroy the remaining copies from merchants all over the Continent.

When Tyndale was told of Tunstall's plan, he rejoiced: "I am the gladder, for these two benefits shall come thereof: I shall get the money of him for these books, to bring myself out of debt and the whole world shall cry out upon the burning of God's word." With the extra money, Tyndale thought, he could print a revised version much improved over the first.

Despite Tunstall's efforts, Tyndale's New Testament was so popular that others pirated the translation and reprinted it with errors and unauthorized changes.

Not only did Tyndale match wits with the Bishop of London, he also incurred the wrath of the Lord Chancellor of England, second only to Henry VIII, Sir Thomas More. During the spring of 1528, Bishop Tunstall had licensed More to read the works of heretics in order to refute them. More, after reading Tyndale's translation, cataloged what he considered errors and published them in an imaginary dialogue against "hereticks," including what he called the "pestilent sect of Luther and Tyndale."

Thomas More recognized Tyndale's scholarly ability, however, and even recognized that Tyndale followed the famous Erasmus in certain word translations. Tyndale liked "elder" or "senior" for the word *presbuteros,* which had been translated "priest" by the traditional church. Instead of "charity," Tyndale preferred "love." Again, he preferred "repentance" over "penance." More may have felt that the weight of evidence for much of the new translation was in Tyndale's favor, since

More basically accused Tyndale of an heretical theology that must give way to the authority of the Roman Catholic church. After all, said More, the English church was not against mere English translations but rather opposed *unauthorized* English translations. Tyndale's translation could not be tolerated because it was Lutheran and heretical.

Tyndale did not quickly respond to More's charges, but he did write an *Answer* published in 1531, in which he accused More of using his pen for political advantage since More himself had formerly attacked some of the very abuses that Tyndale now attacked. At the very heart of the issue was the doctrine of Scripture as the final authority which alone could lead to a personal faith in Jesus Christ. Therefore, Tyndale was willing to undergo all manner of personal deprivation, even expatriation, in order to continue translating the Bible faithfully from the original Hebrew and Greek languages.

Meanwhile, Tyndale continued translating from the Hebrew and published the first five books of the Old Testament (Pentateuch) in 1530. The Book of Jonah followed, and most probably a contemporary translation of Joshua to 2 Chronicles is attributable to Tyndale, as well. Tyndale translated other portions of the Old Testament to be read as "epistles" in church liturgy.

His Old Testament was far more conversational—one might even say zestier—than John Purvey's. Consider Tyndale's translation of Satan's answer to Eve in the garden, "Tush, ye shall not dye." Or Moses's declaration that "the Lorde was with Joseph and he was a luckie felowe." Or the Pharoah's "jolly captaynes (captains) are drowned in the Red Sea."

The greatest of Tyndale's works, without doubt, is the 1534 revision of the English New Testament, characterized by an utmost fidelity to the Greek text as well as an excellent English style. It became the model for most subsequent English translations of the Bible. One of the interesting differences between the 1534 and 1526 editions is found in Luke 2:3. In the earlier edition, everyone went to his own "shiretown," but in the later version "shiretown," is replaced by "city," as is found in most English translations today. The 1534 edition also replaced the "under captain" of 1526 for a Roman officer with the word "centurion," the original term used and the one which has remained in the English Bible ever since.

The King James and subsequent major English Bibles owe very much, perhaps 70 to 90 percent of their phraseology and wording, to Tyndale's 1534 New Testament. To Tyndale we are indebted for such beautiful phrases as "singing and making melody in your heart to the Lord" (Eph. 5:16) and "in him we live and move and have our being." (Acts 17:28) These were taken from Tyndale by the King James Version, with the addition of the "and" in the latter passage. There are Tyndale translations which the King James has rejected but which later versions have reincorporated. Thus, while the King James Version chose "charity" over Tyndale's "love" in First Corinthians 13, the Revised and other major versions returned to Tyndale's "love." Or, the King James incorporates Purvey's "only begotten son" in John 3:16, whereas the Revised and later versions use Tyndale's "only son." With such examples of reliance upon Tyndale by modern versions, it is not difficult to see how some experts place the total influence of Tyndale upon the King James and other modern versions as high as 90 percent of all usage.

It is certainly no exaggeration to say at Tyndale's translations also are greatly responsible for modern English prose. The development runs from Tyndale through the King James Version, through Milton, Bunyan, and other prose writers, to a more or less standard modern English.

Aside from its great literary value, Tyndale achieved his goal of translating so that the "ploughboy" could indeed read the Bible. His Bible translations were not only the first English Bibles to use the printing press but, more important, the first English translations from the original Greek and Hebrew languages. Moreover, Tyndale's work set in motion efforts to render the entire Bible into English so that all might read them.

His achievement was, of course, very costly to Tyndale personally. As a fugitive "heretick," he was hounded by the authorities in Western Europe and finally was treacherously kidnapped in the free city of Antwerp and conveyed to the fortress castle of Vilvorde, where he was charged with heresy and imprisoned for nearly a year and a half. Meanwhile, Thomas Cromwell, the English Lord Chancellor, did his best to secure Tyndale's release. Even Henry VIII now made some conciliatory efforts, but without success.

One of history's most poignant appeals from a prisoner was made by Tyndale to those in authority over him. He requested warmer clothing and a Hebrew Bible, grammar and dictionary for "study." His letter expressed concern for the salvation of those in authority and showed a patient resignation to God's will.

In October 1536, after having been judged guilty as a heretic, Tyndale was strangled and burned. John Foxe, in his *Book of Martyrs,* tells us that Tyndale cried out at the stake "with a fervent zeal and loud voice, 'Lord, open the King of England's eyes'." Little did Tyndale know that his prayer had been answered before he prayed. Some months before his death, an entire English Bible based largely upon Tyndale's own work was now circulating freely with the king's approval in England.

Credits/ Acknowledgments

Cover design by Charles Vitelli

1. The Earliest Civilizations
Facing overview—WHO photo. 13, 15-16—British Museum. 14—(top) Michael Holford. 14—(bottom) *History Today* Archives.

2. Greece and Rome
Facing overview—Painting found in a tomb at Thebes, *Harper's*. 54, 60—Weidenfeld Archives. 56, 79—*History Today* maps by Ken Wass. 57—*History Today* Archives. 58-59—(top) Weidenfeld Archives. 59—(bottom) Mansell Collection. 71, 73—Mansell Collection. 72—Mansell-Alinari.

3. The Judeo-Christian Heritage
Facing overview—United Nations photo by Chen.

4. Muslims and Byzantines
Facing overview—Dover *Pictorial Archives* series. 123, 128-130—Weidenfeld Archives.

5. The Medieval Period
Facing overview—WHO photo. 165—Wellcome Institute. 166—(top) Royal Academy; (bottom) *History Today* Archives. 169—National Gallery of Arts, Washington, DC. 180-181—Mansell Collection. 183-184—Weidenfeld Archives.

6. Renaissance and Reformation
Facing overview—Reproduction from the collection of the Library of Congress. 215, 219—*History Today* maps by Ken Wass. 227—Mansell Collection.

ANNUAL EDITIONS ARTICLE REVIEW FORM

■ NAME: _____ DATE: _____

■ TITLE AND NUMBER OF ARTICLE: _____

■ BRIEFLY STATE THE MAIN IDEA OF THIS ARTICLE: _____

_____

_____

_____

_____

■ LIST THREE IMPORTANT FACTS THAT THE AUTHOR USES TO SUPPORT THE MAIN IDEA:

_____

_____

_____

_____

_____

_____

■ WHAT INFORMATION OR IDEAS DISCUSSED IN THIS ARTICLE ARE ALSO DISCUSSED IN YOUR TEXTBOOK OR OTHER READING YOU HAVE DONE? LIST THE TEXTBOOK CHAPTERS AND PAGE NUMBERS:

_____

_____

_____

_____

_____

_____

_____

■ LIST ANY EXAMPLES OF BIAS OR FAULTY REASONING THAT YOU FOUND IN THE ARTICLE:

_____

_____

_____

_____

_____

■ LIST ANY NEW TERMS/CONCEPTS THAT WERE DISCUSSED IN THE ARTICLE AND WRITE A SHORT DEFINITION:

_____

_____

_____

_____

_____

*Your instructor may require you to use this Annual Editions Article Review Form in any number of ways: for articles that are assigned, for extra credit, as a tool to assist in developing assigned papers, or simply for your own reference. Even if it is not required, we encourage you to photocopy and use this page; you'll find that reflecting on the articles will greatly enhance the information from your text.

We Want Your Advice

ANNUAL EDITIONS:
WESTERN CIVILIZATION, Volume I
Article Rating Form

Here is an opportunity for you to have direct input into the next revision of this volume. We would like you to rate each of the 48 articles listed below, using the following scale:

1. **Excellent: should definitely be retained**
2. **Above average: should probably be retained**
3. **Below average: should probably be deleted**
4. **Poor: should definitely be deleted**

Your ratings will play a vital part in the next revision. So please mail this prepaid form to us just as soon as you complete it.
Thanks for your help!

Annual Editions revisions depend on two major opinion sources: one is our Advisory Board, listed in the front of this volume, which works with us in scanning the thousands of articles published in the public press each year; the other is you—the person actually using the book. Please help us and the users of the next edition by completing the prepaid article rating form on this page and returning it to us. Thank you.

Rating	Article	Rating	Article
	1. Civilization and Its Discontents		26. The World of Islam
	2. Egypt and the Mediterranean World		27. The Rise of the Umayyad Dynasty in Spain
	3. Precincts of Eternity		28. The Viking Saga
	4. Hatshepsut: The Female Pharaoh		29. The Golden Age of Andalusia under the Muslim Sultans
	5. Grisly Assyrian Record of Torture and Death		30. Crusade's Strange Twist
	6. Early Civilizations and the Natural Environment		31. In France, an Ordeal by Fire and a Monster Weapon Called 'Bad Neighbor'
	7. Out of Egypt, Greece		32. Studying the Lives of Medieval Women
	8. American Democracy through Ancient Greek Eyes		33. Margery Kempe and the Meaning of Madness
	9. The Martial Republics of Classical Greece		34. The Cid of History and the History of the Cid
	10. Herodotus—Roving Reporter of the Ancient World		35. Horsemen of Cruel Cunning
	11. Love and Death in Ancient Greece		36. The Myths of Medieval Warfare
	12. The Oldest Dead White European Males		37. How a Mysterious Disease Laid Low Europe's Masses
	13. Greek Gifts?		38. Jan Hus—Heretic or Patriot?
	14. Why Brutus Stabbed Caesar		39. How Jacques Coeur Made His Fortune
	15. Nero, Unmaligned		40. Machiavelli
	16. Everyday Life for the Roman Schoolboy		41. Women of the Renaissance
	17. Friends, Romans or Countrymen? Barbarians in the Empire		42. Bess of Hardwick Was a Woman to Be Reckoned With
	18. Jews and Christians in a Roman World		43. Hungary's Philosopher King: Matthias Corvinus, 1458–90
	19. Who Wrote the Dead Sea Scrolls?		44. Columbus—Hero or Villain?
	20. Who Was Jesus?		45. Luther: Giant of His Time and Ours
	21. Jesus and the Teacher of Righteousness		46. The Forming of German Identity
	22. Women and the Bible		47. Explaining John Calvin
	23. Handmaid or Feminist?		48. That Others Might Read
	24. Byzantium: The Emperor's New Clothes?		
	25. War by Other Means: The Legacy of Byzantium		

(Continued on next page)

ABOUT YOU

Name_____ Date_____

Are you a teacher? ☐   Or student? ☐

Your School Name _____

Department _____

Address _____

City_____ State _____ Zip _____

School Telephone # _____

YOUR COMMENTS ARE IMPORTANT TO US!

Please fill in the following information:

For which course did you use this book? _____

Did you use a text with this Annual Edition?   ☐ yes   ☐ no

The title of the text? _____

What are your general reactions to the Annual Editions concept?

Have you read any particular articles recently that you think should be included in the next edition?

Are there any articles you feel should be replaced in the next edition? Why?

Are there other areas that you feel would utilize an Annual Edition?

May we contact you for editorial input?

May we quote you from above?

ANNUAL EDITIONS: WESTERN CIVILIZATION, Volume I, 8th Edition

BUSINESS REPLY MAIL

First Class   Permit No. 84   Guilford, CT

Postage will be paid by addressee

No Postage
Necessary
if Mailed
in the
United States

The Dushkin Publishing Group, Inc.
Sluice Dock
DPG **Guilford, Connecticut 06437**